A New Star-Rating System & Other Exciting News from Frommer's!

In our continuing effort to publish the savviest, most up-to-date, and most appealing travel guides available, we've added some great new features.

Frommer's guides now include a new **star-rating system.** Every hotel, restaurant, and attraction is rated from 0 to 3 stars to help you set priorities and organize your time.

We've also added **seven brand-new features** that point you to the great deals, in-the-know advice, and unique experiences that separate travelers from tourists. Throughout the guide look for:

Finds	Special finds—those places only insiders know about
Fun Fact	Fun facts—details that make travelers more informed and their trips more fun
Kids	Best bets for kids—advice for the whole family
Moments	Special moments—those experiences that memories are made of
Overrated	Places or experiences not worth your time or money
Tips	Insider tips—some great ways to save time and money
Value	Great values—where to get the best deals

We've also added a **"What's New"** section in every guide—a timely crash course in what's hot and what's not in every destination we cover.

Other Great Guides for Your Trip:

Frommer's Europe

Frommer's Europe from $70 a Day

Frommer's Western Europe's Best-Loved Driving Tours

Frommer's®

Switzerland
10th Edition

by Darwin Porter & Danforth Prince

Here's what the critics say about Frommer's:

"Amazingly easy to use. Very portable, very complete."
—*Booklist*

"The only mainstream guide to list specific prices. The Walter Cronkite of guidebooks—with all that implies."
—*Travel & Leisure*

"Complete, concise, and filled with useful information."
—*New York Daily News*

"Hotel information is close to encyclopedic."
—*Des Moines Sunday Register*

"Detailed, accurate, and easy-to-read information for all price ranges."
—*Glamour Magazine*

Hungry Minds™

Best-Selling Books • Digital Downloads • e-Books • Answer Networks
e-Newsletters • Branded Web Sites • e-Learning
New York, NY • Cleveland, OH • Indianapolis, IN

About the Authors

A native of North Carolina, **Darwin Porter** was a bureau chief for *The Miami Herald* when he was 21 and later worked in television advertising. Since then, he has written numerous best-selling Frommer guides, notably to France, Italy, England, and Germany. He is joined in his research efforts across Switzerland by **Danforth Prince,** formerly a resident of Zurich, who has also worked for the Paris bureau of the *New York Times.* They have traveled in and written extensively about Switzerland.

Published by:

Hungry Minds, Inc.

909 Third Avenue
New York, NY 10022

ISBN 0-7645-6562-1
ISSN 1044-2294

Editors: Kimberly Perdue, Kendra L. Falkenstein
Production Editor: Ian Skinnari
Cartographer: John Decamillis
Photo Editor: Richard Fox
Production by Hungry Minds Indianapolis Production Services

Front cover photo: Passenger train crossing land bridge on the Bernina Pass
Back cover photo: A view of skiers and the Matterhorn from Zermatt

Special Sales

For general information on Hungry Minds' products and services please contact our Customer Care department; within the U.S. at 800-762-2974, outside the U.S. at 317-572-3993 or fax 317-572-4002. For sales inquiries and reseller information, including discounts, bulk sales, customized editions, and premium sales, please contact our Customer Care department at 800-434-3422.

Manufactured in the United States of America

5   4   3   2

Contents

List of Maps

An Invitation to the Reader

In researching this book, we discovered many wonderful places—hotels, restaurants, shops, and more. We're sure you'll find others. Please tell us about them, so we can share the information with your fellow travelers in upcoming editions. If you were disappointed with a recommendation, we'd love to know that, too. Please write to:

Frommer's Switzerland, 10th Edition
Hungry Minds, Inc. • 909 Third Avenue • New York, NY 10022

An Additional Note

Please be advised that travel information is subject to change at any time—and this is especially true of prices. We therefore suggest that you write or call ahead for confirmation when making your travel plans. The authors, editors, and publisher cannot be held responsible for the experiences of readers while traveling. Your safety is important to us, however, so we encourage you to stay alert and be aware of your surroundings. Keep a close eye on cameras, purses, and wallets, all favorite targets of thieves and pickpockets.

New! Frommer's Star Ratings & Icons

Every hotel, restaurant and attraction listing in this guide has been ranked for quality, value, service, amenities, and special features using a star-rating scale. In country, state, and regional guides, we also rate towns and regions to help you narrow down your choices and budget your time accordingly. Hotels and restaurants in the Very Expensive and Expensive categories are rated on a scale of one (highly recommended) to three stars (exceptional). Those in the Moderate and Inexpensive categories rate from zero (recommended) to two stars (very highly recommended). Attractions, towns, and regions are rated according to the following scale: zero stars (recommended), one star (highly recommended), two stars (very highly recommended), and three stars (must-see).

In addition to the rating system, we also use seven icons to highlight insider information, useful tips, special bargains, hidden gems, memorable experiences, kid-friendly venues, places to avoid, and other useful information:

(Finds (Fun Fact (Kids (Moments (Overrated (Tips (Value

The following abbreviations are used for credit cards:

AE	American Express	DISC	Discover	V	Visa
DC	Diners Club	MC	MasterCard		

FROMMERS.COM

Now that you have the guidebook to a great trip, visit our website at **www.frommers.com** for travel information on nearly 2,000 destinations. With features updated regularly, we give you instant access to the most current trip-planning information available. At Frommers.com, you'll also find the best prices on air fares, accommodations, and car rentals—and you can even book travel online through our travel booking partners. At Frommers.com, you'll also find the following:

- Daily Newsletter highlighting the best travel deals
- Hot Spot of the Month/Vacation Sweepstakes & Travel Photo Contest
- More than 200 Travel Message Boards
- Outspoken Newsletters and Feature Articles on travel bargains, vacation ideas, tips & resources, and more!

What's New in Switzerland

Faced with the majestic mountain scenery of Switzerland, you at first think that it is eternal. But there are always changes—a new resort opening up or an old favorite shutting down. The roster of what's hot in dining can shift from year to year. Here are some highlights of the latest developments in Switzerland.

ZURICH Dining New food and beverage laws in this banking city have made it easier to open restaurants. An explosion of new dining places, often funkier and more irreverent than before, has burst onto the scene. Typical of this new type of restaurant is **Reithalle,** Gesserneralle (✆ 01/212-07-66), installed in a former stable on a small island in the center of Zurich. In summer, picnic tables are set out. Stylish and hip, **Blue Note,** Stockerstrasse 45 (✆ 01/202-17-17), is a seductive restaurant more fusion than Asian. It draws a chic young crowd not only to its cuisine but its affordable prices. **Crazy Cow,** Leonhardstrasse (✆ 01/261-40-55), spoofs Switzerland's obsession with dairy products and is a hip version of an old-fashioned inn, lying at the base of a hill that contains Zurich's university. It's an amusing choice for inexpensive dining. See chapter 3.

BASEL Accommodations A novel hotel has opened in this city called **Hotel Brasserie Au-Violon,** Im Lohnhof (✆ 061/269-87-11). From 1835 to 1995 this was the city's best-known prison, but the reception is far more inviting today after its transformation

into an offbeat hotel of charm and grace. See chapter 5.

BERN Accommodations The most famous hotel in the Swiss capital, **Bellevue Palace,** will be closed for most of the life of this edition, but there are many other worthy choices ready to fill the gap. One of the best choices will be the new **Allegro Bern,** Kornhausstrasse 3 (✆ 031/133-95-50), one of the city's top three hotels, enjoying a panoramic view from the medieval town center. There is grand comfort here. See chapter 6.

Dining The most fashionable restaurant in Bern, **Wein & Sein,** Münstergasse 50 (✆ 031/311-98-44), is set in a historic structure in the medieval center. Celebrity chef Beat Blum (don't you love that name?) is wowing the taste buds of the most discerning citizens with his sharply cultivated international cuisine. See chapter 6.

INTERLAKEN Accommodations Built in 1907, the **Royal St. George,** Höheweg 139 (✆ 033/822-75-75), has been newly restored. The Victorian hotel still retains its traditional character in its up-to-date bedrooms, but includes plenty of Art Nouveau touches as well. See chapter 7.

ZERMATT Accommodations A real find in this resort overlooking the Matterhorn, the new **Riffelalp Resort 222,** at Riffelalp (✆ 027/966-05-55), lies a 20-minute cog railway ride north of the resort. A government-rated five-star hotel, it's a mountain stunner, lying in some of the region's best ski country. See chapter 8.

LAUSANNE Attractions One of the most dramatic tours from this lakeside resort town is to the alpine village of **Les Diablerets,** where you can take a cable car ride to towering Col du Pillon. At the summit you encounter an aerie that evokes either an Inca temple or a spacecraft. Snow fights in July are possible. See the sidebar "A Dramatic Ascent to Les Diablerets" in chapter 9.

GENEVA Accommodations Discerning hotel shoppers are making their way to the Left Bank to check into the restored **Les Armures,** 1 rue Puits-Saint-Pierre (© 022/310-91-72), in a building that dates originally from the 17th century. A quirky antique charm prevails, and the place is becoming better known. See chapter 10.

LUCERNE Accommodations This city has never witnessed anything like **The Hotel,** Sempacherstrasse 14 (© 041/226-86-86), a luxurious boutique hotel designed by Jean Nouvel, the greatest modern architect of France. A statement of artful simplicity, it is also luxury personified. See chapter 11.

Attractions This much-visited city is blossoming with new museums, chief of which is the **Neus Kunstmuseum** (Modern Art Museum), Europaplatz 1 (© 041/226-78-00), in the new Culture and Convention Centre also designed by Jean Nouvel (see above). Although there is a permanent collection of art, the real interest here is centered on the Class A temporary exhibits. Also being newly discovered are the improved exhibits at the **Museum of Swiss History,** Pfistergasse 24 (© 041/228-54-24), a showcase for medieval and Renaissance art and sculpture. See chapter 11.

MORCOTE Accommodations & Dining An exciting discovery along scenic Lake Lugano, **Bella Vista,** Strada de Vigh 2, Morcote (© 091/996-11-43), is a secluded hideaway in a vineyard setting, an idyllic stopover for rooms or food. It not only serves some of the best cuisine in the Ticino, but is a charming place to stay for those with nostalgic tastes. See chapter 14.

The Best of Switzerland

You're visiting Switzerland to relax and have a good time, so you don't want to waste precious vacation hours searching for the best deals and experiences. So take us along and we'll do the work for you. Throughout our years spent traveling in Switzerland, we've tested the best lake shores, reviewed countless restaurants, inspected hotels ranging from remote alpine inns to luxurious city palaces, and sampled the best skiing, mountain climbing, and hiking. We've even learned where to get away from it all when you want to escape the crowds. The following is a very personal, opinionated list of what we consider to be the best Switzerland has to offer.

1 The Best Travel Experiences

- **Hiking the Swiss Mountains:** From the time the snows melt in spring until the late autumn winds blow too powerfully, visitors head for the country's alpine chain to hike its beautiful expanses. Well-trodden footpaths through the valleys and up the mountains are found in all the resorts of Switzerland. Hiking is especially enjoyable in the Ticino and the Engadine, but quite wonderful almost anywhere in the country. You'll find fewer visitors in some of the less-inhabited valleys such as those in the Valais. Every major tourist office in Switzerland will give you a free list of the best trails in their area. If you go to one of the area's local bookstores, you can also purchase topographical maps of wilderness trails.

- **Viewing Castles & Cathedrals:** There is so much emphasis on outdoor sports in Switzerland that many visitors forget that it is rich in history and filled with landmarks from the Middle Ages. Explore at random. Visit the castle at Chillon where Lord Byron wrote *The Prisoner of Chillon.* Everyone knows Gruyères for the cheese, but it's also the most craggy castle village of Switzerland, complete with dungeon and spectacular panoramic views. Both Bern and Basel have historic Münsters of cathedrals—the one in Bern dates from the 14th century. Among the great cathedrals, St. Nicholas's Cathedral, in the ancient city of Fribourg near Bern, dominates the medieval quarter, and Schloss Thun, on Lake Thun in the Bernese Oberland, was built by the dukes of Zähtingen at the end of the 12th century.

- **Joining the Revelers at Fasnacht (Basel):** Believe it or not, Switzerland has its own safe and very appealing version of Carnival, with origins dating back to the Middle Ages. It begins the Monday after Ash Wednesday (usually in late February or early March). The aesthetic is heathen (or pagan), with a touch of existentialist absurdity. The horse-drawn and motorized parades are appropriately flamboyant, and the cacophonous music that accompanies the spectacle includes the sounds of fifes, drums, trumpets, and trombones. Sometimes as many as 20,000 people participate in the raucous festivities, which might change your image of straight-laced Switzerland. See "Basel" in chapter 5.

• **Summiting Mount Pilatus:** The steepest cogwheel train in the world—with a 48° gradient—will take you to the top of Mount Pilatus, a 7,000-foot (2,100m) summit overlooking Lucerne. Once at the top you'll have a panoramic sweep that stretches all the way to Italy. Until the 1600s it was forbidden to climb this mountain because locals feared that Pontius Pilate's angry ghost would provide trouble. His body, or so the legend says, was brought here by the devil. Queen Victoria made the trip in 1868 and did much to dispel this long-held myth. You can follow in the queen's footsteps. See "Lucerne" in chapter 11.

• **Discovering the Lakes of Central Switzerland:** Experience the country's sparkling lakes with a tour through central Switzerland on the William Tell Express. Begin in Lucerne on a historic paddle-wheel steamer that chugs across the lake while you have lunch. Before the tour is over, you'll have boarded a train on the lake's most distant shore, traversed one of the most forbidding mountain ranges in central Europe (through the relative safety of the St. Gotthard Tunnel), and descended into the lush lowlands of the Italian-speaking Ticino district. See chapter 14.

• **Wandering the Waterfront Promenades:** One of the greatest summer pleasures of Switzerland is wandering the palm-lined promenades in the Ticino, the Italian-speaking southern section of the country. The best resorts—and the best promenades—are found at Ascona, Locarno, and Lugano. You'll have not only lake scenery, but the rugged Italian Alps as a backdrop on your stroll. Of course, you can do more than just walk. There's swimming, boating, cafe sitting, people-watching, and even shopping. At night, when the harbor lights shine, you can join the Ticinese in their evening stroll. See chapter 14.

2 The Best Scenic Drives

• **The Road over the Great St. Bernard Pass:** Of the many mountain passes of alpine Europe, this is the most famous. Since the days of the Roman Empire, much of the commerce between northern Italy and the rest of Europe has navigated this low point in one of the most forbidding mountain ridges in the world. Modern-day pilgrims follow in the steps of Napoleon and his armies, who traversed the perilous pass in 1800 to invade Italy. Since 1964 a tunnel beneath the mountains has allowed traffic to move unhindered for at least half of every year. Technically, the Swiss section of the pass road begins in French-speaking Martigny and ends in Italian-speaking San Bernardino, 35 miles (56km) away. In reality, most motorists use the pass road as a slow but scenic midsummer diversion on long drives that begin near Basel or Zurich and end in the Italian cities of Aosta or Milan. See "Verbier" in chapter 8.

• **The Road over the Furka Pass:** Traveling in a southwest-to-northeast line for only 20 miles (32km), from the hamlet of Gletsch, northeast of Brig, to the mountain resort of Andermatt, the road follows the high-altitude frontier between German-speaking and Italian-speaking Switzerland. En route you'll see the frozen mass of the glacier that feeds the Rhône and scenery that's absolutely magnificent. Any number of scenic highlights radiate out from here. See "Andermatt" in chapter 11.

- **St. Gotthard Pass Road:** One of the most vital roads in Europe stretches for 40 miles (64km) between German-speaking Andermatt and the Italian-speaking village of Biasca. It shares many characteristics of the above-mentioned St. Bernard Pass, which lies about 25 almost-impassable miles (40km) to the east. Some historians have suggested that the tolls collected since the 1300s along this road helped finance the continued independence of Switzerland itself. Since 1980 a 10-mile (16km) tunnel has allowed motorists to travel the route year-round. Traffic on the high road, however, remains clogged with summer vacationers who come for the stunning views. The landscape is mournful and bleak throughout much of this adventure, a testimony to the savage climactic conditions that exist at these high altitudes. See "Andermatt" in chapter 11.
- **The Road over the Bernina Pass:** During the Middle Ages, merchants led horse and donkey caravans over this pass, risking their lives to carry supplies between what are now the German-speaking and Italian-speaking regions of Switzerland. Frostbite was commonplace, and many died in the snows en route. Today cars can navigate the pass as part of a 2-hour, 34-mile (55km) drive between St. Moritz and Tirano. Be warned, this drive is never problem free. The road is winding, and ice patches have a way of surfacing even in summertime. Snow usually closes the pass completely between mid-October and late April, although trains can usually get through except during the worst midwinter blizzards. But the views are truly spectacular. See "Pontresina" in chapter 13.

- **The Simplon Pass Road:** Unlike the St. Gotthard Pass Road, which is interspersed with artfully engineered bridges, hairpin turns, and retaining walls, the Simplon Pass Road gracefully conforms to the natural topography of some of the most scenic mountainsides in Europe. It stretches about 40 miles (64km), from German-speaking Brig over the Italian border to Domodossola. Napoleon demanded a low-altitude pass for his artillery, and the present road follows the 1805 plan designs. Napoleon's grip on power, ironically, crumbled before his armies could ever use the pass. Despite the best efforts of the Swiss Department of Highways, the road is often closed between December and early May, with automobiles diverted onto flatbed trains instead. These are rather awkwardly carried through one of the longest railway tunnels in the world, the Simplon Tunnel. See chapter 14.

3 The Best Train Trips

- **The *Glacier Express*:** It's advertised as the slowest express train in the world, requiring more than 7½ hours to pass through southeastern Switzerland. Despite that, its 170 miles (274km) of track are an awesome triumph of engineering (of which Switzerland is justifiably proud). Beginning every day in Zermatt, in southwest Switzerland, and ending in St. Moritz, in Switzerland's east, it crosses more than 291 bridges and goes through 91 tunnels, traversing some of the country's most inaccessible mountains with an ease that medieval pilgrims would have considered an act of God. You can also take the train from St. Moritz to Zermatt. Naturally, the scenery is breathtaking. The windows are large enough to allow clear views, and a dining car serves lunch with civilized efficiency. Advance reservations are required; for more information, call **Rail Europe** (© **800/438-7245**). See chapters 8 and 13.

• **The** *Palm Express:* This 2-day itinerary of bus and rail routes takes travelers from St. Moritz (in the rugged Engadine district, near Switzerland's eastern frontier) to either Brig or (for a supplemental fee) Zermatt, in Switzerland's southwest. More leisurely than either of the two rail routes described above, it includes a

hotel night en route. The scenery is spectacular. For more information, call **Rail Europe** (© **800/438-7245**). See chapter 13.

• **The** *Bernina Express:* Like the *Glacier Express,* this railway excursion offers sweeping views of otherwise inaccessible alpine landscapes. A 4-hour trip (each way), it begins in the German-speaking capital of Zurich, traverses isolated regions where the native tongue is the ancient Romansh language, and ends in Italian-speaking Lugano. The rugged, high-altitude landscapes near Chur give way to the verdant, palm-lined lake districts near Tirano. It's the only train route in Switzerland that crosses the Alps without the benefit of tunnels en route. (It also travels some of the steepest railway lines in the world, negotiated without the benefit of racks and pinions.) Consider extending this trip with bus connections from Tirano—the end of the rail line—to the resort town of Lugano. For more information, call **Rail Europe** (© **800/438-7245**). See chapter 14.

4 The Best Walks

• **Mount Säntis:** At 8,209 feet (2,463m), Säntis is the northern outpost of the Alps and the most towering peak in the Alpstein massif. The quaint village of Appenzell is a good place to base yourself. The walk itself begins in the village of Wasserrauen, which is linked to Appenzell by hourly trains. After 5.5 miles—4½ to 5½ hours, depending on your stamina—it ends at the village of Schwägalp, from which you can take a cable car to the viewing platform overlooking the summit of Säntis. Schwägalp is the terminus of the roads coming in from

Urnäsch and Neu-St-Johann. See "Appenzell" in chapter 4.

• **Grosse Scheidegg:** "The great watershed" in English, this popular walk takes you through some of the most dramatic scenery in the Jungfrau region of central Switzerland, known for stunning white glaciers and soaring summits. One of the highlights of the walk is the awesome beauty of the Wetterhorn's massive gray rock walls. Setting out from the village of Meiringen, the walk ends 13 miles (21km) away (6½ to 9 hr.) in the resort of Grindelwald. If you get tired, take advantage of the bus stops along the way. See "Grindelwald" in chapter 7 for more details.

- **The Bürgenstock Felsenweg:** In the Lake Lucerne area, this dramatic hike passes through one of the beauty spots of Switzerland, filled with numerous vistas and alpine foothills. From the ritzy resort of Bürgenstock it is 4.5 miles (7km and a 2½-hr. walk) to Ennetbürgen. Along the way you'll come upon spectacular views of Mount Pilatus and serene Lake Lucerne. The walk ends in Ennetbürgen, one of the most scenic resorts along Lake Lucerne. See "Bürgenstock" in chapter 11.
- **The Upper Engadine Lakes:** The four highland lakes of the Upper Engadine are 5,904 feet (1,771m) above sea level; but as you walk along, it's like traversing the floor of a valley. Craggy ranges and scenic lake vistas greet you at every turn as you make your way along the 8.5 miles (14km and a 3- to 3½-hr. walk) from Maloja to the resort of Silvaplana. You'll pass through the enchanting village of Segl-Maria, one of the most charming of the Romanesch-style villages in eastern Switzerland, eventually arriving at the western edge of Lej da Silvaplana, a lake of unsurpassed beauty. See chapter 13.
- **The Sottoceneri:** It takes its name from the 1,820-foot (546m) watershed of Monte Ceneri, lying about 6 miles (10km) southwest of the town of Bellizona. This is the most southerly part of the Ticino (the Italian-speaking section of Switzerland). Lake Lugano is one of the dominant features of the terrain and presents a panoramic backdrop as you stroll along. The town of Lugano makes an ideal base for walks in the area. The best walk is from Monte Bré, at 3,034 feet (1,011m), all the way to the village of Soragno, a distance of some 7 miles (3 to 3½ hr.). See "Lugano" in chapter 14.

5 The Best Bike Trips

- **Around the Katzensee:** If you're in Zurich on a hot summer day and you're longing for the perfect place to swim, try cycling from Seebach station through the shaded woods to Katzenruti (picnic spot) and then on to the Katzensee, a lake with a beach and Waldhaus restaurant. Return via Affoltern. Duration: 1½ hours, 8 miles (13km). See "Attractions" in chapter 3.
- **Around the Lake of Murten:** Start out at the small medieval town of Murten (stroll down the main street and visit the castle). Carry on to Faoug, Salavaux, Bellerive (a perfect lookout point), and Vully. Duration: 4 hours, 25 miles (40km). See "Murten" in chapter 5.
- **In the Rhône Valley, Lower Valais:** Cyclists on this route through the Valais set off from Martigny station then cross the Rhône River to the villages of Fully, Chataigner, Mazembroz, and Saillon. The cable-car ride to Iserables from the terminus of Riddes is well worth the trip. Duration: 1½ hours, 12 miles (20km). See chapter 8.
- **Through the Lake Geneva Vineyards:** Before leaving from the station at Morges, take a look at the castle (military museum). The route then leads up to Lully and, via Bussy and Ballens, to Biere. Continuing down a small valley to Begnins and Fechy (a scenic lookout point), you'll find yourself in Aubonne. Finally, take

the second-class road, via Lavigny, Villars-sous-Yens, and Lully, back to Morges. Duration: 5½ hours, 35 miles (56km). See "Attractions" in chapter 10.

- **Along the Shore of Lake Lucerne:** This trip can last a whole day, as there are so many spots worth stopping at along the way. Set off from Lucerne station and head for St. Niklausen and Kastanienbaum in the direction of Tribschen (Richard Wagner Museum). The most beautiful stretch is along the lake to Winkel-Horw Beach. Return to Lucerne. Duration: 1½ hours, 8 miles (13km). See "Lucerne" in chapter 11.

- **Lugano's Hinterland:** To discover the small villages around Lugano, set off from the station for the nature reserve at Origlio Lake, and then proceed to Ponte Capriasca (a parish church with a well-preserved copy of da Vinci's *Last Supper*). Continue to Tesserete and Colla, along the left valley side of Cassarate, through the woods to Sonvico, and then on to Dino, Ponte di Valle, and Lugano. Duration: 4 hours, 23 miles (37km). See "Lugano" in chapter 14.

6 The Best Small Towns & Villages

- **Appenzell:** Nowhere is folkloric Switzerland as well preserved. At the base of the green foothills of the Alpstein, this old-fashioned country town still has cowmen in yellow breeches and scarlet waistcoats walking its streets. People in other parts of Switzerland tend to call locals "hillbillies"; and for many Americans attracted to the quirky and the quaint, it evokes the Ozarks. As you wander its centuries-old streets, sampling pear bread and honey cakes while in pursuit of local embroidery, you'll know why Appenzell is called the most authentic of Swiss villages. See "Appenzell" in chapter 4.

- **Wengen:** On a sheltered terrace high above the Lauterbrunnen Valley, this ski resort is one of the gems of the Bernese Oberland. No cars are allowed in this idyllic village, and from its streets (cleared of snow even in winter) and hotel windows, magnificent panoramic views greet you at every turn. The sunsets—over crags and waterfalls—are the most memorable we've ever seen in Switzerland. The village is best known for hosting the World's Cup (for skiing), with the longest and most dangerous downhill race staged every January. See "Wengen" in chapter 7.

- **Sion:** Although it's the small capital of the Valais, this old Roman town with a French-speaking population is often neglected by those rushing to sample the pleasures of Zermatt and Verbier. But sleepy Sion has its own rewards. The town is dominated by the castles of Valère and Tourbillon, and, in its greater days, Sion's bishops were big players on the medieval stage. The moody, melancholy look of the town has inspired such luminaries as Rilke, Goethe, and Rousseau. See "Sion" in chapter 8.

- **Andermatt:** At the crossroads of the Alps, in the Urseren Valley, this picture-postcard town lies at the junction of two alpine roads—the St. Gotthard highway and the road to Oberalp and Furka. From the top of Gemstock, reached by cable car, you can see 600 alpine peaks. Hikers, cross-country skiers, and mountain bikers are attracted to this little backwater.

The life of the town is centered on the main street, some sections of which are still paved with granite stones. See "Andermatt" in chapter 11.

- **Morcote:** Seven miles (11km) south of Lugano, at the southernmost tip of the Ceresio peninsula, stands Switzerland's most idyllic village. Built in the Lombard style familiar to those who have toured the environs of Milan, Morcote's arcaded houses, often clay colored, open directly on the water, with everything set against a backdrop of vineyards and cypresses. For the best view of this cliché of Ticino charm, climb the 400 steps to the Chiesa di Madonna del Sasso, which dates from the 13th century. See "Morcote" in chapter 14.

7 The Best Romantic Getaways

- **Mürren:** It's so isolated that you can only get here by cog railway or cable car. Set on a rocky, high-altitude ledge hundreds of feet above the Lauterbrunnen Valley, Mürren has a handful of chalet-style hotels, excellent ski and hiking trails, and sweeping views over the mountains of the Bernese Oberland. It's as picture-perfect a Swiss village as you'll find. See "Mürren" in chapter 7.
- **Gstaad:** Lying at the junction of four alpine valleys midway between the Bernese Oberland and the Vaud Alps, Gstaad is a winter capital of the European glitterati. You can't get any more stylish, and the skiing is good too. Regardless of their price range, all the hotels seem to have cozy bedrooms, blazing fireplaces, and enough schnapps to set the mood. See "Gstaad" in chapter 7.
- **Verbier:** It lies at the bottom of an enormous alpine bowl ringed with spectacular ski slopes. Although many British travelers appreciate Verbier's charms, the language and atmosphere of the resort are unpretentious and very, very French. You can have a lot of fun in Verbier, and if you didn't happen to import your own romance, you're likely to find one here. See "Verbier" in chapter 8.
- **Bürgenstock:** The only road leading here is so treacherous that almost everyone opts to travel by cog railway or cable car. The town, set on a densely forested limestone ridge high above Lake Lucerne, shelters some of the most luxurious hotels in Switzerland. Reserve part of every day here for climbs along the well-maintained hiking paths, at least one of which skirts the edge of a very steep and panoramic cliff. See "Bürgenstock" in chapter 11.
- **Arosa:** One of the highest (6,000 ft./2,000m) ski resorts in Switzerland, Arosa is less expensive and less forbiddingly elegant than its nearest competitor, St. Moritz. Although the skiing here is excellent, you might consider a romantic getaway in midsummer, when a network of hiking trails leads to lush forests and small lakes. When you tire of these, cable cars can carry you and your companion to alpine heights and sublime vistas. See "Arosa" in chapter 12.

8 The Best Skiing

The jagged borders of Switzerland contain dozens of worthwhile ski resorts; the most popular are described in detail in the chapters that follow. But before heading off to the mountains for a bit of downhill racing, ask yourself some important questions: Do you prefer to schuss down a Swiss mountainside in relative isolation or accompanied by many other skiers? How chic and how expensive do you want your vacation to be? Do you pursue sports other than skiing (perhaps hang-gliding, curling, ice skating, or tobogganing)? And after a day in the great outdoors, do you prefer to retire early to a simple mountain hut with a view of the stars, or do you yearn for late nights with the glittering demimonde of Europe? Read through the list below and discover the resort that's right for you.

- **Grindelwald:** This is one of the few resorts in the Bernese Oberland that occasionally mistakes itself for a genuine city rather than an artificial tourist creation. It offers a healthy dose of restaurants, bars, discos, and, unfortunately, traffic. There are a lot of affordable accommodations here—it's not nearly as snobby as some of the other resorts. Many skiers use it as a base camp for long-haul excursions to the slopes of First, Männlichen, and Kleine Scheidegg. From Grindelwald, the resorts of Wengen and Mürren are accessible by cog railway and/or cable car (no traffic!). See "Grindelwald" in chapter 7.

- **Gstaad/Saanenland:** Gstaad is the most elegant pearl in the larger ski region of Saanenland, on the western edge of the Bernese Oberland. Although a few inexpensive lodgings can be found if you're lucky, don't count on it. The jet set come here to see and be seen, and there's a lot to do off the slopes: music festivals, shopping, people-watching. The architecture is stubbornly alpine, and the interior decorations range from baronial and woodsy in the most expensive hotels to kitschy in the cheaper ones. Opportunities for skiing are widespread, but the slopes are hardly the most difficult in Switzerland. Skiing is best for beginners and intermediates. See "Gstaad" in chapter 7.

- **Mürren:** One of the most oddly positioned resorts in Switzerland, Mürren sits on a rock ledge high above the Lauterbrunnen Valley of the Bernese Oberland. Accessible only by cable car, it's among the most picture-perfect resorts, full of chalet-style architecture and completely free of traffic. Though its isolation makes it charming, it also tends to make the cost of staying here somewhat higher. Mürren is closer than any other resort to the demanding slopes of the Schilthorn. From here, experienced skiers are offered nearly 20 miles (32km) of some of the finest powder in Europe—and eagle-eyed panoramas over some of the most dramatically beautiful landscapes in Europe. See "Mürren" in chapter 7.

- **Verbier:** This is the premier ski resort of French-speaking Switzerland, with an unpretentious panache and a fun-filled atmosphere. Its restaurants serve some of the finest creative cuisine in the region; others make do with simple alpine fare for hearty appetites. If you don't speak French, you won't feel uncomfortable—many of the resort's nightlife options cater to Brits. (Throughout the town, English-style pubs compete cheerfully with French cafes.) Verbier lies at the heart of a sprawling, high-tech network of cable cars and gondolas that will connect you to such relatively unknown satellite resorts as Veysonnaz, Versonnaz, and La Tzoumaz. The resort is favored by world-class athletes for the difficulty of many of its slopes. See "Verbier" in chapter 8.

- **Zermatt:** It's the most southwesterly of the great Swiss ski resorts, occupying a high-altitude plateau at the foot of Switzerland's highest and most-photographed mountain, the Matterhorn. Much of the resort's charm derives from its strict building codes—you'll rarely see a modern-looking building here—and its almost complete lack of traffic. Access is only via cog railway from the valley below. Known for over a century as the party town of the Alps, Zermatt has always been a place where the beer drinking and hedonistic—sometimes raunchy—revelry last into the early-morning hours. The skiing, incidentally, is superb. A complicated network of chairlifts, cog railways, and gondolas carries skiers to such peaks as Stockhorn, Rothorn, Riffelberg, Trockner Steg, and Testa Grigia. See "Zermatt & the Matterhorn" in chapter 8.

- **Arosa:** One of the most isolated of eastern Switzerland's resorts, Arosa is a relative newcomer to the country's ski scene. Drawing a young crowd, it's filled with contemporary buildings rather than traditional, chalet-inspired architecture. Ample annual snowfall, vast alpine meadows, and only one steeply inclined road into town make Arosa ideal for escapists and nature lovers. Families with children usually like the place too. Not as stratospherically expensive or pretentious as St. Moritz, Arosa offers lots of runs for intermediate skiers. Some of the resort's most dramatic slopes, which drop more than 3,000 feet (1,000m) from beginning to end, are only for very experienced athletes. See "Arosa" in chapter 12.

- **Davos:** It's larger, with many more hotels, restaurants, après-ski bars, and discos than its neighbor, Klosters (see below), with which it shares access to a sweeping network of ski lifts and slopes. Davos attracts a sometimes-curious mixture of the very wealthy and the more modest. It has slopes that appeal to advanced skiers, intermediates, and beginners. One of the most challenging runs descends from Weissfluhgipfel at 9,330 feet (2,799m) to Küblis at 2,670 feet (801m). See "Davos" in chapter 12.

- **Klosters:** Named after a 13th-century cloister founded on the site, this resort is smaller, more intimate, and less urban than its nearest major competitor, Davos (see above). A favorite of the royal families of both Sweden and Britain, it offers at least two easily accessible ski zones, the snowfields of the Gotschna-Parsenn and the Madrisa. There's a wide range of trails and facilities, offering challenges to all skill levels. See "Klosters" in chapter 12.

- **St. Moritz:** The premier ski and social resort of eastern Switzerland, St. Moritz draws a lot of folks familiar with the art of conspicuous consumption. This is as close as you'll get to Hollywood in Switzerland. It's more distinctly Austrian than French in its flavor. Although only one or two authentic buildings remain from the town's medieval origins, vast amounts of money have been spent installing folkloric fixtures, carved paneling, and accents of local granite in the public and private areas of most hotels. Skiing in the region is divided into distinctly different areas, the most popular of which is Corviglia, on the mountains above St. Moritz. Adventurers seeking diversion farther afield head for the slopes above the satellite resort of Sils Maria (Corvatsch) and the slopes

Impressions

A Swiss artist living in the south of France said it: "Switzerland does not exist." This made some Swiss upset. Though Switzerland doesn't exist, every Swiss citizen has his assault rifle at home (with ammo). Of course they very rarely use their rifle to attack a bank or to hurt their wives. The Swiss used to be mercenaries, but today they don't want to get involved in other countries' feuds. Although they use migrant workers, they don't like foreigners (tourists are okay). Switzerland is this Disney-land of order and social harmony. It is a secure and peaceful place. It is not part of Europe. It might not even really be part of the world. This, I guess, should be good for the banking business.

—Olivier Mosset, 1994

above the nearby village of Pontresina (Diavolezza). There are plenty of difficult slopes in the region if you seek them out, but intermediate-level skiers enjoy taking a cable car from St. Moritz-Dorf to the top of Piz Corvatsch, almost 11,000 feet (3,300m) above sea level. From here, with only one cable-car connection en route, you can ski a network of intermediate-level trails all the way back down to the resort's lake. St. Moritz boasts some of the most dependable annual snowfalls in Switzerland. See "St. Moritz" in chapter 13.

9 The Best Festivals

• **Vogel Gryff Volksfest:** This colorful tradition has a griffin, a lion, and a "wild man of the woods" floating down the Rhine followed by dancing in the streets. It occurs alternately on January 13, 20, or 27 (changes every year). On a wintry day in January, a raft, laden with two drummers, two men with large flags, and two cannoneers, who repeatedly fire gun salutes, floats down the Rhine. The principal figure is a savage masked man carrying an uprooted pine tree. At Mittlere Brücke (the middle bridge) he's met by a lion and a bird with an awesome beak. At noon the three figures dance on the bridge to the sound of drums. The savage man or Wilder Mann, the Leu (lion), and the Vogel Gryff (griffin) are old symbols for three Basel societies that could be called neighborhoods today. Throughout the afternoon and evening there's street dancing in Basel to honor the occasion, which originated in the 16th century. The purpose of all this madness? Ostensibly, to strengthen community ties. See "Basel" in chapter 5.

• **Celebrating the Onion:** If your favorite sandwich consists of only bread, mayonnaise, and onions, or your idea of humor is to poke fun at buffoons disguised as onions, you'll love the Swiss capital's celebration of Zibelemärit, held annually on the fourth Monday of November. During the festival, huge sections of the city's historic center are filled with vegetable stalls featuring plaited strings of onions (more than 100 tons might be sold in a day here) and other winter vegetables. The barrels of confetti thrown by competing camps of high-spirited students offer endless photo ops. Facetiously dressed jesters appear in bars and restaurants to poke fun (usually in Swiss-German) at the sometimes-pompous political posturing of their governmental elders. See the introduction to chapter 6 for more information.

- **L'Escalade:** Way back on December 11, 1602, the city of Geneva was attacked by Savoyard soldiers trying to scale its ramparts. The duke of Savoy had lost his former possession and wanted it back. Alas, it was not to be. The denizens of Geneva valiantly held

out, and one brave amazon, Mère Royaume, scaled the ramparts and poured a pot of hot soup on the head of a Savoyard soldier. For 3 days and nights beginning December 11, normally staid Geneva becomes virtually Rabelaisian, staging torchlight marches, country markets, and fife-and-drum parades, as a festive crowd in period costumes marches through the streets of the old city. Many present-day Mère Royaumes—armed with soup pots, of course—can be seen. See "When to Go" in chapter 2.

10 The Best Museums

- **Rietberg Museum:** Some of Europe's most interesting collections were amassed by gifted amateurs with enough money to pursue their hobbies. This museum honors the acquisitive skill of Baron von der Heydt, who donated his collection to the city of Zurich in 1952. It includes sculptures and artworks from the Americas and North and South Asia, archaic Buddhist art, carpets from Armenia, and masks from Africa and Oceania. See p. 95.
- **Landesmuseum (Swiss National Museum, Zurich):** This museum traces the growth and development of Swiss civilization from prehistory to the modern age. The collections include prehistoric artifacts, mementos from the Roman and Carolingian empires, and artworks from Romanesque, Gothic, and Renaissance periods. There are also unusual collections of Swiss clocks, Swiss armor and weapons, and folkloric costumes and artifacts from each of the country's cantons. See p. 94.
- **Kunstmuseum (Fine Arts Museum, Basel):** Its first acquisition goes back to 1662. Since then, the bulk of the museum's

3,000 artworks have included works by Swiss and German artists from the 15th and 16th centuries. Despite the excellence of its old master paintings, the museum is especially known for its large collections of modern works, only a fraction of which can ever be exhibited at the same time. See p. 142.
- **Kunstmuseum (Fine Arts Museum, Bern):** Bern's premier museum, this civic showcase contains everything from 13th-century Italian primitives to one of the most complete collections of works by Paul Klee anywhere. See p. 184.
- **Musée d'Art et d'Histoire (Art and History Museum, Geneva):** Geneva's premier museum devotes equal space to exhibits on the history of civilization, the civic history of Geneva, archaeology, and world-class painting—everything from medieval to modern art. See p. 330.
- **Verkehrshaus der Schweiz (Swiss Transport Museum, Lucerne):** One of Switzerland's newer museums, founded in 1959, this collection pays homage to the railway, auto, and airplane

industries that helped propel Europe into the modern age. It contains more than 60 historic locomotives, 40 automobiles, 50 motorcycles, and dozens of other conveyances. Other exhibitions are devoted to cable cars, steamships, and spaceships. There's even a planetarium. See p. 357.

11 The Best Luxury Hotels

- **Baur au Lac (© 01/220-50-20):** Prestigious and historic, it's one of the country's grandest hotels, welcoming prosperous guests since 1844. Richard Wagner, Franz Liszt, and John Lennon are some of the artists who have experienced its charms. Today, the international business community considers it a favorite. See p. 65.
- **Widder Hotel (© 01/224-25-26):** In the heart of the city's Old Town, 10 historic buildings dating from the 15th century have been transformed into an intimate luxury inn. Massive wooden beams and 16th-century frescoes still exist from the days when these buildings were part of the butchers' guild, but now they're juxtaposed with glass elevators and stainless-steel furniture. It's an off-beat, fun choice in a staid city, made especially inviting because of the live jazz in the bar. See p. 69.
- **Hotel Drei Könige (© 061/261-50-50):** Claiming to be the oldest hotel in Europe, the Hotel Drei Könige has operated continuously as an inn since 1026. It was the site of a meeting between two Holy Roman emperors and a Burgundian king that eventually established the southwestern borders of present-day Switzerland. Voltaire, Queen Victoria, and Kaiser Wilhelm II were only a few of this hotel's famous guests. Today there's live jazz in the bar and a cosmopolitanism that permeates every part of this very comfortable hotel. See p. 144.
- **Hotel Schweizerhof (© 031/326-80-80):** A favorite of diplomats, this grand hotel, built in 1859, is filled with antiques and offers great comfort in its state-of-the-art bedrooms. Richly accessorized, it evokes grand luxury in the style of the 19th century. See p. 174.
- **Royal Park Hotel (© 800/874-4002):** Guests wear dinner jackets or semiformal gowns every night at dinner at this very discreet and upper-class hotel. The same family has maintained solidly impeccable standards for at least three generations, and the decor, which has lots of chiseled stone and timbers, seems as solid as the Central Bank of Switzerland itself. Although guests can have a very good time here, this is a seriously elegant hotel known for perfect manners and an utter lack of frivolity. See p. 227.
- **Palace Hotel Gstaad (© 800/223-6800):** Every winter this becomes one of the most sought-after hotels in the world, attracting the chic and fabulous who create what's been called the most amusing and expensive annual house party in Europe. Built in 1912, the hotel sits on a promontory above Gstaad (not exactly a village unfamiliar with luxury). Everything is very, very luxurious. See p. 232.
- **Beau-Rivage Palace (© 800/223-6800):** This is the most prestigious hotel in Lausanne. Undeniably beautiful, it's a beaux-arts masterpiece richly associated with

the city's cultural and social elite. Service is impeccable. Although it has long catered to wealthy and conservative French-speaking Swiss, it has made great efforts in recent years to attract a younger, more international clientele. See p. 273.

- **Le Richemond (℡ 022/715-70-00):** Built in 1875 in the style of a neoclassical palace, Le Richemond drips with Gobelin tapestries, French antiques, and a sophisticated, hardworking staff for whom absolutely nothing is a surprise. It also has the most fascinating bar in town; but if you decide to have a drink here, don't even think of showing up in torn jeans. See p. 307.
- **The Bürgenstock Hotels (℡ 800/874-4002):** If you're tired of waiting in lines at museums to admire paintings by Rubens and Tintoretto, try this hotel. Composed of three different buildings placed behind the trees of a 12-acre park, it shelters the world-class art collection of the present owner's father. Plush and comfortable, the hotel has elaborate gardens, lots of blazing fireplaces, and very good service. See p. 376.
- **Kulm Hotel (℡ 800/223-5695):** This is the great bastion of luxury of the Engandine, rivaling even Suvretta House and Badrutt's Palace Hotel for supremacy. The greats and near-greats of the world have found refuge from the snows here in this trio of buildings, the oldest of which dates from 1760. See p. 425.

12 The Most Charming Small Hotels

- **Hotel Romantic Florhof (℡ 01/261-44-70):** The most charming of the little boutique hotels of Zurich, this was originally the home of a wealthy 15th-century merchant before its transformation. At the edge of Old Town, the hotel represents superb value. See p. 73.
- **Belle Epoque (℡ 031/311-43-36):** The most sophisticated small-scale hotel in the Swiss capital was created out of two historic town houses from the Middle Ages. The hotel celebrates Jugendstil or a Teutonic Art Nouveau. The place is a jewel. See p. 174.
- **Hotel-Restaurant Adler (℡ 052/742-61-61):** Although its bedrooms are comfortable and clean, the location, in one of the most colorful cities on the Rhine, is what gets our vote. We love the hotel's frescoed facade, which depicts characters and plots derived from medieval Rhenish legends. See p. 132.
- **Hotel Appenzell (℡ 071/788-15-15):** Set on the main square of the most folkloric town in Switzerland, this hotel is outfitted in a rustic country-Swiss theme with touches of marble and walnut in the bedrooms. Check out the elaborate antique paneling in one of the dining rooms, rescued from a much older building just before it was demolished. See p. 125.
- **Hostellerie des Chevaliers (℡ 026/921-19-33):** A Relais & Châteaux property, this atmospheric inn stands conveniently aloof from the overrun tourist center but offers the same panoramic views as the chateaux at Gruyères. The decor is the warmest and most old-fashioned in town, rich with antiques, woodwork, and ceramic stoves. See p. 161.

- **Hotel Krafft am Rhein** (© 061/ 690-91-30): It's inexpensive and conveniently located a short walk from the historic core of the city. Its outdoor terrace overlooks the river, the town hall, and the cathedral. The bedrooms have the kind of worn but decent early-20th-century furnishings that remind us of these old-fashioned family-run pensions of postwar Europe. See p. 148.
- **Hotel Olden** (© 033/744-34-44): Set on the town's main thoroughfare, the Olden is a great deal compared to other Gstaad hotels. It enjoys a solid reputation, especially among the many skiers and mountain guides who patronize the restaurant and cafe on the hotel's ground floor. The rooms are cozy and a bit cramped, but comfortable—perfect if you're planning to spend your time out and about. See p. 233.
- **Hotel Antika** (© 027/967-21-51): It's one of the few hotels in Zermatt that won't gobble up most of your travel budget. You wouldn't really guess that it's an affordable option at first glance: Each room has its own covered loggia, and the lobby is carefully paneled with weathered planks. This is a good choice for exploring the most famous resort town of Switzerland's Valais district. See p. 259.
- **The Hotel** (© 041/226-86-86): This is Central Switzerland's most charming boutique hotel. Designed by Jean Nouvel, France's most famous architect, it is exclusive and elegant, luxury personified yet artfully simple at the same time. See p. 363.
- **Hotel Drei Könige und Post** (© 041/887-00-01): Located directly north of the St. Gotthard Pass at 6,920 feet (2,076m), this hotel was built on the site of an inn that has been showing wayfarers hospitality since 1234. Even Goethe spent a night at this family-run place in 1775. Some of the rooms open onto balconies, and the hotel's regional Swiss cuisine attracts both locals and visitors. See p. 386.
- **Hotel Drei Könige** (© 081/252-17-25): Its foundations were laid in the 1300s, and the same hardworking family has owned and managed the place since 1911. It provides a note of cheer in an industrialized, high-altitude town where the temperatures can sometimes plummet. Of special note is its restaurant, one of the most consistently popular in town. See p. 391.

13 The Best Restaurants

- **Peter's Kunststuben** (© 01/910-07-15): Come here for the sublime cuisine of chef Horst Petermann. Since he opened this acclaimed restaurant south of Zurich, demanding diners have been heading here to partake of the constantly changing specialties. After you've sampled his herby Tuscan dove with pine nuts or his lobster with artichoke and almond oil, you'll know that this is as good as it gets in the Zurich area. See p. 87.
- **Kronenhalle** (© 01/251-66-69): It has a hearty, rustic alpine theme, but a glance at its menu, its clientele, and its artwork will quickly convince you that this is a supremely distinctive restaurant. Enjoy paintings by such luminaries as Kandinsky, Matisse, Klee, and Braque as you dine. See p. 82.

- **Restaurant Stucki Bruderholz** (✆ **061/361-82-22**): There's a garden, a collection of upscale antique furniture, a clientele speaking every conceivable European language, and some of the best cuisine in northwestern Switzerland, all based on modern interpretations of French and German recipes. See p. 149.
- **Roland Pierroz** (✆ **027/771-63-23**): You'd never know that the simple chalet-style facade of this place shelters one of the most legendary restaurants in the Valais. One of the finest meals we've ever had in Switzerland was served here on a snowy night. It included a platter of sea bass with sea urchins, followed by couscous of crawfish and pigeon with truffles. Gourmets and epicures will cross any number of national borders to sample the creative cuisine of Roland Pierroz. See p. 243.
- **Hotel de Ville** (✆ **021/634-05-05**): Philippe Rochat is the chef of the moment in Switzerland, having taken over from Alfred (Frédy) Girardet, who was hailed as the world's greatest chef. That was some chef's toque for Rochat to wear, but he has succeeded in retaining the international acclaim that Girardet enjoyed. Occupying a building originally designed as the town hall of a village outside Lausanne, the master continues to please the hundreds of devoted gastronomes who often travel great distances at great expense to dine here. See p. 280.
- **Le Pont de Brent** (✆ **021/964-52-30**): No one had even heard of Brent until this restaurant opened in a late-19th-century house in the heart of the village. Today the restaurant has put the village on the map, in part because of the excellence of such dishes as

mussel-and-leek soup and roast rabbit with mustard sauce. See p. 294.
- **La Favola** (✆ **022/311-74-37**): This is the best Italian restaurant in Geneva, and possibly the city's best restaurant of any kind. The chefs' tender pillows of tortellini would be hard to find this side of Bologna. The cuisine has authentic flavor, the service is skilled and smooth, and only the freshest ingredients go into the kitchen's skillets and stewpots. See p. 323.
- **Le Cygne** (✆ **022/908-90-85**): When the Noga Hilton decided to open a restaurant in its lakefront hotel, neither expense nor effort was spared to make it the best in Geneva. This is no small feat, considering the tough local competition. In a plush, upholstered setting of lacquered wood and deep banquettes, attended by a well-trained army of waiters, you can enjoy a cuisine that ranks among the most sophisticated in Europe. The desserts are a triumph of the pastrymaker's art. See p. 315.
- **Le Chat-Botté** (✆ **022/716-69-20**): Richly sheathed with tapestries and accented with the kind of art and accessories that would have made Louis XVI feel right at home, this restaurant attracts some of the wealthiest and most jaded clients in the world. Everything works smoothly, with nary a glitch, but you can only imagine how hard the staff labors to maintain its position as one of the best restaurants in Switzerland. See p. 315.
- **Le Béarn** (✆ **022/321-00-28**): It's the best restaurant in Geneva's business and financial district, and attracts a who's who of international financiers and their clients. The food is delicious—one of the best dishes, according to Le Béarn's

many fans, is the Provence-style roast lamb. See p. 320.

- **Chesa Grischuna** (Ⓒ **081/422-22-22**): This restaurant succeeds every evening at creating a genuine sense of unpretentious, old-fashioned warmth. Over the years it has hosted such showbiz and political types of yesterday as Winston Churchill, the Aga Khan, Truman Capote, and Audrey Hepburn. The food is hearty and nourishing—perfect for the cold-weather climate of Klosters. See p. 400.

- **Chesa Veglia** (Ⓒ **081/837-28-00**): This business is located in what's said to be the only authentic Engadine-style house—built in 1658—that remains in all of St. Moritz. It contains three different dining rooms, one of which is an informal pizzeria. The other two are rustically elegant hideaways, redolent with warmth and comfort, which cater to an international and very prosperous clientele. See p. 429.

14 The Best Websites for Switzerland

- **Switzerland Tourism** (www.myswitzerland.com): Click here to view photo galleries of Switzerland sights and for a list of upcoming events. You can also book reservations and purchase tourist passes through this helpful site.

- **ZentralSchweiz** (www.centralswitzerland.ch): For beautiful photos and the latest winter and summer "sports reports" throughout central Switzerland, check here.

- **Switzerland** (www.switzerland.com): For the latest news from Switzerland, check out this site's "News and Info Services" option.

- **Geneva—Welcome to Networld** (www.geneva.ch/tourism.htm): For a list of important links and general information for tourists and business travelers in Geneva, try this site.

- **About Switzerland/Austria for Visitors** (http://goswitzerland.about.com): This site offers general information about Switzerland, plus Swiss cams and area maps.

- **All Travel Switzerland** (www.alltravelswitzerland.com): For complete booking options throughout Switzerland, you can try this site, brought to you by the European Travel & Tourism Bureau.

2

Planning Your Trip to Switzerland

This chapter is devoted to the where, when, and how of your trip—the advance planning required to get it together and take it on the road. Browse through this section before you hit the road to ensure you've covered all the bases.

1 The Regions in Brief

The Swiss landscape has been shaped by glaciation. Glaciers hollowed out the valleys and led to the creation of a multitude of magnificent lakes, a large part of Switzerland's beautiful scenery.

The Swiss plateau, set between the Jura and Alps mountain chains and extending from Lake Geneva in the southwest to Lake Constance in the northeast, represents about 30% of the country's surface area. The country's main cities and industries are concentrated on this plateau, making Switzerland one of the world's most densely populated countries. Most of the Swiss live in this zone, with half the population based in the urban areas of Geneva, Lausanne, Basel, Bern, Olten, Aarau, Zurich, and Baden. The plateau is also the country's center of agricultural production.

Within its borders Switzerland has nearly every variety of landscape, vegetation, and climatic condition known in Europe. Only a few dozen miles, as the crow flies, separate the lowest point in Switzerland, the shores of Lake Maggiore (where palm trees thrive in a Mediterranean climate) from the highest, the Dufourspitze (where the climate is one of eternal snow and ice).

Of course, the Alps have become the main tourist attraction of Switzerland,

with about a hundred peaks above 12,000 feet (3,600m). Some 1,800 glaciers offer the sight of an awesome and sometimes-savage nature. The view south from the Jungfraujoch, the highest rail station in Europe, is one of windswept rock and ice, majestic and dramatic.

The Swiss Alps form the centerpiece of Europe's alpine range. They're broken by the great valleys of the Rhône in the canton of the Valais and the Rhine in the canton of the Graubünden, as well as by many lateral valleys. To the north, the alpine chain ends in the Bernese Alps (Finsteraarhorn) and to the south in the Valais Alps (the Monte Rosa range). To the east the Alps end at Piz Bernina. In the canton of Ticino, which on the map looks like a triangular section of northern Italy, Switzerland also possesses part of the southern face of the Alps as well.

Zurich Close to the northern border of Switzerland, Zurich is the country's largest city, spreading across 36 square miles (58 sq. km), with a population of 380,000. The fiscal and business center of the country, it was also the political capital until 1848, when that honor was transferred to Bern.

Switzerland & Liechtenstein

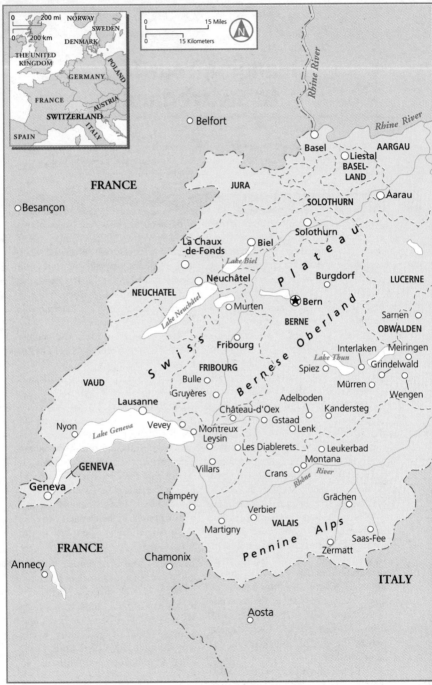

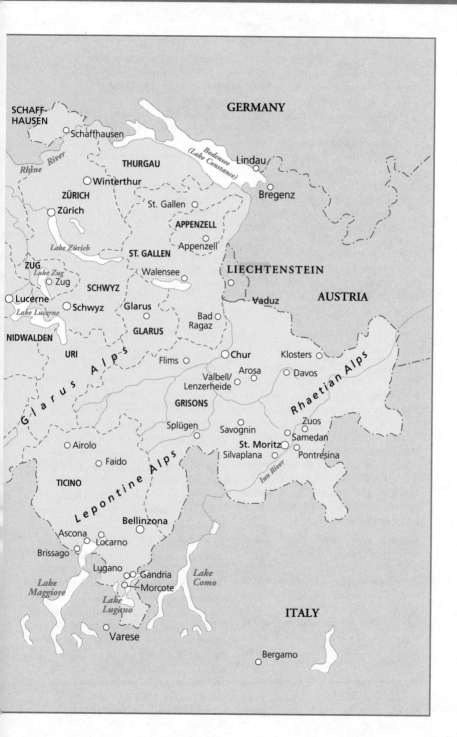

(Fun Fact **Did You Know?**

- More than 3.5% of the working population of Switzerland is employed in the country's controversial banking industry.
- As a financial center, Switzerland ranks in importance behind only New York, London, and Tokyo.
- Since the late 18th and early 19th centuries, there has been no foreign invasion of Swiss territory, despite the devastating conflagrations that surrounded it.
- Until the early 19th century, Switzerland was the most industrialized country in Europe.
- Famous for its neutrality, Switzerland once was equally known for providing mercenaries to fight in foreign armies. The practice was ended by the constitution of 1874, with the exception of the Vatican's Swiss papal guard, dating from 1505.
- In 1986, the Swiss electorate voted against membership in the United Nations, and continues to oppose joining.
- Switzerland drafts all able-bodied male citizens between the ages of 20 and 50 (55 for officers). These soldiers, who continue to live at home, form a reserve defense corps that can be called to active duty at any time.

The Bernese Oberland Switzerland's best-known alpine region is named after its largest city, Bern, the Swiss capital. Known for the beauty of its mountains, it includes many famous resorts, the largest of which is Interlaken, popular mainly in the summer. At its higher altitudes, where the snowfall is more consistent, you'll find such chic and elegant ski resorts as Gstaad, Grindelwald, Kandersteg, Mürren, and Wengen.

Northeastern Switzerland Relatively neglected by tourists, this region is separated from southern Germany and Austria by the waters of the Rhine and Lake Constance. Its highlights include St. Gallen, a lace-making center and the economic center of the region, certain sections of the Rhine valley, and the Rhine Falls, near Neuhausen.

Basel & the Jura In northwestern Switzerland, Basel, the capital of the region, is an ancient university town and trading center on the Rhine, set midway between French Alsace and the Jura canton in Switzerland. The Jura is a range of "folded" limestone ridges set between two great rivers, the Rhône and the Rhine.

The Valais This is the rugged valley of the upper Rhône, encompassing such geographic attractions as the Matterhorn and the Great St. Bernard Pass. Equally divided between French- and German-speaking residents, it's rich in alpine folklore. Its most frequented ski resort is Zermatt.

Lausanne & the Shores of Lake Geneva Called Lac Léman by the Swiss, Lake Geneva is the largest freshwater body in central Europe, embracing some 225 square miles (411 sq. km). It's partially fed by the alpine waters of the Rhône and is emptied by a continuation of the same river, which eventually pours into the Mediterranean. Lausanne, the cultural center of the region, is the second-largest city on Lake Geneva and the fifth largest in Switzerland.

Geneva   Geneva is distinctly different from the rest of Switzerland and culturally more attuned to France. Switzerland's second-largest city, it's built on the Rhône, at the lower end of Lake Geneva, and is bordered on three sides by French territory. A center of world banking and commerce, it's celebrated for its prosperity, elegance, and sophistication. Geneva is also the site of many world organizations, such as the Red Cross.

Lucerne & Central Switzerland
The heartland of Switzerland, this region takes in four different cantons: Lucerne, Uri, Unterwalden, and Schwyz, from which the country's name is derived. The region's only major city is Lucerne, a medieval town made famous as a resort in the 19th century. It sits at the northern edge of the lake that bears its name. Despite Switzerland's wealth of attractions, Lucerne is the Swiss city that most North Americans prefer to visit.

The Grisons & the Engadine   This area is the largest and most easterly of the cantons of Switzerland. It's also one of the least populated, taking in about 140 square miles (225 sq. km) of glaciers and legions of jagged, windswept mountain peaks. Its capital is Chur, the oldest town in Switzerland, but most visitors bypass it en route to the ski resorts of Arosa, Klosters, and Davos. The Engadine stretches for 60 miles (97km), from the Maloja Plateau to Finstermünz. The region's chief attraction is the glamorous winter resort of St. Moritz.

The Ticino   The Italian-speaking part of Switzerland, the Ticino is the most southerly, and therefore the warmest, of the country's regions. Not surprisingly, it's the object of the retirement dreams for many residents in the northern cantons. The region includes the major cities of Lugano and Locarno, which share, respectively, the lakes of Lugano and Maggiore with Italy. The Italian influence is most strongly felt in the region's relaxed tempo.

2 Visitor Information

SWITZERLAND TOURISM OFFICE   You can get the latest tourist information before leaving home from the nearest branch of the Swiss tourism office. In the United States, the center now has an office only at 608 Fifth Ave., New York, NY 10020 (© 212/757-5944). In Canada, it has an office at 926 The East Mall, Etobicoke, ON M9B 6K1 (© 416/695-2090). In Great Britain, contact the Swiss Centre, Swiss Court, New Coventry Street, London W1V 8EE (© 020/7734-1921). In Australia you have to contact the Embassy of Switzerland, 7 Melbourne Ave., Forrest (Canberra), ACT 2603 (© 02-6-273-3977).

3 Entry Requirements & Customs

ENTRY REQUIREMENTS
Every traveler entering Switzerland must have a valid passport, although it's not necessary for North Americans to have a visa if they don't stay longer than 3 continuous months. For information on permanent residence in Switzerland and work permits, contact the nearest Swiss consulate.

PASSPORT SAFETY   Safeguard your passport in an inconspicuous, inaccessible place, like a money belt. If you lose it, visit the nearest consulate of your native country as soon as possible for a replacement. Passport applications are downloadable from the Internet sites listed below.

FOR RESIDENTS OF THE UNITED STATES If you're applying for a first-time passport, you need to do it in person at one of 13 passport offices throughout the United States; a federal, state, or probate court; or a major post office (though not all post offices accept applications; call the number below to find the ones that do). You need to present a certified birth certificate as proof of citizenship, and it's wise to bring along your driver's license, state or military ID, and social security card as well. You also need two identical passport-sized photos (2x2 in.), taken at any corner photo shop (not one of the strip photos, however, from a photo-vending machine).

For people over 15, a passport is valid for 10 years and costs $60 ($45 plus a $15 handling fee); for those 15 and under, it's valid for 5 years and costs $40. If you're over 15 and have a valid passport that was issued within the past 12 years, you can renew it by mail and bypass the $15 handling fee. Allow plenty of time before your trip to apply; processing normally takes 3 weeks but can take longer during busy periods (especially spring). For general information, call the **National Passport Agency** (© 202/647-0518). To find your regional passport office, call the **National Passport Information Center** (© 900/225-5674; http://travel.state.gov).

FOR RESIDENTS OF CANADA You can pick up a passport application at one of 28 regional passport offices or most travel agencies. The passport is valid for 5 years and costs C$60. Children under 16 may be included on a parent's passport but need their own to travel unaccompanied. Applications, which must be accompanied by two identical passport-sized photographs and proof of Canadian citizenship, are available at travel agencies throughout Canada or from the central **Passport Office,** Department of Foreign Affairs and International Trade, Ottawa, ON K1A 0G3 (© 800/567-6868; www.dfait-maeci.gc.ca). Processing takes 5 to 10 days if you apply in person, or about 3 weeks by mail.

FOR RESIDENTS OF THE UNITED KINGDOM A passport is necessary to enter Switzerland. To pick up an application for a regular 10-year passport (the Visitor's Passport has been abolished), visit a passport office, major post office, or travel agency, or contact the **London Passport Office** at © 0990/210-410 or www.open.gov.uk. Passports are £21 for adults and £11 for children under 16.

FOR RESIDENTS OF IRELAND You can apply for a 10-year passport, costing IR£45, at the **Passport Office,** Setanta Centre, Molesworth Street, Dublin 2 (© 01/671-1633; www.irlgov.ie/iveagh/foreignaffairs/services). Those under age 18 and over 65 must apply for a IR£10 3-year passport. You can also apply at 1A South Mall, Cork (© 0214/272-525) or over the counter at most main post offices.

FOR RESIDENTS OF AUSTRALIA Apply at your local post office or passport office or search the government website at **www.dfat.gov.au/passports/**. Passports for adults are A$126 and for those under 18 A$63.

FOR RESIDENTS OF NEW ZEALAND You can pick up a passport application at any travel agency or Link Centre. For more information, contact the **Passport Office,** P.O. Box 805, Wellington (© 0800/225-050). Passports for adults are NZ$80 and for those under 16 NZ$40.

CUSTOMS

You can take personal effects into Switzerland, such as clothing, toilet articles, sports gear, photographic and amateur movie or video cameras (including film), musical instruments, and camping equipment. Medicine must be for your personal use only. You can also take 2 liters of alcohol (up to 15% proof) or 1 liter of more than 15% proof. You are also allowed 400 cigarettes, 100 cigars, or 500 grams of tobacco if you're flying in from outside Europe. Those entering from other European countries are allowed 200 cigarettes, 50 cigars, or 250 grams of tobacco.

IMPORT RESTRICTIONS

Returning U.S. citizens who have been away for 48 hours or more are allowed to bring back, once every 30 days, $400 worth of merchandise duty-free. You'll be charged a flat rate of 10% duty on the next $1,000 worth of purchases. Be sure to have your receipts handy. On gifts, the duty-free limit is $100. You cannot bring fresh foodstuffs into the United States; tinned foods, however, are allowed. For more information, contact the **U.S. Customs Service,** 1301 Constitution Ave. (P.O. Box 7407), Washington, DC 20044 (© **202/ 927-6724**), and request the free pamphlet "Know Before You Go." It's also available on the Internet at www. customs.ustreas.gov.

U.K. citizens returning from a non-EC country have a Customs allowance of: 200 cigarettes; 50 cigars; 250g of smoking tobacco; 2 liters of still table wine; 1 liter of spirits or strong liqueurs (over 22% volume); 2 liters of fortified wine, sparkling wine, or other liqueurs; 60cc (ml) perfume; 250cc (ml) of toilet water; and £145 worth of all other goods, including gifts and souvenirs. People under 17 cannot have the tobacco or alcohol allowance. For more information, contact **HM Customs & Excise,** Passenger Enquiry Point, 2nd Floor Wayfarer House, Great South West Road, Feltham, Middlesex TW14 8NP (© **020/8910-3744,** from outside the U.K. 44/20-8910-3744), or consult their website at www.hmce.gov.uk.

For a clear summary of Canadian rules, write for the booklet **"I Declare,"** issued by Revenue Canada, 2265 St. Laurent Blvd., Ottawa K1G 4KE (© **506/636-5064**). Canada allows residents a C$750 exemption, and you're allowed to bring back duty-free 200 cigarettes, 2.2 pounds of tobacco, 40 imperial ounces of liquor, and 50 cigars. In addition, you're allowed to mail gifts to Canada from abroad at the rate of C$60 a day, provided they're unsolicited and don't contain alcohol or tobacco (write on the package "Unsolicited gift, under $60 value"). All valuables should be declared on the Y-38 form before departure from Canada, including serial numbers of valuables you already own, such as expensive foreign cameras. *Note:* The $750 exemption can only be used after an absence of 7 days.

The duty-free allowance in Australia is A$400 or, for those under 18, A$200. Personal property mailed back from Switzerland should be marked "Australian goods returned" to avoid payment of duty. Upon returning to Australia, citizens can bring in 250 cigarettes or 250 grams of loose tobacco, and 1,125ml of alcohol. If you're returning with valuable goods you already own, such as foreign-made cameras, you should file form B263. A helpful brochure, available from Australian consulates or Customs offices, is "Know Before You Go." For more information, contact **Australian Customs Services,** GPO Box 8, Sydney, NSW 2001 (© **02/9213-2000**).

The duty-free allowance for New Zealand is NZ$700. Residents over 17 can bring in 200 cigarettes, or 50 cigars, or 250 grams of tobacco (or a mixture of all three if their combined weight doesn't exceed 250 grams); plus 4.5 liters of wine and beer or 1.125 liters of liquor. New Zealand currency does not carry import or export restrictions. Fill out a certificate of export, listing the valuables you are taking out of the country, to avoid paying duty upon return. Most questions are answered in a free pamphlet, "New Zealand Customs Guide for Travellers, Notice no. 4," available at

New Zealand consulates and Customs offices. For more information, contact **New Zealand Customs,** 50 Anzac Ave., P.O. Box 29, Auckland (© **09/ 359-6655**).

4 Money

The prices in Switzerland are often higher than those found in the United States and Canada. Nevertheless, this book will try to help you stretch your national currency. There are many good-value hotels and restaurants, but don't expect to find them in the expensive cities of Zurich and Geneva or in such chic resorts as St. Moritz and Arosa. If you're watching your budget, try to stay in small villages, such as Klosters, on the periphery of celebrated resorts.

The basic unit of Swiss currency is the Swiss franc (SF), which is made up of 100 centimes. Banknotes are issued in denominations of 10, 20, 50, 100, 500, and 1,000 francs, and coins are minted as 5, 10, 20, and 50 centimes, and 1, 2, and 5 francs.

If you need a check denominated in Swiss francs before your trip, say, to pay a deposit on a hotel room, you can contact **Ruesch International,** 700 11th St. NW, 4th floor, Washington, DC 20001-4507 (© **800/424-2923**; www.ruesch.com). Ruesch performs a wide variety of conversion-related services, usually for $3 per transaction. You can also inquire at a local bank.

ATMs   ATMs are linked to a national network that most likely includes your bank at home. **Cirrus** (© **800/424-7787**; www.mastercard. com) and **PLUS** (© **800/843-7587**; www.visa.com) are the two most popular networks; check the back of your ATM card to see which network your bank belongs to. Use the 800 numbers to locate ATMs in your destination.

If you're traveling abroad, ask your bank for a list of overseas ATMs. Be

sure to check the daily withdrawal limit before you depart, and ask whether you need a new personal ID number. Often your PIN must be a 4-digit number.

CREDIT CARDS   Credit cards are invaluable when traveling. They are a safe way to carry money and provide a convenient record of all your expenses. You can also withdraw cash advances from your credit cards at any bank (though you'll start paying hefty interest on the advance the moment you receive the cash, and you won't receive frequent-flyer miles on an airline credit card). At most banks, you don't even need to go to a teller; you can get a cash advance at the ATM if you know your PIN number. If you've forgotten your PIN number or didn't even know you had one, call the phone number on the back of your credit card and ask the bank to send it to you. It usually takes 5 to 7 business days, though some banks will provide the number over the phone if you tell them your mother's maiden name or pass some other security clearance.

TRAVELER'S CHECKS   Traveler's checks are something of an anachronism from the days before the ATM (automated teller machine) made cash accessible at any time. The only sound alternative to traveling with dangerously large amounts of cash, traveler's checks were as reliable as currency and could be replaced if lost or stolen.

These days, traveler's checks seem less necessary because most cities have 24-hour ATMs that allow travelers to withdraw small amounts of cash as needed—avoiding the risk of carrying

The Swiss Franc

For American Readers At this writing, $1= approximately 1.80 Swiss francs (or 1SF = approximately 55¢), and this was the rate of exchange used to calculate the dollar values given in this book.

For British Readers At this writing, £1 = approximately 2.50 Swiss francs (or 1SF = approximately 40p) and this was the rate of exchange used to calculate the pound values in the table below.

Regarding the Euro Despite the willingness of many countries within Europe to adopt the euro as their currency of choice, Switzerland, at press time, remained resolutely committed to maintaining the Swiss franc as their currency of choice. As a benchmark indicator, however, the rate of exchange between the euro and the Swiss franc, at this writing, was 1€ = 1.50SF. *Note:* Although the Swiss franc is relatively stable, international exchange rates fluctuate frequently, and this may not be the same when you travel to Switzerland. Therefore, please use this table only as a reflection of approximate, rather than current values. For the latest on exchange rates, you can go online at **www.x-rates.com**.

SF	US$	UK£	€	SF	US$	UK£	€
1	0.55	0.40	0.67	100	55.00	40.00	67.00
2	1.10	0.80	1.34	125	68.75	50.00	83.75
3	1.65	1.20	2.01	150	82.50	60.00	100.50
4	2.20	1.60	2.68	175	96.25	70.00	117.25
5	2.75	2.00	3.35	200	110.00	80.00	134.00
6	3.30	2.40	4.027	225	123.75	90.00	150.75
7	3.85	2.80	4.69	250	137.50	100.00	167.50
8	4.40	3.20	5.36	275	151.25	110.00	184.25
9	4.95	3.60	6.0	300	165.00	120.00	201.00
10	5.50	4.00	6.70	350	192.50	140.00	234.50
15	8.25	6.00	10.05	400	220.00	160.00	268.00
20	11.00	8.00	13.4	500	275.00	200.00	335.00
25	13.75	10.00	16.75	1000	550.00	400.00	670.00
50	27.50	20.00	33.50				

a fortune around an unfamiliar environment. Many banks, however, impose a fee every time a card is used at an ATM in a different city or bank. If you're withdrawing money every day, you might be better off with traveler's checks—provided that you don't mind showing identification every time you want to cash a check.

You can get traveler's checks at almost any bank. American Express offers denominations of $10, $20, $50, $100, $500, and $1,000. You'll pay a service charge ranging from 1% to 4%. You can also obtain traveler's checks issued in Swiss francs, if you think the exchange rate is temporarily in your favor. Get **American Express** traveler's checks over the phone by calling © **800/221-7282;** www.american express.com. By using this number, Amex gold and platinum cardholders are exempt from the 1% fee. AAA members can obtain checks without a fee at most AAA offices.

Visa offers traveler's checks at Citibank locations nationwide, as well as several other banks. The service charge ranges between 1.5% and 2%; checks come in denominations of $20, $50, $100, $500, and $1,000. **MasterCard** also offers traveler's checks. Call ⑦ **800/223-9920** for a location near you.

THEFT Almost every credit card company has an emergency 800 number that you can call if your wallet or purse is stolen. They may be able to wire you a cash advance off your credit card immediately, and in many places, they can deliver an emergency credit card in a day or two. You can't make toll-free calls without using a U.S.-based carrier, but most companies do have a number for you to dial collect. Call your credit card company to

find out in advance what it is. Dial Citicorp Visa's emergency number collect at ⑦ **800/336-8472.** American Express cardholders and traveler's check holders should call collect ⑦ **800/233-5439** for all money emergencies. MasterCard holders should call collect ⑦ **800/307-7309.**

If you opt to carry traveler's checks, be sure to keep a record of their serial numbers, separately from the checks, so you're ensured a refund in just such an emergency.

Odds are that if your wallet is gone, the police won't be able to recover it for you. However, after you realize that it's gone and you cancel your credit cards, it is still worth informing them. Your credit card company or insurer may require a police report number.

5 When to Go

THE WEATHER

The temperature range is about the same as in the northern United States, but without the extremes of hot and cold. Summer temperatures seldom rise above 80°F in the cities, and humidity is low. Because of clear air and lack of wind in the high alpine regions, sunbathing is sometimes possible even in winter. In southern Switzerland, the temperature remains mild year-round, allowing subtropical vegetation to grow.

June is the ideal month for a tour of Switzerland, followed by either September or October, when the mountain passes are still open. During summer, the country is usually overrun with tourist traffic.

HOLIDAYS

The legal holidays in Switzerland are New Year's (Jan 1–2), Good Friday, Easter Monday, Ascension Day, Whit Monday, Bundesfeier (the Swiss "Fourth of July;" Aug 1), and Christmas (Dec 25–26).

Low season airfares are usually offered from November 1 to December 14 and from December 25 to March 31. Fares are slightly higher during shoulder season (during Apr and May, and from Sept 16 to the end of Oct). High-season fares apply the rest of the year (from June 1 to Sept 15), presumably when Switzerland and its landscapes are at their most hospitable and most beautiful.

Keep in mind, it's most expensive to visit Swiss ski resorts in winter, and slightly less so during the rest of the year. Conversely, it's cheaper to visit lakeside towns and the Ticino in winter. Cities such as Geneva, Zurich, and Bern don't depend on tourism as a major source of capital, so prices in these cities tend to remain the same all year.

SWITZERLAND CALENDAR OF EVENTS

The festivals mentioned below, unless otherwise specified, fall on different dates every

Switzerland's Average Temperatures (°F)

		Jan	Feb	Mar	Apr	May	June	July	Aug	Sept	Oct	Nov	Dec
Geneva	High	40	43	50	59	67	74	77	76	70	58	47	40
	Low	29	31	36	41	49	56	59	58	54	45	38	32
Lugano	High	43	49	56	63	70	77	81	81	74	61	52	45
	Low	29	31	38	45	50	58	61	59	56	47	38	32
Zermatt	High	26	26	27	36	46	52	58	53	52	38	33	26
	Low	20	19	19	28	36	42	48	44	42	32	27	20
Zurich	High	36	41	50	59	67	74	77	76	68	58	45	38
	Low	27	29	34	40	47	54	58	56	52	43	36	29

year. Inquire at the Swiss National Tourist Office or local tourist offices for an updated calendar. See "The Best Festivals" in chapter 1 for more information.

January

Vogel Gryff Festival (The Feast of the Griffin), Basel. The "Wild Man of the Woods" appears on a boat, followed by a mummers' parade. For more information call ℂ 061/268-68-68. Mid-January.

February

Basler Fasnacht, Basel. Called "the wildest of carnivals," with a parade of "cliques" (clubs and associations). Call ℂ 061/268-68-68 for more information. First Monday after Ash Wednesday.

March

Hornussen ("Meeting on the Snow"), Maloja. A traditional sport of rural Switzerland. For information call ℂ 081/824-31-88. For a description of the sport, see box below under "Outdoor Adventures." Mid-March.

April

Primavera Concertistica Music Festival, Locarno. Beginning of a series of music concerts that lasts through October. For information call ℂ 091/921-46-64. Mid-April.

Sechseläuten ("Six O'Clock Chimes"), Zurich. Members of all the guilds dress in costumes and celebrate the arrival of spring, which is climaxed by the burning of Böögg, a straw figure symbolizing winter. There are also children's parades. The **Zurich Tourist Office** (ℂ 01/215-40-00) shows the parade route on a map. (Böögg is burned at 6pm on Sechseläutenplatz, near Belevueplatz.) Third Monday of April.

May

Corpus Christi. Solemn processions in the Roman Catholic regions and towns of Switzerland. End of May.

June

Fête à Lausanne, Lausanne. Beginning of an international festival, showcasing weeks of music and ballet. For information, call ℂ 021/613-73-73. Mid-June.

July

Montreux International Jazz Festival, Montreux. More than jazz, this festival features everything from reggae bands to African tribal chanters. Monster dance-fests also break out nightly. The festival concludes with a 12-hour marathon of world music. For more information, write to the **Montreux Jazz Festival,** Case Postale Box 97, CH-1820 Montreux, or call ℂ 021/

Expo 02

Not officially called a "world's fair," the **Expo 02** on the Swiss calendar will actually be close to it. With 4,000 shows and 12,000 performances, the expo will take place from May 15 through October 20, 2002, in three lake towns: Murten, Biel, Neuchatel, and Yverdon-les-Bains. The whole event will cost Switzerland $800 million. For more information contact Switzerland Tourism, 608 Fifth Avenue, New York, NY (✆ 212/757-5944; www.expo.02-ch).

962-84-84. Lasts 2½ weeks and is held in the beginning of July.

William Tell Festival Play, Interlaken. Performances of the famous play by Schiller. Call ✆ 033/822-21-21 for more information. End of July through August.

August

Fêtes de Genève, Geneva. Highlights are flower parades, fireworks, and live music all over the city. Call ✆ 022/909-70-00 for more information. Early August.

International Festival of Music, Lucerne. Concerts, theater, art exhibitions, and street musicians. Call ✆ 041/227-17-17 for more information. August 19 through September 16.

September

Fribourg Braderie, Fribourg. A popular festival and onion market with a citywide sidewalk sale and folk entertainment. Call ✆ 026/321-31-75 for more information. Late September.

October

Wine Growers' Festival, Lugano. A parade and other festivities mark harvest time. Little girls throw flowers from blossom-covered floats and oxen pull festooned wagons in a colorful procession. For information call ✆ 091/921-46-64. October 3 through 5.

Aelplerchilbi, Kerns and other villages of the Unterwalden Canton. Dairymen and pasture owners join villagers in a traditional festival to mark the end of an alpine summer. For more information call the **Saren Tourismus,** Hofstrasse 2 (✆ 041/666-50-40). Late October or the beginning of November.

November

Zibelemärit, Bern. The famous "onion market" fair. Call ✆ 031/311-66-11 for more information. Mid-November.

December

Christmas Festivities. Ancient St. Nicholas parades and traditional markets are staged throughout the country to mark the beginning of Christmas observances, with the major one at Fribourg. Mid-December.

L'Escalade, Geneva. A festival commemorating the failure of the duke of Savoy's armies to take Geneva by surprise on the night of December 11 and 12, 1602. Brigades on horseback in period costumes, country markets, and folk music are interspersed with Rabelaisian banquets, fife-and-drum parades, and torch-lit marches. Geneva's Old Town provides the best vantage point. Call ✆ 022/909-70-00 for more information. Three days and nights (nonstop) in mid-December.

6 Outdoor Adventures

Chapters 3 through 15 of this book are full of specific details on local ski trails, hiking trails, boating, fishing, and more. But in addition, we've assembled the following roundup of sports highlights—some of the very best ways to get outdoors and enjoy Switzerland's magnificent scenery. Most of these activities can be enjoyed independently, but for those of you who like to have someone else sweat the details, we've also listed some of the region's best outfitters.

BALLOONING Balloon rides over Switzerland are even more spectacular than those in France. Contact **Buddy Bombard European Balloon Adventures,** 333 Pershing Way, W. Palm Beach, FL 33401 (© **800/862-8537** or 561/837-6610; fax 561/837-6623; www.bombardsociety.com).

BIKING Biking is a great way to see the Swiss countryside. You can rent a bike for a small fee at one railroad station and return it at another. In addition, bikes can be transported on passenger trains for a nominal fee. You should reserve your bike a day or so in advance at the station from which you plan to start.

Swiss Touring Club (TCS) maintains 10 cycling centers that rent bicycles and offer brochures and maps of nearby bike routes. The club will direct you along the least-congested routes, taking you through villages and past castles and manor houses that you would not otherwise discover. Even in remote areas, you can usually find someone who speaks English to help you if you have a problem or get lost. The head office of the touring club is in a suburb of Geneva at 21, rue Fontenette, 1127 Carouge (© **022/ 342-2233;** fax 022/301-3711; www. tcs.ch).

The most elegant bike tours in Switzerland are offered by **Butterfield & Robinson,** 70 Bond St., Toronto, Ontario, Canada M5B 1X3 (© **800/ 678-1147** or 416/864-0541; www. butterfield.com). Their best route is from Montreux to Gstaad. Every ride is set against the backdrop of the Swiss Alps, from the shores of Lake Geneva to the summit of Diablerets Glacier. A classic 7-day trip, averaging 20 to 30 miles (32–48km) a day in rolling terrain, costs $4,475 per person, with a single supplement of $175. Tours are conducted June through September.

CURLING & SKATING Curling is currently a hot team sport in Switzerland, particularly popular in Davos, Villars, Gstaad, and Zermatt. Curling, of course, is a game played by sliding a large, smooth stone along the ice at a mark (called the tee) 38 yards (35m) away.

Ice skating is one of the leading winter sports of Switzerland, and nearly all major resorts have natural ice rinks. Also, there are dozens of artificial ones, of which Davos has the best.

FISHING In this relatively small country there are at least 20,000 miles (32,000km) of rivers and streams, as well as 521 square miles (839 sq. km) of lakes. These waters are situated at heights between 700 and 6,550 feet (210 and 1,965m) above sea level, and vary in configuration and fauna as much as in altitude. Such a wide choice of conditions certainly puts anglers on their mettle, for they're presented with a fascinating range of challenges. For those who know how to adapt themselves, there is excellent sport in store. Angling techniques and bait must be suited to the particular water one happens to be fishing. With few exceptions, fly-fishing, spinning, and ground fishing, with natural or artificial bait, are permitted in most waters. Trout can be found in most

Fun Fact **Hornussen, Schwingen & Waffenlaufen**

For the majority of the Swiss, the sport of choice is walking, followed by swimming, and only then, skiing. The Swiss are fond of some uniquely Swiss sports as well: "hornussen," "schwingen," and "waffen-laufen." And while these sports may not be seen in the Olympics, they do call for a certain amount of athletic prowess.

One of Switzerland's greatest writers, Jeremias Gotthelf, praised "hornuss" in 1840. He wrote, "There is not any game which calls for as much strength, agility, and coordination between hand, foot, and eye as 'Hornuss.'" The sport was first practiced in the 17th century and stems from war games that had the objective of avoiding projectiles sent flying in the air. Today, hornuss can be most accurately described as a cross between lacrosse and cricket. The whistling sound the disk makes as it flies through the air is similar to the sound of a hornet. The German word for hornet is hornuss, hence the name of the game. The opposing team must try to stop the flying disk as quickly as possible with heavy wooden bats.

In the wrestling game, "schwingen," strength counts above all. Two wrestlers or "schwingers" face each other in the middle of a pit with the goal of grabbing the adversary's oversized shorts, to unbalance him, and bringing both his shoulders down to touch the ground. This sport of attack and defense was once a training technique for soldiers preparing for war.

One sport that exists exclusively in Switzerland is called "waffen-laufen." Runners in military uniform must carry a mountain rucksack to which a rifle is fixed. Together, the rucksack and rifle must not weigh less than 16.5 pounds (7.5km). Thus equipped, thousands of Swiss race along courses ranging from 11 to 26 miles (28–26km) each year.

waters up to altitudes of 6,000 feet (1,800m), and lake trout have been known to weigh up to 22 pounds (10kg). You need a license to fish, but they're easily acquired through municipal authorities, beginning at 50SF ($27.50) per day. Regulations vary from place to place, so to be sure you're legal, inquire at a hotel or local tourist office.

For a complete overview, including places where fishing licenses may be obtained, contact **Schweizerischer Fischereikalender** (Swiss Fishing Calendar), Alte Landstrasse 19, 8596 Scherzingen, Switzerland (© **0041/ 72-75-65-75**).

GOLF There are more than 30 golf courses in Switzerland, 24 of them with 18 holes. Not a lot for a whole country, you may think, but they're located so strategically that, wherever you happen to be in Switzerland, you'll always find one nearby. As regards the vertical—well, there is golfing at a wide range of altitudes: The lowest course is in Ascona, which lies a mere 700 feet (210m) above sea level; among the highest are St. Moritz, at 5,640 feet (1,692m), and Riederalp, at 6,400 feet (1,920m). All the local clubs cater to visitors, who, incidentally, have the advantage of being able to play on weekdays while the locals are busy earning their daily bread. If you left your clubs at home, a set can be rented locally. Should you want to improve your swing, "pros" are available, too.

For more information, contact the **Swiss Golf Association,** 19, place de la Croix-Blanche, CH-1066, Epalinges VD, Switzerland (© **021/784-35-31;** www.asg.ch).

Some of the top courses include **Golf Club Davos** at Davos Dorf (© 081/4165634); **Golf Club de Genève,** Route de la Capite 70, Cologny (© 022/7357540); **Golf Club de Verbier,** Verbier (© 079/4128648); and **Golf Club Interlaken-Unterseen** at Interlaken (© 036/226022).

HIKING With 30,000 miles (48,000km) of well-marked and well-maintained walking paths, Switzerland is a Valhalla for hikers. The paths lead through alpine valleys, over lowlands, up hills to meadows, and into the heart of the Alps. Whether you choose a gentle walk or a rigorous trek, you're sure to see miles and miles of unspoiled beauty.

Many hotels offer walking or hiking excursions, with a serious hiking tour possibly entailing 4 to 7 hours of hiking each day.

Topographic maps, hiking maps, and books can be ordered from such outlets as Amazon.com and various bookstores. These include *Walking Switzerland—The Swiss Way,* which describes numerous hikes and a selection of inn-to-inn tours in the mountain areas. Also of interest is *100 Hikes in the Alps,* containing an interesting section on Switzerland. *Walking Easy in the Swiss Alps* is a 192-page book featuring day walks in six alpine villages, including Zermatt, Saas-Fee, Champex, Kandersteg, Lauterbrunnen, and Samedan/St. Moritz.

HIKING TOURS A specialist in walking and hiking tours is **Mountain Travel—Sobek,** 6420 Fairmount Ave., El Cerrito, CA 94530-3606 (© **800/MTSOBEK** or 510/527-7710; www.mtsobek.com). You can wander with this adventure company across the full landscape of Switzerland, from alpine mountains of the Bernese Oberland to lakeside vistas in Mediterranean-like Ticino. Most nights are spent in old-fashioned hotels or hikers' lodges, and at least 1 night is in an alpine refuge. Hikes are ranked as easy, moderate, or strenuous; one of the most challenging tours, the "Mount Blanc Circuit," is a 13-day hike that covers parts of Switzerland along with areas of Italy and France. The company will provide complete details about all tours.

HORSEBACK RIDING Both St. Moritz and Arosa are good places for horseback riding. Switzerland has 230 riding centers that will rent horses. The only riding stable in St. Moritz, but one of the country's finest, is **Reithalle,** via Ludains 3 (© **081/833-5733**), a 10-minute walk from town center. Rides are conducted either in the rink or in the nearby forests. For more information, refer to St. Moritz in chapter 13. Another large concentration of top riding horses is in and around Arosa at **Fuhrhalterei,** Wierhof (© **081/377-4196**). Rain or snow, these horses take visitors for scenic rides year-round. For more information, refer to Arosa in chapter 12.

MOUNTAINEERING Recognizing the allures (and the very real dangers) of climbing up the rocky crags that dot the surface of Switzerland, the 86,000-member Swiss Alpine Club (SAC), founded in 1863, promotes mountaineering and ski tours in the high Alps. Although its primary function is to organize alpine rescue services, it also lobbies politically to protect the alpine ecology. Working closely with equivalent associations in Austria, Germany, France, and Italy, the club has built mountain huts at strategic spots throughout the country, often hauling in building supplies by helicopter during the short summer season when construction is possible. The huts are modest, with bunk rooms sleeping 10 to 20 people. The average rate for a night's lodging (without food) for members of the club is from 25SF to 35SF ($13.75–$19.25) per person per night. You can write the club and reserve space.

Applicants for membership in the club must be at least 10 years of age and should mail their applications, along with a passport-size photo and a check covering membership fees, to whatever branch of the club interests them the most. (Membership in any regional club grants the right to discounted accommodations at huts throughout the country). To learn of branch offices, contact the organization's headquarters in Bern: **The Swiss Alpine Club,** Mombionstrasse 61, P.O. Box 3000, Bern, Switzerland 23 (© **031/370-18-18;** www.sac-cas.ch). If you're looking for a particularly active regional branch, consider joining the group in Zermatt. Their address is the Swiss Alpine Club, Sektion Zermatt, c/o Herr Kreiger, Haus Golomit, CH-3920 Zermatt, Switzerland (© **027/967-26-10**). Membership fees range from 75SF to 125SF ($41.25–$68.75), depending on the individual branch you join. Checks should be drawn on a Swiss bank (contact Ruesch International; see "Money," earlier in this chapter). Membership includes a subscription to the organization's German- or French-language magazine, *Die Alpen,* and the above-mentioned discounted accommodations at each of the mountain shelters maintained by the club.

The organization is affiliated with mountain-climbing schools throughout the country, including branches in Andermaer, Champéry, Crans, Davos, Les Diablerets, Fiesch, La Fouly, Glarus, Grindelwald, Kandersteg, Klosters, Meiringen, Pontresina, Riederalp, Saas-Fee, Saas-Grund, Schwende, Täsch, Zermatt, and Zinal. Guides that are accredited by the Swiss Alpine Club are available at many other resorts as well, and usually remain in close contact with the staffs at the local tourist offices.

SKIING Skiing in Switzerland, a tradition that goes back 2 centuries, is big business—an estimated 40% of the tourist dollar is spent on it. There are more than 1,700 mountain railways and ski lifts, and ski schools, ski instructors, and the best ski equipment in the world are available throughout the country.

Switzerland, which faces heavy competition from Austria (for a complete guide to resorts, see *Frommer's Austria*), has been called Europe's winter playground. What were once simple alpine farming villages have been transformed into bustling ski resorts, and there are more than 200 throughout the country. Nearly all of them have ski-rental shops.

All the cantons have skiing centers, most of which are in the Bernese Oberland, the Grisons, and the Valais. The ideal ski season is from January to late March. At the very highest resorts the season begins around mid-December. Even at some of the resorts at lower elevation, there is a ski season that begins before Christmas if there are adequate weather conditions and snow is adequate. February is the peak month, in which reservations are most difficult to come by. Skiing in some areas of the country continues until late April or, in other areas such as Zermatt, throughout the summer around the Klein Matterhorn.

Most slopes are nothing short of spectacular in Switzerland, as are the facilities, which cater to every type of skier from the beginner to the Olympic champion.

> **Tips   Ski Rentals**
>
> If you're flying Swissair, you can reserve your ski equipment in advance.

Europeans have always sought out family-oriented villages for inexpensive ski vacations, whereas Americans have traditionally preferred the more famous meccas such as St. Moritz and Gstaad. Happily, that is changing now, and many Americans (and Canadians) are choosing ski packages in the smaller alpine villages.

At the tourist office of most resorts, ask for an area map depicting the various slopes. These maps also grade the ski trails for difficulty. Be sure to familiarize yourself with the resort's signs before hitting the slopes. Obviously, avalanche zones are particularly important to learn.

At more than 50 resorts in Switzerland, the Swiss Rent-a-Ski program prevails. This service allows you to rent skis (either downhill or cross-country), poles, and boots on a weekly basis.

Founded in 1863, the **Swiss Alpine Club** promotes ski tours and mountaineering at lofty alpine altitudes. For more details about membership, see "Mountaineering" above.

Swiss Ski School is the most famous such institution in Europe. Federally run, it provides on-site instruction for beginners as well as advanced skiers. The majority of instructors speak English. Most of these ski schools—found at all major resorts—reduce their charges for five half-day classes. However, all-day classes are usually recommended.

Warning: Always carry plenty of sunscreen, even in winter. The reflection of sunlight off the snow is intense.

Summer skiing, or glacier skiing, takes place on glaciers that retain their snow throughout July and August, and ski schools and lifts are open all summer. Locals say that glacier skiing is best before lunch, especially the early-morning hours. The best glacier ski resorts are Zermatt, St. Moritz, Engelberg, Saas-Fee, Gstaad, and Pontresina.

Experienced skiers may wish to take a popular spring ski tour, the Haute Route, which crosses the French Alps into Switzerland; it's a week-long tour that is usually offered between March and May. Led by a professional guide, skiers stop overnight and for noon rests at cabins maintained by the Swiss Alpine Club (see "Mountaineering," above, for more information on this club).

Cross-country skiing, or *langlauf,* is the fastest-growing sport in Europe, especially at St. Moritz, Pontresina, and Montana. You go at your own speed and are not at the whim of slope conditions. There are no age limits nor charges for use of the well-marked cross-country trails.

From December 18 to March 31 you can get information on conditions in major Swiss ski areas by linking up with Switzerland Tourism Office's **snow report** at **www.switzerland tourism.com**. A phone contact for this data is no longer available.

The best resort for families is **Arosa** (see chapter 12). It is very family oriented and offers runs suitable for every level of skier, especially beginners. Most of the runs, however, are intermediate.

Expert skiers head for the resort of **Zermatt** (see chapter 8). In just minutes skiers can be more than 12,000 feet (3,600m) up on the Klein Matterhorn. Zermatt claims that it can guarantee a skier a vertical drop of some 7,200 feet (2,700m) regardless of the snowfall.

Beginning skiers, often those with families, find the resort of **Grindelwald**

Spa Vacations

Switzerland has 22 resorts with natural curative springs. Most of these spas, which have been approved by the Association of Swiss Health Spas and the Swiss Society of Balneology and Bioclimatology, include a medical examination, along with thermal baths and excursions, in their package plans for visitors. Many of them are open all year. All the spas offer various treatments, along with Turkish baths, mud baths, whirlpools, exercise/weight-loss programs, anti-stress programs, massages, and diets. You can request information from **Switzerland Tourism,** Tours Dept., 608 Fifth Ave., New York, NY 10020 (© **212/757-5944**). You can also phone **Switzerland Vacations** for details (© **800/688-7947**). For very specific data about individual spas, phone **Great Spas of the World** (© **800/772-8463;** www.greatspas.com).

For a spa vacation in Switzerland, one resort towers over all the rest— chic **St. Moritz** in the Engadine. Its thermal springs were known 3,000 years ago. St. Moritz-Bad was the original spa resort lying at the base of the lake, although modern housing has spoiled much of its former character. For more details, refer to "Spas" under St. Moritz in chapter 13.

(see chapter 7) ideal, the best base for skiing the Jungfrau area. It offers cable cars, lifts, funicular railways, and more than 100 miles (160km) of downhill runs.

A great center for intermediates is the resort of **Davos** (see chapter 12) along with its twin resort of **Klosters.** The ski terrain at Davos extends for some 22 miles (35km) in a relatively sheltered valley floor. Of course, these resorts have peaks for the more daring expert skier but offer miles of easy terrain for the intermediate as well.

The chic resort of **St. Moritz** in the Engadine (see chapter 13) has more nightlife possibilities than any resort in Switzerland. All the major ski resorts have an active après-ski life, but St. Moritz offers more diversity, from pubbing to high casino action.

In a virtual ski valley, **Verbier** (see chapter 8) is ideal for early or late-season skiing. Its upper ski area, which culminates at Mont-Fort at 10,850 feet (3,255m), is filled with a widely varied set of pistes. The snow falls early and lingers late into the spring.

FOR THE NONSKIER   The number of nonskiers at ski resorts is growing. It's estimated that at such fashionable resorts as Gstaad, Pontresina, Arosa, and Davos, one out of two guests is a nonskier. Most resorts offer a host of other activities, such as sunbathing on mountain terraces, day hikes in the forest, sleigh rides, sightseeing excursions, and of course, partying in the local bars and clubs. So if some of your family members ski and others don't, everyone will still be happy and entertained.

SNOWBOARDING   All the resorts mentioned under skiing offer snowboarding. The best centers are Celerina, Grindelwald, Gstaad, Kandersteg, St. Moritz, Wengen, and Zermatt. However, the top snowboard resort of Europe is Davos, which offers ideal slope conditions, snowboard schools, and a snowboard hotel. The resort also hosts national and international snowboarding events. Snowboarders will find a wide range of equipment to hire in all the resorts mentioned, with the largest concentration of sports shops in Davos.

OUTFITTERS

Be it rafting, canoeing, sea kayaking, sailing, biking, hiking, paragliding, or horse-and-wagon trips, **Eurotrek,**

Vulkanstrasse 116, CH-8048 Zurich (© **01/434-33-66;** www.eurotrek.ch), has a tour for you. All ages, tastes, and levels of fitness participate in these tours, from absolute beginners to experienced athletes. The outfit uses skilled travel guides, instructors, skippers, and coach drivers. Rafting adventures, for example, are arranged in the Bernese Oberland or on the Lütschine, the wild river at the foot of the Eiger and Jungfrau. Sailing trips are arranged on both Lake Thun and Lake Maggiore, and horse-and-wagon treks explore both the Emmental and the Jura in covered wagons. You can bungee jump in the alpine regions around Davos, or book a 3-day bike tour through the Ticino.

Some of the most dramatic cycling adventures are offered by **Adventure Quest,** 482 Congress St., Suite 101, Portland, ME 04101 (© **800/643-5630** or 207/871-1684). As you bike along you're treated to panoramic vistas of deep forests, snowcapped peaks, and blue lakes.

Biking, walking, and hiking tours are also offered by **Europeds,** 761 Lighthouse Ave., Monterey, CA 93940 (© **800/321-9552**). One of their most thrilling tours is in the Bernese Oberland, averaging some 10 miles (16km) per day.

Walking the World, P.O. Box 1186, Fort Collins, CO 80522 (© **800/340-9255;** 970/498-0500; www.walkingtheworld.com), offers 11-day hiking trips through Switzerland, averaging 6 to 10 miles (10–16km) daily at medium to high elevations.

7 Health & Insurance

STAYING HEALTHY
Medical care and health facilities in Switzerland are among the best in the world. As a result, no endemic contagious diseases exist. Swiss authorities, however, require immunization against contagious diseases if you have been in an infected area during the 14-day period immediately preceding your arrival in Switzerland. Take along an adequate supply of any prescription drugs that you'll need, as well as a written prescription that uses the generic name—rather than the brand name—of the drugs (in general, French and German, not U.S., drugs are available in Switzerland). You may want to include some motion-sickness medicine as well. Be sure to carry your vital medicines and drugs in your carry-on luggage, in case your checked luggage is lost.

WHAT TO DO IF YOU GET SICK AWAY FROM HOME
It can be hard to find a doctor you can trust when you're in an unfamiliar place. Try to take proper precautions the week before you depart, to avoid falling ill while you're away from home. Amid the last-minute frenzy that often precedes a vacation break, make an extra effort to eat and sleep well—especially if you feel an illness coming on.

If you worry about getting sick away from home, you may want to consider medical travel insurance (see the section on travel insurance below). In most cases, however, your existing health plan will provide all the coverage you need. Be sure to carry your identification card in your wallet.

If you suffer from a chronic illness, consult your doctor before your departure. For conditions like epilepsy, diabetes, or heart problems, wear a **Medic Alert Identification Tag** (© **800/825-3785;** www.medicalert.org), which will immediately alert doctors to your condition and give them access to your records through Medic Alert's 24-hour hotline. Membership is $35, plus a $15 annual fee.

If you wear contact lenses, pack an extra pair in case you lose one.

Contact the **International Association for Medical Assistance to Travelers** (IAMAT) (℗ **716/754-4883** or 519/836-0102; www.sentex.net/~iamat). This organization offers tips on travel and health concerns in the countries you'll be visiting, and lists many local English-speaking doctors. When you're abroad, any local consulate can provide a list of area doctors who speak English. If you do get sick, you may want to ask the concierge at your hotel to recommend a local doctor—even his or her own. This will probably yield a better recommendation than any 800 number would. If you can't find a doctor who can help you right away, try the emergency room at the local hospital. Many emergency rooms have walk-in clinics for emergency cases that are not life threatening. You may not get immediate attention, but you won't pay the high price of an emergency room visit.

INSURANCE

There are three kinds of travel insurance: trip cancellation, medical, and lost luggage coverage. **Trip cancellation insurance** is a good idea if you have paid a large portion of your vacation expenses up front. The other two types of insurance, however, don't make sense for most travelers. Rule number one: Check your existing policies before you buy any additional coverage.

Your existing health insurance should cover you if you get sick while on vacation (though if you belong to an HMO, you should check to see whether you are fully covered when away from home). If you need hospital treatment, most health insurance plans and HMOs will cover out-of-country hospital visits and procedures, at least to some extent. However, most make you pay the bills up front at the time of care, and you'll get a refund

after you've returned and filed all the paperwork. Members of **Blue Cross/ Blue Shield** can now use their cards at select hospitals in most major cities worldwide (℗ **800/810-BLUE** or www.bluecares.com for a list of hospitals). For independent travel health-insurance providers, see below. Your homeowner's insurance should cover stolen luggage.

The differences between travel assistance and insurance are often blurred, but in general the former offers on-the-spot assistance and 24-hour hot lines (mostly oriented toward medical problems), while the latter reimburses you for travel problems (medical, travel, or otherwise) after you have filed the paperwork. The coverage you should consider will depend on how much protection is already contained in your existing health insurance or other policies. Some credit and charge card companies may insure you against travel accidents if you buy plane, train, or bus tickets with their cards. Before purchasing additional insurance, read over your policies and agreements carefully. Call your insurers or credit/charge card companies if you have any questions.

Some credit cards (American Express and certain gold and platinum Visa and MasterCards, for example) offer automatic flight insurance against death or dismemberment in case of an airplane crash.

If you do require additional insurance, try one of the companies listed below. But don't pay for more than you need. For example, if you need only trip cancellation insurance, don't purchase coverage for lost or stolen property. Trip cancellation insurance costs approximately 6% to 8% of the total value of your vacation.

Among the reputable issuers of travel insurance are:

Access America, 6600 W. Broad St., Richmond, VA 23230 (℗ 800/284-8300; www.accessamerica.com);

Travel Guard International, 1145 Clark St., Stevens Point, WI 54481 (© 800/826-1300); **Travel Insured International, Inc.,** P.O. Box 280568, East Hartford, CT 06128 (© 800/243-3174; www.travel insured.com); **Columbus Direct,** 279 High St., Croydon CR0 1QH (© 020/7375-0011 in London; www. columbusdirect.net); **International SOS Assistance,** P.O. Box 11568, Philadelphia PA 11916 (© 800/523-8930 or 215/245-4707), strictly an assistance company; and **Travelex Insurance Services,** P.O. Box 9408, Garden City, NY 11530-9408 (© 800/228-9792; www.travelex-insurance.com).

Medicare only covers U.S. citizens traveling in Mexico and Canada. For Blue Cross/Blue Shield coverage abroad, see "Insurance" above. Companies specializing in accident and medical care include:

MEDEX International, P.O. Box 5375, Timonium, MD 21094-5375 (© 888/MEDEX-00 or 410/453-6300; fax 410/453-6301; www.medex assist.com); and **Travel Assistance International** (Worldwide Assistance Services, Inc.), 9200 Keystone Crossing, Suite 300, Indianapolis, IN 46240 (© 800/821-2828 or 202/331-1596; fax 202/828-5896; www. specialtyrisk.com).

For information on **car renter's insurance,** see "By Car" under "Getting Around," later in this chapter.

8 Tips for Travelers with Special Needs

TIPS FOR TRAVELERS WITH DISABILITIES

A few helpful tips:

- A fact sheet and special hotel guide for persons with disabilities are available from the Swiss National Tourist Office.
- On Swiss trains, wheelchair passengers travel in a special section of the passenger car. Certain trains cannot accommodate them there, in which case they travel in a specified area of the luggage car.
- Hertz Rent-a-Car offers minibuses accessible to wheelchair passengers. Arrangements should be made well in advance with **Hertz AG,** Morgartenstrasse 5, Zurich (© 01/242-8484).
- A car-rental company for wheelchair-bound drivers is **Schweizer Paraplegiker-Vereinigung** (Swiss Paraplegic Association), Kantonstrasse 40, 6207 Nottwil (© 041/939-5404).

The Moss Rehab Hospital (© 215456-9600) has been providing friendly and helpful phone advice and referrals to disabled travelers for years through its **Travel Information Service** (© 215/456-9603; www.moss resourcenet.org).

You can join the **Society for Accessible Travel & Hospitality** (SATH), 347 Fifth Ave., Suite 610, New York, NY 10016 (© 212/447-7284; fax 212/725-8253; www.sath.org) for $45 annually, $30 for seniors and students, to gain access to their vast network of connections in the travel industry. They provide information sheets on travel destinations and referrals to tour operators that specialize in traveling with disabilities. Their quarterly magazine, *Open World for Disability and Mature Travel,* is full of good information and resources. A year's subscription is $13 ($21 outside the U.S.).

Travelers with disabilities may also want to consider joining a tour that caters specifically to them. One of the best operators is **Flying Wheels Travel,** 143 W. Bridge (P.O. Box 382), Owatonna, MN 55060 (© 800/535-6790; www.flyingwheelstravel.com). They offer various escorted tours and cruises, with an emphasis on sports, as well as private tours in minivans with lifts. Other reputable specialized tour operators include **Access Adventures** (℃ 716/889-9096), which offers sports-related vacations; **Accessible Journeys** (℃ 800/TINGLES or 610/521-0339; www.disabilitytravel.com), for slow walkers and wheelchair travelers; **The Guided Tour, Inc.** (℃ 215/782-1370); **Wilderness Inquiry** (℃ 800/728-0719 or 612/379-3858); and **Directions Unlimited** (℃ 800/533-5343; www.travel cruises.com).

You can obtain a copy of *Air Transportation of Handicapped Persons* by writing to Free Advisory Circular No. AC12032, Distribution Unit, U.S. Department of Transportation, Publications Division, M-4332, Washington, DC 20590.

Vision-impaired travelers should contact the **American Foundation for the Blind,** 11 Penn Plaza, Suite 300, New York, NY 10001 (℃ 800/232-5463; www.afb.org), for information on traveling with Seeing Eye dogs.

TIPS FOR BRITISH TRAVELERS WITH DISABILITIES   The **Royal Association for Disability and Rehabilitation** (RADAR), Unit 12, City Forum, 250 City Rd., London EC1V 8AF (℃ 020/7250-3222), publishes two annual vacation guides. "European Holidays and Travel Abroad" and "Long Haul Holidays and Travel" each costs £5. RADAR also provides a number of vacation fact sheets on such subjects as sports and outdoor vacations, insurance, financial arrangements for persons with disabilities, and accommodations in nursing-care units for groups or for the elderly. Each of these fact sheets is available for 75p. Fact sheets for the above-mentioned vacation guides can be mailed outside the United Kingdom for a nominal fee.

Another good service is the **Holiday Care Service,** Imperial Building, 2nd Floor, Victoria Road, Horley, Surrey RH6 7PZ (℃ **01293/774-535;** fax 01293/784-647), a national charity that advises on accessible accommodations for the elderly and persons with disabilities. Annual membership costs £30. Members receive a newsletter and access to a free reservations network for hotels throughout Britain and (to a lesser degree) Europe and the rest of the world. The organization's Holiday Care Awards recognize people, hotels, and travel wholesalers in the tourism industry who provide excellent service for persons with disabilities.

If you're flying around Europe, the airlines and ground staff will help you on and off planes, and reserve seats for you with sufficient leg room, but it's essential to arrange for this assistance in advance by contacting your airline.

TIPS FOR GAY & LESBIAN TRAVELERS

Basel, Zurich, and Geneva are the centers of gay life in Switzerland, although such chic resorts as Gstaad, St. Moritz, and Arosa are also (mostly in winter). The national organization for gays in Switzerland is **Pink Cross,** Zinggstrasse 16, P.O. Box 7512, 3001 Bern (℃ **031/372-33-00**).

Before you go, you might pick up the second edition of *Frommer's Gay & Lesbian Europe.* Although Switzerland is not specifically included in this guide, it will be helpful if you're planning to combine a visit to Switzerland with stopovers in such gay meccas as London or Paris.

The **International Gay & Lesbian Travel Association** (IGLTA), (℃ **800/448-8550** or 954/776-2626; fax 954/776-3303; www.iglta.com), links travelers with the appropriate gay-friendly service organization or tour specialist. With around 1,200 members, it offers quarterly newsletters, marketing mailings, and a membership directory that's updated quarterly. Membership often includes gay or lesbian businesses but is open to individuals for $150 yearly, plus a $100 administration fee for new members. Members are kept informed of gay and gay-friendly hoteliers, tour operators, and airline and cruise-line representatives. Contact the IGLTA for a list of its member agencies, who will be tied into IGLTA's information resources.

General gay and lesbian travel agencies include **Above and Beyond Tours** (© **800/397-2681;** www.above beyondtours.com; mainly gay men).

There are also two good, biannual English-language gay guidebooks, both focused on gay men but including information for lesbians as well. You can get the *Spartacus International Gay Guide* or *Odysseus* from most gay and lesbian book stores, or order them from **Giovanni's Room** (© **215/923-2960;** www.giovannis room.com). Both lesbians and gays might want to pick up a copy of *Gay Travel A to Z* ($16). **The Ferrari Guides** (www.q-net.com) is yet another very good series of gay and lesbian guidebooks.

Out and About, 657 Harrison St., San Francisco, CA 94107 (© **800/ 929-2268** or 415/229-1793; www. outandabout.com) offers guidebooks and a monthly newsletter packed with good information on the global gay and lesbian scene. A year's subscription to the newsletter costs $49. **Our World,** 1104 North Nova Rd., Suite 251, Daytona Beach, FL 32117 (© **904/441-5367;** www.ourworld mag.com), is a slicker monthly magazine promoting and highlighting travel bargains and opportunities. Annual subscription rates are $35 in the United States, $45 outside the United States.

TIPS FOR SENIORS

Many discounts are available for seniors (women over age 62 and men over 65). Be advised, however, that you often have to be a member of an association to obtain certain discounts.

Note: Seniors (whom Swissair and American Airlines define as age 62 and older) receive a 10% discount on midweek travel on any of these airlines' promotional economy fares, but only between October and April— and not during Christmastime.

Some 450 hotels in almost 200 Swiss towns and resorts also offer special off-season rates for seniors. When making a reservation, you should indicate that you are a senior and present your passport or ID card at the hotel desk upon arrival. A special guide, **"Season for Seniors,"** listing all the participating hotels, can be obtained from the Swiss National Tourist Office.

Members of the **American Association of Retired Persons** (AARP), 601 E St. NW, Washington, DC 20049 (© **800/424-3410** or 202/ 434-AARP; www.aarp.org), get discounts not only on hotels but on airfares and car rentals, too. AARP offers members a wide range of special benefits, including *Modern Maturity* and *My Generation* magazines as well as a monthly newsletter.

Sears Mature Outlook, P.O. Box 9390, Des Moines, IA 50306 (© **800/336-6330**), began as a travel organization for people over 50, though it now caters to people of all ages. Members receive discounts on hotels and receive a bimonthly magazine. Annual membership is $39.95, which entitles members to discounts and, often, free coupons for discounted merchandise from Sears.

The Mature Traveler, a monthly 12-page newsletter on senior citizen travel, is a valuable resource. It is available by subscription ($32 a year) from GEM Publishing Group, Box 50400, Reno, NV 89513-0400. Another helpful publication is *101 Tips for the Mature Traveler,* available from Grand Circle Travel, 347 Congress St., Suite 3A, Boston, MA 02210 (© **800/ 460-6676** or 617/350-7500; fax 617/ 346-6700).

Tips Rail Bargains

In Switzerland, children under age 16—if accompanied by at least one adult—travel free on national rail lines. This family travel plan is valid for the purchase of Swiss Passes, Swiss Flexi Passes, Swiss Cards, and point-to-point tickets (see "By Train" in "Getting Around," later in this chapter).

Grand Circle Travel is also one of the hundreds of travel agencies specializing in vacations for seniors (347 Congress St., Suite 3A, Boston, MA 02210 (© **800/221-2610** or 617/350-7500; www.gct.com). Many of these packages, however, are of the tour-bus variety, with free trips thrown in for those who organize groups of 10 or more. Seniors seeking more independent travel should probably consult a regular travel agent. **SAGA International Holidays,** 222 Berkeley St., Boston, MA 02116 (© **800/343-0273;** www.saga holidays.com), offers inclusive tours and cruises for those 50 and older. SAGA also sponsors the more substantial "Road Scholar Tours" (© **800/621-2151**), which are fun-loving but with an educational bent.

If you want something more than the average vacation or guided tour, try **Elderhostel,** 75 Federal St., Boston, MA 02110-1941 (© **877/426-8056;** www.elderhostel.org), or the University of New Hampshire's **Interhostel** (© **800/733-9753**), both variations on the same theme: educational travel for senior citizens. On these escorted tours, the days are packed with seminars, lectures, and field trips, and the sightseeing is all led by academic experts. Elderhostel arranges study programs for those aged 55 and over (and a spouse or companion of any age) in the United States and in 77 countries around the world. Most courses last about 3 weeks and many include airfare, accommodations in student dormitories or modest inns, meals, and

tuition. Write or call for a free catalog, which lists upcoming courses and destinations. Interhostel takes travelers 50 and over (with companions over 40), and offers 2- and 3-week trips, mostly international. The courses in both these programs are ungraded, involve no homework, and often focus on the liberal arts. They're not luxury vacations, but they're fun and fulfilling.

TIPS FOR FAMILIES
Several books on the market offer tips to help you travel with kids. Most concentrate on the U.S., but two, *Family Travel* (Lanier Publishing International) and *How to Take Great Trips with Your Kids* (The Harvard Common Press), are full of good general advice that can apply to travel anywhere. Another reliable tome, with a worldwide focus, is *Adventuring with Children* (Foghorn Press).

Family Travel Times is published six times a year by TWYCH (Travel with Your Children), 40 Fifth Ave., New York, NY 10011 (© **888/822-4322** or 212/477-5524), and includes a weekly call-in service for subscribers. Subscriptions are $40 a year for quarterly editions. A free publication list and a sample issue are available by calling or sending a request to the above address.

The University of New Hampshire runs **Familyhostel** (© **800/733-9753**), an intergenerational alternative to standard guided tours. You live on a European college campus for the 2- or 3-week program, attend lectures and seminars, go on lots of field trips, and sightsee—all of it guided by a team of experts and academics. It's designed for children (aged 8 to 15), parents, and grandparents.

A hotel guide, **"Hotels Specially Suited for Families,"** is published by the Swiss Hotel Association and is available from the Swiss national tourist office. It lists more than 100 hotels in the country that cater to families. These hotels each have a supervised children's playroom, a play area or garden, a children's menu served before normal mealtimes, and organized family activities.

TIPS FOR STUDENTS

The best resource for students is the **Council on International Educational Exchange,** or CIEE (☏ **212/ 822-2700;** www.ciee.org). They can set you up with an ID card (see below), and their travel branch, **Council Travel Service** (☏ **888/ COUNCIL;** www.counciltravel.com), is the biggest student travel agency operation in the world. It can get you discounts on plane tickets, rail passes, and the like. Ask them for a list of CTS offices in major cities so you can keep the discounts flowing (and aid lines open) as you travel.

From CIEE you can obtain the student traveler's best friend, the $20 **International Student Identity Card** (ISIC). It's the only officially acceptable form of student identification, good for cut rates on rail passes, plane tickets, and other discounts. It also provides you with basic health and life insurance and a 24-hour help line. If you're no longer a student but are still under 26, you can get a GO 25 card from the same people, which will get you the insurance and some of the discounts (but not student admission prices in museums).

In Canada, **Travel CUTS,** 200 Ronson St., Suite 320, Toronto, ON M9W 5Z9 (☏ **800/667-2887** or 416/614-2887; www.travelcuts.com), offers similar services. **Campus USIT,** 52 Grosvenor Gardens, London SW1W 0AG (☏ **020/7730-3402;** www.usitcampus.co.uk), opposite Victoria Station, is Britain's leading specialist in student and youth travel.

9 Getting There

BY PLANE

Switzerland is situated at the center of Europe and thus is a focal point for international air traffic. The busy intercontinental airports of Zurich and Geneva can be reached in about 8 hours from the east coast of North America and in less than 2 hours from London or Paris. The country is also the crossroads of Europe—all rail lines, road passes, and mountain tunnels lead to it. Similarly, the main European route for east-west travel passes through Switzerland, between Lake Constance and Geneva.

FROM NORTH AMERICA

From New York, it takes about 7 hours to fly to either Geneva or Zurich; from Chicago, about 10 hours; and from the West Coast, about 14 hours.

The Major Airlines Swissair (☏ **800/221-4750** in the U.S. for reservations and information; www. swissair.com), Switzerland's national carrier, offers service from Atlanta, Boston, Chicago, Los Angeles, New York (JFK & Newark), San Francisco, Washington, Montreal, and Miami to Switzerland and to some 110 destinations worldwide. For data on Swissair's tour packages, or to obtain a copy of the airline's winter brochure "The Alpine Experience" or summer offerings in "The European Travel Invention," call ☏ **800/688-7947** in the United States.

American Airlines (☏ **800/433-7300;** www.im.aa.com) makes one daily nonstop flight from Dallas/Fort Worth (DFW) to Zurich, one direct flight from DFW through Chicago, and one direct flight from DFW through Miami.

As part of an arrangement known as a "code share," **Delta Airlines** (© 800/221-1212; www.delta-air. com), prebooks blocks of seats on Swissair flights to Zurich from both New York and Atlanta, as well as blocks of seats on Swissair flights from New York's JFK to Geneva. Frequent-flyer mileage is credited to either Delta or Swissair, and transfers of passengers and luggage from other parts of Delta's vast domestic network are facilitated.

Air Canada (© 888/247-2262; www.aircanada.com), flies nonstop daily from Toronto to Zurich and also flies five evenings a week (Monday through Friday) nonstop from Montreal to Zurich. Flight time from Toronto is about 8 hours; from Montreal, about 7 hours.

FROM BRITAIN

From London's Heathrow Airport, **British Airways** (© 0845/773-3377; www.british-airways.com) offers three daily nonstop flights to Zurich; on Saturdays, there are four flights. The airline also provides between three and five daily flights from Heathrow to Geneva. From Gatwick, BA offers at least three daily nonstops to Geneva. In addition, Swissair and British Airways combine their services and networks, offering one daily nonstop flight from Manchester to Geneva, as well as some other less-frequent flights.

British newspapers are always full of classified advertisements touting bargain airfare. Although competition is fierce, one well-recommended company that consolidates bulk ticket purchases and then passes the savings on to its consumers is **Trailfinders** (© 020/7937-5400 in London; www.trailfinders.com), which offers discounted tickets on major airlines.

BY TRAIN
FROM PARIS

One of the busiest rail links in Europe stretches from Paris to Geneva and Lausanne. Almost as busy are the rail routes between Paris and Zurich. Most of the trains assigned to these routes are part of Europe's network of high-speed trains. (The French refer to them as *trains à grande vitesse,* or TGV). From Paris's Gare de Lyon, about four trains a day depart, respectively, for both Geneva and Lausanne. Travel time to Geneva is about 4 hours; travel time to Lausanne is about 4½ hours.

Trains from Paris to Zurich depart three times a day from Paris's Gare de l'Est. Ironically, kilometers traveled by train within Switzerland are proportionately more expensive than equivalent distances within France, so ongoing fares from Zurich or Geneva to other points within Switzerland might come as an unpleasant surprise. Consequently, many travelers who anticipate lots of rail travel are well-advised to consider the purchase of any of Rail Europe's passes, or one of the Swiss Passes.

Schedules, prices, departure times, and confirmed reservations can be arranged before you leave North America through **Rail Europe, Inc.,** © 800/438-7245 or 914/682-5172; www.raileurope.com.

FROM LONDON

Rail links are also convenient between London and Switzerland. Both the following routes are easy, but the route through France is considerably more scenic (plus, you'll get the thrill of crossing the Chunnel—one of the world's engineering marvels).

VIA THE HOOK OF HOLLAND The standard EuroCity express route sets out from London's Liverpool Street Station, sails from Harwick to the Hook of Holland, and then proceeds by train via Cologne, Germany, to either Basel or Zurich. Once here, it's easy to find rail links to the rest of Switzerland.

ACROSS OR UNDER THE CHANNEL THROUGH PARIS It's also possible to take the rail link from London across or under the English Channel to Paris, where you can make ongoing rail connections to Switzerland. If you depart London at 10am, you can arrive in Geneva or Lausanne before 10pm the same day.

One of the most convenient ways to reach Paris from London is the Citylink rail-hovercraft-rail service. English trains originate at London's Victoria Station and chug through the English countryside to the port of Folkestone. Passengers disembark and board a hovercraft or, in some cases, a conventional ferryboat, and continue across the channel to the French port of Boulogne. Once you reach the continent, there will be a train waiting, on which you'll proceed south through France into Paris's Gare du Nord. In Paris, passengers must travel by taxi or metro (subway) across town to either the Gare de Lyon, for ongoing transfers to Geneva and Lausanne, or the Gare de l'Est, for Basel and Zurich. Trains then depart for Switzerland at regular intervals.

For information, timetables, and confirmed reservations (which are required on certain segments of these routes), contact **Rail Europe, Inc.,** (© **800/848-7245** or fax 800/432-1329).

In 1994, the *Eurostar Express* began twice-daily passenger service between London and both Paris and Brussels. The $15-billion Channel tunnel, one of the great engineering feats of all time, is the first link between Britain and the Continent since the Ice Age. The 31-mile (50km) journey between Great Britain and France takes 35 minutes, although actual Chunnel time is only 19 minutes.

Rail Europe (© **800/94-CHUNNEL** for information) sells tickets for Eurostar service between London and Paris or Brussels. A round-trip first-class fare between London and Paris costs $598, $298 in regular second class. You can make reservations for **Eurostar** at © **0990/186-186** in the United Kingdom; in France at © **01-49-70-01-75;** and in the United States at © **800/387-6782.**

Chunnel train traffic is roughly competitive with air travel, if you calculate door-to-door travel time. Trains leave from London's Waterloo Station and arrive in Paris at Gare du Nord, where fast rail connections can be made to whatever Swiss city you want.

The tunnel trains also accommodate passenger cars, charter buses, taxis, and motorcycles under the English Channel from Folkestone, England, to Calais, France. They operate 24 hours a day, 365 days a year, running every 15 minutes during peak travel times and at least once hourly at night. Tickets may be purchased at the toll booth. With Le Shuttle, gone are weather-related delays, seasickness, and a need for reservations.

You'll drive onto a half-mile-long train and travel through an impermeable underground tunnel.

Before boarding Le Shuttle, you must stop at a toll booth and pass through Immigration for both countries at one time. During the ride, you'll stay in bright, air-conditioned carriages, remaining inside your car or stepping outside to stretch your legs. When the trip is completed, simply drive off toward your destination—in our case, heading southeast to Switzerland.

BY CAR
Situated in the middle of the continent, Switzerland has a network of express highways linking it to other European countries. You can drive all the way from Britain to Switzerland

by taking a northerly route through Belgium or the Netherlands and then Germany. British motorists tend to prefer this express auto route, which is free, to going through France and paying expensive toll charges.

The route through France is also much slower. It begins a few miles south of Calais and leads directly to the Périphérique, or ring road around Paris, where you can pick up the Autoroute du Soleil to Switzerland. In Britain, the best connection for those planning a road link across France is from Portsmouth to Le Havre.

From the south of Germany, Autobahn E35 leads directly into Basel. From Basel, head east to Zurich on E60.

BY BUS

Because of its location at the crossroads of Europe, Switzerland lies astride several important bus routes. The largest bus lines in Europe, **Eurolines,** Ltd., 4 Cardiff Rd., Luton, Bedfordshire, England LU1 1PP (© **0990/143-219** or 020/7730-8235; www.eurolines.com), offers routes into Switzerland from several major European cities, including London. Departing from London's Victoria Coach Station, buses contain toilets, air-conditioning, and reclining seats, and maintain a strict nonsmoking policy. They stop about every 4 hours for a brief rest and refreshments. Other buses depart two evenings a week for Zurich at 8pm, arriving, without a change of equipment, the next day at 1:15pm. One-way fares from London to Zurich go for 53SF ($29.15) one-way and 96SF ($52.80) round-trip. Persons under 26 pay 43SF ($23.65) each way, and 83SF ($45.65) round-trip.

ESCORTED & PACKAGE TOURS

Some of you may want to go on a good vacation tour whose organizers will look after your needs from the moment you arrive at the airport to the time you depart for your return flight. Booking a tour is almost always cheaper than the cost of exploring a country on your own and has the advantage of including a running commentary on sights and monuments. Moreover, you save on both transportation and meals.

U.S. TOUR OPERATORS   There are many different tour operators eager for a share of your business, but one of the most unusual is **Abercrombie & Kent International, Inc.,** 1520 Kensington Rd., Oak Brook, IL 60521 (© **800/323-7308;** fax 630/954-2944; www.abercrombiekent.com), a Chicago-based company established more than 30 years ago. It specializes in deluxe 10-day train tours of Switzerland which, despite all the extras they offer, still cost less than any personally arranged tour.

Abercrombie & Kent's "Great Switzerland Express" tour is a rail trip through the tourist gems of Switzerland. Tour members spend the night either in the mountains, at such resorts as Zermatt and St. Moritz, or beside one of the country's magnificent lakes. Only the finest hotels are selected. Among the stops along the tour are Lugano, Lake Como, Montreux, Lausanne, Geneva, Gruyères, and Zurich, as well as Liechtenstein. Tours depart June through September; the cost for 11 days is $5,745 per person, double occupancy, with a supplement of $1,105 for single occupancy. Included in the price are daily Swiss-style buffet breakfasts, at least seven other meals (European dinners in formal dining rooms or mountain inns), first-class rail transport throughout the country, a boat journey across Lake Geneva, entrance fees to museums, sightseeing commentaries by multilingual guides, and assistance with the tasks of checking in and out of hotels. The agency also offers walks in the Engadine Valley and private ski chalets in Klosters.

SwissPak (© 800/688-7947 in the U.S.) is the land agent for Swissair tours, offering tours to 27 destinations in Switzerland and throughout Europe in both summer and winter.

Other well-recommended tour operators include outfits endorsed and approved by two of North America's largest airlines. These include **Delta Vacations** (© 800/872-7786; www. deltavacations,com) and **American Airlines Vacations** (© 800/321-2121; www.aa.com). Both outfits factor inexpensive airfare into land or hotel packages that can save substantial amounts of money over what you'd have paid if you'd booked the arrangements yourself.

Consider contacting one of the world's largest travel organizers, **American Express Travel** (© 800/446-6234; www.americanexpress. com). Favored treatment and special discounts are probably offered to holders of gold or platinum American Express cards (if you have one of these, call © 800/525-3355); but a wide array of interesting and unusual tours are offered to the general public as well.

Other organizations that offer both escorted and package tours are: **Trafalgar Tours**, 11 E. 26th St., New York, NY 10010 (© 800/854-0103; www. trafalgartours.com); **Brendon Tours**, 15137 Califa St., Van Nuys, CA 91411 (© 800/421-8446; www. brendantours.com); **Globus & Cosmos**, 5301 S. Federal Circle, Littleton, CO 80123 (© 800/221-0090;

www.globus.com); and **Caravan Tours**, 401 N. Michigan Ave., Chicago, IL 60611 (© 800/227-2826; www.caravantours.com).

A number of specialty tours are also possible in Switzerland. Swiss national tourist offices keep up-to-date lists of these constantly changing theme trips. Some of the best adventure tours in the Swiss Alps are offered by **Himalayan Travel**, 112 Prospect St., Stamford, CT 06901 (© 203/743-2349, or 800/225-2380), and **Europeds**, 761 Lighthouse Ave., Monterey, CA 93940 (© 800/321-9552; www.europeds.com).

For river cruises (also barge tours), the most reliable agency, for both Switzerland and Germany, is **KD River Cruises of Europe**, 2500 Westchester Ave., Purchase, NY (© 800/346-6525 or 415/392-8817).

BRITISH TOUR OPERATORS
An array of tour companies operate out of the United Kingdom.

HF Holidays, Imperial House, Edgware Road, Colindale, London NW9 5AL (© 020/8905-9388 for a brochure), offers a range of 1- to 2-week packages to Switzerland, and an array of some 150 special-interest offerings throughout Europe.

One of the best purveyors of Swiss vacations in England is **Waymark Holidays**, 44 Windsor Rd., Slough, SL1 2EJ (© 01753/516-477). Walking and cross-country skiing are primarily featured, with destinations including the Engadine, Kandersteg, S-chanf, and Santa Maria.

10 Getting Around

BY TRAIN
The Swiss Federal Railway is noted for its comfort and cleanliness. Most of the electrically operated trains have first-class and second-class compartments. International trains link Swiss

cities with other European centers. Intercity trains coming from Holland, Scandinavia, and Germany require a change at Basel's station, where a connection is usually available on the same platform. Most intercity trains offer the fastest connections, and since trains leave the Basel station hourly, there's never too long a wait.

It's advisable to purchase European train tickets before leaving home, especially when your itinerary is specific and complicated. All tickets are available through your travel agent.

SWISS PASS/SWISS FLEXIPASS The most practical and convenient ticket for your trip to Switzerland is the **Swiss Pass,** which entitles you to unlimited travel on the entire network of the Swiss Federal Railways, as well as on lake steamers and most postal motor coaches linking Swiss cities and resorts. The Swiss Pass is good for a predetermined number of consecutive days.

An 8-day pass goes for $330 for first class and $220 for second class, a 15-day pass is $400 for first class and $265 for second class, and a 1-month pass costs $525 for first class and $345 for second class. The Swiss Pass is issued at half price to children ages 6 to 15. Free 5 and under. The pass can be purchased in Switzerland.

A variation of the Swiss Pass is the **Swiss Flexipass.** A 3-day pass—valid for any 3 days within a 30-day period—costs $234 for first class and $136 for second class. The **Swiss Family Card** is just for families traveling together. This card allows children under 16 to travel free when accompanied by a parent. It's valid when traveling on a Swiss Pass or a Swiss Flexipass. Probably the best part of all about the Swiss Family Card is that it is free. Just request it when you purchase your Swiss Pass from Rail Europe.

SWISS REGIONAL RAIL PASSES One of the country's most unusual transportation bargains is offered in the form of regional passes that divide Switzerland into about half a dozen districts. Passes, most of which are good for 5 days of unrestricted rail travel, are offered for the Lake Geneva region, the Graubunden (Grisons), the

Ticino, central Switzerland, and the Bernese Oberland. If you plan to devote a block of days to exploring one of these specific regions, you might find one of these passes a great savings.

One of the most popular of these passes is the **Bernese Oberland Regional Pass** (Regional Pass für das Berner Oberland) which comes in variations of 3 travel days out of 7 calendar days, and 5 travel days out of 15 calendar days. They're available from any railway station in the Bernese Oberland. The 3-day option sells for 165SF ($90.75) in second class and 202SF ($111.10) in first class. The 5-day option costs 205SF ($112.75) in second class and 251SF ($138.05) in first class. Either variation allows free transport during the appropriate time frames on all but a handful of the cog railways, buses, cable cars, ferryboats, and SBB trains within the region. Note to holders of either the Swiss Pass or the Swiss Card: If you present either of those documents at the time of purchase, you'll get a 20% discount off the above-mentioned prices.

SWISS CARD This pass is valid for 1 month, entitling the holder to a free transfer from any Swiss airport or border point to any destination within Switzerland and a second free transfer from any destination in Switzerland to any Swiss airport or border point. Each transfer has to be completed within 1 day. Additionally, the Swiss Card gives the holder unlimited half-fare trips on the entire Swiss travel system, including trains, postal coaches, lake steamers, and most (not all) excursions to mountaintops. The pass costs 145SF ($79.75) for first class or 110SF ($60.50) for second class. Children are charged half price.

For more information on Swiss railway passes, call **Switzerland Tourism** at © 212/757-5944.

EURAILPASS The Eurailpass entitles travelers to unlimited first-class travel over the 100,000-mile

(161,000km) national railroad network in all western European countries, except Britain, and including Hungary in eastern Europe. It's also valid on some lake steamers and private railroads. A Eurailpass may be purchased for as short a period as 15 days or as long as 3 months. The passes are not available to residents of the countries where the pass is valid or to residents of the United Kingdom.

Eurailpass, which is ideal for extensive trips, eliminates the hassles of buying tickets—just show your pass to the ticket collector. You should note, however, that some trains require seat reservations. Also, many of the trains have couchettes, or sleeping cars, for which an additional fee is charged.

The pass cannot be purchased in Europe, so you must secure one before leaving on your trip. It costs $554 for 15 days, $718 for 21 days, $890 for 1 month, $1,260 for 2 months, and $1,558 for 3 months. Children under 4 travel free if they don't occupy a seat (otherwise they are charged half fare); children under 12 are charged half fare.

If you're under 26, you can obtain unlimited second-class travel, wherever Eurailpass is honored, on a **Eurail Youthpass,** which costs $623 for 1 month, $882 for 2 months.

Groups of two or more people can purchase a **Eurail Saverpass** for 15 days of discounted travel in first class for $470. To be entitled to the discount, the members of the group must travel together.

The **Eurail Flexipass** allows passengers to visit Europe with more flexibility. It's valid in first class and offers the same privileges as the Eurailpass. However, it provides a number of individual travel days that can be used over a much longer period of consecutive days. That makes it possible to stay in one city and yet not lose a single day of discounted travel. There are two passes: $654 for 10 days of travel

within 2 months and $862 for 15 days of travel within 2 months. Children 4 to 11 are charged 50% of the adult fares.

In addition, a **Eurail Youth Flexipass** is good for travelers under 26. Two passes are available: $458 for 10 days of travel within 2 months and $599 for 15 days of travel within 2 months.

These passes are available from travel agents in North America, or call ✆ **800/848-7245;** www.raileurope.com.

INTERAIL European travelers can travel throughout Europe for up to 1 month by train with the InterRail ticket. In your home country you get a 50% reduction on the normal price. Only supplements, reservations, and special trains like the Eurostar must be paid extra. The ticket is sold at all European travel agents. All you need is a passport and the fee, of course.

BY CAR

Switzerland has excellent roads and superhighways, all marked by clear road signs. Alpine passes are not difficult to cross, except in snowstorms, when they may shut down suddenly. Special rail facilities are provided for drivers wishing to transport their cars through the alpine tunnels of the Albula, Furka, Lotschberg, and Simplon. A timetable, highlighting the various rates, is available from the Swiss National Tourist Office.

CAR RENTALS Several American companies operate in Switzerland. One of the most reliable firms is **Budget Rent-a-Car** (✆ **800/472-3325;** www.budgetrentacar.com); its prices are competitive with those offered by **Avis** (✆ **800/331-2112;** www.avis.com) and **Hertz** (✆ **800/654-3131;** www.hertz.com). Under certain circumstances, the companies offer a discount if you prepay your rental 21 days or more in advance. Budget offers one-way rentals between any two of its more than 20 Swiss offices with no extra drop-off charge. **Kemwel Holiday Autos** (© 800/678-0678; www.kemwel.com) offers a sometimes viable alternative to more traditional car rental companies, such as Budget, Hertz, and Avis, that actually own their automobiles outright. Kemwel leases entire blocks of cars a year in advance at locations throughout Switzerland, then rents them to qualified customers who pre-pay the entire rental in advance. Kemwel, along with its competitor, Auto Europe (see below), offers the advantage of issuing vouchers in advance of your departure, the price of which includes taxes, airport surcharges, unlimited mileage and—if you ask for it—insurance premiums. The company's address is 106 Calvert St., Harrison, NY 10528.

Auto Europe (© 800/223-5555; www.autoeurope.com) is an equivalent company that leases cars, on an as-needed basis, from larger car rental companies throughout Europe. They represent at least 100 car rental locations throughout Switzerland, including all the major cities and airports, at rates that are sometimes less than what's being offered at Hertz and Avis. In a system that's equivalent to the one used by Kemwel (see above), vouchers are issued in advance for car rentals, with most or all incidentals included. Prepayment of between 20% and 60%, depending on the value of the car, is required in advance. Their address is 39 Commercial St., Portland, ME 04101.

Note that there is a 6.5% government tax on car rentals in Switzerland, in addition to a tax of 12% of the total rental usually imposed for rentals at many of the country's airports, including Zurich. With this in mind, you might choose to skip getting a car at the airport and pick up a vehicle at one of the hundreds of downtown rental agencies run by Budget, Hertz, and Avis.

Demystifying Renter's Insurance
Private auto insurance policies do not extend outside of the United States. You are not covered in Switzerland for loss of or damage to a rental car, and liability in case of injury to any other party involved in an accident.

Most major credit cards offer some degree of coverage—provided they were used to pay for rental. Terms vary widely, however, so be sure to call your credit card company directly before you rent. If you are uninsured and driving abroad, your credit card may provide primary coverage as long as you decline the rental agency's insurance. This means that the credit card will cover damage or theft of a rental car for the full cost of the vehicle. Credit cards will not cover liability, or the cost of injury to an outside party and/or damage to an outside party's vehicle. If you are driving in Switzerland, you may seriously want to consider purchasing additional liability insurance from your rental company. Be sure to check the terms, however: some rental agencies only cover liability if the renter is not at fault; even then, the rental company's obligation varies.

The basic insurance coverage offered by most car rental companies, known as the **Loss/Damage Waiver** (LDW) or Collision Damage Waiver (CDW), can cost more than $25 per day. It usually covers the full value of the vehicle with a deductible if an outside party causes an accident or other damage to the rental car. In Switzerland, you have the option to purchase or decline theft insurance. Liability coverage varies according to the company policy, but the minimum is usually $15,000. If you are at fault in an accident, however, you will be covered for the full replacement value of the car but not for liability. Swiss companies allow you to buy additional liability coverage for such cases. Most rental companies will require a police report in order to process any accident-related claims you file, but your private insurer will not be notified of the accident.

Package Deals Many packages are available that include airfare, accommodations, and a rental car with unlimited mileage. Compare these prices with the cost of booking airline tickets and renting a car separately to see if these offers are good deals.

Arranging Car Rentals on the Web Internet resources can make comparison shopping easier. **Microsoft Expedia** (www.expedia.com) and **Travelocity** (www.travelocity.com) help you compare prices and locate car rental bargains from various companies nationwide. They will even make your reservation for you once you've found the best deal.

AUTOMOBILE PERMIT Apart from the auto and train tunnel trips mentioned above, and a toll on the road through the Great St. Bernard Tunnel, there are no toll roads in the country. Instead of tolls, Switzerland levies a single annual fee of 40SF ($22) per car, or 80SF ($44) for trailers, motor homes, and RVs, for use of the nation's superhighways; when the fee has been paid, a permit sticker is affixed to the car. Drivers of cars without the permit sticker face a fine of more than twice the permit's cost. Most rental cars come equipped with this certificate. Otherwise, the appropriate permits may be purchased at any post office in Switzerland, at the Customs office at any Swiss border, or from one of the automobile associations.

If you didn't rent your car in Switzerland, you'll probably have to purchase the permit. Permits are available at border crossings and are valid for multiple re-entries into Switzerland within the licensed period. To avoid long lines at border crossings, you can buy the permit sticker in advance at the Swiss National Tourist Office in Italy, Austria, or Germany (it is not sold in France). *Note:* If you drive into Switzerland on a secondary road, you don't need a permit sticker, but if you drive on a Swiss superhighway without one, you risk facing that heavy fine.

GAS The cost varies across the country. Gas stations are usually open daily from 8am to 10pm. U.S. gasoline credit cards generally are not accepted for payment. At stations along Swiss autobahns, gas prices are higher than along secondary roads. Autobahn stations usually give 24-hour service, and electronic machines accept 10- and 20-franc Swiss notes.

DRIVER'S LICENSE U.S. and Canadian driver's licenses are valid in Switzerland, but if you're at least 18 and touring Europe by car, you might want to invest in an international driver's license. Although you might not actually need one, many travelers like the added security blanket of having one, as they are recognized worldwide whereas your local driver's license isn't. In case of an accident, an international driver's license is easier to read among parties who may not understand your local license. In the United States you can apply for one at any local branch of the **American Automobile Association** (AAA); for a list of local branches, contact their national headquarters, 1000 AAA Dr., Heathrow, FL 32746-5063 (© **800/AAA-HELP** or 407/444-4300; www.aaa.com). Include two 2x2-inch photographs, a $10 fee, and a photocopy of your state driver's license. Canadians can get the address of the nearest branch of the **Canadian Automobile Club** by phoning its national office (© **613/247-0117**).

Note that your international driver's license is valid only if accompanied by your home state or provincial driver's license.

In Switzerland, as elsewhere in Europe, to drive a car legally you must have in your possession an international insurance certificate, known as a **Green Card** (Carte Verte). Your car rental agency will provide one as part of your rental contract.

DRIVING RULES The legal minimum age for driving in Switzerland is 18. Note, however, that car rental companies often set their own minimum age, usually 20 or 21.

Drive on the right side of the road and observe the speed limit for passenger vehicles; it's 120kmph (about 75 mph) on superhighways, 80kmph (about 50 mph) on other highways, and 50kmph (about 30 mph) in cities, towns, and villages, unless otherwise posted. Non-Swiss drivers who exceed the speed limit by 50kmph (about 30 mph) or more are fined 1,130SF ($621.50) on the spot. Swiss citizens similarly caught have their driver's licenses revoked.

When driving through tunnels, be sure to turn on and dim your headlights, as required by law. Never pass another car from the right, even on superhighways. Always wear your seatbelt. Don't permit children under 12 to ride in the front seat. And, needless to say, don't drink and drive; driving while under the influence of alcohol is a serious offense in Switzerland.

BREAKDOWNS/ASSISTANCE
The Automobile Club of Switzerland and its branch offices will assist motorists at all times. For help, contact **Automobile-Club der Schweiz,** Wassergasse 39, CH-3000 Bern 13 (ⓒ **031/328-31-11**), or **Touring Club Suisse,** 9, rue Pierre-Fatio, CH-1211 Geneva 3 (ⓒ **022/417-2727**). The Automobile Club der Schweiz offers 24-hour **breakdown service.** Motorists in need of help can call ⓒ **031/312-1515.** Most mountain roads have emergency call boxes.

MAPS The best maps, available at major bookstores, are *Michelin 427*

Switzerland and the various Michelin regional road guides. An excellent map for those who plan extensive touring is published by Hallwag (1:303000). Local tourist offices provide city maps.

BY PLANE
Switzerland does not have an abundance of airports, partly because of the alpine terrain and partly due to the Swiss people's own resistance to having planes disturb their peace and quiet. To compensate, Switzerland has one of Europe's best railway systems, linking every major city in the country. This is particularly advantageous for cities such as Bern, the capital; it relies almost exclusively on rail transport to Zurich, Geneva, and Basel for air connections to the rest of the world.

If you want to fly within Switzerland, or from Switzerland to about 30 regional cities in Austria, Italy, Germany, or France, **Crossair** (ⓒ **0848/85-2000;** www.crossair. com), a domestic airline operated by Swissair, schedules flights from and to Basel and Amsterdam, Geneva and London, and Lugano and Geneva.

BY BUS
The extremely dense network covered by the Swiss postal buses is useful for trips into the mountains. Hopping on one of the popular yellow buses is a much safer and more comfortable way of seeing the Alps than trying to do your own driving in those regions.

BY BOAT
In the summer, passenger boats sail on Switzerland's major lakes and rivers. More than 100 boats, with accommodations for 60,000 passengers, operate on the lakes and along stretches of the Rhine and the Aare; most of them have dining. Evening trips, with music and dancing, are also quite popular. The old paddle-steamers on the lakes of Brienz, Geneva, Lucerne, and

Zurich, dating from before World War I, are particularly attractive and romantic.

Remember that your Swiss Pass or Swiss Card (half-fare travel card) entitles you to unlimited travel on lake steamers.

11 Tips on Accommodations

HOTELS

Most hotels in Switzerland are clean, comfortable, and efficiently run. Many in the luxury category are among the finest in the world (two in Zurich, in fact, are regarded as the best in Europe). After all, César Ritz came from Switzerland.

There are several categories of hotels. An *alkoholfrei* hotel is one that doesn't serve liquor. A hotel *garni* is one that serves breakfast and beverages but no other meals. You can judge a hotel and its prices by its stars: Five stars signify deluxe; four stars, first class; three stars, superior; and two stars, standard. One star indicates "minimum." A minimum hotel, with the most limited of facilities, can nevertheless be clean and reasonably comfortable, and standard hotels are among the best travel values in the country.

Reservations may be made directly with the hotel, through any recognized travel agency, or through various reservations systems that have 800 numbers. The hotel is entitled to request a deposit when you make your reservation; the amount will vary from hotel to hotel.

If you want a total deluxe hotel chain trip, you'll find the Hilton with more choices, each ideally located. These include the Basel Hilton and the Noga Hilton in Geneva, which is one of the finest chain hotels in Switzerland. The latter hotel occupies an entire city block.

The chains do not dominate the hotel scene in Switzerland as they do in some countries. The Inter-Continental weighs in with such heavy-duty choices as the Royal Plaza Inter-Continental

Montreux but we find this one often filled with convention people as the convention center is just next door.

A much finer choice is the Hotel Inter-Continental Zurich, which lies at the western edge of the business district near an industrial park—not exactly a choice location.

The Sheraton is not a major presence in Switzerland, although Zurich is home to the Sheraton Atlantis Hotel, but it lies in a hard-to-find commercial district at the edge of Uetliberg Forest, some 3 miles (5km) from the city center. Again, it is popular with the convention crowd.

If you're looking for a chain bargain, and your tastes aren't too demanding, you can book into any Novotel (there's one at the Zurich airport, for example).

Among the leading German chains, with minor but choice representation in Switzerland, is the German-owned Steigenberger. Two exceptional hotels in this chain include the Steigenberger Belvedere at Davos Platz and the chic Steigenberger Gstaad-Saanen outside Gstaad.

All accommodations listed in this guide have private bathrooms, unless otherwise noted.

To cut costs, you might consider a package tour (or book land arrangements with your air ticket). You'll often pay 30% less than individual rack rates (off-the-street, independent bookings). Also, be sure to ask about winter discounts. Some hotels won't grant them, but many will, especially if bookings that week are light. The price you'll pay in inexpensive hotels depends on the plumbing. Rooms with showers are much cheaper than

---

Impressions

The Swiss managed to build a lovely country around their hotels.
—George Mikes, *Down with Everybody,* 1951

---

those with private bathrooms. Even cheaper is a room with only a sink and a *cabinette de toilet* (toilet and bidet).

When you check in, remember to ask if there's a surcharge on local or long-distance telephone calls (these can often be lethal, up to 40%).

ALTERNATIVES TO HOTELS

BED-AND-BREAKFASTS The Swiss concept of a bed-and-breakfast is different from that in the United States and Canada. In Switzerland, many bed-and-breakfast places are more like small, cozy hotels than like private homes. Called "E + G Hotels"—a voluntary chain of 220 guesthouses—they can be found throughout the country. A folder listing addresses and phone numbers of E & Gs is available from the Swiss National Tourist Office.

PRIVATE HOMES In Swiss mountain and rural areas, a list of private accommodations can be obtained from most local tourist offices. Look for the following signs advertising such an accommodation (generally, a single room): *zimmer frei* in German, *chambre a louer* in French, and *affitasi camera* in Italian.

CHALET, HOUSE & APARTMENT RENTALS For a list of U.S. agencies handling such rentals, contact the Swiss National Tourist Office. Local tourist offices in Switzerland also provide listings of apartments and chalets to rent. The Swiss prefer to do business in writing rather than on the phone, so it's strongly recommended that you write to the home owners directly; allow about 20 days for a reply.

The best agency for arranging vacation homes in Switzerland is a Swiss-based company, **INTER-HOME,** representing some 20,000 properties throughout Europe—some 4,000 of these in Switzerland. Travelers have easy access to chalets and condos in all the major resort areas, from modest studio apartments at budget prices to luxurious chalets with all the modern amenities. The U.S. branch of INTERHOME, Inc., is at 1990 NE 163 St., Suite 110, North Miami Beach, FL 33162 (✆ **800/882-6864;** fax 305/940-2911; www.interhome.com). Contact them for a catalog of vacation homes outlining some 4,000 listings in almost 200 locations.

In addition, **Hometours International, Inc.,** P.O. Box 11503 Knoxville, TN 37939 (✆ **423/690-8484,** or 800/367-4668 outside New York State), offers chalet apartments and apartment hotels in Zermatt overlooking the Matterhorn. Hometours also rents chalet apartments in the center of the resort in Interlaken.

FARM VACATIONS A unique way to get to know Switzerland, this program lets you experience firsthand the working world and home life of a Swiss farming family. A brochure, "Swiss Farm Holidays," tells exactly how it can be done; it's available from the Swiss National Tourist Office.

YOUTH HOSTELS About 75 youth hostels exist in Switzerland, open to single people, families, or both. Fees range from $18 to $30 per person including bed linen and breakfast, depending on the hostel. There is no upper age limit, but in peak season travelers 25 and younger have priority. For more information, contact **Hostelling International-American**

Youth Hostels, 733 15th St. NW, Suite 840, Washington, DC 20005 (☏ **202/783-6161;** fax 202/783-6171; www.hiayh.org).

12 Recommended Reading

Read a few of the books below to get a feel for Switzerland—its people, atmosphere, and history—before you visit.

- *Why Switzerland?* (Cambridge University Press, by Jonathan Steinberg), provides the best look at Swiss society, culture, and history.
- *A Tramp Abroad* (Oxford Press, by Mark Twain) is the eternal tongue-in-cheek travelogue for "Innocents Abroad" touring the Swiss Alps.
- *Scrambles Amongst the Alps* (Dover Publishers, by Edward Whymper) is the latest reprint of this classic mountaineer's account of his conquest of the Matterhorn.
- For some light reading, *Ticking Along with the Swiss* (Bergli Books, by Dianne Dicks), is an amusing collection of personal tales from travelers to Switzerland.
- For the reader who wants to explore Switzerland in depth and on foot, *Walking Switzerland—The Swiss Way* (Mountaineers Books, by Marcia and Philip Lieberman) is a useful guide for those who want to walk through the tiny country, as hundreds do.

FAST FACTS: Switzerland

American Express American Express has offices in Geneva, Zurich, and Bern (see the individual city chapters for specific locations).

Business Hours **Banks** are usually open Monday through Friday from 8:30am to 4:30pm (closed on legal holidays). Foreign currency may be exchanged at major railroad stations and airports daily from 8am to 10pm. Most **business offices** are open Monday through Friday from 8am to noon and 2 to 6pm. **Shops** are usually open Monday through Friday from 8am to 12:15pm and 1:30 to 6:30pm, and on Saturday from 1:30 to 4pm. In large cities, most shops don't close during the lunch hour, although many do so on Monday morning.

Climate See "When to Go," earlier in this chapter.

Currency/Currency Exchange See "Money," earlier in this chapter.

Driving Rules See "Getting Around," earlier in this chapter.

Drug Laws A word of warning: Penalties for illegal drug possession are more severe in Switzerland than they are in the United States and Canada. You could go to jail or be deported immediately.

Drugstores Switzerland has excellent pharmacies. Yet, outside the main cities it can be difficult to get a prescription filled after business hours.

Electricity Switzerland's electricity is 220 volts, 50 cycles, AC. Some international hotels are specially wired to allow North Americans to plug in their appliances, but you'll usually need a transformer for your electric razor, hair dryer, or soft-contact-lens sterilizer. You'll also need an adapter plug to channel the electricity from the Swiss system to the flat-pronged

American system. Don't plug anything into the house current in Switzerland without being certain the systems are compatible.

Embassies & Consulates Most embassies are located in the national capital, Bern; some nations maintain consulates in other cities such as Geneva. There's an **Australian consulate** in Geneva at Chemins des Fins 2 (℃ **022/799-9100**). The **Canadian embassy** is at 5 Avenue Del 'Ariana, Bern (℃ **031/357-32-00**). In Geneva the consulate is at 1 chemin du Pré-de-la-Bichette (℃ **022/919-92-00**). **New Zealand** has no embassy in Switzerland, but there's a consulate in Geneva at 28A chemin du Petit-Saconnex (℃ **022/734-9530**). The embassy of the **United Kingdom** is at Thunstrasse 50, Bern (℃ **031/359-77-00**), and there is a British consulate in Geneva at 37–39 rue de Vermont (℃ **022/918-24-00**). The embassy of the **United States** is located at Jubilaumstrasse 93, Bern (℃ **031/357-70-11**), with consulates in Zurich at Dufourstrasse 101 (℃ **01/422-25-66**) and in Geneva at World Trade Center Building no. 2 (℃ **022/798-16-05**).

Emergencies Dial ℃ **117** for the police (emergencies only) and ℃ **118** to report a fire.

Gasoline See "Getting Around," earlier in this chapter.

Language The three major languages are German, French, and Italian, although most people in the tourist industry speak English. The best phrase books are published by Berlitz: *French for Travellers, German for Travellers,* and *Italian for Travellers.*

Legal Aid This may be hard to come by in Switzerland. The government advises foreigners to consult their embassy or consulate (see "Embassies & Consulates," above) in case of a dire emergency, such as an arrest. Even if your embassy or consulate declines to offer financial or legal help, it will generally offer advice on how to obtain help locally.

Liquor Laws The official drinking age is 16. As in many European countries, the application of laws governing drinking is flexible and enforced only if a problem develops or if decorum is broken. Driving while intoxicated, particularly if it results in damage to property or persons, brings swift and severe punishment, involving sizable fines and possible imprisonment.

Mail Post offices in large cities are open Monday through Friday from 7:30am to noon and 2 to 6:30pm, and on Saturday from 7:30 to 11am. If you have letters forwarded to a post office to be collected after you arrive, you'll need a passport for identification. The words *"Poste Restante"* must be clearly written on the envelope. Letters not collected within 30 days are returned to the sender. Letters are either first class, meaning air mail, or surface mail, rated second class. To send letters and postcards to America, weighing up to 20 grams, the cost is 1.80SF ($1) in first class or 1.40SF (75¢) for surface. To Great Britain, the charge is 1.30SF (70¢) in first class or 1.20SF (65¢) for surface.

Newspapers/Magazines Swiss papers are published in German, French, or Italian (depending on the region). Most news kiosks in major cities stock the British dailies, plus the latest editions of the *International Herald Tribune,* which, although edited in Paris, is printed in Zurich. *USA*

Today, the latest copies of *Time and Newsweek,* and other U.S. and British magazines are also widely available.

Pets Dogs and cats brought into Switzerland will require veterinary certificates stating that the animals have been vaccinated against rabies not less than 30 days and not more than 1 year prior to entry into the country. This regulation also applies to dogs and cats returning after a temporary absence from Switzerland, but is not applicable to animals transported through the country by rail or air traffic.

Police Dial ⓒ **117** for emergencies.

Radio/TV Television programming transmits in German, French, or Italian (again, depending on the region), but films in English are often shown, with the local language appearing in subtitles. Most hotels have radios on which you can hear British news broadcasts. The BBC can often be picked up on transistor sets, as can the American Forces Network. First-class hotels often subscribe to CNN.

Restrooms Most Swiss public restrooms are clean and modernized. However, in this multilingual country you'll have to know what you're looking for. Depending on which part of Switzerland you find yourself in, public restrooms may be WC (water closet), *Toiletten, toilettes,* or *gabinetti.* Women's rooms may be identified as *"Damen"* or *"Frauen," "Signore"* or *"Donne," "Femmes"* or *"Dames;"* and men's rooms may be labeled *"Herren"* or *"Manner," "Signori"* or *"Uomini," "Hommes"* or *"Messieurs."* Public restrooms can be found at bus stations, railway terminals, and cable-car platforms. If these aren't handy, use the restrooms in cafes. Most public lavatories are free, but have a 20-centime or 50-centime piece ready just in case.

Safety Crimes of violence, such as muggings, are rare in Switzerland. It is generally safe to walk the streets of cities day and night. The most common crime reported by visitors is a picked pocket.

Taxes No taxes are added to purchases in Switzerland. Swiss merchants pay tax to the government, and the percentage is included in the price marked on any object.

In addition, drivers entering Switzerland are required by law to purchase a windshield sticker for 40SF ($22), valid for travel on Swiss roads for 1 year. Stickers are sold at all Customs posts upon entering Switzerland.

Telephone/Telex/Fax The telephone system is entirely automatic and connects the entire country. **Helpful numbers** to know are: **111** for directory assistance, **120** for tourist information and snow reports, **140** for help on the road, **162** for weather forecasts, and **163** for up-to-the-minute information on road conditions. Hotels add substantial service charges for calls made from your room; it's considerably less expensive to make calls from a public phone booth.

To use a **coin-operated telephone,** lift the receiver and insert 40 centimes to get a dial tone. Be sure to have enough coins on hand, as you must insert more for each message unit over your initial deposit. If you insert more coins than necessary, the excess amounts will be returned. A pay phone will accept up to 5SF ($2.75).

To make a local call, dial directly after you hear the dial tone (no area code needed); for other places in Switzerland, dial the area code and then the number. To call a foreign country, dial the code of the country first, then the area code, and then the number.

The country code for Switzerland is **41**. When calling from the United States dial **011**, the country code, the city code dropping the zero, then the number. For example, the city code for Zurich is **1**; use this code if calling from outside Switzerland. If you're within Switzerland but not in Zurich, use **01**. When calling within Zurich, leave off the code and dial the regular phone number.

Time Switzerland's clocks are usually 6 hours ahead of eastern standard time in the United States, and 1 hour ahead of Greenwich mean time. However, because Switzerland and the United States switch their clocks every spring and fall during different weeks, the time difference is sometimes only 5 hours.

Tipping A 15% service charge is automatically included in all hotel and restaurant bills, although some people leave an additional tip for exceptional service. For taxis, a tip is usually included in the charges (a notice will be posted in the cab).

Tourist Offices See "Visitor Information," earlier in this chapter.

Water Tap water is safe to drink in all Swiss towns and cities. But don't drink from rivers or mountain streams, regardless of how clean the water may appear.

Weather American Express Travel Related Service Company provides hourly reports on current weather conditions and 3-day forecasts for more than 900 cities in Europe. For Switzerland, dial ✆ **900/WEATHER** (there's a 95¢-per-minute charge for the call) and press the first three letters of the desired city: BAS (Basel), BER (Bern), GEN (Geneva), LUC (Lucerne), STM (St. Moritz), or VAD (Vaduz, Liechtenstein).

Zurich

Switzerland's largest city is surely among the most beautiful in all of Europe, and even today, Zurich retains much of its 19th-century charm. Situated on the northern shore of Lake Zurich in the heart of the country, the city is both large enough to offer all amenities to its visitors and small enough for you to discover on your own.

Zurich is the capital of a canton of the same name that joined the Swiss Confederation in 1351. Most of the 380,000 residents speak a form of German called Schwyzerdütsch (Schweizerdeutsch, in standard German). A former seat of the Reformation, Zurich is a staunchly Protestant—some say Puritan—city.

Although Zurich is highly industrialized, its skies remain relatively unpolluted because the factories run on electricity. Zurich is also a major center of international finance; the headquarters of five major banks are on Bahnhofstrasse, in the heart of the city. The bankers here are sometimes referred to as gnomes because many of the banks store mountains of gold in underground vaults.

Zurich produces one-fifth of the nation's income, but it's far from being a dreary city of commerce. It's long been a great center of liberal thought, attracting such scholars as Lenin, Carl Jung, James Joyce, and Thomas Mann. The Dadaist school was founded here in 1916. And, the increase of visitors in the last 2 decades has spurred the development of a livelier nightlife and entertainment scene.

Built between the wooded slopes of the Uetilberg and the Zurichberg, Zurich is split by the River Limmat. There is no finer pleasure to be had in Zurich than walking along its quays, which line the banks of the Limmat and Lake Zurich. Sailboats and motorboats take visitors across Lake Zurich. Zurich's Alstadt or Old Town is one of the most intriguing in Switzerland, with two giant cathedrals and dozens of streets ideal for exploring at leisure. It is also a city of parks and gardens, with a particularly outstanding botanical garden.

While based in Zurich you can also take easy side trips to some of the most panoramic views of Switzerland, including to the Uetilberg, the king of picnic spots and known as the "top of Zurich."

1 Orientation

ARRIVING

BY PLANE **Kloten Airport** (📞 **01/ 816-22-11**), the international airport of Zurich, is the biggest airport in Switzerland and the most popular gateway to the country; in fact, it's among the 10 busiest airports in Europe. Located approximately 7 miles (11km) north of the city center, the trip by taxi costs between 52SF and 57SF ($28.60–$31.35). The train service offered by the Swiss Federal

Railways is much cheaper; for 6.70SF ($3.70), you'll arrive in less than 10 minutes at the Zurich Hauptbahnhof, the main railway station. The train runs every 15 to 20 minutes between 5:36am and 12:20am. You can also take bus no. 768 (Zurich Airport–Seebach), but you'll have to change to tram no. 14 to get to the center of town.

BY TRAIN   Several trains bound for Switzerland leave from the Gare de l'Est in Paris. Without a stop, a train departs **Paris** at 10:43pm daily, arriving in Zurich at 6:45am. Other connections are via Basel. One train leaves Paris daily at 2:43pm, arriving 9:22pm in Zurich; yet another leaves Paris at 5:19pm, also going via Basel, arriving in Zurich at 12:06pm. From **Munich,** the Gottfried Keller Express departs daily at 6:15pm with a 10:23pm arrival in Zurich. The Bavaria leaves Munich daily at 8:15am, arriving in Zurich at 12:26pm. All trains arrive at the **Zurich Hauptbahnhof** (© **0900/300-300**).

BY BUS   Zurich's bus routes function only as feeder lines from outlying suburbs, which lie off the train lines, into the vicinity of the town's railroad station.

BY CAR   From Basel, take N3 east, and from Geneva, take N1 northeast, going via Bern, where you'll connect with E4 and E17 heading east into Zurich.

BY BOAT   The **Zurichsee-Schiffahrtsgesellschaft,** Mythenquai 333 (© **01/ 482-10-33**), offers regularly scheduled service on modern passenger ships as well as old steamers plying both sides of Lake Zurich. The service is operated from Easter to October, going from Zurich as far as Rapperswil.

VISITOR INFORMATION

The **Zurich Tourist Office,** Bahnhofplatz 15 (© **01/215-40-00**), is based in the main railway station. It's open November through March, Monday through Friday from 8am to 7pm and on Saturday and Sunday from 9am to 6:30pm; April through October, Monday through Saturday from 8am to 8:30pm and on Sunday from 8:30am to 6:30pm. There's also a branch at the Zurich Airport (Terminal B), open daily from 10am to 7pm year-round.

CITY LAYOUT

Zurich is situated on both shores of the Limmat River, which flows from the northern end of Lake Zurich. The Sihl River, a tributary of the Limmat, also flows through the city, and quays line the riverbanks and the lake. The city spreads across a ravine in the eastern hills between the wooded slopes of the Zürichberg and Käferberg hills into the Glatt River valley.

Zurich is said to have begun at the **Lindenhof,** which is where you, too, might begin your orientation to the city. This square is the architectural center of historic Zurich. From here, you can survey the city as it rises on both banks of the Limmat from Bahnhofbrücke (*brücke* means bridge) to Quailbrücke. Between these two bridges are four other spans over the river: Muhle-Steg, Rudbrunbrücke, Rathausbrücke, and Münsterbrücke.

Below this square runs **Bahnhofstrasse,** one of the most elegant and expensive shopping streets in the world. It begins in the west, at the Hauptbahnhof, the railway station, opening onto Bahnhofplatz, and runs east to the lake. It crosses **Paradeplatz,** a converging point for trams and the modern center of the city. From Paradeplatz you can continue east, passing Fraumünster church and crossing Münsterbrücke to reach the right bank of the river. Here, the narrow streets of the **Limmatquai** are the second-best place in the city to shop. Running parallel to Limmatquai is **Niederdorfstrasse,** in the so-called red-light district of Zurich.

Impressions
Zurich's relationship to the world is not of the spirit, but of commerce.
—C. G. Jung

Old Town, or **Altstadt,** was developed during the early medieval period and is focused on Lindenhof, Fraumünster, Grossmünster, and St. Peter's. It expanded to **Weinplatz,** the oldest market square, and **Strehlgasse.** By the 11th century, the city continued its development on the right bank with such centers as **Kirchgasse** and **Neumarkt.**

FINDING AN ADDRESS In a system that developed during the Middle Ages, all Swiss cities, including Zurich, begin their street-numbering system with the lowest numbers closest to the center of town. In Zurich, the center is the **Hauptbahnhof.** All even numbers lie on one side of the street, and all odd numbers are on the other.

MAPS The best map, published by Falk, is a pocket-size Stadtplan (city plan) with an index. Copies are available at various newsstands and bookstores. Try the **Travel Book Shop,** Rindermarkt 20 (*C* **01/252-38-83**). Hours are Monday 1 to 6:30pm, Tuesday through Friday from 9am to 6:30pm, and Saturday 9am to 4pm.

NEIGHBORHOODS IN BRIEF
Zurich is divided by the Limmat River into the following two general areas:

West or Left Bank This district is dominated by Bahnhofplatz, center of rail connections, and Bahnhofstrasse, which is the main commercial and banking thoroughfare. This is the Zurich world of high finance and elegant shops. The venerable Fraumünster church, on Fraumünsterstrasse, dominates the west bank.

East or Right Bank Opposite Fraumünster, on the other side of the river, rises Grossmünster church, on Grossmünsterplatz; its two Gothic towers are an east-bank landmark. The historic guildhalls of Zurich, such as the Zunfthaus zur Saffran, rise on the east bank of the river. So, too, does the Rathaus, the city's town hall, completed in 1698. On the east bank you can explore the eastern part of Altstadt, strolling along Neumarkt, one of the best preserved of the old streets. The area beyond is Niederdorf, the center of the town's "hot spots."

2 Getting Around

Zurich is an easy city to navigate, and the trams (streetcars) and buses are reliable.

BY PUBLIC TRANSPORTATION
The public transport system of Zurich is operated by VBZ Züri-Linie, or **Zurich Public Transport** (*C* **01/212-37-37** for information). The modern and extensive network of trams and buses (there is no subway) runs daily from 5:30am to midnight. You should have to wait no longer than 6 minutes during rush hours. Most trams and buses connect at the Zurich Hauptbahnhof, in the heart of the city.

You can buy tickets from automatic vending machines located at every stop. You must have a ticket before you get on a vehicle; if you're caught without one, you'll pay a fine of 50SF ($27.50).

For a trip of up to four stops, the fare is 3.10SF ($1.70), and 3.90SF ($2.15) for longer journeys. Visitors can get the most for their money by ordering a Tageskarte (1-day ticket), which costs 7.20SF ($3.95) and allows you to travel on all city buses and trams for 24 hours.

BY TAXI

Traveling by taxi is very expensive. The budget-conscious will only want to use them as a last resort. Your hotel will usually be glad to call a taxi for you, but if you're making the call yourself, call **Taxi-Zentrale Zurich** (✆ **01/272-44-44**). The basic charge before you even get into the vehicle is 6SF ($3.30), plus 3.20SF ($1.75) for each kilometer you travel.

BY CAR

We don't recommend attempting to see Zurich by car—the city is way too congested, and parking is too scarce and too expensive. Save the car for exploring the environs.

RENTAL CARS   All the major car-rental firms are represented in Zurich, with offices at both Kloten Airport and downtown. Representative firms include **Avis,** with offices at Gartenhofstrasse 17 (✆ **01/296-87-87**) or at the airport (✆ **01/800-77-33**); **Budget,** with an office only at the airport (✆ **01/800-77-30**); and **Hertz,** with a base at Morgartenstrasse 5 (✆ **01/242-84-84**) and at the airport (✆ **01/814-05-11**).

PARKING   You should get a street plan (see "Maps" under "Orientation," above), which indicates parking garages with a "P" sign; a similar leaflet is available from the Zurich police. Some hotels have their own parking garages, for which there is an extra charge; others, especially those in congested Old Town, do not. You'll have to inquire at your hotel for the location of the nearest public garage. Parking costs range from 6SF to 10SF ($3.30–$5.50) per hour in most of the city's public garages.

BY BIKE

Biking is a good way to get around Zurich, especially in the outlying areas. Bicycles can be rented at the baggage counter of the railway station, the **Hauptbahnhof** (✆ **0512/22-29-04**), for 27SF ($14.85) per day for a city bike or 21SF ($11.55) for a half day. Hours are daily from 7am to 7:30pm.

ON FOOT

Zurich and its quays are ideal for walking, and many of the places of interest, such as the sights of Altstadt on both sides of the Limmat, are conveniently grouped together.

✆ **FAST FACTS: Zurich**

American Express   The office is at Schützengasse 1 (✆ **01/226-20-73**), open Monday to Friday 9am to noon and 1 to 6pm.

Babysitters   If enough advance notification is given (at least a day in advance), virtually any hotel in Zurich can arrange for a babysitter.

Another option is the child-care facilities at one of Zurich's largest department stores, **Jelmoli**, Bahnhofstrasse 69 (© **01/220-44-11**).

Banks Banks are generally open Monday through Wednesday and on Friday from 8:15am to 4:30pm and on Thursday from 8:15am to 6pm. Two well-known banks are the **Union Bank of Switzerland**, at Shop Ville (© **01/234-11-11**), and the **Swiss Bank Corporation**, Bahnhofstrasse 70 (© **01/224-21-42**). Both banks are open Monday through Friday from 8am to 7pm.

Bookstores See "Books" under "Shopping," later in this chapter.

Climate Summers in Zurich are not as warm as on the French Riviera, but the lake is usually warm enough to swim in during July and August. Many days are chilly, and spring and fall can be quite cold. In winter, the temperature rarely goes below zero. The average temperature in January is 30°F (-1°C); in July, the average is only 61°F (16°C). On cloudy days, the view of the Alps is obscured.

Consulates If you lose your passport or have another emergency, go to the **U.S. Consulate**, Zollikerstrasse 101 (© **01/422-2566**). The **Consulate of the United Kingdom** is at Minervastrasse 117 (© **01/383-65-60**). Canadians and Australians should contact their respective embassies in Bern, and New Zealanders should apply to their consulate-general in Geneva (see "Fast Facts: Switzerland" in chapter 2).

Currency Exchange Most banks and travel agencies will exchange money for you. There's also an exchange office of **Credit Suisse** at the Zurich Hauptbahnhof, the main railway station, open daily from 6:30am to 11:30pm at Minervastrasse 117. Incidentally there are ATMs all over the city, most of the machines taking only MasterCard.

Dentists Emergency dental problems can be solved by calling © **01/269-69-69**. An appointment with an English-speaking dentist can be arranged for you.

Doctors Contact the **Zurich Universitätsspital** (University Hospital), Rämistrasse 100 (© **01/269-69-69**).

Drugstores For 24-hour service, **Bellevue Apotheke**, at Theaterstrasse 14 (© **01/266-62-22**), lies off Bellevueplatz.

Emergencies Call the **police** at © **117**. For **first aid**, phone © **47-47-00**; for the **City Ambulance Service**, dial © **144**. There's an accident center at the **University Hospital**, Rämistrasse 100 (© **01/255-11-11**).

Eyeglasses Your eyeglasses can be replaced or repaired at **Götte Optics**, Bahnhofstrasse 100 (© **01/211-37-80**).

Hairdressers & Barbers Women do not need a reservation at **Gidor**, Theaterstrasse 8 (© **01/251-90-18**). Men can get their hair cut at the Hauptbahnhof, the rail station.

Hospitals See "Doctors" or "Emergencies," above.

Information See "Visitor Information," earlier in this chapter.

Internet Access Head for the **Internet Café**, Uraniastrasse 3 (© **01/210-33-11**), in the Urania Parkhaus. Open Monday to Thursday 9am to midnight, Friday and Saturday 9am to 2am, and Sunday 10am to 11pm.

Laundry/Dry Cleaning One of the best and most centrally located of Zurich's self-service laundries is **Waschbär,** Mühlegasse 11 (℃ **01/ 252-37-95**). On its premises there's also a dry-cleaning service.

Libraries The main branch of the **Pestalozzi Bibliothek** (Pestalozzi Library), the largest in Zurich, is at Zähringerstrasse 17 (℃ **01/261-78-11**). You must maintain a permanent address in Switzerland to be able to borrow books; but even if you don't, you're welcome to browse the stacks and read anything you want on-site. It's open Monday through Friday from 10am to 7pm and Saturday from 10am to 2pm (till 4pm from Sept to May).

Lost Property There is a lost property office at Werdmühlestrasse 10 (℃ **01/216-51-11**), open Monday through Friday from 7:30am to 5:30pm.

Luggage Storage/Lockers These are available at several locations throughout the vast Hauptbahnhof (℃ **01/211-25-51**).

Newspapers/Magazines The major newspaper of Zurich is the *Neue Zürcher Zeitung,* in German. The *International Herald Tribune* is printed in Zurich. Several German-language magazines are published in Switzerland, and the latest copies of *Newsweek* and *Time* (European editions) are available at most newsstands and in big-hotel lobbies.

Photographic Needs A wide supply of all types of film is available at **Jelmoli Department Store,** Bahnhofstrasse 69 (℃ **01/220-44-11**). Jelmoli also offers 1-hour developing service at its "Mister Minit."

Police See "Emergencies," above.

Post Office The main post office is the **Sihlpost,** Kasernenstrasse 95–97 (℃ **01/296-21-11**), across the Sihl River from Löwenstrasse; an emergency-service window is open from 6:30am to 10pm daily. Most post offices—listed under "Post" in the phone directory—are open Monday through Friday from 7:30am to 6:30pm and on Saturday from 6:30 to 11am.

Restrooms Public toilets are located at all central points, including the Hauptbahnhof and such locations as Bellevueplatz, Paradeplatz, and Heimplatz. They are open daily, generally from 5am to midnight.

Safety Zurich is one of the safest cities in Europe, both during the day and at night. The most potentially dangerous place is Niederdorf, the red-light district in Altstadt.

Taxes A 7.5% VAT (value-added tax) is added to hotel and restaurant bills. There are no other special taxes.

Taxis See "Getting Around," above.

Telephone/Telex/Fax A telephone, telex, and fax office is open at the **Zurich Hauptbahnhof,** the main railway station, Monday through Friday from 7am to 10:30pm and on Saturday and Sunday from 9am to 9pm.

Transit Information For bus and tram information, call ℃ **01/212-37-37**.

Weather See "Climate," above.

3 Where to Stay

Zurich is an ideal place to get acquainted with Swiss hospitality. Its more than 120 hotels offer accommodations ranging from the most sumptuous suites in Europe to simple, clean pensions (boardinghouses). Finding a room can be a problem, however. The top hotels are usually filled with businesspeople, and the city is a frequent host to conventions and fairs. So, if possible, make a reservation in advance.

For top-rate comfort in Zurich, you'll have to pay. Inexpensive hotels are often spartan and definitely have no frills. Furthermore, many of the budget hostelries are in dire need of renovation. The myth that you can't find a bad hotel in Switzerland is no longer true, and probably never was.

The division between the left bank and the right bank of Zurich isn't as sharply divided as it is in Paris, for example. You stay on the left bank for greater convenience, as it is the site of the rail terminus, all the major banks, and some of the grandest shops and restaurants. However, the right bank is the site of the Altstadt or Old Town, and for many visitors this section of Zurich has far greater atmosphere. It is also the site of some of the historic guildhalls of Zurich (some of which are now restaurants). A stay here is for those who seek ambience and an old-style atmosphere when lodging in a European capital.

Note: Rooms in all our recommended hotels have private bathrooms with tub and shower unless otherwise indicated.

ON THE LEFT BANK
VERY EXPENSIVE

Arabella Sheraton Atlantis Hotel ⓐ   Situated 5 miles (9km) south of the center of Zurich in the wooded park at the foot of the Uetliberg, the Sheraton provides enough amenities to satisfy most needs. Motorists often prefer it instead of a stay in the congested city center. Because of its isolated position, it has acres and acres for jogging trails and is also known for its convention space, yet it is much less expensive than the also suburban Dolder Grand. The hotel has undergone significant renovations, and the spacious bedrooms are mono-chromatically soothing and well upholstered. The least expensive accommodations lie at the far end of an underground tunnel in the 62-room "Guesthouse" annex and do not receive room service, though they contain the same facilities as in the rest of the hotel. The fifth floor accommodations are your best choice, as they contain balconies with views of the surrounding forests and the spires of Zurich in the distance.

Döltschiweg 234, CH-8055 Zurich. ⓒ **01/454-54-54.** Fax 01/454-54-00. www.starwood.com. 244 units. Main building, 365SF–495SF ($200.75–$272.25) double. Annex, 275SF ($151.25) double; from 1,200SF ($660) suite. AE, DC, MC, V. Free parking outdoors, 20SF ($11) inside. Shuttle bus leaves every hour from Hauptbahnhof, or train S10 to Schweighos Station. **Amenities:** 2 restaurants; bar; health club; sauna; room service; babysitting; laundry/dry cleaning. *In room:* A/C, TV, minibar, hair dryer, safe (in some).

Baur au Lac ⓐⓐⓐ   One of the world's great hotels, owned by the same family since its opening in 1844, Baur au Lac is ideally located at the end of Bahnhofstrasse, right next to the Schanzengraben Canal. Renovated in 1997, the three-story stone building is surrounded by a private park that's filled with red geraniums in summer. In style, grandeur, service, and amenities, it is superior to its nearest competitor, the Widder. The dining facilities here are among the finest in Zurich.

In rooms where Richard Wagner and Franz Liszt once entertained at the piano, guests today are treated to Jugendstil glass, tapestries, antiques, marble floors, and Oriental carpets. All bedrooms and suites are luxuriously and uniquely furnished. Suites have the best antiques, but regular rooms might have an Empire piece, a style from one of the Louis periods, or even modern furnishings. Try for a room with a lake view.

Where to Stay in Zurich

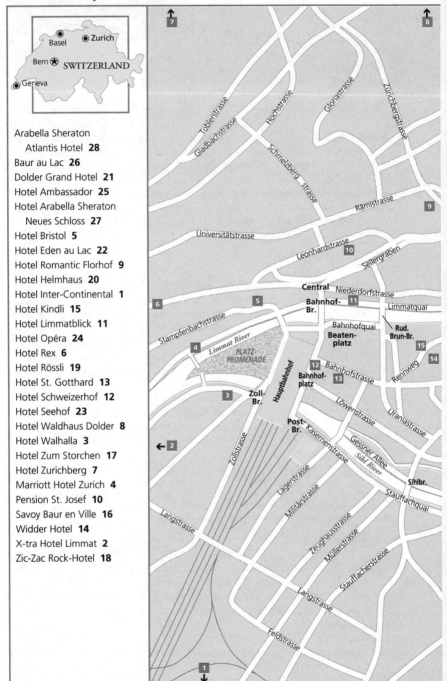

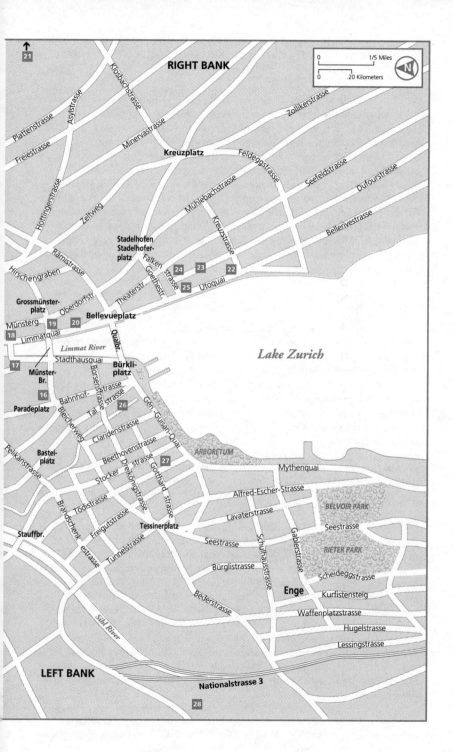

RIGHT BANK

0   1/5 Miles
0   .20 Kilometers

N

Klosbachstrasse
Asylstrasse
Plattenstrasse
Freiestrasse
Minervastrasse
Zollikerstrasse
Kreuzplatz
Feldeggstrasse
Seefeldstrasse
Dufourstrasse
Hottingerstrasse
Zeltweg
Mühlebachstrasse
Kreuzstrasse
Bellerivestrasse
Rämistrasse
Hirschengraben
Stadelhofen
Stadelhofer-
platz
Falken
Goethestr.
24 23   22
Oberdorfstr.
Theaterstr.
25   Utoquai
Grossmünster-
platz
Münsterg.   19   20   Bellevueplatz
18   Limmatquai
Quaibr.
17   Limmat River
Stadthausquai
Bürkli-
platz
Lake Zurich
16   Münster-
Br.
Bahnhof-
Borsenstrasse
strasse
Gen. Guisan-Quai
Paradeplatz
Talstrasse
Bleicherweg
26
Pelikanstrasse
Clarienstrasse
ARBORETUM
Bastei-
platz
Beethovenstrasse
Dreikönig-
strasse
Stocker
strasse
27
Gotthard
strasse
Mythenquai
Brandschenk
estrasse
Tödistrasse
Freigutstrasse
Alfred-Escher-Strasse
BELVOIR PARK
Stauffbr.
Tessinerplatz
Lavaterstrasse
Seestrasse
Tunnelstrasse
Seestrasse
Schulhausstrasse
Gablerstrasse
RIETER PARK
Bürglistrasse
Enge
Scheideggstrasse
Kurfistensteig
Bederstrasse
Waffenplatzstrasse
Hugelstrasse
Sihl River
Lessingstrasse
LEFT BANK
Nationalstrasse 3
28

Talstrasse 1, CH-8022, Zurich. ✆ **01/220-50-20.** Fax 01/220-50-44. www.bauraulac.ch. 127 units. 650SF ($357.50) double; from 1,880SF ($1,034) suite. AE, DC, MC, V. Parking 25SF ($13.75). Tram: 4. **Amenities:** 3 restaurants; bar; small exercise room; room service; massage; laundry/dry cleaning. *In room:* A/C, TV, minibar, coffeemaker, hair dryer, iron, safe (in some).

Hotel Schweizerhof ⭐⭐ Located in one of the city's busiest areas, the landmark Schweizerhof is accessible from anywhere in town by tram. This is a grand old station hotel in turn-of-the-century tradition, although recent major renovations have kept it in step with the times. When stacked up against the Baur auf Lac, Widder, and Savoy, it would definitely be number four, although the Schweizerhof is far superior to the average station hotel in a European capital. The stone building has gables, turrets, and columns and is decorated with flags. Inside, the public rooms are pleasant and unpretentious. The ideal rooms are the semicircular corner units. The fifth floor is nonsmoking. In spite of its central location, rooms are generally quiet because of the triple glazing on the windows. Most units are roomy and filled with many thoughtful extras, including spongy carpeting, alarm clocks, fruit baskets, and deluxe toiletries. They even provide umbrellas.

Bahnhofplatz 7, CH-8023 Zurich. ✆ **01/218-88-88.** Fax 01/218-81-81. www.hotelschweizerhof.com. 115 units. 490SF–660SF ($269.50–$363) double; 690SF ($379.50) junior suite; 1,080SF ($594) suite. Rates include buffet breakfast. AE, DC, MC, V. Parking 25SF ($13.75). Tram: 3 or 4. **Amenities:** 2 restaurants; bar; room service; babysitting; laundry/dry cleaning. *In room:* A/C, TV, minibar, coffeemaker, hair dryer, iron.

Hotel St. Gotthard ⭐ A longtime favorite of the Swiss, Hotel St. Gotthard is located on the main shopping street, only a block from the railroad station. For more than a century, it has been convenient for shops, transportation, business centers, bus terminals, and restaurants. Rooms and suites, including a new collection of business-class units, are generously furnished in various styles and come in a range of sizes. Amenities include voice mail and videos, along with deluxe toiletries in the bathrooms. Suites and business-class rooms have fax machines. The welcome here is warmer and more personal than it is at the giants already recommended.

Bahnhofstrasse 87, CH-8023 Zurich. ✆ **800/457-4000** in the U.S., or 01/227-77-00. Fax 01/227-77-50. www.hotelstgotthard.ch. 150 units. 445SF–560SF ($244.75–$308) double; 730SF ($401.50–$522.50) suite. AE, DC, MC, V. Parking 35SF ($19.25). Tram: 6, 7, 11, or 13. **Amenities:** 3 restaurants; 3 bars; health club; sauna; room service; massage room; babysitting; laundry/dry cleaning; nonsmoking rooms. *In room:* A/C in half the rooms, TV, minibar, coffeemaker, hair dryer, iron (in some).

Hotel Zum Storchen ⭐⭐ This hotel claims to be the oldest in Europe, with origins going back to 1357. However, it was completely rebuilt in 1939, just at the outbreak of World War II. A traditional government-rated four-star hotel, it is an unusual choice for Zurich. Although Zurich's deluxe hotels are far better known, this is the only one directly on the Limmat River and seems more overrun with tourists than the more prestigious Eden au lac, which also lures discerning clients seeking an Old-World ambience. Supposedly named for the storks that nested on the roof, the Storchen is undeniably romantic. A favorite feature is the cafe terrace, which provides a sweeping panorama of Old Zurich. The mid-sized rooms are warmly and invitingly decorated and maintained in state-of-the-art condition. The most desirable units have French windows opening onto the water, across to the floodlit Rathaus. Be sure to reserve ahead of time, especially in summer.

Am Weinplatz 2, CH-8001 Zurich. ✆ **800/457-4000** in the U.S. or 01/227-27-27. Fax 01/227-27-00. www. storchen.ch. 74 units. 545SF–650SF ($299.75–$357.50) double; 950SF ($522.50) suite. Rates include buffet breakfast. AE, DC, MC, V. Parking 30SF ($16.50). Tram: 4 or 15. **Amenities:** 2 restaurants; bar; room service; babysitting; laundry/dry cleaning. *In room:* A/C, TV, minibar, coffeemaker, hair dryer.

Savoy Baur en Ville ✿✿✿   Savoy Baur en Ville is a Zurich landmark and has been since 1838. It's a grand and elegant choice, although coming nowhere near the grandeur of Bauer au Lac. In 1994, the hotel completed a thorough and expensive set of renovations, which almost immediately sparked its leading competitors to renovate as well. It has kept in great shape since. A conservative and refined hotel, it's one of the premier spots of Zurich. Its six stories are conspicuously located amid stores on Paradeplatz, a 5-minute walk from the lake. The public rooms contain high ceilings and are decorated with occasional touches of gilt and expensive accessories. The bedrooms are quietly dignified and decorated in a wide range of styles. Rooms on the sixth floor have balconies, with space for sunbathing or breakfast.

Am Paradeplatz, CH-8022 Zurich. ✆ **01/215-25-25.** Fax 01/215-25-00. www.savoy-baurenville.ch. 112 units. 700SF ($385) double; 1,400SF ($770) suite. Rates include continental breakfast. AE, DC, MC, V. Parking 25SF ($13.75). Tram: 4, 6, 11, or 13. **Amenities:** Restaurant; bar; salon; room service; babysitting; laundry/dry cleaning. *In room:* A/C, TV, minibar, coffeemaker, hair dryer, safe (in some).

Widder Hotel ✿✿✿   Today this is Zurich's most up-to-date deluxe hotel, rivaled in the neighborhood only by the superior Baur au Lac, but well ahead of the Savoy in overall tranquility and comfort. In the early 1990s, the Union Bank of Switzerland managed to acquire 10 interconnected buildings—some associated with the city's medieval butchers' guild—clustered around a central courtyard in the capital's historic core. The well-respected architect they hired, Ms. Tilla Theus, successfully emphasized, rather than diminished, their individual differences when they were combined into this sophisticated international hotel, creating an architectural ensemble that has been praised by architects and cultural authorities ever since.

During the renovations, great care was used to retain the original stone walls, murals, frescos, and ceilings. The result is a unique hotel where every room is different—sometimes radically so—from its neighbors, and where the color scheme (pastel beige, pink, blue, or yellow) reflects the color of the exterior of whichever of the 10 buildings you happen to be in. Interior furnishings range from the metallic, minimalist, and very modern to the traditional. Views from the bedrooms extend out over either the Rennweg, the Augustinergasse, or the buildings' inner courtyard, and some enjoy vistas of the stately Augustinerkirche nearby.

Rennweg 7, CH-8001 Zürich. ✆ **01/224-25-26.** Fax 01/224-24-24. www.widderhotel.ch. 49 units. 575SF–695SF ($316.25–$382.25) double; 825SF–1,400SF ($453.75–$770) suite. Rates include breakfast. AE, DC, MC, V. Parking 28SF ($15.40). Tram: 6, 7, or 11. **Amenities:** Restaurant; bar; health club; room service; babysitting; laundry/dry cleaning. *In room:* TV, fax machine, minibar, coffeemaker, hair dryer, safe (in some).

EXPENSIVE

Hotel Arabella Sheraton Neues Schloss ✿   A modern, government-rated four-star hotel, this well-respected choice lies south of Paradeplatz between Bahnhofstrasse and the lake, near the Tonhalle/Kongresshaus. In this price category it's a far more comfortable and pleasing choice than the equally ranked Inter-Continental Zurich and the Atlantis Sheraton. Owned by the Arabella group, the hotel is small and discreet with a helpful staff. The lobby, restaurant, and public rooms, all recently renovated, have a bright, welcoming atmosphere, as do the well-furnished bedrooms (which have soundproof windows). The rooms are exceedingly well maintained and comfortable.

Stockerstrasse 17, CH-8002 Zurich. ✆ **01/286-94-00.** Fax 01/286-94-45. www.arabellasheraton.com. 58 units. 470SF–610SF ($258.50–$335.50) double; 900SF–1,100SF ($495–$605) suite. Rates include buffet breakfast. AE, DC, MC, V. Parking 30SF ($16.50) outside, 40SF ($22) in a garage. Tram: 6, 7, or 13 to Stocker-strasse. **Amenities:** Restaurant; bar; room service; babysitting; laundry/dry cleaning; nonsmoking rooms. *In room:* A/C, TV, minibar, hair dryer, safe.

Hotel Inter-Continental ⚜   The largest government-rated four-star hotel in Switzerland is a modern complex decorated with sculpture, paintings, and a stark color scheme. In this category, only the Atlantis Sheraton has a slight edge. Guests have access to a good network of bus and tram lines as the hotel is only 10 minutes from the center of town. This hotel makes special efforts to market itself to the international business community, as it lies at the western edge of the business district near an industrial quarter. The rooms are equipped with double-glazed windows and small tiled bathrooms and follow typical Inter-Continental standards—tasteful and always comfortable. Each room contains pay TV, which can receive films in seven languages, including English.

Badenerstrasse 420, CH-8040 Zurich. ℂ **800/327-0200** in the U.S., or 01/404-44-44. Fax 01/404-44-40. www.interconti.com. 364 units. 305SF–370SF ($167.75–$203.50) double; 623SF ($342.65) suite. AE, DC, MC, V. Rates include breakfast. Parking 20SF ($11). Tram: 2 or 3. **Amenities:** Restaurant; cafeteria; bar; health club; sauna; room service; babysitting; laundry/dry cleaning. *In room:* A/C, TV, minibar, coffeemaker (in some), hair dryer, safe.

MODERATE

Hotel Kindli ⚜   Set at the end of a steep street (Rennweg) in Old Town, in a pedestrian zone, this 16th-century building is one of Zurich's most well-recommended middle-bracket hotels. In the '90s it was completely renovated, with a different color scheme designed for each of the nice-sized bedrooms, and a flowery overlay of Laura Ashley fabrics throughout. Each room contains an eclectic blend of old and new furniture and an efficient bathroom.

Pfalzgasse 1, CH-8001 Zurich. ℂ **01/211-59-17.** Fax 01/211-65-28. 20 units. 320SF–340SF ($176–$187) double. Rates include continental breakfast. AE, DC, MC, V. Parking 30SF ($16.50). Tram: 7, 11, or 13. **Amenities:** Restaurant. *In room:* A/C, TV, minibar.

Hotel Zurichberg ⚜ *(Kids*   This hotel stands on a hillside 1¼ miles east of Zurich's center. In 1994, a team of architects and entrepreneurs radically reno-vated a century-old, brick-sided hotel, and added a futuristic-looking annex, interconnecting them with an underground tunnel stretching beneath a lavish garden. Views from the spacious bedrooms encompass either the forest or the lakes and mountains. Because of the convenient and frequent tram service, you do not need a car to stay here. Since its inauguration, several prestigious archi-tectural awards have been lavished upon the property for its successful merging of late-Victorian and avant-garde styles. The curved sides of the annex have been compared to the exterior of the Guggenheim museum in New York. Separating the buildings are two children's playgrounds, the above-mentioned garden, and a warm-weather terrace where tables from the hotel's cafe, Colibri, and its more substantial restaurant, the Kiebitz, are placed during clement weather. Bedrooms are minimalist, accented with as much full-grained wood as possible and occa-sional touches of bamboo.

Orellistrasse 21, CH-8044 Zürich. ℂ **01/268-35-35.** Fax 01/268-35-45. www.zuerichberg.ch. 67 units. 215SF–260SF ($118.25–$143) double. Rates include breakfast. AE, DC, MC, V. Parking 10SF ($5.50). Tram: 6. **Amenities:** Restaurant; cafe; room service; laundry/dry cleaning. *In room:* TV, minibar, hair dryer (in some).

INEXPENSIVE

Hotel Bristol ⚜ *(Value*   This small hotel stands on a hill near the main train station, behind the major road to the airport. For many years, Hotel Bristol has been one of Zurich's best-known and most successful small hotels despite its lack of amenities. The bedrooms are well maintained, frequently renovated, and furnished to a high standard of comfort. The helpful staff makes you feel right at home in the center of Zurich. No alcoholic beverages are sold, and only breakfast is served. The hotel is accessible to travelers with disabilities, equipped with an elevator and an entrance ramp.

Stampfensbachstrasse 34, CH-8035 Zurich. ℂ 01/258-44-44. Fax 01/258-44-00. www.hotelbristol.ch. 53 units. 175SF–195SF ($96.25–$107.25) double; 220SF ($121) triple. Rates include cold buffet breakfast. AE, DC, MC, V. Tram: 11 or 14. **Amenities:** Room service; laundry/dry cleaning. *In room:* TV, iron, hair dryer, safe.

Hotel Rex   Set close to the railway station, Hotel Rex is a white-painted, relatively nondescript-looking hotel offering clean yet simple bedrooms and a well-informed staff. Originally built in the 1940s, the hotel rises five stories above a busy commercial neighborhood. Bedrooms are conservatively outfitted in a modern style and are equipped with neat, organized bathrooms.

Weinbergstrasse 92, 8006 Zurich. ℂ **01/360-25-25.** Fax 01/360-25-52. hotelrex@swissonline.ch. 38 units. 195SF ($107.25) double. Rate includes breakfast. AE, DC, MC, V. Tram: 7. **Amenities:** Restaurant. *In room:* TV, minibar.

Hotel Walhalla *(Value*   Set close to the railway station, this hotel is one of the relatively cheap bargains in central Zurich. It occupies two five-story buildings, one of which was renovated in 1997 (and which contains the better-looking and more comfortable bedrooms). The other is older and a bit dowdier, with high-ceilinged bedrooms and very little architectural flair. All rooms and bathrooms, however, are comfortable and clean. The dining room here serves only breakfast.

Limmatstrasse 5, 8005 Zurich. ℂ **01/446-54-00.** Fax 01/446-54-54. valhalla-hotel@bluewin.ch. 48 units. 200SF ($110) double. AE, DC, MC, V. Tram: 3 or 14. **Amenities:** Restaurant. *In room:* TV.

X-Tra Hotel Limmat *(★ (Finds*   The Limmat is one of the most durable of the cost-conscious hotels of downtown Zurich. The hotel occupies part of a four-story building erected in 1935 in the Bauhaus style as a convention center, and whose boxy-looking façade is today protected as a historic monument. You can expect more here than just a place to stay: Its management, in place since 1997, is one of the largest organizers of rock-and-roll concerts in Switzerland, often staging their acts in the cavernous restaurant and night club that occupies the ground floor. Consequently, members of the bands that play here are often in residence within the hotel, a policy that adds to the cachet of the place for counterculture rock-and-roll enthusiasts across Switzerland. (Residents of the hotel receive a 15SF discount off their admission to the nightclub.) Accommodations are streamlined, partially paneled, and outfitted in a style you might identify as Danish modern. Eight single units do not contain private bathrooms, but toilets and showers lie just off the corridors.

In the Limmathaus, Limmatstrasse 118, CH-8005 Zurich. ℂ 01/448-15-95. Fax 01/448-15-96. www.x-tra.ch. 43 units (35 with bathroom). 185SF ($101.75) double without bathroom; 205SF ($112.75) double with bathroom. Rates include breakfast. Parking 15SF ($8.25) per night. AE, DC, MC, V. Tram: 4 or 13 to Limmatplatz. **Amenities:** Restaurant; bar; cafe with outdoor terrace; nightclub; discounted admission at a nearby health club; laundry. *In room:* Minibar, TV.

ON THE RIGHT BANK
VERY EXPENSIVE

Dolder Grand Hotel *(★*   Sad to say, but the Baur au Lac and the Widder now surpass the standards of this revered monument. When Einstein, Winston Churchill, Arturo Toscanini, and Henry Kissinger were checking in, the Dolder Grand was one of the grandest hotels in Europe. Today it is going through a transitional period; with new owners cutting back and rumors of a future sale, the hotel still enjoys the showcase of a government-rated five-star hotel, but not the grand service. Only 6 minutes from the center of Zurich, it is reached by tram and funicular. The hotel itself is part medieval fortress, part Renaissance chateau, and part 19th-century palace. The cogwheel funicular that connects the hotel to the center of Zurich is only one of its unusual features. Built atop a 50-acre wooded promontory, the hotel is located in a conservative residential section of Zurich and is surrounded by gardens. It consists of two balconied wings, with half-timbered replicas of watchtowers on the far ends. Public rooms include the Gobelin salon, with an enormous tapestry. The 1899 main building contains the original bedrooms; the 60-room modern wing was added in 1964. The newer wing contains the better rooms, although loyalists still prefer the more traditional units of the older building, which evoke the grand hotel style, with artifacts from the gilded age of the haute bourgeoisie. In contrast, bedrooms in the modern wing are painted in light colors and outfitted with conservative modern furnishings.

Kurhausstrasse 65, CH-8032 Zurich. © 01/269-30-00. Fax 01/269-30-01. www.doldergrand.ch. 183 units. 540SF–620SF ($297–$341) double; 707SF ($388.85) junior suite, from 1,000SF ($550) suite. Rates include buffet breakfast. AE, DC, MC, V. Parking 25SF ($13.75). Tram: 3, 8, or 15; then the Dolderbahn funicular to the hotel itself. **Amenities:** Restaurant; 2 bars; pool; 9-hole golf course; 5 tennis courts; health club; sauna; skating rink; room service; babysitting; laundry/dry cleaning. *In room:* A/C (in most), TV, minibar, hair dryer, safe.

Hotel Eden au Lac *Finds*   A grand government-rated five-star hotel with an ornamented facade, Eden du Lac resembles the Paris Opéra, with neoclassical columns, pediments, corner urns, and wrought-iron garlands of fruits and flowers. It comes nowhere near the grandeur of the Baur au Lac, yet is "the sleeper" among the grand hotels of Zurich. Like the hotel Zum Storchen (see above), but far more impressive and deluxe, the Eden au Lac is for the client who prefers an old-fashioned, traditional hotel. The walk from the hotel to downtown Zurich resembles an old-fashioned promenade. Accommodation prices here are based on the size of the room, not the view. So sometimes if you'll settle for a slightly smaller room, you will be rewarded with a lake view. The guest rooms and bathrooms aren't spacious but each is comfortable with many amenities.

Utoquai 45, CH-8023 Zurich. © 01/266-25-25. Fax 01/266-25-00. www.edenaulac.ch. 53 units. 570SF–630SF ($313.50–$346.50) double; 900SF–1,200SF ($495–$660) suite. Rates include buffet breakfast. AE, DC, MC, V. Free parking. Tram: 2 or 4. **Amenities:** Restaurant; bar; room service; laundry/dry cleaning. *In room:* TV, minibar, hair dryer.

EXPENSIVE

Hotel Ambassador   The grand and ornate façade of this government-rated four-star hotel is in sharp contrast to a stripped-down interior, which is more efficiently decorated, and more streamlined, than you might have thought. Built late in the 19th century, in beige stone with lots of beaux-arts-style carvings, it rises from a point near the tramway junction at the Bellevueplatz, near the Opera House. Bedrooms are high-ceilinged and generally spacious. Inside, a well-trained staff attends to your comfort, providing all the services that a traveling business representative might need. In this category, the Ambassador lacks the frills and flourish of its competitors, Florhof and Waldhaus Dolder, but still has its devotees who prefer the simplified no-nonsense atmosphere.

Falkenstrasse 6, CH-8008 Zurich. © 01/261-76-00. Fax 01/251-23-94. www.ambassadorhotel.ch. 46 units. 360SF–480SF ($198–$264) double; 420SF–580SF ($231–$319) suite. Rates include buffet breakfast. AE, DC, MC, V. Parking 25SF ($13.75). Tram: 4. **Amenities:** Restaurant; room service; laundry/dry cleaning. *In room:* A/C (in some), TV, minibar, coffeemaker, hair dryer.

Hotel Romantic Florhof ★★★ (Value)   This is the most charming and tranquil of the little boutique hotels of Zurich, located on the eastern edge of the Old Town. Originally built in the 15th century as a merchant's home, these premises became a hotel during the 1920s. The Florhof represents top value in Zurich and is known as a gracious and well-managed hotel with a loyal clientele. Although the public rooms retain much of their antique glamour (including a noteworthy blue-and-white kachel often used long ago for heating), many of the bedrooms are modern and functional in their inspiration. The single units are a bit small but most doubles are of decent size and are nicely outfitted with plaster work on the ceilings, exceedingly comfortable beds, stone-topped night stands, and generous bathrooms.

Florhofgasse 4, CH-8001 Zurich. © 01/261-44-70. Fax 01/261-46-11. www.romantikhotels.com/zuerich. 33 units. 350SF–410SF ($192.50–$225.50) double; 480SF–580SF ($264–$319) junior suite. Rates include continental breakfast. AE, DC, MC, V. Parking 15SF ($8.25). Tram: 3. **Amenities:** Restaurant; room service; laundry/dry cleaning. *In room:* TV, minibar.

Hotel Waldhaus Dolder ★ (Finds)   Surrounded by forest in the Dolder residential section of Zurich, this hotel offers an experience in country living, yet is only 15 minutes from the center of town and easily accessible by public transportation. It is preferred by many because of its resort-like facilities, almost completely lacking, of course, in hotels in the city center. The hotel consists of two towers, one housing 75 rooms and a suite, the other 25 apartments. All doubles have a kitchenette and a balcony. Apartments, on the other hand, offer a kitchenette and terrace and are mainly for long-term clients (they can be rented nightly if available). Accommodations above the tree line offer panoramic views of the lake.

Kurhausstrasse 20, CH-8030 Zurich. © 01/269-10-00. Fax 01/269-10-01. www.dolderwaldhaus.ch. 100 units. 350SF–450SF ($192.50–$247.50) double; 650SF ($357.50) suite; 850SF ($467.50) apt. for 2. AE, DC, MC, V. Tram: 3, 8, or 15. **Amenities:** Restaurant; indoor pool; minigolf course; sauna; massage; room service; babysitting; laundry/dry cleaning. *In room:* A/C (in some), TV, minibar, coffeemaker, hair dryer. Nearby nine-hole golf course, tennis courts, and outdoor pool are a 10-minute walk away, but use included in hotel rates.

Marriott Hotel Zurich ★   Situated high above the banks of the Limmat a 5-minute walk across the river from the railway station, this hotel is connected to its luxurious modern wing, La Résidence, by a walkway. Its nice-sized bedrooms are up-to-date and comfortable, with such amenities as a cosmetic box, oversize working desk, and direct-dial phone. You can enjoy a view over the lake from anywhere in the main house above the 10th floor.

Neumühlequai 42, CH-8001 Zurich. © 800/228-9290 in the U.S., or 01/360-70-70. Fax 01/360-77-77. www.marriotthotels.com. 260 units. 330SF–450SF ($181.50–$247.50) double; from 850SF ($467.50) suite. AE, DC, MC, V. Parking 30SF ($16.50). Tram: 11 or 14. **Amenities:** 3 restaurants; bar; heated indoor pool; sauna; business center; salon; room service; massage; babysitting; laundry/dry cleaning. *In room:* A/C, TV, minibar, hair dryer, iron.

MODERATE

Hotel Helmhaus ★   In the center of Zurich, Helmhaus is 5 minutes from Paradeplatz/Bahnhofstrasse, the opera house, major museums, and the lake. Set on a boat-landing square, it stands a block from the river at the corner of Limmatquai. Renovated in 1992, the hotel is one of the best in the moderately priced category with a pleasantly personal atmosphere. The bedrooms are newly furnished, often in bright florals, and the bathrooms are a nice size.

Schiffländeplatz 30, CH-8001 Zurich. © 01/251-88-10. Fax 01/251-04-30. www.helmhaus.ch. 24 units. 280SF–360SF ($154–$198) double. Rates include buffet breakfast. AE, DC, MC, V. Parking 25SF ($13.75). Tram: 4 from the Hauptbahnhof. **Amenities:** Shuttle-bus service between the hotel and the airport; business center; laundry/dry cleaning. *In room:* A/C, minibar, hair dryer, iron, safe.

Hôtel Opéra   This cozy choice, next to the Opera House, may be short on facilities, but it's a favorite among many business travelers seeking a central location. Try for one of the corner rooms or an accommodation on the fourth or fifth floor. The Opéra boasts a large, carpeted lobby, with an assortment of armchairs, where you can purchase beer and soft drinks. Although the Opéra doesn't have a restaurant of its own, guests walk across the street to the Hotel Ambassador to use their restaurant, which features fondue and fish dishes.

Dufourstrasse 5, CH-8008 Zurich. ℂ **01/251-90-90.** Fax 01/258-99-00. www.operahotel.ch. 62 units. 340SF–420SF ($187–$231) double; 400SF–480SF ($220–$264) triple. Rates include buffet breakfast. AE, DC, MC, V. Parking 28SF ($15.40) nearby. Tram: 4. **Amenities:** Laundry/dry cleaning. *In room:* A/C, TV, minibar, hair dryer, safe.

Hotel Rössli 🎯   The result of a 1990 radical restoration of a very old house in Oberdorf, this hotel is hip, youthful, stylish, and appealing. The mid-sized bedrooms are high-tech and comfortable, each with its own monochromatic color scheme. The suite is rather special. It doesn't have a separate living room, but offers three bedrooms and a Dachterrasse (terrace on the roof) opening onto a panoramic view of Zurich. Breakfast is the only meal served. There's an in-house bar attracting a clientele of artists and musicians, among others.

Rössligasse 7, CH-8001 Zurich. ℂ **01/256-70-50.** Fax 01/256-70-51. www.hotelroessli.ch. 18 units. 280SF ($154) double; 350SF ($192.50) suite. Rates include breakfast. AE, DC, MC, V. Parking 36SF ($19.80). Tram: 4 or 15. **Amenities:** Bar. *In room:* TV, minibar, hair dryer.

Hôtel Seehof   Set close to the opera house and the promenade that parallels the lake, this small-scale, postmodern hotel was opened in 1999 after a radical renovation and modernization of the original 1930s-era private house. Whereas the hotel retains the original russet-colored exterior, the interior decor is angular and efficient, with stark white walls and the kind of black furniture that you'd expect in a trendy art gallery. Fortunately, the angularity is softened, in both the public areas and the bedrooms, with varnished and beautifully crafted oaken floors and a revolving series of artworks, usually photographs, by Swiss artists. Many of the rooms are reserved by opera singers performing at the nearby Opera House.

Seehofstrasse 11, CH-8008 Zurich. ℂ **01/254-57-57.** Fax 01/254-57-58. www.hotelseehof.ch. 19 units. Mon–Thurs 280SF ($154) double; Fri–Sun 256SF ($140.80) double. Rates include breakfast. AE, DC, MC, V. Tram: 4. **Amenities:** Restaurant (open Mon–Fri for lunch only); bar (closed weekends July–Aug); room service; laundry/dry cleaning. *In room:* TV, minibar, hair dryer, safe (in some).

INEXPENSIVE

Hotel Limmatblick   This hotel, owned by the Leonhard family, is located in the Old Town, a 2-minute walk from the main railroad station. The hotel underwent a major renovation in 2000, but the rooms are small. They contain twin beds and are equipped with rather cramped bathrooms with shower. In contrast to the bedrooms, the hotel's inviting restaurant, Arvenstube, is cozy and traditional, like something you'd find in the Tyrol. In summer, there's a terrace overlooking the water. In addition, a coffee shop, Wyss-Müllirädli, serves such Zurich specialties as bratwurst with onions and rösti (Swiss hash browns).

Limmatquai 136, CH-8001 Zurich. ℂ **01/254-60-00.** Fax 01/252-38-70. 16 units. 190SF ($104.50) double; 220SF ($121) junior suite. Rates include continental breakfast. AE, DC, MC, V. Closed Dec 15–Jan 6. Tram: 4 or 15. **Amenities:** Restaurant; room service; laundry. *In room:* TV, minibar, hair dryer, safe.

Pension St. Josef   Set within two adjacent, rather nondescript-looking houses, this simple pension is run by an offshoot of the Catholic Church, and fills about half of its accommodations with students during the school year. In summer, however, the full complement of 81 beds, scattered among 43 rooms, is available for rentals. It's particularly appropriate for women traveling alone, thanks to a strict staff that doesn't tolerate any behavior too raucous. Located within a 6-minute walk from the railway station, it's clean, comfortable, and well maintained. A 1998 renovation upgraded about half the rooms.

Hirschengraben 64–68, CH-8001 Zurich. ℂ 01/250-57-57. Fax 01/251-28-08. www.st-josef.ch. 81 beds arranged into 43 units (20 with bathroom). 180SF ($99) double with bathroom, 110SF ($60.50) double without bathroom; 210SF ($115.50) triple with bathroom, 160SF ($88) triple without bathroom; 245SF ($134.75) quad with bathroom. Rates include buffet breakfast. AE, DC, MC, V. Parking 15SF ($8.25). Tram: 3 and 10. Bus: 31. *In room:* No phone.

Zic-Zac Rock Hotel   Funky, hip, and trendy, this budget hotel and hangout isn't everyone's bag, but it's unique in Zurich. All the rooms are named after rock-and-roll superstars. You can request your favorites: Led Zeppelin, Pink Floyd, Mick Jagger and The Rolling Stones, Bryan Adams. The place is clean, and the furnishings, although comfortable, are as eclectic and funky as the artists they honor. Only four doubles and the quad have private bathrooms (showers, not tubs), but the corridor bathrooms are generally adequate unless the hotel is completely full. The clients are obviously young, as befits such a theme hotel, and the location is also convenient—right in the heart of Zurich's party scene. This is not the quietest or most tranquil hotel in Zurich.

Marktgasse 7, CH-8001 Zurich. ℂ 01/261-21-81. Fax 01/261-21-75. www.rockhotelziczac.ch. 50 units, 5 with bathroom. 115SF ($63.25) double without bathroom, 165SF ($90.75) double with bathroom; 170SF ($93.50) triple without bathroom; 255SF ($140.25) quad with bathroom. AE, MC, V. Tram: 4. **Amenities:** Restaurant; laundry. *In room:* TV.

4 Where to Dine

Zurich restaurants feature both a selection of international and Swiss specialties. The local favorite is *rösti* (potatoes grated and fried). You should also try *zürigschnätzlets* (shredded veal cooked with mushrooms in a cream sauce laced with white wine) and *kutteln nach Zürcherart* (tripe with mushrooms, white wine, and caraway seed). Another classic dish is *leberspiesschen* (liver cubes skewered with bacon and sage and served with potatoes and beans).

Among local wines, the white Riesling Sylvaner is outstanding and great with fish. The light Clevner wines, always chilled, are made from blue Burgundy grapes that grow around the lake. You should be able to order wine by the glass, even in first-class restaurants.

In 2000, new food and beverage laws were passed by the canton of Zurich that had long-reaching implications for the city's restaurant trade. The new laws made it easier and cheaper to establish a restaurant. Gone were the labyrinth of qualifications and red tape that until then had been necessary for restaurant-owner wanna-bes. Since then, new restaurants—many of them funkier and more irreverent than anything the city had ever seen before—have been established, often in unexpected places that include former factories, foundries, boatyards, and warehouses.

ON THE LEFT BANK
VERY EXPENSIVE

Sukhothai ★★ THAI   With a deliberately simple interior graced with photographs of the royal family of Thailand and a discreet scattering of Thai objets d'art, this restaurant is the premier Thai restaurant in Switzerland. Food is presented in varying degrees of spiciness, and might include lemongrass soup

Where to Dine in Zurich

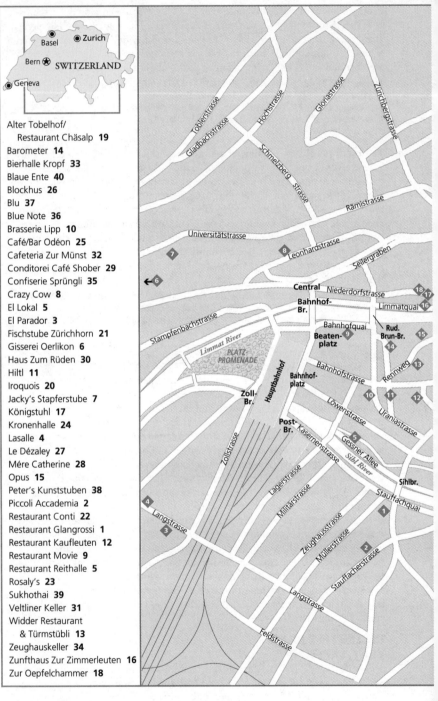

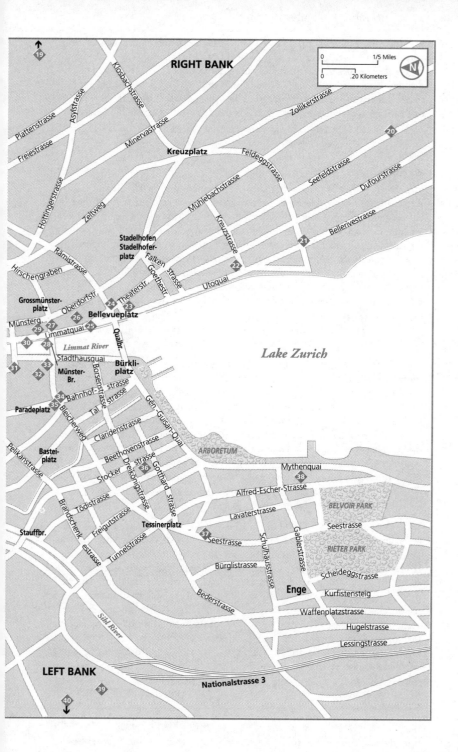

RIGHT BANK

Plattenstrasse
Freiestrasse
Asylstrasse
Klosbachstrasse
Minervastrasse
Zollikerstrasse
Kreuzplatz
Feldeggstrasse
Seefeldstrasse
Dufourstrasse
Hottingerstrasse
Zeltweg
Mühlebachstrasse
Bellerivestrasse
Ramistrasse
Kreuzstrasse
Stadelhofen
Stadelhofer-
platz
Falken strasse
Goethestr.
Hirschengraben
Utoquai
Grossmünster-
platz
Oberdorfstr.
Theaterstr.
Münsterg.
Limmatquai
Bellevueplatz
Quaibr.
Limmat River
Stadthausquai
Bürkli-
platz
Münster-
Br.
Bahnhof- strasse
Börsenstrasse
Tal strasse
Lake Zurich
Paradeplatz
Bleicherweg
Claridenstrasse
Gen.-Guisan-Quai
ARBORETUM
Mythenquai
Basteiplatz
Beethovenstrasse
Stocker strasse
Dreikönigstrasse
Gotthard strasse
Alfred-Escher-Strasse
BELVOIR PARK
Pelikanstrasse
Brandschenk-
estrasse
Tödistrasse
Freigutstrasse
Tessinerplatz
Lavaterstrasse
Seestrasse
RIETER PARK
Stauffbr.
Tunnelstrasse
Seestrasse
Schulhausstrasse
Gablerstrasse
Scheideggstrasse
Bürglistrasse
Enge
Kurfistensteig
Bederstrasse
Waffenplatzstrasse
Hugelstrasse
Sihl River
Lessingstrasse
LEFT BANK
Nationalstrasse 3

0   1/5 Miles
0   .20 Kilometers
N

studded with chicken, a papaya-based Thai salad, brochettes of chicken or shrimp, a selection of rice-based dishes, and a varied array of exotic fish flown in from the waters of East Asia and prepared according to traditional Thai recipes. The chef does an admirable job with all of these dishes, and the flavors are bracing and aromatic, a marvelous change of pace from the typical Swiss cuisine. In the words of one habitué, this restaurant has awakened the sleepy taste buds of Zurichers.

Erlachstrasse 46. ℂ 01/462-66-22. Reservations recommended. Main courses 55SF–85SF ($30.25–$46.75); menu surprise 150SF ($82.50). AE, MC, V. Tues–Fri 11am–2:30pm and Tues–Sat 5:30–11pm. Closed July 12–Aug 10. Tram: 9 or 14.

EXPENSIVE

Piccoli Accademia ★★ ITALIAN The finest and most elegant Italian restaurant in Zurich, Piccoli Accademia is much appreciated at lunchtime by bankers and businesspeople, who use it to entertain their clients. In an Art Deco setting scattered with a collection of oil paintings, a uniformed staff politely serves Italian regional dishes, ranging from Venetian to Neapolitan. Specialties include several succulent versions of pasta, risotto with mushrooms, and veal liver alla Veneziana. Daily specialties, when in season, might include various game dishes, including pheasant, venison, wild boar, and partridge. You are almost never disappointed with the offerings here. It may not be imaginative cuisine, but it's certainly good.

Rotwandstrasse 48. ℂ 01/241-42-02. Reservations recommended, especially in summer. Main courses 45SF–62SF ($24.75–$34.10). AE, DC, MC, V. Mon–Fri noon–2pm; Mon–Sat 6:30–10pm. Tram: 2, 3, 9, 10, or 14.

Restaurant Glangrossi ★ ITALIAN One of Zurich's leading Italian restaurants, this establishment continues to thrive. Dine inside one of three pink and cream-colored dining rooms outfitted somewhat coyly in the Louis XV style, or, during clement weather, sit in the meticulously landscaped garden. They serve typical Italian cuisine including gnocchi with tomato sauce and basil; several kinds of risotto, most of them with mushrooms; and such dishes as roasted sea bass with fresh vegetables and rack of lamb with wine and rosemary sauce. Excellent ingredients are deftly handled by the kitchen staff, and the food is always nicely prepared and fresh tasting. The restaurant remains deservedly popular.

Rebgasse 8. ℂ 01/241-20-64. Reservations required. Main courses 32SF–55SF ($17.60–$30.25). AE, DC, MC, V. Mon–Fri noon–2pm; Mon–Sat 7pm–midnight. Tram: 2, 9, or 14.

Veltliner Keller ★ SWISS/ITALIAN/FRENCH If endurance and longevity are hallmarks of a good restaurant, this dining room would emerge near the top. Veltliner Keller has been a restaurant since 1551; before that it was a wine cellar. Located next to St. Peter's Church in Old Town, it has an ancient interior of carved mountain pine wood called arve (grown only in Switzerland). The chef prepares familiar Swiss specialties, and does so exceedingly well, including the classic chopped-veal dish of Zurich. Several Italian dishes are also featured, including veal piccata and osso buco. A lot of the seafood is grilled or poached, including salmon. Ingredients change with the season, but you can always count on the house's signature dish, a Veltliner pot—baked macaroni with meat and beef liver cooked in a casserole.

Schlüsselgasse 8. ℂ 01/225-40-40. Reservations recommended. Main courses 41SF–54SF ($22.55–$29.70). AE, DC, MC, V. Mon–Fri 11:30am–2pm and 6:30–9:30pm. Closed July 18–Aug 15. Tram: 2, 9, 11, or 13.

Widder Restaurant & Türmstübli ★ INTERNATIONAL When this restaurant opened in the mid-1990s, many of its clients came as an excuse to view the iconoclastic architecture of the hotel that contained it. (See "Where to Stay," earlier.) But since then, these twin dining rooms have taken on a life of their own, and are now sought out as independent eateries in their own right. Although the Widder Restaurant is outfitted in a rustic, folksy style, while the Türmstübli is angular, minimalist, and devoid of most alpine reminders, the same menu is served in both. Look for a clientele from Zurich's financial community, along with a scattering of wealthy bohemians. Menu items include well-prepared versions of chicken mousse served in crepe-style pastry with applesauce, a sumptuous breast of Barbary duckling in an orange-flavored crust served with a pumpkin-and-lettuce-based piccata sauce and galettes of sweet corn, a delectable scampi with morel-stuffed ravioli in a pepper-flavored butter sauce, and a particularly delicious gratin of salmon-trout with cucumber sauce, dillweed, and new potatoes.

In the Widder Hotel, Rennweg 7. ℂ **01/224-2526.** Reservations recommended. Main courses 30SF–49SF ($16.50–$26.95). AE, DC, MC, V. Daily 11:30am–2pm and 6:30–11pm. Tram: 6, 7, 11, or 13.

MODERATE

Brasserie Lipp FRENCH/SWISS   Everything about this place emulates the decor and seating configuration of Lipp, one of Paris's most famous Art Nouveau brasseries. So authentic is the duplication, in fact, that the Zurich version paid a royalty to the original in Paris for the right to use the name and a recreation of its decor. The venue is loud, fast paced and, during the noon rush, frenzied as waiters squeeze between narrowly spaced tables bearing trays of choucroute (sauerkraut); platters of fresh fish such as sole meunière, pepper steaks, smoked salmon, and filets of herring in cream sauce; terrines; many kinds of cold salad; and such daily specials as Moroccan couscous. Don't expect an ambience where you can linger for hours at a table. Nonetheless, the French-inspired ambience is a refreshing change from the Teutonic overtones of many of this restaurant's competitors. The bar, the Jules Verne, is separately recommended under "Zurich After Dark," later.

Uraniastrasse 9. ℂ **01/211-11-55.** Reservations recommended, especially Fri–Sat. Main courses 28SF–48SF ($15.40–$26.40). AE, DC, MC, V. Mon–Sat 11:30am–11pm (1am Fri–Sat). Tram: 6, 7, 11, or 13.

El Parador ✦ SPANISH   The best Spanish restaurant in Zurich is just off Limmatplatz. You'll receive a warm welcome from the English-speaking staff. The small restaurant is known for its cozy atmosphere and well-prepared specialties. We suggest that you begin with a glass of sherry, such as Tío Pepe. Appetizers include garlic soup and Catalàn salad with ham, eggs, sardines, olives, tuna, and asparagus tips. For a main course, we recommend the paella (made with chicken, mussels, squid, scampi, and shrimp) or a zarzuela (boiled seafood, fisher's style). Another specialty is parrillada, a mixed seafood grill, and an old favorite is pollo al estilo de la Abuelita (chicken with garlic and onions).

Luisenstrasse 43. ℂ **01/272-48-64.** Reservations required. Main courses 30SF–48SF ($16.50–$26.40). MC, V. Mon–Fri noon–1:30pm; Mon–Sat 6–11pm. Closed late Aug to late Sept, Mon in mid-winter. Tram: 4, 13, or 32.

Opus ✦ INTERNATIONAL   In this historic neighborhood, Opus, which opened in 1993, continues to impress local residents with its reasonable prices and superb cuisine. In an ambience sheathed with paneling and marble, and filled with marble-top tables similar to what you might expect in a French cafe, you can drink coffee, beer, or whisky; order light snacks or full meals; or simply while away a sunny afternoon at one of the 10 outdoor tables. A handful of popular dishes are available throughout the year. About five times a month, usually on a Friday or Saturday, cultural performances, ranging from opera to theater, are presented.

Pfalzgasse 1, Rennweg. ☎ 01/211-41-82. Reservations recommended. Main courses 32SF–48SF ($17.60–$26.40). AE, DC, MC, V. Mon–Sat 11:30am–midnight. Closed end of July to Sept. Tram: 6, 7, 11, or 13.

INEXPENSIVE

Barometer ☆ CONTINENTAL/PROVENÇAL   Named after the antique barometer that adorns the space above one of its entrances, this is an upscale bistro whose food is much, much better than you might think at first glance. The success of the food here is in large part due to its France-born chef, Ludovic, who spent years training within some of Switzerland's greatest gastronomic citadels, most notably the Ermitage in Zurich's suburb of Kusnach. Within a postmodern decor of warm golds and blacks, you'll enjoy selections from a sophisticated menu that changes weekly. Stellar examples include a tart garnished with fresh tomatoes and semi-cooked tuna; magret of sweet-and-sour duckling; and semi-frozen peaches with peach sorbet and Baumes-de-Venise dessert wine. Some items on the menu remain constant, including braised shoulder of lamb with saffron-flavored zucchini (served every Monday); and fresh codfish with olives and confit of tomatoes (served every Wednesday).

Glockengasse 16. ☎ 01/211-56-65. Reservations recommended. Main courses 19SF–34SF ($10.45–$18.70). Set menu 44SF ($24.20). AE, DC, MC, V. Mon–Fri 11am–midnight, with a limited menu offered 2–6pm. Tram: 6, 7, 11, or 13.

Bierhalle Kropf ☆ *Kids* SWISS/BAVARIAN/AUSTRIAN   Everyone in Zurich goes to "Der Kropf" for its old-fashioned ambience and generous portions at reasonable prices. The restaurant is in one of the oldest burgher houses in town, a few steps from Paradeplatz. Its dining room has stained-glass windows, polished paneling, chandeliers, and plaster columns. On the walls hang stag horns and painted hunting scenes. You get authentic and well-prepared dishes here. Almost no one, including visiting personalities, local political figures or finicky children, leaves disappointed. Bring along a healthy appetite. Specialties include chopped veal with rösti, stewed meats, pork shank, and pot-au-feu Zurich style. For dessert, we recommend *palatschinken* (a chocolate crêpe) or *apfelstrudel* (apple strudel).

In Gassen 16. ☎ 01/221-18-05. Reservations recommended. Main courses 20SF–40SF ($11–$22). AE, MC, V. Mon–Sat 11:30am–11:30pm. Closed Easter, Dec 25, and Aug 1. Tram: 2, 8, 9, or 11.

Hiltl VEGETARIAN/INDIAN   Founded in 1898 but completely redecorated in 1993, this bright, inviting place is Zurich's leading vegetarian restaurant. Its main attraction is a large salad bar, containing more than 40 different types of freshly prepared vegetables. House creations include vegetable paella, mushrooms Stroganoff, and curry colonial. There's a vast choice of fruit juices, teas, draft beer, and wines priced by the glass. The restaurant is also known for its vegetarian Indian specialties, and after 6pm it features an Indian buffet.

Sihlstrasse 28. ☎ 01/227-70-00. Reservations recommended. Main courses 20SF–30SF ($11–$16.50); 42SF–68SF ($23.10–$37.40) Indian buffet. AE, MC, V. Mon–Sat 7am–11pm, Sun 11am–11pm. Tram: 6, 7, 11, or 13.

Restaurant Kaufleuten *Finds* INTERNATIONAL   Despite its location in the heart of one of Europe's most gilt-edged neighborhoods, a few steps from the Bahnhofstrasse, there's something artfully disheveled and happy-go-lucky about this restaurant. You'll find a deliberately mismatched collection of tables and chairs. The menu is just as eclectic, with offerings derived from virtually everywhere. These include favorites from Thailand (including *tom kha kai*, made of chicken, coconut, and fiery spices); Japan (sushi and miso soup); and Austria (Wiener schnitzel). Also available are tender steaks and several kinds of saltwater and freshwater fish, including salmon, sole, and sea bass. The setting is pleasant, and the place is a fine cost-conscious alternative to more formal spots nearby. The site contains a worn, heavily trafficked bar area that's open daily from 9am till whenever the restaurant closes, and a nightclub that's separately recommended in "Zurich After Dark," later.

Pelikanstrasse 18. ☎ 01/225-33-33. Reservations recommended. Main courses 20SF–45SF ($11–$24.75). AE, DC, MC, V. Mon–Fri 11:30am–2pm; daily 7pm–2am (till 3am Fri–Sat). Tram: 6, 7, 11, or 13.

Restaurant Reithalle INTERNATIONAL   One of Zurich's most genuinely unpretentious restaurants occupies the battered premises of what was originally built as a stable and horseback-riding rink. Cost-conscious locals frequent the Reithalle, which is set on a small island in downtown Zurich, bordered by the Schanzengraben creek and the Seil canal. It's at its most fun in midsummer, when picnic tables are set up on the quiet, cobblestoned inner courtyard, which is mobbed every day at lunch and dinner. The rest of the year, tables are moved into the severe-looking, heavily timbered interior that once sheltered horses and riding equipment from the city and weather outside. Menu items are hearty and generous, and include beef curry; peppered paillard of veal; Iranian-style lamb stew; grilled squid with lemon sauce; and several kinds of pastas and salads. Incidentally, every Saturday night, from 11pm till around 3am, the interior of this place becomes a disco, charging an entrance price of 15SF ($8.25) per person. (Patrons of the restaurant enter free.)

In the Theaterhaus Gessnerallee, Gessnerallee 8. ☎ 01/212-0766. Reservations not necessary. Lunch main courses 15.50SF–30SF ($8.55–$16.50). Dinner main courses 19.50SF–30SF ($10.75–$16.50). AE, DC, MC, V. Mon–Fri 11am–midnight, Sat–Sun 6pm–midnight. Tram: 3.

Zeughauskeller SWISS   This mammoth restaurant, dating from 1487, was once an arsenal; its vast dining room now seats 200. Large wooden chandeliers hang from cast-iron chains, and the walls are decorated with medieval halberds and illustrations of ancient Zurich noblemen. Generous portions of traditional and tasty Swiss dishes are served with steins of local beer. Owners Kurt Andreae and Willy Hammer say that patrons consume some 30 tons of potato salad a year. Hurlimann draft beer is poured from 1,000-liter barrels. Specialties, and excellent ones at that, include calves' liver, Wiener schnitzel, and regional sausages, such as saucisson of Neuchâtel. For 77SF ($42.35), you can order a yard-long sausage— enough to feed four hungry people. Service is quick and efficient.

Am Paradeplatz. ☎ 01/211-26-90. Reservations recommended. Main courses 18SF–38SF ($9.90–$20.90). AE, MC, V. Daily 11:30am–11pm. Tram: 2, 6, 7, 8, 9, 11, or 13.

ON THE RIGHT BANK
VERY EXPENSIVE

Haus Zum Rüden ✦✦ SWISS/FRENCH   The Gothic room in this historic guild house dating from 1295 contains one of the best restaurants in the city. It's especially popular with foreign visitors, even though they often get a somewhat stuffy greeting from the staff. The spacious yet intimate dining room has a hardwood ceiling and stone walls decorated with medieval halberds and stag horns. The chef specializes in *cuisine du marché* (market-fresh cuisine). Foie gras sautéed with a salad makes a stunning opening, followed by salmon prepared in the style of Carcassonne or aromatic roast Scottish lamb delectably flavored with mustard grains.

Limmatqual 42. (©) 01/261-95-66. Reservations required. Main courses 48SF–60SF ($26.40–$33); fixed-price lunch 58SF ($31.90). AE, DC, MC, V. Mon–Fri noon–2pm and 6:30–9:30pm (closed Sat–Sun). Tram: 4 or 15.

Jacky's Stapferstube ★★ SWISS   In a 200-year-old manor house near the university, this restaurant is famous throughout the city for its beef and veal dishes. Manager Jacky Donatz is well known among a crowd of fashionable regular clients. In a typically Swiss dining room with white walls, oil paintings, and darkened beams, you can enjoy perfectly prepared veal cutlets, veal shanks, boiled beef, and a wide array of tender steaks. Meat is priced according to its weight, but the staff can advise you on sizes and cuts. Many diners begin with a mini-platter of stuffed mushrooms. Other dishes include pasta and lobster salad, and there's a well-chosen wine list.

Culmannstrasse 45. (©) 01/361-37-48. Reservations required. Main courses 35SF–105SF ($19.25–$57.75). AE, DC, MC, V. Tues–Sat 11:30am–3pm and 6–10pm. Closed mid-July to mid-Aug. Tram: 9 or 10.

EXPENSIVE

Königstuhl ★ INTERNATIONAL   Königstul occupies two floors of a medieval guildhall that was originally the headquarters of the city's tailors' union. Despite the age of the building, the decoration is very modern, very soothing, and filled with amusing references to old-fashioned Swiss tastes. Note the large carved throne—*königstuhl*—which occupies a prominent position in the restaurant.

Although the food is sophisticated and elegant (and based on whatever fresh ingredients are available in the marketplace), the intricacy of the service rituals are more pronounced in the upper floor restaurant than in the street-level bistro. Prices are higher upstairs as well. Despite that, financial and business leaders seem to love it up there, especially at lunchtime. Menu items include such dishes as cream of herb soup with roasted bacon and croutons; homemade terrine of chicken with black truffles and apple salad; medallions of beef in a pine-nut crust served with a sauce of aged port; rack of lamb with eggplant and basil-permeated vegetables, served with homemade noodles; and veal steak with mango curry. The desserts are delicious.

Stüssihofstatt 3. (©) 01/261-76-18. Reservations required for restaurant, recommended in bistro. Bistro, main courses 18SF–40SF ($9.90–$22). Restaurant, main courses 30SF–56SF ($16.50–$30.80). AE, DC, MC, V. Bistro, Sun–Thurs 11am–midnight, Fri–Sat 11am–2am. Restaurant, Sun–Thurs 11am–2pm and 6pm–mindight, Fri–Sat 11am–2pm and 6–11:30pm. Closed July 17–30. Tram: 4 or 15.

Kronenhalle ★ SWISS/FRENCH   This is one of Zurich's most famous restaurants, and it also serves some of the best cuisine. This celebrity favorite has attracted such greats as Thomas Mann, James Joyce, Joan Miró, Georges Braque, Pablo Picasso, Richard Strauss, and Igor Stravinsky. More recent guests have included Plàcido Domingo, Catherine Deneuve, and Yves Saint-Laurent.

The restaurant is in a five-story, gray Biedermeier building with gold crowns above the six windows on the first floor. Traditional Swiss cuisine and international dishes are served in the two dining rooms. The decor includes original paintings by Klee, Chagall, Matisse, Miró, Kandinsky, Braque, Bonnard, and Picasso. Regional specialties are served on a trolley and include smoked pork with lentils and *bollito misto* (boiled beef, chicken, sausage, and tongue). For a main dish, try shredded calves' liver with rösti or filet of sole baked with olives and tomatoes. You might also enjoy *bündnerfleisch*—thinly sliced, smoked, dried beef. This is one of the most outstanding and consistently reliable restaurants in Zurich. In the Kronenhalle Bar, the specialty is the Ladykiller.

Rämistrasse 4. © **01/251-66-69**. Reservations required. Main courses 42SF–60SF ($23.10–$33). AE, DC, MC, V. Daily noon–midnight. Closed Dec 24. Tram: 2, 4, 5, 9, 11, or 15.

Lasalle ✦ INTERNATIONAL   One of the most hip and sought-after restaurants in Zurich today is set within a severe-looking factory built during the 19th century to manufacture boats and lake cruisers. Today, it's the centerpiece of an urban renewal known as Zuri-West, wherein affluent hipsters congregate in ways you might have expected in New York's Soho or Tribeca. A team of architects labored to maintain the original battered shell of the red-brick factory. Their avant-garde solution involved enclosing the restaurant within an enormous but delicate-looking high-tech box of steel beams and Plexiglass, all of it suspended from the building's ceiling and red-brick walls. Centered within the area's core is a massive blown-glass (Murano) chandelier whose delicacy is in ironic contrast to the industrial muscle that otherwise surrounds you on all sides. Menu items seen deceptively simple when listed on the stark white menu, and except for an occasional gaffe, are incredibly flavor-filled and artful upon delivery. Examples include Indian-style entrecote of lamb with raita; grilled filet of salmon with artichokes, tomatoes, and herbs; and a vegetarian version of tortilla with guacamole and sour cream. Either of these might be accompanied with an all-vegetarian gratin of celeriac and potatoes.

Schiffbaustrasse 4. © **01/258-7071**. Reservations necessary. Main courses 24SF–42SF ($13.20–$23.10). Mon–Fri 11:30am–10:45pm, Sat–Sun 5:30–10:45pm. AE, DC, MC, V. Tram: 4 or 13.

Restaurant Conti ✦ ITALIAN   This Belle Epoque restaurant lies just behind the Opera House. Many people eat dinner here, see a show, and then return for dessert and coffee. The menu is based on seasonal specialties. Try a dish of homemade pasta, followed by either scaloppine al limone or entrecôte Robespierre. The menu includes freshwater and ocean fish, as well as game dishes, such as pheasant. You can always count on a warm welcome and good food at this crowded, cheerful spot. The cuisine is fine-tuned and served in abundant portions.

Dufourstrasse 1. © **01/251-06-66**. Reservations required. Main courses 35SF–58SF ($19.25–$31.90); fixed-price lunch 38SF ($20.90). AE, DC, MC, V. Mon–Fri 11:30am–2:30pm; Mon–Sat 6pm–midnight. Closed 1 month during July–Aug (dates vary). Tram: 2 or 4.

Rosaly's ✦ SWISS/INTERNATIONAL   Set about a block from the Bellevueplatz and the clamor of its tram junctions, this restaurant occupies what looks like a mountain chalet that's incongruously perched on a narrow alleyway amid the mid-town urban sprawl. There's a bar on the premises—a half-moon-shaped affair whose clients spill out into the dining room as the evening gets late—but the real appeal here is the reasonably priced, well-prepared food. Part of its allure lies in the hints of California you might detect in the cuisine and the relaxed charm of the staff. (The owner named the restaurant after one he once visited in San Francisco.) The chef here is particularly proud of his butter-braised calf's liver; braised strips of veal prepared "Zurich-style" in cream sauce; and a wide range of salad, vegetarian, and fish dishes. A particularly well-received side dish is "Rosaly's rice," prepared with herbs and cheese. During clement weather, consider dining at one of the geranium-flanked tables lined up along the alleyway outside.

Freieckgasse 7. © **01/261-4430**. Reservations recommended. Main courses 19.50SF–39SF ($10.75–$21.45). AE, MC, V. Daily noon–2pm and 6–10pm (till 11pm Thurs–Sat). Bar stays open to between midnight and 1am, depending on business. Tram: 2, 4, 7, 9, 11, 13.

Zunfthaus Zur Zimmerleuten ⚐ SWISS   With foundations dating from 1336, when it was originally the carpenters' guildhall, the building you see today is from 1708, with few changes made since then. An architectural showpiece of Zurich, it now functions as one of the city's most enduring restaurants. A flight of baroque stairs leads from the street level to the elegant dining room, which is decorated with rows of leaded-glass windows and an impressive collection of hunting trophies. Menu items include "Lake Zurich fish soup" served with a garlic rouille; morel toasts; freshwater bouillabaisse with local catch; filet of pike-perch poached in Savoy cabbage; and a local specialty, *ratsherrentopf,* composed of three different filets with rösti and butter sauce. The reward for the kitchen's vigilance is a loyal clientele of discerning palates, who enjoy the full-bodied dishes.

Limmatquai 40. ⓒ 01/252-08-34. Reservations recommended. Main courses 30SF–55SF ($16.50–$30.25). AE, DC, MC, V. Mon–Sat 11:30am–2pm and 6–11pm. Closed mid-July to mid-Aug. Tram: 4 or 15.

MODERATE

Blue Note ASIAN/INTERNATIONAL   Stylish, hip, and with a cuisine that's more fusion and Asian than anything else we've seen in Zurich, this restaurant is often selected by advertising agencies as the setting for the kinds of breezy, seductive photographs that are likely to be parts of ads for upscale booze or cigarettes. Its centerpiece is a rectangular, slate-topped bar, site of prolonged cocktail-drinking. Ringing that are dining tables where the preferred choice is sushi, sashimi, and sukiyaki. Nighttime lighting is artfully exotic, contributing to a fluid setting, in which dialogue and other nocturnal adventures might conceivably follow.

Stockerstrasse 45. ⓒ 01/202-17-17. Reservations recommended. Lunch main courses 29SF–49SF ($15.95–$26.95). Main courses 29SF–49SF ($15.95–$26.95). Set-price menus 36SF–46SF ($19.80–$25.30). AE, MC, V. Daily 11:30am–2pm and 5:30–11pm. Bar stays open to between 2 and 4am, depending on business. Tram: 7, 8, 13.

Fischstube Zürichhorn (Kids) SWISS   Ideal on a summer evening, this seafood restaurant with outdoor tables is built on pilings over the lake. The scenery, service, and cuisine make it a worthy choice if the weather is balmy. We recommend the lake trout, filet of Dover sole Champs-Elysées, grilled lobster with curry butter, and lake fish sautéed in butter and served with market-fresh vegetables. The cuisine here has a sprightly, original taste, flavored with a dash of this or a dab of that. The chefs rely on the sound principles of simplicity and accurate timing in all their dishes, and the servings are generous. Kids delight at sitting outside overlooking the lake and even like the vegetables cooked here since they're so fresh and delectably cooked.

Bellerivestrasse 160. ⓒ 01/422-25-20. Reservations required. Main courses 28SF–40SF ($15.40–$22); fixed-price lunch 37SF ($20.35). AE, MC, V. Daily 9:30am–11pm. Closed Sept 26–Easter. Tram: 2 or 4.

Mère Catherine PROVENÇAL/FRENCH   This small courtyard restaurant nestled among the back streets of Old Town offers quiet cafe tables, ivy, and, at times, a lot of sun. Anybody who knows backstreet Paris or a small town in France will feel at home here. Unpretentious French, especially Provençal bistro, food is served here. Fresh sea fish is a feature, but the specials change every day. You can always find various meatless platters on the menu. Salade paysanne with a Roquefort sauce is the most popular appetizer, and you can usually order snails en brioche or something more exotic, terrine of quail. The dishes are painstakingly prepared and usually get diners salivating in no time flat. You might want to arrive before your reservations to have an apéritif at the Bar Philosophe, the cozy marble bar next to the restaurant.

Nägelihof 3. ☎ 01/250-59-40. Reservations required. Main courses 22SF–36SF ($12.10–$19.80); surprise lunch Mon–Fri 15.50SF–22.50SF ($8.55–$12.40). AE, MC, V. Daily 11:30am–2:30pm and 6–11:30pm. Tram: 4 or 15.

Zur Oepfelchammer SWISS/FRENCH   This is a historic restaurant. Although for many years it was considered little more than a battered student hangout, it has gained prestige recently as a warmly atmospheric place. In a building erected in 1357, you'll find three different rooms, one of which is a smoke-stained and sometimes boisterous bar, another a rustic, carved-oak dining room, and the last a beerhall tavern. Don't be surprised if you're asked to share one of the long tables with strangers—it's part of the allure. Menu items include air-cured or smoked alpine beef, shredded calves' liver with rösti, shredded veal Zurich style, and fresh salads. No one claims to be a creative chef around here, but the deceptively simple food is quite satisfying to the stomach and taste buds. The cellar contains an unusual collection of relatively unknown but worthwhile wines from local vineyards.

Rindermarkt 12. ☎ 01/251-23-36. Reservations recommended. Main courses 22SF–40SF ($12.10–$22); fixed-price lunch 24SF–27SF ($13.20–$14.85). AE, MC, V. Tues–Sat 11am–12:30am. Closed mid-July to mid-Aug. Tram: 4 or 15.

INEXPENSIVE

Blockhus 🎮 *Value* SWISS/FRENCH   On the richly paneled street level of a wooden, 200-year-old house, this restaurant emulates the glamour and flair of a French bistro. You'll get a warm welcome and be offered well-prepared dishes such as steak au poivre, rack of lamb with rosemary and a touch of garlic, mussels in white wine and herb sauce, and what might be the widest assortment of French cheeses in Zurich. The food is rustic yet urbane, and flavors are well matched. No dish is ever smothered in sauces but is prepared so that its true flavor asserts itself.

Schifflande 4. ☎ 01/252-14-53. Reservations recommended. Main courses 20SF–35SF ($11–$19.25); fixed-price lunch 25SF ($13.75). AE, MC, V. Mon–Sat 11:30am–2pm and 6pm–midnight. Tram: 2, 4, 8, or 11.

Crazy Cow *Finds* SWISS   Set at the base of the hill where Zurich's university is found, this is a hipster's version of an old-fashioned Swiss inn, with a strong sense of satire and a menu that makes virtually everyone laugh. It's one of the most visible places in Zurich where you can see the Swiss poking fun at their own sense of folksy isolationism, as portrayed in the decor with replicas of drug-tripping cows and crazed versions of Heidi looking for a goatherd. Even if your knowledge of German is rudimentary, spend some time deciphering the Swiss dialect in which the menu is printed, since even the Swiss find it irreverently amusing. (Grilled duck breast with olive-lemon sauce is listed as Äntäpüppi; gratin of shredded potatoes with vegetables and cream sauce is listed as Röschti mit G'mües.) The alpine version of macaroni comes with onions and apple wedges, and drinks of choice include all-Swiss versions of hard cider, beer, or wine.

Leonhardstrasse 1. ☎ 01/261-40-55. Reservations recommended. Main courses 17.50SF–32SF ($9.65–$17.60). AE, DC, MC, V. Daily 11am–11:30pm. Tram: 6, 7, 10, or 15.

El Lokal INTERNATIONAL   This restaurant, set within a 150-year-old warehouse beside the Siel canal near the railway station, represents Zurich's counterculture at its most confident and rebellious. Hip, breezy, and artsy, with a waitstaff that's as heavily pierced (noses, tongues, or whatever) as that of any other restaurant in Zurich, it's a rustic-looking hideaway for anyone seeking refuge from the industrial sprawl of central Zurich. Tables, in summer, spill onto the cobble-covered courtyard and, in winter, onto an upper balcony inside. Live music is presented here about five times a month, but otherwise, expect a somewhat disorganized cafe and restaurant where insights into counterculture Zurich are virtually everywhere. Simple platters include spicy grilled chicken; tagliatelle with air-dried alpine beef; salads; and for snacking or dessert, heaping bowls of organic strawberry yogurt.

Gessnerallee 11. ℂ **01/226-1939.** Reservations not necessary. Main courses 16.50SF–22SF ($9.10–$12.10). No credit cards. Daily noon–2:30pm and 6:30–11pm. Tram: 3.

Le Dézaley ★ *Finds* VAUDOIS   Named after a remote corner of the Vaud region of French-speaking Switzerland, this restaurant celebrates the food and traditions of the countryside north of Lake Geneva. Many of the regular clients speak French as they dine on an array of fondues (cheese, chinoise, and bourguignonne) or other dishes such as minced liver, veal kidneys with rösti, pork sausages flavored with leeks, and shredded veal Zurich-style. The chefs are more obsessed with flavor than novelty, and they certainly succeed. Many wines, some rather rare, from the Dézaley region are offered. The large, wood-paneled dining room is set in a pair of interconnected houses originally built during the late 13th century. In summer you can dine in a little garden out back. The restaurant is located close to the Grossmünster church.

Römergasse 7–9. ℂ **01/251-61-29.** Reservations recommended. Main courses 20SF–25SF ($11–$13.75); fondues 24SF–37SF ($13.20–$20.35). AE, DC, MC, V. Mon–Sat 11:30am–2pm and 6pm–midnight. Tram: 4 or 15.

Restaurant Movie AMERICAN/INTERNATIONAL   This is one of the most consistently popular theme restaurants in Zurich. Hip, artful, and fun, and positioned adjacent to one of the city's biggest movie theater complexes, it boasts a campy faux-Hollywood decor that includes a gilded version of the Statue of Liberty, industrial-style ventilation tubes, and the kind of lighting fixtures you'd expect on the original sound stage of *Gone with the Wind*. Even the place mats are emblazoned with publicity stills from about-to-be-screened American movies, with menus printed on round aluminum canisters that traditionally hold a reel of celluloid. Many of the dishes are named after movies and actors. All of this would be hopelessly corny if the food weren't genuinely well-prepared and the place packed, especially during the dinner and after-dinner bar hour. Menus include pastas, sandwiches, salads, quesadillas, fajitas, and grills. Don't overlook the bar area at this place as a California-inspired (and very popular) nightlife option. Outfitted with a black-and-gold ancient Egyptian theme, it has tables spilling out onto the Beattenplatz and dance music that might actually encourage you to rock and roll.

Bahnhofquai 7 at Beattenplatz. ℂ **01/211-66-77.** Reservations not necessary. Main courses 18.50SF–26SF ($10.20–$14.30). AE, MC, V. Daily 11:30am–midnight. Tram: 6, 10.

SOUTH OF THE CENTER

Blaue Ente CONTINENTAL   Set near the edge of Lake Zurich about half a mile southwest of the city's center, this restaurant is in a 300-year-old mill, which was gracefully converted in 1985. Its name comes from a long-defunct inn, the Blaue Ente (Blue Goose), which was established in 1675 in a different location by an ancestor of one of the present owners. The modern incarnation of the place is popular with Zurich artists and trendsetters, who seem to imbue the place with big-city glitter and a hip, bemused cosmopolitanism.

The menu changes every 5 weeks, with new dishes based on the season's ingredients and the whim of the chef. Stunning examples include a salad of bitter greens with strips of confit de canard, a medley of whiting and crayfish in a champagne sauce, rack of lamb with eggplant and potato blinis, and crisp duck fresh from the oven. The flavors are solidly classic and perfectly balanced.

Mühle Tiefenbrunnen. ℭ 01/388-68-40. Reservations recommended. Main courses 30SF–45SF ($16.50–$24.75). AE, DC, MC, V. Daily 11:30am–1:30pm and 6–11:30pm. Closed late July to Aug 7 and Dec 25–Jan 6. Tram: 2 or 4.

Peter's Kunststuben ★★ CONTINENTAL   Since it opened in the early 1980s, this restaurant has attracted most of the well-heeled gastronomes in Zurich, as well as such notables as the emperor of Japan, the Swiss president, and Anthony Quinn. Relentlessly elegant, but with a staff that's more hip and alert than you may expect, it lies 6 miles (10km) south of Zurich in the hamlet of Küsnacht, near Rapperswil, within a house whose date of construction (1873) is marked above a wood-burning stove in the dining room.

There's room for only 55 diners most of the year, but in summer an outdoor terrace ringed with flowering shrubs and flowers adds another 20 places. Amid a collection of upscale accoutrements and well-rehearsed service rituals, you can enjoy such inventive dishes as a tartare of beef and caviar with a potato galette, lobster-studded potato salad with a leek-based cream sauce, stuffed squid with a confit of fennel, and young hen stuffed with shrimp. Dessert might include a gratin of wild strawberries with cannelloni stuffed with almond paste. You'll find almost anything you order irresistible.

Seestrasse 160, Küsnacht. ℭ 01/910-07-15. Reservations required. Main courses 52SF–75SF ($28.60–$41.25); fixed-price menu 210SF ($115.50). AE, DC, MC, V. Tues–Sat noon–2pm and 7pm–midnight. Closed 2 weeks in Feb and 2 weeks Aug–Sept. Take a taxi or the train from Zurich's Hauptbahnhof to Küsnacht, then walk for 5 minutes.

EAST OF THE CENTER

Blu INTERNATIONAL   This is an offbeat choice. The site of this restaurant and shopping complex originated in the late 1800s, when a Swiss entrepreneur assembled a flotilla of barges to take in laundry, using the waters of Lake Zurich to flush the dirt out of clothes and bedding. Later, the boats were permanently moored to the lakeside, and an enormous clothes-washing complex was built beside the lake, centered around a red brick smokestack that still remains in place today, a 15-minute drive from the center of town. In the 1990s, a team of trend-conscious architects transformed the site into a complex of boutiques, offices, and condominiums, one of the highlights of which is this artfully minimalist restaurant that's favored by the young, the arts-conscious, and the upwardly mobile. It's at its most relaxing in summer, when tables are lined up beside a marina that's loaded with tall-masted sailboats. People travel here from far away in any season to experience the unusual design of the starkly minimalist duplex-style dining room. Menu items are deeply entrenched in the seasons, and include, among others, gnocchi with grilled shrimps and cherry tomatoes; slow-braised rack of lamb with herbs; several preparations of fresh fish; meal-sized salads; and a deliberately undercooked version of bittersweet chocolate cake.

Seestrasse 4–7. ℭ 01/488-6565. Reservations recommended for dinner. Main courses 23SF–39SF ($12.65–$21.45). Daily 11:30am–2pm and 4:30–11pm. AE, DC, MC, V. Bus: 861, 865.

WEST OF THE CENTER

Iroquois INTERNATIONAL   The Swiss have never really gone ga-ga over American-style bars and grills, but of the several that exist within Zurich, this is the busiest and most popular. Always crowded and sometimes mobbed, it's a neighborhood tavern whose rough edges and spilled beer add to its image as a rough-and-ready burger and fajitas joint that just happens to have a distinctive Swiss accent. Come here for sports TV and the possibility of striking up a neighborhood friendship. The house cocktail is an Iroquois, made with vodka, Galliano, maracuja (star fruit), and orange juice. If you come with a group that tends to get the munchies, consider a "surfer's platter" prepared for multiple diners at a time, that mixes chicken wings, tortilla chips, quesadillas, and guacamole. Other food choices include ostrich-meat fajitas, burritos, chicken chiliburgers, and turkey tacos. Don't expect grandeur, as virtually everything and everyone here is aggressively unpretentious.

Seefeldstrasse 120. ℭ 01/383-70-77. Reservations not necessary. Main courses, burgers, and salads 19SF–30SF ($10.45–$16.50). Daily 11am–2pm and 6–10pm. Bar open daily 5pm–midnight. AE, MC, V. Tram: 2, 4.

NORTH OF THE CENTER

Alter Tobelhof/Restaurant Chäsalp *Finds* SWISS   Either of these two restaurants would be excellent choices for anyone who wants a taste of folkloric, rural Switzerland without driving very far from Zurich. Its owners refer to them as Wirtschafts, a word that emphasizes a prolonged exposure, and enjoyment, of a leisurely, relaxing meal near the Great Outdoors. The more formal and elaborate of the two is the Alter Tobelhof, a 300-year-old farmhouse devoted to cozy dining, often on seasonal fare that emphasizes whatever is fresh and in season at the time. Look for savory preparations of asparagus, fish, game, and mushrooms, in the form of, for example, grilled freshwater fish with grappa sauce, sauerkraut, and potato dumplings; sautéed perch from the nearby lake served with seasonal vegetables; roasted and truffled chicken with fresh spinach; and a platter piled high with filets of lamb and rabbit in balsamic gravy.

Immediately adjacent, and much more folkloric, is the Chäsalp, a rustic converted stable with rough-hewn timbers and exposed stone like what you'd expect in the high Alps. Here, within a *gemütlich* (warm and cozy atmosphere) and nostalgically Teutonic setting, air-dried beef and cheese are elevated to high art forms, sometimes as part of about a dozen kinds of bubbling fondues. Other menu items include risottos; grilled steaks; salads; and at least 15 different preparations of macaroni, six of them vegetarian. The most popular and savory version is "moonlight macaroni" made with sliced veal, cream sauce, fresh basil, and port wine. Come here for an adventure, knowing that it will take a car ride of about 20 minutes from downtown Zurich to reach this high plateau well beyond the city's borders. If you opt to come, especially in summer, you'll be joined by a mob of other urban residents, all escaping the city's urban congestion.

Tobelhofstrasse 236. ℭ 01/251-1193 (Alter Tobelhof) or 01/260-7575 (Chäsalp). Reservations recommended. Alter Tobelhof main courses 18SF–42SF ($9.90–$23.10); Chäsalp main courses 20SF–39SF ($11–$21.45). DC, MC, V. Daily 9am–midnight. Train 6 to Kirchflunten, then bus 751.

Gisserei Oerlikon *Finds* INTERNATIONAL   It's fun and funky. Until early in 2000, the battered-looking building containing this place had lain empty, a former foundry whose grimy walls had once reverberated with the sound of hammers and heavy machinery. Today, despite a setting that might remind you of a prison camp in Siberia, it's a sought-after address for Zurich's trendsetters, who seek it out as a change from a usual diet of manicured efficiency and predictable Swiss comforts. Don't be dismayed by the concrete and cinder-block severity of the setting. (Some local wits—who invariably have a good time here—compare it to dining in the Gulag.) A tongue-in-cheek team of decorators enhanced the Sputnik-era angularity with a stainless-steel bar, artful lighting, and occasional touches of whimsy. The menu, which will be recited in English or German by the waitstaff, changes daily, and will usually include a choice of only three starters and three main courses. On the evening of our visit, well-prepared menu choices included grilled eggplant with air-dried beef and taboule; fresh cantaloupe with Serrano ham; a "summer salad" with shrimp; a terrine of chanterelle mushrooms; and a ragout of swordfish.

Birchstrasse 108, in Oerlikon. (©) **01/311-7044.** Reservations recommended. Main courses 36SF–42SF ($19.80–$23.10). Mon–Fri noon–2pm; Sun–Thurs 6–10:30pm. AE, MC, V. Tram 11.

CAFES

Café/Bar Odéon   This legendary 1912 bohemian landmark is a popular singles and gay hangout in the evening. Lenin came here during World War I to make such pronouncements as, "The neutrality of Switzerland is a bourgeois fraud and means submission to the imperialist war." Thornton Wilder also sloshed down a few here, as did Mussolini and Mata Hari. The intimate, Art Nouveau cafe has banquettes and cubbyholes. It also sports a curved bar and many sidewalk tables.

Limmatquai 2. (©) **01/251-16-50.** Light meals 14SF–25SF ($7.70–$13.75); coffee 3.50SF–7SF ($1.95–$3.85). Mon–Thurs 7am–2:30am, Fri–Sat 7am–4:30am, Sun 9am–2:30am.

Cafeteria Zur Münst   This unusual coffeehouse in Old Town has fanciful chandeliers by Swiss artist Jean Tinguely. They resemble funny creatures—half human, half robot—that spin, wave feathers, and pivot at each other. The coffeehouse is on a quiet street that runs into Bahnhofstrasse. Delectable pastries, ice cream, and light meals are served in a chatty atmosphere.

Münzplatz 3. (©) **01/221-30-27.** Ice cream from 3.50SF ($1.95); light meals 15SF–80SF ($8.25–$44). Mon–Fri 6:30am–8pm, Thurs 6:30am–9pm, Sat 8am–5pm.

Conditorei Café Schober   One of the most select cafes in Zurich is located in Zum grossen Erker (The Great Alcove), a building dating from 1314 that was turned into a confectionery and coffee shop by Theodor Schober after 1875. When the last Schober retired, the well-known meeting place was bought and renovated by Teuscher, the epicurean name brand in chocolates. The old-fashioned cafe, with its beautiful lighting fixtures and molded ceilings, is known for its hot chocolate. It also offers an array of homemade pastries, cakes, and ice cream.

Napfgasse 4. (©) **01/251-80-60.** Hot chocolate 6.70SF ($3.70). Mon–Fri 8am–6:30pm, Sat 8am–5:30pm, Sun 10am–5:30pm.

A PASTRY SHOP

Confiserie Sprüngli   This old-fashioned pastry shop on Bahnhofstrasse, founded in 1836, is comparable to the legendary Demel in Vienna. Many Zurichers remember this place fondly from their childhood. A variety of pastries and chocolates are sold on the ground floor. The famous Lindt chocolates and the house specialties are about the best you'll ever find. You'll also find fixed-price lunches, tea, and coffee. Many old-time Zurichers journey across town for a cup of hot chocolate.

Am Paradeplatz. (©) **01/224-47-11.** Fixed-price lunches 21SF–26SF ($11.55–$14.30); tea or coffee from 3.80SF ($2.10). Mon–Fri 8:30am–8pm, Sat 8am–4pm.

5 Attractions

Zurich has a rich history and many reminders of its past. There are 20 museums, nearly 100 galleries, and 24 archives, including one devoted to Thomas Mann. The historic buildings, religious monuments, and quays are worth discovering, as are the well-preserved homes of rich burghers, lovely parks, and gardens. Even if you don't have time to visit all those museums and galleries, a walk along the quays of Zurich shouldn't be missed.

You can also visit Uetliberg, southwest of Zurich, the northernmost peak in the Albis ridge (see "Side Trips from Zurich," later in this chapter).

SUGGESTED ITINERARIES

If You Have 1 Day

Take **"Walking Tour 1: Bahnhofstrasse"** to Lake Zurich, where you can board a streamer for a 1½-hour ride on the lake. Return to shore and visit either the **Kunsthaus Museum** or the **Landesmuseum.** In late afternoon, take **"Walking Tour 2: Alstadt,"** along the famous quays of Zurich and through Old Town, where you might have a raclette dinner in an old tavern. (See the walking tours later in this section.)

If You Have 2 Days

Spend the first day as suggested above. In the morning, visit **Fraumünster** or **Grossmünster,** the two most famous churches of Zurich. Enjoy lunch in a typical Zurich cafe. In the afternoon, leave Zurich for **Uetliberg** for a panoramic view of the Alps and the city. Have a beer and listen to the oompah band at the **Bierhall Wolf** in the evening.

If You Have 3 Days

Spend the first 2 days as outlined above. On the third day, see all the attractions you've missed before, including two museums: the **Rietberg,** with its great non-European art collection, and the **Bührle,** with its collection of modern art. Visit the **Botanic Garden** and the **Zoo** in the afternoon, if time remains.

If You Have 4 Days

Spend the first 3 days as outlined above. On the morning of the fourth day, go to **Winterthur,** only a 25-minute ride from Zurich, to see its many attractions, including the Oskar Reinhart Foundation, Am Römerholz, the Kunstmuseum, and the Schloss Kyburg.

THE TOP ATTRACTIONS

The **quays of Zurich** 🐾🐾, with their promenades, are among the city's most popular attractions. They're made for walking. The most famous is **Limmatquai,** in the center of Zurich. It begins at the Bahnhof Bridge and extends east to the Rathaus or town hall and beyond. Many of the quays have lovely gardens. **Uto Quai** is the major promenade along Zurichsee (Lake Zurich), running from Badeanstalt Uto Quai (a swimming pool) to Bellevueplatz and Quai Brücke. The pool is open daily from 8am to 7pm. If you stroll as far as **Mythen Quai,** you'll be following the lake along its western shore and out into the countryside.

Fraumünster   This church, with its slender, blue spire, is on the left bank overlooking the former pig market, Münsterhof. Münsterhof is one of the historic old squares of Zurich and is well worth a visit. A Benedictine abbey was founded at the site in 853 by Emperor Ludwig (Louis the German), the grandson of Charlemagne. His daughter became the first abbess. The present church dates from the 13th and 14th centuries, but the crypt of the old abbey church is preserved in the undercroft.

Fun Fact **Did You Know?**

- Lenin sat out part of World War I in Zurich, plotting the Russian Revolution.
- Because of Zurich's proximity to Germany, a few Allied bombs in World War II rained down on it by accident.
- James Joyce wrote much of *Ulysses* in Zurich, not Ireland.
- Zurich, a well-known financial center of stability, gave birth to the revolutionary artistic movement of dadaism, whose aim was to destroy order.
- As you walk down Bahnhofstrasse, you're only a few feet away from where much of the world's gold and silver is stored underground.
- Marc Chagall completed the modern stained-glass windows in Fraumünster when he was 83 years old.

The chief attractions of Fraumünster are five **stained-glass windows** ✦— each with its own color theme—designed by Marc Chagall in 1970. They are best seen in bright morning light. The Münster is also celebrated for its elaborate organ. The basilica has three aisles; the nave is in the Gothic style. There is no official phone number for the church. Visitors seeking information should inquire at the tourist office.

From Fraumünster you can cross the Münsterbrücke, an 1838 bridge that leads to Grossmünster. On the bridge is a statue of Burgomaster Waldmann, who was beheaded in 1489 when his political enemies seized power. During his rule, the city gained influence over much of the surrounding lands.

Fraumünsterstrasse. Free admission. May–Sept Mon–Sat 9am–noon and 2–6pm, Sun 2–6pm; Oct, Mar–Apr Mon–Sat 10am–noon and 2–5pm, Sun 2–5pm; Nov–Feb Mon–Sat 10am–noon and 2–4pm, Sun 2–4pm. Tram: 4 to City Hall.

Grossmünster This Romanesque and Gothic cathedral was, according to legend, founded by Charlemagne, whose horse bowed down on the spot marking the graves of three early Christian martyrs. The cathedral has two three-story towers and is situated on a terrace above Limmatquai, on the right bank. Despite the legend, construction actually began in 1090 and additions were made until the early 14th century. The choir contains stained-glass windows completed in 1932 by Augusto Giacometti. (Augusto is not to be confused with his more celebrated uncle, Alberto Giacometti, the famous Swiss abstract.) In the crypt is a weather-beaten, 15th-century statue of Charlemagne, a copy of which crowns the south tower.

The cathedral is dedicated to the patron saints of Zurich: Felix, Regula, and Exuperantius. In the 3rd century, the three martyrs attempted to convert the citizens of Turicum (the original name for Zurich) to Christianity. The governor, according to legend, had them plunged into boiling oil and forced them to drink molten lead. The trio refused to renounce their faith and were beheaded. Miraculously, they still had enough energy to pick up their heads and climb to the top of a hill (the present site of the cathedral), where they dug their own graves and then interred themselves. The seal of Zurich honors these saints, depicting them carrying their heads under their arms. The remains of the saints are said to rest in one of the chapels of the Münster (cathedral).

Zurich Attractions

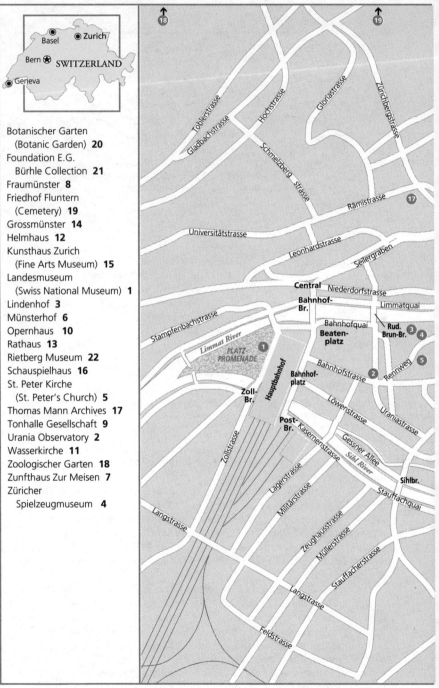

Botanischer Garten
  (Botanic Garden) **20**
Foundation E.G.
  Bürhle Collection **21**
Fraumünster **8**
Friedhof Fluntern
  (Cemetery) **19**
Grossmünster **14**
Helmhaus **12**
Kunsthaus Zurich
  (Fine Arts Museum) **15**
Landesmuseum
  (Swiss National Museum) **1**
Lindenhof **3**
Münsterhof **6**
Opernhaus **10**
Rathaus **13**
Rietberg Museum **22**
Schauspielhaus **16**
St. Peter Kirche
  (St. Peter's Church) **5**
Thomas Mann Archives **17**
Tonhalle Gesellschaft **9**
Urania Observatory **2**
Wasserkirche **11**
Zoologischer Garten **18**
Zunfthaus Zur Meisen **7**
Züricher
  Spielzeugmuseum **4**

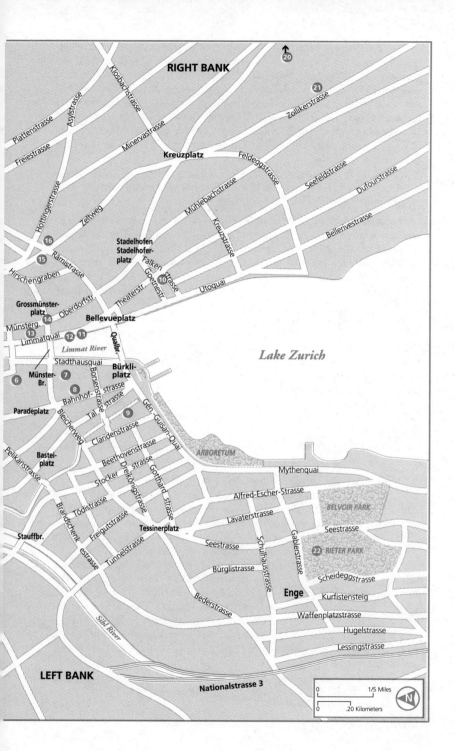

RIGHT BANK

Klosbachstrasse

Plattenstrasse

Freiestrasse

Asylstrasse

Minervastrasse

Hottingerstrasse

Zeltweg

Kreuzplatz

Feldeggstrasse

Zollikerstrasse

Seefeldstrasse

Dufourstrasse

Mühlebachstrasse

Kreuzstrasse

Bellerivestrasse

Stadelhofen
Stadelhofer-
platz

Falken strasse

Goethestr.

Rämistrasse

Hirschengraben

Oberdorfstr.

Theaterstr.

Utoquai

Grossmünster-
platz

Münsterg.

Limmatquai

Bellevueplatz

Qualbr.

Lake Zurich

Limmat River

Stadthausquai

Bürkli-
platz

Münster-
Br.

Börsenstrasse

Bahnhof- strasse

Tal strasse

Paradeplatz

Bleicherweg

Gen. Gusan-Quai

ARBORETUM

Claridenstrasse

Mythenquai

Beethovenstrasse

Basteiplatz

Pelikanstrasse

Stocker

DreiKönigsstrasse

Gotthard strasse

Alfred-Escher-Strasse

BELVOIR PARK

Tödistrasse

Lavaterstrasse

Seestrasse

Brandschenk estrasse

Freigutstrasse

Tessinerplatz

Seestrasse

Schulhausstrasse

Gablerstrasse

RIETER PARK

Stauffbr.

Tunnelstrasse

Bürglistrasse

Bederstrasse

Enge

Scheideggstrasse

Kurfistensteig

Waffenplatzstrasse

Hugelstrasse

Lessingstrasse

Sihl River

LEFT BANK

Nationalstrasse 3

0   1/5 Miles

0   .20 Kilometers

N

The cathedral was once the parish church of Huldrych Zwingli, one of the great leaders of the Reformation. He urged priests to take wives (he himself had married) and attacked the "worship of images" and the Roman sacrament of mass. In 1531, Zwingli was killed in a religious war at Kappel. The hangman quartered his body and soldiers burnt the pieces with dung. The site of his execution is marked with an inscription: "They may kill the body but not the soul." In accordance with Zwingli's beliefs, Zurich's Grossmünster is austere, stripped of the heavy ornamentation you'll find in the cathedrals of Italy. The view from the towers is impressive.

Grossmünsterplatz. 𝄐 01/252-59-49. Cathedral, free; towers, 3SF ($1.65). Cathedral, Mar 15–Oct daily 9am–6pm; Nov to Mar 14 daily 10am–4pm. Towers, Mar–Oct daily (when weather permits); off-season Sat–Sun when weather permits. Same hours as cathedral. Tram: 4.

Landesmuseum (Swiss National Museum) ★★★   This museum offers an epic survey of the culture and history of the Swiss people. Its collection, housed in a feudal-looking, 19th-century building behind the Zurich Hauptbahnhof, contains works of religious art, including 16th-century stained glass from Tanikon Convent and frescoes from the church of Mustair. Some of the Carolingian art dates back to the 9th century. The altarpieces are carved, painted, and gilded.

The prehistoric section is also exceptional. Some of the artifacts are from the 4th millennium B.C. There's a large display of Roman clothing, medieval silverware, 14th-century drinking bowls, and 17th-century china, as well as painted furniture, costumes, and dollhouses of various periods. A display of weapons and armor shows the methods of Swiss warfare from 800 to 1800. There's also an exhibit tracing Swiss clockmaking from the 16th to the 18th centuries.

Special exhibitions are presented twice annually, lasting between 3 and 6 months. Themes are always different; a recent one was devoted to Swiss fashion design.

Museumstrasse 2. 𝄐 01/218-65-11. Admission 5SF ($2.75), 3SF ($1.65) students and seniors; special exhibitions 8SF–12SF ($4.40–$6.60). Tues–Sun 10:30am–5pm. Tram: 3, 4, 5, 11, 13, or 14.

Kunsthaus Zurich (Fine Arts Museum) ★★   One of the most important art museums in Europe, the Zurich Kunsthaus is devoted mainly to the 19th and 20th centuries, although the range of paintings and sculpture reaches back to antiquity. The museum was founded in Victorian times and was overhauled in 1976. Today it's one of the most modern and sophisticated museums in the world, both in its lighting and its display of art.

Our favorite exhibits include Rodin's *Gate of Hell*, near the entrance, and the Giacometti wing, showing the development of this Swiss-born artist. The collection of modern art includes works by all the greats—Bonnard, Braque, Chagall, Lipschitz, Marini, Mondrian, Picasso, Rouault. The gallery owns the largest collection outside Oslo of works by the Norwegian artist Edvard Munch. Two old masters, Rubens and Rembrandt, are also represented. To brighten a rainy day, come see the pictures by Cézanne, Degas, Monet, Toulouse-Lautrec, and Utrillo.

Heimplatz 1. 𝄐 01/253-84-97. Admission 6SF ($3.30) adults, 4SF ($2.20) children, free for children 5 and under; special exhibitions 14SF ($7.70) adults, 7SF ($3.85) children. Tues–Thurs 10am–9pm, Fri–Sun 10am–5pm. Tram: 3 (marked "Klusplatz").

MORE ATTRACTIONS

Botanischer Garten ★   The gardens contain 15,000 living species, including some rare specimens from New Caledonia and Southwest Africa. The

herbarium contains three million plants. The gardens, owned by the University of Zurich, were laid out on the site of a former private villa.

Universität Zurich, Zollikerstrasse 107. (℃ 01/634-84-61. Free admission. Park, Mar–Sept Mon–Fri 7am–7pm, Sat–Sun 8am–6pm; Oct–Feb Mon–Fri 8am–6pm, Sat–Sun 8am–5pm. Greenhouses, daily 9:30–11:30am and 1–4pm. Tram: 11 to Hegibachplatz, or 2 or 4 to Höschgasse. Bus: 33 to Botanischer Garten.

Friedhof Fluntern (Fluntern Cemetery) James Joyce, the author of *Ulysses*, lived in Zurich from 1915 to 1919, at Universitätsstrasse 38. In 1941 he returned to Zurich from Paris, only a month before his death. Near his tomb is a statue depicting the great Irish writer sitting cross-legged with a book in his hand. Elias Canetti, winner of the Nobel Prize for literature in 1981, died in August 1994; his grave lies to the left of Joyce's. The grave of Johanna Spiri (1827–1901), who wrote the famous story *Heidi*, is in the Central Cemetery.

Friedhof Fluntern (Fluntern Cemetery). Zurichberg district. Free admission. May–Aug daily 7am–8pm; Mar–Apr and Sept–Oct daily 7am–7pm; Nov–Feb daily 8am–5pm. Tram: 6 to zoo.

Foundation E. G. Bührle Collection 🏛🏛 This jewel of a collection is most popular for its French impressionist works, including those by Monet, van Gogh, Cézanne, Gauguin, Degas, Renoir, and Manet. See Picasso's *The Italian Girl*. The private collection also includes paintings by Rubens, Rembrandt, and Guardi. There's a limited but very special section of 24 sculptures from the Middle Ages.

Zollikerstrasse 172. (℃ 01/422-00-86. Admission 9SF ($4.95) adults, 7SF ($3.85) students and seniors. Tues and Fri 2–5pm, Wed 5–8pm, Sun 2–5pm. Tram: 2 or 4.

Rietberg Museum 🏛🏛 The Rietberg contains a collection of non-European art, most of which was assembled by Baron Eduard von der Heydt and donated to the city of Zurich in 1952. The collection is housed in the former Wesendonck Villa, constructed in 1857 by a German industrialist, Otto Wesendonck. Modeled after Villa Albani in Rome, the building is located in a garden in Rieter Park and overlooks Lake Zurich. Richard Wagner came here and fell in love with the hostess, who inspired his tragic opera *Tristan und Isolde*.

The eclectic collection was gathered from the South Sea islands, the Near East, Asia, Africa, and pre-Columbian America. Of all the treasures, our favorite is the *Dancing Shiva*, a celebrated Indian bronze. You will also find a collection of stunning Japanese prints, along with art from Tibet and pre-Columbian America, paintings from the Near East and the Far East, and a collection of Armenian and Flemish carpets.

Gablerstrasse 15. (℃ 01/202-45-28. Admission 6SF ($3.30) adults, 4SF ($2.20) students and seniors; free for children 14 and under. Tues–Thurs 10am–8pm, Fri–Sun 10am–5pm. Tram: 7 from the town center (a 12-min. ride).

St. Peter Kirche (St. Peter's Church) Built in the 13th century, St. Peter's—on the left bank south of Lindenhof—is the oldest church in Zurich. It has the largest clock face in Europe: 28½ feet (9m) in diameter; the minute hand alone is 12 feet (almost 4m) long. Inside, the choir is Romanesque, but the three-aisle nave is baroque.

St. Peterhofstatt 1. (℃ 01/211-25-88. Free admission. Mon–Fri 8am–6pm, Sat 9am–4pm.

Thomas Mann Archives Thomas Mann, the German writer who won the Nobel Prize for literature in 1929 for such works as *Death in Venice* and *The Magic Mountain*, died in Kilchberg, near Zurich, in 1955. An opponent of the Nazi regime, he had lived outside Germany after 1933—in the United States and Switzerland during most of the period. The archives, located next to the university, contain manuscripts and mementos.

Swiss Federal Institute of Technology, Schönberggasse 15. ℂ **01/632-40-45.** Free admission. Wed and Sat 2–4pm. Tram: 5, 6, or 9.

Urania Observatory   The observatory is halfway between Bahnhofstrasse and the Limmat River on Uraniastrasse. On clear days, you can look through the telescope, while on bad days the observatory doesn't open. Call in advance to find out. The observatory has been at this site since 1907. Because of its central location, you have a panoramic view not only of Zurich but of the lake and the distant Alps. You can see the stars, planets, and galaxy through a big Zeiss telescope that weighs 20 tons.

Uraniastrasse 9. ℂ **01/211-65-23.** Admission 10SF ($5.50) adults, 5SF ($2.75) children. Apr–Sept Tues–Sat noon–4pm and 7–11pm; Oct–Mar Tues–Sat noon–4pm and 6–9pm. Tram: 7, 11, or 13.

Zunfthaus Zur Meisen   Across the bridge from the Wasserkirche is one of the city's famous old guild houses. It has a wrought-iron gatehouse that opens onto Münsterhof. Dating from 1752, it's a branch museum of the overstuffed Swiss National Museum. It's devoted mainly to 18th-century Swiss ceramics, the porcelain of Zurich, and several antiques. The beauty of the stuccoed rooms competes with the exhibits.

Münsterhof 20. ℂ **01/221-28-07.** Admission 3SF ($1.65) adults; free for children under 16. Tues–Sun 10:30am–5pm. Closed holidays. Tram: 3.

ESPECIALLY FOR KIDS

There are 80 playgrounds in Zurich. For the one nearest your hotel, inquire either at your hotel or at the local tourist office (see "Visitor Information," earlier in this chapter). Most boat trips (see below) leave from the end of Bahnhofstrasse on the right. You might also combine a train ride with a trip to an attraction outside Zurich.

Select theaters also offer changing programs for children. Ask at the tourist office or get a copy of *Zurich Weekly Official*, available at most newsstands.

Several stores may be fun spots to visit with your kids. The largest toy shop in Europe is **Franz Carl Weber,** Bahnhofstrasse 62 (ℂ **01/211-29-61**), named for the famous toy collector. There's also a specialist toy shop, **Pastorini,** Weinplatz 3 (ℂ **01/228-70-70**). Pastorini specializes in wooden toys and is one of the biggest toy stores in Zurich, spread over five floors.

The best-stocked children's bookstore in Switzerland is **Kinderbuchladen Zurich,** Oberdorfstrasse 32 (ℂ **01/261-53-50**), which carries many English-language books

In addition, the following two attractions may be of special interest to children:

Zoologischer Garten (Zoological Garden) ✦   One of the best-known zoos in Europe, Zurich's Zoological Garden contains some 2,200 animals of about 260 species. It also has an aquarium and an open-air aviary. You can visit the Africa house, the ape house, and the terrariums, along with the elephant house and the giant tortoise house. There are special enclosures for red pandas, otters, and snow leopards, and a house for clouded leopards, tigers, Amur leopards, and Indian lions.

Zurichbergstrasse 221. ℂ **01/254-25-00.** Admission 16SF ($8.80) adults, 8SF ($4.40) children 6–16, students 5SF ($2.75); free for children 5 and under. Mar–Oct daily 8am–6pm; Nov–Feb daily 8am–5pm. Tram: 6 from the Hauptbahnhof; the zoo is in the eastern sector of the city, called Zurichberg, on a wooded hill.

Zürcher Spielzeugmuseum (Zurich Toy Museum)   This museum, in one of the oldest parts of the city, contains more than 1,200 antique toys from all over Europe. The collection is displayed on the fifth floor of a house.

Fortunagasse 15. ℂ **01/211-93-05.** Free admission. Mon–Fri 2–5pm, Sat 1–4pm. Tram: 13.

Frommer's Favorite Zurich Experiences

Shopping Along Bahnhofstrasse   It has been called the most beautiful shopping street in the world, and perhaps it is. Built a century ago on the site of the ancient moat, it's a stroller's paradise. In stores on both sides of the street is some of the world's greatest merchandise.

Taking a Boat Trip on Lake Zurich   On a sunny day, this is the best way to spend time in Zurich. Cruises on one of Europe's most beautiful lakes last 1½ to 4 hours. Boats depart from Bürkliplatz, the lake end of Bahnhofstrasse.

Visiting Uetliberg   If the day is sunny, you can take an electric train to this parklike, 2,800-foot (840m) hill. Once here, you can wander about, enjoying the natural surroundings and scenic vistas at every turn. It's best to take a picnic.

Meeting a Swiss Family   Zurich can seem cold and impersonal unless you get to meet some of the locals. The tourist office will arrange for you to get in touch with a family of your own age and occupation. It's a close-up view of how Zurichers live in their safe, prosperous city. The experience is genuine and not something hyped up for visitors.

Biking and Swimming on the Lake   In July and August, one of the most peaceful experiences is to bike from Seebach station through the forest to Katzenruti where you'll find several places ideal for a picnic. After lunch, you can cycle to the Katzensee with its sandy beach, returning later via Affoltern. The tourist office in Zurich will help you plot this course, which takes about 1½ hours to go the full 8 miles (13km).

WALKING TOUR 1   **ZURICH'S BAHNHOFSTRASSE**

Start	Bahnhofplatz.
Finish	Bellevueplatz.
Time	1 hour.
Best Times	Monday through Friday from 9am to 5pm or on Saturday from 9am to 1am (when most stores are open).
Worst Times	Rush hours, Monday through Friday from 8 to 9am and 5 to 6pm.

If you do nothing else in Zurich, walk along world-famous Bahnhofstrasse. One of the most beautiful shopping streets on earth was built on the site of a "frogs' moat." The street is free from all traffic except trams.

Begin the tour at:

❶ Bahnhofplatz

The site of the Hauptbahnhof, the central railroad station, this is the beginning of Bahnhofstrasse. The square itself is rather drab, but the scenery improves as you go along (the street extends almost a mile to the lake). The Hauptbahnhof was built in 1871.

Escalators take you from Bahnhofplatz past an underground shopping mall, Shop Ville, to:

❷ Bahnhofstrasse

With your back to the railway terminus, you can head up Bahnhofstrasse, which is lined with linden trees, as well as some of the world's most prosperous banks and expensive shops, selling such luxury merchandise as Swiss watches and jewelry.

Continue up the street to:

❸ Pestalozzi Park

The park appears on your right, 2 blocks from Bahnhofplatz, between Schweizergasse and Usteristrasse. You can stop here and rest on one of the park benches by a statue of Johann Heinrich Pestalozzi (1746–1827), an educational reformer who had import on school standards in the United States.

TAKE A BREAK
At Bahnhofstrasse 21 (Am Paradeplatz) is the **Confiserie Sprünli** (✆ 01/224-47-11), the most elegant and fashionable place on this chic shopping street to meet for tea and pastries, which are the best in the city. You can also enjoy daily lunch specials.
Farther along, near Augustinergasse and Pelikan Strasse, you'll see a small pedestrian walkway where you can stop to admire the sculpture in the area.

After you pass St. Peter Strasse and Baren-gasse, you'll reach:

❹ Paradeplatz

This is the hub of Zurich and the central tram interchange. In the 18th century, it was a cattle market. The square is dominated by the 1876 mansion of Crédit Suisse. East of the plaza is the Hotel Baur-en-Ville, the first hotel constructed in Zurich, in 1838. The facade was reconstructed in 1978.

Continue along Bahnhofstrasse until you reach:

❺ Bürkliplatz

On the shore of Lake Zurich, this is the point where the Limmat River empties into the lake. This square overlooks Quaibrücke, the bridge across the Limmat that connects the left bank with the right bank. After stopping to admire the lake, you might also consider a boat excursion if it's summer.

If you cross Quaibrücke, you'll arrive on the right bank at:

❻ Bellevueplatz

Here you can enjoy the view of the lake and river as you rest on a park bench and watch all of Zurich pass by.

WALKING TOUR 2   ZURICH'S ALTSTADT

Start	Münsterhof.
Finish	Helmhaus.
Time	1½ hours.
Best Times	Any sunny day between 10am and 4pm (when there's less traffic).
Worst Times	Rush hours, Monday through Friday from 8 to 9am and 5 to 6pm.

Situated on both sides of the Limmat River, Altstadt (Old Town) is known for its squares, narrow cobblestone streets, and winding alleys. There are fountains, medieval houses, art galleries, boutiques, quaint restaurants, hotels (many moderately priced), and antiques shops. To walk its old streets is to follow in the footsteps of such famous figures as Charlemagne, Goethe, Einstein, and Lenin. The oldest houses date from the 1100s.

A former swine market, a good place to begin your exploration of Altstadt is:

❶ Münsterhof

This square, on the left bank, is near such landmarks as Fraumünster and

the Rathaus. You can reach it by walking along Schlüsselgasse. At Münsterhof 8 is the guildhall Zunfthaus zur Waag, erected in 1637, with late Gothic windows and a gabled facade.

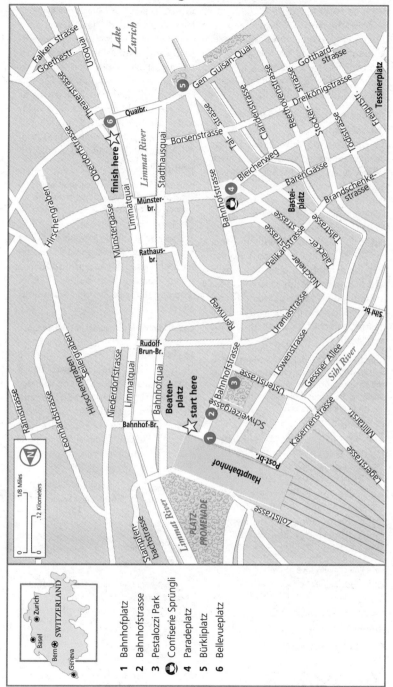

1. Bahnhofplatz
2. Bahnhofstrasse
3. Pestalozzi Park
4. Confiserie Sprüngli
5. Paradeplatz
6. Bürkliplatz
7. Bellevueplatz

Across the square is:

② Fraumünster

The entrance is on Fraumünsterstrasse. A church has stood on this site since 853, when it was a convent for noblewomen. It contains artwork by Chagall and Giacometti, among others.

After the church, your next target can be:

③ Lindenhof

To get here, you must climb narrow medieval alleyways from Fraumünster. Continue north along Schlüsselgasse, heading in the direction of the railroad station. Shaded by trees, the belvedere square of Lindenhof is one of the most scenic spots in Zurich, especially romantic at twilight. Once the site of a Celtic and later a Roman fort, Lindenhof is a good place from which to view the Limmat River; the lookout point has a fountain. There's also a good view of the medieval old quarter, which rises in layers on the right bank.

From Lindenhof, head down Pfalzgasse, forking left onto Strehlgasse to Waggengasse and Rathausbrücke, the city hall bridge spanning the Limmat. You have arrived at the landmark square:

④ Weinplatz

The site of the Corn Exchange until 1620, this is presumably the oldest market square in Zurich. It's named for its 1909 Weinbauer fountain, which depicts a Swiss winegrower with a basket of grapes in hand. Most visitors pause to photograph the Flemish-roofed burghers' houses on the opposite bank.

Here you can also look at the:

⑤ Rathausbrücke

The present City Hall Bridge spanning the Limmat was built in 1878, at the site of the first span in Zurich.

Cross the bridge to visit the:

⑥ Rathaus

Here you'll find the late Renaissance town hall of Zurich, which opens onto Limmatquai. Built in the late 17th century, it has darkly paneled rooms and antique porcelain stoves. Canton councils still meet here in a setting of rich sculptural adornment. The town hall is open on Tuesday, Thursday, and Friday from 10am to 11:30am. Admission is free, but you should tip your guide.

Walk south along Limmatquai until you reach Münsterbrücke, a bridge across the Limmat, and the site of:

⑦ Wasserkirche

Wasserkirche is also known as Water Church. This church got its unusual name because it was surrounded by water when it was built in 1479. There's a statue of Zwingli, the famous Swiss reformer.

Directly north of the church at Limmatquai 31 is the:

⑧ Helmhaus

Built in 1794, the Helmhaus has a fountain hall and a gallery on the second and third floors, where the city shows changing exhibitions of Swiss art. The gallery is open Tuesday through Sunday from 10am to 6pm and also on Thursday from 8 to 10pm.

At the end of your walking tour, you can continue over to Zurich's most famous cafe.

> **WINDING DOWN**
> The Belle Epoque **Café Odéon**, Limmatquai 2 (© **01/251-16-50**), is the place where Lenin sat out most of World War I, plotting the Russian Revolution. It was also popular with the iconoclastic Dada artists of the same era. Stop for a cup of coffee in this historic setting.

ORGANIZED TOURS

TRAM TOURS The quickest and most convenient way to get acquainted with Zurich is with a 2-hour trolley tour, which rolls through various neighborhoods

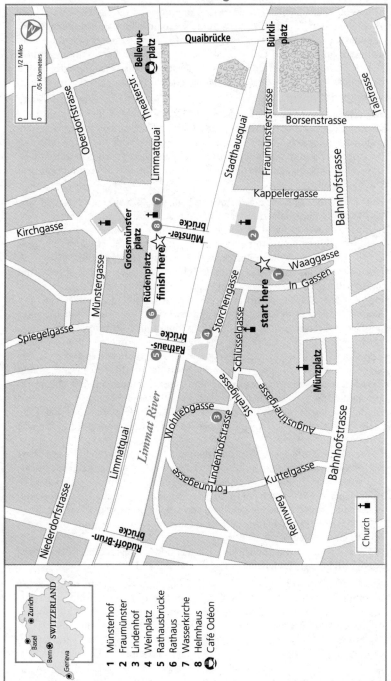

N

1/2 Miles

.05 Kilometers

0

0

Bürkli-
platz

Quaibrücke

Bellevue-
platz

Theaterstr.

Oberdorfstrasse

Borsenstrasse

Talstrasse

Stadthausquai

Fraumünsterstrasse

Limmatquai

Kappelergasse

Bahnhofstrasse

Kirchgasse

Grossmünster
platz

8

Münster-
brücke

7

2

Münstergasse

Rüdenplatz
finish here

Waaggasse

1

In Gassen

start here

Spiegelgasse

6

Rathaus-
brücke

5

Storchengasse

Schüsselgasse

4

Münzplatz

Strehlgasse

Limmat River

Limmatquai

Wohllebgasse

3

Lindenhofstrasse

Augustinergasse

Bahnhofstrasse

Fortunagasse

Kuttelgasse

Rennweg

Niederdorfstrasse

Rudolf-Brun-
brücke

Church

SWITZERLAND

Zurich

Basel

Bern

Geneva

1 Münsterhof
2 Fraumünster
3 Lindenhof
4 Weinplatz
5 Rathausbrücke
6 Rathaus
7 Wasserkirche
8 Helmhaus
8 Café Odéon

of interest. There's no live spokesperson pointing out the sights, but you'll be given a headset, which delivers a running commentary in seven languages. Between May and October, for a fee of 32SF ($17.60) per person, there are tours daily at 10am and 2pm. The tour takes in the commercial and shopping center and Old Town, and goes along the lakefront for a visit to Fraunmünster or one of the historic guildhalls beside the Limmatquai.

CABLEWAY TOUR   Another tour of Zürich is by boat and aerial cableway ascending to the Felsenegg at 2,650 feet (795m). From here, there's a panoramic view over the lake and the Alps beyond. It departs daily at 9:30am between May and September. Make your arrangements in advance with the tourist office in the main hall of Zurich's railway station, although your actual departure will be from a bus parked beside the Sihlquai, at a point that will be communicated to you in advance.

BOAT TOURS   At some point during your stay in Switzerland's largest city, you'll want to take a lake steamer for a tour around Lake Zurich. Walk to Bahnhofstrasse's lower end and buy a ticket at the pier for any of the dozen-or-so boats that ply the waters from late May to late September. The boats are more or less the same so it doesn't matter which one you take. Most of the steamers contain simple restaurant facilities, and all have two or three levels of decks and lots of windows for wide-angle views of the Swiss mountains and shoreline. During peak season, boats depart at approximately 30-minute intervals. The most distant itinerary from Zurich is to Rapperswil, a historic town near the lake's southeastern end. A full-length, round-trip tour of the lake from Zurich to Rapperswil will require 2 hours each way, plus whatever time you opt to explore towns en route. This trip is the highlight of the boat tours offered and if you can spare the time, you'll find it a rewarding way to see the area in and around Zurich. Many visitors opt for shorter boat rides encompassing only the northern third of the lake; the total trip takes about 90 minutes.

The full-length tour of the lake costs 20SF ($11) in second class and 33SF ($18.15) in first class. The shorter boat ride on the northern third of the lake costs 5.40SF ($2.95).

You might also want to take a 55-minute boat trip along the Limmat River for a closer view of Zurich's historic bridges and riverfront buildings. Boats depart daily at 30-minute intervals in the summer months, costing 4.60SF ($2.55) per person. Boats depart from a pier in front of the Landesmuseum, near Zurich's main railway station, and travel downriver to the lake as far as the Zurichhorn or the Wollishofen railway station before retracing their paths upriver back to the pier.

For more information on all the boats mentioned above, contact the **Zürichsee Schiffahrtsgesellschaft** by calling 📞 01/487-1333.

WALKING TOURS   One of the most appealing walking tours in Zurich is a 2-hour guided stroll through the Old Town. If you're interested in participating, meet in the main hall of Zurich's railway station, at the Tourist Service office (📞 01/215-4000). The cost of the tour is 20SF ($11) for adults, 10SF ($5.50) for children 6 to 16, and free for children under 6. From May through October, tours are operated Monday to Friday at 2:30pm (in German and English), and on Saturday and Sunday at 10am (in German and English) and at 2:30pm (in Spanish and English). From November to February, they are offered only at 10am on Wednesday and Saturday, and only in German and English.

ACTIVE PURSUITS

Zurichers are not big on spectator sports—they like to get out and participate.

Many of the larger hotels have added swimming pools and tennis courts or handball and racquetball facilities to their attractions. Some also have fitness centers. The best ones for the sports minded are **Atlantis Sheraton Hotel, Hotel Inter-Continental, Dolder Grand,** and **Waldhaus Dolder.**

GOLF The premier golf club in Switzerland, **Golf & Country Club Zurich,** Wied 9, Aiderstrasse, in the suburb of Zumikon (© **01/918-00-50**), 7½ miles (12km) southeast of the center, was laid out in 1931, and has the most prestigious reputation in the country. An 18-hole, par-72 course, it welcomes nonmembers who phone in advance, but only if they have a handicap of 30 or less, and only if they present a membership at a golf club in another part of the world. Greens fees are 200SF ($110) per person, and clubs can be rented for 30SF ($16.50) per set. To get there from downtown Zurich, take the Forchbahn tram from the Stadelhofen Bahnhof, near the Zurich opera house, then ride for 20 minutes to the tram station in the suburb of Zumikon. From there, it's a 6-minute walk to the golf course.

HIKING Zurich has seven "Vita-Parcours," or keep-fit trails. Someone at the Zurich Tourist Office, Bahnhofplatz 15 (© **01/215-4000**), will map these trails for you.

JOGGING The nearest woodland jogging route is on the **Allmend Fluntern,** which is a wide-open public park, crisscrossed with jogging paths, on the northeastern outskirts of Zurich, near the Zoo. To get here from the center, take tram 6. Joggers are also seen frequently along the quays and elsewhere in the city.

SKIING The closest ski region to Zurich is **Hoch-Ybrig,** about an hour's journey from the Hauptbahnhof. Take the train to Einsiedeln, where you can transfer to a bus to Weglosen and the aerial cableway that will take you to Hoch-Ybrig. Hoch-Ybrig has five ski lifts and two chairlifts.

SWIMMING You can go swimming in Lake Zurich, which has an average summer temperature of 68°F. The finest beach is the **Tiefenbrunnen.** To get to Tiefenbrunnen (which is also popular with the gay crowd), take tram 4 from central Zurich (Bahnhofplatz) to Tiefenbrunnen Bahnhof, a ride of about 15 minutes. The city and many hotels offer indoor and outdoor swimming pools. The **public pool** at Sihlstrasse 71 also has a sauna with its indoor swimming facilities.

6 Shopping

In the heart of Zurich is a square kilometer (about 25 acres) of shopping, including the exclusive stores along **Bahnhofstrasse,** previewed in the sightseeing section. Your shopping adventure might begin more modestly at the top of the street, at Bahnhofplatz. Below this vast transportation hub is a complex of shops known as **Shop Ville.**

Most shops are open Monday through Friday from 8am to 6:30pm and on Saturday from 8am to 4pm. Some of the larger stores stay open until 9pm on Thursday, and other shops are closed on Monday morning.

ART

Art-Repro *(Value* If you've always wanted a Degas or a Renoir but not been able to afford one, this trove of high-quality reproductions of the world's famous masterpieces might provide a reasonably priced alternative. There's an impressive array of artists' works available, including copies of paintings by Picasso, Miró, Chagall, and van Gogh, as well as such old masters as Rembrandt. Scheideggstrasse 95. ℭ 01/482-60-45.

Wuehre 9-Art Deco *Finds*   This shop is noted as one of Europe's richest repositories of objects crafted in the increasingly valuable Art Deco and Art Nouveau styles. The inventory includes everything from furniture to decorative accessories. There are no copies, and the establishment's buyers comb the art markets of France, Italy, England, and North America to replenish the stock. Wühre 9. ℭ 01/221-18-70.

BOOKS

Orell Füssli   Zurich's premier book department store stocks a large inventory of German and English books. In addition to books on Switzerland, you'll find everything from the latest novels to your favorite classics, as well as many contemporary nonfiction titles on every subject. Füsslistrasse at Bahnhofstrasse. ℭ 01/455-56-17.

The Travel Book Shop   This shop has a complete selection of travel books, as well as one of Europe's best map collections. Many of the books are German, but about half the stock is in English. Maps for trekking and mountaineering from all over the world are also sold. Rindermarkt 20. ℭ 01/252-38-83.

CHOCOLATES

Gennoni   Established in the 1970s, this is one of the city's major competitors for the sweet-tooth cravings of Zurich-based chocolate lovers. The displays are as tempting visually as they are gastronomically, and include an array of freshly made truffles flavored with kirsch or with marc de champagne. Any purchase can be shipped abroad. Seefeldstrasse 4. ℭ 01/261-35-30.

Sprüngli   In a country famous for its chocolates, Sprüngli is the most famous chocolatier, although we still consider it second best to Teuscher (see below). The inventory of virtually everything dark and "meltable in your mouth" is featured at this temple to chocolate. Adjacent to the store, you'll find a coffee shop, a small restaurant with a limited menu, and a room designated exclusively for mailing your next high-caloric gifts to friends and family abroad. Additional outlets of Sprüngli are located at Bahnhofstrasse 67, Löwenplatz, Stadelhoferplatz, and, to tempt last-minute buyers, the Zurich International Airport. Paradeplatz. ℭ 01/224-47-11.

Teuscher   Located on a narrow cobblestone street in Old Town, this small store is the original epicurean chocolate shop. You can tell you're in the area by the smell of chocolate truffles, which come in such flavors as champagne, orange, and cocoa. Storchengasse 9. ℭ 01/211-51-53.

CRAFTS

Schweizer Heimatwerk *Finds*   In 1930, in an effort to help economically distressed areas, a nonprofit society, Schweizer Heimatwerk, was created to keep traditional crafts alive. Today, Heimatwerk shops sell only items designed and made in Switzerland, most of them handcrafted. Items include copperware, ceramics, wood carvings, ironwork, jewelry, toys, nave paintings, crystal, tinware, baskets, music boxes, and paper-cutout pictures. Puzzles, games, puppets, even a Noah's ark with its carved wooden animals, are sold here as well. The headquarters shop and four other outlets of Schweizer Heimatwerk are in Zurich. The prices range from reasonable to expensive. Other branches are at Bahnhofstrasse 2 (ℭ **01/221-08-37**), at Rennweg 14 (ℭ **01/221-35-73**), at the

Hauptbahnhof, and at the Zurich airport (**✆ 01/816-40-85**) in Transit Halls A and B. Rudolph Brun-Brücke. ✆ 01/217-83-17.

Teddy's   Swiss-made handicrafts here evoke a nostalgia for old-fashioned Switzerland with the type of gifts a Teutonic Santa Claus might stuff into his bag of Christmas gifts. Items for sale include cuckoo clocks, T-shirts with an assortment of Swiss-inspired sayings, an impressive array of music boxes and beer steins, Swiss army knives, and wood carvings. Anything you buy can be shipped abroad. Limmatquai 34. ✆ 01/261-22-89.

DEPARTMENT STORES

Grieder les Boutiques   This is one of the best department stores in Switzerland, offering both ready-to-wear and couture by such designers as Valentino, Dior, Escada, and Montana. The store fills two floors of a stone building on Zurich's most fashionable commercial street, where the salespeople tend to be bilingual and formidably well dressed. The accessories, including purses, scarves, and leather goods, are well selected. There's a wide choice of shoes—many Swiss-made—for both men and women, plus a good men's department. Bahnhofstrasse 30. ✆ 01/211-33-60.

Jelmoli Department Store   This Zurich institution has everything a large department store should have, from cookware to clothing. Founded more than 150 years ago by the Ticino-born entrepreneur Johann Peter Jelmoli, the store is a legend in the Zurich business community. Bahnhofstrasse 69. ✆ 01/220-44-11.

FASHIONS

Milano-Zurich *(Value)*   Believe it or not, in high-priced Zurich, there are still ways to buy men's and women's clothing at discounted prices. This sophisticated shop maintains a direct pipeline to upscale manufacturers in Milan at prices much less than you'd pay retail in either city. Suits, blazers, trousers, and shirts for men, and dresses and sportswear for women, are routinely stocked from manufacturers that include Moschino, Issey Miyake, Mugler, and Cerruti 1881, as well as shoes from such distributors as Prada. Unless you're a very tall, very muscular, or very bulky man, the store will probably have something to fit you. Ask the multilingual staff for guidance—they're genuinely charming and willing to help. Usteristrasse 23. ✆ 01/212-0068.

Modeshaus Feldpausch   Spread across four floors, this outlet is devoted mainly to women's wear. However, some menswear is found in the basement. On the street level they sell casual wear along with a selection of clothing for young women. On the next level is the house's selection of designer clothing, with cocktail dresses and ensembles on the floor above. Check for sales in late summer and late winter. Bahnhofstrasse 88. ✆ 01/225-11-11.

Sormustin   This is one of the most sophisticated clothing stores of Zurich, lying in the gentrified Aussersihl district. A genius in textiles, Anne Koskiluoma, has teamed with Barbara Egg, a leading fashion designer, to create this clothing store for women. Among some of their more intriguing selections are pants and coats with patterns and colors inspired by the kimono designs of Tokyo. Ankerstrasse 41. ✆ 01/240-2606.

GIFTS

Meister Silber   This elite shop, on prestigious Paradeplatz in the center of Zurich, has one of the widest selections of gift items in Switzerland. The prices are high but reasonable, considering that every article is either exquisitely

Chocolate Superpower

Cocoa beans, which look rather unappetizingly like shriveled almonds, are chocolate's raw ingredient. First publicized in Europe by Columbus, who noticed them growing on trees in Nicaragua in 1502, they were traded as currency by the conquistadors in the New World, who viewed them as an elixir of physical strength. Cortés, oppressor of Mexico, believed that a foot soldier could march for many hours with renewed energy after consuming some of the beans. Back in Spain, royal cooks mixed the pulverized beans with sugar and hot water and served them with great success to the royal family. The Spanish-born Anne of Austria introduced it to the French court at her dinner parties after her marriage to Louis XIII. And in a kind of chain reaction to the bean's original "discovery," London's first chocolate shop was established by a Frenchman in 1657.

The 19th-century attitudes about chocolate as perceived in North America and in Europe were widely different. In 1825 the leading culinarian of the French-speaking world, Brillat-Savarin, declared that chocolate was one of the most effective restoratives of physical and intellectual powers known to man. In contrast, Harriet Beecher Stowe, the American-born moral crusader and woman of letters, declared chocolate unfit for proper American tables, and—in a burst of prudishness—commented suspiciously on its French and Spanish origins.

Despite Ms. Stowe's invectives, the market for chocolate continued to grow, as consumers searched for inexpensive alternatives to their bland, homegrown diets. This fact was immediately noticed by the canny Swiss from their politically neutral bastion in the Alps.

From the early 1800s the Swiss began investing heavily in what they perceived as a long-range money maker. Pioneers of the industry opened the country's first chocolate factory in 1819 at Corsier, near Vevey. What's now a massive multi-national concern, Suchard, was established near Neuchâtel in 1824. In 1875 Swiss-born Daniel Peter invented milk chocolate by adding condensed milk to his brew of pulverized cocoa and sugar. In 1879 the first chocolate bar was created: the Lindt Surfin bar. In 1899 the Sprungli and Lindt empires merged into a Zurich-based chocolate-making dynasty whose success has been likened by Swiss patriots to that of Henry Ford and the Wright brothers. The

handcrafted or comes from producers internationally known for quality and fine design. Bahnhofstrasse 28A. ✆ **01/221-27-30.**

JEWELRY

Les Ambassadeurs   Benefiting from a stylish location on the city's most prestigious shopping street, this well-known jeweler sells gemstones and such watches as Breitling, Cartier, Longines, Omega, and Constantin. Also featured are the baubles of Italian jeweler Mandredi and the Cleopatra line. Bahnhofstrasse 64. ✆ **01/211-18-10.**

Tiffany & Co.   The Swiss branch of America's most famous jeweler, this well-upholstered boutique sells the full line of products originally made famous in

Tobler and Nestlé organizations were founded shortly afterward, just before a host of new inventions followed in relentless succession. One of the most spectacular of these included liqueur-filled chocolate cups whose manufacturing process is considered an engineering marvel. Ironically, improvements in dentistry have always paralleled the increased proficiency of the chocolate industry's blending and marketing techniques.

Switzerland today is the largest chocolate superpower in the world, leading the globe in production. Both secrecy and precision have always been cited as Swiss virtues, and both these qualities are required during a complicated blending process that transforms the raw ingredients into the final product. Every chocolate lover has his or her favorite, ours being Confiserie Tschirren, founded in 1919 by Jean Tschirren. The firm uses 12 tons of chocolate a year. Our all-time to-die-for chocolates from Confiserie Tschirren are the truffle dark, truffle cream, truffle honey, and truffle champagne.

The allure of Swiss chocolate is aesthetic as well as gastronomic: Swiss consumers expect new artwork on their chocolate wrappers at frequent intervals, and an army of commercial artists labors at yearly intervals to comply. The Swiss eat and drink more chocolate per capita than any other nation in the world, fueling their bodies for the bone-chilling temperatures of the alpine climate. No self-respecting mountain climber ever embarks without the requisite chocolate bars. Swiss factories maintain "chocolate breaks" for sugar-induced bursts of energy. Swiss housewives usually don't buy less than a kilo of chocolate at a time, and a fortune is almost guaranteed to anyone who can invent transparent and translucent chocolate. The challenge of producing white chocolate was already conquered—in Switzerland—many years ago.

Swiss chocolate makers, however, face a troubled future. European Union trade protections and high taxes, and the high value of the Swiss franc, threaten much of the chocolate production here. Many of those Nestlé bars today are produced in Spain and Greece. Swiss chocolate production is increasingly located outside Switzerland. This is one of the prices Switzerland pays for staying out of Europe's free-trade zone.

New York, including those by artists such as Paloma Picasso. No crystal or china is offered, but small gift items are sold, as well as a choice of the famous gold and silver chains. Bahnhofstrasse 14. ℂ 01/211-10-10.

Türler   On the ground level of the Savoy Hotel, this outlet has a goldsmith and a watchmaker on staff and is known throughout Zurich for its custom-made watches and jewelry. If you have a special design, they'll make it for you. They also carry a wide variety of watches from other designers—some 30 different brands in all—and they sell both these and a selection of jewelry in a wide range of prices. Bahnhofstrasse 28, edge of Paradeplatz. ℂ 01/221-06-08.

LEATHER GOODS

Leder-Locher   Established 150 years ago, this venerable leather store has maintained high standards despite the changing tides of fashion throughout the years. Its inventory includes handbags, purses, wallets, suitcases, garment bags, and an unusual collection of small but charming gift items and accessories. The store maintains another branch at Bahnhofstrasse 91 (✆ 01/211-70-82). Münsterhof 18–19. ✆ 01/211-18-64.

Mädler   Stephanie Mädler and her family have owned this leather-goods shop since 1951. The store, which specializes in leather bags, wallets, and suitcases, has a massively stocked second floor. Bahnhofstrasse 26. ✆ 01/211-75-70.

LINENS & COTTONS

Albrecht Schläper   Everything for the table and bed are the order of the day at this emporium of sheets, pillowcases, towels, pillows, blankets, and bathroom accessories. Fabrics include silks, linens, cottons, and a well-chosen array of everything in between. Lintheschergasse 10. ✆ 01/211-57-47.

Spitzenhaus   An air of old-fashioned charm permeates this store specializing in carefully crafted linens, cottons, and silks for the dining table. Most of the linen comes from Bern and Zurich (both specialists in linen), while most of the lace is handmade in either St. Gallen or Appenzell. The place also sells embroidered blouses and table scarves. Börsenstrasse 14. ✆ 01/211-55-76.

Sturzenegger   This century-old, wood-paneled store is a good place to buy all kinds of delicate hand-embroidered items, including Swiss-made lace. Several rooms contain a variety of intricately patterned tablecloths, place mats, doilies, and napkins. Also sold are blouses, handkerchiefs, shawls, scarves, and children's frocks. Upstairs is a large assortment of nightgowns, pajamas, and women's lingerie. Bahnhofstrasse 48. ✆ 01/211-28-20.

MUSIC

Musik Hug   This is the largest branch of the best music chain in Switzerland. Conveniently located in the center of Zurich, it stocks thousands of tapes from around the world and has a helpful staff. Its selection of Swiss folkloric music, classical recordings, and modern jazz is especially rich and varied. Limmatquai 28–30. ✆ 01/251-68-50.

PERFUMES

Parfumerie Schindler   This store is devoted exclusively to one of the city's most comprehensive selections of perfumes and fragrances. If you can name it, this store will probably have it. Paradeplatz (Bahnhofstrasse 26). ✆ 01/221-18-55.

PORCELAIN

Ursula Riedi   Whatever you do, don't make any sudden moves in this shop. It's loaded from floor to ceiling with some of the most exquisite and valuable antique Meissen porcelain in Zurich. Everything is breathtakingly fragile, and breathtakingly valuable, a safe haven for aficionados of Europe's most ephemeral art form—antique porcelain. Leave the kids at home. Torgasse 5. ✆ 01/252-35-10.

SHOES

Andy Jllien   This is the quintessential boutique, with a carefully chosen but limited inventory of shoes that might appeal to fashion-conscious women. Torgasse 5–6. ✆ 01/252-19-11.

Bally Capitol This is the place to buy Bally shoes. The prominently situated store is the world's largest official outlet of this famous Swiss chain. The store carries the complete line, along with accessories and clothing for men, women, and children. Bahnhofstrasse 66. ☎ 01/224-39-39.

Graziella Graziella's inventory of shoes comes from throughout Europe. There's everything from sensible oxfords to the kind of flimsy but oh-so-attractive footwear a woman might wear to a Hollywood premier or a glamorous casino. Löwenstrasse 30. ☎ 01/221-11-93.

SPORTSWEAR
Bachtold Sport Everything you'll need for aerobics to ballet and skydiving to grand slalom skiing is on sale here. There's even a department for snorkeling enthusiasts. Clothing and sports equipment are equally featured, and the staff is knowledgeable about both European and North American sizes. Ramistrasse 3 (Bellevue). ☎ 01/252-09-34.

WATCHES
Beyer If you have your heart set on buying a timepiece in Zurich, try this well-established store midway between the train station and the lake. Besides carrying just about every famous brand of watch made in Switzerland—Rolex, Corum, Cartier, and Patke Philippe—it also has a museum in the basement, containing timepieces from as early as 1400 B.C. Exhibitions include all kinds of water clocks, sundials, and hourglasses. Bahnhofstrasse 31. ☎ 01/221-10-80.

Bucherer A longtime name in the Swiss watch industry, this store also carries an impressive collection of jewelry. Some of the most famous names in watch-making are represented in their latest offerings, including Chopard, Rado, and Rolex. Bahnhofstrasse 50. ☎ 01/211-26-35.

7 Zurich After Dark

The city's nightlife is becoming less conservative, but don't expect it to be too wild. Most of the nightspots in Zurich close down early, so you should begin early. Concerts, theater, opera, and ballet all flourish here.

To learn what's on during your visit, pick up a copy of *Zurich News,* available free at the tourist office and distributed at the front desks of most hotels.

THE PERFORMING ARTS
No special discount tickets are granted, but for regular tickets to operas, theaters, and concerts go to **Billettzentrale** (BiZZ for short), Bahnhofstrasse 9 (☎ 01/ 221-22-83), open Monday through Friday from 10am to 6:30pm and on Saturday from 10am to 2pm.

The **Zurich Opera** is the most outstanding local company, performing at the Opernhaus. The **Zurich Tonhalle Orchestra,** performing at Tonhalle, also enjoys an international reputation.

Opernhaus Zurich Opera House, near Bellevueplatz in the center of the city, was founded in 1891. The history of the opera house forms part of the cultural history of Europe; the house was the venue of several world premiers, including performances of *Lulu* by Alban Berg and *Mathis der Maler* by Hindemith. The opera house is also a repertory theater, hosting ballets, concerts, and recitals. The hall is dark in July and August. Falkenstrasse 1. ☎ 01/268-66-66. Tickets 30SF–200SF ($16.50–$110). Box office open daily 10am–6:30pm.

Schauspielhaus   This is one of the most important theaters in Switzerland, generally performing plays in German that range from classic to modern. It's a repertoire theater that performs different works nearly every evening, not long-running shows. Rämistrasse 34, at Heimplatz. ℂ 01/268-66-66. Tickets 10SF–100SF ($5.50–$55). Box office open daily 10am–7pm. Closed mid-June to Sept.

Tonhalle Gesellschaft   This concert hall facing Bürkliplatz is the biggest and most famous concert hall in Zurich, with 1,500 seats in the big hall and 700 seats in the small hall. Brahms opened Tonhalle Gesellschaft in 1895 with a presentation of "Song of Triumph." It's home to the Zurich Tonhalle Orchestra and the venue for appearances by many internationally known soloists. Recitals and chamber music presentations are also staged here. Try to purchase your tickets as early as possible because many seats are sold by subscription. Reservations can be made 2 weeks prior to any concert. Claridenstrasse 5. ℂ **01/206-34-34.** Tickets 16SF–155SF ($8.80–$85.25). Box office open daily 10am–6pm, except concert days when it closes at performance time.

THE CLUB & MUSIC SCENE

Adagio/La Boule   In the city building most frequently used for public meetings (the Kongresshaus), this three-in-one nightclub sets strict standards of respectability for its relatively conservative clientele, generally attracting an over-35 crowd. Its centerpiece is a small-stakes casino, where the roulette and black-jack tables limit bets to 5SF ($2.75), so that gambling is just an amusement. Connected to the casino are two rustically decorated nightclubs. Formerly called Joker, Adagio is a dance club. The dancing is mainly ballroom stuff in a big hall decorated like a church. The staff wears ancient costumes, and fresh flowers and burning candles abound. The club is extremely crowded on weekends. There's no dining except for what is called "the smallest restaurant in the world," seating four persons at a table on a small platform. Of course, you must reserve 4 to 5 months in advance, and if you're granted the table, you get "menu surprise" for 155SF ($85.25). At La Boule, you can play mini-roulette. In the Kongresshaus, Gothardstrasse 5. ℂ 01/206-36-66. Cover 10SF ($5.50) Thurs, 15SF ($8.25) Fri–Sat; free otherwise. Complex open Sun–Thurs 5pm–2am and Fri–Sat 5pm–4am. Adagio and La Boule are open year-round, but the casino vacations from mid-July to mid-August.

Bierhalle Wolf   With 160 seats, this is the best-known beer hall in Zurich, drawing people of all ages and all walks of life. It features "evergreen music" in a sometimes rowdy but safe environment. Folk music is played by an oompah band in regional garb whose instruments include a tuba, accordion, saxophone, clarinet, and bass. The large beer hall is decorated with pennants and flags of different cantons. Beer is available in tankards costing 5SF ($2.75) and up. Live music is presented every day from 4 to 6:30pm and from 8:30pm to midnight, and every Sunday morning from 10am to noon. During the breaks, slides of alpine scenery are shown. You can also dine here on hearty robust fare, with main courses starting at 14SF ($7.70). Limmatquai 132. ℂ **01/251-01-30.** Cover 4SF–5SF ($2.20–$2.75). Daily 11am–2am.

Casa Bar   When Zurichers want to hear New Orleans–style, Dixieland jazz, they head here. Some rhythm and blues from the '50s and '60s is regularly featured as well. The dark-paneled decor is inspired by the forests of Switzerland. On a busy night, at least 60 patrons of varying ages can crowd in here. A beer costs 8.50SF ($4.70) and up. Or you can order hard liquor beginning at 15SF ($8.25). Wine by the glass costs from 14SF ($7.70). Münstergasse 30. ℂ **01/261-20-02.** Daily 5pm–2am.

Kaufleuten   This club attracts one of the widest cross sections of Zurich society, partly because of the central location and partly because of the comfortably battered, old-fashioned interior whose mismatched tables and chairs imply a certain unstructured comfort. Once inside, you'll find four different bar areas with mostly house and garage music playing. The Restaurant Kaufleuten is separately recommended in "Where to Dine," earlier in the chapter. Pelikanstrasse 18. ✆ 01/ 225-33-00. Cover 15SF–25SF ($8.25–$13.75), depending on the night of the week. Sun–Thurs 11pm–2am; Fri–Sat to 4am.

THE BAR SCENE

Blaue Ente   Although Blau Ente is best known as a restaurant, many locals, especially young professionals, come here for its bar. In a high-tech setting, you can enjoy beer beginning at 3.50SF ($1.95), or whisky at 10.50SF ($5.80). Although the restaurant is open daily, the bar is closed on Sunday. Seefeldstrasse 442 at Mühle Tiefenbrunnen. ✆ 01/388-68-40. Bar area open Mon–Fri 10:30am–midnight (until 2am on Sat). Both the bar and its restaurant are closed July 25–August 17.

James Joyce Pub   The furnishings and paneling of this pub were acquired in the early 1970s by the Union Bank of Switzerland, when Jury's, an 18th-century hotel in Dublin, was demolished. The Union Bank reassembled the bar (with slightly more comfortable banquettes) near Bahnhofstrasse to entertain business clients and named it after famous Dubliner James Joyce, who had described its decor in certain passages of *Ulysses*. The blackboard menu lists the daily specials (*plattes*). In December, Irish stew is traditionally served. Other fare includes fish-and-chips, hamburgers, and fried chicken legs. Pelikanstrasse 8. ✆ 01/221-18-28. Mon–Fri 11am–midnight and Sat 11am–6pm.

Jules Verne   To reach the bar, you'll have to ride an elevator to the 11th floor, after passing through the street-level restaurant (Brasserie Lipp—see "Where to Dine," earlier) with which it's associated. Views from the windows encompass the center of Zurich and some of the surrounding scenery, and the decor includes nostalgic references to what the bar's namesake envisioned as the technology of the future. The place can get crowded with talkers and drinkers in their 30s and 40s as music plays in the background. You can expect conviviality but not necessarily intimacy here. It's a great happy hour spot. Uraniastrasse 9. ✆ 01/211-11-55. Daily 11:30am–midnight (till 1am Fri–Sat).

Oliver Twist Pub   Although its friendly bartenders speak a total of 15 languages, making it probably the most cosmopolitan pub in Zurich, this place is Irish to the very core, with framed photographs of Irish landscapes decorating the paneled walls. The pub attracts a young, fun-loving crowd. There's a courtyard with stone pavement and a modern statue of a crouching laborer. Warm snacks and sandwiches are available, and the bar has more than four kinds of draft beer and 20 brands of bottled beer, starting at 6.90SF ($3.80). Rindermarkt 6. ✆ 01/ 252-47-10. Mon–Fri 11am–midnight, Sat 3pm–midnight, and Sun 4pm–midnight.

Rosaly's   The structure looks a lot like a geranium-studded alpine chalet that's oddly positioned on a narrow alleyway near the most congested part of the Bellevueplatz, a busy downtown tram junction. During the dinner hour, patrons huddle around a half-moon-shaped bar area, leaving most of the tables to diners. Later in the evening, however, more and more of the tables—both indoor and outdoor—become devoted to the bar. There's a sense of hipness and whimsy to this place, and an occasional subtle reference to big-city life in faraway California. The list of cocktails include Kamikazes, Rob Roys, Side Cars, and Margaritas. Freieckgasse 7. ✆ 01/261-4430. Daily 4pm–midnight or 1am, depending on business.

Schmuklerski   There isn't that much to the decor of this place, other than a sheathing of mirrors, a kind of glossy minimalism, and tables that spill out into a garden in back during clement weather. But it rates as one of the bars of the minute in trend-conscious Zurich, thanks to its ownership by a local soccer star, Thomas Bickel, whose cachet and contracts draw in a bevy of sports stars and fans, models and mannequins, graphic designers and media people. Look for such cocktails as caipirinhas and mojitos, many kinds of beer, and a contagious sense of hip. 101 Badenerstrasse. ℰ 01/241-1541. Mon 4pm–12:00am, Tues–Wed 9am–12am, Thu–Fri 9am–2am, Sat 12pm–2am, Sunday 12pm–12am.

2 Akt   By daylight, this place resembles a simple bistro, with varnished pine paneling, high ceilings, and accessories that hint at its beerhall-style origins around the turn of the century. A simple menu of Wiener schnitzels and roasted chicken accompanies mugs of beer and glasses of wine. By nightfall, however, the place is filled with the young and the restless, and on nights when a DJ spins state-of-the-art dance music, the place is mobbed. It isn't a disco per se, but rather, a bar and restaurant that just happens to play dance music, and which just happens to attract a crowd of TV announcers, journalists, and artists in modern-day Zurich. As such, you'll probably be tapping your feet to the music, but not actually dancing, unless a group of rowdies breaks loose from their drinking and spontaneously begins to gyrate. The weekly schedule of what spin-meister will be on duty is clearly marked on a blackboard several days in advance, adding an element of star quality to the artist who's actually selecting the music. Food is served Monday to Saturday 9am to 10pm, and Sunday 5 to 10pm. A DJ plays Thursday to Saturday 9pm to 4am. Seinaustrasse 2. ℰ 01/201-6564. No cover. Mon–Sat 9am–2 or 4am, Sun 5pm–2am.

THE GAY SCENE

Barfüsser   This is the premier jeans-and-leather bar for gay men in Zurich. It proudly lays claim to being the oldest continuously operated gay bar in Europe, with a well-worn dark and woodsy decor and a loyal clientele who have patronized the place since its establishment in 1956. Most show up after 8pm, and it's especially popular on weekends. The interior contains two different bar areas, the larger of which tends to serve gay men; the smaller focuses on the bar's growing contingent of gay women. Spitalgasse 14. ℰ 01/251-40-64. Daily 2pm–2am.

Bar Carroussel   Established in 1980, this is Zurich's second-most-important gay bar, catering almost exclusively to men. There's no food or dancing, and many patrons consider it a neighborhood hangout. It lies in the heart of the Old Town, a short walk from the Barfüsser. Fähringerstrasse 33. ℰ 01/251-46-01. Sun–Thurs 4pm–2am and Fri–Sat 4pm–4am.

Predigerhof   This is a warm, friendly, and sometimes very busy men's pub that makes every effort to welcome the widest possible cross section of the local gay community. Despite its attempts at even-handedness, it tends to attract the kind of machos you might have expected in a high-altitude hut in the Swiss Alps. Mühlegasse 15. ℰ 01/251-29-85. Sun–Thurs 2pm–midnight; Fri–Sat 2pm–4am.

8 Side Trips from Zurich

Zurich is surrounded by some of the most interesting sightseeing areas in Switzerland. The following are a few of exceptional interest. All these attractions can easily be reached on a short trip from your hotel in Zurich, either by train or lake steamer.

GREAT RIDES THROUGH THE ENVIRONS

A few fun, quick tours you can take on your own make use of funiculars and trains. If you have time for only one of these trips, make it the Uetliberg (see below).

THE DOLDERBAHN 👉 Take the Dolderbahn for a short aerial cable ride to the **Dolder Recreational Area,** 1,988 feet (596m) above the city. Trains leave every 10 minutes from Römerhofplatz, which you can reach by taking tram no. 3, 8, or 15. The recreational area is open year-round and has restaurants, nature trails, old rustic taverns, a path to the zoo, a miniature golf course, and, from October to March, a huge ice-skating rink. There's a place to swim, the **Dolder Schwimmbad** (✆ 01/267-70-80), which is carved into a hillside with a view of Zurich. The swimming area is a 5-minute walk along a forest trail from the end of the cable-car line; follow the signs to Dolder Wellenbad. Admission to the pool with its artificial waves is 8SF ($4.40) or 4SF ($2.20) for children under 6. The Dolderbahn funicular ride costs 2.50SF ($1.40); buy your tickets from the machine.

THE FORCHBAHN For a close-up view of some of the most desirable residential real estate in Zurich, consider a ride on the Forchbahn, a short-haul railway line originating in downtown Zurich at the Stadelhofen Bahnhof, which lies at the junction of the Bellevueplatz and the Limmatquai, adjacent to the Quaibrucke (✆ 01/918-01-08 for more information). The Forchbahn travels through the capital's staid and endlessly respectable suburbs (local wits refer to it as "The Gold Coast") to end points at Esslingen and Forch, both of which lie within 30-minute rides south of the city center. The area is noted for its sunlight, and as such, gardening seems to be a passionate pastime for local residents. You can get off the train at any of the stops, and pick any of the signposted trails that meander to nearby points of scenic interest. (The tourist office in Zurich is a good source of information. Otherwise, just ask a local or set out on a brief excursion on your own.) The shores of both the Griefensee and the Zurichee are good bets for a walk, with paths that meander down from many points en route. Trains on the Forchenbahn run without conductors, so you must buy your tickets from a machine at whatever point you happen to get on.

A round-trip ticket from Stadelhofen Bahnof to Forch costs 14.40SF ($7.90); a round-trip ticket from Stadelhofen Bahnof to Esslingen costs 17.60SF ($9.70). Trains depart from downtown Zurich (Bellevueplatz) at 30-minute intervals throughout the day and evening.

FELSENEGG 👉 An excursion to the alpine aerie at Felsenegg isn't as vertiginous as other mountain stations in higher-altitude regions of Switzerland, but its proximity to Zurich makes it one of the most consistently popular. To reach it, take one of the frequent (every 25 minutes) trains from Zurich's Hauptbahnhof for the 14-minute ride to the residential suburb of Adliswil, 6 miles (10km) south, for a cost of 7SF ($3.85) each way. Get off in Adliswil, then embark on a brisk, 10-minute uphill climb to an aerial cable car, the Luftseilbahn Adliswil-Felsenegg (LAF; ✆ 01/710-7330), for a 6-minute uphill ride to the top of Felsenegg, at 2,650 feet (795m) above sea level. Expect to pay 7.20SF ($3.95) round-trip. From here, it's a 10-minute hike to the **Restaurant Felsenegg** (✆ 01/710-6306), serving typical alpine food on a panoramic outdoor terrace or indoors. From May to September, the restaurant is open daily from 8am to 10pm; from October to April, from 9am to 8pm. Every Saturday night, year-round, it stays open till 11pm. It's closed 2 weeks in early November.

ALPAMARE   We also recommend a visit to Alpamare (© **055/415-15-87**), Europe's largest water park as certified in the *Guinness Book of World Records.* It lies at Churstrasse 111, in the village of Pfäffikon on Lake Zurich, offering year-round fun in and around the water on four body flumes and both indoor and outdoor tube slides. There's also an indoor swimming pool with breakers, a bubbling hot spring, and an open-air pool with underwater music and massage jets, as well as 300 feet (90m) of lazy river. An outdoor thermal pool contains iodine. The attraction is open daily from 10am to 10pm. Weekdays adults pay 35SF ($19.25) for a visit of up to 4 hours, and 43SF ($23.65) for a visit of up to 8 hours. Children ages 6 to 15 are charged 29SF ($15.95) for a visit of up to 4 hours, and 34SF ($18.70) for a visit of up to 8 hours. Weekends adults pay 37SF ($20.35) and 48SF ($26.40), respectively, and children 31SF ($17.05) and 37SF ($20.35). Children under 6 enter free, but children 2 and under are not allowed in the water.

KILCHBERG   If you're an admirer of Thomas Mann, we recommend a visit to Kilchberg, 4 miles (6km) from Zurich along the southwestern shore of the lake. Mann spent the last years of his life here and was buried on the south side of the small church in the village in 1955. His wife died here in 1980. Fans of the author still flock here to see the grave site, but Kilchberg is more famously associated with the 19th-century Swiss author Conrad Ferdinand Meyer. Train S8 departs from Zurich Hauptbahnhof station every half hour for an 11-minute ride to the village. If traveling by car, proceed along the southwestern shore route of Lake Zurich following the signposts to Kilchberg.

UETLIBERG   Southwest of Zurich, Uetliberg, the northernmost peak in the Albis ridge, is one of the most popular excursions from the city, reached in only 15 minutes. Take the mountain railway Uetlibergbahn from the Selnau station in Zurich. A round-trip costs 14.40SF ($7.90) and takes half an hour. You arrive near the Sihl River, at an elevation of 2,800 feet (840m).

From the station, you can hike 10 minutes to the summit, where there's a cafe and restaurant. The tower is a climb of about 170 steps; from the lookout, on a clear day, you can see as far away as the Black Forest. For more information about the train, call © **01/206-45-11.**

WINTERTHUR

This industrial town in the Toss Valley, 12 miles (20km) northeast of Zurich, is also a music and cultural center, with an art collection that makes the 15-minute train trip from Zurich worthwhile. Winterthur was once a Roman settlement and became the seat of the counts of Kyburg. It later was a stronghold of the Hapsburgs, until it was sold to Zurich. In the United States, the name Winterthur conjures up the du Pont mansion in Delaware with its museum of Americana or else a reference to the financial giant, Winterthur Insurance. Both of these take their name from this Swiss industrial city.

Winterthur is best explored on foot. City officials have signposted an itinerary that takes in the history, architecture, and culture of the town.

A **tourist office** is at Im Hauptbahnhof (© **052/267-67-00**), open Tuesday to Friday 8:30am to 6:30pm, and on Saturday from 8:30am to 4pm.

From Zurich's Hauptbahnhof, trains depart about every 20 minutes throughout the day (trip time: 20 to 26 minutes).

SEEING THE SIGHTS

The skyline of Winterthur is dominated by the twin towers of its parish church, the Stadkirche, built from 1264 to 1515 (the towers were added later).

Museum Oskar Reinhart am Stadtgarten ☆☆   Oskar Reinhart, a famous art collector who died in 1965, willed many of his treasures to the city. Displayed in this gallery are works of Austrian, German, and Swiss artists, with a fine representation of the Romantic painters, including Blechen, Friedrich, Kersting, and Runge. Many canvases are by Hodler. There are some 600 works in all, from the 18th to the 20th century.

Stadthausstrasse 6. ☎ 052/267-51-72. Admission 8SF ($4.40) adults, 6SF ($3.30) children under 8. Wed–Sun 10am–5pm, Tues 10am–8pm. Bus: 1, 3, or 6.

Kunstmuseum ☆   Located a 10-minute walk north of the Stadthaus on Stadthausstrasse and Lindstrasse, this fine-arts museum contains an impressive collection of European and American art and sculpture from the late 19th century to the present. Giacometti and such French artists as Bonnard and Vuillard are well represented. Highlights are works by van Gogh, Miró, Magritte, Mondrian, Kokoschka, Calder, and Klee. There are sculptures by Rodin, as well as works by Medardo Rosso and Maillol. The permanent collection is on display from June to August; temporary exhibits are presented the rest of the year.

Museumstrasse 52. ☎ 052/267-51-62. Admission 10SF ($5.50) adults, 7SF ($3.85) seniors, 5SF ($2.75) children. Tues 10am–8pm, Wed–Sun 10am–5pm. Bus: 1, 3, or 6 to Stadthaus.

Schloss Kyburg   Four miles (6km) from Winterthur, Schloss Kyburg is the largest castle in eastern Switzerland, dating from the Middle Ages. The stronghold was the ancestral home of the counts of Kyburg until 1264, when the Hapsburgs took over. These counts were local rulers and of little interest to visitors today, as their history has long been overshadowed by the more powerful and more famous Hapsburg dynasty. It was ceded to Zurich in the 15th century and is now a museum of antiques and armor. There's a good view from the keep. You may also visit the residence hall of the knights, parapet, and chapel.

Kyburg 8314. ☎ 052/232-46-64. Admission 8SF ($4.40) adults, 6SF ($3.30) students and seniors, 3SF ($1.65) children 6–16; free for children 5 and under. Feb–Nov, Tues–Sun 10:30am–4:30pm. Closed Dec–Jan. From Zurich, take the Winterthur rail line, get off at the Fretekon stop, and transfer to a bus for the 10-min. ride to the castle; buses depart every hour throughout the day. The castle is not on a street (or road) map.

Swiss Technorama   Technorama is the Swiss National Center for Science and Technology. Its permanent exhibition is divided into eight areas, with many interactive experiments and phenomena: Physics, Energy, Water/Nature/Chaos, Mechanical Music, Mathe-Magic, Materials, Textiles, and Automation. Technorama also boasts the world's greatest tin-plate train collection. In the hands-on Youth Laboratory, children can learn from some 100 experiments about science, mathematics, and biology. A self-service restaurant is at the site, and a big park features a steam train and muscle-powered flying machines.

Technoramastrasse 1. ☎ 052/243-05-05. Admission 17SF ($9.35) adults, 11SF ($6.05) students and seniors, 9SF ($4.95) children 6–19; free for children 5 and under. Tues–Sun 10am–5pm. Closed Dec 25. Take motorway N1, exit at Oberwinterthur, and drive a mile toward Winterthur. Or take a train to the Winterthur main station and switch to bus no. 5 marked "Technorama."

WHERE TO DINE

Schloss Wulflingen SWISS   This long-enduring favorite lies 2½ miles west of the center. The rustic stone, stucco, and slate building was built in 1644 and still has many of its original ceramic stoves in the dining rooms. In the summer, the owners adorn the intricate shutters of the step-gabled house with garlands, and cafe tables are set out in front. Specialties include beef in red- and green-pepper sauce with gratin potatoes, sole, catfish, salmon, giant shrimp, and other seafood. A simpler menu is offered at lunch, including veal stuffed with country ham, a mousse of foie gras served with tiny homemade noodles, and fresh fish dishes.

Wulflingerstrasse 240, Winterthur-Wulflingen. ℂ 052/222-18-67. Reservations recommended. Main courses 35SF–63SF ($19.25–$34.65). AE, DC, MC, V. Wed–Sun 10am–midnight. Bus: 2 from Winterthur.

RAPPERSWIL ✪
A lake steamer from Zurich will take you to the "town of roses," on the northern shore of Lake Zurich, 19 miles (31km) away, in about half an hour. To get to Rapperswil from Zurich, you can also take the conventional train, S-5, from the Hauptbahnhof to Rapperswil, a ride of 30 minutes. If you're in Zurich for just a short time and have no other chance to visit the rest of the country, then spend a half-day going to Rapperswil to see an ancient Swiss town. Rapperswil has kept its medieval appearance in its upper town, and is an ideal place for walks and drives around the north shore of Lake Zurich.

The **Tourist Information office** is at Fischmarktplatz (ℂ **055/220-57-57**), open April to October daily 10am to 5pm, November to March Tuesday to Sunday 1 to 5pm.

EXPLORING THE TOWN
The Rathaus (town hall), in the main square, dates from 1471. It has a richly embellished Gothic portal. Many of the town's streets date from the Middle Ages.

Heimatmuseum   Located east of the parish church, this museum is devoted to local history. The museum reflects the history of Rapperswil from the time knights in armor roamed the town to the present. The museum is installed in what was once the residence of a noble family. It contains Roman artifacts, a weapon collection, paintings, and antiques.

Herrenberg, 40. ℂ 055/210-71-64. Admission 3SF ($1.65) adults, 1SF (55¢) children 6–13; free for children under 6. Mid-March to late Oct only. Sat 2–5pm, Sun 10am–noon and 2–5pm; July–Aug also Wed 2–5pm.

Knies Kinderzoo (Children's Zoo) *Kids*   On the north side of the castle hill (see below) is a children's zoo, run by the Knie National Circus; it's on a road that runs along the lake, south of the railroad station. Trained dolphins and other acts perform here. Children can go on pony rides and ride on a miniature railway. Nearby is the Hirschgarten (or deer park), in the Linderhof.

Oberseestrasse. ℂ 055/220-67-60. Admission 8SF ($4.40) adults, 6SF ($3.30) students and seniors, 4SF ($2.20) children 4–16; free for children under 4. Daily 9am–6pm. Closed Nov to mid-Mar.

Rapperswil Castle   Built by the young Count of Rapperswil when he returned from the First Crusade in about 1200, Rapperswil Castle is an imposing medieval stronghold on a rocky hill above the town. In 1875, badly in need of restoration, it became the home of Graf Plater, exiled leader of the resistance against the 19th-century occupation of Poland by the Russian tsars. From Rapperswil, Graf Plater continued to play an active role in Polish politics for another 40 years. Today, the castle contains a museum devoted to mementos of 19th- and 20th-century Polish politics, including portraits of Chopin and Kosciuszko. Occasionally, the castle shows art exhibits on temporary loan from museums in Warsaw or Crakow. Though the castle has no street address, it towers over the town and is impossible to miss.

ℂ 055/210-18-62. Castle and Polish museum 5SF ($2.75); special exhibitions 8SF ($4.40) adults, 4SF ($2.20) students. Free children 15 and under. Apr–Oct daily 1–5pm. Closed Nov–Mar.

WHERE TO DINE

Schloss Restaurant Rapperswil ⚜ CONTINENTAL   Swiss-born entrepreneur Lucia Penner is your hostess at a restaurant that occupies a tiny portion
(only 40 seats) within the brooding medieval mass of the town's 13th-century
feudal castle. Set on a hill above the rest of the Rapperswil, she directs a staff in
preparing an oft-changing cuisine based exclusively on fresh ingredients, many
of them from nearby farms.

Food is slow cooked, and served beneath an elaborate antique wooden ceiling
that scores of workmen labored to complete. There's additional seating during
clement weather within the castle's garden. Menu items include lamb carpaccio
drizzled with herbs and olive oil; filets of tuna in an Asian marinade; hand-rolled
maccheroncini, Mediterranean-style lamb filets; and locally raised veal steaks
served with fresh chanterelles. Available only in late summer and autumn is a
succulent version of venison stuffed with mushrooms and served with
dumplings on a bed of puréed celeriac. The wine cellar contains at least 250
types of wine from around the world.

Lindenhügel. ℂ **055/210-18-28.** Reservations recommended. Main courses 28SF–52SF ($15.40–$28.60);
38SF–58SF ($20.90–$31.90) set lunch; 80SF–125SF ($44–$68.75) set dinner. AE, DC, MC, V. Tues–Sat
11am–2:30pm and 6–10pm. Closed 2 weeks in Jan–Feb.

4

Northeastern Switzerland

The northeastern region of Switzerland—one of the country's most unspoiled areas—contains the cantons of Appenzell, Glarus, St. Gallen, Schaffhausen, and Thurgau, and such wondrous natural sights as St. Gallen's Rhine Valley and the Rhine Falls. St. Gallen is the region's bustling cultural and economic center, and some of the most abundant orchards in the country dot the shores of Lake Constance.

For the athletic, there's plenty of sports and adventure to be found. Skiing, snowboarding, tobogganing, and hiking are easily accessible in the mountain areas. Sailing schools abound in the lakeside communities of Rorschach and Kreuzlingen, and the flat countryside along the lake is perfect for biking.

The northeastern region is also a sensible destination economically, as food and lodging prices are among the lowest in the country.

In seeking a choice for an overnight stopover in the area, our money is on Stein-am-Rhein, one of the most perfectly preserved medieval villages in Europe and also one of the most charming of all Swiss towns. It lies at the point where the Rhein leaves Lake Constance. It also has the most charming Old-World hotels.

However, that doesn't mean that other towns in northeastern Switzerland are without their allure. If you like your cities historic, make it St. Gallen, the largest city in eastern Switzerland. However, if you've come to the area for its folkish charm, head for Appenzell, the country's most traditional town (some Swiss speak of locals here as virtual hillbillies).

If boating and views of Lake Constance are your passion, take a promenade along the seafront, then settle into one of the resorts along Lake Constance—Rorschach has the widest choice of hotels and restaurants.

1 St. Gallen ★★

53 miles (85km) E of Zurich, 97 miles (156km) E of Basel, 9 miles (15km) SW of Rorschach

At 2,200 feet (660m) above sea level, this valley is one of the primary stops in northeastern Switzerland. St. Gallen, which is the highest city of its size in Europe, serves as a good base for exploring Lake Constance (a 15-min. drive away), Mount Säntis, and the Appenzell countryside. This ancient town in the foothills of the Alps was founded by Gallus, an Irish monk who built a hermitage here in 612. By the 13th century his humble cell had developed into an important cultural outpost. St. Gallen became a free imperial city in 1212, and in 1454 it joined the Swiss Confederation. With a population of approximately 75,000, St. Gallen is the capital of a canton of the same name.

St. Gallen is the embroidery and lace capital of Europe, and it was here that three dozen seamstresses worked for a year and a half to make a lace gown for Empress Eugénie, the wife of Napoleon III. Today, most of the embroidery is

Jugglers, dancers and an assortment of acrobats fill the street.

She shoots you a wide-eyed look as a seven-foot cartoon character approaches.

What brought you here was wanting the kids

to see something magical while they still believed in magic.

America Online Keyword: Travel

With 700 airlines, 50,000 hotels and over 5,000 cruise and vaca-

tion getaways, you can now go places you've always dreamed of.

Travelocity.com
A Sabre Company
Go Virtually Anywhere.

WORLD'S LEADING TRAVEL WEB SITE, 5 YEARS IN A ROW" WORLD TRAVEL AWARDS

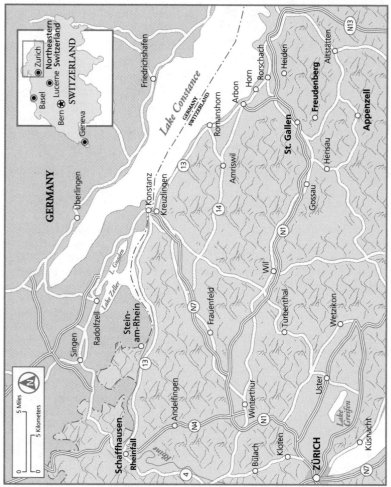

done by computer-driven machines. However, you can still purchase handmade items (see "Shopping," below).

Freudenberg, 2 miles (3km) south of St. Gallen, at an altitude of 3,000 feet (900m), offers a panoramic view of Mount Säntis, St. Gallen, and Lake Constance (known in this part of the country as Bodensee).

ESSENTIALS

GETTING THERE   St. Gallen is on the main train lines connecting Zurich with Munich. At least a dozen trains per day arrive from both directions. Trip time from Zurich is about 75 minutes. St. Gallen is the railway lynchpin for at least four local lines. Call ✆ **0900-300-300** (no area code) for more information.

As in most other Swiss cities, bus connections in St. Gallen are meant to supplement railroad service. Buses connect St. Gallen mainly with such outlying villages as Rorschach and Appenzell, with many stops at local villages along the way. Call the tourist office (see below) for more information.

By car from Zurich, head east on N1 (also called E17).

VISITOR INFORMATION   The **St. Gallen Tourist Office** is located at Bahnhofplatz 1A (© **071/227-37-37**). It's open Monday to Friday 9am to noon and 1 to 6pm, Saturday 9am to noon.

EXPLORING THE TOWN

The **Old City** ✿ is the thing to see here, with its restored, half-timbered houses and their turrets and oriels. Wander the lanes and alleys laid out during the Middle Ages; some of them are closed to traffic.

The Protestant Reformation was victorious in St. Gallen, but the **Benedictine monastery at Klosterhof** remained virtually unaffected. The monastery contains the Catholic bishop's residence, the abbey library, and the canton's government offices. This area is also the site of the Domkirche (see below). The buildings that remain of the abbey date from the 17th and 18th centuries. Its walls were razed, and the best view is from the abbey yard, called the Klosterhof. To reach the abbey from Marktplatz in the center of town, take Marktgasse south, past St. Lawrence's Church, to the large Klosterhof.

St. Gallen offers many sports facilities, including tennis courts and three outdoor swimming pools. The region's best golf course lies 2½ miles from St. Gallen at the **Säntis Park Golfplatz,** Golfpark Waldkirch, St. Gallen (© **071/ 434-6767**). To get here, follow the road signs to Gosau. An 18-hole round of golf costs from 60SF to 70SF ($33–$38.50) per person. Since much of the area is relatively flat, consider renting a bicycle (available at the federal rail station). The tourist office (see "Essentials," above) is helpful in outlining bike routes that aren't too strenuous.

Serious climbers tend to dismiss the region around St. Gallen as being too flat, and they will consequently direct you to loftier altitudes near Appenzell. But if you don't mind a softly undulating landscape that's forested with deciduous trees, and accessible even to those not in the best shape, consider a 5-mile trip that incorporates the best and most panoramic of the local low-lying hills. From the center of St. Gallen, take bus no. 5 to the satellite hamlet of Reithüsli. From there, you'll climb a low hill, **Bernegg,** whose views sweep out over the Bodensee. There's a cozy wood-sheathed restaurant near its summit (the **Falkenburg Restaurant;** © **071/222-55-81**), where air-dried beef and hearty stews and steaks are the norm every day at lunch and dinner. From here, you can walk about a mile to **Drei Weiher,** a trio of small, clear lakes, where you can swim. Afterwards you can walk back to St. Gallen directly, or retrace your steps to the hamlet of Reithüsli. The complete excursion can last between a half-day and about 6 hours, depending on how much you dawdle en route. For more information on this and other treks near St. Gallen or Appenzell, contact the local tourist office.

Domkirche (Cathedral)   The twin-towered Domkirche at Klosterhof is Switzerland's best example of baroque architecture. It was erected in 1756, on the site of the celebrated 14th-century Gothic abbey. Be sure to check out the cathedral chancel, one of its more interesting architectural features.

Klosterhof. © **071/227-34-88.** Free admission. Daily 9am–7pm.

Stiftsbibliothek (Abbey Library) ★★★   This world-famous library contains some 130,000 volumes, including manuscripts dating back to the 8th through the 15th centuries (several of the Renaissance manuscripts have well-preserved illustrations). The library hall is built in a rococo style, with stucco art and ceiling paintings. A plan of the St. Gallen Abbey in the year 830 is displayed, preserved under glass.

Klosterhof 6. (*C* 071/227-34-16. Admission 7SF ($3.85) adults, 5SF ($2.75) students and seniors; free for children 15 and under. Apr–Nov, Mon–Sat 10am–5pm, Sun 10am–noon and 1:30–4pm; Dec–Mar, Mon–Sat 10am–noon and 1:30–4pm, Sun 10am–noon and 1:30–4pm.

SHOPPING

Many shoppers come to St. Gallen seeking embroideries. The best place to look is **Sturzenegger Broderie,** Spisergasse 2 (*C* **071/222-45-76**), established in 1883. Here you'll find a large variety of tablecloths, place mats, doilies, and napkins, both hand- and machine-made. Sturzenegger also sells blouses, handkerchiefs, shawls, scarves, and children's frocks, as well as a large assortment of nightgowns, pajamas, and women's lingerie.

You can find real bargains when the local textile factories have clearance sales, usually in January and July. The tourist office (see "Essentials," above) will advise.

Another good source for textiles and embroidery is **Saphir,** Bleichestrasse 9 (*C* **071/223-62-63**), which sells high-quality goods, including the finest table linens and hand-embroidered handkerchiefs. They also sell bolts of St. Gallen lace and tasteful fabrics by the yard.

If you'd like to see how the famous embroideries—both hand- and machine-made—of St. Gallen are produced, call **Försterhoner Embroiderie,** Flurhofstrasse 150 (*C* **071/243-15-15**), which is 10 minutes by car from the center of town in the direction of Bodensee. You need an appointment, but they'll show you the factory and explain the process to you.

Finally, **Graphica Antiqua,** Marktgasse 26 (*C* **071/223-50-16**), is a real shopping find, selling an array of antique prints of Swiss landscapes, including the Alps and "Heidi meadows." Prints are available from all parts of Switzerland, and each region is clearly identified in the shop.

WHERE TO STAY
EXPENSIVE

Einstein Hotel ★★   The most desirable hotel in town, the Einstein is near the center of the historic district. Built some 150 years ago, originally as a Swiss embroidery factory, it was renovated in 1983 into a stylish provincial hotel. It has a gray-and-white neoclassical facade and a marble lobby, and you're likely to hear live piano music playing in the pub/cocktail bar. The mid-sized guest rooms are conservatively furnished and well maintained, each fitted with neatly kept bathrooms.

Berneggstrasse 2, CH-9001 St. Gallen. (*C* **071/227-55-55**. Fax 071/227-55-77. www.einstein.ch. 65 units. 330SF–360SF ($181.50–$198) double; 550SF ($302.50) suite. AE, DC, MC, V. Parking 20SF ($11) in the garage, free outside. Bus: 1, 3, or 11. **Amenities:** Restaurant; bar; room service; laundry/dry cleaning. *In room:* TV, minibar, hair dryer.

Hotel Walhalla ★   This modernized Best Western is a first-class hotel in the shopping district. It faces the main railroad station and parking garage, and is about a 3-minute walk from the Old Town. Many visitors use the Walhalla as a base for excursions to Appenzellerland and the Lake Constance area. The rooms are nicely furnished and include well-scrubbed bathrooms. The hotel has a lovely Mediterranean-style restaurant, which also serves typical Swiss cuisine.

Bahnhofplatz, CH-9001 St. Gallen. (*C* **800/528-1234** in the U.S. and Canada, or 071/222-29-22. Fax 071/222-29-66. www.hotelwalhalla.ch. 57 units. 260SF ($143) double; 370SF ($203.50) suite for 2. Rates include buffet breakfast. AE, DC, MC, V. Parking 20SF ($11) in the garage (only 2 spaces), 12SF ($6.60) outside. Bus: 1. **Amenities:** Restaurant; bar; room service; laundry/dry cleaning; nonsmoking floors. *In room:* TV, minibar, hair dryer.

MODERATE

Hotel Ekkehard   Located in the center of town, this typical government-rated three-star Swiss hotel is neat and well maintained, with small but pleasant rooms. All are equipped with tidily kept bathrooms. The hotel offers a wood-trimmed restaurant with modern decor serving Austrian food at reasonable prices (closed from July 13 to August 9), as well as a more upscale option.

Rorschacher Strasse 50, CH-9000 St. Gallen. ✆ **071/222-47-14.** Fax 071/222-47-74. 29 units. 226SF ($124.30) double. Rates include buffet breakfast. AE, DC, MC, V. Bus: 1 or 7. **Amenities:** 2 restaurants; room service; laundry. *In room:* TV, minibar, hair dryer, safe.

Hotel Gallo   This hotel lies along a busy traffic artery, about a 10-minute walk from the town center. Some of the details of its Art Nouveau facade are still visible. The recently renovated rooms have tall windows and contain private bathrooms.

St. Jacobstrasse 62, CH-9000 St. Gallen. ✆ **071/242-71-71.** Fax 071/242-71-61. www.hotelgallo.ch. 24 units. 210SF ($115.50) double; 250SF ($137.50) triple. Rates include buffet breakfast. AE, DC, MC, V. Parking 12SF ($6.60). Bus: 3. **Amenities:** Lounge; laundry/dry cleaning. *In room:* A/C, TV, minibar, hair dryer, trouser press.

INEXPENSIVE

Hotel Dom   This simple but adequate hotel is one floor above street level, near the cathedral in the center of town. Originally built in 1966, it has been renovated slowly and gradually many times since. Silvia Lendi and her very helpful staff offer small, basic units with comfortable furniture, some with private bathrooms. No meals other than breakfast are served, but many restaurants and taverns can be found nearby.

Webergasse 22, CH-9000 St. Gallen. ✆ 071/223-20-44. Fax 071/223-38-21. www.hoteldom.ch. 40 units (32 with bathroom). 110SF ($60.50) double without bathroom, 190SF ($104.50) double with bathroom. Rates include continental breakfast. AE, DC, MC, V. Parking 10SF ($5.50). Bus: 1. **Amenities:** Lounge; room service. *In room:* TV.

WHERE TO DINE

In the restaurants recommended below, as well as in the area's tearooms and inns, make an effort to try the famous local sausage, bratwurst, and to sample St. Gallen's rich regional pastries.

Am Gallusplatz 🌟🌟 FRENCH/SWISS   Am Gallusplatz is the most famous restaurant in the old town, and has a dining room that dates from 1606. Finding it is part of the pleasure of dining here. It's opposite the cathedral, behind a low wall and a pink facade. The five- or seven-course "menu surprise" dinner includes wine and champagne, and the regular menu changes frequently and is always based on fresh ingredients. If available, we recommend bouillabaisse "chef," pot-au-feu of fish, garnished goose liver with fresh herbs, grilled sole and salmon Florentine style, and lamb medallions Provençal. The savory dishes are prepared with flair, with perfectly balanced flavors and textures. The wine list, one of the most extensive in Switzerland, includes 450 choices, the oldest dating back to 1893. The restaurant also offers a nice selection of armagnacs and brandies.

Gallusstrasse 24. ✆ **071/223-33-30.** Reservations recommended. Main courses 28SF–65SF ($15.40–$35.75); fixed-price lunch 58SF ($31.90); 5-course menu surprise 155SF ($85.25), 7-course menu surprise 277SF ($152.35). AE, DC, MC, V. Tues–Fri and Sun 11:30am–2:30pm and 6pm–midnight, Sat 6pm–midnight. Closed last week of July to the first 2 weeks of Aug. Bus: 1.

Hotel Einstein Restaurant FRENCH/SWISS   One of the finest restaurants in the city is located on the fifth floor of the Hotel Einstein, with the best panoramic view in town. The decor blends rustic timber with marble trim.

Specialties include calves' liver with garden herbs, grilled veal schnitzels, cream of spinach soup with salmon strips, and filet of sole with artichokes and sherry-flavored butter. The food is rather hearty but often prepared with a sense of delicacy too.

Berneggstrasse 2. ✆ 071/227-55-55. Reservations recommended. Main courses 35SF–60SF ($19.25–$33); fixed-price lunch 40SF ($22), fixed-price dinner 89SF ($48.95). AE, DC, MC, V. Daily noon–2pm and 6–10pm. Bus: 1, 3, or 11.

Restaurant Neubad ✶✶✶ SWISS/FRENCH/ITALIAN   Set in a 300-year-old house in the historic center of St. Gallen, this restaurant contains a street-level bistro and a more formal (and expensive) restaurant upstairs, which is one of the finest in northeastern Switzerland. The setting's antique charm is most visible in the two dining rooms upstairs. Here, a *cuisine du marché*, featuring menu items that change with the seasons, might include roast haunch of venison with fresh spätzle, several preparations of fresh fish, filet of veal with alpine herbs and vegetable risotto, and roast lamb with rosemary sauce and garlic. Wild-game dishes are featured in autumn, and the salads are usually very, very fresh. The dishes prepared here seem more engaging year after year, and you can always count on first-rate cuisine.

Bankgasse 6. ✆ 071/222-86-83. Reservations recommended for the restaurant, not required for the bistro. Restaurant, main courses 36SF–55SF ($19.80–$30.25); fixed-price 3-course lunch 54SF ($29.70); fixed-price 4-course menu dégustation 89SF ($48.95); fixed-price 5-course surprise menu 99SF ($54.45). Bistro, main courses 18SF–48SF ($9.90–$26.40). AE, DC, MC, V. Mon–Fri 10am–2pm and 6–10:30pm. Closed 2 weeks in July.

ST. GALLEN AFTER DARK

Many locals head for the town's main hotel, **Einstein** (see "Where to Stay," above) which has the best pub/cocktail bar in town. If you're lucky, you'll catch a set of live piano music in this dark, leathery enclave.

Another good spot on the after-dark circuit, for those who like a bustling, noisy Teutonic atmosphere, is the **Weinstube zum Bäumli,** Schmiedgasse 18 (✆ **071/222-11-74**), which has been in business for 5 centuries. It has the town's best wine collection, and you can order inexpensive food here, mainly regional fare such as bratwurst. Tables are shared and it has a very cozy atmosphere. The location is convenient to the Old Town. It's closed Sunday and Monday.

You can also check the program at the local tourist office to see what might be presented at the **Stadttheater,** Museumstrasse 24 (✆ **071/242-06-06**), which presents at least 200 concerts and dramatic performances during its annual season from September to June. Ticket prices depend on the presentation.

Local bands often appear at the **Trischli,** Brühlgasse 18 (✆ **071/226-09-00**), which also sponsors the occasional karaoke or theme night. The club is open in July and August daily from 10pm to 5:30am, and from September to June daily from 9pm (closing hours vary). There's a cover charge of 7SF ($3.85) on Friday and Saturday. A DJ spins different kinds of music every night at the **Ozon,** Goliathgasse 28 (✆ **071/224-81-24**), with its flashing lights and steep beer prices. The club is open Sunday and Wednesday to Thursday from 10pm to 2am and Friday and Saturday from 10pm to 3am. Cover is from 15SF to 25SF ($8.25–$13.75).

2 Appenzell ✶

11.3 miles (18km) S of St. Gallen, 12 miles (20km) SW of Altstätten

In the rolling, verdant foothills of the Alpstein, south of Lake Constance, the Appenzell district retains some of Switzerland's strongest folklore. However, in recent years, in an attempt to attract the tourist purse, it has become somewhat self-conscious and commercial about its traditions. Its hamlets contain intricately painted houses whose colorful decorations are distinctive to the region. The inhabitants, proud of their cultural distinctions, sometimes wear folk costumes, which include an elaborate coif with large wings made of a fabric called tulle. Local men are known for their rakish earrings and their habit of going barefoot in the summer.

Appenzell is famous for three reasons: for its baked goods such as pear bread and chocolates, for the artists who adhere to a certain school of naive art (which some observers compare to paintings by the late American primitivist Grandma Moses), and for its status as the yodeling headquarters of Switzerland. For centuries the district was relatively isolated from the rest of Switzerland, but modern roads and trusty cable cars now ferry sightseers across the otherwise inaccessible terrain.

Appenzell is an excellent base for exploring two nearby peaks, the **Ebenalp** and **Mount Säntis.**

Appenzell's main square, **Landsgemeindeplatz,** and its main street, **Hauptgasse,** are lined with traditional painted houses. Here, shops sometimes sell the famous embroidery of the area—but examine items carefully before you buy, as some embroideries are made in China or Portugal.

ESSENTIALS

GETTING THERE   From Zurich, you can take a slow local train without transferring; you'll reach Appenzell in about 2 hours. A faster way is to take an express train from Zurich to Gossau, a satellite village of St. Gallen, and transfer to the local train. Trip time from St. Gallen or Gossau to Appenzell on one of the 30 or so daily locals is about 45 minutes. Call ℭ **0900-300-300** for information.

The town's only bus line goes between Appenzell and St. Gallen, via a meandering path through local villages not serviced by the rail lines. From St. Gallen, you'll have to transfer buses in a village called Teufen. For more **information** call ℭ **071/227-37-37.**

By car from St. Gallen, drive south from the city toward Teufen, where the road is signposted south to Appenzell.

VISITOR INFORMATION   The **Appenzell Tourist Office** is at Hauptgasse 4 (ℭ **071/788-96-41**), and is open Monday to Friday 9am to noon and 2 to 6pm, Saturday and Sunday 10am to noon and 2 to 5pm.

SHOPPING

The main street is filled with shops hawking souvenirs and gifts, some of dubious origin. However, for the best and most authentic handicrafts, head for **Trachtenstube,** Hauptgasse 23 (ℭ **071/787-16-06**). On the second floor of this outlet you'll find a wide array of traditional Appenzeller clothing, along with farmers' floral work shirts and hand-embroidered handkerchiefs. A wide selection of lace, embroidery, and crafts are sold here as well. Proof of the pudding? Even the locals come here to shop for costumes during festivals.

Another outlet on the main street, **Margreiter,** Hauptgasse 29 (ℭ **071/ 787-33-13**), offers machine-made work produced in neighboring factories that's often quite stunning. Embroideries decorated with edelweiss or other alpine flora seem to be the fastest-moving items.

WHERE TO STAY

Hotel Appenzell ✿ Located on the town's main square, this modern hotel built in 1983 is painted with whimsical folk colors on its gabled facade with shuttered windows. The comfortable rooms include conservative, modern walnut furniture, and the bathrooms are lined with marble. The hotel's street-level cafe, with an outdoor terrace, is a comfortable stop for daily meals. Through the cafe is an elaborately paneled dining room, which is suitable for a more intimate experience.

Landsgemeindeplatz, CH-9050 Appenzell. ✆ **071/788-15-15.** Fax 071/788-15-51. www.hotel-appenzell.ch. 16 units. 194SF–205SF ($106.70–$112.75) double. Rates include buffet breakfast. AE, DC, MC, V. Free parking. Closed 3 weeks in Nov. **Amenities:** 2 restaurants; bar; lounge; room service; babysitting; laundry/dry cleaning. *In room:* TV, minibar, hair dryer.

Hotel Hecht This 300-year-old hotel, in the center of town opposite the Catholic church, is the biggest alpine inn in Appenzell. The Knechtle family has owned the place for more than 50 years, keeping it clean, attractive, and conservative. The overall effect is cheerful and comfortable. Bedrooms are small but tastefully furnished with private bathrooms, most of which contain shower-tub combinations.

Hauptgasse 9, CH-9050 Appenzell. ✆ **071/787-10-25.** Fax 071/787-47-83. www.hechtappenzell.com. 42 units, 32 with bathroom. 180SF–198SF ($99–$108.90) double. Rates include buffet breakfast. AE, DC, MC, V. **Amenities:** Restaurant; room service; laundry/dry cleaning. *In room:* TV, hair dryer.

Romantik Hotel Säntis ✿✿ Appenzell's best hotel in the town center is decorated with dozens of stenciled, symmetrical designs. Its traditional rooms are cozy, and many are filled with regional antiques. Try for a room in the old wing, dating from 1835, if you like painted beams and provincial wooden furnishings. Some accommodations have four-poster or canopy beds. There's a small Appenzell-style dining room with a wood ceiling and colorful tablecloths (see "Where to Dine," below). The Heeb family offers a cordial welcome.

Landsgemeindeplatz 3, CH-9050 Appenzell. ✆ **071/788-11-11.** Fax 071/788-11-10. www.romantikhotels. com/appenzell. 37 units. 220SF–260SF ($121–$143) double; 300SF ($165) suite. Rates include buffet breakfast. Parking 5SF ($2.75). AE, DC, MC, V. **Amenities:** Restaurant; room service; laundry/dry cleaning. *In room:* TV, hair dryer.

WHERE TO DINE

Hotel Hecht Restaurant ✿ SWISS Located in the oldest part of town, this restaurant (ca. 1650) is famous for its excellent cuisine and wine cellar. Cherry paneling and paintings by local artists add a homey touch to the rustic dining room. Specialties include trout (served au bleu or meunière), rice Casimir, veal with mushrooms in a cream sauce, and filet Gulyas Stroganoff. Filet of pike, battered and sautéed in oil, is the preferred dish, although the cheese fondue is also very good.

In the Hotel Hecht, Hauptgasse 9. ✆ **071/787-10-25.** Reservations recommended. Main courses 18SF–45SF ($9.90–$24.75). AE, DC, MC, V. Daily noon–2pm and 6:30–11pm.

Restaurant Säntis ✿✿ SWISS Located on the first floor of the popular Romantik Hotel Säntis, this restaurant offers a view over the elaborately detailed houses of the main square. The menu changes frequently. Typical appetizers include a nourishing bouillon or alpine dried beef garnished with pickles and onions. Main courses might include loin of lamb Provençal or roast filet of pork. Some of the meat and fish dishes are accompanied by homemade noodles, served with al dente carrots and spinach.

> ### ⸝Tips⸍ A Must-Have Picnic Item
>
> If you're planning a picnic in the mountains, stock up on some of the local Appenzeller cheese at **Sutter**, Industriestrasse 2 (✆ **071/787-12-27**). This cheese tastes like nothing else found in Europe.

In the Romantik Hotel Säntis, Landgemeindeplatz 3. ✆ 071/788-11-11. Reservations recommended. Main courses 34SF–53SF ($18.70–$29.15); fixed-price meal 22SF–28SF ($12.10–$15.40) for lunch, 59SF ($32.45) for dinner. AE, DC, MC, V. Daily 11am–2pm and 6:30–11pm. Closed Jan 15 to Feb.

EASY EXCURSIONS

Either of the following excursions would be ideal for a picnic, with some of the most dramatic mountains in eastern Switzerland as your backdrop. Before heading here, pick up supplies in Appenzell and the day is yours. We hope it's a sunny one.

EBENALP ⸝⸍⸝⸍ Visit Ebenalp, 4 miles (6km) away, for a spectacular view of the hills and pastures of the Appenzell district. The jagged promontory is at an elevation of 5,400 feet (1,620m). Wear sturdy walking shoes so that you can walk down to **Wildkirchli**—a chapel in a grotto, inhabited by hermits from the mid-17th to the mid-19th century. Paleolithic artifacts discovered here at the turn of the century indicate that it is the oldest prehistoric settlement found in Switzerland so far.

To get there, drive to the end of the Weissbad-Wasserauen road, then take a cable car for an 11-minute ride to the summit. The cable car leaves every 45 minutes in season; a round-trip costs 22SF ($12.10). For information, call ✆ **071/799-12-12**.

MOUNT SÄNTIS ⸝⸍⸝⸍⸝⸍ The major attraction in the area is Mount Säntis, the highest peak (8,209 ft./2,463m) in the Alpstein massif. It offers a panoramic view of eastern Switzerland, including the Grisons, the Bernese Alps, the Vorarlberg mountains, Lake Constance, and even Lake Zurich. On a clear day you can see as far as Swabia in southern Germany.

To reach the departure point for the cable car (whose German name is Säntis Schwebebahn), drive 9 miles (14km) west of Appenzell, following the signs pointing to Urnesch and Schwagalp. Year-round, the cable car departs at 30-minute intervals; round-trip passage costs 33SF ($18.15). For more information, call ✆ **071/365-65-65**.

Instead of driving all the way, you can take one of the most dramatic walks in the area from the village of Wasserrauen to the village of Schwägalp, at which point you can take a cable car to the belvedere overlooking Säntis. Hourly trains from Appenzell will take you to Wasserrauen. The walk between Wasserrauen and Schwägalp is 5½ miles, taking anywhere from 4½ to 5½ hours, depending on your stamina. As you hike along, you'll see some of the most scenic panoramas in this part of Switzerland.

3 Lake Constance ⸝⸍⸝⸍⸝⸍

Lake Constance is divided into three parts, although the name is frequently applied to Bodensee, the largest part. At the western end of Bodensee, the lake splits into two branches: a long fjord called Überlingersee and an irregular marshland known as Untersee. Untersee is connected to the rest of the lake by a narrow channel of water, which is actually the young Rhine River. The blue felchen, a pike-like fish found only in Lake Constance, furnishes the district with a tasty and renowned specialty.

The 162-mile-long (261km) shoreline of the lake is shared by three countries—Switzerland, Germany, and Austria. The surrounding hills are covered with vineyards and orchards and are dotted with many farming villages. Vacationers are drawn here by the sunny, mild climate and nice beaches.

The Swiss gateway to Lake Constance is **Rorschach,** 7 miles (11km) northeast of St. Gallen. You can get here by train from Zurich in 1½ hours (the train departs every hour) or from St. Gallen in 20 minutes. From Rorschach, you can continue on—by frequent local trains or buses along the lake—to the three major centers: **Arbon, Horn,** and **Romanshorn.** A well-organized network of modern passenger ferries links all these towns along the shore and connects Switzerland with Germany and Austria.

The **Rorschach Tourist Office,** Hauptstrasse 63 (✆ **071/841-70-34**), provides an up-to-date timetable for all forms of transportation. They are open Monday to Friday 9:30am to 5:30pm. You can also contact one of the most popular boat lines, **Schiffahrtsbetrieb Rorschach** (✆ **071/846-60-60**), the best and most economical way to cruise from one town along the lake to another, thereby transforming a commuter trip into a cruise. This is easiest to do from May to September.

Your choice of towns along Lake Constance will depend almost entirely on your selection of a hotel. The towns and attractions are so similar that it is hard to tell where one town ends and another begins. All of them offer lakeside promenades and flower gardens overlooking the lake, and all of them can become centers for pleasure boating and trips on the lake. The towns are also so close together that even if you're in Romanshorn in the west, you can arrive at Rorschach in the east in minutes. Because it has a greater choice of hotels, we'd give the nod to Rorschach.

Once at Lake Constance, you'll find dozens of bike trails, each marked with a red sign, and each running around the southern tier (the Swiss side) of the lake.

RORSCHACH

This medieval harbor town is located at the foot of the Rorschacher Berg, at the southern tip of the lake. It offers lakeside gardens, an extensive promenade, a good choice of hotels, and facilities for sailing, rowing, swimming, fishing, and windsurfing. Passenger ships pass through Rorschach en route to Germany, Austria, and Liechtenstein.

Rorschach's illustrious past is reflected in its buildings, which include the **Kornhaus,** a granary built in 1746; the former **Mariaberg cloister;** and **18th-century painted houses** with oriel windows along Hauptgasse. If you'd like to bike along the lake, you can go to the railway station and rent a bike for the day for 26SF ($14.30).

WHERE TO STAY & DINE

Hotel Mozart   Opened in 1986, this comfortable hotel with its own garage is situated between the main street of town and the lake. The polished-granite building has well-maintained, mid-sized rooms, eight overlooking the lake.

The old-world ambience of the hotel's Café Mozart complements its variety of famous pastries. Another specialty is tea—19 varieties, including essence of kiwi, linden blossom, and tea leaves grown on the foothills of Mount Everest. The cafe also offers simple meals.

Hafenzentrum, CH-9400 Rorschach. © 071/841-06-32. Fax 071/841-99-38. www.mozart-rorschach.ch. 33 units. 155SF–178SF ($85.25–$97.90) double; 195SF ($107.25) suite. Rates include buffet breakfast. AE, DC, MC, V. Free parking. **Amenities:** Restaurant; lounge. *In room:* TV, minibar.

Parkhotel Waldau 🐾🐾   This country manor was built after World War II as a private school for boys, then transformed into a government-rated five-star hotel, the best in town. The hotel sits on a hill overlooking the lake 4 miles (6km) southwest of the center. As a first-class hotel, Parkhotel Waldau, as opposed to its more modest and smaller competitor, the Mozart, has far larger and better furnished rooms and more spacious and well-equipped bathrooms. In addition, it has all the amenities of a deluxe hotel (including two swimming pools as well as tennis courts and a health club), with which no other hotel in town can compete. And if that wasn't enough, Parkhotel Waldau also has the finest and most varied cuisine in town.

Seebleichestrasse 42, CH-9400 Rorschach. © 071/855-01-80. Fax 071/855-10-02. 42 units. 199SF ($109.45) double, 260SF ($143) junior suite. Rates include buffet breakfast. AE, DC, MC, V. Free parking. **Amenities:** 2 restaurants; 2 pools; tennis courts; health club; sauna; room service; babysitting; laundry/dry cleaning. *In room:* TV, minibar, hair dryer, safe.

HORN

This old fishing hamlet is a 5-minute drive east of Arbon. Set in the canton of Thurgau, it provides another base for exploring the shores of Lake Constance. The large port of Rorschach is only a 10-minute car or bus ride to the east. Frankly, the main reason to visit is to stay or dine at the Hotel Bad Horn; otherwise, you'll find more facilities at Rorschach.

WHERE TO STAY & DINE

Hotel Bad Horn 🐾 *Finds*   This large blue-and-white hotel is located in the town center at the end of a small peninsula on the lakefront. Built in 1827, it is fully restored with big windows, gables, a tile roof, rooftop terraces, and an expanse of lawn extending almost to the lake. The mid-sized bedrooms are well furnished and comfortably appointed, each with a neatly kept bathroom.

The hotel has two restaurants. We recommend the Captain's Grill, with its nautical decor. Specialties include aiguillettes of pink duck, quenelles of local fish, scampi with calvados, and filet of beef with armagnac. Less formal is the Glottasteube, with a rustic alpine decor.

Seestrasse 36, CH-9326 Horn. © 071/841-55-11. Fax 071/841-60-89. 54 units. 240SF ($132) double; 320SF ($176) suite. Rates include buffet breakfast. AE, DC, MC, V. Free parking. **Amenities:** 2 restaurants; room service; laundry/dry cleaning. *In room:* TV, minibar, hair dryer, safe.

ARBON 🐾

One of the best spots along the lake is Arbon, the lakefront promenade that offers a view of Constance, the German shore, and the Alps. It has far more facilities than Horn (see above), although the views and ambience are pretty similar. If lakeside walks appeal to you, this might be the place, as most of the town lies on a promontory jutting out into Lake Constance. In summer you're surrounded by orchards and lake meadows, so strolling is what to do here. Facilities include a large boat harbor, swimming pools, and a school for sailing and surfing. The town was built on the site of an ancient Celtic community and was called Arbor Felix by the Romans.

After leaving Rorschach, continue northwest along Route 13 for 15 minutes until you reach Arbon. The town is also a major stopover for all the trains and buses running along the southern tier of Lake Constance.

The town's most visible monument is its 13th- or 14th-century castle, **Schloss Arbon,** Hauptstrasse (© **071/446-60-10**), which broods over the town from its hilltop. Most of its interior is devoted to a technical school for adults, but you can visit the small-scale museum during its limited open hours. Exhibits include ancient Roman artifacts unearthed in the region, and displays relating to the once-potent, now defunct industries that used to call Arbon home. Premier among these is the Saurer Truck Company, which employed up to 3,000 local workers between its 1906 founding and its merger with Mercedes-Benz in 1982. Frankly, unless you're terribly interested in the history of the local region, you can skip this museum entirely. Between May and September, the museum is open daily from 2 to 5pm; the rest of the year it's open only on Sunday, from 2 to 5pm. It's completely closed from December 1 to the end of February. Admission costs 2SF ($1.35) for adults and 1SF (65¢) for children 14 and under.

For tourist information, go to **Verfkehrsverein,** Bahnhofstrasse 40 (© **071/ 447-85-15**), open Monday to Friday 8am to noon and 2 to 5:30pm, Saturday 9am to noon.

WHERE TO STAY & DINE

Hotel Metropole ⚸   This concrete Best Western hotel, across from the train station, is part of a lakeside complex that exemplifies creative urban planning. It's Arbon's best choice for overnighting. The complex includes a department store, a grocery store, and a busy cafeteria. The hotel lobby is Nordic modern, and the rooms are comfortable but plain, each with a loggia facing the lake and well-maintained bathrooms. The best place to dine is the second-floor restaurant, serving Swiss cuisine and specializing in fish caught in the lake.

Bahnhofstrasse 49, CH-9320 Arbon. © 071/447-82-82. Fax 071/447-82-80. www.metropole-arbon.ch. 42 units. 230SF–245SF ($126.50–$134.75) double; 260SF–290SF ($143–$159.50) suite for 1–3. Rates include buffet breakfast. AE, DC, MC, V. Free parking. **Amenities:** 2 restaurants; bar; pool; health club; Jacuzzi; sauna; room service; laundry/dry cleaning; . *In room:* TV, minibar, hair dryer, safe.

Hotel Rotes Kreuz   This is a stucco house with a lake terrace built in 1760. The handful of rooms it contains are simple, small, and well scrubbed. All contain a private bathroom. You can dine in a glass-enclosed solarium or a cozy pine-paneled room. Specialties include a variety of lake fish.

Hafenstrasse 3, CH-9320 Arbon. © 071/446-19-14. Fax 071/446-24-85. 28 units. 145SF ($79.75) double. Rates include continental breakfast. MC, V. Free parking. **Amenities:** Restaurant; lounge. *In room:* TV.

ROMANSHORN

This industrial town is the largest port on the lake and the base for Swiss steamers. In spite of the industrial overlay, Romanshorn is also a successful summer lakeside resort. Popular with Swiss, German, and Austrian tourists, it's set against a backdrop of panoramic views of the Austrian and Swiss mountains nearby. The resort offers a swimming pool, a sailing school, a waterskiing school, and tennis courts. There's also a park as well as a zoo.

A year-round ferry service links Romanshorn with Friedrichshafen, Germany. Boats operated by the **Schweizerische Bodensee Schiffahrtsgesellschaft** (© **071/446-78-88** in Romanshorn) make hourly transits to Friedrichshafen, beginning at 8:30am daily between May and October, and ending between 6:30 and 7:30pm, depending on the day of the week. One-way transit, which requires about an hour, costs 11SF ($6.05). The attractions on the German side of the lake are actually far more interesting than anything on the Swiss border, and there's no hassle or fees to cross, so we recommend you take the chance to visit **Friedrichshafen.** Here you can stroll its lakefront promenade, with a sweeping view of the Swiss Alps. Biking along the broad Seestrasse is also a delight. A kiosk within the Stadtbahnhof or local rail station rents bikes. You can also visit the **Zeppelin Museum** in the Hafenbahhof on Seestrasse 22, with its fascinating re-creation of the historic Hindenburg, which exploded in a fire in New Jersey in 1937, possibly because of sabotage.

In summer, boat trips are organized to Mainau, a German island about 4 miles (6km) north of Constance that was once the home of the grand duke of Baden. Boats operated by the **Schweizerische Bodensee Schiffahrtsgesellschaft** (© **071/446-78-88** in Romanshorn) make two daily transits every day from May to October, from Romanshorn to Mainau. Transit takes 90 minutes each way and costs 27SF ($14.85) round-trip. You'll have to pay an entrance free of 14SF ($7.70) to gain access to the island. **Mainau Island,** 4 miles (6km) north of the German city of Konstanz (Constance), is well worth your time. Because of the mild climate, the island is almost tropical, filled with palms and orange trees, along with fragrant flowers in bloom year-round—even though the island lies practically in the shadow of the snow-covered Alps. In the center of the island is a botanical garden, set on the site of an ancient castle, once a residence of the Knights of the Teutonic order.

In Romanshorn, two other worthy options involve hopping aboard any boat operated by Schweizerische Bodensee Schiffahrtsgesellschaft (see above). If you go on the one bound for Rorschach (three departures per day), you'll pay about 11SF ($6.05) one-way. Then you can explore the town of Rorschach before returning to Romanshorn by any of the many trains (a 20-minute ride).

A second option involves sailing from Romanshorn to **Kreuzlingen** or the German town of **Konstanz,** a 1-hour ride (between two and three departures per day), and taking the train back (a 20-min. ride). One-way boat transit to either Kreuzlingen or Konstanz costs 12SF ($6.60).

For tourist information in Romanshorn, contact **Verkehrsbüro,** Bahnhofplatz (© **071/463-32-32**), open Monday to Friday 8am to noon and 2 to 6pm, Saturday 9am to noon. If you'd like to bike along the lake, you can go to the railway station where a kiosk rents bikes from 27SF to 35SF ($14.85–$19.25) per day.

WHERE TO STAY & DINE

Park-Hotel Inseli ✦   This model hotel, the best in town, is secluded in a grove of trees a 10-minute walk from the center, directly on the lake. Its comfortable and spacious bedrooms offer views of the park or the lake; the public rooms are decorated with chrome and plush carpeting. Manager Anton Stager and his family keep up the hotel's informal ambience.

There's a sunny, indoor-outdoor cafe and a more formal rotisserie where French cuisine is served daily. There's a pretense to grandeur, and those in the know order the local fish caught from Lake Constance. The cafe offers a panoramic view all the way to Austria.

Inselistrasse 6, CH-8590 Romanshorn. © **071/463-53-53.** Fax 071/463-14-55. www.inseli.ch. 39 units. 250SF–275SF ($137.50–$151.25) double. Rates include buffet breakfast. AE, DC, MC, V. Free parking. **Amenities:** 2 restaurants; bar; lounge; room service; laundry/dry cleaning. *In room:* TV, minibar, hair dryer, safe.

4 Stein-am-Rhein ✦/✦

12 miles (20km) E of Schaffhausen, 17 (27km) miles N of Winterthur

Dating from 1094, Stein-am-Rhein is pure Old Town, one of the most authentic and best-preserved medieval towns in Switzerland. It's on the right bank of the Rhine, west of Untersee, an arm of Lake Constance. The town is blessed with the finest half-timbered houses in northeastern Switzerland, and the foundations of some of them dip into the river itself. Flower-decked fountains and oriel-windowed houses are grace notes. The facades, which are often fully painted, invite the photographer in all of us. Nearby was the first Roman bridge ever built over the Rhine.

ESSENTIALS

GETTING THERE   Stein-am-Rhein lies midway along the railway link connecting Schaffhausen with Kreuzlingen, on the edge of Lake Constance. From Zurich, passengers take an express train to Schaffhausen, then change for a less frequent local train to Stein-am-Rhein; trip time from Zurich is just under 2 hours. There are also good train connections to Stuttgart, Germany. For rail schedules or more information, call © **0900/300-300.**

The only bus connection to Stein-am-Rhein crosses the border into a German village named Singen, from which there are rail connections to Stuttgart, Germany. Call © **0900-300-300** for information.

By car the trip from Zurich takes less than an hour. Head north on N1 until a point near Winterthur, where you connect with E41 going north to Schaffhausen. This route becomes N4, connecting with Route 13, heading east toward Stein-am-Rhein.

VISITOR INFORMATION   The Stein-am-Rhein **Tourist Office,** at Oberstadt 10 (© **052/741-28-35**), maintains up-to-date bus and rail schedules. It's open Monday to Friday 9 to 11am and 2 to 5:30pm.

SEEING THE SIGHTS

A number of quaint houses line **Rathausplatz** (Town Hall Square) and **Hauptstrasse** (Main Street). Many have oriel windows, rich frescoes, timberwork, and fountains.

Historische Sammlung (Historical Museum) is in one of the rooms of the town hall, on Rathausplatz (© **052/741-21-42**). The collection includes weapons, banners, and stained glass. Admission is 3SF ($1.65). The exhibit keeps no set hours; you have to call and arrange for an appointment to view it.

A Benedictine abbey was built near Rathausplatz during the 11th century; it was abandoned during the Protestant Reformation in 1524. Today it's the **Kloster-museum St. Georgen** (St. George's Abbey Museum) (© **051/741-21-42**), devoted to local history and art. The rooms, because of their rich ceilings, paneling, and 16th-century murals by Thomas Schmid and Ambrosius Holbein, are often more interesting than the exhibits. Admission to the museum is 3SF ($1.65) for adults, 1.50SF (85¢) for children. The museum is open Tuesday to Sunday from 10am to noon and 1 to 5pm, only from March to October. The restored Convent Church of St. George, a Romanesque basilica built by the Catholics and later transformed into a Protestant church, has sections dating from the 12th century.

Wohnmuseum Lindwurm, Understadt 33 (© **052/741-25-12**), lies in an old, 19th-century *bürgerhaus.* With exhibits and artifacts, it re-creates life here in that century. You learn how the townspeople and their servants lived, and something about their farming methods. It's open March to October, Wednesday to Monday from 10am to 5pm, charging 5SF ($2.75) for adults and 3SF ($1.65) for children.

If riding a bike appeals to you, consider renting one from the kiosk (© **052/741-21-34**) within the railway station, and then heading off for a 12½-mile (each way) westbound excursion to Schaffhausen, or an 18-mile (each way) eastbound excursion to Kreuzlingen. The cost is about 27SF ($14.85) per day. The edges of both the Rhine and the Bodensee are flanked with "velo-routes" (bicycle paths) that are clearly marked with red-and-white signs that display a bicycle.

Ecologically and panoramically, the area where the Rhine widens into a lake is particularly interesting for sightseeing and cruising. If you're in Stein-am-Rhein, you'll find yourself midway along the route of a series of cruises that depart from Schaffhausen, to the west, and meander their way into the Untersee, the lake just to the west of the Bodensee. The terminus of the cruise is in the Swiss town of Kreuzlingen, just across the water from the German city of Konstanz. If you opt for a full round-trip excursion from Schaffhausen to Kreuzlingen, a travel time of 4 hours each way, you'll spend a full day in some of the most appealing waterways of central Europe. The cost is 29SF ($15.95) round-trip. There are between three and four departures per day from both Schaffhausen and Kreuzlingen, but only between April and early October. For reservations and more information, contact **Schiffahrt Untersee und Rhein,** Freierplatz 7, 8202 Schaffhausen (© **052/634-08-88**).

SHOPPING

Most of the town's shopping options line either side of the **Understadt,** a thoroughfare that some old-time residents still refer to as Hauptstrasse. Set near the town's railway station and Rathaus, its most appealing shop is **Heimatwerk,** Understadt 28 (© **052/741-33-92**). Devoted to the merchandizing of artifacts made exclusively in Switzerland, it inventories glass, ceramics, wood carvings, textiles, Swiss army knives and watches, and lots of small and usually inexpensive art objects guaranteed to collect dust after you display them in your home.

WHERE TO STAY

Hotel Chlosterhof ✸✸✸ The finest hotel in town, situated on the Rhine east of Rathausplatz, was created from an abandoned shoe factory and now has a brick facade with angled glass. Its interior includes an open fireplace and a lobby with a cruciform vault. The rooms, which come in various shapes and sizes, are stylized; 10 have four-poster beds and most of the suites open onto the Rhine. All units contain neatly kept bathrooms. The restaurant, Le Bâteau, offers fine dining amid a nautical decor, and Le Jardin is a little in-house bistro.

Oehningerstrasse 201, CH-8260 Stein-am-Rhein. © 052/742-42-42. Fax 052/741-13-37. chlosterhof@ bluewin.ch. 69 units. 265SF–310SF ($145.75–170.50) double; 370SF–600SF ($203.50–$330) suite. Rates include buffet breakfast. AE, DC, MC, V. Free parking. **Amenities:** 2 restaurants; bar; pool; health club; sauna; room service; laundry/dry cleaning. *In room:* TV, minibar, hair dryer, safe.

Hotel-Restaurant Adler ✸ *Finds* This tasteful, comfortable hotel has one of the most flamboyant facades in the old city: It's painted with characters from Rhenish legends, depicting such medieval scenes as a tree of life, martyrs at the stake, and characters groveling before Asian potentates. The hotel has two sections: One dates from 1461, and the other, less interesting guest house annex was built in 1957. The rooms, streamlined with a Nordic design and equipped with firm beds, often attract traveling families.

Rathausplatz, CH-8260 Stein-am-Rhein. © 052/742-61-61. Fax 052/741-44-40. 25 units. 170SF ($93.50) double. Rates include continental breakfast. AE, DC, MC, V. **Amenities:** Restaurant; lounge; laundry. *In room:* TV.

Hotel Rheinfels ✸ This is a large and commodious building built in 1448 near the entrance to Stein-am-Rhein beside the Rhine. It's well known for its pleasantly decorated bedrooms and for its popular restaurant with family-style tables. Bedrooms range from small to mid-sized, and each is traditionally furnished with comfortable beds. Upstairs from the restaurant is an antique room with wide, creaking floorboards, massive chandeliers, old portraits, and a collection of medieval armor.

Rhygasse 8, CH-8260 Stein-am-Rhein. © 052/741-21-44. Fax 052/741-25-22. 16 units. 180SF ($99) double. Rates include continental breakfast. AE, MC, V. **Amenities:** Restaurant; lounge; room service; laundry. *In room:* TV, hair dryer.

WHERE TO DINE

Hotel Rheinfels Restaurant SWISS   This regional restaurant offers a view of the head of the Rhine, where it exits from Lake Constance. Typical dishes include filet of fera (a lake fish) with lemon and capers, fricassée of Rhenish fish with baby vegetables, hot Bauernschinken (farmer's ham), and grilled veal steak. A potpourri of desserts is offered. The cuisine is based on very fresh and quality ingredients that are deftly handled by the kitchen staff.

Rathausplatz. © 052/741-21-44. Reservations recommended. Main courses 35SF–52SF ($19.25–$28.60). AE, MC, V. Thurs–Tues 11am–2pm and 6–9:30pm.

Restaurant Sonne ★★★ SWISS/FRENCH   Located near the well-preserved marketplace, the Sonne, set in a 15th-century building, is the most famous—and best—restaurant in town. Chef/owner Philippe Combe prepares cuisine moderne for guests in the intimate dining room decorated with damask and Biedermeier. Typical dishes include delectable fresh river crabs in a vinaigrette sauce, a savory wild game in a beaujolais sauce served with wild mushrooms sautéed in butter, and a tender roast hare with mustard sauce. The menu might also include ravioli stuffed with lobster or a superb sea bass with fresh asparagus. Good wines complement the fine food, and smooth desserts, such as chocolate mousse, provide the perfect finish.

Rathausplatz 127. © 052/741-21-28. Reservations required. Main courses 32SF–53SF ($17.60–$29.15); fixed-price menu 55SF–105SF ($30.25–$57.75). AE, MC, V. Thurs–Mon 11:30am–2pm and 6–9:30pm.

STEIN-AM-RHEIN AFTER DARK

Most city residents head home after work in a city that's not noted for its raucous nightlife. But the bar that attracts more business than any other, **Le Papillon,** is in the Hotel Chlosterhof (see above), Oehningerstrasse (© 052/742-42-42). It opens every night at 6pm and offers lots of varnished paneling, a woodsy kind of coziness, and views of the river. They will happily stay open until the last customer leaves.

5 Schaffhausen ★ & the Rheinfall ★★

32 miles (51km) N of Zurich, 17 miles (27km) N of Winterthur

Once a major depot for river barges, Schaffhausen is built on terraces along the steeply inclined right bank of the Rhine. Although many sections of the city are modern and heavily industrialized, Schaffhausen retains its medieval spirit, exemplified by its romantic fountains and old, brown-roofed houses, dotted with oriel windows and decorated with statues in niches. It's a center for visiting the Rhine Falls (Rheinfall), one of the most popular sights in northeastern Switzerland.

Once ruled by the Hapsburgs, Schaffhausen became an imperial free city and later the capital of a Swiss canton of the same name. Germany borders the canton on three sides, heavily influencing the Teutonic flavor of much of the city's architecture.

ESSENTIALS

GETTING THERE   Schaffhausen is on all major north-south train lines between Stuttgart and Milan. There are at least 14 express trains from Zurich every day (trip time is 40 min.). Call ☎ **0900-300-300** for more information.

If you're driving from Zurich, head north on Route 4 all the way, taking about 1 hour.

VISITOR INFORMATION   The Schaffhausen **Tourist Information Office** is at Fronwagturm (☎ **052/625-51-41**), open in summer Monday to Friday 10am to 6pm, Saturday 10am to 4pm, Sunday 10am to 1pm; winter Monday to Friday 10am to 5pm, Saturday 10am to 2pm.

SEEING THE SIGHTS

Spend a morning touring the **Old Town** ✿ on foot. There's a good view of the town from the battlements of the **Munot,** which dates from 1564. The round fortress has a tower, platform, and parapet walks. It can be reached by stairs and has a covered footbridge across the moat. The Munot is the only fortress to be based on a book by Albrecht Dürer, published in Nürnberg in 1527. It's open May to September daily from 9am to 8pm; October to April daily from 10am to 5pm. Admission is free.

The crowning glory of the old town is the **Münster** (All Saints' Church), on Münsterplatz. Now Protestant, it was formerly a Benedictine monastery, consecrated in 1052. Its Romanesque architecture is stern and plain. In a nearby courtyard is the 15th-century bell that inspired Schiller's poem "Song of the Bell" and the opening of Longfellow's "Golden Legend."

The most characteristic street is **Vordergasse** ✿, where visitors usually stop to photograph the frescoed Haus zum Ritter, dating from 1485. On Fronwegplatz, you'll find two outstanding fountains from the 1520s.

Museum zu Allerheiligen (All Saints' Museum) ✿, Baumgartenstrasse (☎ **052/625-43-77**), is one of the most important national museums in Switzerland. The former abbey has exhibits ranging from prehistoric times to the present, including traditional garb of the province, old weapons, and period furnishings. Visit the "Treasury" in the former abbots' salon. The museum is open year-round, Tuesday to Sunday from 10am to noon and 2 to 5pm (10am–5pm Sat and Sun Mar–Oct). Admission is free.

A SPECTACULAR WATERFALL

The Rheinfall (or Rhine Falls) is the most celebrated waterfall in central Europe. It's also the most powerful—700 cubic meters of water per second rush over a width of 150 yards (137m). The water falls 70 feet (21m), a sight that inspired Goethe to liken it to the "source of the ocean." This natural wonder is most spectacular in early summer, when it's fed by mountain snows.

From the bus station at Schaffhausen, take bus no. 1. There are frequent departures for the 10-minute ride. A train runs every 30 minutes during the day from the station at Schaffhausen to Rheinfall.

To get to the Rheinfall from Zurich, take a train from the Hauptbahnhof to Neuhausen and get off at the Rheinfall stop. The trip takes less than an hour. It's a 15-minute walk from the train depot at Neuhausen to the waterfall. To further enhance the experience, you can take a 6.20SF ($3.40) boat trip to the rock in the center of the Rheinfall from April to October.

In addition, the falls can be viewed from the belvedere of **Laufen Castle** on the left bank. The castle has been converted into a restaurant with a staircase that leads to the view. Bring a raincoat.

You can also take a ferry across the river to Neuhausen and the little castle of **Schlöseli-Wörth** (✆ 052/672-24-21), built in the 12th century as a customs post. Today it's a restaurant, open daily from March through November.

SHOPPING

Consistent with its role as a hardworking, industry-conscious border town, Schaffhausen doesn't place too much emphasis on folklore, so the handful of kitschy souvenirs you're likely to find will probably be sold from small shops around the railway station, or from nondescript outlets beside either of the town's main shopping streets, **Vordergasse** and **Fronwegplatz.** More appealing are two shops that specialize in equipment designed for climbing, skiing, and virtually every other sport you can think of. These are **Benz,** Fronwegplatz (✆ 052/624-56-93), and **Elite Sport,** Vorstadt 3 (✆ 052/625-18-43). In addition to everything from tennis racquets to snowshoes, each of these sells clothing suitable for any weather Switzerland can dish out.

WHERE TO STAY

Hotel Park Villa ✦   This chiseled gray hotel is located near the train station in a municipal park with massive trees. Originally built as an opulent private home around 1900, it was converted into a hotel in the 1960s. It's designed very much like a castle, with towers and steep roofs. The interior is as graceful as the exterior is rough, containing crystal chandeliers and several public rooms with fresh flowers, comfortable chairs, and oil paintings. A few bedrooms are decorated regally with antiques; others are in an uninspired modern style. All units are well maintained.

Parkstrasse 18, CH-8200 Schaffhausen. ✆ 052/625-27-37. Fax 052/624-12-53. www.parkvilla.ch. 20 units. 175SF–229SF ($96.25–$125.95) double; 309SF ($169.95) suite. Rates include breakfast. AE, DC, MC, V. Free parking. **Amenities:** Restaurant; lounge; tennis court; room service; laundry/dry cleaning. *In room:* TV, minibar, hair dryer.

Rheinhotel Fischerzunft ✦✦✦   Located on Freier Platz next to a promenade along the Rhine, this is an inviting inn that was formerly occupied by the fishermen's guild. The Jaeger family converted it to a hotel in 1898. The main public room has Chinese decor. Since there are so few bedrooms, and this place is so well known, reservations are especially important in summer. The chateau-style, contemporary bedrooms at first appear out of place in such a medieval city, but they're soothingly comfortable. The six with views of the Rhine carry higher price tags.

The excellent restaurant mixes classic European and Asian influences, featuring curried chicken consommé with Chinese ravioli, filet of venison with five Chinese spices and sautéed mustard cabbage, ravioli of crayfish, and an assortment of dim sum. Aside from the spaghetti, the kitchen chefs make all the pastas themselves. The dishes are rich in taste, texture, and presentation. The desserts include a medley of passion fruit and papaya.

Rheinquai 8, CH-8202 Schaffhausen. ✆ 052/632-05-05. Fax 052/632-05-13. www.relaischateauz.ch. 10 units. 270SF–310SF ($148.50–$170.50) double; 415SF ($228.25) junior suite. Rates include buffet breakfast. AE, DC, MC, V. **Amenities:** Restaurant; lounge; room service; laundry/dry cleaning. *In room:* TV, minibar, hair dryer, safe.

WHERE TO DINE

Consider an elegant dinner at the Rheinhotel Fischerzunft (see above), which is one of the top three restaurants in Switzerland.

Restaurant Gerberstube ITALIAN   The Guidi family runs the finest Italian restaurant in Schaffhausen. The dining room is in a 17th-century guildhall, which contains a changing exhibit of modern paintings. You might begin with stracciatella, the famous egg-and-consommé soup of Rome, and follow it with spaghetti, cannelloni, or a veal schnitzel pizzaiola. They also serve many classic dishes, including chateaubriand with béarnaise sauce and various preparations of veal and pasta. The cooking, although not exactly innovative or exciting, is always reliable and satisfying and is prepared with quality ingredients.

Bachstrasse 8. ℂ **052/625-21-55.** Reservations required. Main courses 40SF–50SF ($22–$27.50); 3-course lunch 62SF ($34.10); 5-course dinner 92SF ($50.60). AE, DC, MC, V. Tues–Sat 11am–3pm and 6pm–10:30pm.

SCHAFFHAUSEN AFTER DARK

Many night owls gravitate toward Schaffhausen's **Saffrangasse,** a narrow historic street with the most crowded and popular bars in town. Two of them stand out. The **Bar Orient,** Saffrangasse 13 (ℂ **052/633-02-02**), a loud, sometimes raucous hangout for folks under 35, offers high-energy, foaming mugs of beer and occasional bouts of live music. Its most visible competitor is the smaller, somewhat calmer **Cuba Club,** Saffrangasse 2 (ℂ **052/625-34-98**), which is also favored by clients under 40. Catering to an older and somewhat more sedate crowd is the **Piano Bar Eckhaus,** Stadthausgasse 1 (ℂ **052/624-55-55**), where stiff drinks, a cozy setting, and live piano music help keep the conversation rolling. Most spots are open 7 days a week.

Basel & the Jura

Northwestern Switzerland, with its valleys, waterfalls, and old-world villages, is one of the most beautiful regions in the country. Most of the region has a medieval feel, reflected mainly in the ancient architecture.

The area lies at the juncture of Germany and France and encompasses the Jura mountain range, Basel, and the surrounding towns. During this part of your journey you'll be zigzagging between two cultures, and the names of the towns—for example, Morat in French and Murten in German—will often confuse you. Most citizens of Basel, for instance, speak German, although many, living so close to France, also speak French and often English as well. To confuse the cultural brew, every weekday some 30,000 commuters from both France and Germany cross into Basel to work, returning to their native countries in the evening.

Some of the towns may sound familiar to you: Gruyères is well known for its cheese. Other places, such as the walled university town of Fribourg and historic Neuchâtel, are also well worth a visit. You'll probably be based in Basel (or Basle), which straddles the Rhine, between Alsace in France and the Jura in Switzerland.

The canton of Jura was established in 1979 as the 23rd member of the Swiss Confederation. A total of 82 communes make up the canton, with Delemont as its capital. Nearly 88% of the population is Roman Catholic, and French is the predominant language.

Situated between the Rhine and the Rhône, the geological folds and faults of the Jura mountain range form the border between Switzerland and France and extend from Geneva, in the southwest, to Schaffhausen, along the northern border. Vastly different in height and character from the Alps, few peaks in the Jura exceed 5,500 feet (1,650m).

The center of the Swiss watchmaking industry is here. Thriving winter-sports resorts can also be found throughout the mountains, although most of them draw a local rather than an international clientele.

1 Basel ✶✶✶

53 miles (85km) NW of Zurich, 61 miles (98km) N of Bern

The third-largest city in Switzerland, Basel stands on the Rhine at the point where the French, German, and Swiss borders meet. At the entrance to the Swiss Rhineland, Basel is the capital of the half-canton of Basel-Stadt. On its borders are the French Vosges, the German Black Forest, and the Swiss Jura Mountains. Grossbasel, or Greater Basel, lies on the steep left bank, and Kleinbasel, or Lesser Basel, is on the right bank. The old imperial city stood at Grossbasel.

The two parts of the city are linked by half a dozen bridges, plus four ferries powered by river currents. The first bridge, erected in 1225, was for centuries the only one spanning the Rhine; it has since been replaced by the Mittlere Rheinbrücke (Middle Rhine Bridge).

The town was a Roman fort in A.D. 374, named Basilia, and was later ruled by prince-bishops for about 1,000 years. The Great Council met in Basel between 1431 and 1448, during which time a pope was crowned here. After Basel joined the Swiss Confederation in 1501, it became a Protestant region. During the onset of the Reformation in 1529, it served as a refuge for victims of religious persecution. They flooded in from Holland, Italy, and France, bringing renewed vitality to Basel and laying the foundation for the city's great golden age in the 18th century.

As one of Switzerland's most important cultural centers, Basel saw the development of the printing press and the book trade. In 1516 Erasmus, the great Dutch humanist and writer, published here the first edition of the New Testament in the original Greek. He is buried in the cathedral. Other notable Basel residents were the painter Holbein the Younger, who made portraits of Erasmus; the German philosopher Friedrich Nietzsche, who taught at the University of Basel; Theodor Herzl, who addressed the first Zionist World Congress here in 1897; and Jacob Burckhardt, a native, who achieved fame with his history of the Italian Renaissance.

Today the cultural traditions of Basel live on in its many museums (27 in all), art galleries, and schools. The city has become known as an international marketplace for art and antiquities. In 1967 its citizens voted by referendum to purchase two well-known works by Picasso, *The Seated Harlequin* and *The Two Brothers*. Picasso was so moved that he donated four other paintings to Basel.

Basel, which is also a banking and industrial center, is headquarters of the Bank for International Settlement. In addition, Basel's chemical and pharmaceutical industry is one of the most important in the world.

Except at carnival, the citizens of Basel are self-restrained and industrious. The German dramatist Rolf Hochhuth has observed: "English understatement looks like megalomania when compared to the people of Basel."

ESSENTIALS

GETTING THERE   Although no flights from North America land directly in Basel, you can arrange for a seat on one of Swissair's frequent commuter flights to Basel from Zurich. Flight time is only about 30 minutes, but most visitors find it more convenient to take the train. For more information, call **Swissair** (© **800/221-4750;** www.swissair.com).

Located on the major rail lines between Paris and Zurich, Basel is the most important railroad junction in the Juras. Trip time from Paris is between 4½ and 5 hours, depending on the train; from Zurich, an express train can take as little as an hour. Call © **0900/300-300** (no area code) for **rail information.**

Basel is a junction point for highways from all over Europe. From Bern, head north on N1, continuing north on N2 at the junction. From Zurich, drive west on the same N1, turning north onto N2 at the junction.

ARRIVING   If you're flying to Basel, your plane will land at the **EuroAirport Basel-Mulhouse-Freiburg** (Basel-Mulhouse airport), which is actually across the French border 5 miles (9km) northwest of Basel. For information, call © **061/325-25-11.** A road links the Swiss sector of the airport with Switzerland. A city bus runs between the airport and Basel's main railway station, departing every 30 minutes daily between 5:10am and 11:30pm; the 15-minute trip costs 2.80SF ($1.55) one-way.

Basel has three railroad stations—Swiss, French, and German—making it one of the largest rail junctions in Europe. The SNCF station is on Centralbahnplatz,

> ### (*Tips*) The Mobility Ticket
>
> Any tourist staying in Basel at paid accommodations is entitled to a **"mobility ticket,"** which allows free use of Basel's public transport for the duration of your stay. The reception desk at your hotel should provide you with your ticket upon check-in.

as is the SBB station. The DB station is across the Rhine and down Richenstrasse.

VISITOR INFORMATION   The **Basel Tourist Office,** Schifflände 5 (© 061/ 268-68-68), is open year-round Monday to Friday from 8:30am to 6pm and Saturday from 10am to 4pm; closed Sunday.

GETTING AROUND   Basel has a good, relatively cheap public transportation system. Bus or tram tickets must be purchased at a station in advance. Clear maps will help you find your way. For 7.50SF ($4.15) you can buy a ticket allowing you unlimited travel in two geographical zones for a 24-hour period. A single, once-only tram ride costs 2.80SF ($1.55) within one zone.

Basel is best covered on foot, as most of its attractions radiate from the historic heart of this ancient city on the Rhine. When you need to go farther afield, you can take public transportation such as a tram. Taxis tend to be expensive.

Another way of getting around is to rent a bike at the kiosk next to the information booth at the rail station in the center of town. The cost is 29SF ($15.95) per day, and an ID deposit is required. Bikes are rented daily from 7am to midnight.

SPECIAL EVENTS   Dating from the Middle Ages, **Fasnacht** is the most exciting time to be in Basel. All the city seems caught up in the revelry beginning the Monday after Ash Wednesday (usually in late Feb or early Mar). Motorized and horse-drawn parades highlight the activities, along with music from dozens of bands—fifes, trumpets, trombones, and drums.

The **Basel Art Fair** in mid-June (© 061/686-20-20 for more information) grows larger every year, with 260 dealers displaying the work of some 1,000 artists. The fair also generally hosts more than two dozen solo shows. Basel's most traditional festival is **Vogel Gryff Volksfest,** when a griffin, a lion, and a "wild man of the woods" float down the Rhine on a raft. This event occurs either on January 13, 20, or 27 (it changes every year). The event is followed by street dancing. The Wilder Mann, the lion, and the griffin are traditional symbols for the three main neighborhoods of Basel.

SEEING THE SIGHTS

As a city Basel is visited primarily for its urban attractions such as museums and shopping. However, if you'd like to escape the congestion and get out and see some countryside, you're at the right place. On the outskirts of the city are 744 miles (1,198km) of **Wanderweg,** which are marked trails crisscrossing the scenic highlights of the area. To get you going on your journey, catch bus 70 to Reigoldswil. Here you can board the Gondelbahn cable to take you to the mountain peak of Wasserfallen at 3,073 feet (922m). Once here, you can set off on hikes in many directions. Call © 061/941-18-81 for information about the best hikes in the Reigoldswil and Wasserfallen region.

THE TOP ATTRACTIONS

Basler Zoologischer Garten ✦✦✦   Established in 1874, the Zoologischer Garten is one of the greatest zoos in the world, famous for breeding endangered species in captivity. Covering 26 acres in an urban setting within a 7-minute walk of the railway station, it has some 4,500 animals of 600 different species. Trained elephants and sea lions perform tricks. The Vivarium is filled with everything from penguins to reptiles.

Binningerstrasse 40. ✆ **061/295-35-35.** Admission 14SF ($7.70) adults, 5SF ($2.75) children, 30SF ($16.50) family ticket. May–Aug daily 8am–6:30pm; Mar–Apr and Sept–Oct daily 8am–6pm; Nov–Feb daily 8am–5:30pm. Tram: 1, 2, 6, 8, 10, or 17.

Historisches Museum Barfüsserplatz ✦   This former 14th-century Franciscan church on "Barefoot Square" (named for the unshod friars) contains many relics of medieval Basel, including rare 15th-century tapestries and specimens of ecclesiastical art. One of the best-known sculptures is in the late Gothic style, depicting a babbling king. Its greatest exhibit is a reliquary bust of St. Ursula, in silver and gold, commissioned by the people of Basel to contain the saint's relics.

Barfüsserplatz. ✆ **061/205-86-00.** Admission 5SF ($2.75) adults, 3SF ($1.65) students; free for children 15 and under. Wed–Mon 10am–5pm. Tram: 1–15.

Museum Jean Tinguely ✦ *Finds*   The museum is dedicated to the work of Jean Tinguely, one of Switzerland's greatest sculptors, who died in 1991. The 70 mechanical sculptures in the collection span 4 decades of artistic evolution beginning with reliefs and printing machines from the 1950s and progressing to later pieces like the Mengele-Totentanz cycle and huge, clanking metaharmonies. Further insight into the artist's life and times can be found in the many drawings and writings that document his projects around Europe and the United States.

The museum is a wonderfully surprising delight. All four levels are alive with ponderous movement, musical with the clean notes of working machinery. "Works of art usually make their statements silently," said Mario Botta, the Swiss architect who designed the museum specifically to house the collection. "These works are the exception, for they communicate through sound engendered by their movements." Many of the exhibits in the museum were donated by Tinguely's wife and fellow artist, Niki de Saint Phalle.

Botta's dramatic architectural vision has made the museum building an attraction in its own right, a modern landmark in Solitude Park on the right bank of the river Rhine. The red sandstone building is topped by the "barca," a bold steel construction.

Grenzacherstrasse 210. ✆ **061/681-93-20.** Admission 8SF ($4.40), 5SF ($2.75) seniors and students; free for children 16 and under. Wed–Sun 11am–7pm. Tram: 2 or 15.

Kunsthalle   Located a 5-minute walk from the Kunstmuseum (see below), this gallery offers experimental works by contemporary artists. Banners displayed throughout the town announce current exhibitions. It has shown a changing program of exhibitions since 1872, featuring many of the leading artists of classical modern and abstract expressionism before they became household names. Since the early 1980s it has been among the leading spaces in Switzerland to exhibit the most recent trends in modern art.

Steinenberg 7. ✆ **061/206-99-00.** Admission 9SF ($4.95) adults, 6SF ($3.30) seniors and children. Tues and Thurs–Sun 11am–5pm, Wed 11am–8:30pm. Tram: 1, 2, 6, 8 or 14. Go left from the Kunstmuseum on St. Alban-Graben, cross Bankenplatz, and follow Theaterstrasse.

Basel Attractions

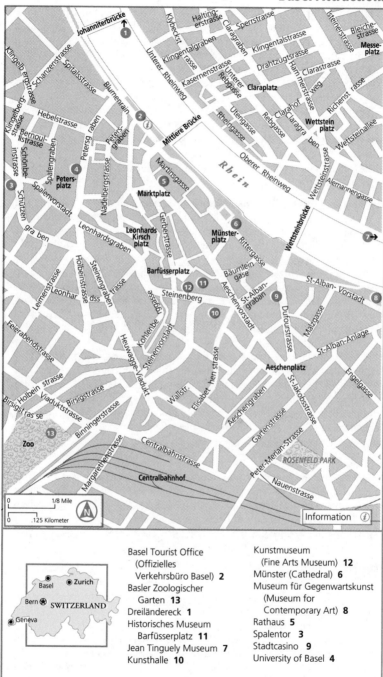

Basel Tourist Office
(Offizielles
Verkehrsbüro Basel) **2**
Basler Zoologischer
Garten **13**
Dreiländereck **1**
Historisches Museum
Barfüsserplatz **11**
Jean Tinguely Museum **7**
Kunsthalle **10**

Kunstmuseum
(Fine Arts Museum) **12**
Münster (Cathedral) **6**
Museum für Gegenwartskunst
(Museum for
Contemporary Art) **8**
Rathaus **5**
Spalentor **3**
Stadtcasino **9**
University of Basel **4**

Kunstmuseum (Fine Arts Museum) ★★★   This is the oldest museum in Switzerland, offering one of Europe's most remarkable collections—everything from the old masters to 20th-century paintings. You approach the massive building through a courtyard graced with sculptures by Rodin, Calder, and others. The collections represent the development of art of the Upper Rhine Valley from the 14th to the 17th century, as well as works by outstanding modern artists.

In addition to paintings by Holbein the Younger (who lived in Basel between 1515 and 1538) and Konrad Witz, the Kunstmuseum contains a collection of impressionist and modern art, including works by van Gogh, Picasso, Braque, Gauguin, Klee, Chagall, and Giacometti.

St. Alban–Graben 16. ℂ 061/206-62-62. Admission 10SF ($5.50) adults, 8SF ($4.40) seniors and children. Tues–Sun 10am–5pm. Tram: 2 or 15.

Münster (Cathedral)   This red sandstone building towering over the old town was consecrated way back in 1019. Destroyed by an earthquake in 1356, it was rebuilt along Romanesque and Gothic lines with a green-and-yellow tile roof. The cathedral has functioned as an Evangelical Reformed church since 1529.

The facade is richly decorated, depicting everything from prophets to virgins. The pulpit, which dates from 1486, was carved from a single block of stone. One of its many treasures, at the end of the south aisle, is an 11th-century bas-relief. There's a monumental slab on one of the pillars honoring Erasmus of Rotterdam, who died in Basel in 1536. The church also contains the tomb of Anna von Hohenberg, wife of Rudolf of Hapsburg.

The double cloister can be entered from Rittergasse; it was erected in the 15th century on the foundations of a much earlier Roman structure. Visitors will find an excellent view from the twin Gothic towers of the cathedral. There are also two famous views of the cathedral—from the right bank of the Rhine and from the back of the Pfalz (palace). This 65-foot (20m) terrace also provides a splendid panorama of the Rhine and Germany's Black Forest.

Münsterplatz. ℂ 061/271-21-82. Admission cathedral, free; towers, 3SF ($1.65). Easter to Oct 15 Mon–Fri 10am–5pm, Sat 10am–4pm, Sun 1–5pm; Oct 16 to Easter Mon–Sat 11am–4pm, Sun 2–4pm.

Museum für Gegenwartskunst (Museum for Contemporary Art) ★   This is one of Europe's leading museums, highlighting artists from the 1960s to the present, with works by Bruce Nauman, Richard Long, Jonathan Borofsky, Joseph Beuys, Frank Stella, and Donald Judd.

Alban-Rheinweg 60. ℂ 061/272-81-83. Admission 10SF ($5.50) adults, 8SF ($4.40) students and seniors; free for children 15 and under. Tues–Sun 11am–5pm. Tram: 2.

MORE ATTRACTIONS

Rathaus (town hall) on Marktplatz dominates the market square of Basel. It was built in 1504 in the lat7 Burgundian style, but additions have been made since. The sandstone building is decorated with shields of the ancient city guildhall and adorned with frescoes.

You may also want to visit the **University of Basel,** on the south side of Peter-splatz. Founded in 1460, it's one of the oldest academic institutions in Switzerland (the school's charter was signed by Pope Pius II). Its library contains a million volumes, including works by Martin Luther, Erasmus, and Zwingli, and a collection of rare manuscripts.

Spalentor (Spalen Gate), west of the university, marks the end of the medieval sector. It's one of the most beautiful gates in the country. Built in the

1400s, it was heavily restored in the 19th century, and has a pointed roof and two towers with battlements.

Finally, **Dreiländereck** (Three Countries' Corner), which juts out into the Rhine, is one of Basel's more unusual sites. If you walk around a pylon marking the spot, in just a few steps you can cross from Switzerland into Germany and then into France—and you don't even need a passport.

ORGANIZED TOURS

Basel is a popular embarkation point for cruises on the Rhine. In summer (between May and October), **Basler Personenschiffahrt,** Blumenrain 2 (© 061/ 639-95-00), conducts cruises to Rheinfelden. Ships leave May to mid-October, Monday to Saturday at 1:45pm and on Sunday at 9:15am. A one-way ticket costs 26SF ($14.30), or 47SF ($25.85) round-trip; children travel for half price. Evening cruises are often conducted, costing 48SF to 72SF ($26.40–$39.60), depending on the cruise. The theme of the night cruise changes daily—a fondue cruise, a captain's dinner, a Gypsy evening. Check with the tourist office or with Basler Personenschiffahrt for last-minute changes in these schedules.

SHOPPING

Cosmopolitan, sophisticated, and prosperous, Basel shelters a medley of shops whose merchandise rivals that found in much larger cities. The finest antiques shop in the region is **Antiquités M. & G. Ségal,** Aeschengraben 14 (© 061/ 272-39-08). Founded in 1862, it's run by the articulate and knowledgeable fourth-generation owner, Georges Ségal, and his North Carolina-born wife, Margaret. Their specialties include 18th-century continental paintings, silver, furniture, ceramics (including antique Meissen porcelain), and art objects, all of which are displayed over four floors of a building bulging with treasures. You'll also find two impressive art galleries in town. The immensely prestigious **Ernest Beyeler Gallery,** Baunleingasse 9 (© 061/272-54-12), is a cultural focal point that's famous throughout Europe for its roster of impressionist, modern, and contemporary paintings. Also, a more avant-garde gallery with more emphasis on minimalist, hyper-contemporary art, is the well-respected **Galerie Gisele Linder,** Elisabethenstrasse 54 (© 061/272-83-77).

Upscale housewares, with an emphasis on grandeur and social correctness, are displayed at a store beloved by brides-to-be, **Füglistaller,** Freie Strasse 23 (© 061/ 261-78-78). Here, in a setting that includes a monumental staircase worthy of Scarlett O'Hara, look for quality porcelain, crystal, silverware, and gift items.

Seeking a suitcase to pack the loot you've already acquired in Basel? Head for **Leder-Droeser,** Eisengasse 11 (© 061/261-42-53), where wallets, valises, purses, handbags, shaving kits, even gym bags, offer leather making at its best. Shoes and clothing for both men and women can be found at **Bally Capitol zum Pflug,** Freie Strasse 38 (© 061/261-18-97), a three-level emporium that works hard at supplying what upscale consumers really want. Men's goods are showcased one floor above street level; women's shoes and clothing lie on street level and in the cellar. And if you have a yen for fine tobaccos, check out **David-off,** Aeschenvorstadt 4 (© 061/272-47-50), where brier-wood and meer-schaum pipes, along with cigarettes and cigars from around the world (including Cuba), are sold along with their appropriate accessories. And finally, dozens of emporiums in Basel are ready, willing, and able to sell you a wristwatch. One of the city's most upscale shops is **Gübelin,** Freie Strasse 27 (© 061/261-40-33). More closely geared to the mass market and less expensive is **Kurz,** Freie Strasse 39 (© 061/261-26-20).

Impressions

*Once people have been to Basel, they keep coming back. The only diffi-
culty we have is in getting them to come for the first time.*
—Urs Hitz, 1992

The best place to shop for handicrafts and gifts is **Heimatwerk,** Schneider-
gasse 2 (© **061/261-91-78**), which carries an array of tasteful merchandise from
all parts of the country. You'll find everything here from ceramics to wooden
toys. Household linens, made at the textile capital of St. Gallen, are sold at
Sturzenegger, Freie Strasse 62 (© **061/261-68-67**).

If you're just seeking general merchandise, head for the leading department
store in Basel, **Globus,** Marktplatz 2 (© **061/268-45-45**).

WHERE TO STAY

Keep in mind that it's almost impossible to get hotel reservations during the
Swiss Industries Fair, which attracts about a million visitors every spring. Rooms
are also impossible to find at carnival time, when hotels often raise their prices
by as much as 40%. Check with the Basel Tourist Office for exact dates.

VERY EXPENSIVE

Hilton Basel International ✸✸ Visitors can expect the customary Hilton
service in this black steel-and-glass hotel built in 1975. In the center of town, it's
connected via an underground shopping arcade to the main railway station.
Bedrooms are generally roomy and comfortable, with built-in furnishings,
blackout draperies, abstract paintings, and easy chairs, plus plenty of work space.
Bathrooms are large and well equipped. Some of the units are smoke-free, others wheelchair accessible. There are even some rooms for tall people. The
Wettstein Restaurant is one of the city's best restaurants.

Aeschengraben 31, CH-4002 Basel. © 00-800/2400-2400 in the U.S. and Canada, or 061/271-66-00. Fax
061/275-66-50. 214 units. www.hilton.com. 295SF–530SF ($162.25–$291.50) double; from 750SF ($412.50)
suite. AE, DC, MC, V. Parking 24SF ($13.20). Tram: 1, 2, or 8. **Amenities:** 2 restaurants, bar; pool; health club;
sauna; room service; massage; babysitting; laundry/dry cleaning. *In room:* A/C, TV, minibar, hair dryer, safe.

Hotel Drei Könige (Hôtel des Trois Rois) ✸✸✸ Established in 1026, this
is the oldest government-rated five-star hotel in Europe, although most of the
building you see today was constructed in the 18th century. Originally named
Zur Blume ("At the Flower"), the white building, situated on the Rhine, houses
a guest book, now a museum piece, containing the names of Voltaire, Napoleon,
Princess (later Queen) Victoria, and Kaiser Wilhelm II. History records that
soon after the establishment of the inn, three kings (Conrad II, emperor of the
Holy Roman Empire; his son, Henry III; and Rudolf III, the last king of Burgundy) drew up a treaty here that divided western Switzerland and southern
France.

A tapestry resembling a Gobelin tapestry hangs in the wood-paneled lobby;
the bar area is accented with pin lights and brass detail. Some of the traditional
guest rooms have their original ornamentation on the ceilings. Even the stables
and old servants' quarters have been converted into comfortable rooms. Most
units are spacious, and all are up to date with soft robes and well-kept bathrooms. Try, if possible, for a room opening onto the river.

Blumenrain 8, CH-4001 Basel. © 061/261-50-50. Fax 061/260-50-60. www.drei-koenige-basel.ch. 88 units.
520SF–695SF ($286–$382.25) double; from 1,200SF ($660) suite. AE, DC, MC, V. Parking 30SF ($16.50). Tram:

Where to Stay in Basel

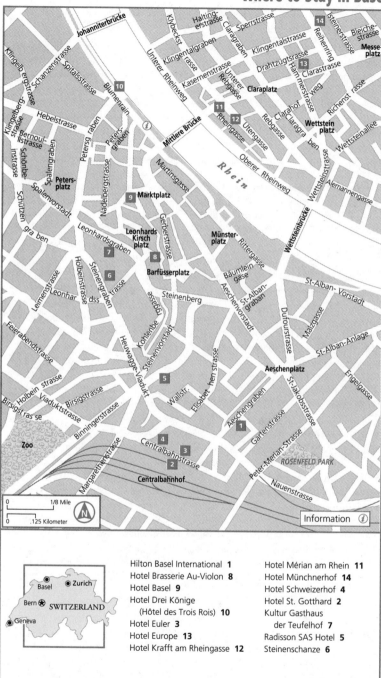

Hilton Basel International **1**
Hotel Brasserie Au-Violon **8**
Hotel Basel **9**
Hotel Drei Könige
   (Hôtel des Trois Rois) **10**
Hotel Euler **3**
Hotel Europe **13**
Hotel Krafft am Rheingasse **12**

Hotel Mérian am Rhein **11**
Hotel Münchnerhof **14**
Hotel Schweizerhof **4**
Hotel St. Gotthard **2**
Kultur Gasthaus
   der Teufelhof **7**
Radisson SAS Hotel **5**
Steinenschanze **6**

1, 6, 8, 14, or 15. **Amenities:** 2 restaurants, bar; room service; babysitting; laundry/dry cleaning. *In room:* A/C, TV, minibar, hair dryer, safe.

Hotel Euler ⚜ This hotel offers everything you'd expect from a grand hotel in Basel. Built in 1865 near the railroad station, it's elegantly detailed in white, with gray stone half columns. The bedrooms are luxuriously paneled and impeccable, having housed everyone from Greta Garbo to Elizabeth Taylor over the years. Rooms have traditional styling with original paintings, some period furnishings, and such extras as spacious closets. All the bathrooms are maintained in excellent condition with heated towel racks. The chandeliered dining room, Le Bonheure, serves first-class dinners. The cuisine is mainly French with a lot of fish and a changing menu that takes advantage of the best of seasonal produce. The famous bar is richly ornamented with leather, wood, and red velvet, and is a favorite of visiting businesspeople and local bankers.

Centralbahnplatz 14, CH-4051 Basel. ℂ **061/272-45-00.** Fax 061/271-50-00. www.hoteleuler.ch. 67 units. 350SF–450SF ($192.50–$247.50) double; 770SF ($423.50) suite. AE, DC, MC, V. Tram: 6, 10, 16, or 17. **Amenities:** Restaurant, bar; room service; babysitting; laundry/dry cleaning. *In room:* TV, minibar, hair dryer, safe.

EXPENSIVE

Hotel Basel ⚜ Since its opening in 1975, this modern hotel keeps abreast of the times and remains one of the best bets for lodgings in the Old Town. On weekdays the hotel fills almost exclusively with businesspeople, but on weekends out-of-town visitors predominate, especially those from both the French and Swiss sides of the Juras. The public rooms are high ceilinged with crystal chandeliers. Coming in a range of shapes and sizes, bedrooms are well furnished with both traditional and modern pieces; each is exceedingly comfortable with well-maintained bathrooms.

Münzgasse 12, CH-4058 Basel. ℂ **061/264-68-00.** Fax 061/264-68-11. 72 units. 240SF–315SF ($132–$173.25) double. Rates include buffet breakfast. AE, DC, MC, V. Parking 25SF ($13.75). Tram: 1, 6, or 8. **Amenities:** 2 restaurants, bar; room service; babysitting; laundry/dry cleaning. *In room:* A/C, TV, minibar, hair dryer.

Hotel Europe ⚜ Centrally located next to the Swiss Industries Fair and within easy access of the Swiss and German railway stations, this recently renovated hotel offers modern comforts and contemporary style. Most of its bedrooms overlook a quiet roof garden, and all units contain neatly kept bathrooms. Some readers have praised these bathrooms—"storage enough for a platoon"— and enjoyed the two 5-foot-wide mirrors. Le Quatre Saisons, the hotel's luxury restaurant, is considered among the top three in Basel, although some find it overrated and overpriced. An international market-fresh cuisine is served.

Clarastrasse 43, CH-4005 Basel. ℂ **800/223-56-52** in the U.S. and Canada, or 061/690-80-80. Fax 061/690-88-80. www.balehotels.ch. 166 units. 250SF–480SF ($137.50–$264) double. Children 12 and under stay free in parents' room. Rates include buffet breakfast. AE, DC, MC, V. Parking generally free, 27SF ($14.85) for fairs and congresses. Tram: 2, 6, or 8. **Amenities:** 2 restaurants, bar, cafe; room service; babysitting; laundry/dry cleaning; nonsmoking rooms. *In room:* TV, minibar, hair dryer, safe.

Hotel Schweizerhof ⚜ Located near the train station across from a landscaped park, this ornate hotel is six stories high, with a terrace and wrought-iron balconies. It has been in the Goetzinger family for three generations. Built in 1864, it was once the most luxurious hotel in Basel, entertaining such greats as Casals, Menuhin, and Toscanini. Today it remains the traditional favorite of town, but is likely to attract more business travelers than its former clientele of the wealthy chic. The salons are decorated with Oriental rugs and some 19th-century antiques, while the bedrooms are both modern and traditional, sometimes blending Biedermeier with pine and beech. Half the accommodations are air-conditioned.

Centralbahnplatz 1, CH-4002 Basel. ℂ **061/271-28-33.** Fax 061/271-29-19. 75 units. 275SF–290SF ($151.25–$159.50) double. Rates include continental breakfast. AE, DC, MC, V. Free parking. Tram: 6, 10, 16, or 17. **Amenities:** Restaurant, bar; room service; laundry/dry cleaning. *In room:* A/C in some, TV, minibar, hair dryer, safe.

Kultur Gasthaus der Teufelhof ★★★ *Finds*   This is one of the most unusual hotels in Switzerland, if not all of Europe. Set in what was originally a 19th-century private home in the Spalen district, near the Academy of Music, it contains two restaurants, a charming bar, and handsomely decorated bedrooms featuring decor that's been written up in newspapers across the city. Each room was entrusted to the artistic inspiration of a different Swiss, Italian, or German "environmental artist." Each artist was given carte blanche to create whatever he or she decided. The result gives you the impression of living inside a work of art that happens to be exceedingly comfortable with cozy chairs and modern plumbing. Even if you don't stay here, consider the hotel's dining possibilities.

Leonhardsgraben 47, CH-4051 Basel. ℂ **061/261-10-10.** Fax 061/261-10-04. www.teufelhof.com. 33 units. 255SF–365SF ($140.25–$200.75) double; 295SF–450SF ($162.25–$247.50) suite. Rates include breakfast. AE, MC, V. Parking 25SF ($13.75). Tram: 3. **Amenities:** 2 restaurants, bar; room service; laundry/dry cleaning. *In room:* Hair dryer.

Radisson SAS Hotel ★   Lying near the Historiches Museum and the Münster, this hotel gives a first impression of an impersonal structure at the airport. However, it's right in the center of Basel. Don't judge it immediately by its bustling lobby, filled weekdays with businesspeople and background music. Its bedrooms have been recently refurbished, and 90% of them are tranquil, with views over the inner court garden. The Basel Hilton's rooms are better, but this is a viable alternative, with built-in furnishings and great comfort. Some units are designed especially for women.

Steinentorstrasse 25. CH-4001 Basel. ℂ **061/227-27-27.** Fax 061/227-28-28. www.radisson.com. 205 units. 300SF–430SF ($165–$236.50) double; from 600SF ($330) suite. Rates include buffet breakfast. AE, DC, MC, V. Parking 25SF ($13.75). Tram: 6, 10, 16, or 17. **Amenities:** 2 restaurants; pool; health club; sauna; steam room; room service; babysitting; laundry/dry cleaning. *In-room:* A/C, TV, minibar, hair dryer, safe.

MODERATE

Hotel Mérian am Rhein ★   This 1972 hotel lies just off the quay where a 13th-century bishop commissioned the construction of the only bridge across the Rhine between Lake Constance and the sea. Located in the oldest part of the city, the Mérian has updated conveniences, including very comfortable beds. Rooms with river-view balconies of the Rhine are more expensive. Ranging from mid-sized to spacious, units are well equipped with modern furnishings, glass-topped cocktail tables, well-lit desk space, and tiled bathrooms.

With its black lacquer and beech furnishings, the Café and Restaurant Spitz on the ground floor of the hotel is famous locally, especially because of its terrace by the Mittlerebrücke and the Rhine.

Rheingasse (at Greifengasse 2), CH-4058 Basel. ℂ **061/681-00-00.** Fax 061/685-11-01. www.merian-hotel.ch. 65 units. 240SF–280SF ($132–$154) double. Rates include continental breakfast. AE, DC, MC, V. Parking 14SF ($7.70). Tram: 6, 8, or 14. **Amenities:** 2 restaurants, lounge; room service; laundry/dry cleaning. *In room:* TV, minibar, hair dryer.

Hotel Münchnerhof   In front of the Basel Fair and Conference Center and close to the railroad station, Hotel Münchnerhof is housed in a brownish-ocher building with white trim and small balconies. Bedrooms are small to mid-sized, each well maintained and comfortable. Furnishings are a combination of modern and traditional. In addition to the hotel, the Früh family also operates a restaurant, known for its French, Swiss, and Italian cuisine.

Riehenring 75, CH-4058 Basel. © 061/691-77-80. Fax 061/691-14-90. 32 units. 170SF–295SF ($93.50–$162.25) double. Rates include buffet breakfast. AE, DC, MC, V. Parking 20SF ($11). Tram: 1, 2, 6, or 14. **Amenities:** Restaurant, Bavarian cellar, bar; laundry/dry cleaning. *In room:* TV.

Hotel St. Gotthard   Opposite the train station, this building is graced with arched canopies stretching above the two doors and three picture windows. The hotel, run by the third generation of the Geyer-Arel family, offers comfortable, well-maintained, and individually decorated bedrooms. All contain neatly kept bathrooms with shower stalls. The hotel was expanded in 1998. The staff is exceedingly friendly and helpful.

Centralbahnstrasse 13, CH-4002 Basel. © **061/225-13-13.** Fax 061/225-13-14. www.bestwestern.ch. 104 units. 280SF–360SF ($154–$198) double; 460SF ($253) junior suite. Rates include buffet breakfast. AE, DC, MC, V. Parking 25SF ($13.75). Tram: 1, 2, or 8. **Amenities:** Lounge; laundry/dry cleaning. *In room:* TV, minibar, hair dryer.

INEXPENSIVE

Hotel Brasserie Au-Violon ★★ *(Finds)*   One tries to avoid overnighting in a prison, but not in this case. This historic site, once a 12th-century cloister for priests and from 1835 to 1995 a famous prison, is now an offbeat hotel of comfort and grace. If you want that jailhouse feeling, ask for one of the bedrooms fronting the courtyard. These units still adhere to their cellblock plan, although space is tight. Accommodations whose windows open onto the Altstadt are larger and more comfortable. All units come with well-maintained but rather small private bathrooms with shower stalls. Some of the doors leading to the bedrooms are 5 feet tall, so be duly warned. Even if you don't stay here, consider a visit to its charming old-world brasserie with its classic French cuisine. Tables are placed outside on a terraced garden in fair weather.

Im Lohnhof, CH-4051 Basel. © **061/269-8711.** Fax 061/269-8712. www.au-violon.com. 20 units. 120SF–180SF ($66–$99) double. **Amenities:** Restaurant, bar; room service; laundry/dry cleaning. *In room:* TV hair dryer.

Hotel Krafft am Rhein ★★ *(Finds)*   Located across the river from the old town's Rathaus and Münster, this elegant little mansion is a real discovery, its terrace cafe and its bedrooms opening directly on the waterfront of Basel's right bank. The public rooms are decorated with 19th-century antiques, oversize gilt mirrors, and Oriental rugs. The comfortable, modernized rooms often have good views, and contain Oriental carpets and artwork. All units offer showers with some containing shower/tub combinations. The Waldmeyer-Schneiter family also manages the well-known restaurant Zem Schnooggeloch (Mosquito's Den) and the Restaurant Petit Bâle, serving French and Swiss cuisine.

Rheingasse 12, CH-4058 Basel. © **061/690-91-30.** Fax 061/690-91-31. www.krafftamrhein.ch. 52 units. 172SF–258SF ($94.60–$141.90) double. Rates include continental breakfast. AE, DC, MC, V. Parking 24SF ($13.20). Tram: 8. **Amenities:** 2 restaurants, lounge; room service; laundry/dry cleaning. *In room:* TV, hair dryer.

Steinenschanze   The location is inconvenient and opens onto a much-trafficked highway artery, but in high-priced Basel it still comes as a welcome relief. On the border of the nighttime district of clubs, bars, and taverns, the Steinenschanze has been renovated. Bedrooms are small and furnished in a minimalist, almost Danish style. But there is comfort here: The beds are fairly new and the bathrooms are welcoming and neatly tiled. The accommodations opening onto a garden in the rear of the building are more tranquil and free of noise. Other than breakfast, small meals can be arranged ahead of time.

Steinengraben 69, CH-4051 Basel. © 061/272-53-53. Fax 061/272-45-73. 55 units. 200SF–260SF ($110–$143) double; 340SF ($187) suite. Rates include breakfast. AE, DC, MC, V. Free parking. Train to Bozsbb station, then tram 1 or 8. **Amenities:** Lounge; laundry/dry cleaning. *In room:* TV, minibar, hair dryer.

WHERE TO DINE

Five centuries ago the humanist Enea Silvio de' Piccolomini (who later became Pope Pius II) said about Baslers: "Most of them are devotees of good living. They live at home in style and spend most of their time at the table." Not much has changed.

VERY EXPENSIVE

La Rôtisserie des Rois ✶ SWISS   This elegant restaurant is famous for its riverside terrace, where in midsummer tables are set close to the waters of the Rhine. The restaurant offers a *cuisine du marché*—that is, a cuisine based on the best of market-fresh ingredients. Original seasonings as well as a sound classic technique characterize this refined cuisine, which is exceptionally flavorful. No wonder the locals flock here for that special celebration. Specialties change with the seasons; you might try homemade terrine of goose liver, guinea fowl with chanterelles, chicken breast with leek-flavored cream sauce, potato pancakes with caviar, or chateaubriand in a confit of shallots.

In the Hotel Drei Könige, Blumenrain 8. © **061/260-50-50.** Reservations recommended. Main courses 52SF–148SF ($28.60–$81.40); 6-course gourmet menu 118SF ($64.90); 4-course seafood menu 92SF ($50.60). AE, DC, MC, V. Daily noon–2:45pm and 7–11pm. Tram: 1, 6, 8, 14, or 15.

Restaurant Stucki Bruderholz ✶✶✶ FRENCH   Located a short distance south of the city limits, Hans and Susi Stucki's gourmet restaurant is renowned throughout Switzerland, an elegant shrine of haute cuisine. Customers may dine inside or on the backyard terrace by the garden. The former private residence is decorated with antiques and oil paintings. Our favorite room is the Salon Vert, with its green napery, Empire chairs, and light-patterned Oriental rug.

The chef produces a refined yet lively cuisine known for its intense flavor and use of top-quality ingredients. Specialties may include a filet of saltwater red mullet with coriander, a terrine of foie gras, sliced veal kidneys in a tarragon vinaigrette sauce, or a lobster ragoût with truffles and baby leeks. The selle d'agneau (lamb) is cooked with a gratin of green beans, and the sweetbreads are masterful. For dessert, we'd suggest a compote of pears or a soufflé made with the fresh fruits of the season.

Bruderholzallee 42. © **061/361-82-22.** Reservations required. Main courses 55SF–65SF ($30.25–$35.75); fixed-price lunch 85SF ($46.75); 6-course menu surprise 130SF–190SF ($71.50–$104.50). AE, DC, MC, V. Tues–Sat noon–3pm and 6pm–midnight. Bus: 15.

Teufelhof Restaurant ✶✶✶ INTERNATIONAL   Monica and Dominique Thommy-Kneschaurek operate the most unusual hotel (see "Where to Stay," above) and the most unusual dining complex in Basel. Their "House of Art and Culture" is in a former 19th-century private home in the Spalen district. Chef Michael Baader, whose philosophy is "The art of cooking starts in the heart, not in the pan," displays more creativity than any other chef in the city and uses only fresh, high-quality ingredients. Before coming to Basel, he was ranked as one of the 10 best chefs in Germany. He oversees the cuisine in the hotel's gourmet restaurant, its Weinstube, and its cafe. The wine list offers more than 350 different wines; a great number can be ordered by the glass.

Some of chef Baader's dishes might be a first for you—for example, carrot soup with mushroom ravioli as an appetizer. Main courses are likely to include grilled filet of beef with a butter-and-pepper sauce, stuffed medallions of venison in a peppery sauce with buttered noodles and kohlrabi, or French rack of lamb in a rosemary sauce with artichokes.

In the Weinstube—sometimes called the Brasserie—Baader and his staff prepare meals, including a fixed-price dinner, with the same attention and care that they do in the formal restaurant. The dress here, as in the cafe and bar, is casual. Simple but high-quality ingredients are used, with a daily menu featuring at least 10 different dishes. The cafe opens at 7am, but after 6pm it becomes a bar, featuring a choice of Highland malt whiskeys and an assortment of sherries, ports, armagnacs, and cognacs. In summer, guests can take their drinks into a small garden.

In addition, the complex has two small theaters, and although many of the presentations are in German, many of the cabaret programs have universal appeal.

In the Kultur Gasthaus der Teufelhof, Leonhardsgraben 47. ② 061/261-10-10. Reservations recommended. Restaurant Bel Étage, main courses 65SF–85SF ($35.75–$46.75); fixed-price menu 128SF–180SF ($70.40–$99). Weinstube, fixed-price menu 72SF ($39.60). AE, DC, MC, V. Restaurant Bel Etage, Tues–Fri noon–2pm and 7–9pm, Sat 7–9pm. Weinstube, daily noon–midnight, with a limited menu offered 2:30–6pm. (Cafe, daily 8am–6pm; bar, daily 6pm–midnight.) Tram: 3.

EXPENSIVE

Kunsthalle Restaurant ✿ FRENCH/ITALIAN   This elegant restaurant houses pictures from the Kunsthalle (art gallery) on its walls to complement the chandeliers, handsome rugs, stone arches leading into the bar, and murals on the walls. In the main dining room, cold specialties are served buffet style, and white-jacketed waiters will take your orders for hot courses. You can order a salad of arugula with mushrooms and cheese, followed by a double entrecôte with risotto or grilled sea bass served with potatoes. You can also eat supper in the bar from the same a la carte menu offered in the main restaurant. Though hardly the best cuisine in Basel, the food is consistently reliable, and diners usually leave satisfied.

Steinenberg 7. ② 061/272-42-33. Reservations recommended. Main courses 45SF–65SF ($24.75–$35.75). No credit cards. Daily 11am–2pm and 6–10pm. Tram: 6 or 14.

Schloss Binningen ✿✿ FRENCH   This 16th-century chateau and its grounds are owned by the township but managed by independent entrepreneurs. The entrance hall is appropriately baronial, and the grand dining rooms contain an antique loggia (presumably used long ago by chamber orchestras). The wine cellar is among the best in the region, with at least 50 vintages not listed on the menu (the wine steward will make appropriate suggestions). The menu changes at least three times a year but is likely to include a *timbale de langoustines* (crawfish served in a pie crust) with caviar, a selle de chevreuil rôsti (saddle of roast roebuck), or fresh lobster, followed by a cold soufflé. Although not ranking in the stellar company of Der Teufelhof or Bruderholz, this restaurant is tranquil and charming. Dishes are carefully prepared, and lighter versions of classic dishes appear frequently.

Schlossgasse 5, Binningen. ② 061/421-20-55. Reservations required. Main courses 38SF–65SF ($20.90–$35.75); fixed-price menu 50SF ($27.50) at lunch, 100SF ($55) at dinner. AE, DC, MC, V. Tues–Sat noon–2pm and 7–9:30pm. Closed 2 weeks in Feb. Tram: 2, 10, or 17.

St. Alban-Eck ⚑ *(Finds)* SWISS/FRENCH Set in the antiques district and filled with architectural charm, this small and intimate restaurant is a 5-minute walk from the Museum of Fine Arts. The historic 750-year-old building has retained its beautiful original stone and oak door. The kitchen is known for its high-quality French and Swiss specialties. You might try the homemade ravioli stuffed with salmon in a creamy truffle sauce, grilled turbot with potatoes and vegetables, or suprême of duckling with honey sauce or coriander. The chef also prepares grilled U.S. beef with arugula and rack of veal with potatoes and chanterelles. We are exceedingly fond of this place, and after sampling the meticulously prepared cuisine, we think you will be too.

Malzgasse-St. Alban-Vorstadt 60. ✆ **061/271-03-20.** Reservations recommended. Main courses 43SF–58SF ($23.65–$31.90); fixed-price 5-course menu 78SF ($42.90). AE, DC, MC, V. Mon–Sat 11:30am–2:30pm and 7–11:30pm. Closed July 16–Aug 16. Tram: 2 or 14.

MODERATE

L'Escargot SWISS/FRENCH L'Escargot, one of the best spots in Basel to try la cuisine bourgeoise, is located in a train station, at the bottom of green terrazzo steps. It's warm and cozy, with discreet lighting and hanging ceramic pots. The bar area is nicely decorated with illustrations of castles and trees. Part of the menu is devoted to French regional cooking, including tripe à la mode de Caen and other dishes. The kitchen prepares snails in three different ways. In season you may order roebuck, and year-round you can try Egyptian-style eggplant gratiné. For dessert, we've always enjoyed the apfelstrudel.

Centralbahnstrasse 14. ✆ **061/295-39-66.** Main courses 27SF–52SF ($14.85–$28.60). AE, DC, MC, V. Mon–Fri 11am–2pm and 6–11pm. Closed July 10–Aug 15 and Sat–Sun. Tram: 1, 2, or 8.

Safran-Zunft *(Value)* SWISS Upon entering this medieval stone building, you'll notice the wrought-iron depiction of the restaurant's logo, a gluttonous monk inhaling the aroma from a goblet of wine. That sets the tone for this time-tested favorite attracting faithful devotees, primarily those drawn by its bargain lunches. Inside, the restaurant is set up tavern style, with red-checked tablecloths, wood paneling, and oversize Gothic windows.

The kitchen serves elaborate specialties and good-tasting appetizers such as caviar and smoked salmon. And while you'll regularly find veal steak and chateaubriand on the menu, most guests order the delectable fondue Bacchus, with veal and all the condiments. The soups are especially good.

Gerbergasse 11. ✆ **061/269-94-94.** Reservations recommended. Main courses 23SF–39SF ($12.65–$21.45); fixed-price lunch 25SF ($13.75). AE, DC, MC, V. Sept–June Mon–Sat 11:30am–11pm, July–Aug Mon–Fri 10am–2pm and 5pm–midnight. Tram: 1, 6, 8, 11, or 14.

Schlüsselzunft ⚑⚑ FRENCH This is one of the oldest guildhouses in Basel, begun in the 12th century by cloth merchants. The restaurant has a menu offering seasonal specialties, including various types of fish and, in the autumn, venison. The cooking is careful, and the talented kitchen delivers on solid flavors, using quality ingredients. Regular specialties include veal curry, tenderloin steak with goose liver and morels, shredded calves' kidney in a madeira sauce, and shredded veal and kidney in a cream sauce with spätzli. It also serves well-prepared traditional soups and a fine selection of pasta, including cannelloni au gratin.

Freie Strasse 25. ✆ **061/261-20-46.** Reservations recommended. Main courses 35SF–50SF ($19.25–$27.50); fixed-price menu 48SF ($26.40) at lunch, 68SF ($37.40) at dinner. AE, MC, V. Mon–Sat 11:30am–3pm and 6pm–midnight. Tram: 6 or 14.

Zum Goldenen Sternen CONTINENTAL   Set near the edge of the Rhine and established in 1421, this is one of the oldest restaurants in Switzerland. Renovated in a conservative mixed style of old and modern architectural elements in the early 1990s, it's known to many different generations of Baslers. The well-prepared dishes are traditional, influenced by neighboring France. Dishes include smoked eel, smoked trout, terrine maison, lobster soup, roast rack of lamb, filet of veal with lemon, and roast guinea fowl with a mushroom ragoût.

St. Albanrheinweg 70. ℭ **061/272-16-66.** Reservations recommended. Main courses 34SF–48SF ($18.70–$26.40); fixed-price menu 59SF–84SF ($32.45–$46.20). AE, DC, MC, V. Daily noon–2pm and 6–10pm. Tram: 6 or 12.

INEXPENSIVE

Da Roberto *Value* ITALIAN   Located on a narrow side street 1 block from the central train station, this restaurant attracts younger Baslers, many of whom appreciate its nonsmoking area. Depending on what you order, you can dine here rather inexpensively, enjoying good food, a lively atmosphere, and polite but informal service. There are three separate seating areas, decorated with checkered tablecloths and paneled walls. At night the young crowd often drops in for the tasty pizzas. The soups are a good value, as are the 15 different spaghetti dishes.

Kuchengasse 3. ℭ **061/205-85-50.** Main courses 22SF–34SF ($12.10–$18.70); pizzas and salads 16SF–27SF ($8.80–$14.85); fixed-price lunch 18SF–28SF ($9.90–$15.40). AE, DC, MC, V. Sun–Fri 11:45am–2pm and daily 5:30–11pm. Tram: 1, 2, 8, 10 or 11.

Zum Schnabelb SWISS/INTERNATIONAL   This restaurant is ideal for simple dining in a nice cozy atmosphere. The rustic decor of the house is enhanced with wood paneling and country tables. The menu has hearty choices like grilled steak, filet of sea bass, roasted chicken, and sautéed veal, all served with the house favorite, rösti, or Swiss hash browns. For finer dining head up to the wood-lined second floor for a candlelit dinner and a more romantic atmosphere.

Trillenásslein 2. ℭ **061/261-49-09.** Reservations required. Main courses 18SF–37SF ($9.90–$20.35). MC, V. Mon–Sat noon–2pm and 6–midnight. Tram: 8 to Marktplatz.

BASEL AFTER DARK

Regardless of which language you speak, you'll find lots of options for nightlife, whether you're looking for a sophisticated cocktail lounge or a funky alternative club. A worthwhile cluster of them are in the **Stadtcasino,** Barfüssenplatz (ℭ **061/226-36-00**), a venue that contains a stage (Musik Halle) for live musical acts, plus at least three other bars and restaurants. The most animated and appealing of them is **Café Galileo's,** Barsussarplatz 6 (ℭ **061/271-36-19**). Although it's open throughout the day as a cafe and simple restaurant, it's at its best after 5pm, when a live pianist creates an ambience conducive to meeting attractive strangers of all possible sexual persuasions and lifestyles. On Steinenberg 14, look for the American-inspired **Papa Joe's** (ℭ **061/272-04-04**), a restaurant containing vague references to Hemingway and a commodious bar area. A few steps away, at Steinenberg 7, directly opposite the whimsical fountain designed by mega-artist Jean Tigueley, is the **Campari Bar** (ℭ **061/272-83-83**), a youthful site for drinking, gossiping, or whatever.

There's a highly appealing, discreetly prosperous bar, **The Old City Bar,** in the previously recommended Basel Hilton International, Aeschengraben 31

(© 061/271-66-22). Its decor evokes a prestigious men's club in London. Here, you'll get the distinct feeling that everything from billion-dollar bank transfers to romantic assignations have been discreetly and stylishly conducted. Several notches upscale, with older and more prestigious antecedents, is the **Euler Bar,** in the Hotel Euler, Centralbahnplatz 14 (© **061/272-45-00**). Popular with the international business community, it contains a lavishly coffered ceiling, a live pianist, lots of leather upholstery, a noise level that rarely rises above a murmur, and stiff drinks. More raucous and earthy is the popular bar in the oldest hotel in Europe, the **Drei Könige,** Blumenrain 8 (© 061/260-50-50), which is smaller and more bohemian than the previously recommended bars.

Next door to the Drei Könige is **Queens,** Blumenrain 10 (© **061/271-00-50**), a safe and well-recommended disco with an appealing cross section of youthful and middle-aged partygoers, both gay and straight. Admission is free. The music is a mix of '60s, '70s, and '80s. Music lovers head for the city's most deeply entrenched bastion of electronic music, avant-garde jazz, and rock and roll, the **Café Atlantis,** Klosterberg 13 (© 061/712-46-31). Favored by rock-star hopefuls and college students, it contains a labyrinth of bars and balconies, and views of the medieval cathedral from the second-floor windows. It's open Monday to Thursday from 11am to 2am, Friday from 11am to 4am, and Saturday from 4pm to 4am. On Friday and Saturday nights it becomes a disco. During the week it has occasional live music. Admission is free.

You're always likely to strike up an interesting conversation when you drop in at any of Basel's gay bars, which tend to get going relatively late at night, around 11pm. Try **Elle et Lui,** Rebgasse 39 (© 061/692-54-79). If you'd like to dine and drink, head for **Dupf,** Rebbasse 43 (© 061/692-00-11), set within a nondescript antique house in the heart of Basel's oldest section, near the Wettstein-platz. This is the premier gay bar of Basel. If you drop in just for a drink, you'll find yourself beneath a stone vaulted ceiling with gay men (women are welcome, but very few ever actually come here) from throughout the surrounding region. There's a restaurant on the premises as well, open only for dinner, nightly from 6pm till midnight Sunday to Thursday, and till between 2 and 4am on Friday and Saturday. Main courses cost from 18SF to 35SF ($9.90–$19.25) each, and include a medley of French, Italian, German, and Thai dishes. The interior decor changes about once a month, usually to reflect whatever holiday or season it is.

On a more cultural note, the **Basel Stadttheater,** Theaterstrasse 7 (© 061/295-11-33), presents an array of opera, operetta, dance concerts, and plays in German. The box office is open Monday to Saturday from 10am to 1pm and 3:30 to 6:45pm, and 1 hour before any performance. It is closed over July and August.

2 Solothurn ★

27 miles (43km) N of Bern, 16 miles (25km) NE of Biel

The capital of a canton by the same name, Solothurn, according to a 16th-century rhyme, is "the oldest place in Celtis save Trier." Located on the banks of the Aare at the foot of the Jura Mountains, it has been fortified many times. Roman inscriptions calling it Salodurum have been found, as have the remains of a Roman castrum. But today the town is celebrated for its baroque architecture—reason enough for a visit.

Many guidebooks ignore the town completely, and many visitors relegate it to a day trip from Bern, but there are rewards to be found here.

ESSENTIALS

GETTING THERE   Solothurn has frequent train connections to the major cities of Switzerland, including Zurich (65 min.), Geneva (2 hr.), and Biel (1 hr.). Call (©) **0900-300-300** (no area code) for **rail information.**

If you're driving, head north from Bern along the N1, veering west at the turnoff to Solothurn.

VISITOR INFORMATION   The Solothurn tourist office, the **Verkehrsbüro,** Hauptgasse 69, am Kronenplatz ((©) **032/626-46-46**), will provide you with a map and pinpoint some of the best hiking in the area. Open Monday to Friday 8am to noon and 2:30 to 6pm, Saturday 9am to noon.

SEEING THE SIGHTS

Solothurn is Switzerland's finest baroque town. It was at its peak from the 16th to the 18th century, when it was the residence of the French ambassadors to the Swiss Confederation. Solothurn became part of the Confederation as early as 1481.

Exploring Solothurn on foot is the typical way to see the town's attractions, although you might opt for a **rental bike** instead. At the Solothurn rail station on Hauptbahnhofstrasse ((©) **032/621-34-74**), you can rent a bike for 29SF ($15.95) daily from 8am to 7pm.

Solothurn's **Old Town** ✦ is on the left bank of the river, partially enclosed by 17th-century walls. Inside those walls you'll find many Renaissance and baroque buildings. The Old Town is entered through the **Biel Gate,** or the Basel Gate. The heart of the old sector is **Marktplatz,** with its clock tower and a produce market on Wednesday and Saturday mornings from 9am to noon. The 15th-century **Rathaus** (town hall) has a notable Renaissance doorway. The two most colorful streets are **Hauptgasse** (Main Street) and **Schaalgasse,** where you'll find many wrought-iron signs and brightly painted shutters.

The baroque **Cathedral of St. Ursus** ✦—said to stand on the spot where its namesake was martyred—dates from the 18th century and has been the seat of the bishop of Basel since 1828. The cathedral, just inside Basel Gate, was constructed by builders from Ticino, which explains its Italian artistry. Try to visit the gardens on the east side.

The **Jesuitenkirche,** or Jesuits' Church, on Hauptgasse between the cathedral and the marketplace, dates from 1680 and contains a frescoed, **three-bay nave** ✦.

After you've absorbed the town's beauty, you might want to see some of the **Juras,** which tower in the background. There are many marked trails in the area for biking or hiking. The most scenic trail leads from the center of Solothurn to the Weissenstein Alpine Center, which will take about 2 hours by foot. Start out at the corner of Wengisteinstrasse and Verenawegstrasse in Solothurn and follow signs leading to Weissenstein. Once there you can board a chairlift that takes you down from Weissenstein to a station in Oberdorf where you can return to Solothurn by rail.

In summer consider a **boat tour** leaving from the quays at Solothurn to the towns of Biel, Murten, or Neuchâtel. A round-trip fare costs 45SF ($24.75), and the tourist office (see above) keeps a list of departure times, which vary depending on the weather.

Kunstmuseum Solothurn (Municipal Fine Arts Museum) Visit this museum if only to see the *Madonna of Solothurn* 🗲, by Holbein the Younger. Also outstanding is a 15th-century painting on wood from the Rhenish school, the *Virgin with Strawberries* 🗲. The museum emphasizes Swiss art from the mid-19th century to the present. A collection of excellent works represent Frölicher, Hodler, Vallotton, Trachsel, Amiet, Berger, Gubler, and others.

Werkhofstrasse 30. ℭ 032/622-23-07. Free admission. Tues–Fri 10am–noon and 2–5pm, Sat–Sun 10am–5pm.

Museum Altes Zeughaus (Old Arsenal) Slightly to the northwest of the cathedral stands this museum, which houses one of the largest collections of weapons in Europe. There are fascinating exhibits of medieval weaponry, flags, and Swiss military uniforms.

Zeughausplatz 1. ℭ 032/623-35-28. Admission 6SF ($3.30) adults, 4SF ($2.20) children and seniors, 10SF ($5.50) family ticket; free for children 7 and under. June–Oct Tues–Sun 10am–noon and 2–5pm; Nov–May Tues–Fri 2–5pm, Sat–Sun 10am–noon and 2–5pm.

WHERE TO STAY

Hotel Krone 🗲 This hotel is clearly the frontrunner. Hotel Krone, near the Clock Tower, is one of the oldest inns in the country and basks in its reputation as the hotel where Napoleon's wife, Josephine, stayed for several days in 1811. Run by the Küng family, the inn is a member of Ambassador Swiss hotels and still attracts history buffs. The gilt lettering on the pink facade spells out the name in French—Hôtel de la Couronne. The bedrooms are old-fashioned but exceedingly comfortable and well maintained. Most of the units are quite spacious, and all contain neatly kept bathrooms.

Hauptgasse 64, CH-4500 Solothurn. ℭ 032/622-44-12. Fax 032/626-44-45. 42 units. 255SF ($140.25) double. Rates include buffet breakfast. AE, DC, MC, V. Parking 12SF ($6.60). **Amenities:** Restaurant, bar; room service; laundry/dry cleaning. *In room:* TV, minibar, hair dryer.

Tour Rouge Parts of this hotel date from the 1100s; others were added throughout the centuries to create the inner labyrinth of rooms and corridors that make the architecture of this place the most complicated and intriguing in town. The site has functioned as an inn since the 1840s, and the current Swiss family owners provide modern, comfortable bedrooms; the largest overlook the front square. Accommodations come in a range of sizes and shapes, and most furnishings are traditional. All units are equipped with well-maintained bathrooms. The staff keeps the place in tiptop shape.

Hauptgasse 42, CH-4500 Solothurn. ℭ 032/622-96-21. Fax 032/622-98-65. 35 units. 185SF–215SF ($101.75–$118.25) double. Rates include breakfast. AE, DC, MC, V. **Amenities:** 2 restaurants, bar; room service; laundry/dry cleaning. *In room:* TV, minibar, hair dryer.

WHERE TO DINE

Zum Alten Stephan 🗲🗲🗲 SWISS This restaurant is the finest in this region of Switzerland. Parts of the structure that contain this place were built 1,000 years ago as housing for the staff of a nearby chapel, St. Stephan's Kappelle. Later it functioned as the point of demarcation from which most of the streets of Solothurn were laid out. Today it's the oldest restaurant in the canton and the most charming and amusing place in town, with two distinctly separate venues, menus, and price scales.

We usually prefer the simpler, street-level dining room, where varnished pine, marble floors, bare wood tables, and oil paintings in gilded frames provide an uncluttered dignity. Upstairs is a smaller, more intimate and hushed ambience where the cuisine is more thoughtful and cerebral (and more fussed over) than in the brasserie. Menu items in the brasserie include several kinds of rösti, which many locals consider a meal in itself. According to your wishes, it will include any combination of ham, onions, cheese, bacon, and fried eggs. There's also pasta, salads, soups, meat, and fish. Upstairs, look for such dishes as Scottish salmon in puff pastry with broad beans and soy sauce, filet of U.S. beef served with vegetables and wild mushrooms, and such desserts as four-fruit sorbet with fresh berries.

Friedhofplatz 10. ℂ 032/622-11-09. Reservations recommended, especially for the upstairs restaurant. Upstairs restaurant, fixed-price meals 55SF ($30.25) at lunch, 155SF ($85.25) at dinner. Street-level brasserie, main courses 16SF–52SF ($8.80–$28.60); fixed-price menu 18SF ($9.90). AE, DC, MC, V. Restaurant Tues–Sat 11am–2pm and 5pm–midnight. Brasserie daily 11am–midnight.

3 Fribourg ★★

22 miles (35km) SW of Bern, 33 miles (53km) NE of Vevey

Once a sovereign republic, set between lakes and mountains, Fribourg was founded in 1157 and today has a population of some 40,000 and a university. It was a stronghold of Catholicism for centuries and was known for its dyers, weavers, and tanners. In 1481 it joined the Swiss Confederation, and today it's the capital of a canton of the same name. Visitors arrive today to see Switzerland's most rural canton, famous for its Holstein cows. It's a charming place with narrow medieval town houses. To wander its ancient precincts is well worth a day or at least an afternoon of your time.

ESSENTIALS

GETTING THERE   Fribourg is on the main train lines that connect Zurich and Bern with Lausanne and Geneva. Travel time from Lausanne is about 45 minutes; from Bern, about 25 minutes. Call ℂ **0900-300-300** for **train schedules** and information.

If you're driving, head southwest from Bern on N12; from Vevey, on Lake Geneva, go northeast on N12.

VISITOR INFORMATION   The **Office du Tourisme** is at 1, place de la Gare (ℂ **026/321-31-75**), open Monday to Friday 9am to 12:30pm and 1:30 to 6pm, Saturday 9am to 12:30pm and 1:30 to 4pm, Sunday 9am to 12:30pm (closed Sat afternoon Oct–Apr).

SEEING THE SIGHTS

Fribourg's major attraction is **St. Nicholas's Cathedral** ★, on place Notre-Dame (ℂ **026/347-10-40**), with its lofty 15th-century Gothic bell tower that dominates the medieval quarter. The most remarkable feature is the main porch **tymphanum** ★★, which is surmounted by a rose window. Depicted are such subjects as "the last judgment" and "heaven and the inferno." The nave dates from the 13th and 14th centuries, although the choir was reconstructed in the 17th century. La Chapelle Saint-Sépulcre, from the 15th century, has some remarkable stained glass and a celebrated organ.

In the vicinity of the cathedral you'll find **old patrician houses.** On foot, you can explore this architecturally interesting part of Fribourg—its Gothic houses, small steep streets, and squares adorned with fountains.

Whether it's called the Rathaus (in German) or the Hôtel de Ville (in French), the **town hall** of Fribourg is a notable 16th-century building. Located on route des Alpes, its best feature is its octagonal clock tower where mechanical figures strike the hours. Outside the town hall, the seat of the parliament of Fribourg, traditionally dressed farmers' wives sell produce on Wednesday and Saturday—the most colorful days to visit the city.

Eglise des Cordeliers, the Franciscan church (© **026/347-11-60**), is another important religious site. It's located north of place Notre-Dame, where St. Nicholas stands. The choir at the Franciscan church is from the 13th century, the nave is from the 18th century, and the church has an outstanding wood triptych carved in 1513. Its chief attraction is an altarpiece that rises from the main altar, the work of the "Masters of the Carnation," 15th-century artists who signed their works with a white or a red carnation.

The city also has an outstanding art and history museum, the **Musée d'Art et d'Histoire** or Museum für Kunst und Geschichte, 12, rue de Morat (© **026/ 322-85-71**). Housed in the 16th-century Hôtel Ratze and a former slaughterhouse, it has archaeological collections of prehistoric, Roman, and medieval objects, as well as a remarkable series of Burgundian belt buckles. The epic sweep of Fribourg's history comes alive in the sculptures and paintings from the 11th to the 20th century. There are also displays on the political, military, and economic life of the canton. Other exhibits include numerous 15th- to 18th-century stained-glass windows and the largest collection in Switzerland of wood sculpture from the first half of the 16th century. The museum is open Tuesday to Sunday from 10am to 6pm (also Thurs 8–10pm). Admission is 6SF ($3.30), 4SF ($2.20) students and seniors.

To reach the upper town of Fribourg, you can take a funicular. At some point, you'll want to see the **Ponte de Berne,** a covered wooden bridge built in 1580.

The best way to sample Fribourg life is to sit at one of the **small cafes** along rue de Romont or rue de Lausanne. Here you can see the parade of city folk pass by—30% calling themselves Freiburger in German, the remaining viewing themselves as Fribourgeois in French.

From a hill rising above the river, Fribourg offers a panoramic view of the **Bernese Alps.** If you're feeling energetic, rent a bike from the train station on place de la Gare for 27SF ($14.85) and go exploring. The best attraction in the environs is Schwarzee or Black Lake, a distance of 17 miles (27km) from the center. It is reached from Fribourg along N74. This is both a summer or winter excursion, and the scenic setting is one of the most memorable in the area.

SHOPPING

The folkloric souvenirs you'll see in Fribourg revolve around the canton's dairy and cheese-making traditions, with lots of emphasis on objects with heraldic shields and coats-of-arms. If you want to buy some, stroll along the town's main shopping streets, **rue de Romont** and **rue de Lausanne,** or head directly to any of the three addresses listed below. A good inventory of handicrafts is stocked in the city's **Office de Tourisme,** 1, place de la Gare (© **026/321-31-75**), and in a shop that's wholeheartedly devoted to French-speaking Switzerland's folklore, **La Clef du Pays,** 1, rue du Tilleul (© **026/322-51-20**). Barring that, consider rummaging through the town's largest department store, **La Placette,** 30, rue de Romont (© **026/350-66-11**), where you'll find everything you want and more, including gift items, clothing, and any necessities you may have overlooked while packing for your trip.

WHERE TO STAY

Golden Tulip Set high on a cliff a few blocks from the main railroad station, this hotel provides a grand view of historic Fribourg. With easy parking and convenience to the city's modern sector, the recently renovated hotel is preferred by many businesspeople. The rooms here are spacious and cheerfully decorated. All are equipped with neatly kept bathrooms. Many of the rooms have Murphy beds.

14, Grand-Places, CH-1700 Fribourg. ✆ 026/351-91-91. Fax 026/351-91-92. www.goldentulip.ch. 122 units. 260SF–300SF ($143–$165) double. Rates include buffet breakfast. AE, DC, MC, V. Free parking. Bus: 1 or 2. **Amenities:** Restaurant, bar; room service; babysitting; laundry/dry cleaning. *In room:* TV, minibar, hair dryer.

Hotel Alpha *Value* Located a 15-minute walk from the train station, this modern hotel is one of the best bargains in town. Each of the modern furnished rooms is simple but adequate, and generally tranquil. Beds are firm, and maintenance is high in all units and bathrooms. A restaurant and bar on the first landing are independent of the hotel. Call ✆ **026/322-69-33** for information about the restaurant.

13, rue du Simplon, CH-1700 Fribourg. ✆ **026/322-72-72.** Fax 026/323-10-00. 20 units. 170SF ($93.50) double. Rates include continental breakfast. AE, DC, MC, V. Bus: 1 or 2. **Amenities:** Restaurant, bar; room service. *In room:* TV, minibar, hair dryer.

Hôtel de la Rose Occupying a grand sandstone building near the cathedral, this is a historic property, which has been renovated in a rather pristine way. The flowered ceiling in the lobby—the hotel's most dramatic feature—contains elements of the original construction from the 1600s. The mid-sized bedrooms are modern and comfortably furnished, each with a firm bed and a neat bathroom.

Place Notre-Dame, 1, rue de Morat, CH-1700 Fribourg. ✆ **026/351-01-01.** Fax 026/351-01-00. 40 units. 190SF–210SF ($104.50–$115.50) double; 250SF ($137.50) suite. Rates include buffet breakfast. AE, DC, MC, V. Bus: 1 or 2. **Amenities:** 2 restaurants, bar; room service; car rental; babysitting; laundry/dry cleaning. *In room:* TV, minibar.

Hôtel Duc Berthold Yes, there was a Duke Berthold, who once lived in this building, although it's unlikely that he'd recognize it after its conversion to a hotel in 1969. It's in a fairly noisy part of town, on a busy street alongside the cathedral and the Zähringen Bridge, which is why the hotel's windows are triple-glazed. Some bedrooms are more modernized than others; many retain an antique aura with reproductions of traditional furniture and soft, cream-colored bed linen. The size and shape of the rooms vary but all are comfortably furnished, with good maintenance. The hotel's major restaurant, La Marmite, deserves a separate recommendation (see "Where to Dine," below).

5, rue des Bouchers, CH-1700 Fribourg. ✆ **026/350-81-00.** Fax 026/350-81-81. www.hotelducberthold.ch. 36 units. 180SF–230SF ($99–$126.50) double. Rates include breakfast. AE, DC, MC, V. Bus: 1 or 2. **Amenities:** 2 restaurants, bar; room service; babysitting; laundry/dry cleaning. *In room:* TV, minibar, hair dryer.

WHERE TO DINE
Auberge de Zähringen ✪ SWISS This 17th-century, former private residence attracts seasoned diners. On the ground floor the owners have established both a brasserie and a more intimate French restaurant. The restaurant offers such seasonal specialties as rack of rabbit and pike-perch, plus a ragoût of fresh mushrooms in a Gruyère-cream sauce and game cock sautéed with fresh mushrooms. The brasserie has drinks, light meals, and platters of food available during the afternoon.

13, rue de Zähringen. ✆ **026/322-42-36.** Reservations required in the restaurant. Restaurant, main courses 25SF–53SF ($13.75–$29.15); fixed-price menu 63SF–115SF ($34.65–$63.25). Brasserie, fixed-price menu 36SF–46SF ($19.80–$25.30). AE, DC, MC, V. Mon 7:30–10:30pm, Tues–Sun noon–1:30pm and 6:30–9:30pm. Closed Sun–Mon July–Aug. Bus: 1 or 2.

La Fleur-de-Lys ★★★ FRENCH   This is the most outstanding restaurant in Fribourg, dwarfing the competition. Elegant and charming, the restaurant is a showcase for the culinary skills of Pierre-Andre Ayer, who offers a magic combination: great food at affordable prices. The service is formal without being stiff, and Ayer shops for only the finest ingredients in any season, which he shapes into an array of specialties that show both inventiveness and a solid technique. Typical seasonal specialties include in May and June a delectable lake perch served with an asparagus-stuffed ravioli and crunchy vegetables. In spring you can also enjoy fresh cherries poached in red wine. From November to March a ravioli stuffed with black sausage appears on the menu, a dish made even more delightful by its accompaniment of wild berries and a cider-flavored butter.

18, rue des Forgerons. ℭ 026/322-7961. Reservations required. Lunch main courses 15SF–45SF ($8.25–$24.75); dinner main courses 62SF–95SF ($34.10–$52.25). AE, DC, MC, V. Tues–Sat noon–2pm and 7–10pm. Closed Feb 25–Mar 6 and Aug.

Restaurant La Marmite ★ *Finds* FRENCH   This restaurant offers perfect continental cuisine and lovely antique decor. It has a ceramic stove, paintings, and intimate lighting. The chef's specialties include a parfait of smoked salmon with langoustines; ravioli with foie gras; sea bass cooked with eggplant, tomatoes, and black olives; and partridge suprême with wild mushrooms. Although La Marmite shuts down on weekends, the brasserie, L'Escargot, remains open with basically the same menu.

In the Hôtel Duc Bertold, 112, rue des Bouchers. ℭ **026/350-81-00.** Reservations required. Main courses 32SF–52SF ($17.60–$28.60); fixed-price menu 52SF ($28.60) at lunch, 95SF ($52.25) at dinner. AE, DC, MC, V. Mon–Fri 11:30am–1:30pm and 6:30–9:30pm. Bus: 1 or 2.

FRIBOURG AFTER DARK

You'll find more cafes and hole-in-the-wall bars around Fribourg's railway station than anywhere else in town, especially along either side of boulevard de Pérolles, rue de Romont, and rue de l'Hôpital. A particularly cozy bar is **La Cave de la Rose,** in the cellar of the also-recommended Hôtel de la Rose, 1, rue de Morat (ℭ **026/322-24-44**). There's also a piano bar, where music begins every night around 10pm, in the previously recommended **Golden Tulip hotel,** and at least two discos. One of these **Le Macumba,** 17, route de Tavel (ℭ **026/ 481-33-88**), is a high-energy, high-volume disco favored by folks under 30. A bit more mellow and sedate is the well-recommended disco in the cellar of the **Restaurant l'Escale,** 3, route de Belfaux, in the suburb of Givisiez (ℭ **026/ 466-27-67**), half a mile west of Fribourg's commercial core.

The latest hot spot is **Planet Edelweiss,** Mariahilf, Düdingen ℭ **026/ 492-0505,** an 18th-century inn converted into a bustling restaurant and dance club. It draws a young crowd to its location a 5-minute ride northeast of the center. At the train depot, in Fribourg, a taxi ride costs 22SF ($12.10). The club keeps the latest hours in the area: until 2am Sunday to Tuesday, 3am Wednesday and Thursday, and 4am Friday and Saturday.

4 Gruyères ★★

4 miles (6km) S of Bulle, 40 miles (64km) SW of Bern, 27 miles (43km) E of Palézieux

This small town, which once belonged to the counts of Gruyères, is known for its castle and its cheese. It's a highlight for anyone taking the "cheese route" through Switzerland. It's also a good base for exploring the district of Gruyère (the region is spelled without an "s").

In the canton of Fribourg, the little town of Gruyères seems to slumber somewhere back in the Middle Ages. Enclosed by 12th-century ramparts, it's dominated by a castle, where the counts lived from the 12th to the 16th century. Their crest, which bears a crane, is still used in Gruyères.

Cars are forbidden to enter between Easter and the first of November (and on Sun year-round). Therefore you must park your car outside the gates and walk into town. Everything can be explored on foot.

ESSENTIALS

GETTING THERE   From either Lausanne or Zurich, most Gruyères-bound passengers transfer at the busy railway junction of Palézieux. From here, a secondary railway spur leads to Gruyères, stopping at about 20 other hamlets along the way. Trip time from Zurich to Gruyères is about 4½ hours; from Palézieux to Gruyères, about 1 hour. For **train information,** call ℭ **0900-300-300.**

About seven buses a day connect Gruyères with the rail and bus junction of Bulle, a 10-minute drive northwest of Gruyères. From Bulle, you can make bus connections to Fribourg and rail connections to the rest of Switzerland. For **bus schedules** and information, call ℭ **026/913-05-21.**

If you're driving from Bern, head southwest along N12 and take the southeast turnoff to Bulle; Gruyères is signposted from there.

VISITOR INFORMATION   The **Office du Tourisme** (ℭ **026/921-10-30**) is in the center of the village, open Monday to Friday 9am to noon and 1:30 to 5pm, Saturday and Sunday 10am to 4pm. Street names aren't used—the village is very small.

SEEING THE SIGHTS

If you're here when the tour buses aren't, you'll discover one of the most charming villages on the Continent.

At the entrance to town, at the foot of a hill near the railway station, the Swiss Cheese Union operates a model dairy, **Fromagerie de Démonstration,** près de la gare, at Pringy (ℭ **026/921-84-00**), for demonstration purposes. Here you can see workers produce the famed Gruyère cheese (a single wheel weighs 75 lb.), which is a more piquant version of the equally famous Emmenthaler. An audiovisual show reveals how the cheese is made. The dairy is open daily from 9am to noon and 1:30 to 7pm, but it's best to go between 10 and 11am or 2 and 3pm, when the cheese is actually being made. In July and August, daily hours are 7am to 7pm. For information, contact the tourism office (see above).

The traditional lunch in all the restaurants here is **raclette.** A machine is usually placed on your table, so you can melt and scrape the cheese at your own speed. You can eat right down to the rind, which is crunchy and considered by many to be the best part of the raclette. In the right season, you can finish with a large bowl of fresh raspberries in thick cream.

You can walk the cobblestone road to the **Château Gruyères** ✦ (ℭ **026/921-21-02**), passing the house of the famed court jester Chalamala. Dating mostly from the 15th century, the castle, or chateau, is owned today by the canton of Fribourg. In 1848 the Bovy family of Geneva acquired it and ordered many of its embellishments. Several famous artists, including Corot, have lived here. The chateau is filled with objets d'art, the most outstanding of which are three mourning copes from the Order of the Golden Fleece—part of the bounty grabbed up in the Burgundian wars. The castle is open to the public June through September daily from 9am to 6pm; March through May and October daily from

9am to noon and 1 to 6pm; and November to February daily from 9:30am to noon and 1:30 to 4pm (till 5pm on weekends). Admission is 6SF ($3.30).

WHERE TO STAY

Hostellerie des Chevaliers ★★   This atmospheric hotel is set at the end of a private driveway near the main town square and thus avoids the bus hordes who descend upon Gruyères. The restaurant section is in a 1950s private villa. The comfortable, conservative, mid-sized bedrooms are situated a few steps away in a more recent addition, and the best rooms offer sweeping views of the valley. All units are well maintained and contain neatly kept bathrooms.

Both guests and nonguests are welcome to visit the three elegant dining rooms. The one with the best view is covered from floor to ceiling with garden lattices. The others have a scattering of antiques, Delft tiles, and paneling.

CH-1663 Gruyères. (C) **026/921-19-33.** Fax 026/921-25-52. www.gruyeres-hotels.ch/chevaliers. 30 units. 160SF–220SF ($88–$121) double. Rates include breakfast. AE, DC, MC, V. Free parking. Closed Jan to Feb 15. **Amenities:** Restaurant, lounge; room service; laundry/dry cleaning. *In room:* TV, minibar.

Hostellerie de St-Georges ★★★   This peaceful hideaway is the best place to stay in the region. The building, which dates from the 1500s, offers well-furnished bedrooms, all with new beds and bathrooms.

✐ An Ode to Cows & Cheese

Their bovine forms enhance many an alpine panorama, but have you ever considered that the cows of Switzerland do more than provide local color? With the help of the farmers who tend them, they produce milk for cheese—lots of it, and in such abundance and variety that the modern Swiss are endearingly thin-skinned about anyone who refers to Switzerland as the land of cheese and whey.

The output is staggering. Annual production of alpine cheeses is around 34,000 metric tons, a satisfyingly profitable amount considering the brutal terrain of the alpine pastures on which the cheese is produced.

Don't think for a moment that cheese production in Switzerland is as automated as, say, the steel or watchmaking industry. Some aspects of the craft defy modernization, and many of the basic needs of the dairy industry are still fulfilled by the time-tested agrarian methods of yesteryear. Many cheese-making families continue to ferment their cows' milk in old-fashioned iron vats over wood-burning fires, form the cheeses in wooden cheese presses on pinewood tables, and immerse the cheese wheels by hand in their obligatory series of saltwater baths.

Our favorite cheese? Gruyère, the tangy yellow cheese with holes, a tough outer rind, and a flavor that's absolutely divine. Hundreds of more esoteric cheeses are loaded onto the country's cheese boards, but Gruyère (produced in the mountains of French-speaking Switzerland) is still a perennial favorite. Despite the aggressive efforts of the Swiss cheese industry to prevent it, Gruyère and its closely related cousin, Emmenthaler, are still referred to rather imprecisely as "Swiss cheese" throughout England and the Americas.

There's a cozy cafe suitable for drinks, snacks, and light lunches. But many guests prefer the old-world charm of the formal dining room in back, where specialties include filet of beef served on a slate platter, breast of duckling with green peppercorns, and a quiche made with—of course—Gruyère cheese.

CH-1663 Gruyères. ℂ 026/921-83-00. Fax 026/921-83-39. Hostellerie-st-georges@swissonline.ch. 14 units. 160SF–280SF ($88–$154) double. Rates include continental breakfast. AE, DC, MC, V. Closed Nov and last 2 weeks of Jan. **Amenities:** 2 restaurants, lounge; laundry. *In room:* TV, minibar.

Hôtel de Ville *Value* Housed in a historic building in the center of the old town, Michel Murith's hotel offers comfortable, pleasantly furnished rooms, all of which contain tidy bathrooms. There is also a terrace cafe in front. The restaurant serves such specialties as ham and trout. Like the hotel housing it, the restaurant is one of the best bargains in town.

CH-1663 Gruyères. ℂ 026/921-24-24. Fax 026/921-36-28. www.hoteldeville.ch. 8 units. 180SF–300SF ($99–$165) double; 280SF ($154) junior suite. Rates include continental breakfast. AE, DC, MC, V. **Amenities:** Restaurant, lounge; laundry/dry cleaning. *In room:* TV, safe.

WHERE TO DINE

Restaurant le Chalet de Gruyères *Finds* SWISS One of the most popular and evocative restaurants in town specializes in any dish that can be made with the region's most famous product—cheese. Built in the 1700s a few paces from the chateau, and functioning as a traditional restaurant since the early 20th century, it counts former U.S. president Jimmy Carter as one of its patrons. Amid aged timbers, honey-colored planks, and polished farm tools, you can order *assiettes gruyèriennes* (Gruyères plates) piled high with ham, cheese, sausages, and air-dried beef; Gruyère salads; *croûtes aux Gruyère* garnished with salad and ham; several kinds of fondues with bread and potatoes; and raclettes. For anyone not interested in cheese, there's a savory mixed grill of meats and sausages.

Rue Principale. ℂ 026/921-21-54. Reservations recommended. Main courses 17SF–42SF ($9.35–$23.10). AE, DC, MC, V. Daily 11am–10:30pm.

5 Murten

11 miles (18km) N of Fribourg, 19 miles (30km) W of Bern

Of the many ancient towns in Switzerland, we find Murten to be one of the most idyllic and beautifully preserved. The town sits on what is called the "language demarcation line," and its residents speak either French or German, quite often both. Lying on the southern side of the lake Murtensee, known in French as Lac de Morat, Murten forms a gateway into French-speaking Switzerland. Outside Murten, on June 22, 1476, a fierce battle was fought between the Confederates and Charles the Bold of Burgundy.

ESSENTIALS

GETTING THERE Murten is connected by direct rail line to Fribourg, a 30-minute ride away. About 20 trains a day make the run, stopping off at about six hamlets along the way. Murten also has good connections to the nearby town of Ins, which lies directly on most of the train routes between Zurich and Paris. For **train information,** call ℂ 0900-300-300. If you'd like to rent a bike, stop in at the station; a kiosk rents bikes for 25SF ($13.75) a day.

A **boat ride** is quite a restful way to reach Murten over the lakes that lie to the north and west. Ferries make the water crossing between Neuchâtel and Murten about five times daily between late May and late September. It takes about 1¾ hours to cross the two lakes (Lac de Neuchâtel and Murtensee) and the canal (La Broye) that connects them; the one-way boat fare is 16.40SF ($9). Call ℂ **026/670-26-03** for more information.

In midsummer, another way to reach Murten is from Biel (Bienne). Between late May and late September, a ferry departs Tuesday to Sunday from the central piers in Biel at 11:20am, arriving in Murten at 3:30pm. One-way transit costs 28.50SF ($15.70) and will take you through three lakes (Bielersee, Lac de Neuchâtel, and Murtensee) and across the canals connecting them.

If you're driving, head west from Bern on Route 10 and turn south to Murten at the junction with Route 22.

VISITOR INFORMATION   The **Murten Tourist Information Office** is at Französische Kirschgasse 6 (ℂ **026/670-51-12**), open Monday to Friday 9am to noon and 2 to 6pm, Saturday 10am to 2pm.

EXPLORING THE AREA

Many houses date from the 15th to the 18th century, and the town itself is surrounded by **medieval ramparts** ⭐⭐ with a wall walk. Today you can stroll along the wall, taking in the view over Altstadt (Old Town) with the castle, lake, and Jura Mountains as a backdrop.

Duke Peter of Savoy built the town's **castle** in the 13th century. It's bleak and foreboding, but impressive nevertheless, and from its inner courtyard (which you can enter for free) there's a vista of the lake and the Jura foothills.

The main street, **Hauptgasse** ⭐, is the major attraction of Murten, running through the center of the old quarter. It leads to the baroque **Bernegate,** which contains one of the oldest clock towers in the country, dating from 1712.

Musée Historique, adjacent to the castle (ℂ **026/670-31-00**), contains everything from archaeological excavations revealing the city's earliest history to a diorama of the 15th-century Battle of Morat. It's housed in an 8-century-old mill a few steps from the walls of the castle. The museum shows a film featuring the Battle of Murten, one of the defining moments in the history of the Swiss cantons. It's open May to September Tuesday to Sunday from 10am to noon and 2 to 5pm; March to April and October to December, Tuesday to Sunday from 2 to 5pm; and January and February, only on Saturday and Sunday from 2 to 5pm. Admission is 4SF ($2.20) for adults, 3SF ($1.65) for seniors, 2SF ($1.10) for students, 1SF (55¢) for children 6 to 16, and free for children 5 and under.

Nearby, **Murtensee** ⭐, or Lac de Morat, spread over nearly 10 square miles, has a maximum depth of 150 feet. Between late May and September, you can take boat trips and circular tours on the three lakes from Murten to Neuchâtel to Biel (Bienne), with trips through the canals in the Great Marshes. Check with the tourist office for information on these excursions.

One of the most enchanting **bike rides** in this part of Switzerland is around Lake Murten. The tourist office (see above) will provide maps, and you can set out on your own. You can rent a bike at the rail station and visit such lakeside villages as Faoug, Salavaux, Bellerive, and Vully. Allow about 4 hours for this 25-mile (40km) jaunt.

WHERE TO STAY & DINE

Hotel Krone (Hôtel de la Couronne) 𝒱𝒶𝓁𝓊ℯ   This is a heavily gabled building in the center of town that was originally a 15th-century inn. It offers well-maintained, orderly accommodations at reasonable prices. All units contain neatly kept bathrooms. Some rooms are small; those opening onto the lake are the most sought after. The owners, Werner and Christine Nyffeler, oversee service at the hotel's five eating areas. You can opt for the street-level pizzeria, which also serves fondue, or the adjacent Café-Brasserie. A large sunny restaurant and open-air terrace can be found one floor above the lobby, offering a salad bar with as many as two dozen varieties of vegetables.

Rathausgasse 5, CH-3280 Murten. ℭ **026/670-52-52.** Fax 026/670-36-10. 33 units. 150SF–180SF ($82.50–$99) double. Rates include continental breakfast. AE, DC, MC, V. Closed Nov 10–Dec 10. **Amenities:** 3 restaurants, bar; room service; laundry/dry cleaning. *In room:* TV, minibar.

Hotel Schiff   Located at the edge of the lake near the harbor, this hotel is surrounded by parks and operates a lakeside cafe. The building, with 19th-century gables and porches, has a modern extension containing well-decorated public rooms, with Persian rugs, antiques, and lots of gilt. All the units are comfortable and well maintained.

The hotel's restaurant, Lord Nelson, has large windows offering a view of lawns and chestnut trees down to the lake. The French menu is changed every 2 months; in September, during the hunting season, it features game selections. The hotel's dance club is yet another option for an evening activity. Indoor and outdoor swimming pools are a short walk away.

Ryf 53, CH-3280 Murten. ℭ **026/670-27-01.** Fax 026/670-35-31. www.hotel-schiff.ch. 15 units. 220SF–240SF ($121–$132) double. Rates include continental breakfast. AE, DC, MC, V. Parking 8SF ($4.40). **Amenities:** 2 restaurants, bar, nightclub; 2 pools; room service; laundry/dry cleaning. *In room:* TV, minibar, hair dryer.

Hotel Weisses Kreuz (Hôtel de la Croix Blanche) ★★   This is a superb, recently renovated, attractive hotel, with a gracious staff. It's situated on the lake about a 10-minute walk from the train station. The historic buildings—one of which was originally a stable—are set behind a screen of roses on a cobblestone street in the center of the old town. The hotel has a scattering of antiques; the mid-sized bedrooms have either a modern or an antique decor. Some of the bedrooms are across the street on a block without views of the lake. However, don't reject these too quickly, as the accommodations here are among the best in Murten, furnished in a combination of styles ranging from Biedermeier to Louis XVI, and from Empire to Art Nouveau.

Rathausgasse 31, CH-3280 Murten. ℭ **026/670-26-41.** Fax 026/670-28-66. www.weisses.krev.ch. 27 units. 180SF–280SF ($99–$154) double. Rates include continental breakfast. AE, DC, MC, V. Closed Dec–Feb. **Amenities:** Restaurant, lounge; room service; laundry/dry cleaning. *In room:* TV, hair dryer.

Le Vieux Manoir au Lac ★★★ *(Finds)*   Located 1½ miles west of the town center (a 5-minute taxi ride from the train station), this is a gabled, stucco building in an idyllic setting. With a sun deck and balconies overlooking Lake Morat, this is the finest place to stay in the entire area. In the Belle Epoque era, a French military officer—homesick for his native Normandy—constructed this manor with the turrets and half-timbers of his homeland. Inside, the decor blends many periods and styles, with objects such as Persian rugs collected from all over the world. The nice-sized bedrooms are comfortable, furnished with individual style and decor. Country prints abound, making for a cozy atmosphere, and the bedrooms open onto either a landscaped park or the lake.

The restaurant, which has a collection of antiques from around the region, serves excellent French cuisine.

Rte. de Lausanne, CH-3280 Murten-Meyriez. ℭ **026/678-61-61.** Fax 026/678-61-62. www.vieuxmanoir.ch. 30 units. 320SF–390SF ($176–$214.50) double; 540SF ($297) suite. Rates include continental breakfast.

AE, DC, MC, V. Free parking. Closed mid-Dec to mid-Feb. **Amenities:** Restaurant, lounge; room service; laundry/dry cleaning. *In room:* TV, minibar, hair dryer, safe.

6 Neuchâtel ★/★

29 miles (46km) W of Bern, 19 miles (30km) SW of Biel

Neuchâtel lies at the border of a lake of the same name and at the foot of the green slopes of Chaumont (3,871 ft/1,161m). It's the capital of the canton of Neuchâtel, created in 1815 out of a Prussian principality that had joined the Swiss Confederation. The majority of Neuchâtel's population are Protestant and French-speaking (indeed, they're said to speak the finest French in Switzerland). They acquired their fame for watchmaking as early as the 18th century.

Situated at the foot of the Jura Mountains, in the midst of vineyards, Neuchâtel enjoys an idyllic setting. Many of its limestone houses have a distinctive yellow or ocher color, which inspired Alexandre Dumas to describe the town as having been carved out of a "block of butter."

Neuchâtel is also a notable seat of culture and learning, with a university that was founded in 1838.

The French influence is evident in its architecture. Many houses in the old town date back to the 16th century; some were built with defensive towers. The spirit of old Neuchâtel is best seen at the **Maison des Halles,** the market square, where you may want to buy some well-known local cheese—de Jura—for a picnic around the lake after you've walked the long promenade.

No cars are allowed in the center of the old sector.

ESSENTIALS

GETTING THERE Neuchâtel lies at the junction of major rail lines linking Geneva with Basel and Zurich with Paris. Travel time to Neuchâtel from Geneva is about 90 minutes; from Zurich, about 2½ hours. For **train information,** call ✆ **0900-300-300.**

Ferries arrive in Neuchâtel about five times a day, in both winter and summer, from Murten (Morat). The trip takes about 1¾ hours. The one-way boat fare is 16.40SF ($9). For **ferry information,** call ✆ **032/729-96-00.** For a longer boat itinerary, available only in the summer, see "Essentials" under section 5 earlier in this chapter.

If you're driving from Bern, take Route 10 west, then Route 5 south to Neuchâtel.

VISITOR INFORMATION For more information, contact the **tourist office** at Hotel des Postes (✆ **032/889-68-90**), open Monday to Friday 9am to noon and 1:30 to 5:30pm, Saturday 9am to noon.

SEEING THE SIGHTS

The medieval core of Neuchâtel is dominated by three architectural attractions: a castle (chateau), a collégial (University Church), and the Prison Tower (Tour des Prisons), standing on the highest peak of the city. Of the three, the building that has been altered most over the centuries is the **castle** ★ (✆ **032/889-68-00**). Its oldest section, the west wing, dates from the 12th century, but most of what you'll see today was added during the 15th, 16th, and 17th centuries. The structure is stern and forbidding; from some of its ramparts you get a panoramic view of the old town. To visit the castle's interior, apply to the building's concierge (you'll find him near the gate to the castle, under an archway). Accompanied visits, for a minimum of two or three people, are conducted Monday to Saturday at 10 and 11am, and 2, 3, and 4pm; and Sunday at 2, 3, and 4pm. The castle is open daily 10am to 6pm. Admission is free.

Next door, the **Eglise Collégial** was built during the 12th and 13th centuries, though sections of it, most notably the western towers, were a 19th-century embellishment, constructed when the church underwent (some say suffered) a major overhaul. The building's highlight, found in the Romanesque choir, is a monument to the counts of Neuchâtel, created during the 14th century. Adorned with 15 painted effigies of almost-forgotten noblemen, this is the most spectacular Gothic memorial in the country. The collégial is open daily from 8am to 8pm (to 6pm in the winter); admission is free.

Tour des Prisons, rue Hochberg, offers a panoramic view. It was a jail until 1850. It's open 24 hours a day every day from Easter to September. Admission, via a Metro-style turnstile, is .50SF (30¢).

The **Griffin Fountain,** from 1664, stands nearby on rue du Château. It's one of the most famous fountains in the country, thanks to Henri II of Orléans, who in 1657 had it filled with 1,300 gallons of red wine to honor his entry into Neuchâtel.

Stroll into the garden of the **Hôtel du Peyrou,** faubourg de l'Hôpital, dating from 1764. This excellent patrician house was constructed for Monsieur du Peyrou, who was a friend of Jean-Jacques Rousseau and published some of his works. *The Bather,* a statue in the pool, is by Ramseyer.

For a view of the Lake of Neuchâtel and the distant Alps, take a funicular to the **Crête du Plan,** a height of 1,962 feet. Approach from rue de l'Ecluse, on the border of the medieval sector.

Neuchâtel doesn't lack for shopping options, many of which lie near the railway station in the heart of town. Three of your best bets for crafts and souvenirs are the **Magazin Cachet,** 2, rue de Saint-Honoré (© **032/721-20-22**); a somewhat less elegant competitor, the **Magazin Naville,** place Pury (© **032/724-47-50**); and a relatively upscale alternative, **Unip,** 3, rue des Epancheurs (© **032/724-79-00**).

In and around Neuchâtel are 250 miles of signposted **mountain bike trails.** Free trail maps are distributed by the tourist office (see above). Mountain bikes are rented at **Alizé,** place du 12-Septembre (© **032/724-40-90**).

WHERE TO STAY

Beau-Rivage ★★★   This is the grandest place to stay in town. A hotel since the 1800s, this graceful lakeside property has been splendidly rejuvenated and should last long into the 21st century. When you pull back the draperies of your bedroom window, you're rewarded with a panoramic alpine view. In the heart of Neuchâtel, this tranquil oasis reopened in 1993 after a long slumber. It's in the grand hotel tradition with luxurious bedrooms, spacious and airy and comfortably furnished. Only one-third of the bedrooms lack lakeside views. Elegant fabrics and cherry-wood furnishings and paneling add to the allure of the hotel. The cuisine at the restaurant here is imaginative, with an array of seasonal produce and fine wines.

1 Esplanade de Mont-Blanc, CH-2001 Neuchâtel. © **032/723-15-15.** Fax 032/723-161-16. 360SF–420SF ($198–$231) double, from 490SF ($269.50) suite. Children up to 16 free in parents' room. AE, DC, MC, V. **Amenities:** Restaurant, bar; room service; laundry/dry cleaning. *In room:* TV, minibar, hair dryer, safe.

Hôtel Beaulac ★   Set near the intersection of quai Léopold-Robert and quai du Port, this hotel's angular modernity strikes a glaring note when compared to the 18th-century sandstone buildings surrounding it. Nevertheless, it's one of the city's leading hotels. Across from the Museum of Art and History, it enjoys a lakefront location, with panoramic vistas extending toward the Alps. The bedrooms are well maintained and comfortable, but not stylish, often containing Formica, 1960s tiles, and vinyls. Guests can watch the activity of the nearby marina from cafe tables on the hotel's waterside terrace.

2, quai Léopold-Robert, CH-2000 Neuchâtel. ℂ **032/723-11-11.** Fax 032/725-60-35. www.beaulac.ch. 80 units. 230SF–300SF ($126.50–$165) double; 550SF–600SF ($302.50–$330) suite. Rates include continental breakfast. AE, DC, MC, V. Parking 10SF ($5.50). Bus: 1. **Amenities:** 2 restaurants, lounge; room service; laundry/dry cleaning. In room: TV, minibar, hair dryer.

Hôtel City _Value_   The hotel, a dignified building erected in the early 1800s, is in the commercial center of town, across the street from Neuchâtel's Art Nouveau post office. Its owners, Thony and Madelein Blaettler, offer carefully scrubbed, mid-sized rooms containing Louis XIV reproductions and modern beds and bathrooms, which for the most part are equipped with shower-tub combinations. Known for its good value, the hotel welcomes a varied clientele, ranging from foreign diplomats and domestic bankers to budget-conscious travelers.

12, place A. M. Piaget, CH-2000 Neuchâtel. ℂ **032/725-25-77.** Fax 032/721-38-69. 35 units. 135SF–150SF ($74.25–$82.50) double; 180SF ($99) suite. Rates include continental breakfast. AE, DC, MC, V. Free parking. Bus: 1. **Amenities:** Restaurant, lounge. In room: TV, minibar.

La Maison du Prussien _Finds_   The setting for this historic inn lies, ironically, within an industrial zone of Neuchâtel, 3 miles (5km) west of the center, but thanks to a protective barrier of trees, you'd imagine yourself in a sylvan corner of the Swiss forest. The site was the setting for a series of mills—at least three of them—that first appeared in 1614, and a brewery that was founded in 1798. In 1991, it was transformed into a hotel and then a restaurant. Today it's a stylish enclave of good food and comfort, with its original ocher-colored stone walls (local geologists refer to it as "stone from Hautrive"), half-timbering, and a sprawling terrace that encompasses a view of the waterfall that used to turn the grinding wheels of the mills. Each of the bedrooms has at least one wall of the exposed original stone, as well as comfortable furnishings. Although the rooms are attractive, most guests come here for the food, which is centered around the local produce, fish, and game, and local wines.

Au Gor du Vauseyon, CH-2006 Neuchâtel. ℂ **032/730-5454.** Fax 032/730-2143. www.hotel-Prussien.ch. 10 units. 165SF–200SF ($90.75–$110) double; 290SF ($159.50) suite. AE, DC, MC, V. From the center, follow the signs to La Chaux-de-Fonds, then turn off toward Pontarlier-Vauseyon. Signs point to the hotel. **Amenities:** Restaurant, lounge. In room: TV, minibar, hair dryer.

WHERE TO DINE

La Maison des Halles _CONTINENTAL_   One of the most appealing and deeply entrenched restaurants in town lies in the pedestrian zone of the commercial center. One floor above street level is the relatively exclusive restaurant gastronomique. Here, amid white walls and pink napery, and with service rituals patterned after the grand bourgeois restaurants of Paris or Lyon, you'll dine on food that's fussier and more delicate (and more expensive) than in the earthier, more raucous, brasserie downstairs. Stellar examples include filet of duckling with orange sauce, or sweetbreads with a mustard sauce. In the street-level brasserie, look for lots of varnished wood, turn-of-the-century-style mirrors, leather banquettes, and such rib-sticking food as freshwater fera from the nearby lake that's served with a sauce Neuchâtelois made from white wine, cream, baby onions, and capers; or filet of lake perch with butter-flavored parsley sauce.

4, rue du Trésor. ℂ **032/724-31-41.** Reservations recommended. Restaurant, main courses 25SF–44SF ($13.75–$24.20); fixed-price menus 78SF–110SF ($42.90–$60.50). Brasserie, main courses 9SF–35SF ($4.95–$19.25); fixed-price menu 12SF–46SF ($6.60–$25.30). MC, V. Restaurant daily noon–2pm and 7pm–midnight; brasserie daily 11am–midnight.

NEUCHÂTEL AFTER DARK

As a university town, Neuchâtel is lively when the sun goes down. The hot spot is the **Casino de la Rotonde,** Faubourg du lac 14 (ℂ **032/724-48-48**), with a trio of dance clubs. The town has popularized the *bar musicaux* in this part of Switzerland, and many places now stay open until dawn, offering food and music. The best of these is **Garbo,** a bar and disco at 5–7, rue de Chavannes (ℂ **032/724-31-81**), where you can eat, drink, and dance the night away from 9pm to 6am daily. Its chief rival, keeping the same hours, is **Dakota,** 3, av. de la Gare (ℂ **032/710-07-05**). A young crowd mostly composed of students flocks nightly to the town's hottest pub, **Le Shakespeare,** 7, rue des Terreaux (ℂ **032/ 725-85-88**). On weekends this pub often imposes a 15SF ($8.25) cover charge.

6

Bern

As the Swiss capital, Bern is an important city of diplomats and the site of many international organizations and meetings. It's one of the oldest and loveliest cities in Europe, with origins going back to the 12th century. Since much of its medieval architecture remains today, Bern evokes the feeling of a large provincial town rather than a city. In 1983, the United Nations declared it a World Cultural Landmark.

Over the years the city landscape has been praised by many famous visitors, including Horace Walpole, who called it "the most Faire city." Dorothy, sister of William Wordsworth, gushed, "There is a beautiful order, a solidity, a gravity in this city, which strikes one at first sight and then never loses its effect."

The modern mingles harmoniously with the old in this charming city, and in recent years residents have discreetly added contemporary-style homes and structures to the historic environment. Such coexistence between the old and new is also evident in Bern's university, known equally for traditional studies and pioneering scientific research.

Bern joined the Swiss Confederation in 1353. In 1848, it replaced Zurich as the seat of the federal government. The city stands on a thumb of land that's bordered on three sides by the Aare River, hence the several bridges connecting various sections of the city.

Market days in Bern—ideal times to visit—are Tuesday and Saturday. People from the outlying areas come to town to sell their produce and wares. If you're fortunate enough to be in town on the fourth Monday of November, you'll witness the centuries-old **Zwiebelmarkt** (*Zibelemärit,* in the local dialect), or Onion Market. This is the city's last big event before the onset of winter, and residents traditionally stock up on onions in anticipation of the first snows. In the historic core of Bern, vendors arrive before dawn to set up stalls featuring plaited strings of onions. It is customary to sell some 100 tons of onions in one day during the festival. It's not all salesmanship either—buffoons disguised as onions run about, barrels of confetti are thrown, and a good time is had by all. Naturally, local restaurants feature all their special dishes made with onions at the time.

Bern is also a popular starting point for many excursions, especially to the lakes and peaks of the Bernese Oberland (see chapter 7)—a vast recreational area only minutes from the capital.

1 Orientation

ESSENTIALS
GETTING THERE
BY PLANE   The **Bern-Belp Airport** (© **031/960-21-11**) is 6 miles south of the city in the town of Belpmoos. International flights arrive from London,

Paris, and Nice, but transatlantic jets are not able to land here. Fortunately, it's a short hop to Bern from the international airports in Zurich and Geneva.

Bern is connected by air links to the rest of the world by **Swissair** (© **0848/ 800-700**). **Crossair Airlines** connects Bern to Basel, Lugano, and Paris. For reservations, call © **031/960-2121. Swisswings Airlines** links Bern to Amsterdam, London City Airport, and Munich. For information, call © **0848/ 848-328.**

A taxi from the airport to the city center costs about 45SF ($24.75), so it's better to take the shuttle bus that runs between the airport and the Bahnhof (train station)—it costs 14SF ($7.70) one-way.

BY TRAIN   Bern has direct connections to the continental rail network that includes France, Italy, Germany, the Benelux countries, and even Scandinavia and Spain. The TGV high-speed train connects Paris with Bern in just 4½ hours. Bern also lies on major Swiss rail links, particularly those connecting Geneva (90 min.) and Zurich (75 min.). For **rail information** and schedules, call © **0900/ 300-300.**

The **Bahnhof** rail station, on Bahnhofplatz, is right in the center of town near all the major hotels. If your luggage is light, you can walk to your hotel; otherwise, take one of the taxis waiting outside the station.

BY CAR   Bern lies at a major expressway junction, with E17 coming in east from Zurich, N2 heading south from Basel, and N12 running north from Lake Geneva.

VISITOR INFORMATION
Bern Tourist Office, in the Bern Bahnhof, on Bahnhofplatz (© **031/ 328-12-12;** www.bernetourism.ch), is open June through September daily from 9am to 8:30pm; October through May Monday through Saturday from 9am to 6:30pm and on Sunday from 10am to 5pm. If you need help finding a hotel room, the tourist office can make a reservation for you in the price range you select.

CITY LAYOUT
MAIN ARTERIES & STREETS   The geography of the city is neatly pressed into a relatively small area, so getting about is quite easy. You can walk to most of the major sights. **Altstadt,** or Old Town, lies on a high rocky plateau that juts out into a "loop" of the Aare River. Most of the major hotels and attractions lie within this loop.

Most arrivals are at the Bahnhof on Bahnhofplatz, in the center of town. From here you can walk along the major arteries of Bern: **Spitalgasse, Marktgasse, Kramgasse,** and **Gerechtigkeitsgasse.** The town's major squares include **Theaterplatz,** with its famed Zytgloggeturm (or Clock Tower), **Kornhausplatz** and its much-photographed Ogre Fountain, and **Rathausplatz,** on which stands the old Rathaus (Town Hall), seat of the cantonal government.

The three major bridges crossing the Aare into this historic loop are **Kirchenfeldbrücke, Kornhausbrücke,** and **Lorrainebrücke.**

FINDING AN ADDRESS   In a system developed during the Middle Ages, street numbers in the city begin in the center of Altstadt, and the numbers increase as they fan out. Even numbers lie on one side of the street, odd numbers on the other.

MAPS   Good local maps are available at the Bern Tourist Office.

NEIGHBORHOODS IN BRIEF

Only two of Bern's many neighborhoods are of particular interest to tourists:

Altstadt   This is the heart of Bern, lying inside a bend of the Aare River. Filled with flower-decked fountains, it encompasses some 3½ miles (6km) of arcades and medieval streets, many reserved for pedestrians only. Its main street is Marktgasse, filled with luxury shops and 17th- and 18th-century houses.

South of the Aare   This sprawling district south of the Aare can be reached by crossing the Kirchenfeldbrücke. The neighborhood contains three major museums, the Swiss Alpine Museum, the Bern Historical Museum, and the Natural History Museum.

2 Getting Around

ON FOOT   This is the only practical means of exploring Altstadt and its many attractions. You can see what there is to see here in about 2½ hours.

Don't overlook the possibility of walks in Greater Bern, including Bern's own mountain, **Gurten,** a popular day-trip destination reached in 25 minutes by tram no. 9 and rack railway. Once here, you'll find walks in many directions and can enjoy a panorama over the Alps. There's also a children's playground.

Walks in and around Bern include 155 miles (250km) of **marked rambling paths.** One of the most scenic runs along the banks of the Aare through the English gardens, the Dählhölzli Zoological Gardens, Elfenau Park, and the Bremgarten woods.

For **jogging and running,** the best spots are the Aare River Run (Dalmaziquai), stretching 2¼ miles (4km), or the Aare River Run—Bear Pits, which is 3 miles (5km) long.

BY BUS & TRAM   The public transportation system, the **Stadtische Verkehrsbetriebe** (SVB), is a reliable, 48-mile (77km) network of buses and trams. Before you board, purchase a ticket from one of the automatic machines (you'll find one at each stop) because conductors don't sell tickets. If you're caught traveling without one, you'll be fined 50SF ($27.50) in addition to the fare for the ride. A short-range ride (within six stations) costs 1.60SF (90¢); a normal ticket, valid for 45 minutes one-way, goes for 2.50SF ($1.40).

To save time and money you might purchase a tourist ticket for 6.50SF ($3.60), which entitles you to unlimited travel on the SVB network. Just get the ticket stamped at the automatic machine before beginning your first trip. One-day tickets are available at the **ticket offices** at Bubenbergplatz 5 (© **031/321-88-88**).

BY TAXI   You can catch a taxi at the public cab ranks, or call a dispatcher; **Nova Taxi** is at © **031/301-11-11, Bären Taxi** at © **031/371-11-11.**

BY CAR   Seeing Bern by car is very impractical due to traffic congestion in Old Town, its confusing layout of one-way streets, and a lack of on-street parking. If you have a car, it's best to park in a public garage and explore the city on foot; its miles of arcades were designed to protect pedestrians from rain, snow, and traffic.

If you want to rent a car to explore the environs, arrangements can be made at **Hertz,** Casinoplatz at Kochergasse 1 (© **031/318-21-60**); or **Avis,** Wabernstrasse 41 (© **031/378-15-15**).

BY BICYCLE   Altstadt is compressed into such a small area that it's better to cover the historic district on foot rather than on a bike (bicycles aren't allowed on many pedestrians-only streets, anyway). However, in Greater Bern and its environs, there are 248 miles of cycling paths. These are marked on a special cycling map available at the tourist office (see above). The narrow yellow lanes throughout the road network are reserved for bikers. The point of departure for most official routes is Bundesplatz in Parliament Square. Special red signs will guide you through a wide variety of landscapes. For 25SF to 27SF ($13.75–$14.85), bikes can be rented at the **SBB Railway Station** (✆ **051/ 20-34-61**). Call a day in advance for a reservation.

✐ *FAST FACTS:* Bern

The following is a quick-reference guide to Bern. For more information, see "Fast Facts: Switzerland," in chapter 2.

Babysitters Babysitting can be arranged through most hotels. Try to make arrangements as far in advance as possible.

Bookstores The best for English-language books is **Stauffacher,** Neuengassan 25 (✆ **031/313-61-36**).

Business Hours Banks are open Monday through Friday from 8am to 4:30pm (on Thurs until 6pm). Most offices are open Monday through Friday from 9am to 5pm, and on Saturday from 9am to noon.

Car Rentals See "Getting Around," above.

Currency Exchange This is available on the lower level of the Bahnhof, on Bahnhofplatz, open daily from 6am to 10pm.

Dentists Call ✆ **0900/57-67-47** for a referral to an English-speaking dentist.

Doctors Call ✆ **0900/57-67-47** for a referral to an English-speaking doctor.

Drugstores Try **Central-Apotheke Volz & Co.,** Zeitglockenlaub 2 (✆ **031/ 311-10-94**). It's near the Clock Tower in Old Town. The staff speaks English and can suggest over-the-counter substitutes for foreign drugs that can't be found in Europe. It's open on Monday from 9am to 6:30pm, Tuesday through Friday from 7:45am to 6:30pm, and on Saturday from 7:45am to 4pm. **Aperto,** at the Bahnhofplatz (✆ **031/311-41-15**), is open daily from 7am to 10pm.

Embassies & Consulates The **U.S. Embassy** is at Jubiläumsstrasse 93 (✆ **031/357-70-11**). Other embassy addresses are: **Canada,** Kirchenfeldstrasse 88 (✆ **031/357-32-00**); and **United Kingdom,** Thunstrasse 50 (✆ **031/359-77-00**). **New Zealand** citizens should call their consulategeneral in Geneva (✆ **022/929-03-50**).

Emergencies Call ✆ **117** for the police, ✆ **144** for an ambulance, ✆ **118** to report a fire, or ✆ **140** for the road patrol, but only for an emergency.

Eyeglasses A large and centrally located optician, **Delta Optik,** Kramgasse 81 (✆ **031/312-11-88**), can replace both eyeglasses and contact lenses.

Hairdressers/Barbers One of the city's best-known hairdressers is **Erminio,** Marktgasse 50 (✆ **031/312-22-33**). There are separate sections for men and women. Hours are Monday through Friday from 9am to 6:30pm and Saturday from 8am to 1pm.

Hospital The city's largest is **Insel Hospital,** Freiburgstrasse ((C) **031/632-21-11**), the clinic affiliated with the University of Bern.

Information See "Visitor Information," above.

Internet Access Internet access is possible at **BTM Medienhaus,** Zeughausgasse 14 ((C) **031/327-11-88**).

Laundry/Dry Cleaning **Jet Wash** is a coin-operated, conveniently located laundry on Dammweg 43 ((C) **031/330-26-30**). For dry cleaning, try **Textilpflege,** Hauptbahnhof ((C) **031/312-00-77**) which is located in the main railway station.

Lost Property The lost property office at Predigergasse 5 ((C) **031/321-50-50**) is open Monday through Friday from 10am to 4pm (until 6pm Thurs).

Luggage Storage/Lockers Storage facilities are available on the lower level of the Bahnhof, on Bahnhofplatz.

Photographic Needs Go to **Coop Ryffihof,** Aarbergergasse 53 ((C) **031/329-71-11**), which has a big film and photography department.

Police The police station is at Waisenhausplatz 32 ((C) **031/321-21-21**).

Post Office The main post office (Schanzenpost), at Schanzenstrasse 4 ((C) **031/386-61-11**), is open Monday through Friday from 7:30am to 7pm, on Saturday from 7:30 to 11:30am. An emergency office at this address is open Sunday from 10am to noon and 4 to 8pm.

Restrooms You'll find public facilities in the Bahnhof and in some squares in Old Town.

Safety Bern is Europe's safest capital. Nevertheless, you should take the usual precautions; protect your valuables. It's generally safe to walk the streets at night, and crimes against women are rare.

Taxes A 7.6% value-added tax (VAT) is included in the price of all goods and services rendered, including hotel and restaurant bills. There are no other special taxes.

Taxis See "Getting Around," above.

Telegrams/Telex/Fax Most hotels will arrange the expedition of faxes and telegrams. If not, head for the main post office (see above).

Transit Information Call (C) **0900/300-300** for **rail information** or (C) **031/370-88-88** for **postal-bus information.**

3 Where to Stay

There are accommodations for most budgets in Bern. As the federal capital, Bern hosts many conventions and international meetings, so the hotels are frequently fully booked. Make a reservation. You can reserve a hotel room in advance either by phone ((C) **031/328-12-10**), or by Internet (www.bernetourism.ch). The service is free.

Altstadt is built on a peninsula so compact that everything is literally "around the corner," including nearly all hotels, more than 150 restaurants, the major sights, 3½ miles (6km) of arcades for shopping—even the weekly farmers' market and the Houses of Parliament.

VERY EXPENSIVE

Hotel Schweizerhof ✮✮✮   This centrally located hotel managed by the Gauer family is popular with diplomats. Built in 1859, it has undergone many renovations since then, and remains one of the grandest hotels in the Swiss capital. It contains many antiques and some of the best decorative art in Bern— 18th-century drawing-room pieces, wall-sized tapestries, and crystal chandeliers. Each room is uniquely decorated, but all offer comfortably upholstered chairs and sofas, with a fairly good chest, desk, or table, as well as neatly maintained bathrooms. There are several formal restaurants, including Yamato, the first Japanese restaurant to open in Bern.

Bahnhofplatz 11, CH-3001 Bern. (✆ **031/326-80-80.** Fax 031/326-80-90. www.schweizerhof-bern.ch. 84 units. 380SF–450SF ($209–$247.50) double; from 590SF ($324.50) suite. AE, DC, MC, V. Parking 26SF ($14.30). Tram: 3, 9, or 12. **Amenities:** 4 restaurants, bar; room service; babysitting; laundry/dry cleaning. *In room:* A/C, TV, minibar, hair dryer.

EXPENSIVE

Allegro Bern ✮✮   We stay here just for the panoramic view of the medieval town center of Bern and the Swiss Alps. That's reason enough to check in—that and the fact that this is one of the top three hotels in town in comfort and grace. The hotel runs as efficiently as a Swiss clock. There is grand comfort everywhere, especially in the mid-sized to spacious bedrooms which are well furnished, immaculately kept, and equipped with combination tubs and showers in the immaculate and well-accessorized bathrooms. The best accommodations are in the Panorama Club at the front of the hotel. These are especially sought out for their view of the Bernese Alps. All units have large beds, modern equipment, and excellent service from a well-trained staff.

Kornhausstrasse 3, CH-3000 Bern. (✆ **031/133-9550.** Fax 031/133-9551. www.srs-worldhotels.com/ Switzerland/bern. 163 units. 300SF ($165) double. AE, DC, MC, V. **Amenities:** 3 restaurants, 2 bars; exercise room; free bike rental; room service; babysitting; laundry/dry cleaning. *In room:* TV, minibar, safe.

Belle Epoque ✮✮✮ *Finds*   This is the hippest, most savvy, and most sophisticated small-scale hotel in town, with a countercultural slant, a charming and hardworking staff, and a flair for elegance and charm. In 1989, an interconnected pair of historic Bern medieval houses were gutted, renovated, and turned into this hotel, devoted to the promotion of Teutonic Art Nouveau (*Jugendstil*). Each of the bedrooms is outfitted with jewel-toned colors, big windows, turn-of-the-century furniture and lighting fixtures, and unusual antique paintings and engravings. Minibars and closets are artfully concealed within trompe-l'oeil replicas of steamer trunks, in a style that's in pleasing contrast to bathrooms that are immaculately tiled (some have Jacuzzis) and very modern, with free condoms on offer. Public rooms are somewhat cramped but beautifully decorated and convivial. They include a cozy bar whose cafe tables extend out under the 17th-century arcades in front. A full renovation of each of the bedrooms in 2000 contributed to this hotel's allure.

Gerechtigkeitsgasse 18, CH-3001 Bern. (✆ **031/311-43-36.** Fax 031/311-39-36. www.belle-epoque.ch. 17 units. 300SF ($165) double; 400SF ($220) suite. Rates include breakfast. AE, DC, MC, V. Bus: 12. **Amenities:** Restaurant, bar; room service; babysitting; laundry/dry cleaning. *In room:* TV, minibar, hair dryer.

Hotel Bern ✮   This six-story hotel, a frequent host to diplomats and business travelers, sits behind one of Bern's most striking Art Deco facades ornamented with arches, columns, and a series of iconoclastic sculptures. The mid-sized guest rooms are comfortable and well furnished, with breakfast areas and firm beds,

Where to Stay in Bern

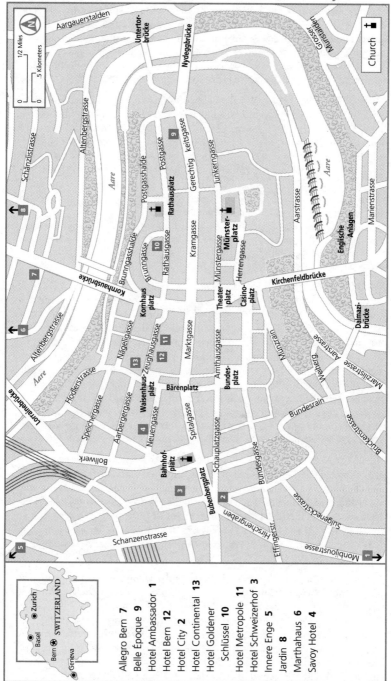

Allegro Bern **7**
Belle Époque **9**
Hotel Ambassador **1**
Hotel Bern **12**
Hotel City **2**
Hotel Continental **13**
Hotel Goldener
  Schlüssel **10**
Hotel Metropole **11**
Hotel Schweizerhof **3**
Innere Enge **5**
Jardin **8**
Marthahaus **6**
Savoy Hotel **4**

plus tidy bathrooms. The best rooms look out onto a garden courtyard. The hotel has nine dining rooms, but most of these are reserved for groups and banquets. The Grill Room is more formal, serving French cuisine.

Zeughausgasse 9, CH-3011. ⓒ 031/329-22-22. Fax 031/329-22-99. 99 units. 220SF–260SF ($121–$143) double; 370SF ($203.50) suite. Rates include buffet breakfast. AE, DC, MC, V. Tram: 9. **Amenities:** 2 restaurants, bar; room service; laundry/dry cleaning. *In room:* TV, minibar, hair dryer, safe.

Innere Enge ★★★ *Finds* When you tire of Bern's impersonal bandbox hotels, head for this converted inn in a building from the 1700s. This small but choice hotel, a 20-minute walk from the center of town, has windows that open onto views of the Bernese Oberland, and the grass and trees around the building make for quite a tranquil setting. The atmosphere in the public rooms is that of Jugendstil or a Teutonic Art Nouveau. The well-kept bedrooms are often spacious and filled with sunshine. Furnishings are traditional, and maintenance meets the high standards set by the manager. The most romantic units are on the top floor, resting under the eaves with sloped ceilings.

Engestrasse 54, CH-3012 Bern. ⓒ 031/309-61-11. Fax 301/309-61-12. www.ghotels.ch. 26 units. 230SF–320SF ($126.50–$176) double. Rates include continental breakfast. AE, DC, MC, V. Free parking. Bus: 21 from the rail station. **Amenities:** Restaurant, bar; room service; babysitting; laundry/dry cleaning. *In room:* TV, minibar, hair dryer.

MODERATE

Hotel Ambassador ★ This nine-story hotel is the tallest building in a neighborhood of old houses with red-tile roofs. The guest rooms come with refrigerators, and many have a view of the federal palace, the Bundeshaus. They tend to be smallish and furnished rather impersonally, but they are well maintained with firm beds and neat bathrooms. Since the hotel caters to business travelers, its rooms offer fax and computer hookups. It's located about a mile from the train station, and easily reached by tram. Dining choices include the Japanese Teppan Restaurant, surrounded by a Japanese garden.

Seftigenstrasse 99, CH-3007 Bern. ⓒ 031/371-41-11. Fax 031/371-41-17. www.fhotels.ch. 97 units. 210SF ($115.50) double. AE, DC, MC, V. Free parking. Tram: 9. **Amenities:** 2 restaurants, lounge; pool; sauna; room service; babysitting; laundry/dry cleaning. *In room:* TV, minibar, hair dryer, safe.

Hotel City Renovated and enlarged in 1993, this six-story, gray-stone, very narrow hotel lies a 2-minute walk from the railway station, attracting both business clients and visitors. It isn't voluptuously ornate or even particularly historic, but it offers well-maintained and simple, modern bedrooms at acceptable prices. All units contain nicely kept bathrooms. Breakfast is the only meal served.

Bubenbergplatz 7, CH-3011, Bern. ⓒ 031/311-53-77. Fax 031/311-06-36. 58 units. 122SF–193SF ($67.10–$106.15) double. AE, DC, MC, V. Free parking. **Amenities:** Lounge; room service; laundry/dry cleaning. *In room:* TV, minibar.

Hotel Continental Another of those fairly anonymous hotels clustered around the Bern rail station, this government-rated three-star choice achieves a grace note with flower boxes blooming in spring at its bedroom windows. The last renovations were in 1997. Filled with shops at ground level, the building lures mainly business travelers during the week, although weekends are more devoted to visitors, often the Swiss themselves. The smallest bedrooms, although a bit lackluster, are still well maintained and furnished with both traditional and modern pieces. Breakfast is served in fair weather under a canopied terrace upstairs.

Zeughausgasse 27, CH-3011 Bern. ⓒ 031/329-21-21. Fax 031/329-21-99. www.hotelbern.ch/continental. 43 units. 140SF–180SF ($77–$99) double. Rates include buffet breakfast. AE, DC, MC, V. Tram: 3 or 9. **Amenities:** Lounge. *In room:* TV.

Hotel Metropole   Located in the city's center, the Metropole offers comfortable if small rooms. Each is furnished with a combination of modern and provincial pieces. Bathrooms are small but tidy and for the most part are equipped with shower-tub combinations. The public rooms are neat and orderly but lack any real style. All of the hotel was entirely refurbished in 1998, but food and bar service has been discontinued. There are plenty of dining choices nearby, as the hotel is well located between the rail station and the Altstadt.

Zeughausgasse 26, CH-3011 Bern. (℃ 031/311-50-21. Fax 031/312-11-53. www.hotelmetropole.ch. 58 units. 195SF ($107.25) double. Rates include buffet breakfast. AE, DC, MC, V. Tram: 9. **Amenities:** Lounge. *In room:* TV, minibar.

Savoy Hotel (*Value*   Close to the main rail depot and the commercial center, this is a traditional Bern hotel of some charm and grace, achieving a four-star rating from the government. The fabled arcaded shopping streets of Bern lie just outside the door. The owners, the Gauer family, have long tired of hearing that this is the "budget version" of the Schweizerhof, a more deluxe choice. This place is more welcoming than many straitlaced Bern hotels; you're even given a free welcome drink. The five-story building shares its entrance with a bank. Rooms are fairly standardized and plain but have recently been renovated and are quite comfortable, with mostly combination tub and shower bathrooms (15 with shower only). Soundproof windows keep the noise outside, and there is also individually adjustable ventilation.

Neuengasse 26, CH-3011 Bern. (℃ 031/311-4405. Fax 031/312-1978. www.ehi.com/travel/ehi/switzerl/ berne-hotels-savoy-hotel.htm. 56 units. 200SF–235SF ($110–$129.25) double; 265SF ($145.75) junior suite. AE, DC, MC, V. **Amenities:** Cafe-bar; room service; laundry/dry cleaning. *In room:* TV, minibar, hair dryer.

INEXPENSIVE

Hotel Goldener Schlüssel *ℛ*   In the heart of Altstadt, opening onto Rathausgasse, the building housing this cozy little inn dates from the 13th century, when it was used as a stable. Any hints of its origins have long been removed, and the house today is beautifully maintained. Some of the carpeted bedrooms have wood-paneled walls. It's fairly busy on the street outside, so ask for one of the rooms in the rear if you prefer it quieter. Immaculate linens on the beds and fresh tiles in the shower-only bathrooms reflect the good housekeeping. If you're a bargain hunter, ask for a room without a shower; the hallway plumbing is adequate. The hotel's sidewalk cafe does a thriving business throughout the summer, and the restaurant (see "Where to Dine," below) offers reasonably priced meals.

Rathausgasse 72, CH-3011 Bern. (℃ 031/311-02-16. Fax 031/311-56-88. 29 units (21 with bathroom). 115SF ($63.25) double without bathroom, 148SF ($81.40) double with bathroom; 155SF ($85.25) triple without bathroom, 190SF ($104.50) triple with bathroom. Rates include continental breakfast. AE, MC, V. Free parking. Tram: 9. Bus: 12. **Amenities:** Restaurant, cafe; room service. *In room:* TV.

Jardin (*Value*   Set about a half mile north of Bern's center, Jardin lies within a leafy residential suburb with lots of parking. This establishment functioned only as a restaurant and apartment building between the year it was built (ca. 1900) and 1985. Then, its apartments were transformed into modern, warmly appealing hotel rooms that are larger than virtually anything else within their price category. All rooms are equipped with private bathrooms. Your hosts are identical twins Andy and Daniel Balz. Joggers and nature enthusiasts appreciate the large verdant spaces (part of a military academy) across the street from this russet-brown, four-story hotel.

Militärstrasse 38, CH-3014 Bern. (℃ 031/333-01-17. Fax 031/333-09-43. www.hoteljardin.ch. 17 units. 141SF ($77.55) double; 205SF ($112.75) triple. Rates include breakfast. AE, DC, MC, V. Free parking. Tram: 9 to Breitenrainplatz. **Amenities:** Restaurant, lounge; laundry/dry cleaning. *In room:* TV.

Marthahaus _Value_   Set within a verdant suburb about a 12-minute walk to the city center, this is a five-story hotel which was originally built around 1900 and has comfortably battered, semi-antique bedrooms that might remind some visitors of a slightly dowdy college dormitory. There's a tiny elevator to carry guests upstairs, and a simple but respectable and clean format that symbolizes good value in an otherwise expensive town. Present management—an organization that directs a pension and retirement fund for women—has been in place here since the 1970s. The most recently renovated rooms contain small private bathrooms, most of which contain shower-tub combinations.

Wyttenbachstrasse 22A, CH-3013 Bern. ✆ **031/332-41-35.** Fax 031/333-33-86. 38 units (6 with bathroom). 95SF ($52.25) double without bathroom; 120SF ($66) double with bathroom. MC, V. Bus: 20. **Amenities:** Lounge. _In room:_ TV.

4 Where to Dine

Bern is a city of international cuisine. There are dozens of specialty restaurants offering everything from paella to porterhouse, in addition to the famous Swiss potato dish, rösti. We recommend sampling one of the charming country inns on the outskirts.

EXPENSIVE

Jack's Brasserie (Stadt Restaurant) ★★ FRENCH/CONTINENTAL Although this restaurant is one of the less formal choices within the Hotel Schweizerhof, it's a nice spot for an important meal or even a celebratory dinner. Decorated along the lines of a Lyonnais bistro, replete with paneling, banquettes, and etched glass, it bustles in a way that's chic, friendly, and matter-of-fact, all at the same time. Menu items include fish soup, the kind of Wiener schnitzels that hang over the sides of the plate, succulent versions of sole meunière and sea bass, veal head _vinaigrette_ for real regional flavor, and smaller platters piled high with salads, risottos, and succulent pastas. You will smack your lips over these luscious and full-flavored dishes inspired by the mood of the chef and what looks good at the market.

In the Hotel Schweizerhof, Bahnhofplatz 11. ✆ **031/326-80-80.** Reservations recommended. Main courses 28SF–63SF ($15.40–$34.65); fixed-price menu 89SF ($48.95). AE, DC, MC, V. Daily 6am–11:30pm. Limited menu daily 1:45–6:15pm.

Restaurant la Terrasse ★ INTERNATIONAL   For a unique gastronomic experience with the Alps as a backdrop, try the refined cuisine in this dining room high above the Aare River. The kitchen is resolutely contemporary, although drawing inspiration from the classic repertoire. All the ingredients are carefully selected and inventively paired. This is the quintessential choice for haute cuisine dining in Bern. The menu might begin with smoked salmon or a mushroom salad, followed by langoustine with olive rice and fresh basil, or else sole in cream sauce with shiitake mushrooms. In fair weather, grilled fish is often served on a summer salad. A pianist adds to the soothing atmosphere.

In the Bellevue Palace, Kochergasse 3. ✆ **031/320-45-45.** Reservations recommended. Main courses 42SF–85SF ($23.10–$46.75). AE, DC, MC, V. Daily noon–2pm and 6–11pm. Closed for dinner in winter. Tram: 3, 9, or 12.

Schulteissenstube ★★★ FRENCH/CONTINENTAL   Set within the august and sometimes sternly formal walls of the Hotel Schweizerhof, this is the kind of restaurant where you could entertain the head of a trade delegation, a well-placed government official, or a top-ranking CEO. Surrounded by carefully maintained paneling and folksy-looking souvenirs, it has an alpine rusticity off-set by some very carefully thought out cuisine. Year after year the discerning palates of Bern are amused and intrigued by the imaginative offerings served here. Once you taste your first bite, you can easily become a loyalist to this well-established place. The menu includes lobster and chive-stuffed ravioli, supreme of guinea fowl with fried scampi and sweet garlic risotto, and a roulade of sad-dle of lamb served with thyme and a medley of fresh tomatoes with red, green, and yellow peppers.

In the Hotel Schweizerhof, Bahnhofplatz 11. ℭ 031/311-4501. Reservations recommended. Main courses 40SF–65SF ($22–$35.75); fixed-price lunch 39SF–120SF ($21.45–$66); fixed-price dinner 75SF–120SF ($41.25–$66). AE, DC, MC, V. Mon–Sat noon–2:30pm and 6–10pm.

Wein & Sein ✿✿✿ INTERNATIONAL   In terms of underground, word-of-mouth chic, this is the most fashionable and hip restaurant in Bern today. Set within the cellar of an historic building in the city's medieval core, it's accessible via a steep staircase that leads you past an open kitchen where a view of the staff comprises part of the allure. Chef and owner Beat Blum, a celebrity whose fame derives from his former administration of a more expensive restaurant near Lucerne, is the impresario who directs the show here. Within a severely spartan-looking dining room, you'll have only one choice—a set-price menu that's writ-ten on a blackboard, and which doesn't allow a lot of room for either variety or indecision. On the night of our latest visit, it consisted of such heavenly con-coctions as braised tuna and free-range chicken served with braised pepperoni in a sweet-and-sour sauce; terrine of melon; beef filet with a vegetable puree; and a quark (white cheese) mousse served with pineapple and homemade ice cream. You'll select your wine from racks at one end of the dining room, a system that affords lots of interplay with the staff over whatever it is that you propose drink-ing with your meal.

Münstergasse 50. ℭ 031/311-98-44. Reservations required. Set-price menu 78SF ($42.90). MC, V. Tues–Sat 6–9pm. Closed 2 weeks in July–Aug. Bus: 12.

MODERATE

Arlequin SWISS/ITALIAN   Bern's society and intelligentsia are attracted to this informal restaurant in the city center rustically decorated with art and bronze pieces. Typical and well-prepared Swiss dishes include chicken pâté with morel mushrooms in puff pastry, farmhouse ham-and-potato salad, and goulash soup. From Wednesday to Friday, the chef is known for turning out Bern's best Wiener schnitzel. There are also the usual offerings of pasta dishes and fresh salads. Dur-ing the summer, tables are set up on the pergola-shaded outdoor terrace.

Gerechtigkeitsgasse 51. ℭ 031/311-39-46. Reservations recommended. Main courses 17SF–35SF ($9.35–$19.25); fixed-price meal 18SF ($9.90). MC, V. Daily 11am–1pm and 5–10pm. Tram: 9.

Churrasco *Kids* ARGENTINIAN   You can imagine yourself in a corny version of Argentina here. The ranchero decor includes cowhide banquettes, hanging lamps fashioned from pierced tin drums, and accessories you might find on the pampas. A chef dressed like a gaucho grills seasoned meats over a wood fire. Por-tions are generous, and the meat is tender and well flavored. Specialties include rumpsteak and entrecôte, along with gazpacho, sangría, fried potatoes, and a spe-cial blend of coffee. Recently they have expanded their menu to include spareribs, fresh fish, and several beef preparations. A special appetizer that kids will appre-ciate is Provolone Dolce, Churrasco's version of the grilled cheese sandwich.

Aarbergergasse 60. ℭ 031/311-82-88. Reservations recommended. Main courses 14SF–45SF ($7.70–$24.75); lunch special 20SF ($11). AE, DC, MC, V. Daily 11:30am–11:30pm. Tram: 9.

Della Casa 🍴 CONTINENTAL Entering the hotel, you'll find yourself immersed in what has been called Switzerland's "unofficial Parliament headquarters." The inner room, often filled with chattering diners, contains the day's newspapers. You'll find a quieter, more formal dining room upstairs. The menu features continental and Italian dishes, such as *bollito misto* (a medley of mixed boiled meats) and rack of lamb. Two local favorites are the *ravioli maison* and the fried zucchini; a popular meat specialty is a filet mignon à la bordelaise with Creole rice. For the more adventurous, try the boiled veal head served with onions, tomatoes, and potatoes with a herbed vinaigrette. The cuisine is very authentic, very savory, and very satisfying.

Schauplatzgasse 16. ☎ **031/311-21-42.** Reservations recommended. Main courses 22SF–38SF ($12.10–$20.90); fixed-price meal 24SF ($13.20). AE, DC, MC, V (downstairs only). Mon–Fri 11am–2pm and 6–9:30pm, Sat 9:30am–3pm. Upstairs level closed July. Tram: 3, 5, or 9.

Frohsinn *Finds* FRENCH/SWISS This little restaurant, containing only a dozen tables, stands in the shadow of the Tour de l'Horioge (Clock Tower). It attracts businesspeople, journalists, and politicians as much for its traditional cuisine as for its cozy atmosphere. The menu might include goose-liver mousse, liver with rösti, or filet of rabbit with watercress. Other dishes reflect a southern Italian influence, especially the homemade ravioli. Sabayon with strawberries is a seasonal specialty. You'll relish most of the dishes, as they are prepared with first-rate ingredients.

Münstergasse 54. ☎ **031/311-37-68.** Reservations required. Main courses 22SF–42SF ($12.10–$23.10). AE, DC, MC, V. Tues–Sat 8am–2pm and 6–11:30pm. Closed July 15–Aug 15. Tram: 54.

Gaumentranz 🍴 *Finds* SWISS/PACIFIC RIM This is a good example of the new and hip restaurants sweeping through the Swiss capital. Small and artsy, it has a decor that leans toward industrial and high-tech design, and a kitchen that's open for viewing. Chef Max Zwahlen prepares a continental menu that's fused with international and Asian overtones, and which changes every 6 weeks. Stellar examples include shrimp with lemongrass, strips of asparagus, and raspberry vinaigrette; pink chicken breast served with salsa verde, galettes of black rice, and spring vegetables; and exotic peppered filets of kangaroo steak with caramelized onions and asparagus in a mustard-flavored cream sauce. Dessert, depending on the inspiration of the chef that night, might include a sumptuous crème brûlée infused with white chocolate.

Gerechtigkeitsgasse 56. ☎ **031/311-64-84.** Main courses 28.50SF–36.50SF ($15.70–$20.10); set-price lunch 17.50SF–18.50SF ($9.65–$10.20). AE, MC, V. Tues–Sat 11am–2pm and 6–10pm.

Goldener Schlüssel 🍴 SWISS As you dine at this very Swiss restaurant, you can relish both the cuisine and the atmosphere. Overhead is the old planking and stonework of a 13th-century building, and you're surrounded by the endless bustle of a workaday restaurant. Serving wholesome and good-tasting food in ample portions, the restaurant is on the street level of a budget-priced hotel of the same name (see "Where to Stay," above). Specialties include a well-flavored *mignon d'agneau au poivre vert* (tenderloin of lamb with green-pepper sauce and corn croquettes), *schweinbratwurst mit zwiebelsauce* (butter-fried sausage with onion sauce), and rösti.

Rathausgasse 72. ☎ **031/311-02-16.** Reservations recommended. Main courses 25SF–35SF ($13.75–$19.25); fixed-price lunch 18SF–22SF ($9.90–$12.10). AE, MC, V. Sun–Thurs 7am–11:30pm, Fri–Sat 7am–12:30am. Tram: 9. Bus 12.

Räblus FRENCH/SWISS REGIONAL The building containing this restaurant is 200 years old, making it the oldest on the street. Centrally located near the Clock Tower, it offers dinner guests a chance to stop for an apéritif in the ground-floor bar before proceeding upstairs to the richly paneled and sculpture-filled dining room. The chef prepares French cuisine with a definite Swiss/German influence. Dishes include potpourri of seafood with Pernod, saffron-flavored sole, citrus-flavored veal, and those old reliables, tournedos Rossini and veal kidney flambé, that have appeared on French menus forever. If not terribly imaginative, the cuisine is satisfying, especially on a cold day. The kitchen is talented, and local produce is deftly handled.

Zeughausgasse 3. © **031/311-59-08.** Reservations required. Main courses 20SF–37SF ($11–$20.35); 3-course fixed-price menus 32SF–57SF ($17.60–$31.35). AE, DC, MC, V. Mon–Wed 6pm–1:30am, Thurs 6pm–2:30am and Fri–Sat 6pm–3:30am. Tram: 3 or 9.

Ratskeller *Kids* SWISS   This historic establishment offers old masonry, modern paneling, and a battalion of busy waitresses serving ample portions of good, rib-sticking food. This dining room has long been the family favorite of locals. Swiss parents who take their children here once were taken here by their parents. Specialties include rack of lamb à la diable for two, an omelet soufflé aux fruits, veal kidneys Robert, and *côte de veau* (veal steak) in butter sauce. Your best bet is the tiny filet of perch ("egli" in German) with white sauce on a bed of spinach. Prized by gourmets, this tiny fish is native to the lakes around Bern.

Gerechtigkeitsgasse 81. © **031/311-17-71.** Reservations recommended. Main courses 20SF–39SF ($11–$21.45). AE, DC, MC, V. Daily 11:30am–2pm and 6–11pm. Tram: 9.

Restaurant Harmonie SWISS/BERNESE   Located at the corner of Münstergasse a few blocks from the Houses of Parliament, this Art Nouveau local favorite evokes 1890s Paris with its grimy overlay. It has been in the hands of the Gyger family since 1915. Service is efficient, and tables are spaced far enough apart to allow a feeling of privacy. There are two separate dining rooms and a handful of sidewalk tables set behind banks of potted geraniums. You get the same regional specialties that Grandmother Gyger might have served between the wars: pork sausage with rösti, tripe with tomatoes, and cheese fondues. If you're not ravenously hungry, go for the simple platter of cooked ham with pickles, pickled onions, and sliced bread.

Hotelgasse 3. © **031/313-11-41.** Reservations recommended. Main courses 20SF–45.50SF ($11–$25.05). MC, V. Mon–Fri 8am–11:30pm. Closed mid-July to mid-Aug. Tram: 9.

Verdi Ristorante, Bar & Enoteca ITALIAN   This is a charmingly decorated Italian hideaway that's more elegant, and more sophisticated, than its reasonable prices would imply. Set near the eastern terminus of one of the most important medieval streets of the old town, it includes at least three different dining areas, simultaneously evoking both a brick-lined trattoria and a grand gourmet restaurant. Accessories include a zinc-topped bar, a vast array of wine that's artfully arranged in a replica of an antique wine cellar, an antipasti buffet, and a fireplace that blazes merrily throughout the winter. Food items are good, classic, and Italian. The best examples include braised artichokes in herb-flavored olive oil, with Parma ham; medallions of angler-fish with white wine and saffron sauce; diced filets of rabbit with mushrooms, olives, and rosemary, served with risotto; and grilled filets of beef with arugula-basil sauce and risotto.

Gerechtigkeitsgasse 5. © **031/312-63-68.** Reservations recommended. Pastas 21SF–27SF ($11.55–$14.85); main courses 29SF–38SF ($15.95–$20.90). AE, DC, MC, V. Daily 11am–2pm and 6–11pm. Bus: 12.

Zum Zähringer ★ *Finds* CONTINENTAL   No restaurant in Bern projects such a high mountain atmosphere. It occupies a weathered chalet that sits across a quiet street from the surging waters of the Aare, at the bottom of the steep cliff whose top contains the cathedral and the rest of medieval Bern. Many aspects, particularly its riverfront terrace, evoke a country inn that's far removed from the politics of the Swiss capital, but with a menu that's much more modern than you might have expected. Menu items are creative and filled with flair. They include asparagus mousse served with a tartare of salmon; house-made terrine with green peppercorn and chutney; braised chicken livers with arugula; pike-perch with chive-flavored cream sauce; an artfully composed "hamburger" of goosemeat with Asian vegetables and Basmati rice; and scallops with spring vegetables served with olive-studded mashed potatoes.

Badgasse 1 (corner of Aaregasse). © 031/311-32-70. Reservations recommended. Main courses 34SF–45SF ($18.70–$24.75); set menus 59SF–69SF ($32.45–$37.95). MC, V. Tues–Fri 11am–2:30pm and 6–11:30pm, Mon and Sat 6–11:30pm.

INEXPENSIVE

Altes Tramdepot Brauerel & Restaurant *Kids* INTERNATIONAL   One of the most visible and popular restaurants on Bern's tourist circuit lies immediately adjacent to the Bear Pits, within what was built around 1900 as a tramway depot. In 1999, the space beneath its soaring, heavily trussed ceiling was transformed into a brewery and brasserie. You'll have to descend into the cellar to see the complicated vats and pipes of the brewery, where any of three kinds of beer—blonde, dark, and white (wheat) beer—are likely to be percolating and fermenting. Many clients gravitate toward the sprawling terrace overlooking a view of the city. Menu items focus on a hearty, wholesome cuisine that goes beautifully with beer. Good-tasting examples include pork sausages with onion sauce and rösti; sliced veal Zurich-style with mushroom sauce and rösti; Wiener schnitzels; beef filet Stroganoff with noodles or rice; grilled spareribs, steak, or shrimp; salads and sandwiches; and at least four different wok-prepared dishes inspired by the cuisine of Thailand. There's even a special menu, each dish of which is named after a species of bear, for children.

Am Bärengraben, Gr. Muristalden 6. © 031/368-14-15. Reservations not necessary. Main courses 17.50SF–34SF ($9.65–$18.70). Children's platters 7.50SF–15SF ($4.15–$8.25). AE, DC, MC, V. Daily 11am–11:30pm. Tram: 12.

Jardin INTERNATIONAL   Set within the Jardin hotel (see above), this is a stately looking restaurant that flourished long before the hotel was established in 1985. Part of its appeal is its ability to be as formal or informal as you want. Consequently, you can snack on cheese croquettes and beer, or dine on something more substantial, such as grilled steaks, minced Zurich-style veal with rösti, and pork schnitzel with braised cabbage.

Militärstrasse 38. © 031/333/01-17. Reservations recommended. Main courses 16SF–45SF ($8.80–$24.75); fixed-price menu 50SF ($27.50). AE, DC, MC, V. Mon–Fri 11am–2pm and 5–10pm. Tram: 9 to Breitenrainplatz.

Kornhaus Keller/Kornhaus Café SWISS/MEDITERRANEAN   This is one of the biggest restaurant and cafe combinations in Bern, with a history going back to the 18th century, when it was a warehouse for grain. It's most famous for its cellar-level beerhall, where you'll find ceilings and walls rich with frescoes, intricate beams and trusses, and baronial trappings of the old-fashioned Teutonic world. Many visitors come down into this cellar (recent renovations added a modern-looking Plexiglass-sided elevator to help access it) just for a drink, but if you want a meal, the venue is old-fashioned, stately, and hearty. Unfortunately, because of its huge size (it holds 462 diners at a time, and the staff can tend to be blasé), it can be just a bit anonymous, although folkloric music at

ALPS   ASPEN

AT&T Direct® Service

The easy way to call home from anywhere.

Global | **AT&T**
connection | direct
with the AT&T | service
Network |

For the easy way to call home, take the attached wallet guide.

nighttime makes things more jovial. Menu items include sautéed breast of chicken with lemon sauce; rack of lamb with fennel; and saltimbocca of sole with saffron-laced risotto. In 1999, management here took over what had originally been a post office, immediately upstairs from the cellar. Today, under soaring vaulted ceilings and a cavernous inner space, you'll find a cafe that's at its most appealing in summer. Then, tables spill out under the arcades that surround the cafe for a replica of something akin to a giant outdoor living room. Menu items in the cafe include salads, sandwiches, salmon with mustard-flavored dill sauce, and bouillabaisse.

Kornhausplatz 18. (*C*) **031/327-72-70.** Reservations recommended in cellar-level restaurant, not necessary in cafe. Main courses in cellar 37.50SF–45.50SF ($20.65–$25.05); platters and snack items in cafe 9.50SF–25SF ($5.25–$13.75); glasses of wine and tea in cafe 4.50SF–5SF ($2.50–$2.75) each. AE, DC, MC, V. Cafe daily 8am–12:30am. Cellar Mon–Sat 11:45am–2pm and daily 6–11pm (last order). Cellar-level bar 6pm–12:30am or 2am, depending on business.

Restaurant Zimmermania (★) (*Value*) FRENCH   This is a small and charming French bistro that's set on a quiet street of Bern's historic core. Inside, you'll find two dining rooms outfitted like something you might have expected in a small French town in the 1920s, a marble-topped service bar, and a menu that emphasizes many classic brasserie-style dishes from France. In addition to a short but well-chosen wine list, you can expect such well-prepared French classics as foie gras of duckling, carpaccio of beef, marinated herring with apple slices and sour cream, fresh oysters, veal kidneys in mustard sauce, rack of lamb with green beans, steak tartare, and guinea fowl roasted with rosemary.

Brunngasse 19. (*C*) **031/311-15-42.** Reservations recommended. Main courses 26.60SF–51SF ($14.65–$28.05); set-price lunch 21.50SF–38.50SF ($11.85–$21.20). Tues–Sat 12:30–2pm and 6–10pm. Closed: July. Tram: 12.

Menuetto VEGETARIAN   Set at a prominent street corner in the heart of Bern's oldest section, this is a well-managed vegetarian restaurant with inventive cuisine. Within a mostly white setting that includes hanging plants and parquet floors, you can order such all-vegetarian dishes as samurai rice (a fancy permutation of tofu); *nasi goreng,* the well-accessorized national rice dish of Indonesia; and a delicious eggplant moussaka. The all-vegetarian broth is superb. Even the wines served here are organic, as is most of the food.

Münstergasse 47 at the Herrengasse. (*C*) **031/311-1448.** Reservations recommended. Main courses 20SF–25SF ($11–$13.75); fixed-price menus 15SF–25SF ($8.25–$13.75). AE, DC, MC, V. Mon–Sat 11:15am–2:15pm and 5:30–10pm. Tram: 3 or 5. Bus: 12.

5 Attractions

Before you rush off to sample the sightseeing attractions of the capital of Switzerland, stop in at the **Brasserie zum Bärengraben,** Muristalden 1 ((*C*) **031/331-42-18**), immediately across the street from the Bear Pits, the town's major attraction (see below). At a table here you can enjoy a slice of local life better than anywhere else. Many habitués settle down to read the morning news, ordering their favorite coffee, a beer, or a glass of wine.

THE TOP ATTRACTIONS

Bärengraben (Bear Pits) (★) is a deep, moon-shaped den where the bears, Bern's mascots, have been kept since 1480. According to legend, when the duke of Zähringen established the town in 1191, he sent his hunters out into the surrounding woods, which were full of wild game. The duke promised to name the city after the first animal slain, which was the *Bär* (bear). Since then, the town has been known as Bärn (Bern). Today, the bears are beloved, pampered, and fed by both residents and visitors (carrots are most appreciated). The Bear Pits lie on the opposite side of the **Nydegg Bridge** (Nydeggbrücke) from the rest of Old Town. The bridge was built over one of the gorges of the Aare River; its central stone arch has a span of 180 feet (54m) and affords a sweeping view of the city. Below the Bear Pits, you can visit the **Rosengarten** (Rose Gardens), from which there's a much-photographed view of the medieval sector of the city.

Zutgloggeturm (Clock Tower) ✯ ("Zeitglocketurm" in standard German), on Kramgasse, was built in the 12th century and restored in the 16th century. Four minutes before every hour, crowds gather for the world's oldest and biggest horological puppet show. Mechanical bears, jesters, and emperors put on an animated performance. Staged since 1530, it's one of the longest running acts in show business.

Cathedral of St. Vincent ✯   The Münster is one of the "newer" Gothic churches in Switzerland, dating from 1421. The belfry, however, was completed in 1893. The most exceptional feature of this three-aisle, pillared basilica is the **tympanum** ✯✯ over the main portal, which depicts the Last Judgment and contains more than 200 figures. You'll see mammoth 15th-century stained-glass windows in the chancel, but the most remarkable window, the *Dance of Death*, can be found in the Matter Chapel. The cathedral's 300-foot-tall (90m) **belfry** ✯✯ dominates Bern and offers a panoramic sweep of the Bernese Alps; to reach the viewing platform, you must climb 270 steps. The vista also includes the old town, its bridges, and the Aare River. Outside the basilica on Münsterplatz is the Moses Fountain, built in 1545.

Münsterplatz. ☎ **031/312-04-62.** Cathedral, free; viewing platform, 3SF ($1.65) adults, 1SF (55¢) children. Cathedral Easter Sun to Oct Tues–Sat 10am–5pm, Sun 11:30am–5pm; off-season Tues–Fri 10am–noon and 2–4pm, Sat 10am–noon and 2–5pm, Sun 11:30am–2pm. Viewing platform closes half an hour before cathedral. Bus: 12.

Kunstmuseum (Fine Arts Museum) ✯✯   The world's largest collection of works by Paul Klee ✯✯✯ is the star attraction here. The painter was born in Switzerland in 1879, the same year that the building housing the collection was constructed. The collection includes 40 oils, 2,000 drawings, and many gouaches and watercolors.

The museum also contains works by other artists, with an emphasis on the 19th and 20th centuries. There's a collection of Italian 14th-century primitives, including Fra Angelico's *Virgin and Child*. Swiss primitives include some from the "Masters of the Carnation." Hodler, the romantic artist, is represented by allegorical paintings depicting *Day and Night*. Impressionists include Monet, Manet, Sisley, and Cézanne, along with Delacroix and Bonnard. Surrealistic painters represented here include Dalí, Seligman, Oppenheim, and Tschumi. You'll also see works by Kandinsky, Modigliani, Matisse, Kirchner, Soutine, and Picasso. The museum also houses works by contemporary Swiss artists.

Hodlerstrasse 12. ☎ **031/328-09-44.** Permanent collection, 7SF ($3.85) adults, 5SF ($2.75) seniors; special exhibitions, 10SF–15SF ($5.50–$8.25) extra. Tues 10am–9pm, Wed–Sun 10am–5pm. Bus: 20.

MORE ATTRACTIONS
IN TOWN
The town's old but dignified **Rathaus** (Town Hall), on Rathausplatz, is still a center of political life. Built in 1406 in the Burgundian Gothic style and restored during World War II, the town hall has a double staircase and a covered porch.

Fun Fact **Did You Know?**

• Bern has the largest covered shopping promenade in Europe, with 3½ miles (6km) of arcades.

• Some of the best examples of European medieval architecture are found in Bern.

• After a fire in 1405 destroyed what had been a city built almost entirely of wood, the city fathers rebuilt Bern in sandstone.

• Eleven bridges span the Aare River, the oldest of which was erected in 1489.

• Bern is the only Swiss city to be listed as a World Cultural Landmark by the United Nations.

• The world's largest collection of works by Paul Klee is in Bern.

• The bear is the heraldic symbol of Bern.

Bernisches Historisches Museum (Bern Historical Museum) ★★   This neo-Gothic castle is built in the Swiss fortress style of the 16th century. The museum contains historical relics, along with archaeological, ethnographic, and numismatic collections. The main attraction is a series of seven 15th-century tapestries. A tapestry called *The Thousand Flowers,* plus four others telling the story of Julius Caesar, once belonged to the dukes of Burgundy. A number of rural and urban rooms, filled with period furnishings and artifacts, are also open to the public.

Helvetiaplatz 5. ✆ **031/350-77-11.** Admission 7SF ($3.85) adults, 5SF ($2.75) students and seniors, free for children 16 years and under. Tues–Sun 10am–5pm. Tram: 3 or 5.

Botanischer Garten (Botanical Garden)   Medicinal and fiber plants, examples of tropical and subtropical alpine plants, woodland and water plants, and a collection of plants from the cold steppes of central Asia are just some of the attractions in this vast garden arranged in descending terraces to the banks of the Aare River. Vegetation from various ecological zones is grown both in greenhouses and outdoors.

Altenbergrain 21. ✆ **031/631-49-44.** Free admission. Garden, Mon–Fri 8am–6pm, Sat–Sun 8am–5pm. Greenhouses, daily 8am–5pm. Bus: 20.

Bundeshaus   This Renaissance building, the Federal Palace, contains the two chambers of Switzerland's Parliament. Inaugurated in 1902, the Parliament building has a glass dome that displays the coats of arms of all 22 Swiss cantons. Of interest are the stained-glass windows, which symbolize education, public works, defense, and justice. In the ground floor rotunda a relief depicts the legend of the origin of Switzerland as dramatized in Schiller's saga of *Wilhelm Tell.* You can also visit the Chamber of the National Council, dominated by a large fresco by Gyron, and the Chamber of the Council of States decorated with a mural painting by Albert Welti. There's a flower market in front of the building on Tuesday and Saturday mornings.

Bundesplatz. ✆ **031/322-85-22.** Free admission. Tours given on the hour Mon–Sat 9–11am and 2–4pm; Sun 10am, 11am, 2pm, and 3pm, except when Parliament is in session. Closed public holidays. Tram: 9.

NEARBY

The most panoramic attraction in the immediate vicinity of Bern is the belvedere atop **Mount Gurten** ★★ at 2,815 feet (844m). There's a children's fairyland and a walking area as well as the lookout point. The belvedere is connected to Bern by the Gurtenbahn, a cable-train that's one of the fastest in Europe. The train departs from a station beside the Monbijoustrasse, about a half mile from Bern's center. To reach the departure platform, take tram 9, costing 2.50SF ($1.40) each way, to the Gurtenbahn station. The trip takes only 4 minutes each way. If you're driving, follow the road signs to Thun. There's a parking lot in the hamlet of Wabern, a short walk from the cable-train station.

Round-trip passage on the cable-train to the belvedere costs 8.50SF ($4.70). The train operates year-round daily from 7:30am to sunset (depending on the season). For information contact **Gurtenbahn Bern,** Eigerplatz (✆ **031/961-23-23**).

ESPECIALLY FOR KIDS

Dählhölzli Tierpark, Tierparkweg (✆ **031/357-15-15**), is one of the most interesting zoos in Europe. It offers a complete range of European creatures, from the tiny harvest mouse to the mighty musk oxen. You can admire more than 2,000 animals, including exotic birds, reptiles, and fish in the vivarium. Admission is 7SF ($3.85) for adults, 3SF ($1.65) for children 6 to 16, free for children under 6. The zoo is open April through September, daily from 8am to 6pm; off-season, daily from 9am to 5pm. Take bus 18.

Kids also enjoy the **Zytgloggeturm** (Clock Tower) and the **Bärengraben** (Bear Pits). The **Naturhistorisches Museum,** with its fascinating reptile collection and gallery of stuffed African beasts, is best for a rainy day, and a picnic at **Mount Gurten** is a good way to cap any visit to Bern with children.

WALKING TOUR	BERN'S ALTSTADT

Start	Bahnhofplatz.
Finish	Swiss Parliament.
Time	2 hours.
Best Times	Any sunny day.
Worst Times	Rush hours, Monday through Friday from 8 to 9am and 5 to 6pm.

Start at Bahnhofplatz, site of the Bern railroad station, the Bahnhof, facing the:

❶ Hotel Schweizerhof

Many ambassadors and presidents have stayed at this famous landmark hotel.

Opening onto Bahnhofplatz is the:

❷ Church of the Holy Ghost

Also called the Heiliggeistkirche, this church dates from 1729 and is somehow out of place in such a traffic-congested area.

From the church, head east up Spittalgasse, coming first to:

❸ Bagpiper Fountain

The Pfeiferbrunnen, which depicts a bagpiper atop a column and capital, was erected in about 1545, presumably by Hans Gieng.

Directly east of the fountain, at Bärenplatz, is the:

❹ Prison Gate

Called the Käfigturm, this gate dates from the 1200s. It now shelters a tiny museum devoted to the cultural and business life of the city.

Continue east along:

❺ Marktgasse

This is the main street of Old Town, filled with fashionable shops and florists. Many of its buildings date from the 17th century.

The street leads into one of the principal squares of Altstadt:

Walking Tour: Bern's Altstadt

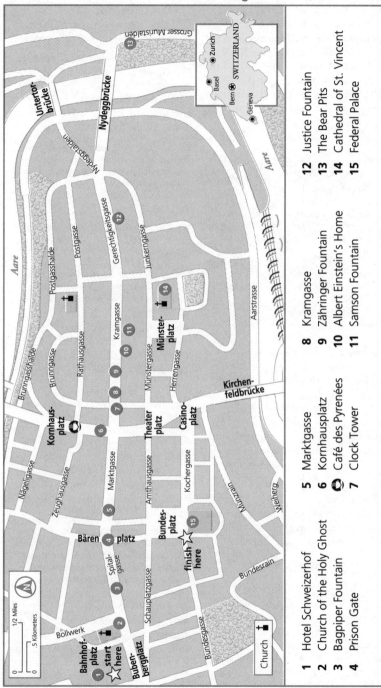

1 Hotel Schweizerhof
2 Church of the Holy Ghost
3 Bagpiper Fountain
4 Prison Gate
5 Marktgasse
6 Kornhausplatz
7 Café des Pyrenées
7 Clock Tower
8 Kramgasse
9 Zähringer Fountain
10 Albert Einstein's Home
11 Samson Fountain
12 Justice Fountain
13 The Bear Pits
14 Cathedral of St. Vincent
15 Federal Palace

⑥ Kornhausplatz

This square is the site of the Ogre Fountain, which is a representation of a carnival figure, with a pillar and capital erected about 1544. The Kornhaus, an old granary from the 1700s, also stands on the square; today it's a restaurant and wine cellar.

In this square you can:

 TAKE A BREAK
The "nerve center" of Bern, Café des Pyrenees, Kornhausplatz (✆ 031/311-30-63), is frequented by international journalists and visitors drawn to its sidewalk terrace. This bistro cafe also attracts many expatriates in Bern. Stop in for a drink—half a dozen types of Spanish brandy, for example—or any of the sandwiches and pasta dishes. Open Monday to Friday 9am to 12:30am and Saturday 8am to 5pm.

Also opening onto this square is the celebrated:

⑦ Clock Tower

Also called the Zytgloggeturm, the Clock Tower was the town's west gate from 1191 to 1250. Its chimes start pealing at 4 minutes before every hour. A picture postcard of this scene is the most popular souvenir of Bern.

Leaving Kornhausplatz, continue east along:

⑧ Kramgasse

A continuation of Marktgasse, this street contains many old houses with corner turrets and oriel windows.

Another major fountain standing on this street is the:

⑨ Zähringer Fountain

This fountain was a monument to the city founder, Berchtold von Zähringen. Here you can see the Bern bear, mascot of the city, along with the Zähringer coat of arms. The pillar, capital, and figure were erected in 1535 by Hans Hiltprand.

Continuing, at Kramgasse 49 you come to:

⑩ Albert Einstein's Home

In 1905, the famous physicist wrote his *Special Theory of Relativity* here.

The next fountain encountered on this same street is the:

⑪ Samson Fountain

This notable fountain is an allegory of strength, with a pillar and capital from 1527 and the figure from 1544.

Continue east along the street, which now changes its name to Gerechtigkeitsgasse. In the center of the street stands yet another famous fountain, the:

⑫ Justice Fountain

This fountain is an allegory of Justice, with worshipping subjects, including the pope, at her feet. The statue was erected in 1543.

Walk to the end of the street and continue across the river, crossing the Nydeggbrücke, until you reach Bern's most visited sight:

⑬ The Bear Pits

The Bärengraben is immediately on your right. The city of Bern is named after the bear (now its official mascot), and bears have resided in these pits since 1480.

Cross back over the bridge, and this time take the street to the left, heading west along Junkerngasse until you reach the:

⑭ Cathedral of St. Vincent

In Münsterplatz, the cathedral's first stone was laid in 1421, but building went on until 1573. From the tower you'll get a panoramic view of Bern.

After leaving the cathedral, continue west along Münstergasse until you reach Theaterplatz, one of Altstadt's major squares. Continue west, following the same street, which has now changed its name to Amthausgasse. You'll then approach Bundesplatz, site of the:

⑮ Federal Palace

Also called the Bundeshaus (Swiss Parliament) and capped with a massive dome, it was inspired by the Italian Renaissance Cathedral in Florence. This is the seat of Swiss democracy and one of the nation's treasured symbols.

ORGANIZED TOURS

We highly recommend the 2-hour **bus tour** that leaves from the tourist office at the railway station at Bahnhofplatz. You'll have an English-speaking guide as you travel through the city's residential quarters, past museums, and down to the Aare River, which flows below the houses of Parliament. You'll see the Rose Gardens and the late Gothic cathedral and stroll under the arcades to the Clock Tower. After visiting the Bear Pits, you'll be led through medieval streets back to the railroad station. Tours are offered June through September daily at 2pm; April, May, and October Monday through Saturday at 2pm; and November through March only on Saturday at 2pm. The cost is 24SF ($13.20) for adults, 12SF ($6.60) for children 6 to 16, free for children 5 and under.

The tourist office also conducts **walking tours** of Bern from May through October. The daily meeting point is either at the tourist office at 11am, or at Zytglogge at 11:15am. The cost is 14SF ($7.70) for adults, 7SF ($3.85) for children 6 to 16, free for children 5 and under.

We also recommend an organized **railway tour**—call © **0900-300-300** for information. The tour is an alpine adventure, traveling first through Interlaken, Lauterbrunnen, Wengen, and Kleine Scheidegg, then over the Jungfraujoch via Grindelwald and Interlaken, and back to Bern. Jungfraujoch, at 11,333 feet (3,400m), has the highest railway station in Europe and offers panoramic views over glaciers and the Alps, including the so-called Ice Palace. The cost of this excursion is 174SF ($95.70) in second class and 210SF ($115.50) in first class.

6 Outdoor Pursuits

The people of Bern are not particularly addicted to spectator sports, but they're very fond of recreational sports. The vast playground of Europe, the Bernese Oberland (see chapter 7) is at their doorstep, and they tend to take full advantage of it.

BIKING There are approximately 1,860 miles of roadway in the Bernese Oberland around Bern. Pick up a bicycle map that outlines the routes at the tourist office, then rent a bike at the Bahnhof and set off on your adventure. See "By Bicycle" in "Getting Around," earlier in this chapter, for more information.

FITNESS, SAUNA, SOLARIUM Go to the **STB Training Center,** Seilerstrasse 21 (© **031/381-02-03**), where full facilities are available to keep you in shape.

GOLF If you're a member of a golf club back home and have your membership card, you can patronize the **Golf and Country Club** in Blumisberg (© **026/496-34-38**), 11 miles west of Bern near Flamatt (on the road to Fribourg). Call for more information.

HIKING There are an estimated 155 miles (250km) of marked walking trails in the area surrounding Bern. You can pick up a rambling map at the tourist office. See "On Foot" in "Getting Around," earlier in this chapter, for more information.

SWIMMING The city's best indoor pool, along with a Turkish bath and sauna, is the **Hirschengraben Indoor Pool,** Maulbeerstrasse 14 (© **031/ 381-36-56**). The pool is open Monday, Wednesday, and Saturday from 8am to 6pm; Tuesday, Thursday, and Friday from 8am to 9pm. Admission is 6.50SF ($3.60) to the pool and 15SF ($8.25) to the sauna. The pool is closed July and August.

TENNIS   Courts are available at **Thalmatt,** Mettlenwaldweg 19, Herren-schwanden (℡ **031/307-33-33**).

7 Shopping

With a few exceptions, stores in the city center are open on Monday from 2 to 6:30pm; on Tuesday, Wednesday, and Friday from 8:15am to 6:30pm; on Thursday from 8:15am to 9pm; and on Saturday from 8:15am to 4pm. They're closed on Sundays.

With 4 miles (6km) of arcades, stores of all types are sheltered in Bern. The main shopping streets are **Spitalgasse, Kramgasse, Postgasse, Marktgasse,** and **Gerechtigkeitsgasse.**

You might begin your shopping excursion at **Globus,** Spitalgasse 17 (℡ **031/ 313-40-40**), a major department store that has been compared to Blooming-dale's, with departments for everything. Many people from the Bernese Oberland come into Bern just to shop at Globus. Also in the center of town, **Loeb ag Bern,** Spitalgasse 47 (℡ **031/320-71-11**), has a little bit of everything but is known chiefly for its high-quality fashions.

The best handcrafts, souvenirs, and gifts are found at **Oberlander Heimat,** Kramgasse 61 (℡ **031/311-30-00**), located on a historic street near the Clock Tower. This outlet sells handcrafts from all over Switzerland, including textiles, wood carvings, music boxes, and jewelry.

A collection of Art Nouveau pewter pieces is found at **Galerie Trag-art,** Gerechtigkeitsgasse 9 (℡ **031/311-64-49**). You'll find toys from all over the world at **Kunsthandwerk Anderegg,** Kramgasse 48 (℡ **031/311-02-01**).

For antiques, dolls, and toys, the best outlet is **Puppenklinik,** Gerechtigkeits-gasse 36 (℡ **031/312-07-71**). Another antiques shop is **Altstadt Galerie,** Kramgasse 7 (℡ **031/311-23-81**), which has two floors of Swiss chests and tables, many from the Bernese Oberland. The owner also exhibits works by Swiss painters.

The coin and stamp collector should head for Bern's most famous dealer, **Zumstein,** Zeughausgasse 24 (℡ **031/312-00-55**).

A good outlet for leather footwear is **Bally,** Spitalgasse 9 (℡ **031/311-54-81**), a branch of the famous Swiss shoe manufacturer that carries the complete line. Spitalgasse lies right off Bahnhofplatz. On the same street, **Gygax Mode,** Spi-talgasse 4 (℡ **031/311-25-61**), is a leading name in leather goods. It sells locally produced items as well as some of the best from neighboring countries such as Italy.

The finest jewelry store in town is **Gubelin,** Bahnhofplatz 11 (℡ **031/ 311-54-33**). This is one of the most reliable places to purchase a Swiss watch.

For fashion, woman gravitate to **Ciolina Modehaus,** Marktgasse 51 (℡ **031/ 328-64-64**), where clothes have fine styles and high prices. A leading men's store is **Zwald,** Neuengasse 23 (℡ **031/311-71-29**). Fashions here reflect a conti-nental flair.

Swiss chocolates (not always made in Switzerland these days) are sold at **Beeler,** Spitalgasse 29 (℡ **031/311-28-08**), one of the city's leading choco-latiers, and **Abegglen,** Spitalgasse 36 (℡ **031-311-21-11**).

Hats and handbags are the specialties at **KB Accessories,** Münstergasse 12 (℡ **031/312-01-15**), as designed by funky fashion iconoclasts Brigitte Keller and Stephan Billeter. Look for the kind of unusual and hip millinery that, if you're brave enough to wear proudly and with good posture, will evoke memo-ries and comparisons to Marlene Dietrich.

Many of the art objects at **Galerie Granero/Erg du Ténéré,** Nydegasse 15 (© **031/311-71-41**), derive from Africa's dusty Sub-Sahara region, especially the arid and folklore-rich countries of Chad and Mali. The Swiss-born owners scour that region for silver jewelry crafted by members of the Tuareg tribes, some of which come adorned with mystical symbols that are believed to ward off evil and empower the wearer.

Chalk **Llhasa,** Münstergasse 51 (© **031/311-61-06**), up to offbeat shopping. Switzerland's status as a neutral nation has encouraged the emigration to Bern of some of Tibet's mystical leaders. This shop acts as a focal point for some of them. You'll find meditative aids, exotic jewelry, carpets and weavings, clothing, incense, and books describing various aspects of Tibet's unique points of view about politics, philosophy, and religion. There's a second branch of this store at Bubenbergplatz 5 (© 031/311-01-88).

Here's a random sampling of funky shops in funky Bern. **Irmak und Wirz,** GmbH, Kramgasse 10 (© **031/312-06-04**), specializes in tribal rugs from Iran, many of them woven high in the Iranian mountains according to age-old geometric designs of the Quashquai tribes. **Trouvaillen am Münster,** Münstergasse 16 (© **031/312-79-82**), is dusty and overcrowded, containing an intriguing, sometimes bizarre collection of African and Swiss hunting trophies, antique lighting fixtures, bric-a-brac, and oddities that include an elephant embryo from the 1950s, and a barely used motorcycle from the 1930s. This is counterculture Bern at its most genuinely eccentric. Visit **Marcopolo,** Münstergasse 47 (© **031/311-88-44**), for artifacts from the developing world, all arranged in glittering arrays of jewelry and weavings from Africa, India, Uzbekhistan, and Afghanistan. Everything here seems exotic and ironically positioned a bit like a cleaned-up version of a Mideastern bazaar.

8 Bern After Dark

Most Bern residents get up early on weekday mornings, so they usually limit their evening entertainment to a drink or two at one of the historic cellars, such as the Kornhauskeller or the Klötzlikeller. Nevertheless, the city offers several late-night clubs, with dancing and cabaret, for the nocturnally active international crowd. *This Week in Bern,* distributed free by the tourist office, keeps a current list of cultural events.

THE PERFORMING ARTS

THE MAJOR CONCERT & PERFORMANCE HALLS   The **Bern Symphony Orchestra,** one of the finest orchestras in Switzerland, is conducted by the acclaimed Russian-born Dmitrij Kitajenko, whose services are supplemented by frequent guest conductors from around the world. Concerts by the orchestra are usually performed at the concert facilities in the **Bern Casino,** Herrengasse 25 (© **031/311-42-42**). Except for a summer vacation usually lasting from July until mid-August, the box office is open Monday through Friday from 12:30 to 3pm. Tickets range from 20SF to 50SF ($11–$27.50).

Concerts with fewer musicians, especially chamber music, are often performed in any of four or five churches; in the auditorium at the **Konservatorium für Musik,** Kramgasse 36 (© **031/311-62-21**); or in the concert and recording facilities of **Radio Studio Bern,** Schwarztorstrasse 21 (© **031/388-91-11**).

Major opera and ballet performances are usually staged in what is generally acknowledged as Bern's most beautiful theater, the century-old **Stadttheater,** Kornhausplatz 20 (© **031/329-51-11**). Performances are usually in German, and to a lesser degree in French, but even if you don't understand those languages, you might want to attend a performance. Other plays and dance programs, including ballet and cabaret, are presented in the **Theater am Käfigturm,** Spitalgasse 4 (℃ **031/311-6100**). Contemporary German-language dramas, comedies, tragedies, and satires are featured in the **Kleintheater,** Kramgasse 6 (℃ **031/320-26-26**).

THE CLUB & BAR SCENE

Bar aux Petits Fours   This is the newest of several contenders for the title of best gay bar in Bern, attracting a multilingual, attractive, and international group of gay people, mostly men. There's no dance floor and no restaurant on the premises, but what you get is a low-key bar, filled with regular clients, where a newcomer with a bit of effort can usually break the glacial freeze of Swiss reserve. Kramgasse 67. ℃ 031/312-73-74. Open daily 5pm–12:30am.

Come Back Bar   This isn't a gay bar in the strictest sense of the word, but a tavern that's cosmopolitan and tolerant, and likely to attract lots of genuinely cool artists and hipsters in Bern. It occupies the cellar vaults below the medieval buildings of the Rathausgasse. Inside, blinking lights frame a discreet dance floor and a long bar functions as a local hangout for many of the gay and gay-friendly residents of the old town. It's especially crowded on weekends, with a calmer, more low-key approach to things during weeknights. Rathausgasse 42. ℃ 031/311-77-13. Open daily 6pm–12:30am (till 3:30am Fri and Sat).

Klötzlikeller   The oldest wine tavern in Bern is near the Gerechtigkeitsbrunnen (Fountain of Justice), the first fountain you see on your walk from the Bärengraben (Bear Pits) to the Zytgloggeturm (Clock Tower). Watch for the lantern outside an angled cellar door. The well-known tavern dates from 1635 and is leased by the city to an independent operator. Some 20 different wines are sold by the glass, with prices starting at 7.50SF ($4.15). The menu is changed every 6 weeks. The appetizing snacks are always traditional, including sliced cheese, with prices ranging from 10SF to 25SF ($5.50–$13.75). The traditional Bernese kitchen produces various dinner plates, reflecting regional specialties and costing 22SF to 45SF ($12.10–$24.75). 62 Gerechtigkeitsgasse. ℃ 031/311-74-56. Open Tues– Sat 4pm–12:30am.

Marians' Jazzroom   The Louis Armstrong Bar, site of this jazz venue, has its own separate entrance from the Innere Enge Hotel. Unique in Bern, it serves up not only food and drink, but the finest traditional jazz performed live by top artists from around the world. From Tuesday through Thursday, hours are 7:30pm to 1am, Friday and Saturday 7:30pm to 2am. On Saturday, there is a Concert Apéro from 4 to 6:30pm, and on some Sundays there is a Jazz Brunch from 10am to 1:30pm. In the Innere Enge Hotel, Engerstrasse 54. ℃ 031/309-61-11. Cover 15SF–45SF ($8.25–$24.75), depending on the act. Closed June 6–Sept 7.

Samurai Club   This gay bar draws people who work in the local embassies, Bern locals, and young men from the Bernese Oberland in for a night on the town. Women are also welcome. Guys gyrating to the sounds of hot music fill the dance floor. Aarbergergasse 35. ℃ 031/311-88-03. Open Sun–Thurs 8pm–2:30am and Fri–Sat 8pm–3:30am.

Temple   One of the biggest and best-known discos in Bern is sweet and sexy, drawing a young crowd (especially on Friday and Saturday nights when there's usually a live band). Wednesday is golden-oldie night; on other days there's a DJ spinning. Aarbergergasse 61. © **031/311-50-41.** Cover (including the first drink) 10SF ($5.50) Mon–Thurs, 15SF ($8.25) Fri–Sat. Open Mon–Thurs 9pm–3am, and Fri–Sat 9pm–3:30am. Closed July–Aug.

GAMBLING

Jackpot Spielcasino, Kornhausstrasse 3 (© **031/333-10-10** or 031/333-18-55), is the only place in town to gamble. Indeed, it's a great spot for novices to learn because serious money rarely changes hands here. Betting is limited to 1SF to 5SF (55¢–$2.75), as required by Swiss law. It's open daily from noon to 3:30am, and admission is free. Drinks cost 10SF to 12SF ($5.50–$6.60). There are three restaurants and two bars, plus a dance hall which charges a 15SF ($8.25) cover. It's open on Thursday from 9pm to 2am, on Friday and Saturday from 9pm to 3:30am, and on Sunday from 3 to 10pm.

7

The Bernese Oberland

The Bernese Oberland is one of the greatest tourist attractions in the world, mainly because it's one of the best areas for winter sports. The region sprawls between the Reuss River and Lake Geneva, with the Rhône forming its southern border. The area contains two lakes, the Thun and the Brienz, and takes in a portion of the Alps (culminating in the Finsteraarhorn at 14,022 ft./4,207m). The canton of Bern, which encompasses most of the area, is the second largest in Switzerland and contains about 100 square miles (160 sq. km) of glaciers.

The best center for exploring the Bernese Oberland is Interlaken, most popular as a summer resort. Other cities in the region, such as Gstaad, Grindelwald, Kandersteg, and Mürren, are both summer and winter playgrounds. You can ski the mountains during winter and swim, sail, and water-ski on Lake Thun in the summer.

EXPLORING THE BERNESE OBERLAND

To compensate for the region's almost impossible geography, Swiss engineers have crisscrossed the Oberland with cogwheel railways (some of them still driven by steam), aerial cableways, and sinuous mountain roads. Though often a confusing experience, getting to a particular resort can be part of the fun. The region's busiest railroad junction, and the point where most travelers change trains for local railways, is **Interlaken.**

You can buy a **transportation pass** for the Bernese Oberland from the Swiss Rail System. The train ticket is valid for 7 days, and costs 180SF ($99) in second class and 220SF ($121) in first class. Another pass, valid for 15 days, costs 220SF ($121) in second class and 265SF ($145.75) in first class. With the 7-day pass, you'll travel free for 3 days and pay a reduced fare for the final 4. With a 15-day pass, you'll travel free for 5 days and pay reduced fares for the rest of the time. Children travel at half price. The pass is valid on most railroads; all mountain trains, cable cars, chairlifts, steamers on Lakes Thun and Brienz; and most postal-bus lines in the area. The ticket also qualifies you for a 25% reduction on the Kleine Scheidegg-Eigergletscher-Jungfraujoch railway, the Mürren-Schilthorn aerial cable line, and the bus to Grosse Scheidegg and Bussalp. You must purchase the pass at least 1 week before you arrive. For information about the pass, call © **212/757-5944** in New York City, © **310/640-8900** in Los Angeles, © **877/794-8037** in Chicago, or © **416/695-2090** in Toronto.

Since Interlaken is the focal point of one of the most complicated networks of ski lifts in the world, most visitors opt to buy a comprehensive pass that allows unlimited access to the cog railways, buses, cable cars, chairlifts, and gondolas (incorporating every mechanical lift in and around Interlaken, Wengen, Grindelwald, and Mürren). Sold at the Interlaken tourist office (see below) and tourist offices at the other leading resorts, it's called the **Jungfrau Top Ski Region Pass.** You can buy the 2-day pass for 110SF ($60.50), the 5-day pass for

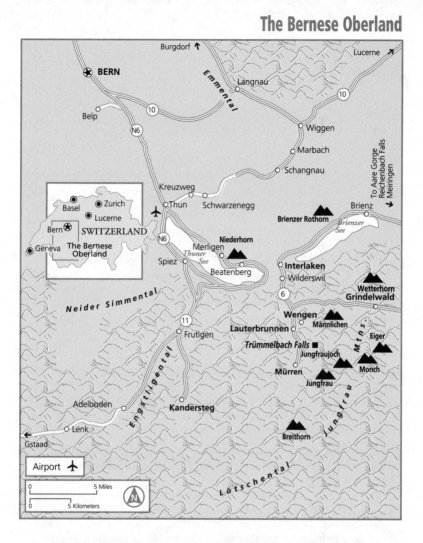

230SF ($126.50), or the 7-day pass for 275SF ($151.25). Discounts of 10% are offered to seniors 62 and older, discounts of 20% to youths aged 16 to 20, and discounts of 50% to children 6 to 15. Kids 5 and under travel for only 10% of the above rates. This pass incorporates access to 45 ski lifts, 127 miles (204km) of well-groomed downhill runs, 60 miles (99km) of prepared walking and cross-country ski paths, and 31 miles of tobogganing runs. It covers the region around Grindelwald, Wengen, and Mürren.

Other passes include the following:

First Region Ski Pass is a small-scale cluster of ski lifts, favored by beginners and intermediates, that includes six lifts and a gondola. It's available only for the region immediately around Grindelwald, and does not include Wengen. A 1-day pass costs 55SF ($30.25), a 2-day pass 100SF ($55).

Kleine Mannlichen and Scheidegg Pass is the same scale of difficulty as the First Region Ski pass, as well as the same price (1- and 2-day passes are the only offerings). Unlike the First Region Pass, it's available to residents of either Wengen or Grindelwald, but residents of Mürren are not invited to this particular cluster of runs.

BY MOUNTAIN BIKE   Hundreds of miles of cycling paths riddle the Bernese Oberland, and most of them begin in Interlaken. Separate from the network of hiking paths, the bike routes are signposted and marked on rental maps distributed at bike-rental agencies. Of course, it's the law to use only specially signposted routes and not destroy plant and animal life or ride across private fields. Hikers, incidentally, are given the right of way over bikers.

There are 13 railroad stations in the Bernese Oberland offering bike-rental services. Rates are reasonable. Families can rent four bikes (two for adults, two for children 15 and under) for an all-inclusive price of 37SF ($20.35) per day or 250SF ($137.50) per week. Individual rentals cost 27SF ($14.85) per day or 180SF ($99) per week. Reservations must be made the evening before the tour. You can make reservations in Interlaken at either of its rail stations, **Interlaken East** (✆ **033/828-73-19**) or **Interlaken West** (✆ **033/826-47-50**).

ON FOOT   The Bernese Oberland is ideal for walkers and hikers. The natural terrain here will satisfy everyone from the most ambitious mountain hiker to the casual stroller.

Trails designed for walkers branch out from almost every junction. Most are paved and signposted, showing distances and estimated walking times. Most tourist offices will suggest itineraries for walkers.

For the more athletic, itineraries include long hikes far afield in the mountains, with suggestions for overnight accommodations en route.

Even if you don't feel up to scaling alpine peaks, you can still go on walks. Take one of the Swiss postal-bus rides uphill to a village, then stroll back down to Interlaken, for example. Be warned, however, that walking downhill in Switzerland can still strain your calf muscles.

1 Interlaken ✮✮✮

34 miles (54km) SE of Bern, 81 miles (130km) SW of Zurich

Interlaken is the tourist capital of the Bernese Oberland. Cableways and cog railways designed for steeply inclined mountains connect it with most of the region's villages and dazzling sights, including the snowy heights of the Jungfrau, which rises a short distance to the south. Excursion possibilities from Interlaken are both numerous and dazzling.

This "town between the lakes" (Thun and Brienz) has been a vacation resort for over 300 years. Although it began as a summer resort, it developed into a year-round playground, altering its allure as the seasons change. During the winter, skiers take advantage of the town's low prices. Interlaken charges low-season prices in January and February, when smaller resorts at higher altitudes are charging their highest rates of the year. The most expensive time to visit Interlaken is during midsummer, when high-altitude and snowless ski resorts often charge their lowest rates.

An Augustinian monastery was founded in Interlaken in 1130 but was later closed during the Reformation; the ruins can still be seen in a park in the center of town. Tourism to the area is said to have begun in 1690, when Margrave Frederic Albert of Brandenburg journeyed into the snow-covered rocks of the Jungfrau massif. However, tourism as we know it today dawned at the beginning of the 19th century, when artists and writers—many of them British—were drawn to the town by its scenery. As the country's railroad and steamer services improved, a steady stream of visitors followed, including such notables as Mark Twain, Goethe (who seems to have lived everywhere), Wagner, Mendelssohn, and representatives of European royal families.

ESSENTIALS

GETTING THERE   There are several trains daily between Zurich and Interlaken (2 hr.) and between Bern and Interlaken (40 min.). Frequent train service also connects Geneva with Interlaken (2½ hr.). For additional **rail information** call ✆ **0900/300-300.**

Note: Although the town has two different railway stations, Interlaken East and Interlaken West, West is most convenient to the city's center.

If you're driving from Bern, head south on N6 to Spiez, then continue east on N8 to Interlaken.

VISITOR INFORMATION   The **Tourism Organization Interlaken** is in the Hotel Metropole at Höheweg 37 (✆ **033/822-21-21**). It's open in July and August, Monday to Friday from 8am to noon and 1:30 to 6:30pm, Saturday from 8am to 5pm, and Sunday from 5 to 7pm; the rest of the year, Monday to Friday from 8am to noon and 2 to 6pm and Saturday from 8am to noon.

A **Visitor's Card** is granted to persons registered at local hotels and confers certain discounts to some of the local attractions.

GETTING AROUND   Train arrivals are at either Interlaken East or Interlaken West. If you're loaded with luggage, you'll want to grab a taxi. However, after you've been deposited at one of the local hotels (nearly all of which are in the city center), you'll rarely need a taxi—the town is closely knit and best explored on foot. Buses are convenient for connections to the satellite towns and villages or heading to the outskirts. The **bus station** is at Areckstrasse 6 (✆ **033/ 828-88-28**).

EXPLORING THE AREA

It's very simple—the best way to see everything in Interlaken is to walk. You can either randomly stroll around, enjoying the panoramic views in all directions, or follow a more structured walking tour. If you'd like some guidance, go to the tourist office (see "Visitor Information" in "Essentials," above) and ask for a copy of *What to Do in Interlaken.* It maps out walks for both young and more mature visitors.

The **Höheweg** ✦✦ covers 35 acres in the middle of town between the two train stations. Once the property of Augustinian monks, it was acquired in the mid-19th century by the hotel keepers of Interlaken, who turned it into a park. As you stroll along Höhenpromenade, admire the famous view of the Jungfrau mountain. Another beautiful sight is the flower clock at the Kursaal (casino). You're also sure to see some *fiacres,* or horse-drawn cabs. The promenade is lined with hotels, cafes, and gardens.

Cross over the Aare River to **Unterseen,** built in 1280 by Berthold von Eschenbach. Here you can visit the parish church, with its late Gothic tower dating from 1471. This is one of the most photographed sights in the Bernese Oberland. The Mönch appears to the left of the tower, the Jungfrau on the right.

Back in Interlaken, visit the **Touristik-Museum der Jungfrau-Region,** am Stadthausplatz, Obere Gasse 26 (✆ **033/822-98-39**), the first regional tourism museum in the country. Exhibitions show the growth of tourism in the region throughout the past 2 centuries. The museum is open from May to mid-October

Tuesday to Sunday from 2 to 5pm. Admission is 5SF ($2.75), or 3SF ($1.65) with a Visitor's Card. Children are charged 2SF ($1.10).

To see the sights of Interlaken, Matten, and Unterseen by *fiacre,* line up at the Interlaken West train station. The half-hour round-trip tour costs 37SF ($20.35) for one or two, plus 10SF ($5.50) for each additional person; children 7 to 16 are charged half fare, and those 6 and under ride free.

Other attractions in the area include animal parks, afternoon concerts, and steamers across Lakes Brienz and Thun. During the summer, visitors can sit in covered grandstands and watch Schiller's version of the William Tell story and the formation of the Swiss Confederation. We also recommend the delectable pastries sold in the local cafes.

OUTDOOR ACTIVITIES

If you're feeling energetic, or just looking to work off an excess of fondue dipping, Interlaken offers many opportunities for sports—sailing, windsurfing, rowing, fishing, golf, tennis, mountain trekking, and glider flying. There's also a swimming pool in town. More information is available at the tourist office.

GOLF   You can play at the **Interlaken-Unterseen course** (© 033/823-60-16) from April to October. The cost is 80SF ($44) Monday to Friday and 90SF ($49.50) Saturday and Sunday. With a Visitor's Card, the cost is reduced to 70SF ($38.50).

HORSEBACK RIDING   There are several bridle paths between Lake Thun and Lake Brienz. The **Voegeli Riding School,** Scheidgasse 66, in Unterseen (© 033/822-74-16), offers guided rides costing 40SF ($22) for 1 hour and 75SF ($41.25) for 2 hours.

SWIMMING   There's a public **indoor pool** and a public open-air pool, **Bödeli** (© 033/822-24-16), behind the Kursaal. The indoor pool has a sauna and a solarium as well as a fitness room. This pool is open year-round Monday from 9am to 9pm, Tuesday through Friday from 9am to 9:45pm, and Saturday and Sunday from 9am to 6pm. Entrance is 8SF ($4.40) for adults, 4.80SF ($2.65) for children 6 to 16, and free for children 5 and under. The outdoor pool, with its changing cabins and 33-foot diving board, is open mid-May through September daily from 9am to 7pm. Keep in mind, though, that even July and August might be too chilly for you. Entrance is 5SF ($2.75) for adults and 3SF ($1.65) for children.

TENNIS   Use of a court at the **Höhematte** costs 24SF ($13.20) per hour, with a Visitor's Card. If you're alone and willing to be matched up with another person, it will cost you half the court fee. For reservations, phone © 033/822-14-72. The courts are open from mid-April to mid-October, daily from 8am to 8 or 9pm.

SHOPPING

True to its role as the nerve center of the entire Oberland region, Interlaken stocks an ample supply of souvenirs and sports equipment. You'll find all the handicrafts and art objects you could possibly need beside the resort's main street, Höheweg, and around the Interlaken West railway station. One of the best of these is **Heimatwerk Interlaken,** Höheweg 115 (© 033/823-16-53). It's been a fixture for tourists since the turn of the century. It stocks only goods manufactured in Switzerland, including a wholesome and comprehensive roster of wood-carved children's toys, tablecloths and linens, cutting boards and cheese boards, ceramics, and glass. A leading competitor, with less emphasis on all-Swiss inventories and a higher percentage of less expensive things (such as

T-shirts) is the **Boutique Edelweiss,** Höheweg 26 (© **033/823-80-60**). Since Interlaken has higher-altitude ski and hill-climbing resorts stretching upward on virtually all sides, you won't lack for purveyors of sporting goods equipment. Two of the best are **Intersport,** Postgasse 16 (© **033/822-06-61**), and **Harry Sport,** Bahnhofstrasse 8 (© **033/822-73-22**).

WHERE TO STAY
VERY EXPENSIVE
Grand Hotel Beau-Rivage ★★★   This government-rated five-star Belle Epoque hotel between Höheweg and the Aare River is one of Interlaken's grand hotels. Only Victoria-Jungfrau is better. The Beau-Rivage sells luxury on a smaller, more intimate scale than its competitors, and is located in a very tranquil spot. It's only a short distance from the Interlaken East rail station, which makes it a good center for excursions in all directions. The central tower has an ascending series of covered loggias decorated with carvings and flowers, a triangular pediment, and a mansard roof. There are two wings with gables and wrought-iron balconies. The renovated rooms are conservatively modern with excellent beds and nicely kept bathrooms. The front rooms open onto the Jungfrau, and the rooms in the rear are not only quieter but front the river.

Höheweg 211, CH-3800 Interlaken. © 800/447-7462 in the U.S. and Canada, or 033/821-62-72. Fax 033/ 823-28-47. www.beau-rivage-interlaken.ch. 101 units. 370SF–414SF ($203.50–$227.70) double; from 450SF ($247.50) suite. Rates include buffet breakfast. AE, DC, MC, V. Free parking outdoors, 20SF ($11) in garage. **Amenities:** 2 restaurants, bar; pool; health club; sauna; room service; babysitting; laundry/dry cleaning. *In room:* TV, minibar, hair dryer.

Victoria-Jungfrau Grand Hotel & Spa ★★★   Since 1865, this grand hotel has reigned as one of the most important resort properties in Switzerland. The owner of the Victoria Hotel, Edouard Ruchti, united it with the Jungfrau Hotel in 1895, and the landmark property has stood ever since. Through its corridors has passed everyone from the emperor of Brazil to the king of Siam to Mark Twain. During World War II the hotel served as headquarters of the Swiss commander in chief, Gen. Henri Guisan. Designed in a richly ornate Victorian style, it sits right in the town center at the foot of rigidly symmetrical gardens. The hotel boasts valuable antiques and one of the best-trained staffs in Interlaken. The most expensive rooms open onto views of the Jungfrau. The mid-sized to spacious accommodations are luxurious.

Höheweg 41, CH-3800 Interlaken. © 800/223-6800 in the U.S., or 033/828-28-28. Fax 033/828-28-80. www.victoria-jungfrau.ch. 216 units. Summer 590SF–660SF ($324.50–$363) double. Winter 440SF–520SF ($242–$286) double. Year-round from 750SF ($412.50) junior suite; from 1,250SF ($687.50) suite. Half board 100SF ($55) per person extra. AE, DC, MC, V. Free parking outside, 20SF ($11) in garage. **Amenities:** 2 restaurants, 2 bars; pool; tennis courts; spa; sauna; Jacuzzi; room service; massage; babysitting; laundry/dry cleaning. *In room:* TV, minibar, hair dryer.

EXPENSIVE
Hotel Interlaken ★   This is the resort's oldest hotel, receiving overnight guests since 1323, first as a hospital, later as a cloister and, beginning in the early 1400s, as a tavern and inn. Guests have included Byron and Mendelssohn. The hotel, directly east of the casino, has been gutted and rebuilt since, with a salmon-colored facade sporting baroque touches. The most expensive rooms have a few 19th-century antiques; the rest have conservative, modern furnishings with excellent beds and well-maintained bathrooms.

Höheweg 74, CH-3800 Interlaken. © 033/826-68-68. Fax 033/826-68-69. www.interlakenhotel.ch. 60 units. 220SF–310SF ($121–$170.50) double. Rates include continental breakfast. Half board 35SF ($19.25) per person extra. AE, DC, MC, V. Free parking. **Amenities:** Restaurant, bar; exercise room; sauna; room service; laundry/dry cleaning. *In room:* TV, minibar, hair dryer.

Hotel Metropole 🎖️🎖️ Americans often prefer this sleek, modern hotel in the city center, the only skyscraper in the Bernese Oberland, to the aging palaces of Interlaken. The 18-story building was built in 1976 and has since been stylishly renovated. It's the most up-to-date and best-managed hotel in town. The small, standardized rooms have plush carpeting, modern furniture, and balconies. All units have neatly kept bathrooms. Those facing south have a panoramic view of Interlaken and the towering mountains. Try to steer clear of the 18 units in the annex, as they are a bit lackluster and have no views.

Höheweg 37, CH-3800 Interlaken. ℂ 800/223-5652 in the U.S., or 033/828-66-66. Fax 033/828-66-33. www.metropole-interlaken.ch. 97 units. May–Oct 310SF ($170.50) double; Nov–Apr 260SF ($143) double. Rates include buffet breakfast. Half board 48SF ($26.40) per person extra. AE, DC, MC, V. Parking 10SF ($5.50) outside, 14SF ($7.70) in garage. **Amenities:** 2 restaurants, 2 bars; pool; sauna; room service; baby-sitting; laundry/dry cleaning. *In room:* TV, minibar, hair dryer.

MODERATE

Hotel Beau-Site 🎖️ A short walk from the Interlaken West train station, this hotel is surrounded by spacious gardens with parasol-shaded card tables and chaise lounges in the summer. Since 1943, the Ritter family has been providing a pleasant and relaxing oasis in the middle of town. The mid-sized rooms are modern, and some open onto mountain views.

Seestrasee 16, CH-3800 Interlaken. ℂ 033/826-75-75. Fax 033/826-75-85. www.beausite.ch. 50 units, 43 with bathroom. 120SF ($66) double without bathroom, 250SF–285SF ($137.50–$156.75) double with bathroom. Rates include continental breakfast. AE, DC, MC, V. Parking free outside, 20SF ($11) in garage. **Amenities:** 2 restaurants, lounge; room service; laundry/dry cleaning. *In room:* TV, minibar.

Hotel Weisses Kreuz This safe and tranquil hotel is located on the famous Höheweg, right in the center of Interlaken. The interior is pleasantly decorated yet simple, and the bedrooms are newly renovated. Each has a well-maintained bathroom. Owned and managed by the Bieri family since 1911, the hotel offers a brasserie-style restaurant with Italian/Swiss cuisine. In summer, guests gravitate to its boulevard terrace for people-watching, drinks, and pastries.

Höheweg (at Jungfraustrasse), CH-3800 Interlaken. ℂ 033/822-59-51. Fax 033/823-35-55. www.weisseskreuz.ch. 60 units. 180SF–210SF ($99–$115.50) double. Rates include buffet breakfast. AE, DC, MC, V. Free parking. **Amenities:** Restaurant, bar; room service; laundry/dry cleaning. *In room:* TV.

Park-Hotel Mattenhof 🎖️ This large, old-fashioned, government-rated four-star hotel is in a secluded area at the edge of a forest 1 mile (2km) south of the center; you can reach it by heading away from the center toward Wilderswil. The exterior looks like a private castle, with its high, pointed roof, tower, loggias, and balconies. It was originally built as a simple and sedate pension in 1897, but adopted most of its mock-medieval form after a massive enlargement in 1906. During World War II it functioned as a hospital for injured soldiers, but for the past 30 years it has been managed by Peter Bühler and his family. They offer a calm retreat with terraces, manicured lawns, and panoramic views of the Alps. The salons are warmly decorated and sunny, and some of the well-furnished but small bedrooms have a view of the Jungfrau and the Niederhorn. All have well-kept bathrooms, and several also are equipped with a balcony.

Hauptstrasse, Matten, CH-3800 Interlaken. ℂ 033/821-61-21. Fax 033/822-28-88. www.park-mattenhof.ch. 76 units. June–Sept and Dec 26–Jan 1 260SF ($143) double. Off-season 190SF ($104.50) double. Rates include buffet breakfast. AE, DC, MC, V. Free parking. Bus: 5. **Amenities:** 2 restaurants, 2 bars; pool; tennis court; health club; sauna; room service; laundry/dry cleaning. *In room:* TV.

Royal St. Georges 🏰   Built in 1907, this oft-restored hotel is a historical landmark structure. In spite of several renovations, it has retained its traditional character. In contrast to the old-style architecture, the bedrooms are as up to date as tomorrow, ranging in size from small to exceedingly spacious. Some of the suites are in the Victorian style. Bathrooms are generous in size and often stylized, such as a special Art Nouveau bathroom. The hotel is divided into two parts, the Royal Wing and the St. Georges Wing, both linked to each other through a gangway. Unlike most peas-in-a-pod hotel rooms, this government-rated four-star choice offers individualized bedrooms—you can hardly find two rooms that are identical. Each unit contains a private bathroom with either shower or combination tub and shower.

Höheweg 139, CH-3800 Interlaken. ℂ **033/822-75-75.** Fax 033/823-30-75. www.royal-stgeorges.ch/ infrastructure/wellness.html. 89 units. 190SF–290SF ($104.50–$159.50) double; 250SF–380SF ($137.50–$209) suite. Rates include breakfast. AE, DC, MC, V. **Amenities:** Restaurant, bar; Jacuzzi; steam room; sauna; room service; laundry/dry cleaning. *In room:* TV, minibar, hair dryer, safe.

INEXPENSIVE

De la Paix   This family-run hotel is a pleasant stopover, a block away from the Westbahnhof (Interlaken West). You'll recognize it by its ornate roofline, which is gabled and tiled like a house in a Brothers Grimm fairy tale. The small rooms are simply but comfortably furnished and are all equipped with private, well-kept bathrooms with shower-tub combinations.

Bernastrasse 24, CH-3800 Interlaken. ℂ **033/822-70-44.** Fax 033/822-87-28. www.interlakentourism.ch. 22 units. 150SF ($82.50) double. Rates include buffet breakfast. AE, DC, MC, V. Closed mid-Oct to mid-Mar. Free parking. **Amenities:** Lounge. *In room:* TV.

Hotel Lötschberg 🏰 *(Finds)*   A hotel that's sure to transmit an old-fashioned sense of Swiss charm is this sprawling villa-style building that rises from the city's commercial core, a 3-minute walk from the railway station. Originally built around 1910 as a cost-conscious pension, and painted a striking shade of blue, it has been frequently improved, repaired, and renovated between 1994 and 1998. All but three of the units have a TV set, and the three that don't are located within a simple, century-old guesthouse a short walk away. Rooms come in a wide variety of sizes, ranging from small units to medium-sized ones (two to three guests), and even very spacious rooms, each comfortable enough for four persons. By far the best part about this place is the personalized attention offered by Susi and Fritz Hutmacher, who pride themselves on providing advice that usually leads guests to less frequently visited sites in and around Interlaken. Breakfast is the only meal served within this hotel, but on the premises, under separate management, is an Asian restaurant that serves lunch and dinner. You can rent mountain bikes from the Hutmachers or even check your e-mail for a small fee.

Général Guisanstrasse 31, CH-3800 Interlaken. ℂ **033/822-2545.** Fax 033/822-2579. www.lotschberg.ch. 23 units. 119SF–180SF ($65.45–$99) double. Rates include breakfast. AE, DC, MC, V. Closed Jan. Free parking. **Amenities:** Restaurant, lounge; laundry/dry cleaning. *In room:* TV.

Swiss Inn *(Value)*   This small Edwardian inn with balconies and gables offers good value. Mrs. Vreny Müller Lohner rents tasteful, simply decorated one- to three-room apartments equipped with good beds and well-kept bathrooms with shower-tub combinations in one half, only showers in the others. They accommodate two to six guests, and children's beds or cots are available. The inn has a lounge, a sitting area with a fireplace, and a grill for barbecues in the garden.

Général Guisanstrasse 23, CH-3800 Interlaken. © **033/822-36-26.** Fax 033/823-23-03. www.swiss-inn.com. 10 units. 120SF–170SF ($66–$93.50) double; 15SF–200SF ($82.50–$110) apt. for 2; 220SF–240SF ($121–$132) apt. for 4. AE, MC, V. Free parking. **Amenities:** Lounge; room service; laundry/dry cleaning. *In room:* TV.

WHERE TO DINE

Most guests dine at their hotels, which partially explains why such a world-famous resort as Interlaken has so few independent restaurants worth noting.

EXPENSIVE

Il Bellini ✿✿ INTERNATIONAL   This is one of the finest restaurants in the Bernese Oberland. Established in 1994, it sits one floor above the lobby in the tallest hotel in Interlaken, the Metropole, and is outfitted in a graceful 19th-century rendition of pale pinks and greens. The fresh, good-tasting food is served with a discreet panache you might have expected in Italy, and includes an assortment of antipasti. You can order individual selections of hors d'oeuvres, including prosciutto with melon or smoked salmon and carpaccio. The soups, especially the homemade minestrone, are tasty, and the main courses include such delectable specialties as tender beefsteak Florentine, saltimbocca, and chicken breasts grilled with tomatoes and mozzarella. The fish selections are limited but well chosen.

In the Hotel Metropole, Höheweg 37. © **033/828-66-66.** Reservations recommended Fri–Sun. Main courses 25SF–50SF ($13.75–$27.50); pastas 14SF–30SF ($7.70–$16.50). AE, DC, MC, V. Daily 11:30am–2pm and 6:30–10pm.

Restaurant Teene (Chez Pierre) ✿ SEAFOOD/SWISS   Locals seem to love this restaurant, which lies just outside the center near the resort's gymnasium. It has a bright, refreshing interior, decorated mostly in white. For a main course, you can order fresh fish from a tank. Other satisfying dishes include filet of sole with freshly made noodles and vegetables, a delicious fried trout, and tender grilled T-bone steaks. The chef specializes in lobster.

Alpenstrasse 58. © **033/822-94-22.** Reservations required. Main courses 20SF–35SF ($11–$19.25); fixed-price dinner 20SF–50SF ($11–$27.50). AE, DC, MC, V. Thurs–Tues 11am–2pm and 6–10:30pm.

MODERATE

Gasthof Hirschen *Value* SWISS   This hotel restaurant offers some of the best and most reasonably priced meals in town. The menu is varied; the potato soup with mountain cheese is the finest we've ever tasted. Another tasty appetizer is the ravioli filled with salmon. For a main dish, we recommend sautéed calves' liver, filet of beef bordelaise, beef goulash, broiled trout, or chateaubriand. The Hirschen also operates its own farm, which supplies Bio-Angus beef, veal, cheese, fresh vegetables, and herbs. Fresh berries and honey are also brought in from the farm during summer.

Hauptstrasse 11, Matten. © **033/822-15-45.** Reservations recommended. Main courses 20SF–55SF ($11–$30.25). AE, DC, MC, V. Wed 6:30–9:30pm, Thurs–Mon 11:30am–2pm and 6:30–9:30pm.

INEXPENSIVE

Pizpaz *Kids* ITALIAN   The central location with many outdoor tables makes this pizzeria a popular place, especially with families. Typical Italian specialties here include calves' liver in marsala, veal marsala, saltimbocca (veal with ham), osso buco, and at least 20 different pizzas (the best in town). The gelato misto, a mixed selection of ice cream, is the most popular dessert—deservedly so.

Bahnhofstrasse 1. © **033/822-25-33.** Main courses 16SF–38SF ($8.80–$20.90); fixed-price lunch 14.50SF ($8); pizzas 12SF–21SF ($6.60–$11.55). AE, MC, V. Tues–Sun 11am–10pm.

Schuh SWISS/CONTINENTAL   This attractive restaurant and tearoom in the center of town has been known for its pastries since 1885. They are still the town's finest. The alpine building has a thick roof arched over the fourth-floor windows and, in back, a sunny terrace with a view of the Jungfrau and a well-kept lawn. The dining room has large windows and a Viennese ambience. A pianist provides music.

Höheweg 56. (*©* **033/822-94-41.** Main courses 21SF–55SF ($11.55–$30.25); fixed-price meal 37SF–43SF ($20.35–$23.65). AE, DC, MC, V. Tues–Sun 8am–11pm. Closed Oct 25–Dec 9.

INTERLAKEN AFTER DARK

Merchants in Interlaken have always known how to inject their town with enough razzle-dazzle to keep visitors coming back. As such, Interlaken boasts one of the highest per-capita rates of nightclubs of any town its size in Switzerland. The town's business is so transient—composed mostly of short-term visitors on their way to somewhere else—the clientele of any particular bar or club is likely to change virtually every week. Given that, here's a roster of those that at this writing were the most animated and/or fun.

You'll usually find a drinking buddy in the folksy, amiably kitschy **Victoria Bar** in the town's stateliest hotel, the Victoria-Jungfrau, Höheweg 41 (*©* **033/828-28-28**). The **Sternen Bar,** set amid a cluster of shops on the all-pedestrian precinct of Jungfraustrasse (*©* **033/822-34-25**), is the closest thing to a big-city wine bar in Interlaken, complete with the requisite platters of food and an alpine version of daytime soap-opera intrigue. **Buddy's Pub,** in the Hotel Splendid, Höheweg 33 (*©* **033/822-76-12**), provides a cozy, richly paneled setting that evokes an upscale version of a smoke-stained pub in Ireland.

If you want to combine drinking with dancing, head to **Johnny's Club,** in the Hotel Carlton, Höheweg 92 (*©* **033/822-38-21**). Although the dance floor is comically small, the music is danceable. Because there are never enough banquettes and chairs for the crowd, everyone seems to mingle extra freely. Its leading competitors include **Hollywood,** in the Hotel Central, Bahnhofstrasse (*©* **033/823-10-33**), where live bands sometimes play. **Disco High-Life,** Rugenparkstrasse 2 (*©* **033/822-15-50**), has been a staple for local residents for many years, especially for off-duty restaurateurs from throughout the surrounding valleys. It plays enough disco tunes from the 1970s and 1980s to unthaw the Big Chill. Somewhat more restrained is the **Black and White,** in the Hotel Metropole, Höheweg 37 (*©* **033/828-66-66**), where a somewhat better-dressed crowd in their 30s and 40s mingles happily together.

Access to virtually every disco in Interlaken costs 7SF ($3.85) on Friday and Saturday nights, and is free every other night. Things begin happening a bit earlier than you might expect—many are rocking by 11pm.

Despite its allegiance to the music coming out of London and Los Angeles, Interlaken also places a lot of emphasis on folklore and alpine schmaltz. The Casino/Kursaal, Höheweg at Strandbadstrasse (*©* **033/827-61-00**), is the venue for the dinner-and-entertainment **Swiss Folklore Show,** a somewhat self-conscious duplication of the quirks and yodels that made alpine Switzerland so unique. The show is in a cavernous convention hall, Monday to Saturday beginning at 7:30pm during July and August, with a less dependable schedule during May and June and again in September and October. Access to the show, which at its most fun can be sudsy and the teeniest bit raucous, costs 20SF ($11); access to the show that includes a fixed-price menu ranges from 39.50SF to 60SF ($21.75 to $33), depending on the meal you order.

Interlaken's most intense doses of folk schmaltz take the form of the **Tell-freilichtspiele,** a secular version of a Teutonic morality play that's presented in an open-air amphitheater in Interlaken's suburb of Matten, a village en route to Grindelwald reached after a brisk 15-minute walk from Interlaken's center. A sweeping cast of as many as 250 presents Schiller's pageant play *William Tell,* complete with galloping horses, flaming torches, flower-draped cows, apple-shooting scenes, and an all-German text delivered in the lilting diphthongs of the Schwyzerdeutsch accent. Tickets for the 2½-hour show cost 23SF to 35SF ($12.65 to $19.25), and are available from **Tellbüro,** Bahnhofstrasse 5 (© **033/822-37-22**). The play is presented at 8pm every Thursday and Saturday between mid-June and early September. Bring a jacket or sweater, or rent one of the blankets from an on-site kiosk, as the alpine chill seems to enhance this epic tale of the struggle for Swiss independence from the tyranny of neighboring Austria.

EASY EXCURSIONS FROM INTERLAKEN

By making the mountains of the Bernese Oberland accessible by train and cable car, Swiss engineers paved the way for visitors to this popular region to explore some of the most scenic and enjoyable spots in the country. There are many organized excursions, as adventurous as they are varied, and Interlaken is the most sensible starting point.

JUNGFRAUJOCH ⋆⋆⋆

A train trip to Jungfraujoch, at 11,333 feet (3,400m), is often considered the trip highlight by visitors. For more than a century it's been the highest railway station in Europe. It's also one of the most expensive: a round-trip tour costs 169.50SF ($93.25) in first class, 159SF ($87.45) in second class. However, families can fill out a Family Card form, available at the railway station, which allows children 16 and under to ride free. Departures are usually daily at 8am from the east station in Interlaken; expect to return around 4pm. To check times, contact the sales office of **Jungfrau Railways,** Höheweg 37 (© **033/828-71-11**).

With luck, you'll get good weather for your day trip; you should always consult the tourist office in Interlaken before boarding the train. The trip is comfortable, safe, and packed with adventure. First you'll take the Wengernalp railway (WAB), a rack railway that opened in 1893. It will take you to Lauterbrunnen, at 2,612 feet (784m), where you'll change to a train heading for the Kleine Scheidegg station, at 6,762 feet (2,029m)—welcome to avalanche country. The view includes the Mönch, the Eiger Wall, and the Jungfrau, which was named for the white-clad Augustinian nuns of medieval Interlaken (Jungfrau means "virgin").

At Kleine Scheidegg, you'll change to the highest rack railway in Europe, the Jungfraubahn. You have 6 miles to go; 4 of them will be spent in a tunnel carved into the mountain. You'll stop briefly twice, at Eigerwand and Eismeer, where you can view the sea of ice from windows in the rock (the Eigerwand is at 9,400 ft./2,830m and Eismeer is at 10,368 ft./3,110m). When the train emerges from the tunnel, the daylight is momentarily blinding, so bring a pair of sunglasses to help your eyes adjust. Notorious among mountain climbers, the Eigernordwand (or "north wall") is incredibly steep.

Once at the Jungfraujoch terminus, you may feel a little giddy until you get used to the air. There's much to do in this eerie world high up Jungfrau, but take it slow—your body's metabolism will be affected and you may tire quickly.

Behind the post office is an elevator that will take you to a corridor leading to the famed **Eispalast** (Ice Palace) ⋆. Here you'll be walking inside "eternal ice" in caverns hewn out of the slowest-moving section of the glacier. Cut 65 feet (19m) below the glacier's surface, these caverns were begun in 1934 by a Swiss guide and subsequently enlarged and embellished with additional sculptures by others. Everything in here is made of ice, including full-size replicas of vintage automobiles and local chaplains.

After returning to the station, you can take the Sphinx Tunnel to another elevator. This one takes you up 356 feet (107m) to an observation deck called the **Sphinx Terraces,** overlooking the saddle between the Mönch and Jungfrau peaks. You can also see the Aletsch Glacier, a 14-mile (23km) river of ice—the longest in Europe. The snow melts into Lake Geneva and eventually flows into the Mediterranean.

Astronomical and meteorological research is conducted at a scientific station here. There's a research exhibition that explains weather conditions, and a video presentation.

There are five different **restaurants** from which to choose. The traditional choice is Jungfraujoch Glacier Restaurant. Top of Europe, opened in 1987, offers several different dining possibilities, and there's also a self-service cafeteria. As a final adventure, you can take a **sleigh ride,** pulled by stout huskies.

On your way back down the mountain, you'll return to Kleine Scheidegg station, but you can vary your route by going through Grindelwald, which offers panoramic views of the treacherous north wall.

HARDER KULM ★★

For a somewhat less ambitious excursion, set out from Interlaken East for this belvedere at 4,337 feet (1,301m). The funicular ride takes 15 minutes and costs 21SF ($11.55) round-trip for adults or 10.50SF ($5.80) for children. From the lookout, you can see Interlaken, the Bernese Alps, and the two lakes, Thun and Brienz, that give Interlaken its name. Departures are every half hour, daily from May until the end of October. The first funicular departs at 9:10am, the last one back leaving at 6pm (6:30pm in July and August). There's a mountain restaurant at Harder Kulm, with observation terraces. For details, call ✆ **033/828-72-16** or 033/822-34-44.

HEIMWEHFLUH ★

You can also take the funicular trip up to Heimwehfluh, at 2,196 feet (659m), where you'll be rewarded with panoramic views of both lakes and the classic trio of Jungfrau, Mönch, and Eiger. In addition to the lookout tower, there's a cafe and restaurant. The funicular station is about a 6-minute walk from the Interlaken West rail station at the southern end of Rugenparkstrasse. The ride takes about 5 minutes and costs 10SF ($5.50) round-trip for adults, 6SF ($3.30) for children. Departures are April to October daily from 9:30am to 5:30pm.

ST. BEATUS-HÖHLEN

According to legend, these caves in the cliffs above Lake Thun were once a dragon's lair until Beatus, a 6th-century Irish missionary, slew the beast and set up residence here. The caves came to be known as Grottes de St-Béat in French and St. Beatus-Höhlen in German. They can be reached by boat, bus, or car, even by foot.

The caves can be explored to a depth of 3,300 feet (990m), along a path lit by electricity. There's a reproduction of a prehistoric cave settlement. The museum section also includes the cell of St. Beatus. Tours are available through the huge caverns and grottoes featuring the striking stalactites and stalagmites. The caves are open from April to October daily from 10:30am to 5pm. Tours depart every 20 to 30 minutes and cost 14SF ($7.70) for adults and 6SF ($3.30) for children. For details, call © **033/841-16-43.**

Just inside the cave entrance is a well-managed restaurant. You can have a meal or a snack inside the cozy dining area or outside on the cave terrace.

The caves can be reached in a number of ways: The bus from Interlaken is the shortest route. From Interlaken bus station, take STI bus no. 21 for a 15-minute ride to the entrance of the caves. Round-trip tickets cost 5SF ($3.35) and buses depart every hour at 15 minutes to the hour. You can drive from Interlaken taking N8 toward Thun. Follow signs leading to the caves. It's a half-hour boat ride to the caves from Interlaken West. The arrival spot is an approximately 20-minute walk from the caves' entrance. Tickets cost 5SF ($2.75) round-trip. Or, walkers and hikers can make it a 2½-hour trip. Start at Interlaken West station and follow signs for the caves.

WILDERSWIL/SCHYNIGE PLATTE ★★★

Less than 2 miles (3km) south of Interlaken, Wilderswil stands on a plain between Lakes Brienz and Thun, at the foot of the Jungfrau Mountains. It's both a summer and a winter resort, and the starting point for many excursions. The resort has 16 levels of accommodations, ranging from hotels to guesthouses, but most tourists stay in Interlaken and visit Wilderswil to take the excursion to **Schynige Platte.** To get to Wilderswil, take the 6-minute train ride from the Interlaken East station. Switch to a cogwheel train for the harrowing, steep ascent to the Schynige Platte, at 6,454 feet (1,936m). The rack railway, which opened in 1893, climbs the 4½-mile (7km) slope in less than an hour, with gradients of up to 25%. There are more than a dozen trips a day in season, June to October, costing 45SF ($24.75) round-trip.

There's an alpine garden in Schynige Platte, containing some 500 species of plants; admission is 3SF ($1.65). From a nearby belvedere, visitors command a splendid view of the Eiger, Mönch, and Jungfrau. The Hotel Restaurant, Schynige Platte, offers good food and drink. For details, call © **033/822-34-31.**

LAKE THUN ★★

Occupying an ancient terminal basin of a glacier, Lake Thun (Thunersee) was once connected to Lake Brienz (Brienzersee). The lake is 17 miles (27km) south of Bern and there is a frequent rail service which continues east to Interlaken. The Lutschine River deposited so much sediment at Interlaken that the one body of water eventually became two. Lake Thun, once beloved by Brahms, is 13 miles (21km) long and 2 miles (3km) wide.

Because of its mild climate, Lake Thun is known as the Riviera of the Bernese Oberland. Popular lake sports include waterskiing, yachting, and windsurfing. On shore there are excellent swimming pools (indoor and outdoor), windsurfing schools, golf courses, tennis courts, horse stables, and caves.

The lake's major resort is **Thun,** a small city that was founded on an island where the Aare River flows out of Lake Thun. The city has since expanded onto the banks of the river to become the political and administrative center of the Bernese Oberland and the gateway to the Bernese mountains.

The most interesting part of the city is on the Aare's right bank. The busy main street, **Hauptgasse,** has walkways built above the arcaded shops. There's a 17th-century town hall on Rathausplatz, where you can climb a covered staircase up to the formidable **Schloss Thun** (Castle Kyburg) ★. The castle is now a historical museum (© **033/223-20-01**). It was built by the dukes of Zähringen at the end of the 12th century. Later it was the home of the counts of Kyburg, as well as the Bernese bailiffs. The massive residential tower has a large Knights' Hall, which contains a Gobelin tapestry from the time of Charles the Bold and a fine collection of halberds and other weapons. Other rooms have important archaeological finds, an exhibit of military uniforms, period furniture, and toys. From the turrets there's a panoramic view of the surrounding area. The museum is open daily April to October from 9am to 6pm and November to March from 10am to 4pm. Admission is 6SF ($3.30) for adults, 2SF ($1.10) for children.

LAKE BRIENZ ✦

Lake Brienz, directly east of Interlaken, is the smaller of the two Oberland lakes. It's about 9 miles (15km) long and up to 2 miles (3km) wide. Most North American visitors bypass the many vacation areas and resorts along its shores in favor of the more traditional resorts on Lake Thun. Europeans, on the other hand, tend to prefer Lake Brienz.

The resort of **Brienz** is at the northern end of the lake, facing Giessbach Falls. The town is famous for its wood carvers, whose work can be found in souvenir shops throughout Switzerland. It's also known for its violin makers.

Brienz has good rail links with Interlaken. Trains run in both directions every hour. For **train schedules** and information, call ✆ **0900-300-300.**

The town's most popular excursion is a cogwheel railway trip to **Brienzer Rothorn,** where you'll get a panoramic vista of the Bernese Alps and Lake Brienz. The tour requires about 2 hours and takes you to an elevation of 7,700 feet (2,310m). Nine trips run each day from June to October. A round-trip costs 66SF ($36.30) per person.

Giessbach Falls ✦✦, some of the most dramatic falls in the Bernese Oberland, are accessible by funicular, which leaves from a platform across the lake. You can get there by car or boat. The funicular costs 5SF ($2.75) for adults, 2.50SF ($1.40) for children 6 to 16, and is free for children 5 and under. The boat to the funicular departs from the lakeshore wharf in the center of Brienz. Allow about 2 hours for the entire excursion. For more information about excursions in the area, call the **Brienz Tourist Office** at ✆ **033/952-80-80.**

For a glimpse of Switzerland's rural history, you can visit the **Swiss Open-Air Museum of Rural Dwellings and Lifestyle** ✦ at Ballenberg, near Brienz (✆ **033/951-11-23**). This is a living, breathing museum—not a dusty, boring complex. Thirteen scenic areas, comprising more than 2,000 acres, lie within the jurisdiction of this museum; they include clusters of typical old farm buildings, tiny settlements, and gardens and fields that Swiss farmers cultivate using time-tested regional methods. The various sections of the museum, which include

---

Lake Tours

A fleet of ships with a total capacity of 6,720 passengers operates on **Lake Thun** daily from April to October. A 4-hour voyage from Interlaken West to Beatenbucht, Spiez, Overhofen, Thun, and back costs 53SF ($29.15) in first class, 35.60SF ($19.60) in second class.

Boat trips on **Lake Brienz** are also available daily from June to September. There are five motor ships and one steamship, with a total capacity of 3,160 passengers. A 3-hour voyage from Interlaken East to Iseltwald, Giessbach, Brienz, and back costs 45.60SF ($25.10) in first class, and 30.40SF ($16.70) in second class. For details, call **B.L.S.** (✆ **033/334-52-11**).

both a nature park and the still alpine waters of Lake Wyssen, are connected by good roads. The museum's acreage lies between the villages of Hofstetten and Brienzwiler, and various sections document architecture specific to different cantons and regions of Switzerland.

A tour of the museum takes about 3 hours. It's open April 15 through October daily from 10am to 5pm. Admission is 14SF ($7.70) for adults and 7SF ($3.85) for children. Guided tours are available by request, but reservations are necessary; plus there's a minimum charge of 100SF ($55).

For those driving to the museum, there's parking at the Hofstetten and Brienzwiler entrances. You can also take a train along the Interlaken-Meiringen-Lucerne line to the Brienz railroad station and transfer there for a bus to the museum.

MEIRINGEN ✦

This resort lies about 8 miles (13km) from Brienz and can be easily visited on a day trip from Interlaken. Several trains headed to Meiringen stop at Interlaken's two railway stations every day. Travel time each way is about 50 minutes.

Strategically centered between three alpine passes (the Grimsel, the Brunig, and the Susten), this old town is a suitable base from which you can explore the eastern sections of the Bernese Oberland and the wild upper reaches of the Aare River. Classified as the major town in the Haslital district and set above the waters of Lake Brienz, Meiringen is famous throughout Europe for its meringue, a dessert that was supposedly invented here.

Rich in scenery and wildlife, the district attracts mountaineers, rock climbers, and hikers. Surrounding the town, you'll find more than 185 miles (298km) of marked hiking trails through unspoiled natural settings, with a complicated network of lifts to reach panoramic vantage points. Destinations for excursions include the Aare Gorge, the Rosenlaui Glacier, and the Reichenbach Falls. The district also has a folklore museum, a crystal grotto, an antique water mill, and a pathway across a glacier. Almost everyone visits the parish church in the upper part of the village. Its crypt was built during the 11th century.

From Meiringen you can set out for Grindelwald, a distance of some 16½ miles (27km) and one of the great walks in the Jungfrau region. Along the way you can absorb the stunning panoramas of the massif, the Eiger, with its massive gray rock walks. Soaring summits and white glaciers form your backdrop as you walk along. If you get tired along the way, there are bus stops where you can board public transportation to take you into Grindelwald. This is also an option should the weather turn bad. Otherwise, depending on your stamina, the walk takes from 6½ to 9 hours.

If you're in the mood for meringue, you can buy one or two at a local bakery. According to legend, the dessert was created when Napoleon visited the town and the local chef in charge of the welcoming banquet had a lot of leftover egg whites. Inspired, he created the puffy mounds and served them in a saucer brimming with sweet mountain cream, much to the general's delight.

Aare Gorge ✦✦ is full of recesses, grottoes, precipices, and arches—all fashioned by the Aare's waters over centuries. The cleft is 1,500 yards long and 650 feet (195m) deep, carved in the Kirchet, a craggy barrier left over from the ice age. In some places the towering rock walls of the gorge are so close together that only a few rays of sunshine can penetrate, just before noon. A unique natural wonder of the Swiss Alps, the gorge can only be reached by car, via the Grimsel-Susten road along the Kirchet. Admission is 6SF ($3.30) for adults and

The Murder of Sherlock Holmes

In 1891, the English writer Sir Arthur Conan Doyle, creator of the most famous detective in all fiction, Sherlock Holmes, acted too hastily in killing off his fictional hero. In a story entitled *The Final Problem,* after a battle with Professor Moriarty (called "the Napoleon of Crime"), Holmes and the fiendish villain were sent plunging to their deaths into Reichenbach Falls at Meiringen.

Although the Sherlock Holmes stories had proven successful, Conan Doyle apparently decided that he'd had enough of Sherlock's sleuthing. His rather outraged public disagreed, so Conan Doyle was forced to virtually call back Sherlock Holmes from the dead, and the detective went on to solve at least 60 more crimes.

The wonder of the falls is reason enough to visit the site, but Holmes devotees wanted more, so in May 1991, the town leaders opened a **Sherlock Holmes Museum,** Bahnhofstrasse 26 (© **033/971-42-21**), in an old Anglican church at Meiringen. There, you can visit a re-creation of Sherlock Holmes's sitting room at 221B Baker Street in London, with exhibits donated by fans from around the world. The museum is open May through September Tuesday through Sunday 3 to 6pm, and October through April Wednesday through Sunday 3 to 6pm. Admission costs 3.80SF ($2.10) for adults and 2.80SF ($1.55) for children.

3.50SF ($1.95) for children. The gorge is open May to October daily from 10am to 5pm; in July and August it's also open from 8am to 6pm.

If you're a fan of Sherlock Holmes, you'll enjoy an excursion to **Reichenbachfall** , where the rivers of the Rosenlaui Valley meet. The impressive beauty of the falls has lured many visitors, beginning with the British in the 19th century. One visitor, Sir Arthur Conan Doyle, creator of Holmes, was so impressed with the place that he used it as the setting for the scene in *The Final Problem,* in which the villain, Professor Moriarty, struggles with the detective and tosses him into the falls. You can see a Sherlock Holmes commemorative plaque near the upper station of the funicular. The falls can be visited from mid-May to mid-September. The funicular takes you to a point at 2,779 feet (834m) near terraces overlooking the water. Handrails provide safety. Departures are every 10 minutes daily from 8:15am to 11:45am and 1 to 6pm. The cost of admission is 7SF ($3.85) for adults and 3.50SF ($1.95) for children. The price includes the cost of the funicular. It's a 10-minute walk from Meiringen to the base of the funicular. If you're driving from Meiringen, take the road to Grimsel and turn right toward Reichenbach Falls and Mervenklinik. For more information, call © **033/971-40-48.**

After admiring the cascade, you can hike through the river valley. The footpath through the **Rosenlaui Valley** is marked. After 90 minutes you'll arrive at the entrance to Rosenlaui Gorge. The surfaces of the sheer rock faces echo the sounds of the many small waterfalls within. The **glacier gorges** which have been hollowed out by the waters from the melting ice of the Rosenlaui Glacier are a spectacular sight. You can walk from one end of this gorge to the other in about 30 minutes. A small hotel and seasonal restaurant are near the entrance.

Most visitors turn around at the uppermost reaches of the gorge and make the 2-hour trek back to Reichenbach Falls to pick up the funicular back to Meiringen. The gorge can be visited May through October daily from 9am to 5pm. The cost is 6SF ($3.30) for adults and 3.50SF ($1.95) for children.

2 Mürren ★★

7 miles (11km) S of Lauterbrunnen, 19 miles (30km) S of Interlaken

This village has a stunning location, high above the Lauterbrunnen Valley. At 5,414 feet (1,624m), Mürren is the highest year-round inhabited village in the Bernese Oberland. It's an exciting excursion from Interlaken in the summer and a major ski resort in the winter. Downhill and slalom skiing were developed here in the 1920s. Mürren is also the birthplace of modern alpine racing.

ESSENTIALS

GETTING THERE   Take the mountain railway from the Interlaken East rail station to Lauterbrunnen (trip time: 1 hour). Once at Lauterbrunnen, you can take a cogwheel train the rest of the way to Mürren. Departures from Lauterbrunnen are every half hour from 6:30am to 8:30pm daily, costing 9.50SF ($5.25) one-way.

A regular postal-bus service goes once an hour from Lauterbrunnen to Stechelberg; the rest of the way you must travel by cable car, costing 28.80SF ($15.85) round-trip. Departures are every half hour, and the trip takes about 10 minutes.

Mürren is not accessible to traffic. You can drive as far as Stechelberg, the last town on the Lauterbrunnen Valley road, and switch to the cable car discussed above.

VISITOR INFORMATION   The **Mürren Tourist Information Bureau** is at the Sportzentrum (✆ 033/856-86-86). There is no street plan—follow the clearly indicated signs to the various hotels and commercial establishments. The office is open Monday to Friday 9am to noon and 2 to 6:30pm, Saturday to Sunday 2 to 6:30pm.

OUTDOOR FUN
IN TOWN
There are miles of downhill runs in the area. Mürren, one of the finest ski resorts of Switzerland, provides access to the Schilthorn at 9,745 feet (2,923m), the start of a 9-mile (15km) run that drops all the way to Lauterbrunnen. It also has one funicular railway, seven lifts, and two cable cars. A 1-day ski pass that includes the area around Schilthorn costs 52SF ($28.60), a 7-day pass goes for 236SF ($129.80). For cross-country skiers there's a 7½-mile track in the Lauterbrunnen Valley, 10 minutes by railway from Mürren.

The alpine **Sportzentrum** (Sports Center), in the middle of Mürren (✆ 033/856-86-86), is one of the finest in the Bernese Oberland. The modern building has an indoor pool, a lounge, a snack bar, an outdoor skating rink, a tourist information office, and a children's playroom and library. There are facilities for squash, tennis, and curling. Hotel owners subsidize the operation, tacking the charges onto your hotel bill. Supplemental charges include 16SF to 22SF ($8.80 to $12.10) per hour for tennis, 16SF to 22SF ($8.80 to $12.10) per 45-minute session for squash, 13SF to 16SF ($7.15 to $8.80) per hour for use of the sauna. The facility is usually open Monday to Friday from 9am to noon and 2 to 6pm, and from Christmas through April and July to mid-September, also on Saturday from 1 to 6:30pm and Sunday from 1 to 5:30pm; but check locally as these times can vary.

On the Trail of James Bond

The **Schilthorn,** with its aerial cableway and steep snow slopes, was the setting for the most exciting scenes in the film *On Her Majesty's Secret Service,* one of the classic Bond thrillers. The incomparable location, the dramatic view of ice-covered peaks, and the fact that the imposing summit house is accessible only by aerial cableway convinced United Artists to select the Schilthorn as the film site.

Between October 1968 and April 1969, an army of volunteers transformed the Schilthorn into the film's "Piz Gloria." A landing pad for helicopters was constructed that was also used as a curling rink in the film and now serves as a sun terrace. The film was the breakthrough that made Schilthorn the world-famous attraction it has become. Today, the imitation-blood trails have long been washed away, the fake bodies carted off, and the revolving restaurant never really exploded. A James Bond video in the Touristorama reminds visitors of this spectacular scenic film adventure.

NEARBY

The famous **Mürren-Allmendhubel Cableway** leaves from the northwestern edge of Mürren. From the destination, there's a panoramic view of the Lauterbrunnen Valley as far as Wengen and Kleine Scheidegg. Between mid-June and late August the alpine meadows are covered with wildflowers. A walk in this hilly region might be a highlight of your trip to Switzerland. The cable car operates daily throughout the year from 8am to 5pm. However, there are annual closings for maintenance in May and November. It costs 14SF ($7.70) per person roundtrip. For information, call ✆ **033/823-14-44.**

The most popular excursion from Mürren is a cable-car ride to the **Schilthorn** ✿✿✿, famous for its 360° view. The panorama extends from the Jura to the Black Forest, including the Eiger, Mönch, and Jungfrau. The Schilthorn is also called "Piz Gloria" after the James Bond film *On Her Majesty's Secret Service* (the most dramatic scenes in the movie were filmed here). Today, Piz Gloria is the name of the revolving restaurant on-site. The summit is the start of the world's longest downhill ski race. The cable car to Schilthorn leaves every 30 minutes, and the round-trip costs 89SF ($48.95). The journey to the top takes 20 minutes. For details, call ✆ **033/823-14-44.**

SHOPPING

Commercial real estate in Mürren is expensive, particularly since the terrain is so inhospitable and supplies have to be hauled up by cable car or helicopter. Consequently, many of the resort's store owners make it a point to cram as much as possible into their shops, hoping to catch impulse buyers during shopping sprees. Therefore, the rule is, don't make any assumptions that shops here won't have what you want, as they're deceptively all-encompassing. Two of the resort's most interesting shops combine displays loaded with both sporting equipment and handicrafts. These are **Sporthaus Abegglen** (✆ **033/855-12-45**) and **Sporthaus Stäger** (✆ **033/855-23-55**).

WHERE TO STAY

EXPENSIVE

Anfi Palace Hotel (★ Built early in the 20th century, this hotel lies under a black mansard roof and indented loggias with wrought-iron balconies. There's a modern extension jutting off to one side. A change of management in the early 1990s arranged the gradual renovation and improvement of this property, which underwent several name changes throughout the 1970s and 1980s. The bedrooms are the most spacious, best furnished, and also the most comfortable in Mürren. The beds are excellent, and the bathrooms are nicely maintained.

CH-3825 Mürren. ℂ 033/855-24-24. Fax 033/855-24-17. www.muerren.ch/palace. 40 units. Summer 320SF ($176) double; winter 340SF–420SF ($187–$231) double. Rates include buffet breakfast. Half board 35SF–45SF ($19.25–$24.75) per person extra. AE, DC, MC, V. **Amenities:** 3 restaurants, 2 bars; pool; sauna; Jacuzzi; room service; babysitting; laundry/dry cleaning. *In room:* TV, minibar, hair dryer, safe.

Hotel Eiger (★ Founded in the 1920s and last renovated in 1994, this chalet is the longest-established hotel in Mürren. The public rooms are warmly decorated, and many of the windows have panoramic views. The bedrooms are small, cozy, and comfortable and decorated in a typical alpine style. All units have tidy bathrooms. The hotel, managed by Annelis Stähli-von Allmen and family, lies across the street from the terminus of the cable car from Lauterbrunnen.

CH-3825 Mürren. ℂ 033/856-54-54. Fax 033/856-54-56. www.muerren.ch/eiger. 44 units. Summer 230SF–320SF ($126.50–$176) double, 480SF–520SF ($264–$286) suite. Winter 240SF–380SF ($132–$209) double, 420SF–620SF ($231–$341) suite. Rates include breakfast. AE, DC, MC, V. Closed Easter to mid-June and mid-Sept to Dec 19. **Amenities:** Restaurant, bar; pool; fitness center; sauna; room service; babysitting; laundry/dry cleaning. *In room:* TV, hair dryer.

MODERATE

Hotel Alpenruh Set in the most congested yet charming section of the village, the Alpenruh possesses an interior that's plusher than its chalet-style facade implies. The old building was upgraded in 1986 to government-rated three-star status without sacrificing any of its small-scale charm. The small rooms have pine paneling and a mix of antique and contemporary furniture, and most of them open onto a view of the Jungfrau. The hotel is owned by the company that operates the aerial cable cars to the Schilthorn's Piz Gloria, and you can get a voucher to have breakfast there.

CH-3825 Mürren. ℂ 033/856-88-00. Fax 033/856-88-88. www.schilthorn.ch. 26 units. 200SF–245SF ($110–$134.75) double. 50% reduction for children 12 and under sharing parents' room. Rates include breakfast. Half board 30SF ($16.50) per person extra. AE, DC, MC, V. **Amenities:** Restaurant, lounge; room service. *In room:* TV, minibar.

Hotel Jungfrau/Haus Mönch This government-rated, three-star, 19th-century building, located a 3-minute walk from the Mürrenbahn, lies under gables behind green shutters, stucco, and brick walls. A comfortable annex was constructed in 1965; both buildings have an inviting, modern decor with open fireplaces, clusters of armchairs, and a shared dining room. The small bedrooms are bright and appealing. Twenty of the rooms are in the Hotel Jungfrau and 25 are across the street in the lodge. Units are equal in comfort. All contain neatly kept bathrooms.

CH-3825 Mürren. ℂ 033/855-45-45. Fax 033/855-45-49. www.hoteljungfrau.ch. 45 units. Off-season 190SF–210SF ($104.50–$115.50) double. Winter 230SF–280SF ($126.50–$154) double. Rates include buffet breakfast. AE, DC, MC, V. Closed mid-Apr to late May and mid-Oct to mid-Dec. **Amenities:** Restaurant, bar; room service; laundry/dry cleaning. *In room:* TV.

INEXPENSIVE

Hotel Blumental *Value*   This centrally located, chalet-type hotel is graced with stone masonry and wood-paneled public areas. Run by the von Allmen family, it offers a cozy atmosphere inspired by the nearby mountains. The small bedrooms have wood walls and new pine furnishings and are decorated in attractive colors. All units have neat bathrooms, and several have private balconies. In summer you can dine outside, enjoying a panoramic view of the mountains.

CH-3825 Mürren. (℃) **033/855-18-26.** Fax 033/855-36-86. 16 units. 160SF–190SF ($88–$104.50) double. Rates include buffet breakfast. Half board 25SF ($13.75) extra. AE, DC, V. **Amenities:** Restaurant, lounge; free admission to nearby Sports Centre; room service; laundry/dry cleaning. *In room:* TV, hair dryer.

WHERE TO DINE

Eigerstübli *★* SWISS   The best food in Mürren is served here in a festive ambience. The Eigerstübli's cuisine includes fondue and an international range of hearty and well-prepared specialties well suited to the alpine heights and chill. Main dishes include a delectable roast lamb shoulder with lentils, a whole sole from the grill, beef Stroganoff, a savory cheese fondue, a perfectly prepared roast breast of duck with orange sauce, or poached filet of trout. All main dishes may be ordered with rösti (Swiss hash browns). Dessert specialties include vodka sherbet and iced soufflé Grand Marnier.

In the Hotel Eiger. (℃) **033/856-54-54.** Reservations recommended. Main courses 23SF–54SF ($12.65–$29.70). AE, DC, MC, V. Daily 11:30am–2pm and 6–9pm. Closed Easter to mid-June and mid-Sept to mid-Dec.

Hotel Alpenruh *★* FRENCH   This small hotel contains one of the finest restaurants in Mürren, offering a large and varied menu. The place is always a reliable bet for lunch or dinner, even during the rainy months of April and May and again in November when many of the other restaurants and hotels in Mürren are closed. Both its dining rooms have attractive alpine themes and wide terraces with a panoramic view of the surrounding mountains. Appetizers include dried tomato strips with sage butter and tortellini with ricotta. You can dive enthusiastically into such dishes as veal steak with a Dijon mustard sauce and lamb cutlet with a garlic-herb sauce. The steaks are delectable. The fish courses might include sole Colbert and anglerfish medallions with jumbo shrimp. For dessert, try the fresh pineapple with caramel mousse or a gratiné of kiwi and oranges.

(℃) **033/856-88-00.** Reservations recommended in winter. Main courses 20SF–40SF ($11–$22); fixed-price menu 42SF ($23.10). AE, DC, MC, V. Daily 7am–11pm.

Restaurant im Gruebi SWISS   This popular restaurant offers a sunny outdoor terrace on the lobby level of the Hotel Jungfrau. The large hexagonal dining room has views of the mountains and ski slopes. You get authentic Swiss flavor here and first-rate ingredients. Some specialties are prepared for two, including chateaubriand, New York steak, rack of lamb flavored with herbs, and veal filets with fruits in a cognac sauce. It also offers the classic fondue bourguignonne. Ten different types of rösti are served, including the classic Jungfrau version—ham, tomatoes, and raclette cheese. The chef also features what he calls "week-hits," a different specialty every night. One night might feature a salad and an all-you-can-eat array of meat fondues. Another night might be pasta night, grill night, and so on. There's even a cheese night, featuring raclette, fondues, and various types of Swiss cheese preparations.

In the Hotel Jungfrau. (℃) **033/855-45-45.** Reservations recommended in midwinter. Main courses 26SF–38SF ($14.30–$20.90); fixed-price menu 32SF ($17.60). AE, DC, MC, V. Daily 7:30am–9:15pm. Closed mid-Apr to mid-June and mid-Oct to mid-Dec.

Restaurant Piz Gloria ⭐ (Finds SWISS   Piz Gloria is the most dramatically located restaurant in Europe, with a setting so inhospitable and an architecture so futuristic that it was used as the setting for the James Bond film *On Her Majesty's Secret Service.* Designed like a big-windowed flying saucer and anchored solidly to the alpine bedrock, it was built at staggering expense in one of Switzerland's highest locations, the Schilthorn. Closed during blizzards, the restaurant has a terrace where newcomers should beware of becoming seriously sunburned by the rays of the high-altitude, unfiltered sunlight. You'll dine inside at long wooden tables, each with a wraparound view. The menu includes hearty dishes suited to the climate. There are both weekly and daily specials, ranging from chicken cordon-bleu to filet of codfish with rice and vegetables. One spaghetti dish is named for James Bond; it's made with peppers, mushrooms, bacon, and Italian veal sausages. Another dish often served is puff pastry filled with veal and served with a white sauce. The 007 for dessert is a bowl of five different scoops of ice cream, topped with fruits.

Schilthorn. © **033/856-21-40.** Main courses 14SF–34SF ($7.70–$18.70); daily special 21.50SF ($11.85). AE, DC, MC, V. Daily from the first cable car's arrival until the last cable car's afternoon departure. The first departure from Stechelberg is at 7:25am in summer and at 7:55am in winter. The cable car's last departure from Schilthorn's summit is at 6pm in summer and 5pm in winter. Closed Nov 15–Dec 4 and 1 week after Easter. The only access is via the Schilthorn cable car, which departs from the relatively low-lying town of Stechelberg and stops at 3 way stations, the most prominent of which is Mürren. Round-trip fare from Stechelberg 89SF ($48.95); round-trip fare from Mürren 60SF ($33).

MÜRREN AFTER DARK

Every hotel in Mürren contains a bar offering maximum amounts of alpine coziness. Two that deserve special mention, however, are the **Bliemlichäller,** a sudsy, popular, and sometimes raucous disco in the Hotel Blumental (© **033/855-18-26**); and an equivalent disco, the **Inferno-Bar,** in the Hotel Palace (© **033/855-24-24**). Both open in the late afternoon, then crank up in midwinter and midsummer around 10:30pm into roaringly high-energy discos. More correctly perceived as a pub for après-skiing or après-hill climbing is the winter-only **Tächi-Bar** in the Hotel Eiger (© **033/855-13-31**).

3 Wengen ⭐⭐⭐

16 miles (26km) S of Interlaken, 3 miles (5km) NE of Mürren

The Mönch, Jungfrau, and Eiger loom above this sunny resort town built on a sheltered terrace high above the Lauterbrunnen Valley, at about 4,160 feet (1,248m). Wengen (pronounced *Ven*-ghen) is one of the more chic and better-equipped ski and mountain resorts in the Bernese Oberland. It has 30 hotels in all price categories, as well as 500 apartments and chalets for rent.

In the 1830s, the International Lauberhorn Ski Race was established here. At that time Wengen was a farm community. The British were the first to popularize the resort, after World War I. Today parts of the area retain their rural charm. The main street, however, is filled with cafes, shops, and restaurants welcoming tourists. Robert Redford is a frequent visitor. No cars are allowed in Wengen, but the streets are still bustling with service vehicles and electric luggage carts.

ESSENTIALS

GETTING THERE   Take the train from Interlaken Ost to Wengen. Departures are every 45 minutes 6:30am to 11:30pm, costing 12SF ($6.60) one-way. After a stopover at Wengen, the train goes on to Kleine Scheidegg and Jungfraujoch. For **rail information,** call © **0900/300-300.**

If you're driving, head south from Interlaken toward Wilderswil, following the minor signposted road to Lauterbrunnen, where you'll find garages and open-air spaces for parking. You cannot drive to Wengen but must take the train (see above). You can park in one of the garages at Lauterbrunnen for 9SF ($4.95) a day. Trains from Lauterbrunnen to Wengen leave at the rate of one every 15 minutes from 6am to midnight, costing 5.60SF ($3.10) one-way.

VISITOR INFORMATION   There are no street names; hotels, restaurants, and other major establishments are signposted with directional signs, which make them relatively easy to find. The **Wengen Tourist Information Office** (© **033/855-14-14**) is in the center of the resort, open mid-June to mid-September and mid-December to Easter only, Monday to Friday 9am to noon and 2 to 5pm, Saturday 8:30 to 11:30am.

EXPLORING THE AREA

The **ski area** around Wengen is highly developed, with ski trails carved into the sides of Mannlichen, Kleine Scheidegg, Lauberhorn, and Eigergletscher. A triumph of alpine engineering, the town and its region contain three mountain railways, two aerial cableways, one gondola, 31 lifts, and 155 miles (250km) of downhill runs. You'll also find a branch of the Swiss Ski School, more than 7 miles (11km) of trails for cross-country skiing, an indoor and outdoor skating rink, a curling hall, an indoor swimming pool, and a day nursery.

During the summer, the district attracts hill climbers from all over Europe. The **hiking trails** are well maintained and carefully marked, with dozens of unusual detours to hidden lakes and panoramas. Wengen also has five public tennis courts available through the tourist office (see "Essentials," above), a natural skating rink (Natureisbahn), and a partially sheltered indoor rink (Kunsteisbahn). The hours these rinks keep are subject to change, so check with the tourist office for details.

NEARBY ATTRACTIONS   From Wengen and Grindelwald, there are a number of excursions up and down the Lauterbrunnen Valley. You can visit **Trümmelbach Falls** ★★★, which plunges in five powerful cascades through a gorge. You can take an elevator built through the rock to a series of galleries (bring a raincoat). The last stop is at a wall where the upper fall descends. The falls can be visited from the end of May through June and in September and October, daily from 9am to 5pm; in July and August, daily from 9am to 5:30pm. They're closed during other months. Admission is 10SF ($5.50) for adults, 4SF ($2.20) for children 6 to 16, and free for children 5 and under. It takes about 45 minutes to reach the falls on foot. For information, call © **033/855-32-32**. A postal bus from Lauterbrunnen (only 15 minutes from Wengen by train) stops at Trümmelbach Falls. It costs only 1.30SF (70¢) for adults, .60SF (35¢) for children, and departs once an hour from Lauterbrunnen. For information, call © **033/828-70-38**.

You might also want to visit the base of the **Staubbach Waterfall** ★★, which plunges nearly 1,000 feet (300m) in a sheer drop over a rock wall in the valley above Lauterbrunnen. Lord Byron compared this waterfall to the "tail of the pale horse ridden by Death in the Apocalypse." Staubbach can be reached from the resort village of Lauterbrunnen, which lies only 15 minutes from Wengen by train (see "Essentials" above). From the center of Lauterbrunnen follow the signposts along a walkway running along a creek and then be prepared for some steep stairs to reach the viewing point for the falls.

SHOPPING

Despite its proximity to the wide, open spaces of the big-sky Alps, don't be disappointed by the distinctly non-alpine-looking shops here. The well-recommended **Boutique zur Vase,** Dorfstrasse (© **033/855-26-27**), offers fragile and exquisite cutlery, porcelain, and flatware. Two of the town's most successful shops for ski and other sports equipment are **Alpia Sport,** Dorfstrasse (© **033/855-26-26**), and **Central Sport,** Dorfstrasse (© **033/855-23-23**). If you're interested in capturing the scenery that unfolds on all sides, head for **Foto-Haus,** Dorfstrasse (© **033/855-11-54**). In addition to film and cameras, it also sells one of the town's widest rosters of handcrafted souvenirs to commemorate your stay in the Oberland.

WHERE TO STAY

All the hotels in Wengen are mobbed most of the winter, so make reservations if you plan to arrive during ski season.

EXPENSIVE

Hotel Regina 🐘🐘 Wengen's most time-honored hotel lies in an embellished Victorian elephant of a building with balconies and lots of charm. Guido Meyer has been known to arrange unusual concerts for his guests (once, during our stay, a group of Oklahoma high school students gave a concert on the front lawn). One of the public rooms has a baronial carved-stone fireplace. The mid-sized to spacious bedrooms are comfortable and cozy, each well furnished and immaculately maintained. All units contain tidily kept bathrooms. Maintenance is high, as is the level of service.

CH-3823 Wengen. © **033/856-58-58.** Fax 033/855-15-74. www.wengen.com/hotel/regina. 95 units. Summer 380SF ($209) double; winter 450SF ($247.50) double. For a suite add 30SF ($16.50) per person. Rates include half board. AE, MC, V. Closed Oct 15–Dec 15. **Amenities:** Restaurant, bar; health club; sauna; room service; babysitting; laundry/dry cleaning. *In room:* TV, hair dryer.

Hotel Silberhorn 🐘 Famous for the cluster of restaurants and nightclubs located on its first two floors, this first-class family-owned hotel also offers comfortable modern rooms filled with pine and chintz, many with wooden balconies, and a few with kitchenettes. The simple Victorian building has been modernly equipped. The most spacious, most comfortable, and most attractive rooms are in the older wing. The restaurants located here shine in mid-winter.

CH-3823 Wengen. © **033/856-51-31.** Fax 033/855-22-44. www.wengen.com/hotel/silberhorn. 61 units. Summer 200SF–246SF ($110–$135.30) double, 300SF–315SF ($165–$173.25) suite for 2. Winter 320SF–380SF ($176–$209) double, 390SF–460SF ($214.50–$253) suite for 2. Children 5 and under stay free in parents' room. Rates include buffet breakfast. Half board 35SF ($19.25) extra. AE, DC, MC, V. **Amenities:** 2 restaurants, 1 nightclub, 1 bar; Jacuzzi; sauna; salon; room service; babysitting; laundry/dry cleaning. *In room:* TV, minibar, hair dryer.

Sunstar Hotel Originally constructed in 1910 as the Metropole Hotel, this present hostelry is from the mid-1970s. Today it's a government-rated four-star hotel in the heart of the village, with wraparound balconies and a modern design inspired by traditional alpine architecture. The Kirche family are the helpful hosts. The nice-sized rooms are well furnished and comfortable, many opening onto balconies with panoramic views of the Alps. All units are equipped with well-kept bathrooms. Guests can relax in the spacious lounge with a fireplace or retreat to the hotel's cozy bar.

CH-3823 Wengen. © **033/856-51-11.** Fax 033/855-32-72. www.sunstarhotels.ch. 76 units. Summer 304SF–334SF ($167.20–$183.70) double. Winter 345SF–450SF ($189.75–$247.50) double. Rates include half board.

AE, DC, MC, V. Closed Easter to end of May and mid-Oct to mid-Dec. **Amenities:** Restaurant, bar; pool; sauna; room service; babysitting; laundry/dry cleaning. *In room:* TV, minibar, hair dryer.

MODERATE

Hotel Eiger ⭐ Rustic timbers cover the walls and ceilings of this attractive hotel behind the railway station. Karl Fuchs and his family offer spacious, attractive rooms with balconies. The suites, which are rented on a weekly basis only, are often sold out a year in advance. All rooms come equipped with well-maintained bathrooms. There's a modern dining room with views of the Jungfrau massif and the Lauterbrunnen Valley. In the hotel lobby you'll find an inviting sitting area with a fireplace.

CH-3823 Wengen. ℂ **800/528-1234** in the U.S. and Canada, or 033/856-05-05. Fax 033/855-10-30. www.eigerhotel.ch. 33 units. Summer 218SF ($119.90) double. Winter 235SF ($129.25) double. Year-round 320SF–342SF ($176–$188.10) suite for 2. Rates include breakfast. Half board 25SF ($13.75) per person extra. AE, DC, MC, V. Closed mid-Apr to June 1 and Nov. **Amenities:** Restaurant, bar; laundry/dry cleaning. *In room:* TV.

Victoria-Lauberhorn This venerable hotel, which accepts bookings by the week, is in the center of Wengen. Built in 1895, the gabled hotel has been enlarged at least twice since then. The cozy rooms are decorated in a wide array of styles, ranging from modern to alpine with painted furniture. The best accommodations open onto a panorama of the mountains.

CH-3823 Wengen. ℂ **033/856-29-29.** Fax 033/856-29-19. www.hovic.ch. 62 units. 660SF–730SF ($363–$401.50) weekly. Rates include half board. AE, DC, MC, V. Closed Easter to June 2 and Sept 26–Dec 19. **Amenities:** Pizza pub, creperie, outdoor cafe, winter-only bar; room service; laundry. *In room:* TV, hair dryer.

INEXPENSIVE

Hotel Eden *Value* You'll find home-style comfort in this economy oasis. The symmetrical villa with red shutters is located among guesthouses and private chalets above the commercial center of town. Kerstin Bucher directs a cooperative staff. Some of the well-furnished but small bedrooms have balconies, and nearly all of them open onto a panoramic view of the mountains. Each comfortable room is cozy and clean, a real snug alpine nest. The few rooms that do contain private bathrooms have well-kept showers.

CH-3823 Wengen. ℂ **033/855-16-34.** Fax 033/855-39-50. 30 units, 6 with bathroom. Summer 150SF ($82.50) double without bathroom, 165SF ($90.75) double with bathroom. Winter 170SF ($93.50) double without bathroom, 190SF ($104.50) double with bathroom. Rates include breakfast. Half board 30SF ($16.50) per person extra. AE, DC, MC, V. **Amenities:** Restaurant, lounge. *In room:* No phone.

WHERE TO DINE

Arvenstube SWISS This is a local favorite with pinewood panels and a polite crew ready to serve you. The well-prepared menu might include smoked trout with horseradish, air-dried alpine beef, smoked breast of goose, Bernese-style beef with mushrooms, filet of fera (a lake fish), and veal steak Alfredo and morels. Three kinds of fondue are also offered. The fondue bourguignonne is particularly stunning with 40 garnitures—you must order it a day in advance. The Valais-style braserade of beef cooks over a small flame at your table.

In the Hotel Eiger. ℂ **033/856-05-05.** Main courses 18SF–55SF ($9.90–$30.25); fixed-price lunch 25SF ($13.75), fixed-price dinner 52SF ($28.60). AE, DC, MC, V. Daily 11am–2pm and 6–9:30pm (open all day in winter). Closed May.

Hotel Bernerhof Restaurant SWISS/ITALIAN The Schweizers run this old family favorite with wine-red shutters. There's an alpine-themed bar, which fills up in the early evening with beer drinkers returning from the slopes. Hearty alpine food, including raclette and fondue, is served in the dining room. Several savory Italian dishes are also featured. Justifiably favorite dishes include grilled trout with horseradish sauce, Burgundy-style snails, and a delectable fondue bourguignonne.

CH-3823 Wengen. ℂ 033/855-27-21. Reservations sometimes required. Main courses 12SF–38SF ($6.60–$20.90); fixed-price menu 30SF ($16.50); lunch dish of the day 16.50SF ($9.10). AE, MC, V. Daily 8am–11:30pm.

Hotel Hirschen Restaurant *(Finds* SWISS   This quiet retreat at the foot of the slopes has true alpine flavor. The rear dining room is decorated with hunting trophies, pewter, and wine racks. Johannes Abplanalp and his family offer a dinner special called Galgenspiess—filet of beef, veal, and pork flambéed at your table. Other dishes include filet of breaded pork, rumpsteak Café de Paris, and fondue Bacchus (in white-wine sauce), *bourguignonne* (hot oil), or *chinoise* (hot bouillon). A hearty lunch is *winzerrösti,* consisting of country ham, cheese, and a fried egg with homemade rösti.

CH-3823 Wengen. ℂ 033/855-15-44. Reservations recommended. Main courses 14.50SF–44.50SF ($8–$24.50); fixed-price menu 39.50SF–69.50SF ($21.75–$38.25). MC, V. Mon and Wed–Fri 5–11pm, Sat–Sun 11:30am–2:30pm and 5–11pm (closed Mon in summer and Tues all year). Closed mid-Apr to May and late Sept to Dec 15.

WENGEN AFTER DARK

Except for the **Disco Carrousel** in the Hotel Regina (ℂ **033/855-15-12**) that's open only 1 week during ski championships, and then 1 week over Christmas and New Year, Wengen has only one disco, the popular **Disco Tiffany.** Set in the cellar of the Hotel Silberhorn (ℂ **033/856-51-31**), near the arrival point for the cog-railway cars from Lauterbrunnen, it's small, crowded, and painted in tones of navy blue and black. Look for nightly openings between mid-December and early April, and openings on Friday and Saturday nights the rest of the year. No cover; show up after 10:30pm.

More reliable and prevalent than discos in Wengen are the resort's hard-drinking bars and sudsy pubs. The two wildest are the **Tanne Bar,** Dorfstrasse (no phone), across the street from the Sunstar Hotel; and **Sina's Pub,** Dorfstrasse (ℂ **033/855-31-72**), where karaoke mikes and monitors are pulled out from storage whenever things begin to look dull. An enduring favorite is the **Pickel Bar,** in the Hotel Eiger (ℂ **033/856-05-05**). Set in a trapezoidal room lined with thick unfinished planks and stout timbers, it's illuminated with candlelight and can take all the punishment a rowdy core of skiers can dish out. At the **Hot Chili Peppers Bar,** Dorfstrasse (ℂ **033/856-68-68**), there's live music on Saturday nights, and drinking, flirting, and gossiping every night. One spot with touches of village-life kitsch is the **Kegelbahn Bar,** Dorfstrasse (ℂ **033/855-24-12**). Associated with the owners of the Hotel Belvédère, it contains three billiard tables, a bowling alley, and some dart boards. It's located in the cellar of Wengen's only movie theater.

4 Grindelwald ⍟⍟⍟

14 miles (22km) S of Interlaken, 120 miles (192km) SW of Zurich

The "glacier village" of Grindelwald at 3,445 feet (1,033m) is set against a backdrop of the Wetterhorn and the towering north face of the Eiger. It's both a winter and a summer resort.

Unlike Wengen and Mürren, it's the only major resort in the Jungfrau region that can be reached by car. Because of its accessibility, Grindelwald is often crowded with visitors, many of whom come just for the day.

Grindelwald is surrounded by folkloric hamlets, swift streams, and as much alpine beauty as you're likely to find anywhere in Switzerland. Although at first the hiking options and cable-car networks might seem baffling, the tourist office will provide maps of the local peaks and valleys and help clear up any confusion.

ESSENTIALS

GETTING THERE   The **Bernese Oberland Railway** (BOB) leaves from the Interlaken East station. The trip takes 35 minutes. Call ℂ **0900-300-300** for information.

If you're driving, take the Wilderswil road south from Interlaken and follow the signs all the way to Grindelwald.

VISITOR INFORMATION   The resort doesn't use street names or numbers; instead of street names, hotel direction signs are used to locate places. If you're booked into a hotel or tourist home in Grindelwald, request a pass at your hotel that will entitle you to many discounts, especially on mountain rides.

The tourist office is at the **Sportszentrum,** on Hauptstrasse, CH-3818 Grindelwald (ℂ **033/854-12-12**), open July and August, Monday to Friday 8am to 7pm, Saturday 8am to 5pm, Sunday 9 to 11am and 3 to 5pm; September to June, Monday to Friday 8am to noon and 2 to 6pm, Saturday 8am to noon and 2 to 5pm.

THE GREAT OUTDOORS

For details about the tours below, including seasonal changes, consult the tourist office.

GLACIER TOURS   The town maintains a sheltered observation gallery, adjacent to the base of the **Lower Grindelwald Glacier** (Untere Gletscher) that offers a close look at the glacier's ravine. The half-mile gallery stretches past the deeply striated rocks, which include formations of colored marble worn smooth by the glacier's powers of erosion. The gallery is easy to reach on foot or by car. Round-trip bus service is available from Grindelwald for 11.20SF ($6.15), and there's a parking lot and restaurant nearby.

The **Blue Ice Grotto** is part of the Upper Grindelwald Glacier (Obere Gletscher), which is a 2-hour hike or a 15-minute bus ride from the Lower Grindelwald Glacier. The two glaciers are separated from one another and flow into different valleys. At midday, the 150-foot-thick (45m) ice walls take on an eerie blue tinge. Local guides will assure you that although the grotto and the glacier that contains it are slowly moving downhill, you'll be perfectly safe. The grotto is open mid-June to October, daily from 9am to 6pm. Round-trip bus service costs 11.20SF ($7.50). *Note:* Once you get off the bus, you'll still have to climb 900 steps to reach the grotto.

HIKING & MOUNTAIN CLIMBING   If you've come to Switzerland to see the Alps, Grindelwald and its surroundings offer dozens of challenging paths and mountain trails that are well marked and carefully maintained. Outdoor adventures range from an exhilarating ramble across the gentle incline of an alpine valley to a dangerous trek with ropes and pitons along the north face of Mount Eiger. The choice depends on your inclination and your skills. A map showing the region's paths and trails is available at the town's tourist office.

If you're adventurous enough to be tempted by peaks 13,000 feet (3,900m) high or higher, or if you'd like to learn the proper way to climb rocks and ice, contact the **Bergsteigerzentrum,** CH-3818 Grindelwald (ℂ **033/853-52-00**), which lies adjacent to the Sunstar Hotel in Grindelwald. Far more modest in its scope is a 1-day hiking tour that's recommended to everybody capable of hiking in boots for 2 or 3 hours. After a scenic mountain train ride from Grindelwald to Eigergletscher, you'll be led by a local mountain guide to the Bergsteigerzentrum Grindelwald, a husky-breeding center. Then you'll hike along the foot of the north face of Mount Eiger. Along the way, your guide will narrate the history of this famous wall, providing interesting stories. Back down in Alpiglen, you can rest and enjoy a lunch of toasted cheese. The train will transport you back to Grindelwald. Try to make reservations 2 to 3 days in advance.

Faulhorn, at 8,796 feet (269m), is an historic vantage point from which you can view a panorama of untouched alpine beauty. Near the summit is the mountain hotel **Faulhorn Hotel** (© 033/853-27-13), which has been here for over 150 years and can be reached in a 7-hour hike from Grindelwald. Less committed hikers usually opt for cable car or bus transfers to Bussalp, to First, or to Schynige Platte, and then continue their hike on to Faulhorn from any of those three points. Hikes to Faulhorn from Bussalp take 2¾ hours; from First, 2½ hours; and from Schynige Platte, 4 hours.

A 30-minute ride on a six-passenger gondola ("bubble car") will take you to **First Mountain** ★★, at 7,113 feet (2,134m). You can stop at the intermediate stations of Bort and Grindd as you cross the alpine meadows to the First Mountain terminal and sun terrace. You'll have many hiking possibilities into the neighboring Bussalp or Grosse Scheidegg area, and you can return by bus. An hour's brisk hike will take you to idyllic Lake Bachalp. Besides the 2½-hour trek to Faulhorn, you can trek on foot to the Schynige Platte in 6 hours. A round-trip gondola ride between Grindelwald and First costs 46SF ($25.30). There's a large restaurant at First, **Bergrestaurant First** (© 033/853-12-84), where you can order lunch.

Grosse Scheidegg ★, at 6,434 feet (1,930m), is a famous pass between the Grindelwald and Rosenlaui valleys. You can hike here in 3 hours from Grindelwald, or take the bus for 40 minutes. Our preference is usually to take a bus to Grosse Scheidegg and then begin our hill walking away from the village traffic and crowds. Round-trip bus passage from Grindelwald to Grosse Scheidegg is 34SF ($18.70) per person.

If you want to climb in the upper regions of the Oberland, you might consider this **itinerary:** Take a bus from Grindelwald to Grosse Scheidegg. Walk for 2½ hours from Grosse Scheidegg to **Schwartzwaldalp.** The peaks of the First and Wetterhorn will loom on either side of you. After a panoramic respite in Schwartzwaldalp, you can take a bus, which will retrace your steps, first to Grosse Scheidegg, then to Grindelwald. This excursion is only possible in the summer; the total bus fare is 39SF ($21.45) per person. Also only in the summer, a short aerial cable-car ride will take you to **Pfingstegg,** at 4,564 feet (1,369m), from which you can hike to the Lower and Upper Grindelwald glaciers. The round-trip cost is 15SF ($8.25). A hike to **Baregg-Stieregg** (1 hr.) is highly recommended as a 1-day journey, as is the trek to **Banisegg** (2 hr.). You'll get a view of the Eismeer and the Fiescherwand, and they're both worth the hike.

An especially popular half-day hike from Grindelwald goes to **Milchbach,** where melting glacial ice forms a milk-colored stream laden with gravel sediment. After about an hour's climb from Grindelwald, you'll find yourself at the base of the Upper Grindelwald Glacier (Obere Gletscher). The Blue Ice Grotto, which is about 45 minutes' walking distance above the Milchbach, can be visited as part of the same half-day excursion. After your visit, you can return by either hiking back to Grindelwald or by climbing aboard any of the postal buses that connect the Blue Ice Grotto to Grindelwald at hourly intervals.

From Grindelwald, it's also easy to visit **Kleine Scheidegg** ✫✫, which is the departure point for the final ascent to Jungfraujoch by train. The rack-and-pinion railway from Grindelwald to Kleine Scheidegg costs 46SF ($25.30) round-trip or 28SF ($15.40) each way. For information on this and all trains departing from Grindelwald, call the **Grindelwald railway station** (✆ 033/828-75-40).

SKIING In winter, Grindelwald is one of the major ski resorts of Europe, perfect as a base for skiing in the Jungfrau ski region. It has 22 lifts, eight funiculars, a trio of cable cars, and more than 100 miles of downhill runs. Snowboarders and novice skiers are also welcome. It's a ski circus for all ages and various skills.

In the winter, skiers take the cableway to **Männlichen,** at 7,335 feet (2,200m), which opens onto a panoramic vista of the treacherous Eiger. From here there is no direct run back to Wengen; however, skiers can enjoy an uninterrupted ski trail stretching 4½ miles to Grindelwald. The cost of the Mannlichen cable car (Grindelwald-Grund to Mannlichen) is 29SF ($15.95) each way, or 46SF ($25.30) round-trip. For information, call the departure point for the **Mannlichen Bahn** in Grindelwald (✆ **033/854-80-80**).

SHOPPING

There are a lot more shops in Grindelwald than the seasonal local economy can sometimes support. Most of them line the crowded edges of the resort's main thoroughfare, a sometimes traffic-clogged highway. A half-dozen of these shops specialize in sporting goods and ski equipment, many stockpiling inventory from prestigious, high-tech manufacturers from around Europe and North America. The best of them include **Buri-Sport,** Hauptstrasse (✆ **033/853-14-27**), and **Bernet Sport,** Hauptstrasse (✆ **033/853-13-09**). If you're in the market for a timepiece, **Casa Grande,** Hauptstrasse (✆ **033/853-50-15**), has a wide inventory of all kinds of Swiss watches and—to a much lesser extent—simple jewelry.

WHERE TO STAY
EXPENSIVE

Belvedere ✫   This is a vastly renovated government-rated four-star hotel dating from 1904. It once declined the offer of a higher rating from the Swiss government so that it could keep its prices within reason. It has the most spectacular view in Grindelwald, and its luxurious public rooms include a fireplace and comfortable armchairs. There's also another lounge for nonsmokers decorated in the antique Louis Philippe style with well-preserved old pieces and Bohemian crystal chandeliers. The attractive and spacious bedrooms all have balconies and private bathrooms. Twenty-two of the double rooms are classified as "luxury twins" or "junior suites." The hotel is a 5-minute walk from the center of the resort and easily accessible by the mountain-railway systems.

CH-3818 Grindelwald. ✆ 033/854-54-54. Fax 033/853-53-23. www.belvedere-grindelwald.co.ch. 57 units. 345SF–475SF ($189.75–$261.25) double; 460SF–530SF ($253–$291.50) junior suite for 2; 860SF–1,000SF ($473–$550) deluxe suite for 4. Rates include half board. AE, DC, MC, V. Free parking. **Amenities:** 2 restaurants, lounge; pool; health club; sauna; Jacuzzi; room service; massage; babysitting; laundry/dry cleaning. *In room:* TV, minibar, hair dryer, safe.

Grand Hotel Regina ✫✫✫   Across from the Grindelwald train station, this hotel is part rustic and part urban slick and dates from the turn of the century. It became a hotel in 1953 and still evokes the glamour of that era. The facade of the oldest part has an imposing set of turrets with red-tile roofs. One of the salons has Victorian chairs clustered around bridge tables, with sculpture in wall niches. The collection of art includes etchings, gouaches, and oil paintings. The large bedrooms, done in various styles, are comfortable and contain well-maintained bathrooms. These elegantly furnished rooms are your finest choice for a vacation here in either summer or winter. Most bedrooms enjoy panoramic views.

CH-3818 Grindelwald. (C) **800/223-6800** in the U.S., or 033/854-86-00. Fax 033/854-86-88. www.grand regina.ch. 98 units. 450SF ($247.50) double; from 1,100SF ($605) suite. AE, DC, MC, V. Free parking outside, 15SF ($8.25) in garage. Closed mid-Oct to Dec 18. **Amenities:** 2 restaurants, 3 bars; 2 pools; 2 tennis courts; sauna; salon; room service; massage; babysitting; laundry/dry cleaning. *In room:* TV, minibar.

MODERATE

Derby Bahnhof   This is a large and modernized mountain chalet, rated three stars by the government. Peter and Christiane Märkle carry on the century-old family tradition. The present building, with a twin-peaked roof and several irregularly shaped balconies, dates from 1973. The pine-paneled bedrooms are brightly furnished and comfortable if a bit small. All contain well-kept bathrooms, which for the most part contain shower-tub combinations. The Derby offers some of the best restaurants and bars in town.

CH-3818 Grindelwald. (C) **033/854-54-61.** Fax 033/853-24-26. 70 units. 178SF–202SF ($97.90–$111.10) double. Rates include buffet breakfast. Half board 35SF ($19.25) per person extra. AE, DC, MC, V. Free parking. **Amenities:** 3 restaurants, bar; room service; laundry/dry cleaning. *In room:* TV, minibar.

Hotel Eiger   This hotel looks like a collection of interconnected balconies from the outside, each on a different plane and built of contrasting shades of white stucco and natural wood. The interior is attractive, simple, and unpretentious, with lots of warmly tinted wood, hanging lamps, and contrasting lights. The small to mid-sized bedrooms are comfortable, well furnished, and alpine cozy. All are equipped with tidily kept bathrooms. Maintenance is high, and the hotel staff is extremely inviting and hospitable.

CH-3818 Grindelwald. (C) **033/856-05-05.** Fax 033/856-05-06. www.eiger-grindelwald.ch. 50 units. Summer 210SF–260SF ($115.50–$143) double; winter 270SF–305SF ($148.50–$167.75) double. Rates include buffet breakfast. Half board 35SF ($19.25) per person extra. AE, DC, MC, V. Free parking outdoors, 6SF–12SF ($3.30–$6.60) in garage. **Amenities:** Restaurant, bar; exercise room; sauna; babysitting; laundry/dry cleaning. *In room:* TV, minibar.

Hotel Kreuz & Post (*)   This angular, modern hotel is ideally located on the main square of town, across from the Sports Center. The Konzett family takes advantage of the location by setting up an outdoor cafe on the sidewalk in front. The interior is decorated in part with 18th-century antiques and engravings. Many of the rooms have balconies. Ranging from small to mid-sized, the tidy units are traditionally furnished and equipped with neatly kept bathrooms. The welcome here is warm in any season. There's a sun terrace on the roof with a panoramic view of the mountains.

CH-3818 Grindelwald. (C) **033/854-54-92.** Fax 033/854-54-99. www.grindelwald.ch/kreuz-post. 42 units. Summer 250SF ($137.50) double. Winter 320SF ($176) double. Rates include buffet breakfast. Half board 40SF ($22) per person extra. AE, DC, MC, V. Free parking. **Amenities:** Restaurant, lounge; fitness center; Jacuzzi; sauna; babysitting; laundry/dry cleaning. *In room:* TV, minibar.

Hotel Restaurant Steinbock (*Value*)   Mentioned as a tavern for the first time in chronicles in 1798, the Steinbock basks in its tradition. It is a cozy, chalet-style, government-rated three-star hotel, just opposite the Sunstar Hotel and lying near the bottom of the First gondola leading to the First skiing area in winter or a hiking Valhalla in summer. The ski bus stop for Klein Scheidegg/Männlichen areas is located just next to the Steinboch. Completely rebuilt in 1992, the hotel is run by the Ponzio family, who also operate the on-site Pizzeria da Salvi where the best pies in town emerge piping hot from a wooden stove. Bedrooms are small but handsomely and comfortably furnished in a modern alpine style. The hotel's Grappa Bar offers 100 different kinds of grappas.

CH-3818 Grindelwald. (C) **033/853-89-89**. Fax 033/853-89-98. www.steinbock-grindewald.ch. 22 units. 240SF–270SF ($132–$148.50) double. Rates include breakfast. MC, V. **Amenities:** Restaurant, bar. *In room:* TV, hair dryer.

Parkhotel Schoenegg   This hotel, established by the Stettler family in 1890, is today a modern expansive property. The bedrooms are cozy and comfortable, some with private balconies. Each is furnished in an alpine decor, and beds are excellent, as is the housekeeping. All units are also equipped with neatly kept bathrooms. The hotel's dining room serves French cuisine. Local ski runs terminate at the hotel; a lift to the ski school is close to the front door.

CH-3818 Grindelwald. (C) **033/854-18-18**. Fax 033/854-18-19. 50 units. Summer 240SF–330SF ($132–$181.50) double, winter 350SF–390SF ($192.50–$214.50) double. Rates include continental breakfast. AE, MC, V. Parking 6SF–12SF ($4–$8.05). Closed May and Nov. **Amenities:** Restaurant, lounge; pool; health club; sauna; room service; massage; babysitting; laundry/dry cleaning. *In room:* Hair dryer, safe.

INEXPENSIVE

Central Hotel Wolter   It's more modern and boxy than the other hotels in town, but its central location just a few steps from several more expensive hotels makes it a solid and reliable choice. On the ground floor there's a popular outdoor cafe and a substantial restaurant. Upstairs is the reception area and a salon that resembles a room in a private home. It has armchairs, a few antiques, and a compact bar. The small bedrooms are simply decorated, all with comfortable beds and well-kept bathrooms.

CH-3818 Grindelwald. (C) **033/854-33-33**. Fax 033/854-33-39. www.grindelwald.ch/wolter. 35 units. 180SF–210SF ($99–$115.50) double. Rates include buffet breakfast. Half board 40SF ($22) per person extra. AE, DC, MC, V. Parking 7SF ($3.85). Closed Nov 7–Dec 17. **Amenities:** 2 restaurants, bar; room service. *In room:* TV, minibar, hair dryer.

Hotel Hirschen *(Value*   In the government-rated three-star Hirschen, the Bleuer family offers one of the best values in town. The hotel, which has an attractive modern facade, is both comfortable and affordable with rooms in a variety of styles. Each is well furnished with good beds and equipped with neatly kept bathrooms.

CH-3818 Grindelwald. (C) **033/854-84-84**. Fax 033/854-84-80. www.grindelwald.ch. 28 units. 150SF–210SF ($82.50–$115.50) double. Rates include continental breakfast. Half board 30SF ($16.50) extra. AE, DC, MC, V. Free parking outside, 8SF ($4.40) in garage. Closed Nov to Dec 19. **Amenities:** Restaurant, bar; room service; laundry/dry cleaning; bowling alley. *In room:* TV.

Hotel Jungfrau Swiss Mountain Lodge   This establishment consists of two hotels, the Jungfrau (with 18 rooms, built in 1903) and the Crystal (with 29 rooms, built in 1972), located across the street from one another at the edge of the village, a 3-minute walk from the railway station. Both the reception area and the dining room, called "Mr. Chicken," are in the Jungfrau, but both offer clean, comfortable rooms at favorable prices with equal extras. The lounge has a view of the fierce north face of the Eiger, and it expands during warm weather onto an outdoor terrace. The bedrooms were recently renovated in a Canadian mountain lodge style. All come equipped with neatly kept private bathrooms, which mostly contain shower-tub combinations.

CH-3818 Grindelwald. (C) **033/854-41-41**. Fax 033/854-41-42. www.jungfraulodge.ch. 47 units. Summer 130SF–170SF ($71.50–$93.50) double. Winter 140SF–200SF ($77–$110) double. Rates include buffet breakfast. AE, DC, MC, V. Free parking. Closed Nov. **Amenities:** Restaurant, lounge; room service; laundry/dry cleaning. *In room:* TV.

WHERE TO DINE

EXPENSIVE

La Pendule d'Or/Jägerstube ⭐ SWISS/FRENCH   Some of the best cuisine in Grindelwald is served in these two dining rooms. In La Pendule d'Or men must wear jackets and ties, but not in Jägerstube, an elegant version of a hunter's retreat, and our preferred choice. Typical dishes include poached eel with crayfish tails, French snails, Russian caviar, steak tartare, scampi flambéed with Chivas Regal, and aiguillettes of veal in a saffron sauce. The cooking, if not always sublime, is exceedingly professional. Flavors are balanced and ingredients are first rate. Both restaurants serve the same menu, but fondue is offered only in the Jägerstube. Service is formal and correct.

In the Grand Hotel Regina. ☎ 033/854-86-00. Reservations recommended. Main courses 45SF–120SF ($24.75–$66); fixed-price menu 85SF ($46.75). AE, DC, MC, V. La Pendule d'Or, daily noon–2pm and 7–10pm. Jägerstube, daily 7–10pm. Closed mid-Oct to Dec 18.

Restaurant Français ⭐⭐ INTERNATIONAL   This is the best restaurant in Grindelwald. The owner, Urs Hauser, is always in the dining room during meal hours to aid and advise diners. Special buffets are a feature of the restaurant. As you listen to the soothing sounds of a live pianist, you can study the menu (which will have changed by the time of your visit). Just to give you an idea, you might be served an appetizer of game terrine, Grindelwald air-dried meat, or thinly sliced lamb carpaccio. Fish dishes might include poached filet of turbot served on zucchini and potato rounds with a yellow-red pepper sauce or fried filet of salmon with a truffle butter sauce. Main dishes are likely to include lamb entrecôte in a coating of peppercorns or breast of guinea fowl with red wine and prunes. The cuisine intelligently blends flavors with imagination and zest. The cooks in the kitchen really know their stuff, and their wine list is among the finest in the area.

In the Hotel Belvedere. ☎ 033/854-54-54. Reservations recommended. Main courses 30SF–48SF ($16.50–$26.40); fixed-price menu 54SF–66SF ($29.70–$36.30). AE, DC, MC, V. Daily noon–1pm and 6:45–9pm.

MODERATE

Il Mercato ITALIAN/SWISS   The decor is elegant and alpine, with Italian touches you might expect in the Ticino. The dining room's visual centerpiece is a large window with a sweeping view over the mountains. During warm weather, tables are set out on a terrace dotted with flowers. Menu items include virtually everything from the Italian repertoire, with an emphasis on cold-weather dishes from the Val d'Aosta (northern Italy's milk and cheese district). There is a tempting array of salads, pizzas, pastas, risottos, and grilled veal, beef, and chicken dishes, always with fresh ingredients.

In the Hotel Spinne. ☎ 033/854-88-88. Reservations recommended. Main courses 15SF–25SF ($8.25–$13.75). AE, DC, MC, V. Daily 11am–2pm and 6:30–11pm. Closed Oct to mid-Dec.

Restaurant Alte Post ⭐ *Finds* SWISS   Often fully booked at least a day in advance, this Swiss, pine-paneled charmer serves traditional specialties, often to local residents of Grindelwald, with efficient service. Typical dishes include a terrine of morels, smoked filet of trout, asparagus with air-dried ham, filet steak with green peppers, scallop of veal cordon-bleu, and beef Stroganoff. Because of the first-rate cooking and the quality ingredients, this is one of the most satisfying choices in town.

CH-3818 Grindelwald. ☎ 033/853-42-42. Reservations required. Main courses 12SF–45SF ($6.60–$24.75). AE, MC, V. Thurs–Tues 11:30am–2pm and 6:30–9pm. Closed end of Oct to mid-Dec.

Restaurant Kreuz & Post SWISS/INTERNATIONAL   Explore this alpine restaurant before choosing a table. Tucked away in the corner is an attractive room, the Challi-Stube; the ceiling and paneling are especially well crafted. Everything in here is made of wood from a farmhouse that was torn down in 1748. The menu here is in English. Hearty alpine flavor and first-class ingredients characterize the cuisine. Typical appetizers are smoked salmon and oxtail soup. For a main course, steak, pork, and fish are offered, including blue trout sautéed in butter. For a traditional Swiss dish, try sliced veal Zurich style with rösti, or veal steak with a morel-cream sauce. The chef specializes in the two classic fondues, *chinoise* and *bourguignonne,* served for two.

In the Hotel Kreuz & Post. ℭ **033/854-54-92.** Reservations recommended. Main courses 14SF–52SF ($7.70–$28.60); 3-course fixed-price lunch 27SF ($14.85); 5-course fixed-price dinner 45SF ($24.75). AE, DC, MC, V. Tues–Sun 11:30am–1:30pm and 6:30–10:30pm. Closed Apr 14–May 21.

Restaurant Sportzentrum SWISS   This rustic, timbered dining room in the modern Sports Center is in the middle of the resort. Windows look down over an indoor swimming pool on one side and an enormous ice-hockey rink on the other. It opens early in the morning and serves snacks and drinks until late. The menu offers many Swiss specialties, including cheese fondue, beef bourguignonne, and Wiener schnitzel. Come here for typically soul-satisfying Swiss food, each dish well prepared and reasonable in price too.

CH-3818 Grindelwald. ℭ **033/853-32-77.** Main courses 16SF–38SF ($8.80–$20.90). MC, V. Daily 7:30am–11:30pm.

INEXPENSIVE

Onkel Tom's Hütte PIZZAS AND SALADS   Set within a rustic-looking A-frame house whose indestructible furniture and plank floors have seen thousands of snow-and-mud-covered boots tramping across its surface, this is Grindelwald's most visible and popular pizza place. There's a wide selection of beer and wine available, and a multilingual staff member will bring any of the three sizes of pizza to your amiably scarred and battered table. Varieties of pizza include the Onkle Tom (tomatoes, cheese, pepperoni, and assorted vegetables), the Rustica (tomatoes, cheese, broccoli, and garlic), and an Al Capone (tomatoes, cheese, braised leeks, bacon, and onion).

At the top of Hauptstrasse, near the Firstbahn cablecar station. ℭ **033/853-5239.** Pizzas 10SF–29SF ($5.50–$15.95); salads 7SF–12SF ($3.85–$6.60). MC, V. Daily noon–2:30pm and 3:30–10:30pm. Closed Nov and June.

GRINDELWALD AFTER DARK

After sundown, Grindelwald transforms itself into one of the liveliest towns in the Bernese Oberland. In addition to the following choices, many of the hotels sponsor get-together parties at least once a week for residents, and each contains at least one bar. Bars that are noteworthy in their attempts at aggressively searching out the patronage of nonresidents include the **Cava Bar,** in the Derby Hotel (ℭ **033/854-54-61**). From their site near the railway station, they throw in the occasional live band. The **Challi Bar,** in the Hotel Kreuz & Post (ℭ **033/ 854-54-92**), does a roaring business—mostly from drinkers, less so from dancers—inside what looks like the re-creation of an alpine barnyard lined with roughly textured planks. Both bars are only open in the winter.

Don't be fooled by the name of the **Espresso Bar,** in the Hotel Spinne (ℭ **033/854-88-88**), a cramped, hot, and crowded venue with the inner walls of a log cabin and a penchant for suds and schnapps. Only a handful of its clients actually opt for coffee. The same hotel is the site of everybody's favorite ethnic hideaway, the **Disco Mescalero.** Here, tacos, tortillas, and refried beans are served until around 10pm, after which lots of very danceable music is unleashed. Over the summer, the Mexican restaurant is closed; however the disco still opens 3 days a week. Offhandedly elegant is **Regina Bar,** the entertainment focal point of the Grand Hotel Regina (© 033/854-86-00), and **Le Plaza-Club,** a prosperous-looking disco favored by prosperous-looking people in the Hotel Sunstar (© 033/854-77-77). A replica of a smoke-stained English pub on the street level of the Bellevue Hotel, Hauptstrasse, is **Ye Olde Spotted Cat** (© 033/853-12-34). Finally, the **Gepsi-Bar,** in the Hotel Eiger (© 033/854-31-31), is appealingly conducive to dialogue and flirtation. There's no dancing here, but live musicians sometimes arrive to perk things up a bit.

5 Kandersteg ✯

16 miles (26km) S of Spiez, 27 miles (43km) SW of Interlaken

Lying between Grindelwald and Gstaad, Kandersteg is a popular resort at one of the southern points of the Bernese Oberland. It's a tranquil, lovely mountain village with rust- and orange-colored rooftops and green Swiss meadows. The summer and winter resort is spread over 2½ miles (4km), so nothing is ever too crowded. The village itself lies at the foot of the Blumlisalp chain (12,000 ft./3,600m) and provides access to six remote alpine hamlets.

Kandersteg developed as a resting point on the road to the Gemmi Pass, which long ago linked the Valais with the Bernese Oberland. The village still has many old farmhouses and a tiny church from the 16th century. It's very proud of its traditions.

ESSENTIALS

GETTING THERE   Kandersteg is at the northern terminus of the 9-mile-long (15km) **Lotschberg Tunnel,** which, ever since the beginning of World War I, has linked Bern with the Rhône Valley. The railroad that runs through the tunnel can transport cars. Trains leave every 30 minutes; no reservations are necessary. The resort is also served by the Berne-Lotschberg-Simplon railway. Call © **0900/300-300** for **rail information.**

If you're driving from Interlaken, take N8 west to Spiez, where the Kandersteg road then heads south into the mountains. The journey from Spiez to Kandersteg takes only 20 minutes along the well-built road.

VISITOR INFORMATION   In lieu of street names, directional signs are used. All guests who have a room in Kandersteg are given a **visitor's card,** entitling them to certain price reductions, including a discount on the town's network of cable cars.

Kandersteg Tourist Office, Hauptstrasse, CH-3718 Kandersteg (© 033/675-80-80), dispenses information. Open Monday to Friday 8am to noon and 2 to 6pm.

EXPLORING THE AREA
IN TOWN

In summer, qualified riders in proper clothes can rent horses at the local riding school at the **Royal Park Hotel** (see below). For walkers there's an extensive network of level footpaths and strategically located benches around Kandersteg. These paths are open year-round.

In winter, the resort attracts cross-country skiers and downhill novices (top-speed skiers go elsewhere). It has a cable car, two chairlifts, and four ski tows; the National Nordic Ski Center offers a ski-jumping station. The 1½-mile (2km) cross-country ski trail is floodlit in the evening. Other facilities include an indoor and outdoor ice rink.

If you select Kandersteg for your winter vacation, don't expect the breadth and diversity of ski slopes that are available in the much larger, more varied Jungfrau region accessible from Wengen, Mürren, Interlaken, and Grindelwald. Kandersteg's ski trails lie on the slopes of a bowl-shaped depression whose sides slope down into the waters of Oeschinensee, and incorporate 8 miles (13km) of downhill runs, 47 miles (76km) of cross-country trails, and eight ski lifts, three of which are short "baby lifts" for beginners. Adults pay 62SF ($34.10) for a 2-day pass, 135SF ($74.25) for a 5-day pass, and 185SF ($101.75) for a 7-day pass. Skiers looking for more far-flung pastures can add access to the Lauchernalp slopes, a neighboring, narrowly defined, and somewhat limited network of ski slopes, for a supplement of around 20%.

Discounts of around 10% are offered to senior citizens over age 62, and discounts of between 20% and 50% are available to children, depending on their ages and whether they buy their passes in conjunction with passes sold to their parents or guardians.

NEARBY

The most popular excursion from Kandersteg is to **Oeschinensee** ★★★, or Lake Oeschinen, high above the village. The lake is surrounded by the snow-covered peaks of the Blumlisalp, towering 6,000 feet (1,800m) above the extremely clear water. You can walk to it from the Victoria Hotel or take a chairlift, costing 17.20SF ($9.45) round-trip or 11.50SF ($6.35) one-way, to the Oeschinen station and walk down from that point. If you opt to walk, allow about 1½ hours, or 2 hours if you'd like to stroll. Many visitors who take the chairlift decide to hike back to Kandersteg. Be warned, however, of the steep downhill grade.

Another popular excursion is to the **Klus Gorge** ★★. Park your car at the cable station's lower platform at Stock and walk 2 miles (3km) to the gorge, which was formed by the abrasive action of the Kander River. The rushing water creates a romantic, even primeval, setting. However, watch your step—the path gets very slippery in places. The spray coats the stones and pebbles and has fostered a layer of moss. There's a tunnel over the gorge. During the winter, the access route is icy and dangerous.

SHOPPING

Kandersteg's small size doesn't allow for too many shops, but of the limited number available, the best include **Käthy Sport,** Hauptstrasse (© **033/675-16-09**), which is in two connected buildings. The smaller is a century-old house dispensing folkloric Oberland souvenirs (wood carvings, glass, ceramics, textiles, and the like); the larger sells sporting equipment, with emphasis on hill climbing and skiing. Its most appealing competitor is **Grossen-Sport,** Hauptstrasse (© **033/675-00-16**), where special emphasis during warm-weather months is on tennis equipment and mountain bikes, and, in winter, on ski and ice hockey equipment.

WHERE TO STAY & DINE
EXPENSIVE
Royal Park Hotel ★★★   The brown-and-white facade of this four-story hotel doesn't adequately convey the luxury you'll find inside. One of the finest

hotels in Switzerland, it has been owned by the Rikli family for three generations. The interior has flagstone floors covered with dozens of Oriental rugs,
Louis XIII-style armchairs, a collection of antiques, and rococo lighting fixtures.
Around the fireplaces are clusters of carved armchairs covered with gray bro-
cades. The spacious bedrooms are sumptuous, each individually furnished in a
classical style with soft colors; large windows open onto views. All the bathrooms
have been recently redone with deluxe appliances.

The lovely grounds include gardens, evergreens, and lawns. From the back
garden there's a mountain vista. In summer, hiking excursions are arranged, and
guests can ride one of the many horses or bicycles. If you love horses, bring your
riding clothes and boots. The hotel operates at least three impressive boats—
both motorized and sailing craft—which are moored nearby and are available
for the use of hotel guests. Lake Thun is 10 minutes away. In winter, alpine and
cross-country skiing are available.

CH-3718 Kandersteg. (℃) **800/874-4002** in the U.S., or 033/675-88-88. Fax 033/675-88-80. www.royal
kandersteg.com. 31 units. 300SF–450SF ($165–$247.50) double; 550SF–900SF ($302.50–$495) suite. AE, DC,
MC, V. Free parking outside, 20SF ($11) in garage. Closed Mar 26 to May and Oct to Dec 17. **Amenities:**
4 restaurants, bar; 2 pools; tennis courts; health club; Jacuzzi; sauna; horseback riding; bike rental; room service; massage; babysitting; laundry/dry cleaning. *In room:* TV, minibar, hair dryer, safe.

MODERATE

Hotel Adler 🍴 An open fire crackling in the foyer sets the tone of this warm,
cozy inn. A wood-sided chalet originally built in 1906, it's set on the main street
near the center of town. The fourth-generation owner, Andreas Fetzer, and his
Finnish-born wife, Eija, offer comfortable mid-sized bedrooms paneled in
pinewood, each with a tidily kept bathroom. At least 90% of the accommodations open onto a private balcony; six rooms have Jacuzzis, and two offer a private fireplace. The Adler-Bar, which fills most of the ground floor, is one of the
most popular après-ski hangouts in town.

CH-3718 Kandersteg. (℃) **033/675-80-10.** Fax 033/675-80-11. www.chalethotels.ch. 24 units. Feb–Mar and
July–Sept 180SF–210SF ($99–$115.50) double. Off-season 170SF ($93.50) double. Rates include breakfast.
Half board 30SF ($16.50) per person extra. AE, DC, MC, V. Free parking. Closed Nov 22–Dec 26. **Amenities:**
2 restaurants, bar; exercise room; sauna; room service; laundry/dry cleaning. *In room:* TV, minibar, hair dryer.

Hotel Victoria Ritter (Kids) This is a longtime favorite. The original part of
this hotel was built as a coaching inn in 1789 and named the Ritter (knight),
after a local nobleman. In 1912, the Victoria, a larger and more opulent hotel,
was added. Today, the two hotels form a single architectural unit, and although
much of the interior has been modernized, they still retain their original exterior
detailing. The mid-sized bedrooms are contemporary, with neatly kept bathrooms. The premises boast a kindergarten for small children as well.

CH-3718 Kandersteg. (℃) **033/675-80-00.** Fax 033/675-81-00. www.hotel-victoria.ch. 75 units. 170SF–250SF
($93.50–$137.50) double. Rates include continental breakfast. Half board (minimum 2 days) 40SF ($22) per
person extra. AE, DC, MC, V. Free parking. Closed mid-Oct to mid-Dec. **Amenities:** Restaurant, bar; pool;
2 tennis courts; room service; massage; babysitting; laundry/dry cleaning; kindergarten. *In room:* TV.

INEXPENSIVE

Hotel Alpenblick Built in 1902, this small chalet in the center of town is a
5-minute walk from the train station. Though small, bedrooms are traditionally
furnished with alpine comfort, each with tidy bathrooms. Register for your
room near the bar of the locally popular hotel brasserie, the Oberlanderstube.
The owner plays the clarinet, and his band performs on Friday nights during the
busy season.

CH-3716 Kandersteg. © 033/675-11-29. Fax 033/675-21-29. 12 units. 110SF–135SF ($60.50–$74.25) double. Rates include continental breakfast. AE, DC, MC, V. Free parking. **Amenities:** Brasserie, bar, lounge. *In room:* No phone.

KANDERSTEG AFTER DARK

Every hotel in the region offers at least one comfortable, often panoramic showcase, usually with a blazing fireplace, perfect for a drink or two on starry evenings. Two of the most convivial and animated deserve mention. The **High Moon Pub,** in the Hotel Alfa-Soleil (© **033/675-84-84**), is a faithful replica of an English pub, replete with battered paneling, billiards, darts, and hints of the Edwardian age. At least twice a month, and sometimes more often, when business justifies the effort, the site is transformed into a disco. The **Adler-Bar,** in the Hotel Adler (© **033/675-80-10**), has textured timbers, pine paneling, a pianist who adds ambience in winter beginning around sundown, and lots of clients mellowing out after a day in the great outdoors.

6 Gstaad ★★

38 miles (61km) SW of Thun, 26 miles (42km) SE of Bulle

Against a backdrop of glaciers and mountain lakes, Gstaad is a haven for the rich and famous. Frequent visitors include King Juan Carlos II of Spain, Elizabeth Taylor, and the Italian auto magnate Giovanni Agnelli. The film director Blake Edwards and his wife, Julie Andrews, own a chalet nearby.

Built at the junction of four quiet valleys near the southern tip of the Bernese Oberland, Gstaad was once only a place to change horses during the grueling voyage through the Oberland. But as the railroad lines developed, it grew into a resort. After the opening of the deluxe Alpina Grand Hotel, wealthy Russian and Hungarian families started coming, bringing their entourages of valets, nannies, and translators. In 1912, 2 years before the outbreak of World War I, a hotel that was to become one of the most legendary in Switzerland, the Palace, opened, promising the ultimate in luxury. In 1916 Le Rosey school (listed in the Guinness Book of World Records as "the most expensive prep school in the world") opened its doors in the satellite town of Tolle. The school contributed to the fame of Gstaad, as prestigious visitors, including King Leopold of Belgium, came to see their children.

The town, by far the most chic in the Bernese Oberland, retains much of its turn-of-the-century charm. Some first-time visitors, however, say that the resort is a bore if you can't afford to stay at the Gstaad Palace or mingle with the stars in their private chalets. Yet the town has many moderately priced hotels, taverns, and guesthouses with an allure of their own. Many of the bistros and cafes close from late April to mid-June and from October to mid-December.

ESSENTIALS

GETTING THERE   Gstaad is on the local train line connecting Interlaken with Montreux and several smaller towns in central-southwest Switzerland. About a dozen trains come into Gstaad every day from both of those cities, each of which is a railway junction with good connections to the rest of Switzerland. Travel time from Montreux can be as little as an hour and 20 minutes; from Interlaken, about 30 minutes, sometimes with a change of train at the hamlet of Zweisimmen. Call © **0900/300-300** for **rail schedules** and information.

If you're driving from Spiez, head southwest on Route 11; from Bulle, head south and then east on Route 11.

VISITOR INFORMATION Some streets have names; others are placed outside street plans, but there are directional signs to lead you to hotels and restaurants. The **Gstaad-Saanenland Tourist Association,** CH-3780 Gstaad (© **033/748-81-81**), is a useful source of information, open July and August Monday to Friday 8:30am to 6:30pm, Saturday 9am to 6pm, Sunday 10am to 5pm; September to June Monday to Friday 8:30am to noon and 2 to 6pm, Saturday 9am to noon.

FUN IN THE OUTDOORS

Gstaad is a resort rich in entertainment and sports facilities. Many skiers stay in Gstaad by night and venture to one of the nearby ski resorts during the day. Cable cars take passengers to altitudes of 5,000 and 10,000 feet (1,500 and 3,000m)—at the higher altitudes there's skiing even in the summer. Other facilities include tennis courts, heated indoor and outdoor swimming pools, and about 200 miles (320km) of hiking trails. Many of these scenic trails are possible to walk or hike year-round (the tourist office will advise). The **Gstaad International Tennis Tournament,** beginning the first Saturday in July, is the most important tennis event in Switzerland.

Skiers setting off from Gstaad have access to 70 lifts, mountain railroads, and gondolas. The altitude of Gstaad's highest skiable mountain is 6,550 feet (1,965m), with a vertical drop of 3,555 feet (1,066m). Most beginner and intermediate runs are east of the village in Eggli, a ski area reached by cable car. Eggli has a sunny, southern exposure. Wispellan-Sanetch is favored for afternoon skiing, with lots of runs down to the village. At its summit is the Glacier des Diablerets, at a height of 9,900 feet (2,970m). Wasserngrat, reached from the south side of the resort, is yet another skiing area. Advanced skiers prize Wasserngrat for its powder skiing on steep slopes.

The **Swiss Ski School at Gstaad** (© **033/744-18-65**) has first-class teachers and qualified mountain and touring guides. Special classes for children are offered. Some 100 private instructors are available. It receives stiff competition from the **Schweizer Schi Schule** (Swiss Ski School) (© **033/744-36-65**) in the nearby satellite resort of Schönried.

Gstaad has several satellite resorts, which many visitors prefer. Saanen and Schönried are both summer and winter resorts, with excellent accommodations. **Saanen,** at 3,450 feet (1,035m), is east of Gstaad; some of its wooden chalets date from the 1500s. The **Menuhin Festival** draws an international music-loving crowd from late July to mid-September. The resort can be reached easily by car or by the Montreux-Oberland railway; there's also a small airfield at Saanen for visitors who fly in. **Schönried,** some 2½ miles (4km) northeast of Gstaad, is appreciated for its arguably better snowfall and accommodations, notably the Alpenrose Hotel.

Whichever resort you choose—Gstaad, Saanen, or Schönried—you'll be surrounded by dramatic glaciers and bucolic alpine pastures. This part of the country, called **Saanenland,** is undoubtedly one of the most beautiful parts of Switzerland.

The funiculars and chairlifts around Gstaad are configured into a system that services the slopes of at least six other resorts scattered over four valleys of the Bernese Oberland. In addition to Gstaad, the region's star, the resorts include Saanen, Saanen-Möser, Schönreid, and Sankt Stephan. An all-inclusive ski pass—known locally as a **"Ski Gstaad Pass"**—is sold at the departure point of any of the region's funicular stations, and allows automatic access to 155 miles (250km) of downhill slopes and 70 chairlifts and gondolas.

All-inclusive passes ("Ski Gstaad Passes") may vary depending on what point in the season you buy them, but generally cost 92SF ($50.60) for 2 days, 185SF ($101.75) for 5 days, and 268SF ($147.40) for 7 days, with a complicated set of discounts for children depending on their age and to what degree they're traveling as part of a family unit.

If you're in Gstaad for only 1 day, it's probably smarter to buy a limited pass for access to just a few slopes and chairlifts. The less comprehensive pass (known as a pass for Eggli-La Vide Manette) is sold only in 1-day increments for a price of 46SF ($25.30). Frankly, for anyone planning on 2 or more days of skiing, it's a lot more appealing, and not that much more expensive, to go for the more comprehensive pass.

SHOPPING

Stores along Gstaad's main shopping street, **Hauptstrasse,** seem more upscale, more lavish, and more aggressively tuned to the big-city affluence of Paris, London, and Munich than in virtually any other ski resort in Switzerland. Most of the shops that sell sporting goods in Gstaad inventory other sorts of casual and formal clothing as well, allowing buyers one-stop shopping for the layered look that keeps you warmer on the slopes. Three worthy outlets are **Brand,** Palace Strasse (© **033/744-17-75**); **Hermen Jat,** Hauptstrasse (© **033/744-15-47**); and in the satellite hamlet of Saanen, **Schneerberger,** Dorfstrasse (© **033/ 744-12-30**). If you want to check out the kinds of jewelry bought by the resort's most glamorous clients, consider a visit to **Villiger,** Promenade (© **033/ 744-11-22**). Barring that, you can always visit any of the aggressively upscale, relentlessly chic luxury boutiques in the Palace Hotel.

A boutique that always has something interesting is **La Vérandah,** Kirchstrasse (© **033/744-20-02**), which sells everything from vintage quilts from Scotland to picture frames covered in dried and lacquered ivy leaves. **Von Siebenthal,** Promenade (© **033/744-12-81**), is a three-story housewares emporium filled with high-performance Swiss-made gadgets, ranging from wooden molds for making anise cookies to fondue sets.

Pernet, Promenade (© **033/744-15-77**), is to Gstaad what Fauchon is to Paris. Even the designer, Valentino, when not in Rome, might be seen shopping here for truffle pâté, smoked salmon, grappa, and more than two dozen different cooking oils. The best bookstore for reading on a cold alpine night is **Buchhandlung,** Hauptstrasse (© **033/744-39-90**).

WHERE TO STAY

Gstaad is not known for its inexpensive hotels. Prices soar in the winter. When business is slow, many of the hotels close; the dates of these closings can vary from year to year.

VERY EXPENSIVE

Grand Hotel Park ★★★   This landmark hotel lives again. In 1990, one of the Oberland's most venerable hotels was demolished and rebuilt in a style that reflects the 1910 original. Associated with and partially owned by investors in the Palace Hotel, it sits astride a hill overlooking the center of the town and across from the Palace. Its design, including the bedrooms, evokes a mixture of the Edwardian age with a posh ski resort you might find in Vail, Colorado. Standard rooms measure a generous 375 square feet, and the more expensive rooms facing south open onto views of the Wispile, Eggli, and Glacier des Diablerets. Each accommodation comes with an immaculately kept bathroom. Although some of the original turn-of-the-century furniture was incorporated into the new design, much of the interior is new, sleekly modern, and richly accessorized with decorative and structural bands of chiseled granite, polished marble, and burnished pine.

CH-3780 Gstaad. (✆ **033/748-98-00.** Fax 033/748-98-08. www.grandhotelpark.ch. 93 units. Summer 530SF–750SF ($291.50–$412.50) double; from 975SF ($536.25) suite. Winter 670SF–810SF ($368.50–$445.50) double; from 1,200SF ($660) suite. Rates include half board. AE, DC, MC, V Parking 18SF ($9.90) in winter, free in summer. Closed Mar 23–June 10 and Sept 26–Dec 17. **Amenities:** 3 restaurants, 2 bars; 2 pools; tennis courts; health club; sauna; salon; room service; babysitting; laundry/dry cleaning. *In room:* TV, minibar, hair dryer, safe.

Palace Hotel Gstaad ✮✮✮ This other landmark hotel on a wooded hill overlooks the center of Gstaad. Opened in 1912, the Palace has mock-fortified corner towers and a neomedieval facade. The designer, Valentino, called the architecture a "brutal Sleeping Beauty castle." It's one of the most sought-after luxury hideaways in the world, attracting corporation heads, movie stars, and fashionable aristocrats, many of whom return every winter and stay a long time, earning the Palace the reputation as "Switzerland's largest family boarding-house." Owner and manager Ernst Scherz's motto is: "Every king is a client, and every client is a king." It's true—if you can afford it.

The nerve center of this chic citadel is an elegantly paneled main salon, with an "eternal flame" burning in the baronial stone fireplace. This flame isn't so eternal—it burns only in winter. Radiating hallways lead to superb restaurants, bars, discos, and sports facilities. The plush, spacious rooms are tastefully furnished and very distinguished; all come equipped with beautifully maintained bathrooms. However, be duly warned: Those facing north open onto a parking lot. Nonetheless, accommodations here are among the most sumptuous in Europe.

CH-3780 Gstaad. (✆ **800/223-6800** in the U.S., or 033/748-50-50. 124 units. Summer 520SF–800SF ($286–$440) double; from 1,720SF ($946) suite. Winter 790SF–1,200SF ($434.50–$660) double; from 2,200SF ($1,210) suite. Rates include breakfast. Half board 85SF ($46.75) per person extra. AE, DC, MC, V. Free parking outside, 20SF ($11) in garage. Closed end of Mar to mid-June and late Sept to shortly before Christmas (dates vary). **Amenities:** 4 restaurants, 2 bars, nightclub; 2 pools; tennis courts; health club; sauna; salon; room service; massage; babysitting; laundry/dry cleaning. *In room:* TV, minibar, hair dryer, safe.

EXPENSIVE

Bellevue Grand Hotel ✮ A venerable favorite still holding its own, this hotel is from 1912. Gstaad's leading government-rated four-star hotel, it stands in a serene park with tall, old trees in the midst of the town. The rooms are spacious and well lit, in a calming color palette. The furnishings are traditional and exceedingly comfortable, as reflected by the deluxe beds and the well-maintained bathrooms.

Hauptstrasse, CH-3780 Gstaad. (✆ **033/748-31-71.** Fax 033/744-21-36. 52 units. 490SF–600SF ($269.50–$330) double. Rates include breakfast. Half board 35SF ($19.25) per person extra. AE, DC, MC, V. Free parking outside. Closed Oct 22–Dec 22. **Amenities:** Restaurant; bar; pool; 2 tennis courts; room service; laundry/dry cleaning; curling hall. *In room:* TV, minibar, hair dryer, safe.

Hostellerie Alpenrose ✮✮✮ *finds* For those who seek the charm of a small inn, this is the preferred choice in the area, the only Relais & Châteaux listing within 30 miles. The pine-paneled rooms are exquisitely decorated with rustic furnishings, and the small bedrooms are comfortable and tastefully appointed. All are equipped with well-maintained bathrooms. Its kindly host, Michel von Siebenthal, is a memorable fellow, setting the fashionable tone of the chalet, which is famous for its restaurant (see "Where to Dine," below).

Hauptstrasse, CH-3778 Schönried-Gstaad. (✆ **033/744-67-67.** Fax 033/744-67-12. www.relaischateaux.fr. 19 units. Summer 380SF–460SF ($209–$253) double. Winter 480SF–710SF ($264–$390.50) double. Half board 45SF ($24.75) per person extra. AE, DC, MC, V. Free parking. Closed Nov. **Amenities:** Restaurant, lounge. *In room:* TV, minibar.

Hotel Bernerhof ★ *Kids*   This hotel lies in the center of the resort town about half a block from the rail station. Built on the site of a hotel dating from 1904, it offers modern comforts and attracts a loyal clientele who keep in touch via a hotel newsletter. Wooden balconies extend across the front. Thomas and Claudia Frei offer well-furnished rooms with neatly kept bathrooms. Children are catered to at the hotel, and many activities are planned for them. The restaurant is recommended in "Where to Dine," below. The Stöckli Bar is a popular place for drinks.

CH-3780 Gstaad. © 033/748-88-44. Fax 033/748-88-40. www.gstaad.ch/bernerhof. 47 units. 250SF ($137.50) double; 320SF–360SF ($176–$198) suite. Rates include breakfast. Half board 32SF ($17.60) per person extra. AE, DC, MC, V. Free parking outside, 10SF ($5.50) in garage. Closed Nov 20–Dec 1. **Amenities:** 3 restaurants; bar; pool; health club; Jacuzzi; sauna; children's activities; room service; babysitting; laundry/dry cleaning. *In room:* TV, minibar, hair dryer.

Hotel Olden ★★   This is one of the most low-key and gracefully unpretentious hotels in Gstaad, a sort of Victorian country inn set amid a sometimes chillingly glamorous landscape—or at least a chillingly expensive landscape. The Olden has a facade painted with regional floral designs and pithy bits of folk wisdom. Embellishments are carved or painted into the stone lintels around many of the doors.

The small to mid-sized rooms are generally furnished in a typical alpine style, although the bathrooms have been modernized. Some guests are housed in the adjacent chalet wing where the comfort level and amenities are the same.

Hauptstrasse, CH-3780 Gstaad. © 033/744-34-44. Fax 033/744-61-64. 15 units. 450SF ($247.50) double. Rates include continental breakfast. AE, DC, MC, V. Free parking. Closed late Apr to late May. **Amenities:** Restaurant, bar; room service; laundry/dry cleaning. *In room:* TV, minibar.

Steigenberger Avance Hotel ★   Constructed in 1981, yet designed like a well-built cluster of traditional wooden chalets set in the hills in Saanen, this hotel blends well into the surrounding evergreen forest about 2 miles (3km) from the center of Gstaad. From the windows of its warm and comfortable public rooms, guests enjoy panoramic vistas over the Saanen Valley. The interiors are crafted with lots of paneling and antique details; the lobby has a lounge, a fireplace, and live jazz or piano music. During the summer, geraniums adorn the balconies that come with all rooms except those with terraces. The spacious bedrooms contain spruce and mountain-pine paneling and traditional furniture, including excellent beds and neatly kept bathrooms. The service is impeccable.

Auf der Halten, CH-3792 Saanen. © 800/223-5652 in the U.S. for reservations, or 033/748-64-64. Fax 033/748-64-66. 135 units. 252SF–370SF ($138.60–$203.50) double; 538SF–675SF ($295.90–$371.25) suite. Rates include breakfast. Half board 60SF ($33) per person extra. AE, DC, MC, V. Parking free outside; 10SF ($5.50) in garage. Closed Nov–Dec 15. **Amenities:** 2 restaurants, bar, lounge; pool; health club; sauna; steambath; salon; table tennis; room service; babysitting; laundry/dry cleaning. *In room:* TV, minibar, hair dryer, safe.

Wellness & Spa Hotel Ermitage-Golf ★★   This is a government-rated five-star hotel designed and built in 1958. Its developers had intended that a golf course surround it on all sides. Although the building permit for the golf course was eventually refused by the city, the name remained in place. There's a nine-hole golf course, however, about 2 miles (3km) away. Today this is a large and comfortable hotel, with a helpful staff and lots of alpine warmth. In the winter it's a toasty, cozy retreat; in the summer it's a pleasure chalet, as red geraniums bloom on its balconies and chaise lounges are set up on its lawns. Heiner Lutz and Laurenz Schmid offer paneled bedrooms, each individually furnished. Some have Oriental rugs and have grand comfort.

Hauptstrasse, CH-3778 Schönried-Gstaad. © **033/748-60-60.** Fax 033/748-60-67. www.ermitagegolf.ch. 69 units. 550SF–700SF ($302.50–$385) double; 630SF–890SF ($346.50–$489.50) suite. Rates include half board. AE, DC, MC, V. Parking 10SF–18SF ($5.50–$9.90). Closed Oct 25–Dec 18. **Amenities:** 3 restaurants, 2 bars; 2 pools; tennis court; health club; Jacuzzi; sauna; Turkish bath; room service; massage; babysitting; laundry/dry cleaning. *In room:* TV, minibar, hair dryer, safe.

MODERATE

Hotel Alphorn *Finds*   Located at the base of the Wispile cable car, this intimate chalet is a small, relatively unpublicized hotel owned by the Bruriswill family. The hotel, built in 1970 and enlarged and upgraded in 1992, has a ski shop on the premises. The small rooms are comfortable and snug, each fitted with a well-kept private bathroom.

Steigstrasse, CH-3780 Gstaad. © **033/748-45-45.** Fax 033/748-45-46. www.alphorn-gstaad.ch. 30 units. 200SF–250SF ($110–$137.50) double. Rates include breakfast. Half board 30SF ($16.50) per person extra. AE, DC, MC, V. Free parking. **Amenities:** Restaurant, lounge; sauna; babysitting; laundry/dry cleaning. *In room:* TV, minibar, hair dryer.

Posthotel Rössli *Value*   The Rössli is an authentic and traditional chalet in the center of Gstaad. Often attracting a young crowd, it's well heated and furnished with modern conveniences in its small but cozy and comfortable bedrooms. All are equipped with neatly kept bathrooms. Every week Ruedi Widmer, mountain guide, ski teacher, and owner of the hotel, organizes walks and grill parties in summer or skiing days in winter. Guests are invited to participate at no extra charge. Locals mix with guests in the *bierstube* (beer tavern), the Stübli.

Hauptstrasse, CH-3780 Gstaad. © **033/748-42-42.** Fax 033/748-42-43. www.posthotelrossli.ch. 26 units. 180SF–220SF ($99–$121) double. Rates include breakfast. AE, DC, MC, V. Free parking. **Amenities:** Restaurant, lounge. *In room:* TV, minibar.

WHERE TO DINE

Most visitors dine at their hotel, so there are few independent restaurants in Gstaad. The following choices are worth venturing out for.

VERY EXPENSIVE

Restaurant Chesery *✦✦✦* FRENCH/SWISS   At an elevation of 3,600 feet, this is one of the 10 best restaurants in Switzerland. The floors are pink marble and the walls are polished pine. The menu changes daily, based on the freshest ingredients available. The chef is a perfectionist and shops far and wide for only the finest of produce with which to dazzle his clients—grouse from Scotland, Charolais beef from France, truffles from Umbria. You might sample his salt-crusted sea bass with wild rice or his chicken Houban (a very special breed from France). Try also his Scottish lamb with a crust of fresh herbs or rack of venison with whortle-berries. In the basement bar, Casino, a piano player entertains nightly, and the bar is open from 6pm to 3am, when the last ski bunny departs.

Lauenenstrasse. © **033/744-24-51.** Reservations required. Main courses 45SF–65SF ($24.75–$35.75); fixed-price lunch 49SF–64SF ($26.95–$35.20), fixed-price dinner 128SF–148SF ($70.40–$81.40). AE, DC, MC, V. Tues–Sun 11:30am–2:30pm and 7pm–midnight. Closed mid-Oct to mid-Dec, Easter to June 10, and in winter (Tues–Fri) for lunch.

The Restaurant *✦✦✦* FRENCH/INTERNATIONAL   The hotel opens up to three different dining rooms, each elegantly paneled and boasting impeccable service and the finest haute cuisine. Some of the finest chefs in the Bernese Oberland create dishes here for an extremely demanding clientele. Formal attire is essential—men without ties will be asked to dine in the Sans-Cravatte.

For an appetizer, caviar and foie gras abound, but there are also superb hors d'oeuvres, including beefsteak tartare, and delicate soups and consommés. Some especially delectable dishes include crisp rack of Scottish lamb with eggplant lasagne, grilled sole flavored with oregano, crispy duck for two, and chicken Taj Mahal with curry and many side condiments. This wide repertoire includes imaginative interpretations of old favorites. Most desserts are elaborate, but if you wish, you can order a simple sorbet.

In the Palace Hotel. ℭ **033/748-50-00**. Reservations required. Main courses 55SF–155SF ($30.25–$85.25); 3-course fixed-price lunch 75SF ($41.25), 5-course fixed-price dinner 105SF ($57.75). AE, DC, MC, V. Daily 12:30–2:30pm and 7:30–10:30pm. Closed end of Mar to mid-June and mid-Sept to shortly before Christmas.

EXPENSIVE

Hostellerie Alpenrose ★★ SWISS/FRENCH   During the summer, the paneled dining rooms are full of local residents and guests from the surrounding chalets. Michel von Siebenthal is your chef; his father built the first ski lift in the region in 1935. He has elevated a modest pension into a culinary citadel known throughout Switzerland for its cuisine.

The varied menu changes every 3 weeks. Lobster is almost always on the menu, but look for marinated salmon, which remains a delectable house specialty. Begin, perhaps, with the duck-liver terrine or a velvety-smooth imaginative soup made of nettles. One savory dish is a cassoulet of mushrooms. The grilled turbot is prepared with several different sauces, including an unusual carrot sauce, and you can also order a superb wild duck in a juniperberry sauce. Consider having an after-dinner drink in the nightclub, Sammy's.

Hauptstrasse, Schönried-Gstaad. ℭ **033/744-67-67**. Reservations recommended. Main courses 37SF–68SF ($20.35–$37.40); 4-course fixed-price menu 78SF ($42.90). AE, DC, MC, V. Daily 6:30–10pm, Wed–Thurs noon–2pm, Fri–Sun noon–2:30pm. Closed mid-Oct to mid-Dec.

MODERATE

D'Halte Beiz SWISS   This is the specialty restaurant of the hotel, designed to accentuate the decor and savory alpine menu of the region. Its name translates as "meadow in the hills." In other hotels it would be defined as the gourmet restaurant, but here the appeal is regional, folkloric, and alpine, with rustic beams and colorful table settings. There's a view of the Rublihorn. In the winter, there's a varied salad buffet with exceedingly fresh choices. A typical meal includes local herb schnapps, Batzi, and Swiss cherry cake. For a main course, try the excellently prepared filet of fera (a fish from Lake Thun), a tender and well-flavored chateaubriand, or a memorable alpine *carré d'agneau* (lamb).

In the Steigenberger Hotel, Auf der Halten, Saanen. ℭ **033/748-64-64**. Reservations recommended. Main courses 20SF–45SF ($11–$24.75); vegetarian dishes 16SF–19SF ($8.80–$10.45). AE, DC, MC, V. Daily 11:30am–2pm and 5:30–10:30pm. Closed Nov to mid-Dec.

Olden Restaurant ★★ MEDITERRANEAN/ITALIAN   This is the most formal restaurant of the several dining choices in this previously recommended hotel. On the street level, it attracts the latest visiting celebrity with its country charm. Meals are formally served in the pine-paneled dining room. The always tempting menu might include smoked salmon, fresh goose-liver terrine, shrimp bisque with green peppercorns, house-style tagliatelle, raclette, veal cutlet Milanese, Scottish lamb, and sea bass with olives, potatoes, tomatoes, and onions. Although there are grander restaurants in Gstaad, as well as dining rooms serving a more haute cuisine, the Olden remains our most satisfying choice year after year.

In the Hotel Olden, Hauptstrasse. ℭ **033/744-34-44**. Reservations recommended. Main courses 28SF–75SF ($15.40–$41.25). AE, DC, MC, V. Tues–Sun noon–2:30pm and 6:30–10:30pm. Closed mid-Apr to mid-May and 2 weeks in Nov.

Restaurant Bernerhof _Kids_ INTERNATIONAL   This tavern-style restaurant at the previously recommended hotel of the same name attracts plenty of discerning devotees. A longtime family favorite, it serves a menu so wide-ranging there's almost always something to please everybody. Along with the standard international dishes, it also offers a selection of excellent Swiss regional specialties, including a fondue with veal liver. Asian culinary delicacies are featured in the blun-chi section, and every day a large variety of succulent fresh pasta dishes are prepared. The hotel also houses the popular après-ski Stöckli Bar.

In the Hotel Bernerhof. © 033/748-88-44. Reservations recommended. Main courses 13SF–48SF ($7.15–$26.40); fixed-price lunch 20SF ($11), fixed-price dinner 59SF ($32.45). AE, DC, MC, V. Daily 11:30am–2:30pm and 6:30–10:30pm. Closed Nov 20–Dec 1.

Ristorante Rialto ITALIAN   One of the finest Italian restaurants in the Bernese Oberland, the Rialto lies in the heart of Gstaad. The proprietors, Peter and Tanja Burri, use only the freshest ingredients, and the menu changes with the season. You might begin with a selection of always tempting antipasti, followed by the luscious salmon carpaccio with a truffle-cream sauce or one of the pasta dishes, including pappardella. The flavor-filled risotto with fresh asparagus and the chef's sea bass Mediterranean style are both excellent.

Promenade. © 033/744-34-74. Reservations recommended. Main courses 21SF–50SF ($11.55–$27.50). AE, DC, MC, V. Open daily 24 hours. Main meals served Mon–Sat noon–2pm and 8:30–11:30pm, Sun noon–2pm. (Light dishes, drinks, and salads through the day.) Closed Mon May–June and Nov.

INEXPENSIVE

Posthotel Rössli SWISS   Set within a 150-year-old chalet in the heart of town, nearly adjacent to the Stadtkirche, this restaurant welcomes many generations of diners, most of whom have appreciated the paneled interior, small windows, and agrarian artifacts scattered throughout. Menu items—most of which are on the lower end of the price scale—are hearty, alpine-inspired, and served in generous portions. Examples include pork and veal schnitzels, tender beefsteaks in a mushroom-flavored cream sauce, velvety fondues, chicken roulades layered with ham and cheese, and several variations on Italian pastas. Salads are fresh, and the beer is cold.

Hauptstrasse 1. © 033/748-4242. Main courses 18SF–45SF ($9.90–$24.75); fixed-price menu 35SF ($19.25). AE, MC, V. Daily 11:30am–2:30pm and 4:30–10pm.

GSTAAD AFTER DARK

Much more than its competitors, Gstaad has been accused of attracting glamorous folk who care more about the resort's social scene than they do about skiing. As such, the resort supports a healthy roster of nightspots that range from boozy to glamorous. In midwinter, your options include alpine coziness in at least two mountain huts accessible only by cable car, the **Berghaus Eggli,** on the Eggli ski slopes (© 033/748-96-12), and the **Berghaus Wispile,** on the Wispile ski slopes (© 033/748-96-32). Access to either requires an 8-minute ascent on the Eggli (south of the center) and Wispile (north of the center) cable cars (gondelbahns). Both are infused with the odors of simmering raclette and fondues, both are open only during the height of the winter season, and both encourage guests to ski home after a night of alpine _gemütlichkeit_ (a Swiss term for cozy, good times shared with sympathetic souls). Don't even think of riding the cable car uphill for a meal or drink at either of these places after dark without a reservation, as their scheduling and priorities are as haphazard as anything at the resort.

More conventional evening diversions include the **Palace Hotel** (© 033/
748-50-00), which contains a supremely upscale bar adjacent to the pine-
sheathed lobby where the comings and goings could fill any Robin Leach production. The hotel also contains the most exclusive—and sometimes somewhat
stuffy—disco in Gstaad, the **Green Go Disco,** where pinpricks of light illuminate
a mysterious semipsychedelic decor of orange, green, and black. Call ahead, as it
operates only during midwinter and selected weekends in the peak of midsummer.

In the heart of Gstaad, there's a bar, the **Hostellerie Chesery,** Lauenenstrasse
(© 033/744-24-51), that hosts both piano music and dance music (later in the
evening). Its main focus, its restaurant, is separately recommended above. An
appealingly battered hangout reminiscent of England is **Richie's Pub,** Hauptstrasse (© 033/744-57-87). Nobody dances here, but the place is a town
favorite. A few steps away is a worthy and much more elegant competitor, the
Rialto Bar, in the Ristorante Rialto, Hauptstrasse (© 033/744-34-74). There
is a large terrace in the summer, and in the winter, there's sometimes live music
in the restaurant.

8

The Valais

The Valais is a region in southern Switzerland that borders on Italy and consists mostly of the valley around the upper Rhône River. The valley was called Vallis Poenina by the Romans, and the Germans refer to it as Wallis. The main attractions here include the Matterhorn, the Great St. Bernard Pass, and Zermatt. The area offers excellent skiing and other winter sports (Zermatt has one of the longest ski seasons in Switzerland).

The Valais is surrounded by the Alps, with more than 50 major mountain peaks, but the Matterhorn at 14,701 feet (4,410m) is by far the most majestic. The Valais contains the largest glacier in Switzerland as well as several others that send tributaries to feed the Rhône, which flows northwest to Lake Geneva, then on through France to the Mediterranean. The Valais also contains about 5 square miles (8 sq. km) of lakes.

Often called the hiking capital of Switzerland, the Valais is riddled with well-maintained and well-marked mountain paths. Some of this former network of alpine mule paths are called Roman roads, because in ancient times the Simplon and Great Saint Bernard passes were the gateways to the Valais from Italy. Walks along irrigation channels—called bisses—are among the most intriguing for nature lovers.

For centuries the Rhône Valley has been a major route through the Alps. The Celts used the Great St. Bernard Pass and Simplon Pass, and then the Gauls held the territory for 500 years. Hannibal and Napoleon both passed through on their way to conquest.

Today, wide highways and tunnels provide a direct route to Italy.

Protected by mountains, the Valais enjoys a sunny, stable climate, with weather comparable to that of northwestern Spain and France's Provence. The vineyards are second only to those of the Vaud, and the local wine is known for its fruity bouquet and delicate flavor. Dairy farming is widespread. Raclette, the classic Swiss dish, is usually made of the rich, unskimmed milk from the Bagnes Valley, near the Great St. Bernard Pass. Just outside most of the regional towns, you'll see *mazots* or *raccards*, small, elevated grain-storage barns.

Most residents in the western part of the Valais, from Lake Geneva to Sierre, speak French, while those living to the east speak a German dialect. Many people speak both languages as well as some English. Most residents of the Valais are Roman Catholic, evident in the number of churches, abbeys, and monasteries.

The Valais is an increasingly popular year-round travel destination, but not to worry. The growth of resorts and recreation facilities has not disturbed the natural splendor and tranquility of the alpine countryside.

Chances are if you're visiting the Valais by train you'll land at the major rail terminus of Martigny, which also attracts visitors heading across the Great St. Bernard Pass. Visitors going to the Ski resort of Verbier (see below) also pass through here. Frequent trains arrive in Martigny from Lausanne every hour, taking 30 minutes; from Montreux, every 30 minutes, taking

30 minutes; and from Sion, every 15 minutes, taking 30 minutes.

If you'd like to take one of the most scenic bike trips in the Valais, rent a bike at the kiosk at the **train station** (© **027/723-33-30**), costing 25SF ($13.75) per day. The **tourist office** at Martigny, 9 place Centrale (© **027/ 721-22-20**), will provide you with maps of the area. The office is open September to June, Monday to Friday from 9am to noon and 1:30 to 6pm and on Saturday from 9am to 2pm; in July and August, hours are daily 9am to 6pm.

From Martigny you can cycle through a beautiful region of the Lower Valais, heading across the Rhône River to the villages of Fully, Chataigner, Mazembroz, and Saillon.

1 Verbier 👓

80 miles (128km) E of Geneva, 25 miles (40km) N of Great St. Bernard Tunnel, 18 miles (29km) E of Martigny, 36 miles (58km) SW of Sion

Verbier sits on a vast, sunny plateau in the Bagnes Valley in Switzerland's southernmost Alps. It looks toward the Combin and Mont Blanc mountains, which are covered with snow year-round, even when the town is bursting with leafy trees and flowers. At 5,000 feet (1,500m), Verbier was a pastureland before developing into an outstanding sports center. The area is protected from harsh winds by the surrounding mountains. The predominant language of the resort is French.

Verbier doesn't have the architectural distinction of Zermatt. Everything from souvenir shops to the fast-food joints to the chalets is modern. But, you don't concentrate on the man-made architecture—the draw is the panoramic site of the resort itself, as its buildings are scattered over a slope of the Bagnes Valley surrounded by snow-covered mountains.

ESSENTIALS

GETTING THERE   From the railway junction of Martigny, take the train along a secondary spur route to Le Châble. Call © **0900-300-300** for **train schedules.** At Le Châble you can transfer to a postal bus. Le Châble is also the departure point for an aerial cableway leading directly to Verbier. The cost of one-way transport on the cable car is 7SF ($3.85) per person.

During the peak of the ski season, a consortium of hotels operates a shuttle bus that travels directly from Martigny to Verbier that's timed to coincide with the arrival of important trains into Martigny. The one-way cost is 15SF ($10.05). Regrettably, it operates only during winter, and only on Friday afternoon (one bus) and on Saturday (three buses). For **shuttle bus information** and reservations, call © **0900-300-300.**

If you're driving, take N9 as far as Martigny on the Great St. Bernard route. Turn left for Verbier at Sembrancher.

VISITOR INFORMATION   Some areas have no street names, so many establishments are signposted. The **Verbier Tourist Office,** place Centrale (© **027/775-38-88**), dispenses information. Open Monday to Friday 8am to noon and 2 to 6:30pm, Saturday 9am to noon and 2 to 4pm.

SKIING & OTHER SPORTS

Skiing tops the list of attractions. The area offers 190 miles (306km) of ski runs, serviced by 47 lifts. Téléverbier, a company founded in 1950, oversees one of the biggest conveyance systems in all of Switzerland. A recent addition, a heavy-duty cable car ("Le Jumbo"), whose cables are strung between the region of La Chaux and the Col des Gentianes, is the largest lift in the country.

In cooperation with neighboring regions, visitors can use their Téléverbier passes on more than 98 additional lifts in the area known as Les 4 Vallées (valleys) and L'Entremont. From Verbier, a single lift ticket can take skiers as high as 11,000 feet (3,300m). The permit also authorizes cross-country skiing, and several circuits are possible. One goes from Verbier to Mont-Gelé, Mont-Fort, and La Chaux and then back to Verbier. Another circuit goes from Verbier to Tortin, Mont-Fort, and La Chaux. For information on skiing in the Téléverbier network, contact **Téléverbier S.A.,** CP 419, CH-1936 Verbier (℡ **027/775-25-11**).

Throughout the winter, comprehensive passes that entitle skiers to access on all the ski lifts and slopes in the 4 Vallées region cost 68SF ($37.40) for 2 days, 156SF ($85.80) for 5 days, and 206SF ($113.30) for a full week. Children ages 6 to 16 and seniors 63 or older pay only 60% of these rates.

The **Swiss Ski School** (Ecole Suisse de Ski) (℡ **027/775-33-63**) has 170 instructors and in winter offers group lessons daily from 9:15 to 11:45am and more individualized lessons every day in winter from 2:10 to 4:30pm. Private lessons can be arranged as well.

The inauguration of **Le Centre Sportif** (Verbier Polysports Center) (℡ **027/771-66-01**) has greatly expanded sports offerings in all seasons. Facilities include a covered swimming pool, 10 indoor curling lanes, an indoor ice rink, nine tennis courts, squash courts, saunas, whirlpools, a solarium, and a games area. The center, open daily from 10am to 9pm, also contains a simple restaurant.

Besides sports, Verbier abounds in alpine beauty. The **Haut Val de Bagnes Nature Reserve** (Haut Val de Bagnes Réserve Naturelle) ⛰⛰, whose terrain can be safely visited only between mid-May and early October, has a rich variety of flora and fauna, including some rare species of plants. You might see alpine aquilegia, white gentian, yellow pond lily, edelweiss, and several kinds of orchids. Botanical walks are organized in the summer; inquire at the tourist office. There's a sweeping view of the Bagnes Valley from the Combe des Violettes. In the distance, you can see Mont-Pleureur, with Italy in the blue mist on the horizon.

There are around 12½ miles (21km) of footpaths in and around Verbier that are open for **hiking** in summer and hiking or cross-country skiing in winter. These are carefully maintained and signposted by the municipality. A bit farther afield from Verbier you'll find almost 250 miles (402km) of hiking trails of varying degrees of difficulty. Maps are available (see the tourist office, under "Essentials," above). There are usually signs posted to indicate the estimated time it takes the average hiker to reach each destination.

If you'd prefer to participate in activities more strenuous than mere walking and hiking, you can try one of several alpine adventures. Trained mountain guides lead jaunts in rock climbing, mountaineering, and cliff climbing, often on excursions of 3 days or more. Call the **Bureau des Guides de Verbier,** a branch of the above-recommended ski school (℡ 027/775-33-63), or one of its competitors, **L'Ecole de Ski Fantastique** (℡ **027/771-41-41**), for more information about hiring a mountain guide.

Golf Club de Verbier (℡ **027/771-5314**) is an 18-hole course open from June to October. It is one of the finest in the Valais, set against a scenic alpine backdrop, at an altitude of 5,248 feet (1,574m). Greens fees Monday to Friday are 65SF ($35.75), going up to 75SF ($41.25) on weekends. Every hole provides stunning views of such mountain ranges as Combin, Rogneux, and even Mont-Blanc.

SHOPPING

Much of the merchandizing that keeps Verbier's economy pumping involves alpine sports, summer or winter, and as such, you'll find half a dozen sporting

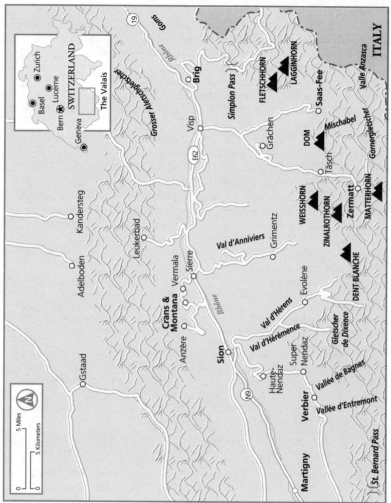

goods stores in town. Three of the best are **Philippe Roux Sport,** place Centrale (© **027/771-47-12**); its nearby competitor, **Médran-Sport,** route de Verbier (© **027/771-60-48**); and located close to the departure point for most of the cable cars and ski lifts, **Boît'Askis,** rue de Médran (© **027/771-34-87**). If you're more interested in handcrafts than state-of-the-art ski and mountaineering equipment, head for Verbier's largest dealer of the ceramic and carved wooden artifacts that the Valais produces in such abundance, **Bagn'Art,** rue de la Poste (© **027/771-5060**).

WHERE TO STAY

In the peak of the winter season, hotels often require Saturday-to-Saturday bookings.

EXPENSIVE

Hôtel Les 4 Vallées 😿😿 The hotel stands near the main square and the Médran lift station, and was built in the early 1980s in a contemporary chalet style. Each of its often sunny rooms has pine paneling, plush carpeting, and a balcony often looking southward toward the mountains. A copious breakfast buffet is served in a room with large windows and paneling.

Rue de Médran, CH-1936 Verbier. ⓒ 027/775-3344. Fax 027/775-3345. www.les4vallees.com. 20 units. Summer 250SF ($137.50) double. Winter 220SF–340SF ($121–$187) double. Rates include continental breakfast. AE, DC, MC, V. Free parking. Closed May–June and Sept–Nov. **Amenities:** Bar; free use of nearby indoor swimming pool; sauna; laundry. *In room:* TV, minibar, hair dryer, safe.

Hôtel Rosalp 😿😿😿 This is the plushest resort here. Roger and Anita Pierroz built the Rosalp in 1945, and Anita's cooking brought early fame to the place. But their son, Roland, put it on Europe's gastronomic map. Today, first-class rooms and refined cuisine are available at this Relais & Châteaux. The suites are excellent, and the small public salon is a tranquil retreat. The bedrooms are decorated with flair and filled with modern comforts and amenities such as state-of-the-art plumbing. Many have dark paneling and some contain a sun deck. Suites for four contain two rooms, two bathrooms, and a private salon. The hotel has the area's premier restaurant, Roland Pierroz (see "Where to Dine," below).

Rue de Médran, CH-1936 Verbier. ⓒ **027/771-63-23.** Fax 027/771-10-59. www.relaischateaux.ch.rosalp. 18 units. Summer 355SF–380SF ($195.25–$209) double; 855SF ($470.25) suite for 4. Winter 460SF–520SF ($253–$286) double; 1,150SF ($632.50) suite for 4. Rates include continental breakfast. Half board 75SF ($41.25) per person extra. AE, DC, MC, V. Parking free outside, 15SF ($8.25) in garage. Closed May–June and Oct–Nov. **Amenities:** 2 restaurants, 1 bar; fitness center; Jacuzzi; sauna; room service; laundry/dry cleaning.

Hôtel Vanessa 😿 One of the biggest hotels in Verbier is also one of the resort's finest. This government-rated four-star hotel dating from 1980 has comfortable and modern mid-sized rooms; most resemble suites and offer bright upholstery and balconies. The beds are exceedingly comfortable, and the maintenance is among the finest in town. Each unit is fitted with a well-maintained bathroom. This large chalet is right off place Centrale.

Place Centrale, CH-1936 Verbier. ⓒ **027/775-2800.** Fax 027/775-2888. 56 units. Summer 250SF ($137.50) double; 390SF ($214.50) suite. Winter 310SF ($170.50) double; 440SF ($242) suite. Rates include breakfast. Half board 48SF ($26.40) per person extra. AE, DC, MC, V. Parking 15SF ($8.25). Closed Apr–June and mid-Oct to Dec 1. **Amenities:** Restaurant, piano bar; exercise room; Jacuzzi; sauna; room service; babysitting; laundry. *In room:* TV, minibar, hair dryer.

MODERATE

Golf Hôtel 😿 The rooms in this government-rated three-star chalet are equivalent to four-star accommodations in other towns. Opened in 1953, the hotel sits in isolated grandeur a short walk below the main square. The public areas, including the lobby, contain architectural details that emulate antique models. Contrary to the hotel's name, it's not affiliated with a nearby golf course—most of its business comes from midwinter skiers. The mid-sized rooms contain Oriental carpets, pine paneling, and conservative furniture. Most have a private balcony.

Rue de Verbier, CH-1936 Verbier. ⓒ **027/771-65-15.** Fax 027/771-14-88. www.verbier.ch. 25 units. Summer 180SF–250SF ($99–$137.50) double; winter 270SF–410SF ($148.50–$225.50) double. Rates include half board. AE, DC, MC, V. Free parking. Closed Apr–June and Oct to Dec 10. **Amenities:** Restaurant, bar; fitness room; sauna/steam bath; room service; laundry service. *In room:* TV, safe.

Hôtel Catogne *Value* Set a 5-minute walk west of the central square, this pleasant, well-scrubbed hotel offers well-maintained, simple, and comfortable accommodations for good value. The upper half looks like a chalet; the lower half consists of masonry and stucco, with big windows and a modern extension containing drinking and dining facilities. Each room comes with a small bathroom. If you're not too demanding, you'll find a certain alpine charm here.

Chemin de la Croix, CH-1936 Verbier. ℰ 027/771-65-05. Fax 027/771-52-05. 24 units. Summer 220SF ($121) double; winter 295SF ($162.25) double. Rates include half board. AE, DC, MC, V. Closed mid-Nov to mid-Dec and for 1 month after Easter. **Amenities:** Restaurant, bar. *In room:* Minibar.

Hôtel de la Poste *(Kids* This red-shuttered chalet on the main street near the central square has long been a family favorite. Despite its lack of special facilities or programming for children, this family-owned and run resort stands out against the other more upscale, adult-oriented hotels in the market as being a family spot. Constructed in 1955, it was rebuilt in 1962 and then drastically renovated in 1980, which accounts for its present look. The small rooms are snug and comfortable with a modern alpine decor, and each comes with an adequate tiled bathroom. The hotel restaurant, La Tana, serves typical Swiss alpine cuisine.

Rue de Médran, CH-1936 Verbier. ℰ **027/771-66-81.** Fax 027/771-34-01. hoteldelaposte@verbier.ch. 30 units. Summer 200SF–230SF ($110–$126.50) double; winter 280SF–320SF ($154–$176) double. Rates include half board. AE, DC, MC, V. Free parking. Closed mid-Apr to mid-June and Sept 15–Dec 10. **Amenities:** Restaurant; pool. *In room:* TV.

WHERE TO DINE

Verbier has several excellent restaurants, many serving traditional Swiss dishes and continental cuisine. Most of the best restaurants are connected with hotels.

EXPENSIVE

Roland Pierroz ✫✫✫ FRENCH The finest food in the Valais is served at this Relais & Châteaux selection. Roland Pierroz is one of the great chefs of Switzerland; gourmets drive across national borders to sample his light cuisine moderne and regional specialties. The menu changes frequently, but could include roulades of carpaccio of sea bream with tomatoes en confit; a theatrical but delicious version of fried foie gras in a beet-and-onion "cage"; red mullet soup studded with shellfish; a divine poached chicken with truffles and baby vegetables (for two); and tournedos of lamb with a mousseline of local potatoes (rattes), garlic, and crispy sauerkraut. The cheese trolley emerges with at least 35 selections, followed by desserts such as a crisp and tasty apple tart with ice cream that was celestial. The finest meal we've ever had in Switzerland was had here.

In the Hôtel Rosalp, rue de Médran. ℰ 027/771-63-23. Reservations required at least a day ahead. Main courses 60SF–80SF ($33–$44); fixed-price menus 150SF ($82.50), 180SF ($99), and 200SF ($110). AE, DC, MC, V. Daily noon–2pm and 7–9:30pm. Closed May–June and Oct–Nov.

MODERATE

Au Vieux Verbier SWISS One of the few restaurants in Verbier not affiliated with any hotel, the Old Verbier is on a hillside a few paces from the town's ski slopes. It's set in a building that functions as the nerve center for the surrounding hillside cable cars. Its decor features brightly polished brassware, ceiling beams, and stone. The kitchen defines its cuisine as *bonne cuisine bourgeoise,* which is rich, traditional, and filling, exemplified by such featured dishes as La Potence—a grilled steak flambéed at your table with a red-wine sauce. Grilled fish and roasted rack of lamb are among the more delectable items to order. The specialty of the house—and it's a delight for connoisseurs—is pigs' feet in madeira with rösti, but it's only served in autumn.

Gare de Médran. ℰ 027/771-16-68. Reservations required for dinner. Main courses 19SF–49SF ($10.45–$26.95); fixed-price menus (summer only) 30SF–45SF ($16.50–$24.75). AE, DC, MC, V. Daily 11:30am–3pm and 6:30pm–midnight. Closed early May to mid-July and Mon in summer and fall.

La Pinte ★ *(Finds)* SWISS   This is master chef Roland Pierroz's second, more reasonably priced restaurant, on the ground floor of the Hôtel Rosalp. The 19th-century paneling is decorated with painted flowers; in the back a snug room displays hunting trophies. The cuisine features simmered and grilled specialties. A typical meal includes a to-die-for tart made with leeks or Gruyére cheese. Meats, ranging from a brochette of lamb to tournedos, are grilled over an open fire. He offers several regional dishes, including a savory sausage with lentils. Specials change daily.

In the Hôtel Rosalp, rue de Médran. ℂ 027/771-63-23. Reservations required. Main courses 25SF–46SF ($13.75–$25.30). AE, DC, MC, V. Daily noon–2pm and 7–9:30pm. Closed May to mid-Dec.

Le Caveau SWISS   Set in a cozy cellar, the entrance to the restaurant overlooks the town's main square. "The Cave" has a warmly rustic decor, a convivial bar near the entrance, and a menu offering the most famous dishes of the French-speaking alpine world. Specialties include five different kinds of fondues, raclettes, pepper steak, peppered filet of lamb, a fondue of chanterelles, and grilled steaks served with *gratin dauphinois* or rösti. The fondues are the resort's finest. No one will mind if you just drop in for a drink. Few other restaurants in town are as willing to close down whenever the weather is clear and sunny. Presumably when that happens, the staff rushes to the slopes because it's almost certain that the restaurant will be empty.

Place Centrale. ℂ 027/771-22-26. Reservations recommended. Main courses 15SF–45SF ($8.25–$24.75); all-you-can-eat raclette 35SF ($19.25). AE, DC, MC, V. Daily 11:30am–1am. Closed May–June.

Le Sonalon ★ *(Finds)* SWISS/CONTINENTAL   Some 2½ (4km) miles northwest of Verbier's center, this discovery lies near the edge of one of Verbier's less frequently used ski slopes (la piste de Savolère). This wood-sided chalet was built in the mid-1980s and has been known as a warm, comfortable dining spot ever since. You can reach it by car, following the directions listed below, or take the cable car to the Savolère station, then trek downhill on a steeply inclined 10-minute walk. In a dining room sheathed in light-colored wood paneling, or on an outdoor terrace with panoramic views encompassing the entire village of Verbier, you'll enjoy well-prepared meals whose gusto seems enhanced by the high altitudes. Menu items include raclette (available at dinner but not at lunch), several kinds of fondue, grilled lamb chops with aromatic herbs, filets of beef prepared with pepper sauce or mushrooms, and such palate-pleasing fish as pike-perch, filet of sole, and salmon. Calorie-conscious dishes such as grilled chicken in a sweet-and-sour sauce are classified as "fitness platters," although their weight-reducing benefits are usually offset by such desserts as crème brûlée, tiramisu, or a particularly succulent version of pears marinated in red wine and spices, served with cinnamon-flavored ice cream.

Piste de Savolère. ℂ 027/771-72-71. Reservations recommended. Main courses 15SF–50SF ($8.25–$27.50). AE, DC, MC, V. Daily 11:30am–2pm and 7–10pm. Closed mid-Apr to May and Nov, and Mon–Tues in June and Sept–Oct. From place Centrale in Verbier, follow the signs to Savolère and Carrefour, then branch off on a dirt road signposted Le Sonalon.

INEXPENSIVE

Pizzeria Fer à Cheval *(Value)* PIZZA/GRILLS   Although it defines itself as a pizzeria, this is among the best cost-conscious restaurants of Verbier, offering more than the dozen types of pizza for which it's best known. Crowded and friendly, with additional seating on another floor, it lies a short walk uphill from the resort's main square. It has an outdoor terrace that's used throughout the summer and on nice days the rest of the year, and an interior with large windows and pinewood paneling. The menu includes pizzas, such pastas as lasagna and spaghetti, all sorts of salads, and grills such as tenderloin of pork and filet steaks. A great between-meals snack is a *croûte au fromage*—a slice of bread covered with melted Gruyére and white-wine sauce, garnished with sliced ham or a fried egg.

Rue de Médran. ℂ 027/771-26-69. Reservations recommended. Salads 5SF–20SF ($2.75–$11); pizzas and pastas 15SF–25SF ($8.25–$13.75); platters 27SF–40SF ($14.85–$22). AE, DC, MC, V. Daily 8am–midnight. Closed May–June and Sept to early Nov.

Restaurant au Robinson SWISS   This stucco-sided brasserie, hidden away on the side of Verbier's main square, is popular with local residents and the maintenance crews who keep the town's ski slopes and tourist facilities running. No one will mind if you order just a drink, but if you want a full-fledged meal, the staff is happy to accommodate you. Among the most popular and tasty items are beefsteaks, fondue *chinoise* or *bourguignonne*, and a regional dish known as La Pirade—morsels of beef, duck, or chicken cooked on a hot platter directly at your table. Accompanying sauces might include curry, calypso, or tartar sauce. Also available is a heaping platter of air-dried alpine beef with pickles and onions (*assiette valaisanne*), filet of beef Stroganoff, and pastas.

Place Centrale. ℂ 027/771-32-13. Reservations recommended. Main courses 18SF–45SF ($9.90–$24.75). MC, V. Tues–Sat noon–2pm and 7–10pm. Closed Aug to Sept 1.

VERBIER AFTER DARK

Partly because of its cosmopolitan mixture of English, French, and Swiss clients, many of whose youthful high spirits rise to alpine levels during ski and hill-climbing vacations, Verbier has more discos (at least four, all open only in the winter) and bars than you'd expect. The disco most popular with English-speaking tourists is the **Farm Club,** route de Verbier (ℂ **027/771-61-21**). Here, amid weathered beams, sturdy and amiably battered furniture, and a modern decor that includes several blazing fireplaces, you can drink, spill beer, and dance to your heart's content. It's open every night between December and April, and things really get going after 10:30pm. Its most visible competitor is the **Tara Club,** route des Creux (ℂ **027/771-45-35**), with loud and danceable music, plank-covered walls, and alpine detailing. It's open only during mid-winter, with hours that depend on how many dance-crazed clients are in Verbier at the time.

Even if you arrive during the off-season when the discos are closed, you can always drink in any of the dozen or so bars and pubs. The most English of the lot is the neo-Victorian **Nelson Pub,** in the Hotel Vanessa, place Centrale (ℂ **027/775-28-00**). Look for cheeseburgers, croque-monsieurs, and platters of air-dried alpine beef, along with at least 40 brands of beer from virtually every-where. A less theme-ish, less aggressively Olde English venue is **Le Crok,** route des Creux (ℂ **027/771-69-34**), with tiny tables, leather-upholstered ban-quettes, and a modern decor. The place offers stiff drinks and frequent live music. The **Bar New Club,** rue de la Poste (ℂ **027/771-22-67**), re-creates the glossy, comfortable living room of an affluent bachelor, with couches perfect for conversation and comfortable drinking. Two noteworthy hotel bars are **Jacky's Bar,** in the Hôtel du Golf, rue de Verbier (ℂ **027/771-65-15**), and the **Bar L'Auin,** in the Hotel Rosalp, rue de Médran (ℂ **027/771-63-23**), which wins as the most conservative, discreet, elegant, and comfortable bar in town. The fireplace there gives a warm glow.

GREAT ST. BERNARD PASS ★★★:
AN EASY EXCURSION FROM VERBIER

Because of the danger of avalanches and road blockage, most winter drivers headed between the Valais and northern Italy travel through the 4-mile-long (6km) Great St. Bernard Tunnel instead of negotiating overland roads that are treacherous or impassable. In the summer, however, many visitors make the pilgrimage over the St. Bernard Pass instead, often to conclude that the drive is one of the highlights of their trip. The overland road is usually open only from mid-June to early October; its highest point lies about an hour's drive from Martigny, 25 miles away. If you're staying in Verbier and you'd like to visit the pass, you can drive east from Verbier along a winding road until you come to the village of Sembranchen. From here, E21 leads directly south to this historic pass. Follow the signs pointing uphill to Hospice St-Bernard. Travel time by car from Verbier is about 1¼ hours.

St. Bernard dogs are beloved in Switzerland, even though they no longer roam the snowy passes on missions of mercy with brandy in their casks. The dogs are still bred by Augustinian monks in one of the oldest monasteries in Europe, the **Great St. Bernard Hospice,** Le Grand-St-Bernard, 1946 Bourg-St-Pierre (© **027/787-12-36**). Set on the Swiss side of the vertiginous Swiss-Italian border, it was founded in 1050, and was mostly rebuilt of somber-looking gray stone in the 1600s. Year-round, the hospice houses only four or five Franciscan monks, many native to the Valais, as well as monks from other parts of Europe who stay for short-term bouts of meditation and prayer. Visitors can arrive by car only between June 15 and early October; the rest of the year, all roads are snowbound and transit is possible only via special skis. (See below for details.)

The monastery shelters a treasury of religious artifacts, a museum showcasing the often-tragic history of the pass, and historic kennels that are devoted to the perpetuation of the bloodlines of the St. Bernard breed of dog. During the winter visitors are forced to make a strenuous 4-mile (6km) uphill trek, on specially accessorized skis, from a parking lot near the Swiss entrance to the St. Bernard Tunnel. Don't even think of trying this without warning the monastery of your plans in advance, as the brothers will discourage you in the event of impending storms or avalanches. Proper equipment is required, including sealskin sheathing for your skis for traction during the uphill trek. In the event of an emergency, midwinter guests can be evacuated by snowmobile or helicopter.

In summer, between June 15 and early October, the kennels and the museum can be visited every day from 8:30am to 7pm. Admission to the public areas of the monastery and its chapel is free; admission to the museum and the kennels costs 5SF ($2.75) per person. The rest of the year, visits can be made only by special arrangement.

During limited warm-weather periods you can stay in the wood-sheathed interior of the **Hôtel de l'Hospice du Grand-St-Bernard,** Le Grand-St-Bernard, 1946 Bourg-St-Pierre (© **027/787-11-53;** fax 027/787-11-92). The four-story, gray-stone building was built in 1899 and restored in 1997. It's owned by the monastery, leased to a private entrepreneur, and contains 33 rooms. None has a TV or phone, and furnishings are simple and vaguely monastic. But views sweep out over both the Swiss and Italian Alps, and the food in the in-house restaurant is plentiful and reasonably priced. The hotel is open only between early June and mid-October, when it welcomes hill climbers, nature lovers, and members of religious organizations. The rest of the year it's locked tight, and the intrepid visitors who make the uphill trek on skis are housed, space and circumstances permitting, in the monastery itself. Per-person rates are 55SF ($30.25), single or double occupancy, with breakfast and dinner included. MasterCard and Visa are accepted.

WHERE TO STAY & DINE

Auberge du Vieux-Moulin *(Finds)*   This is a remote oasis. Part of a rocky hill was blasted away to make room for this small roadside inn in the hamlet of Bourg-St-Pierre, which lies on the way to the monastery (see above). Built in 1964 and recently renovated, the small rooms are streamlined and comfortable, with good beds. Guests in a room without private bathroom will find clean corridor facilities. Private bathrooms are small but neat with shower stalls.

CH-1946 Bourg-St-Pierre. © 027/787-11-69. Fax 027/787-11-92. 19 units, 9 with bathroom. 90SF ($49.50) double with or without bathroom. Rates include continental breakfast. AE, DC, MC, V. **Amenities:** Restaurant; gas station; currency exchange. *In room:* No phone.

2 Sion *(★★)*

17 miles (27km) E of Martigny, 33 miles (53km) W of Visp

The capital of the Valais, the ancient city of Sion is known for its glorious springs and autumns and for its ancient status as a trading post on the trails between France and Italy. Dating from Roman times, the town is dominated by the silhouettes of the castles of Valère and Tourbillon. Most of its population speaks French.

Most of the towns of the Valais are sports oriented, but Sion is one of the exceptions. Come here if you want to see a beautifully preserved old Swiss town with a lot of history and plenty of impressive walks in all directions. It's not as tourist oriented as such cities as Verbier, and even though it's a capital, it's still off the beaten path for most visitors. The stone streets of the Vieille Ville, or Old Town, are flanked with cafes and restaurants.

ESSENTIALS

GETTING THERE   Sion lies on the major rail lines that connect Milan and Turin (via the Simplon Tunnel) with Geneva and Paris. Trains arrive from both directions every day. Call © **0900-300-300** (no area code) for **rail schedules.**

If you're driving, head east from Martigny, and from Visp go west, on E2.

VISITOR INFORMATION   The **Sion Tourist Information Office** is on place de la Planta (© **027/327-77-27**), open July 15 to August 15, Monday to Friday 8:30am to 6pm, Saturday 10am to 4pm; off-season Monday to Friday 8:30am to noon and 2 to 5:30pm, Saturday 9am to noon. During high season, the office is also open Sunday 9am to noon.

SEEING THE SIGHTS

Château de Tourbillon (© **027/606-47-45**) is perched on a steep rock on a hill overlooking the northern periphery of the town. It's the broodingly impressive ruin of a medieval stronghold built by a 13th-century bishop to defend Sion against the House of Savoy. Destroyed by a fire in 1788, it has never been reconstructed, but you can still make out the remains of a keep, watchtower, and chapel. There's a **panoramic view** *(★)* of the Rhône Valley from its base, which sits at an elevation of 2,149 feet (645m).

Atop the town's other steep hill are the deeply weathered walls of an unusual Gothic church, the **Eglise-Fortresse de Valère** *(★)* (also known as the Château de Valère), whose foundations were built as a fortress by the ancient Romans. In much better shape than the previously mentioned castle, the three-aisle basilica dates from the 12th and 13th centuries. It contains 17th-century choir stalls and what has been called "the oldest playable organ in the world," dating from the 14th century.

Valère Museum ★, in the Eglise-Fortresse de Valère (✆ **027/606-47-10**), is in the former residence of the cathedral chapter and is now the cantonal museum of history and ethnography. It contains fine works of medieval religious art, ancient arms and armor, uniforms, Roman and Gothic chests, and interesting ethnological collections. Both the museum and the fortified church that contains it are open Tuesday to Sunday from 10am to noon and 2 to 6pm (to 5pm Oct–Apr). Admission to both the church and museum costs 7SF ($3.85) for adults and 4SF ($2.20) for children 12 and under. A family pass costs 14SF ($7.70). *Note:* There's a steep uphill climb between the parking lot and the church.

Back in town, the **Hôtel de Ville** (town hall), rue du Grand-Pont, whose inner chambers cannot be visited, has a facade embellished with 17th-century doors and columns. The foundations were laid by the ancient Romans in A.D. 377. On Sion's main street, rue du Grand-Pont, is an **astronomical clock.**

Northeast of the Hôtel de Ville is the **Cathédrale Notre-Dame-du-Glarier,** 13, rue de la Cathédral (✆ **027/322-80-66**). It was reconstructed in the 15th century, although the **Romanesque belfry** ★ remains, dating from the 11th and 13th centuries. Inside, look for the triptych in gilded wood, called *The Tree of Jesse.*

Although Sion has the monuments mentioned above, you can connect more intimately with regional life by taking an organized **wine-tasting excursion** (the tourist office—see above—will provide details). A long marked **footpath,** the most impressive walk in the area, is called *le chemin du vignoble,* and it passes through vineyards on the outskirts of the city. Our favorite vintner is the **Varone Vineyard,** a *centre de dégustation* at av. Grand-Champsec 30 (✆ **027/203-56-83**), across the river. It is open Monday from 2 to 6:30pm, Tuesday to Friday 10am to noon and 2 to 6:30pm, Saturday 10am to noon and 2 to 5pm. Before beginning your hike, pick up the makings of a picnic at **Co-op City,** place du Midi, right off avenue de la Gare.

WHERE TO STAY

Hôtel du Castel Modern and boxy, this government-rated three-star hotel is at the edge of the road to Simplon at the northeast edge of town. Built in 1968, it was recently renovated. The small rooms have modern furniture and soundproof windows, and each comes with a good bed and tidy bathroom. Many units have views of the jagged cliffs that support the medieval chateau.

36, rue du Scex, CH-1950 Sion. ✆ **027/322-91-71.** Fax 027/322-57-24. 29 units. 150SF–165SF ($82.50–$90.75) double. Rates include buffet breakfast. AE, DC, MC, V. Free parking. **Amenities:** Restaurant. *In room:* TV.

Hôtel du Rhône This cinder-block hotel allows you to escape the traffic congestion of the Old City, lying at its outer border. The small rooms are furnished with angular contemporary furniture and full bathrooms. In spite of its no-frills atmosphere, the hotel is the best place to stay in town.

10, rue du Scex, CH-1950 Sion. ✆ **027/322-82-91.** Fax 027/323-11-88. www.bestwestern.ch. 45 units. 162SF ($89.10) double. Rates include continental breakfast. AE, DC, MC, V. Free parking. **Amenities:** Restaurant; limited room service. *In room:* TV, minibar, hair dryer.

WHERE TO DINE

Caves de Touts-Vents *Finds* VALAISIAN This restaurant occupies several levels of a 13th-century cellar, whose vaultings were originally built to store wine. You descend a steep flight of stairs to reach the first room, much of which is devoted to a well-stocked bar. Claustrophobics might elect to go no farther. The lack of windows, the ancient stones, the flickering candles, and the effect of the wine work together to make the room cozy. The specialties—and good-tasting ones at that—include tagliatelle with salmon, mushrooms in puff pastry, calves' liver with shallots, and, of course, fondue and raclette.

16, rue des Châteaux. ⓒ 027/322-46-84. Reservations recommended. Main courses 25SF–36SF ($13.75–$19.80); raclette 31SF ($17.05); fondue 20SF–25SF ($11–$13.75). AE, MC, V. Restaurant, daily 7–10:30pm. Cafe and bar, Tues–Sat 5pm–midnight. Closed mid-July to Aug.

Enclos de Valère ★★ FRENCH   It's sometimes unnerving to drive a car up the steep and narrow street leading to this restaurant, but once you reach it, you'll find a site loaded with charm and one of the best-regarded restaurants in Sion. Located near the edge of the gardens that surround the Eglise-Fortresse de Valère, the restaurant is small and intimate, with an outdoor dining area. The dining room has a regional decor, with flagstone floors and a beamed ceiling. The menu changes monthly, but might include lamb with garlic and thyme; crawfish salad; filets of perch with white-butter sauce; magret of duckling with raspberry-vinegar sauce; and an "assiette Clos de Valérie" loaded with dried meats, pâtés, shredded duckmeat, and salads. Dessert might include a slice of lemon tart or a crème brûlée. The cooking is seductive with over-the-top flavors.

18, rue des Châteaux. ⓒ 027/323-32-30. Reservations recommended. Main courses 27SF–42SF ($14.85–$23.10); fixed-price menus 40SF ($22) lunch, 70SF ($38.50) dinner. DC, MC, V. Daily 11:45am–1:30pm and 6:30–9:30pm. Closed Jan to Feb 15 and Sun–Mon in Apr and Oct.

Le Jardin Gourmand ★★★ VAUDOISE   Established in 1996, this is the town's finest restaurant. Set near the railway station, it occupies a trio of rooms outfitted in Louis XVI furniture, with complicated wooden ceilings, floors of Carrara marble, and a glassed-in winter garden that's air-conditioned in summer. If you're absolutely committed to cutting costs, you might opt to dine in the cafe-style brasserie near the entrance, where lunchtime fixed-price menus are rock-bottom inexpensive at 19SF to 25SF ($10.45 to $13.75) each. It's much more appealing, however, to pass into the inner sanctum, where the owner and chef, Pascal Fantoli, prepares food equivalent to what you'd expect from a culinary citadel in Lausanne or Geneva. Examples include a crawfish- and scallop-studded couscous infused with saffron and served with an aromatic court bouillon, a salad of wild greens with quail meat and foie gras, baby turbot with an anisette-flavored cream sauce, strips of filet of lamb with Provençal-derived aïoli (garlic mayonnaise), and a particularly succulent dessert that combines frozen nougat, almonds, caramel, and rum sauce.

22, av. de la Gare. ⓒ 027/323-23-10. Reservations recommended. Main courses 25SF–48SF ($13.75–$26.40); fixed-price menus 65SF ($35.75) lunch, 80SF–95SF ($44–$52.25) dinner. AE, DC, MC, V. Mon–Sat 11:30am–2pm and 7–10pm. Closed 4 weeks in July–Aug.

Supersaxo ★ FRENCH/SWISS   This particularly appealing restaurant, outfitted with a modernized decor vaguely inspired by Louis XV architecture, lies within a sheltered, pedestrian-only passageway in the heart of Sion. Inside, you'll find a cosmopolitan staff that prepares a seasonal menu filled with culinary nuances and rare delicacies. The dishes are likely to include a roasted and stuffed rabbit, grilled filet of veal, filet of beef stuffed with foie gras and truffles, and tender roasted rack of alpine lamb. Any of these might be preceded with carpaccio or foie gras. Desserts are appropriately rich and tempting; service suitably attentive.

In the Passage Supersaxo, between rue de la Lausanne and rue de Couthey. ✆ **027/288-2109.** Reservations recommended. Main courses 45SF–58SF ($24.75–$31.90). Fixed-price menus 90SF–110SF ($49.50–$60.50). MC, V. Mon–Sat noon–2:30pm and 7–9:30pm.

3 Crans-Montana ★★

9 miles (14km) N of Sierre, 13 miles (21km) E of Sion, 99 miles (158km) E of Geneva

Crans and Montana-Vermala, at 4,985 feet (1,494m), are twin ski resorts; both are modern and fashionable and long associated with an upscale Italian clientele. Set on a handsome plateau where the air is said to be "lighter than champagne," they enjoy excellent snowfall and views as far as the Rhône valley. Crans, whose hotel construction began in 1912, is composed for the most part of colonies of apartments and hotels, many in the half-timbered mountain style. Montana, clustered around the shores of Lac Grenon, is the older section, begun in 1892. Connected to them both, at a slightly lower altitude, is Aminona, still an infant resort but rising rapidly.

Note that the lack of street names in many cases is confusing, although restaurants and hotels often have directional signs. It seems that all the residents want to erase the distinctions between Crans and Montana, as the resort has become virtually one over the years.

ESSENTIALS

GETTING THERE   From Geneva, take a direct train to Sierre; call ✆ **0900-300-300** for **rail information.** At Sierre, change to a funicular or bus, each of which charges around 10.80SF ($5.95) per person each way to Crans-Montana. Telephone the **Crans-Montana Service des Buses et Funiculaires** (✆ **027/481-33-55**) for departure times.

A postal bus from Sion makes the run up the mountain to Crans-Montana.

If you're driving, the resorts are accessible by good roads from Sion or the market town of Sierre. From Sion, take E2 east to Sierre; from here, follow the signs up the winding mountain road until you reach Crans-Montana.

VISITOR INFORMATION   Not all thoroughfares have street names; to find establishments that lie off the street plans you should look for directional signs. The **Tourist Information Office** is at Immeuble Scandia, in Crans (✆ **027/485-08-00**). In Montana, an equivalent organization is on avenue de la Gare (✆ **027/485-04-04**). Open Monday to Friday 8:30am to noon and 2pm to 5:30pm, Saturday 8:30am to noon. During high season, open till 6:30pm Monday to Friday, Saturday 9:30 to noon and 2 to 4pm, Sunday 9am to noon.

FUN IN THE OUTDOORS

Neither resort limits its allure to wintertime diversions. During the summer Montana tends to focus on spa cures and general health and well-being, and Crans transforms itself into a golf center. Nearby facilities include the 18-hole Plan-Bramois course, on the western outskirts of town, and the 9-hole Jack Nicklaus (formerly known as the Xires course), on the resort's southern perimeter. For golf information, call ✆ **027/481-121-68.** The Swiss Open, held at Crans, draws top golfers from all over the world. Tennis, hiking, and mountain climbing are the main summer sports at Crans-Montana; others include horseback riding, hiking, and fishing. Winter sports include skating, ski-bobbing, and ice-hockey matches. Skiing is available year-round.

There's a spectacular ascent to **Point Plaine-Morte** ★★, at nearly 10,000 feet (3,000m); but even at such a great height there are still runs suitable for novice skiers. To get here, take the gondola from Montana-Barzettes to the east of Montana, stopping at Les Violettes first. There's a restaurant at Plaine-Morte.

Cry d'Err, which looms north of the resort, rises to 7,430 feet and has a large restaurant and a sunbathing terrace. To get here, take the Grand Signal gondola from Montana or the Crans-Cry d'Err gondola from Crans.

Piste Nationale is known for its steep, narrow runs, which attract many skiers. **Mount Tubang,** especially its La Toula run, is another slope only for the advanced skier.

All-inclusive ski passes that provide access to all the cable cars and chairlifts in the Crans-Montana district cost 112SF ($61.60) for 2 days, 236SF ($129.80) for 5 days, and 295SF ($162.25) for a full week. Children between the ages of 6 and 15 are charged 68SF ($37.40) for 2 days, 143SF ($78.65) for 5 days, and 180SF ($99) for a week. A passport-size photo is required for anyone who wants to buy a ski pass.

SHOPPING

The crisp air and the dozens of outdoor diversions here might inspire purchases of sporting equipment rather than kitschy souvenirs. The accessories and paraphernalia you'll need to do anything in the Alps will jump out at you from virtually every local shop. Two of the best, however, are **Alex Sports,** rue du Prado, in Crans (© **027/481-40-61**); and **Ski Rinaldo,** route de Rawyl, in Montana (© **027/481-89-17**).

WHERE TO STAY
VERY EXPENSIVE

Grand Hôtel du Golf ★★★   This government-rated five-star hotel, a 5-minute walk from the center of Crans, is on an 18-hole golf course, where in winter you can practice cross-country skiing. The hotel, however, does not operate the golf course. The landmark hotel in Crans, the Grand was constructed by British golfers in 1907 and has been run by the same family since World War I. From the bedrooms facing south, you can enjoy views of the Alps and of the Rhône Valley. The ample guest rooms have tidy bathrooms attached. The hotel attracts not only sports people, but also the "genteel" crowd who don't like to exert themselves too much.

CH-3963 Crans. © **027/485-42-42.** Fax 027/485-42-43. www.grand-hotel-du-golfe.ch. 80 units, 8 suites. Winter and July 20–Sept 8 540SF–670SF ($297–$368.50) double; 1,180SF ($649) suite for 2. Off-season 470SF–550SF ($258.50–$302.50) double; 850SF ($467.50) suite for 2. Rates include half board. AE, DC, MC, V. Free parking. Closed Apr 15 to May and end of Sept to mid-Dec. **Amenities:** 2 restaurants; bar; pool; spa; sauna; salon; room service; massage; babysitting; laundry. *In room:* TV, minibar, coffeemaker (on request), hair dryer.

EXPENSIVE

Aïda-Castel ★★   Known for its Valasian decor, this government-rated four-star hotel is composed of two separate chalet-style buildings united during a series of massive renovations in the early 1990s. They lie on either side of the hotel's driveway, connected by a quiet passageway that passes above the underground piano bar. Set midway between Montana and Crans, near the flashier Hôtel Crans-Ambassador, it offers spacious bedrooms with lots of exposed wood and small seating areas that give the fleeting impression that the rooms are equivalent to small suites. Most accommodations have private balconies, and each comes with a clean bathroom. This is one of the few hotels of Crans-Montana that remains open the entire year.

CH-3962 Montana-Crans. ✆ **027/485-41-11.** Fax 027/481-70-62. 61 units. Summer 250SF ($137.50) double; winter 310SF ($170.50) double. Rates include breakfast. Half board 35SF ($19.25) extra. AE, DC, MC, V. **Amenities:** 3 restaurants, bar; pool; sauna; room service; laundry service. *In room:* TV, minibar, hair dryer.

Hôtel Alpina & Savoy ⭐ This is the oldest hotel in Crans, built in 1912. Owned by three generations of the Mudry family, it has been frequently modernized and expanded. The hotel remains consciously unfashionable but venerable, lying a short walk from the departure point for the Cry d'Err gondola. The bedrooms come in different shapes and sizes, but each is exceedingly comfortable with alpine decor, excellent plumbing, and a tidy bathroom.

Rte. touristique de Crans, CH-3963 Crans. ✆ **027/481-21-42.** Fax 027/481-61-75. www.alpina-savoy.ch. 50 units. 260SF–320SF ($143–$176) double. Rates include breakfast. Half board 40SF ($22) per person extra. AE, DC, MC, V. Free parking. Closed Apr 15 to mid-June and Sept 15 to mid-Dec. **Amenities:** Restaurant, bar; pool; saunas; concierge; room service; laundry/valet. *In room:* TV, minibar, hair dryer.

Hôtel Crans-Ambassador ⭐⭐ Lying between the twin resorts of Crans and Montana, this is a stylized château built in the 1970s with a contemporary roofline that resembles three connected alpine peaks. It's only a short walk uphill from Lake Grenon and a nearby sports center. The staff members are conscious of their roles as emissaries of one of Crans-Montana's most prestigious hotels. From the bedrooms and public areas, guests have a view over the Alps and Rhône Valley. Despite the iconoclastic architecture of the exterior, the mid-sized bedrooms are conservatively modern, each with a balcony or terrace. In the summer you'll enjoy the public outdoor terrace brimming with flowers. There are two ski lifts about 100 yards (91m) from the hotel, Grand Signal and Cry d'Err, as well as the end of one of the ski runs. The hotel has the most complicated rate schedule in Crans; make sure you check in with your accountant.

CH-3962 Montana. ✆ **027/485-48-48.** Fax 027/485-48-49. www.crans-ambassador.ch. 70 units, 10 suites. 290SF–330SF ($159.50–$181.50) double; 480SF–720SF ($264–$396) suite for 2. Rates include buffet breakfast. AE, DC, MC, V. Parking 10SF ($5.50). Closed Dec 4–20. **Amenities:** Restaurant, bar; pool; health club; steam bath; room service; babysitting; laundry service. *In room:* TV, minibar, coffeemaker, hair dryer, iron, safe.

MODERATE

Hôtel de la Forêt *(Value)* This is one of the better bargains. Some kind of hotel has stood on this site, about half a mile east of Montana's center, since the turn of the century. Skiers appreciate the hotel's proximity to the slopes—only 200 yards (182m) from the cable car of Les Violettes-Plaine Morte. Alain and Serge Morard throw weekly raclette parties for their guests. The mid-sized bedrooms facing south have balconies and some barely perceptible noise from the road; those rooms facing north don't have balconies and get less sun, but are quiet and offer views of the forest. Each unit comes with an efficiently organized bathroom.

CH-3962 Montana. ✆ **027/480-21-31.** Fax 027/481-31-20. 60 units. Summer 190SF ($104.50) double; winter 200SF–300SF ($110–$165) double. Rates include half board. AE, DC, MC, V. Parking 15SF ($8.25). Closed mid-Apr to June 1 and mid-Oct to mid-Dec. **Amenities:** Restaurant, bar; pool; sauna; room service; laundry service. *In room:* TV, hair dryer, safe.

INEXPENSIVE

Hôtel des Mélèzes *(Finds)* If you're looking for relative isolation, you'll like this place about half a mile from the town's commercial district in a forest of pines that the French call *mélèzes*. Built in 1959, the hotel is a solid, well-recommended, government-rated, three-star choice run with a personal touch. Marie-Louise Lamon offers well-furnished and comfortable, though small, alpine rooms with balconies, plus private bathrooms with shower. The hotel has one of the most appealing sun terraces and greenhouse-style dining rooms in town. Breakfast is served outdoors in the summer, near the seventh hole of an 18-hole golf course.

CH-3963 Crans. ✆ 027/483-18-12. Fax 027/483-16-08. 20 units. 150SF–160SF ($82.50–$88) double. Rates include buffet breakfast. MC, V. Free parking. Closed Apr to June 20 and Sept 15–Dec 20. **Amenities:** Restaurant, bar; golf course. *In room:* TV, minibar, hair dryer.

WHERE TO DINE
EXPENSIVE
Le Cervin/La Bergerie ✿ SWISS/VALAIS   Set in a meadow above the twin resorts, this red-shuttered, barnlike restaurant offers two different sections, both simply decorated. The more formal Le Cervin, on the street level, is a well-upholstered *maison bourgeoise* with lots of emphasis on the nuances of gastronomy. Here the French and Swiss specialties are likely to include salmon steak with fresh mushrooms, tournedos with onions, and salads studded with quail eggs and foie gras. La Bergerie, in the building's basement, features *la cuisine valaisanne* and platters of raclettes, fondues, grilled steaks, salads, and brochettes. The daily buffet in the brasserie is especially appealing.

Quartier Vermala, Crans. ✆ 027/481-21-80. Reservations required in the evening. Le Cervin, main courses 32SF–62SF ($17.60–$34.10); fixed-price meal 85SF–120SF ($46.75–$66). La Bergerie, platters 30SF–40SF ($16.50–$22). AE, DC, DISC, MC, V. Daily noon–2:30pm and 7:30–10pm. Closed Mon–Tues mid-Apr to mid-June and mid-Oct to mid-Dec.

Restaurant de la Côte ✿✿ FRENCH   The best restaurant in the district lies in isolated and panoramic splendor in an alpine house whose facade is surprisingly modest. Inside, there's an apéritif lounge and a modernly decorated space for up to 50 well-dressed diners at a time. The restaurant's location, 2 miles from Sierre and 7½ miles from Montana, guarantees that you'll need your car (or a taxi) to reach it. As you gaze over faraway vineyards and valleys below, you can enjoy such smooth and perfectly flavored dishes as a gelée of foie gras with braised sweetbreads and a compôte of Granny Smith apples, roast wild duck on a bed of juniperberries, and in season, a lightly larded haunch of rabbit stuffed with sage. Desserts are suitably delectable, and service is discreet and polite.

Corin-sur-Sierre. ✆ 027/455-13-51. Reservations recommended. Main courses 35SF–55SF ($19.25–$30.25); fixed-price meal 45SF–95SF ($24.75–$52.25) lunch, 85SF–135SF ($46.75–$74.25) dinner. MC, V. Wed–Sun noon–2pm and 6:30–9:30pm. Closed 3 weeks in June.

MODERATE
Auberge de la Diligence *Value* VALAIS/LEBANESE   This relatively inexpensive alpine tavern is on the highway beside the road leading in from Sierre. It specializes in flavor-filled combinations of cuisine from both the Valais and faraway Lebanon, whose spices and succulent flavors are much appreciated in the cold alpine air. The outdoor terrace is popular on fine days, and there's ample parking nearby. Dishes include couscous and fondues, grilled fish and steaks, well-spiced kebabs of chicken and lamb, and a succulent platter of Lebanese appetizers.

The hotel housing the tavern maintains nine bedrooms upstairs, five with a bathroom and all with TV and phone. Each has a balcony and, although they're larger than you might have expected, they come with almost no amenities or extra services. That fact contributes to their reasonable value at 130SF ($71.50) for a room with a bathroom, and 120SF ($66) for a room with shared facilities. Rates include breakfast. Both the hotel and its restaurant are open year-round.

Quartier La Combaz, CH-3963 Crans-Montana. © 027/485-99-85. Fax 027/485-99-88. Reservations recommended in the evening. Main courses 23SF–47SF ($12.65–$25.85). AE, DC, MC, V. Restaurant, daily
11:30am–2pm and 7–9:30pm. Cafe, daily 8am–11:30pm.

Le Pavillon ✦ SWISS   Le Pavillon is graced with a delightful lakeside locale—
a verdant setting near the Migros grocery store in the lowlands of "downtown"
Montana—and an expansive terrace that make it popular in both winter and
summer. You can drop in for snacks and drinks at any time; at mealtimes, the
chef presents a *cuisine du marché,* featuring fresh ingredients from the marketplace. Perfectly prepared menu items are likely to include grilled filet of lamb
with Provençal sauce, magret of duckling with orange sauce, filet of beef with
green peppercorns, a savory version of fondue *chinoise,* and trout and perch from
nearby lakes. Dessert includes a sorbet *valaisan,* flavored with apricots and
locally distilled apricot liqueur.

Montana. © 027/481-24-69. Reservations recommended. Main courses 25SF–47SF ($13.75–$25.85). AE,
DC, MC, V. Daily noon–2pm and 7–10pm. Closed Mon–Tues in April–May and Oct, and 2–3 weeks in Nov
(dates vary).

CRANS-MONTANA AFTER DARK

Here's how the night scene works in the twin playgrounds of Montana and
Crans: Head for a pub both before and after dinner. Suitably rowdy choices with
a bit of flair and humor include **Amadeus Pub,** in the Olympic Hotel, rue
Louis-Antille, in Montana (© **027/481-29-85**); and the woodsy and British-
looking **George & Dragon,** rue du Grand-Place, in Crans (© **027/481-54-96**).
After your obligatory pints of beer, which cost around 5.50SF ($3.05) each,
head off to any of the resort's discos, preferably after midnight. The best of them
is **l'Absolut Club,** rue Centrale, in Crans (© **027/481-65-96**); and **400
Coupe,** in Montana (© **027/481-16-80**). Both charge a cover of around 20SF
($11), which includes the first drink, and both mingle—in ways that can be a
lot of fun—electronic dance music with bouts of folkloric evergreen.

4 Zermatt ✦✦✦ & the Matterhorn ✦✦✦

41 miles (66km) SE of Sierre, 30 miles (48km) SW of Brig, 151 miles (242km) E of Geneva

Zermatt, 5,315 feet (1,594m) above sea level, is a small village at the base of the
Matterhorn. It made its debut as a hiking and hill-climbing resort more than
150 years ago, when it was discovered by English tourists. World attention was
turned on the **Matterhorn** in the 1860s, when Edward Whymper, the English
explorer and mountaineer, made a series of attempts to ascend it. Approaching
the Matterhorn from the Italian side, he tried six times to climb it and failed.
Then, on July 14, 1865, after changing his strategy and approaching the mountain from the Swiss side (using Zermatt as his departure point), he succeeded,
and—accompanied by two of his guides—became the first person to reach the
summit of the Matterhorn. During the process, however, four climbers in his
team had fallen to their deaths.

Three days later, an Italian guide, Jean-Antoine Carrel, spurred on by the
acclaim of Whymper's feat, successfully made the climb from the Italian side.
Since then, the Matterhorn (known as Mont Cervin to the French-speaking
Swiss) still lures mountain climbers, although only a few of them attempt to
reach its summit. Two of the most memorable hikes are the climb up to the **Met-
telhorn** (11,000 ft./3,300m) and the hike up to the **Matterhorn Hut,** a few
thousand feet below the wind-blasted cliffs that surround the summit.

Impressions

If St. Moritz is Cary Grant in To Catch a Thief, *then Zermatt is Hugh Grant in* Four Weddings and a Funeral—*equally charming and handsome, perhaps, but far less sophisticated than it would like to think.*

—Mark Orwoll, 1998

Zermatt is a world-renowned resort with many luxurious accommodations and dozens of fashionable boutiques. You can walk from one end of the town to the other in about 15 minutes, which is handy because no cars are allowed on the local streets. The town does, however, have one of the best networks of alpine cable cars, gondolas, and cog railways in Switzerland—36 of them operating in the winter and 21 in the summer. In the peak season it's mobbed with hundreds of tourists.

Because more snow falls on Zermatt than on many other winter resorts in Europe, high-altitude skiing—especially at the Théodul Pass—continues throughout the spring and early summer. As for winter skiing, skiers can choose between wide, gentle slopes and difficult runs only for world-class champion skiers. Zermatt's **ski school** (𝄞 **027/966-24-66**) offers certified instruction and mountain guides.

From Zermatt, you can take one of the grandest and most scenic train rides in Europe. The **Glacier Express** might be the slowest express train in the world, taking 7½ hours to pass through southeastern Switzerland, but it's the most panoramic. A stunning feat of mountain engineering, the train begins its daily run in Zermatt, heading for the resort of St. Moritz in the Engadine. Along the way it crosses 291 bridges and goes through 91 tunnels. Windows on the train are designed to take in these stunning mountain panoramas. There's also a dining car aboard. Make advance reservations by calling **Rail Europe** at 𝄞 **800/438-7245,** or see their website at www.raileurope.com.

ESSENTIALS

GETTING THERE   Take a train to Visp or Brig, where you can transfer to a narrow-gauge train to Zermatt. Departures are every 20 minutes daily between 6am and 11:30pm. It's about a 4-hour trip from Geneva. For Swiss **rail information,** call 𝄞 **0900-300-300.**

In addition, buses run from Visp and Brig to Täsch hourly, which is the departure point for the cog railway that ascends frequently to Zermatt. Call the tourist office (see below) for more information.

If you're driving, head to Täsch, 3 miles from Zermatt, and park your car in an open lot or a garage. A rail shuttle in the center of the village will then take you to the resort for 14.80SF ($9.90) per person round-trip.

VISITOR INFORMATION   The **Zermatt Tourist Office** is on Bahnhofplatz (𝄞 **027/966-81-00**), open mid-June to mid-Oct Monday to Saturday 8:30am to 6pm, Sunday 9:30am to noon and 4 to 7pm; otherwise Monday to Saturday 8:30am to noon and 1:30 to 6pm.

Only a few of Zermatt's streets, notably Bahnhofstrasse, have names—most don't. To find your way around, you can rely on the dozens of signs pointing the way to the various hotels and restaurants at the resort.

SEEING THE SIGHTS

There are many diversions in Zermatt, including a popular curling center, with eight rinks, each equipped with precision-crafted curling stones. There are also two natural ice-skating rinks, unusual shops, and a variety of bars and restaurants.

You might also pay a visit to the **Alpine Museum** (© 027/967-41-00), which details Whymper's race to climb the Matterhorn. Exhibits include climbing equipment, relief models of the great mountain, and artifacts discovered near Zermatt from prehistoric and Roman times. The museum is open June to October, daily from 10am to noon and 4 to 6pm; December to May, Sunday to Friday from 4:30 to 6:30pm (closed in November). Admission costs 6SF ($3.30) for adults, 2SF ($1.10) for children ages 6 to 16, and is free for children 5 and under. To find the museum, get on Hauptstrasse (main street) and find the Hotel Mount Cervin. Across from it is the train station; the museum is in back.

SKIING & HIKING

The skiing and hiking areas of Zermatt are divided between the Gornergrat, the Blauherd-Rothorn, and the Klein Matterhorn regions. There are a number of ski-lift passes sold in various combinations, but there isn't much savings regardless of the plan you select. A 2-day pass covering all the lifts in the Zermatt area costs 110SF ($60.50), while day passes cost 62SF ($34.10). The one break that ski-pass holders get is free rides on the ski bus linking all three ski areas. To purchase tickets, visit the tourist office (see "Essentials," above).

GORNERGRAT ★★★   Gornergrat is perched at a lofty altitude of 10,170 feet. To get here, take a cogwheel train, the highest open-air railway in Europe, to its terminus. En route, you'll stop at **Riffelberg,** which offers a panoramic view of both the Matterhorn and Mount Rosa. The complete ride from Zermatt to Gornergrat is 63SF ($42.20) round-trip. At Gornergrat, an observatory looks out on the bleak expanses of the Gorner glacier and over the heights of the Dom, which, at nearly 15,000 feet, is the highest mountain entirely within Switzerland.

At Gornergrat, you can take a cable car to other elevations. A two-stage cable car reaches a point near the top of the **Stockhorn,** at 11,180 feet; the cost is an additional 24SF ($13.20) round-trip from Gornergrat.

BLAUHERD-UNTER ROTHORN ★★   To get to Blauherd-Unter Rothorn, take a cog railway through a tunnel from Zermatt to the alpine meadows of Sunegga, and then transfer to a cable car. After changing cable cars at Blauherd (which offers many hiking and skiing options of its own), you'll continue by cable car to the flat, rocky summit of the Unter Rothorn, where possibilities for alpine rambles or ski descents abound.

SCHWARZSEE-THEODUL   To reach Zermatt's third major ski area, take a cable car from Zermatt to **Furi-Schweigmatten** (usually abbreviated to Furi). Here you'll find a variety of cross-country skiing and hiking trails, and downhill skiing even in midsummer across the Théodul Pass and the border into Italy. In the winter you can continue downhill on skis to the Italian ski resort of Breuil-Cervinia for lunch, on the opposite side of the Matterhorn from Zermatt. At Furi, a cable car carries you downhill to the calm waters of Schwarzsee (Black Lake) at 8,480 feet. Here the **Schwarzseehotel** (© 027/967-22-63) offers vistas plus lunch or a drink on its terrace. Some skiers depart from Schwarzsee for another series of lonely but spectacular downhill runs. The round-trip excursion from Zermatt via Furi to Schwarzsee costs 33SF ($18.15).

KLEIN MATTERHORN ★★★   To reach the "Little Matterhorn" from Furi, you must take two additional cable cars (the first of which will transfer at an alpine junction named Trockenersteg) before reaching an elevator that will carry you up to one of the highest mountain terraces in the world (12,533 ft./ 3,760m). If the sky is clear, you'll be able to see both the French and the Italian Alps and breathe a rarefied air usually reserved for the hardiest of alpine climbers. The excursion to Klein Matterhorn from Zermatt costs 75SF ($41.25) round-trip.

SHOPPING

Zermatt's critics accuse it of combining a hard-nosed commercialism, shrewdly calculating the value of every snowflake, with a less harsh obsession with Swiss folklore. Consequently, the town's main shopping thoroughfare, **Bahnhofstrasse,** contains branches of stores you might have expected only in much larger cities, with an emphasis on luxury goods, alpine souvenirs, and sporting goods. Ski and mountaineering equipment here tends to be state-of-the-art. Stores selling the stuff appear virtually everywhere, but worthwhile examples include **Slalom Sport,** Steinmatt (very close to the village church; © 027/966-23-66). Well-recommended competitors, both on Bahnhofstrasse near the Gornergrat cable car, include **Glacier Sport** (© 027/968-13-00) and **Bayard Sport** (© 027/966-49-60).

Local souvenirs in Zermatt include everything from the genuinely artful to the hopelessly kitschy. One of the biggest outlets is **Haus der Geschenke** (House of Presents), on Bahnhofstrasse near the Gornergrat railway station (© 027/967-30-51). A nearby competitor, **WEGA,** on Bahnhofplatz (© 027/967-17-87), is just as folkloric. As an antidote to all the folk souvenirs, some visitors make it a point to search out more universal, or international, forms of art at one of the several art galleries. At the **Galerie Capricorn,** Bahnhofstrasse, near the village church (© 027/967-19-41), you'll find oil paintings, watercolors, lithographs, and engravings, as well as inexpensive posters.

Snow and ice aren't the only things that sparkle in Zermatt, so if you're susceptible to impulse purchases of jewelry, be aware that there are a lot of shops to avoid. One of the most visible is **Bijouterie Schindler,** Bahnhofstrasse (© 027/967-11-18), which stockpiles both Swiss watches and gemstones.

WHERE TO STAY

Zermatt has something for most budgets. It contains more than 120 hotels and guesthouses, plus a growing array of private apartments and condominiums. Some hotels make arrangements to meet clients at the cog-railway station if you inform them in advance of your arrival.

VERY EXPENSIVE

Alex Schlosshotel Tenne ⭐   The chiseled stonework and baroque-style stepped roofs, coupled with the Art Nouveau decor of its bedrooms and public rooms, make this hotel a welcome change from the many chalet-style hotels that surround it. Comfort and service are the keynote here, and you live well in alpine surroundings, with stunning views in most directions. Beds are exceedingly comfortable, and the private tiled bathrooms are of a good size. Each of its junior suites contains a whirlpool bath and a separate sitting room with fireplace. All south-facing rooms have private balconies.

CH-3920 Zermatt. © 027/966-44-00. Fax 027/966-44-05. www.zermatt.com. 38 units. Summer 320SF–440SF ($176–$242) double; 520SF ($286) junior suite for 2. Winter 360SF–480SF ($198–$264) double; 610SF ($335.50) junior suite for 2. Rates include half board. AE, MC, V. Closed mid-Oct to mid-Dec. **Amenities:** Restaurant, bar; fitness center; Jacuzzi; steam bath; sauna; room service; laundry service. *In room:* TV, minibar, hair dryer.

Grand Hotel Zermatterhof ☆☆☆   This white-walled 1879 hotel, Zermatt's grandest resort, pointedly refuses to imitate a chalet. Rated five stars by the Swiss government, it's more plush and comfortable than anything in town. The bedrooms are paneled and well upholstered, with vivid colors. Alpine-style furnishings add a warm, cozy ambience, and each room is equipped with deluxe beds, plus marble and tile bathrooms boasting dual basins, robes, and heated towel racks. In summer a carriage awaits guests at the rail station at Täsch.

Bahnhofstrasse, CH-3920 Zermatt. © 027/966-66-00. Fax 027/967-66-99. www.zermatt.ch. 86 units. Winter 580SF–760SF ($319–$418) double; 960SF ($528) suite. Off-season 510SF–630SF ($280.50–$346.50) double; 810SF ($445.50) suite. Rates include half board. AE, DC, MC, V. Closed Oct 10–Nov 28. **Amenities:** 3 restaurants, 2 bars; pool; tennis court; health club; Jacuzzi; sauna; steam bath; children's playroom; room service; massage; babysitting; laundry/dry cleaning. *In room:* TV, minibar, coffeemaker, hair dryer, iron.

Hotel Monte Rosa ☆   According to Edward Whymper, the Englishman who conquered the Matterhorn, this is the best hotel at Zermatt. Of course, he made that pronouncement back in 1865. Monte Rosa has long since lost that position but still holds its own beautifully as one of the most welcoming and traditional hotels in the Valais. Located on the main street, the Monte Rosa has stone posts, lintels, and red shutters around its windows. The lounges have parquet floors, thick rugs, and crackling fireplaces; the antique armchairs are beautifully upholstered in stripes and patterns. The mid-sized to spacious bedrooms, decorated with Victorian prints and cabinetry, are among the most comfortable in Zermatt. Rooms facing south are the most desirable, the most expensive, and the hardest to come by. Each unit comes with a good-sized, immaculately kept private bathroom.

CH-3920 Zermatt. © 800/223-6800 in the U.S., or 027/966-03-33. Fax 027/966-03-30. www.zermatt.ch. 49 units. Winter 338SF–484SF ($185.90–$266.20) double; 568SF–736SF ($312.40–$404.80) suite. Summer 284SF–368SF ($156.20–$202.40) double; 484SF–568SF ($266.20–$312.40) suite. Rates include breakfast. Half board 100SF ($55) extra. AE, DC, MC, V. Closed Apr 18–June 24 and Oct 24–Dec 17. **Amenities:** Restaurant, bar; use of nearby pool and fitness center; room service; babysitting; laundry/dry cleaning. *In room:* TV, minibar, hair dryer, safe.

Hotel Walliserhof ☆☆ *(Finds)*   Originally a Valaisian farmhouse, this hotel is one of the most successful conversions in town. It enjoys much German patronage, ever since the German newspaper *Bunte* named it "Swiss hotel of the year" a few years back. Renovations have made it worthy of a four-star government rating. In the center of town, it is easy to spot with its red shutters and balconies. It offers a large terrace out front, and inside you'll find stone fireplaces, thick walls, masonry columns, and flagstone floors. The mid-sized carpeted bedrooms have wooden furniture and good beds, plus neat bathrooms.

Bahnhofstrasse, CH-3920 Zermatt. © 027/966-65-55. Fax 027/967-65-50. www.reconline.ch. 30 units. Winter 340SF–370SF ($187–$203.50) double; 420SF ($231) suite. Summer 240SF–280SF ($132–$154) double; 360SF ($198) suite. Rates include breakfast. Half board 25SF ($13.75) per person extra. AE, MC, V. **Amenities:** 2 restaurants, bar; limited room service; babysitting (on request); laundry service. *In room:* TV, minibar, hair dryer.

Riffelalp Resort 222 ☆☆ *(Finds)*   Set within a 20-minute cog-railway ride north of Zermatt, this resort sits on sloping terrain midway up the mountain, in the midst of some of the region's most venerated skiing. It originated in 1884, when ancestors of the present owners (the Seiler family) erected a Victorian-style summer-only hotel, which was eventually damaged in a disastrous fire in 1961. Since then, the original building (the "Nostalgia wing") has been repaired and enlarged with a modern annex ("The Chalet"). Each accommodation comes with a mid-sized bathroom. This government five-star resort offers quick access to the region's spectacular hiking, skiing, and views. The Gornergrat cable car will carry you even higher into the Alps (all the way to the Stockhorn) if you want more altitude, or down into Zermatt if you're looking for a rowdy good time in the town's bars, discos, or restaurants.

Riffelalp, 3920 Zermatt. ℂ **027/966-05-55.** Fax 027/966-05-50. 68 units. Summer 480SF–540SF ($264–$297) double. Winter 690SF–870SF ($379.50–$478.50) double. AE, DC, MC, V. Closed: mid-Oct to mid-Dec and mid-Apr to mid-June. From Zermatt, take the Gornergrat cablecar to its halfway point, Riffelalp. **Amenities:** 2 restaurants (1 with an outdoor terrace), lobby bar with piano music; indoor swimming pool; health club with sauna; room service (7am–11pm); child-care facilities; bowling alley; in-house movie theater; billiard room. *In room:* TV, minibar.

Seiler Mont Cervin 🏔🏔🏔 This has remained one of Zermatt's leading hotels since it was established in 1872. The rooms are often sunny and spacious, with fine craftsmanship. Units in the old quarter are more old-fashioned and still preferred by traditionalists. Accommodations in the newest wing have a restrained classic decor, and some are decorated in regional stucco along with hand-carved blond-wood pieces. All the units except nine have a tub and shower combination; the remaining nine have only a shower. You and your bags will be picked up at the rail station by a horse-drawn sleigh in the winter or by an old-fashioned horse-drawn carriage in the summer.

Bahnhofstrasse, CH-3920 Zermatt. ℂ **800/223-6800** in the U.S. and Canada, or 027/966-88-88. Fax 027/967-28-78. www.zermatt.ch/montcervin. 132 units. Summer 430SF–690SF ($236.50–$379.50) double; 619SF–810SF ($340.45–$445.50) junior suite; 730SF–1,030SF ($401.50–$566.50) suite. Winter 489SF–890SF ($268.95–$489.50) double; 690SF–1,000SF ($379.50–$550) junior suite; 810SF–1,450SF ($445.50–$797.50) suite. Rates include half board. AE, DC, MC, V. Closed mid-Apr to mid-June and mid-Oct to end of Nov. **Amenities:** 2 restaurants, bar; pool; fitness center; steam bath; sauna; salon; room service; massage; baby-sitting; laundry service. *In room:* TV, minibar, hair dryer, safe.

MODERATE

Hotel Antika 🏔 Set behind an attractive chalet facade, each of the bedrooms of this hotel opens onto its own covered loggia with flower boxes and wooden trim. Making use of wood furnishings, rooms have an alpine charm and cozy comfort, with excellent beds and most often mountain views. The interior is accented with Oriental carpets and a partial sheathing of weathered planks. A large garden behind the hotel is great for quiet contemplation of the Matterhorn.

CH-3920 Zermatt. ℂ **027/967-21-51.** Fax 027/967-57-83. www.antica.ch. 28 units. Winter 150SF–220SF ($82.50–$121) double; summer 150SF–165SF ($82.50–$90.75) double. Rates include buffet breakfast. AE, DC, MC, V. Closed May 5–June 10 and Oct 7–Nov 11. **Amenities:** Restaurant; Jacuzzi; sauna; room service. *In room:* TV, hair dryer.

Hotel Butterfly This Best Western hotel lies under a peaked roof, with large windows and flower boxes. The Alps loom in the distance. The interior is warm and cozy, with arched windows, Oriental rugs, and knotty-pine furniture. Mrs. Gunda Woischnig offers small to mid-sized rooms with balconies facing south, all of them renovated in 1995. The well-stocked hotel bar serves as an intimate rendezvous point, and buffet breakfast is served.

CH-3920 Zermatt. ℂ **800/528-1234** in the U.S. and Canada, or 027/966-41-66. Fax 027/966-41-65. 40 units. Winter 340SF ($187) double; summer 250SF ($137.50) double. Rates include buffet breakfast. Half board 25SF ($13.75) per person extra. AE, DC, MC, V. Closed Apr 20–May 20 and Oct 20–Dec 20. **Amenities:** Restaurant, bar; fitness center; steam bath; sauna; room service; laundry service. *In room:* TV, minibar, hair dryer.

Hotel Darioli 🏔 This five-story, balconied hotel is on the main street near the train station. Built in 1964, the hotel was completely overhauled in 1979 and has been often renovated since. It's one of the few hotels in Zermatt to remain open all year, although its restaurant closes in November. This is one of the best government-rated three-star hotels in town; many guests prefer it to some hotels with higher ratings. The reception area is upstairs. The hotel has Oriental rugs and an attractive wooden bar. The Darioli family offers comfortable mid-sized rooms with regional furniture, usually painted in vivid colors with stenciled floral patterns. Most of the rooms have private bathrooms. One of the most consistently popular restaurants in Zermatt, Le Gitan (see "Where to Dine," below), is on this hotel's street level.

Bahnhofstrasse, CH-3920 Zermatt. ℭ **027/967-27-48.** Fax 027/967-12-37. www.reconline.ch/darioli. 22 units, 18 with bathroom. Winter 175SF ($96.25) double without bathroom, 210SF ($115.50) double with bathroom. Summer 130SF ($71.50) double without bathroom, 180SF ($99) double with bathroom. Rates include buffet breakfast. AE, MC, V. **Amenities:** Restaurant, 2 bars; laundry service. *In room:* TV (in some).

Hotel Post ⟨★ ⟨*Finds*   Built in 1880 and extensively rebuilt in the 1950s when American-born Karl Ivarsson and his family acquired it, this hotel is better known for its sprawling restaurant and nightlife facilities than for its bedrooms. There's a definite Anglo influence here, not only from the Americans attracted to the place but the increasing numbers of Brits as well. The small to mid-sized bedrooms have unusual floor plans, deliberately mismatched pieces of antique furniture, modern plumbing, and in some cases, a TV. By no means should you assume that the Hotel Post falls into the predictable mold of the typical Swiss hotel. Its clients tend to be the most iconoclastic in Zermatt, and have included many of the great names in British rock and roll, including David Bowie. Fittingly, the Post's labyrinth of nightlife facilities are the loudest, the most irreverent, and the most fun in Zermatt.

Bahnhofstrasse, CH-3920 Zermatt. ℭ **027/967-19-32.** Fax 027/967-41-14. www.postzermatt.com. 21 units. Winter 210SF–280SF ($115.50–$154) double; 365SF ($200.75) suite. Summer 150SF–230SF ($82.50–$126.50) double; 270SF ($148.50) suite. Rates include buffet breakfast. 7-day minimum stay in midwinter. AE, DC, MC, V. **Amenities:** 2 restaurants, 3 bars; limited room service; babysitting (by arrangement). *In room:* TV, hair dryer.

Hotel Riffelberg ⟨*Finds*   Set in an alpine meadow 8,200 feet (2,460m) above sea level, a 90-minute trek or a 30-minute cog-railway ride from Zermatt, this isolated hotel sits amid natural splendor in the shadow of the Matterhorn. Built in 1853 by a local clergyman and purchased by the city of Zermatt in 1873, it has served ever since as a well-maintained hotel and restaurant, with the kind of views that restore health to bodies and minds. Because of its altitude, the area gets 8 full hours of sunlight in December, and even more in midsummer. Skiing between December and April, thanks to the nearby Gornergrat cableway, is excellent. Despite several recent renovations, the Riffelberg retains a simple alpine decor in its comfortable but small bedrooms. Round-trip transit from Zermatt on the cog railway costs 60SF ($33) per person, and the last train from Zermatt departs at 6pm. The Riffelsee is not far from the train stop; an ibex colony lives nearby as well.

CH-3920 Zermatt-Umgebung. ℭ **027/966-65-00.** Fax 027/966-65-05. 30 units. Winter 270SF–320SF ($148.50–$176) double; summer 220SF ($121) double. Rates include half board. AE, DC, MC, V. Closed Apr 15–June 20 and Oct 18–Dec 20. **Amenities:** Restaurant, bar; Jacuzzi; sauna; limited room service. *In room:* TV, minibar.

Romantik Hotel Julen ⟨★★   Across the river from Zermatt's historic cemetery, this hotel (ca. 1937), with its weathered balconies, is Zermatt's most romantic.. The mid-sized bedrooms are furnished in mountain-resort style with carved pine beds and ceramic-tile bathrooms. Try for one on the south side— those have balconies with views of the Matterhorn. The main dining room features French cuisine and has an ornate ceiling and paneled walls. In addition, the Schaferstube offers more informal fare in a setting of pinewood, ceiling beams, and the inevitable cowbells. The hotel has installed an entire spa, and on the third floor is a "dreamshower" (you select what you want, from warm tropical to ice-cold glacier).

CH-3920 Zermatt. © 027/966-76-00. Fax 027/966-76-76. www.zermatt.ch/julen. 32 units. Summer 280SF–360SF ($154–$198) double; 382SF–530SF ($210.10–$291.50) suite. Winter 318SF–424SF ($174.90–$233.20) double; 530SF–648SF ($291.50–$356.40) suite. Rates include half board. AE, DC, MC, V. **Amenities:** 2 restaurants, bar; pool; health club; spa with sauna, steam bath, and mud baths; room service; babysitting; laundry service. *In room:* TV, minibar, hair dryer, safe.

INEXPENSIVE

Hotel Alphubel ⓥalue   Located near the train station, this is a large chalet with a solid stone foundation and curved stairs leading to the entrance. The Julen family named it after a local mountaintop. The small rooms are decorated in a functional, modern style with tub-equipped bathrooms. The restaurant is open for half-board guests only and serves good, moderately priced dishes.

CH-3920 Zermatt. © 027/967-30-03. Fax 027/967-66-84. 30 units. Summer 180SF–206SF ($99–$113.30) double; winter 200SF–246SF ($110–$135.30) double. Rates include half board. AE, MC, V. Closed Oct to the end of Nov. **Amenities:** Restaurant, bar; sauna. *In room:* TV, hair dryer.

Hotel Garni Tannenhof ⓥalue   The hotel is located in the center of the village, just a 3-minute walk from the train station and lying just off the Bahnhofstrasse (follow the signposts onto a pathway). The atmosphere is rustic and the rooms are simple and a bit small, but the place fills up quickly in winter. The hotel has simple alpine furnishings, including good beds, along with thick, cozy rugs.

Bahnhofstrasse, CH-3920 Zermatt. © 027/967-31-88. Fax 027/967-21-73. www.rhone.ch/tannenhof. 25 units, 15 with bathroom. 100SF ($55) double without bathroom, 130SF ($71.50) double with bathroom. Rates include breakfast. AE, DC, MC, V. Closed Oct to Dec 15. **Amenities:** Laundry service.

Hotel Weisshorn   Convenient for frugal travelers arriving at the train station, this is a bargain in this otherwise high-priced resort area. However, if you're planning a winter visit, make reservations as far in advance as possible, as the hotel fills up quickly. You don't get luxury here but are provided with alpine comfort in a setting of low-paneled ceilings and winding staircases. The place is snug and cozy as the blizzards rage outside. The bedrooms are small but adequate, with plush comforters and, in some cases, small balconies.

Bahnhofstrasse, CH-3920 Zermatt. © 027/967-11-12. Fax 027/967-38-39. 17 units, 7 with bathroom. 86SF–110SF ($47.30–$60.50) double without bathroom, 112SF–150SF ($61.60–$82.50) double with bathroom. Rates include continental breakfast. MC, V. **Amenities:** Restaurant. *In room:* TV, hair dryer.

WHERE TO DINE
EXPENSIVE

Alex Grill ⚜ SWISS   This stylish basement restaurant is decorated with carved paneling, leaded windows, flagstone floors, bright upholstery, and rich accessories. The chefs concoct appetizing dishes based on regional and Swiss recipes prepared with market-fresh ingredients. As an appetizer, try a platter of three kinds of smoked fish or fresh Atlantic oysters. The main courses include grilled lobster, grilled salmon scallop, and giant shrimp with a chive-flavored cream sauce. The meat dishes include veal kidneys in mustard sauce, grilled rack of lamb, chicken breast filled with a salmon-and-herb mousse, and a variety of game in season.

In the Hotel Alex. © 027/966-70-70. Reservations recommended. Main courses 45SF–60SF ($24.75–$33); fixed-price menus 75SF–82SF ($41.25–$45.10). AE, MC, V. Daily 7–9:30pm. Closed May to mid-June and mid-Oct to mid-Nov.

Alex Schlosshotel Tenne ✦ SWISS/INTERNATIONAL   In the lobby level of the previously recommended hotel of the same name, this duplex restaurant includes an upper wraparound gallery and a ceiling fresco covered with a representation of the zodiac. The kitchen continues to steer a steady course between rich, regional specialties and the subtler flavors of an international repertoire. Ingredients are first rate, and the restaurant is known for its grill specialties. The menu might include herb-flavored shrimp soup, whole-meal noodles, roast salmon in a white-wine sauce, or rack of lamb from the grill. For dessert, try cherries flambé with a honey parfait.

In the Alex Schlosshotel Tenne. ✆ 027/967-44-00. Reservations required in winter. Main courses 25SF–56SF ($13.75–$30.80). AE, MC, V. Daily 7–9:30pm. Closed mid-Oct to mid-Dec.

The Grill Room/The Stübli ✦ ITALIAN/SWISS   In what was originally built as a farmhouse, in the heart of town, these restaurants—unlike many of their competitors—remain open every day throughout the year. The Grill Room is the more elegant of the two, serving French, German, and Italian fare. There's an especially elegant collection of hors d'oeuvres, including smoked salmon, and main courses, such as veal cutlets and brook trout with almonds or veal piccata with risotto. The commendable regional dishes are filled with rich, subtle flavors. The less formal Stübli serves basically the same menu but concentrates on alpine Swiss specialties, such as fondues, raclettes, and grilled meats, in a cozy setting.

In the Hotel Walliserhof, Bahnhofstrasse. ✆ 027/966-65-55. Reservations recommended. Main courses 25SF–42SF ($13.75–$23.10). AE, DC, MC, V. Daily 11am–2pm and 7–11pm.

Le Gitan ✦ SWISS   This is neither the most formal restaurant in town, nor the most glamorous. Despite that, reservations during the winter ski season are sometimes booked a week in advance, and virtually everyone in town seems to pick Le Gitan as their favorite restaurant. Set on the street level of a well-managed three-star hotel, the interior is very cozy, with an open fireplace and room for no more than 50 diners. With a wide selection of Swiss and regional specialties available, the array of grilled meats is the house specialty. The grilled beef, veal, game, and pork dishes are all richly garnished and impressively presented. Of special note is an excellent *gigot d'agneau* (lamb) with garlic, and a selection of savory fondues served in the bistro in front of the restaurant.

In the Hotel Darioli, Bahnhofstrasse. ✆ 027/968-19-40. Reservations required. Main courses 23SF–44SF ($12.65–$24.20). AE, MC, V. Daily 6:30–10pm.

MODERATE

Arvenstube SWISS/INTERNATIONAL   A tempting variety of international and Swiss dishes is served in this paneled dining room with a corner bar. The chefs here continue to please visitors year after year with their skill. As an appetizer, try the *assiette valaisanne*, a plate of air-dried meats from the Grisons. Other specialties include *riz Casimir* (a curry rice dish), tournedos in a savory-mustard sauce, and sliced veal in a mushroom-cream sauce. These dishes are often served with rösti or Swiss hash browns. Trout with almonds is another favorite.

In the Hotel Pollux, Bahnhofstrasse. ✆ 027/966-40-00. Reservations recommended. Main courses 27SF–75SF ($14.85–$41.25). AE, DC, MC, V. Daily 11:30am–2pm and 6–9pm. Closed 2 or 3 weeks in Nov.

Findlerhof ✦✦ (Finds) SWISS/ITALIAN   The Findlerhof is the best mountain restaurant near Zermatt. Despite its remote location—in the small hamlet of Findeln, on a steep mountainside—the place is very popular. It has a sun terrace and a roof terrace facing the Matterhorn. Your hosts are Franz and Heidi Schwery, who offer such delights as meat and salmon carpaccio, salads laced with salmon and scampi, and excellent pasta dishes.

Findeln. ℭ **027/967-25-88.** Reservations required. Main courses 25SF–40SF ($13.75–$22); fixed-price menu 25SF–35SF ($13.75–$19.25). No credit cards. Daily 9am–6pm. Take the Sunnegga chairlift to the first stop, then hike across the fields; leave your skis in the snow and head down the steep, winding pathway, past the plastic palm trees.

Grillroom Stockhorn ⭐ SWISS

This is one of the few restaurants of Zermatt not located in a hotel, and it's one of the two or three best dining rooms in town. A fireplace extends into the dining room of this elegant chalet owned by Emil Julen. The decor includes an alpine wedding chest and regional chairs, as well as travertine floors, heavy beams, varnished pine, earth-tone accents, and stained stucco walls. The savory, rib-sticking specialties include raclette, piccata with spaghetti, fondue *bourguignonne,* and grilled meats. There's also a bar.

Riedstrasse. ℭ **027/967-17-47.** Reservations required. Main courses 25SF–40SF ($13.75–$22). AE, MC, V. Daily 11:30am–1pm and 6:30–10pm. Closed May to mid-June and Oct to mid-Nov.

Portofino Grill INTERNATIONAL

Decorated in tones of marine blue with lots of highly varnished wood, this is the most elegant of the several dining choices in the Hotel Post. A fresh antipasto buffet is laid out in what used to be a boat, and the cuisine—which some visitors consider a welcome change from a constant diet of Swiss alpine food—features seafood and Italian choices. Menu items include a selection of homemade pastas with savory sauces, and freshly prepared veal, poultry, and meat dishes. Many diners opt for a before- or after-dinner drink in the Boathouse Bar. Crafted from the cabin of a once-glamorous three-masted schooner, it seats only a dozen drinkers in cozy, knee-rubbing proximity. The spillover from the main bar moves into what's affectionately known as "The Disaster Room," where photos of the 20th century's greatest marine disasters are prominently displayed.

In the Hotel Post. ℭ **027/967-19-32.** Reservations recommended. Main courses 26SF–48SF ($14.30–$26.40). AE, DC, MC, V. Open Dec–Apr daily 7pm–midnight. Closed Easter–Nov.

Schäferstübli SWISS

This moderately priced restaurant offers atmospheric dining amid plank-covered walls, heavy beams, flickering candles, and leaded-glass windows. If you're not already a convert of Swiss cuisine, you may easily become one after a meal here. The house specialty is lamb, served in a variety of styles. You can also order grilled veal and beef dishes, traditionally prepared. The restaurant is part of the Romantik Hotel Julen but has its own separate entrance.

In the Romantik Hotel Julen. ℭ **027/967-76-05.** Reservations required. Main courses 16SF–45SF ($8.80–$24.75); lamb fondues 40SF ($22) per person; cheese fondues 23SF ($12.65) per person; all you can eat raclette 35SF ($19.25) per person; fixed-price meal 40SF ($22). AE, DC, MC, V. Daily 6–9:30pm. Closed May and 2 weeks in Nov.

INEXPENSIVE

Walliserkanne SWISS/ITALIAN

This rustic family restaurant is 2 minutes from the Zermatt train station. Walliserkanne is divided into three main dining rooms and a second restaurant in the basement. The elegant rooms are large and feature paintings by local artists on the walls. The restaurant offers a delectable menu of Italian dishes such as antipasto *misto della casa* (variety of Italian starters), carpaccio *d'agnello con rucola e parmigiano* (thin slices of raw lamb served with arugula and Parmesan), or *vitello tonnato* (slices of roast veal with tuna fish sauce). Pizzas and pastas round out the succulent fare. The menu also offers a wide choice of desserts.

Bahnhofstrasse. ✆ 027/966-46-10. Reservations recommended. Main courses 15SF–40SF ($8.25–$22). AE, MC, V. Daily 10am–midnight.

ZERMATT AFTER DARK

Zermatt is known for its après-ski activities, which include tea dances, restaurants, bars, nightclubs, and discos. It has more nightclubs than any other resort in the Valais.

AN ENTERTAINMENT COMPLEX

Hotel Post (✆ 027/967-19-32), where everybody shows up after recovering from Elsie's Irish coffee (see below), has a virtual monopoly on nightlife in Zermatt. The owner, Karl Ivarsson, an American, has gradually expanded it into one of the most complete entertainment complexes in Zermatt, with a number of restaurants and nightspots under one roof. Photographs of former guests, including famous athletes and models, are displayed under glass at the reception desk. On the way to the restaurant, in the basement, you'll pass a series of murals telling the story of a lonely tourist looking for love in Zermatt.

Take your pick of the various venues, including the **Jazz Bar,** open December to Easter and 1 month in summer. In winter, they import a different band every year, although there's only a piano player in summer. The **Broken Bar,** located in the basement, is where the most hardened ski bums listen to hard rock music at very high volumes, drink heavily, and generally raise hell. **Le Village** is the most interesting disco in Zermatt, built in a 19th-century alpine barn, with Edwardian palms, leather couches, candles, and bentwood chairs. David Bowie has performed here. For hunger pangs, head for the **Brown Cow** at street level, a rustic room with 19th-century farm implements hanging from the ceiling. The menu includes hamburgers, goulash soup, sandwiches, and salads. **The Spaghetti Factory** is also open year-round, until midnight.

THE BAR SCENE

Elsie's Place, at Kirchplatz (✆ 027/967-24-31), is a small house, dating from 1879, that packs in a large crowd around 6pm. It's comfortable, sedate, and bourgeois. Skiers show up for hot chocolate or Elsie's famous Irish coffee, for 12.50SF ($6.90). The house is on the main street, near the Zermatterhof Hotel. During the day, the menu includes ham and eggs, hot dogs, and even escargots. They also serve caviar and oysters (a special luxury in this area). The cafe is open in the winter daily from 11am to 2am and in the summer daily from 4pm to 2am.

One of the most animated and energetic bars is **Grampy's Pub,** Bahnhofstrasse (✆ 027/967-77-88), across from the Post Hotel, a pub and disco favored by the resort's army of off-duty waiters, bartenders, chambermaids, and ski instructors. A roughly equivalent competitor is the **Papparia Pub** (✆ 027/967-40-40), near the Hotel Julen, where live music produced by Swiss folk and North American country/western bands gets your blood pumping.

Hotels that contain relatively animated pubs include the Hotel Bristol, the Schlosshotel Tenne, and the Hotel Excelsior. The least pretentious of the lot is the **Kegelstube** (the "Bowling Alley Bar") in the Hotel Bristol (✆ 027/966-33-66), where the resort's only bowling alleys add visual distraction to the large bar area. Upstairs, a more formal bar (the **Bristol Bar**) has a dance floor, a fireplace, and a view of the attached restaurant. The Alex Schlosshotel Tenne's most appealing after-dark spot is the **Bar Tenne** (✆ 027/967-18-01), whose Art Nouveau decor is a welcome change from the relentless emphasis on Swiss chalets everywhere else. Here, near a bar that resembles an ambulatory in a monastery, and a DJ booth that might have been a church pulpit, you can relax on comfortable sofas or dance beneath the kleig lights of a circular dance floor. In the Hotel Excelsior (℃ 027/967-30-17), you can head for the sometimes rowdy and garrulous Ex-Bar or seek refuge in the somewhat calmer, somewhat more upscale, winter-only Luna Bar, which is shielded from the noise nearby by thick doors and masonry walls.

Hotel Schwyzerhof (℃ 027/967-67-67), with its restaurant, and the Hotel Simi (℃ 027/966-46-00), with its Dancing Simi, both combine a regime of Swiss folklore and oompah music with alpine warmth, a busy bar area, platters of food, and—in the case of the Hotel Simi—some emphasis on disco. You'll find a rough approximation of big-city, urban life in the form of the Scotch Corner Bar, in the Hotel Aristella (℃ 027/967-20-41). You can always grab a beer and a shot or two of schnapps in the cozy setting of the Hotel Walliserhof's Stübli (℃ 027/966-65-55).

9

Lausanne & Lake Geneva

For decades, visitors have sought the scenic wonders of Lake Geneva (Lac Léman) in the southwestern corner of Switzerland. Native son Jean-Jacques Rousseau popularized the lake among the Romantics, and Lord Byron and Shelley both made pilgrimages here.

Formed by the Rhône, Lac Léman is the largest lake in central Europe. It consists of a Grand Lac to the east and a Petit Lac to the west, near Geneva (for a description of Geneva and its environs, see chapter 10). The lake covers 225 square miles (411 sq. km); more than half belongs to Switzerland, the rest to France. The French own most of the southern shore, except for Geneva in the west and the Valais in the east; the Swiss hold the entire northern shore, which forms a large arc. The water is limpid blue, except where the muddy Rhône empties into it.

Famous people who chose to live on the lake's shores have included the historian Edward Gibbon; the writers Honoré de Balzac, George Eliot, and André Gide; the composers Richard Wagner and Franz Liszt; the aviator Charles Lindbergh; and the actors Charlie Chaplin, Yul Brynner, Audrey Hepburn, James Mason, Noel Coward, William Holden, David Niven, and Sophia Loren (many of whom went here originally for tax reasons but liked the area so much that they stayed on until their deaths). Some of these actors, such as Chaplin and Hepburn, adopted Switzerland as their permanent home and were buried here.

Since 1823 steamer trips have been the most popular way to tour the lake. Nearly all the cities, hamlets, and towns along the lake have schedules posted at the landing quays, and service usually runs from Easter to October. If possible, though, we recommend touring by car or bus so that you can stop and visit sights along the way. Railways also run along both shores. Our exploration will begin with Lausanne.

1 Lausanne ★★

41 miles (66km) NE of Geneva, 134 miles (214km) SW of Zurich

Lausanne, whose 127,000 inhabitants make it the second-largest city on Lake Geneva and the fifth-largest in Switzerland, is built on three hills overlooking the lake, called Lac Léman by the city's inhabitants. The upper and lower towns are connected by a small *metro* (subway).

Lausanne has been inhabited since the Stone Age (it was the ancient Roman town of Lousanna). In 1803 the canton of Vaud, of which Lausanne is the capital, became the 19th to join the Swiss Confederation.

For centuries Lausanne has been a favorite spot for exiles and expatriates, attracting, among others, deposed monarchs. Lausanne flourished particularly in the Age of Enlightenment, when it was associated with Rousseau and Voltaire, two of the leading writers in the 18th century. Even today the city is

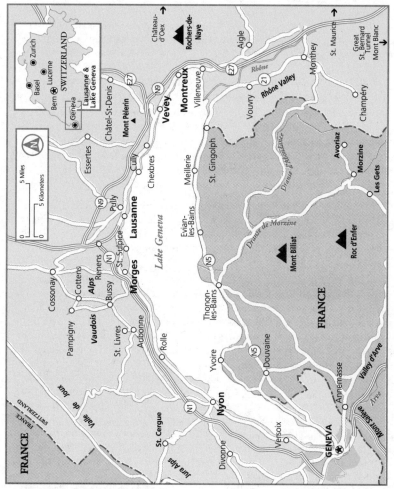

cited by many French-speaking Swiss as the place they would most like to live because of its low-key elegance and sense of grace. Regrettably, it's no longer a center of the intellectual or artistic elite. Voltaire and the likes have given way to water-skiers, swimmers, and "Sunday sailors," most of whom have never heard of Rousseau, much less read him. Even so, Lausanne retains an aesthetic charm and a cultural tradition—today it's the headquarters of the International Olympic Committee.

ESSENTIALS

GETTING THERE   Lausanne doesn't have an airport, so most visitors fly to Cointrin Airport in Geneva (see chapter 10) and then travel on to Lausanne. The train from Geneva leaves for Lausanne every 20 minutes and the trip takes 45 minutes. Call ⓒ **0900/300-300** for **train** schedules.

In addition, between late May and late September a lake steamer cruises several times a day in both directions between Geneva and Saint-Gingolph, Lausanne, Vevey, Montreux, and Nyon. Sailing time from Geneva is about 3½ hours.

Round-trip transit from Geneva costs 72SF ($39.60) in first class, 52SF ($28.60) in second class, with 50% discounts for children 16 and under. For information, contact the **Compagnie Générale de Navigation (CGN)**, 17, av. de Rhodanie (*©* **0848-811-848**).

If you're driving, Lausanne is connected by motorway (N1) to Geneva. The Great Saint Bernard road tunnel is 70 miles (113km) to the southeast, reached along E2, which becomes E21 during your final approach.

VISITOR INFORMATION   The **Office du Tourisme et des Congrès**, 2, av. de Rhodanie (*©* **021/613-73-21** or 021/613-73-73), is open from Easter to mid-October, Monday to Friday from 9am to 7pm, Saturday from 9am to 6pm, and Sunday from 9am to noon and 1 to 6pm; off-season, Monday to Friday from 8am to 6pm and Saturday from 8am to noon and 1 to 5pm.

CITY LAYOUT

Lausanne is spread out along the shore of Lake Geneva, surrounded by suburbs. There are two sections in particular that attract the most visitors—the **Upper Town** (Haute Ville), which is the old part of the city, and the **Lower Town** (Basse Ville), or **Ouchy;** the two sections are connected by a small subway (*metro*).

HAUTE VILLE *★★*   Lausanne's UpperTown still evokes the Middle Ages—a nightwatchman calls out the hours from 10pm to 2am from atop the cathedral's belfry. A visit to the Haute Ville takes about 2 hours and is best done on foot. In fact, walking through the old town of Lausanne is one of its major attractions. It's easy to get lost—and that's part of the fun. This area is north of the railroad station; you can reach it by going along rue du Petit-Chêne. The focal point of the Upper Town, and the shopping and business heart of Lausanne, is **place Saint-François.** The Church of St. François, from the 13th century, is all that remains of an old Franciscan friary. Today the square is filled with office blocks and the main post office; regrettably, La Grotte, the villa with the terrace on which Edward Gibbon completed *The History of the Decline and Fall of the Roman Empire* in 1787, was torn down in 1896 to make room for the post office. While vehicles are permitted south of the church, the area to the north is a pedestrian-only zone; it has more than 1¼ miles of streets, including **rue de Bourg,** northeast of the church, the best street for shopping. Rue de Bourg leads to the large, bustling rue Caroline, which winds north to **Pont des Bessières,** one of the three bridges erected at the turn of the century to connect the three hills on which Lausanne was built. From the bridge, you'll see the Haute Ville on your right, with the 13th-century **cathedral of Lausanne,** opening onto place de la Cathédrale. From the square, rue du Cité-de-Vant goes north to the 14th-century **Château Saint-Marie,** on place du Château—once the home of bishops and now containing the offices of the canton administration.

From here, avenue de l'Université leads to **place de la Riponne,** with the **Palais de Rumine** on its east side. From place de la Riponne, rue Pierre-Viret leads to the **Escaliers du Marché,** a covered stairway dating back to the Middle Ages. You can also take rue Madeleine from the place de la Riponne, continuing south to place de la Palud. On the side of place de la Palud stands the 17th-century **Hôtel de Ville** (town hall).

South of place de la Palud is rue du Pont, which turns into rue Saint-François (after crossing rue Centrale). Nearby, at **place du Flon,** you can catch the subway to Ouchy. In recent years place du Flon, with its cafes and bars, has become a favorite evening hangout.

OUCHY ⚑⚑ Ouchy, once a sleepy fishing hamlet, is now the port and hotel resort area of Lausanne. The lakefront of Lausanne consists of shady quays and tropical plants spread across a lakefront district of about half a mile. The **Château d'Ouchy** stands on place de la Navigation; from here, place du Port adjoins immediately on the east. **Quai de Belgique** and **quai d'Ouchy** are lakefront promenades bursting with greenery and offering the best views of the lake.

GETTING AROUND

BY METRO To avoid the crawling pace of the city's trams, take the metro. The trip between the heart of the Haute Ville and Ouchy takes 6 minutes. Departures are every 7½ minutes Monday to Friday from 6:15am to 11:45pm. During off-hours and on weekends and holidays, trains run every 15 minutes. A one-way ride from the town center to Ouchy costs 2.20SF ($1.20); a 24-hour ticket sells for 6.50SF ($3.60).

BY BUS & TRAM The TL (Lausanne Public Transport Company) has a well-designed network of trams and buses whose routes complement the city's subway line. The tram or bus fare is 2.20SF ($1.20), regardless of the distance, for a single trip completed within 60 minutes on lines 1 to 50 of the TL urban network on the Lausanne-Ouchy metro.

You can purchase or stamp your tickets at the automatic machines installed at most stops, or just ask the driver. (A surcharge is collected if you get your ticket from the driver at a stop that has a machine.) A 1-day ticket for unlimited rides costs 6.50SF ($3.60) for adults, 3.50SF ($1.95) for children.

BY TAXI Lausanne contains dozens of taxi stands, where you'll usually find a line. Alternatively, you can telephone **Taxibus** (✆ **0800/800-312**) or **Taxi-phone** (✆ **0800/80-18-02**) for a cab. The meter starts at 6SF ($3.30); each kilometer (.62 miles) traveled adds 2.50SF ($1.40) during daylight hours in town, or 3SF ($1.65) in town on weekends or at night between 8pm and 6am. For trips outside the town limits, each kilometer traveled costs 3.75SF ($2.05), regardless of the time of day. The first 10kg (22 lb.) of luggage is free, with 1SF (55¢) charged for every suitcase thereafter.

BY CAR If you drive to Lausanne or rent a car while here, wearing seatbelts is required, and children 11 and under are not allowed to ride in the front seat. In Lausanne there are four types of parking zones: a white zone, in which parking is free and unlimited; a red zone and a blue zone, in which parking is free but variously limited (15 hours in the red zone and 90 minutes in the blue zone); and a fourth zone with parking meters. To park, you must display a parking disk on the dashboard of your car; parking disks are free and can be obtained at police stations, automobile clubs, and most gas stations.

BY BIKE You can rent bikes at the baggage-forwarding counter of the **railroad station** (✆ **0900-300-300**). It's open daily from 6:50am to 7:50pm. The cost is 30SF ($16.50) per day. Bikes can be transported by train from Lausanne to any of the region's outlying districts (or anywhere in Switzerland) for an extra fee.

BY BOAT To rent boats or *pédalos* (pedal boats), try various rental kiosks at Ouchy and Parc Bourget at Vidy. One of the best of these is **Ste. C. Barke,** place du Vieux-Port, Lausanne-Ouchy (✆ **021/616-08-44**).

ON FOOT This is the only way to see the old Upper Town effectively. Afterward, you can take the subway to Ouchy and resume your walk along the lakefront quays. Lausanne's civic authorities conduct a **guided walking tour** of their city, lasting 1 to 2 hours, Monday through Saturday. Departure is from place de

To France by Lake Steamer

With its scenic beauty, it's hard to depart Switzerland. But for a change of pace you can visit **Evian-les-Bains** in France. It lies on one of the southern shores of Lake Geneva and is the leading spa resort in eastern France, its lakeside promenade fashionable since the 19th century. Bottled Evian is, of course, one of the great French table waters.

Lake steamers to Evian are operated by **CGN** (Compagnie Générale de Navigation; ✆ **021/614-62-22** for reservations). They depart from the lakefront quays of Lausanne every hour in summer (May 20 to September 17), and about 3 times per day in the dead of winter. Transit takes only 35 minutes each way. Once you get to Evian, you can wander, lunch, and kibbutz on your own, as there are no guided tours available. Round-trip cost of passage from Lausanne to Evian is 32SF ($17.60) in second class, or 44SF ($24.20) in first class. Note that the midsummer departures that leave either city around noon (there's usually a 12:30pm departure from Lausanne) offer more comprehensive restaurant service than what's available at other times, when there's just a snack bar operational.

la Palud, adjacent to the city hall, at 10am and 3pm. The cost is 10SF ($5.50) for adults, 5SF ($2.75) for seniors, 3SF ($1.65) students and children. For more information, call the city's tourist office (see "Essentials," above).

SEEING THE SIGHTS

The **cathedral of Lausanne,** place de la Cathédrale, is the focal point of the Upper Town and one of the finest medieval churches in Switzerland. North of the cathedral, at the end of the Upper Town, is the **Château Saint-Marie.** It was built of brick and stone in the 14th and early 15th centuries. Powerful bishops lived here until they were replaced by the Bernese bailiffs, who turned Lausanne into a virtual colony of Bern. Today the chateau is used for the canton's administrative offices.

In the center of town is **place de la Palud.** Located on the square is the **Hôtel de Ville** (town hall), which has a 17th-century Renaissance facade; it was completely restored in the late 1970s. Today it's the headquarters of the Communal Council. Also on the square is the **Fountain of Justice,** dating from 1726. A clock with animated historical scenes presents a drama daily every hour on the hour from 9am to 7pm. A traditional market is held here every Wednesday and Saturday. To visit the cathedral, take the **Escaliers du Marché,** a covered flight of medieval stairs on one side of the square.

North of place de la Palud is **place de la Riponne,** where you can visit the Italianate **Palais de Rumine,** built in 1906. It contains several museums, a university founded in 1537, and the university and cantonal library with some 700,000 volumes.

On the east side of town, **Mon Repos Park** contains landscaped gardens and the **Empire Villa,** where Voltaire performed his work *Zaïre* for a group of friends. The **Tribunal Fédéral** is in the northern area of the park; it was constructed in the 1920s and today houses Switzerland's highest court.

To the north, the **Signal de Sauvabelin,** known popularly as *le signal,* rises above the town. At 2,125 feet (637 meters), it has a restaurant and a belvedere opening onto Lake Geneva, with the Fribourg Alps in the distance. It's a 20-minute hike from town.

Ouchy is the lakeside resort and bustling port of Lausanne. Its tree-shaded quays have flower gardens that are nearly half a mile long. The small harbor contains a 700-boat marina, and the Savoy Alps are visible on the opposite shore. The **Château d'Ouchy** is now a hotel and restaurant. The Allies, Greece, and Turkey signed a peace treaty here in 1923. The 13th-century keep is still standing. In the **Hôtel d'Angleterre,** formerly the Auberge de l'Ancre, is a plaque commemorating the stay of Lord Byron, who wrote *The Prisoner of Chillon* here. In the **Beau-Rivage,** the Treaty of Lausanne was ratified in 1923; it settled the final reparations disputes after World War I.

THE TOP ATTRACTIONS

Cathedrale de Lausanne ★★   One of the most beautiful Gothic structures in Europe, the cathedral stands 500 feet above Lake Geneva. Construction began in 1175; in 1275 the church was consecrated by Pope Gregory X. While in Lausanne, the pope met Rudolph of Hapsburg, emperor of Germany and the Holy Roman Empire. The doors and facade of the cathedral are luxuriously ornamented with sculptures and bas-reliefs. The architect Eugène Viollet-le-Duc began a restoration of the cathedral in the 19th century—and it's still going on! The interior is relatively austere except for some 13th-century choir stalls; the rose window also dates from the 13th century. The cathedral has two towers; you can climb the 225 steps to the observation deck of one of the towers.

Place de la Cathédrale. ✆ **021/316-71-61.** Admission cathedral, free; tower, 2SF ($1.10). Apr–Sept Mon–Fri 8am–6:30pm, Sat 8:30am–6pm, Sun 2–7pm; Oct–Mar Mon–Fri 7:30am–6pm, Sat 8:30am–5pm, Sun 2–5:30pm. Visits not permitted Sun morning during services. Bus: 7 or 16.

Musée Historique de Lausanne/Ancien-Evêché   A bishop's palace until the early 15th century, the Ancien-Evêché has a 13th-century fortified tower and a collection of historical studies of Old Lausanne. You can see a 250-square-foot scale model depicting the old city as it was in the 17th century.

4, place de la Cathédrale. ✆ **021/331-03-53.** Admission 4SF ($2.20) adults, 2.50SF ($1.40) seniors, free for students and children 16 and under. Tues–Thurs 11am–6pm, Fri–Sun 11am–5pm. Bus: 7 or 16.

Musée Cantonal des Beaux-Arts (Cantonal Museum of Fine Arts)   The chief city museum is devoted to the works of 19th-century artists who painted in western Switzerland, but it also has an impressive collection of French paintings, including works by Degas, Renoir, Bonnard, Matisse, and Utrillo. This complex also houses the Geological Museum, the Museum of Paleontology, the Archaeological and Historical Museum, and the Zoological Museum.

In the Palais de Rumine, 6, place de la Riponne. ✆ **021/316-34-45.** Admission 6SF ($3.30) adults, 4SF ($2.20) students and seniors, and free for children 16 and under. Tues–Wed 11am–6pm, Thurs 11am–8pm, Fri–Sun 11am–5pm. Bus: 5, 6, or 8.

Château de Beaulieu et Musée de l'Art Brut ★   Located on the northwestern side of town, this chateau dates from 1756 and was once occupied by Madame de Staël. The museum displays what the artist Jean Dubuffet called *art brut* in the 1940s. This curious melange of artwork was collected by the painter from prisoners, the mentally ill, and the criminally insane. It's like a bizarre twilight zone of art, often dubbed "psychopathological," especially the art by schizophrenics. Dubuffet despised the pretentiousness of the avant-garde art scene around him, and as a form of protest decided to begin this collection of the works of "non-artists," many of whom he found superior to the more established artists of his day.

11, av. des Bergières. © 021/647-54-35. Admission 6SF ($3.30) adults; 4SF ($2.20) seniors, students, and children. Tues–Fri 11am–noon and 2–6pm, Sat–Sun 11am–6pm. Bus: 2 to Beaulieu.

Musée Romain de Lausanne-Vidy   At Vidy, west of Ouchy, lying off the Lausanne-Maladière exit from N1/E25, is one of the more intriguing Roman museums of Switzerland. This museum of antiquities is filled with findings from excavations at the site of Lousonna, a Roman settlement that lasted from about the 15th century B.C. into the 4th century. Once a private home, this place now shows Roman treasures—everything from votive figures to ancient coins, even the tools of daily life, right down to the pins that held up those togas. Guided tours of nearby archaeological digs are conducted on the last Sunday of every month for another 3SF ($1.65).

24, chemin du Bois-de-Vaus. © 021/625-10-84. Admission 4SF ($2.20). Tues and Thurs–Sun 11am–6pm, Wed 11am–8pm.

Olympic Museum   Seeing that the Comité International Olympique has been installed in Lausanne since 1915, the city decided in 1993 to open a museum recalling the history of the games since ancient Greece. The largest information center for the Olympic movement in the world, it's a tribute to the union of sport, art, and culture, with a coin and stamp collection, an Olympic Study Center, a library, an information center, and a video library recalling some of the games' most historic moments. There's even a scattering of artifacts commemorating the sporting triumphs of South America's Aztec empire. Advanced audiovisual, computer, and robotic technology allows visitors to share in the great feats and the emotions of the athletes. An Olympic flame burns alongside a column that lists the venues where the games have been held over the years.

1, quai d'Ouchy. © 021/621-65-11. Admission 14SF ($7.70) adults, 9SF ($4.95) for senior citizens and students, 7SF ($3.85) children 10–18, free for children 9 and under, 34SF ($18.70) family ticket. May–Sept daily 9am–6pm (till 8pm Thurs); Oct–Apr Tues–Sun 9am–6pm. Closed Jan 1 and Dec 25. Take bus no. 8 from the center of Lausanne or the metro from the rail station to Ouchy, then walk for 15 mins. with the lake on your right, passing the Beau-Rivage Place Hotel en route.

THE ACTIVE VACATION PLANNER

The Lausanne tourist office (see "Essentials," above) will acquaint you with the best places for **jogging** in and around the city. Vita Parcours trails, broken up by various stops for exercising, are found at Vidy, at Chalet-à-Gobet, and above Pully, the last lying between Lausanne and Montreux. The tourist office will also advise about the best transportation connections to reach starting points, and provide maps showing their various locations.

Following in the footsteps of such celebrities as the late Charlie Chaplin, you can go **hiking**—some call it strolling—through vineyard and chateau country along the north shore of Lake Geneva. Literally millions have been here before you. Not only the Lausanne tourist office but various town and village offices will advise you of the best itineraries and supply detailed maps to guide you on your way. If you enjoy planning this sort of thing even before your arrival in the Vaud, consider contacting the **Association Vaudoise de Tourisme Pédestre** (Vaudois Association of Trekkers and Hill Climbers), 23, Grand St-Jean, CH-1003 Lausanne (© **021/323-10-84**).

For more vertiginous and higher-altitude adventures, you can take **mountain wilderness trails** cutting into the Alpes Vaudoises. You can also explore the canyons and heavily wooded areas around Château-d'Oex, or the alpine meadows above Villars.

SHOPPING

Shoppers in Lausanne tend to be much more concerned with the commercialized glamour of Paris than with kitschy mountain souvenirs. That being the case, you'll find lots of emphasis on high-profile outfits such as luggage and leather maker **Louis Vuitton,** 30, rue de Bourg (© **021/312-76-60**); or haute jeweler **Cartier,** 6, rue de Bourg (© **021/320-55-44**).

But if handmade souvenirs from the Vaud region appeal to you, head for **Heidi's Shop,** 22, rue du Petit-Chêne (© **021/311-16-89**). For artifacts with deeper patinas that sell for a lot more money, check out the art and antiques at two intriguing, relentlessly upscale antiques shops: **Antiquités R.S.,** 17, av. de la Gare (© **079/210-45-61**), and the **Galerie du Château,** 2, place du Tunnel (© **021/647-2142**), both of which specialize in 18th- and 19th-century furniture. A worthy competitor, with a greater emphasis on paintings and sculpture, is the **Galerie de la Belle Fontaine,** 9–13, rue Cheneau-de-Bourg (© **021/ 323-47-87**). The biggest and best bookstore in Lausanne is the **Librairie Payot,** 4, place Pepinet (© **021/341-33-31**), which carries English-language titles. The biggest jeweler in Lausanne, with a well-established international recommendation, is **Bucherer,** 5, place St-François (© **021/320-63-54**). Competitors, especially for Swiss watches, include **Roman Mayer,** 12, place St-François (© **021/ 312-23-16**), which has especially good buys in Omega watches, and **Junod,** 8, place St-François (© **021/312-27-45**), carrying Blancpain watches among others.

The major tobacco outlet is **Besson,** 22, rue de Bourg (© **021/312-67-88**), known for its Davidoff cigars. A branch of the famous **Franz Carl Weber,** 23, rue de Bourg (© **021/320-14-71**), carries a complete line of international toys, among the finest in the world. The best Swiss-made linen, including embroidered handkerchiefs, is sold at **Langenthal,** 8, rue de Bourg (© **021/ 323-44-02**). Some 12 miles west of Lausanne, about 20 antiques dealers have assembled a widely divergent trove of antique (and in some cases, merely old) furniture and art objects, **Château Allaman** (© **021/808-82-39**), in the hamlet of Aubonne. Hours are erratic, varying widely with the season and the whims of each dealer, so an advance phone call is strongly recommended.

WHERE TO STAY

The luxury and elegance of the top hotels in Lausanne have made the city a favorite destination of the wealthy. In the summer space is tight, so try and make a reservation. Trade fairs and conventions also keep the better hotels booked. The annual International Tourism Fair is in March. The tourist office can help you find a hotel. If you want to stay directly on the lake, we recommend a hotel in Ouchy.

VERY EXPENSIVE

Beau-Rivage Palace ★★★   One of the leading hotels in the world, the Beau-Rivage Palace is surrounded by 10 acres of lush gardens, with cedar, begonia, and sculptures. Built in 1861 and extended in 1908, the hotel has been renovated with respect for its original period architecture. The hotel is among the last bastions of formal Europe, attracting both aristocrats and *la grande bourgeoisie,* but not forgetting the demands of the world's business travelers. In the tradition of the grand hotels of yesterday, rooms come in a wide range of styles. The less

A Dramatic Ascent to Les Diablerets

For a high-alpine view of Switzerland's highest heights, consider a day trip from Lausanne to the high-alpine village of **Les Diablerets,** which is rather confusingly designated as the geographical and spiritual center-piece of a high-altitude and rocky **Les Diablerets region** ★★. To reach the village of Les Diablerets, visitors take a conventional train from Lausanne to the town of Aigle—a 30-minute relatively high-speed ride, priced at 28SF ($15.40) per person round-trip. In Aigle, they transfer onto a relatively slow narrow-gauge train that carries them to the village of Les Diablerets—a 46-minute ride priced at 20SF ($11) per person round-trip.

In Diablerets, you can wander around the alpine village, site of about 10 hotels, including two in the government-rated four-star category. There's an attempt to maintain old-fashioned aesthetics in this town, and it does have some alpine charm. Diablerets "Village" is the center-piece of three distinct regions: the D'Ifenau ski region, the Le Meilleret ski region (which funnels into yet another ski region known as the Villarf region); and the Glacier region ("Les Diablerets Glacier 3000"). It's also the site of a 7.2-kilometer bobsled ride (*piste de luge*) that's among the most thrilling (terrifying?) in the region.

After visiting "Les Diablerets Village," you can either return to Lausanne, or continue on to see the **Glacier des Diablerets** at 9,835 feet. In winter, a free minibus will haul you to the door of most of the hotels in Les Diablerets Village, then continue to the base of one of Switzerland's newest (inaugurated in 1999) cable cars at Col du Pillon, which will carry you on to the Glacier des Diablerets. The minibuses take 15 minutes for

desirable are somewhat sparsely furnished and open onto the parking area, while the more luxurious have Oriental carpeting, wing chairs, and private balconies overlooking Lake Geneva. The hotel is air-conditioned through an ingenious system using water pumped from nearby Lake Geneva.

One of the hotel's restaurants, La Rotonde, offers a panoramic view of lakes and mountains. The Café Beau-Rivage is recommended separately (see "Where to Dine," below).

17–19, place du Port, CH-1006 Lausanne-Ouchy. ✆ **800/223-6800** in the U.S., or 021/613-33-33. Fax 021/ 613-33-34. www.brp.ch. 169 units. 440SF–720SF ($242–$396) double; from 2,500SF ($1,375) suite. AE, DC, MC, V. Parking 20SF ($11). Metro: Ouchy. **Amenities:** 3 restaurants, 2 bars; 2 pools; tennis courts; fitness center; salon; room service; babysitting; laundry. *In room:* A/C, TV, dataport, minibar, hair dryer, iron, safe, Jacuzzi in 8 suites.

Lausanne Palace ★★★ The "Palace" is as grand and elegant a hotel as you'll find anywhere in Europe. The columns, plaster details, and marble floors date from the 19th century; the public rooms are decorated with tapestries, crystal chandeliers, and gilded rococo furniture. The hotel, in the center of Lausanne, offers a grand view of Lake Geneva and the Savoy Mountains. Many of the rooms reflect the hotel's turn-of-the-century style; others are in a more contemporary mode. The best units have Empire reproductions, and some even have marble fireplaces. The front rooms open onto urban streets; the rooms to the

the ride. In summer, there are no free minibuses: instead, you'll board any of five daily departures aboard a Swiss Postal Bus for the 15-minute ride to the base of the cable car at Col du Pillon, and pay 10SF ($5.50) per person each way. Or if you want to walk through the village, it will take you about 90 minutes from the railway station to the base of the cable car.

Once you reach Col du Pillon, departures on the cable car to the glacier are continuous between 8:30am and 9am (depending on the season), ending at between 4 and 5:30pm (depending on the season). The 15-minute uphill ride (very steep, very dramatic) requires one change of car at a midway point up the mountain. The cost is 49SF ($26.95) per person round-trip. For **cable car information** and confirmation that the car is running, call $\textcircled{C}$ **024/492-33-77** (the cashier) or 024/492-28-14 (the administration).

The summit is the site of a futuristic-looking aerie designed by Mario Botta, resembling an angular Inca temple or a spacecraft, depending on your point of view. Inside, there are two eateries (a self-service restaurant and a more formal sit-down restaurant); and the departure point for winter skiing (December to mid-April), summer skiing (late June to late July), and lots of hiking trails on or near the edges of the glaciers. There's also a "snow-bus" excursion, priced at 10SF ($5.50) for a 30-minute outing, in a vehicle with very big snow tires and big windows. There might be a group of husky dogs on-site, practicing dog sledding, Alaskan-style, but this is unpredictable and iffy. The entire site, including the cable car, is closed during May for annual maintenance.

rear face the lake, and most have private balconies. All come with luxurious marble bathrooms.

7–9, rue du Grand-Chêne, CH-1002 Lausanne. $\textcircled{C}$ **800/223-6800** in the United States, or 021/331-31-31. Fax 021/323-25-71. www.lausanne-palace.ch. 150 units. 450SF–670SF ($247.50–$368.50) double; 700SF–2,620SF ($385–$1,441) suite. AE, DC, MC, V. Parking 20SF ($11). Bus: 7 or 16. **Amenities:** 3 restaurants, 2 bars; pool; health club; sauna; Turkish bath; business center; room service; babysitting; laundry. *In room:* TV, minibar, hair dryer, safe.

EXPENSIVE

Hôtel de la Paix $\textcircled{R}$ Opened in 1910, this is a landmark, which has seen a lot of changes in the past decades, including recent renovations. With its elaborate balconies and loggias, many with wrought-iron details, the hotel retains its original facade, although the interior has been vastly renewed. In the heart of the city, it faces the lake and the Alps beyond, and is convenient for shopping in the old town. A favorite with business clients, it offers completely modern mid-sized bedrooms, either opening onto the lake or, less desirably, onto one of the city's urban landscapes. About one-quarter of the bedrooms are refurbished every year.

5, av. Benjamin-Constant, CH-1002 Lausanne. $\textcircled{C}$ **800/528-1234** in the U.S. and Canada, or 021/310-71-71. Fax 021/310-71-72. www.hoteldelapaix.net. 115 units. 340SF ($187) double; 530SF ($291.50) suite. Rates include buffet breakfast. AE, DC, MC, V. Parking 25SF ($13.75). Metro: St-François. **Amenities:** Restaurant, bar; business center; salon; limited room service; babysitting; laundry/dry cleaning. *In room:* TV, minibar, hair dryer, safe.

La Residence ⊛ At the edge of Lake Geneva, a trio of elegant villas from the 18th and 19th centuries combine to form this little hotel on the Ouchy waterfront, standing next to the most luxurious Beau-Rivage. The famous Beau-Rivage hotel in fact owns La Residence, but this hotel is less expensive and even closer to the water. Many guests who can afford the grander palace actually prefer to stay here. There are intimate and cozy touches, including a lounge with a fireplace, Oriental rugs, chintz curtains, and dining in summer on a deck that stretches toward the water. One part of the hotel, L'Angleterre, housed Lord Byron when he was writing *The Prisoner of Chillon*. In 2001 the property was completely renovated, and the bedrooms are better than ever.

15, place du Port, CH-1006 Lausanne. ℂ 021/613-34-34. Fax 021/613-34-35. 60 units. 380SF–410SF ($209–$225.50) double; 410SF–450SF ($225.50–$247.50) junior suite. AE, DC, MC, V. Free parking. **Amenities:** 2 restaurants, bar; pool; exercise room; sauna. *In room:* A/C, TV, minibar, hair dryer, safe.

Le Château d'Ouchy ⊛ Built around 1900, this first-rate hotel uses a medieval (12th-century) tower as its core. The chateau has housed countless travelers throughout the 20th century. Many of its die-hard fans consider it the best location in all of Lausanne, across from the flower-bedecked pedestrian walkway of the lakefront. Its once-fortified tower, ideal for a honeymoon, is capped with a black-and-red-tile roof and surrounded by wings, dungeons, Renaissance-style gables, and Romanesque arches—all crafted from gray stone. Massive renovations have upgraded the restaurants and public areas. Your opinion of this relic will depend almost entirely on what room you're booked into. Some are faded and in need of renovations; others are exquisite. Request to see the rooms before checking in, if possible. All units come with good-sized bathrooms. If you're in a romantic mood and would like to stay in a castle, and if you aren't too demanding about your modern comforts, this is certainly the most nostalgic and evocative choice in town.

2, place du Port, CH-1006 Lausanne-Ouchy. ℂ 021/616-74-51. Fax 021/617-51-37. www.chateau-d-ouchy. com. 39 units. 270SF ($148.50) double. Rates include buffet breakfast. AE, DC, MC, V. Free parking. Metro: Ouchy. **Amenities:** 2 restaurants; pool; room service; babysitting; laundry. *In room:* TV, minibar, hair dryer, safe.

MODERATE

Hôtel Agora ⊛ Set just 300 yards from the railroad station, this is a government-rated, four-star, six-story hotel that opened in 1987 after a total renovation of an older hotel on the site. The new look is startlingly unique to Lausanne. Locals often compare its architecture, with a facade of sculpted marble, to a spaceship. "ET has landed," wrote one columnist. The small to mid-sized bedrooms are comfortable and contain modern furniture and firm beds. Amenities include soundproof windows. The accommodations often have a futuristic aura, in glowing silver or glittering metallic.

9, av. du Rond-Point, CH-1006 Lausanne. ℂ 021/617-12-11. Fax 021/616-26-05. www.fhotels.ch. 85 units. 243SF–263SF ($133.65–$144.65) double; 326SF ($179.30) junior suite. AE, DC, MC, V. Free parking. Bus: 1, 3, or 5. **Amenities:** Restaurant; concierge; car rental; business center; limited room service; laundry/dry cleaning. *In room:* A/C, TV, dataport, minibar, coffeemaker, hair dryer, safe (on request).

Hôtel Carlton In the summer, awnings decorate the arched windows of this white Mediterranean-style four-story villa with a red-tile roof, located in a park near the lake. Built in 1909, it was renovated in 2001. The soundproof, mid-sized bedrooms are comfortable, with modern decor. Try, if possible, for a room with a balcony, although they don't open onto the lake.

4, av. de Cour, CH-1007 Lausanne. ℂ 021/616-32-35. Fax 021/616-34-30. 47 units. 145SF–250SF ($79.75–$137.50) double; 270SF–310SF ($148.50–$170.50) junior suite. Rates include buffet breakfast.

AE, DC, MC, V. Free parking. Bus: 2 or 5. **Amenities:** 2 restaurants; limited room service; laundry/dry cleaning. *In room:* TV, minibar, hair dryer.

INEXPENSIVE

Hôtel AlaGare   A government-rated, three-star stucco hotel a block from the rail station, this building dates from the turn of the century but was last renovated in the 1990s. Access to the hotel is via a pedestrians-only street in the town center, but any resident can drive up to the front door of the hotel and deposit luggage. In summer, flowers bloom in the window boxes of the hotel, adding a nice touch. The interior has pine paneling stained in several different tones. The well-maintained bedrooms have sleek modern styling and are generally small.

14, rue du Simplon, CH-1006 Lausanne. ℂ 021/617-92-52. Fax 021/617-92-55. 46 units. 180SF–210SF ($99–$115.50) double. Children under 12 stay free in parents' room. Rates include buffet breakfast. AE, DC, MC, V. Bus: 1, 3, or 5. Closed Dec 25–Jan 9. **Amenities:** Restaurant. *In room:* TV, safe.

Hôtel Aulac *Value*   This lakefront Ouchy hotel has a baroque yellow façade with white trim and a three-story Renaissance porch flanked by two elaborate columns. Originally built around the turn of the century, it was renovated in the 1990s. The mansard roof is inlaid with tiles in a geometric design and topped with a tall Victorian clock tower. Sailboats bob in the lake nearby. The hotel is, in fact, the least expensive accommodation right on the water in Lausanne. It is hardly the best, and most of its bedrooms rarely rise above a standard motel offering. The standardized accommodations are somewhat tacky and battered but reasonably comfortable. Request a room with a lake view and balcony. In spite of its drawbacks, this hotel is a favorite and is often heavily booked because of its location.

4, place de la Navigation, CH-1006 Lausanne-Ouchy. ℂ 021/617-14-51. Fax 021/617-11-30. 84 units. 175SF–235SF ($96.25–$129.25) double. Rates include continental breakfast. AE, DC, MC, V. Metro: Ouchy. **Amenities:** Restaurant. *In room:* TV, minibar.

Hotel Continental *Value*   Opposite the main rail station, this hotel is ideally located for both business travelers and visitors. A modern, first-class hotel, it is also convenient to the shopping area. While it doesn't have the grand style of some of the palaces recommended, it is most affordable and up to date in its amenities. Bedrooms are mid-sized to spacious, each with an efficiently organized private bathroom.

2, place de la Gare, CH-1001 Lausanne. ℂ 021/321-88-00. Fax 021/321-88-01. www.tophotels.ch/continental/index.asp. 120 units. 295SF ($162.25) double, 306SF ($168.30) junior suite. AE, DC, MC. Rates include buffet breakfast. **Amenities:** 2 restaurants, bar; limited room service; laundry. *In room:* TV, minibar, hair dryer, safe.

Hôtel Elite *Finds*   The large, illuminated sign on the front lawn obscures the neoclassical details of this white, five-story hotel with balconies and a flat roof. You'll find this mid-city location just uphill from the rail terminal. Even though it's right in the heart of things, this small hotel provides a tranquil atmosphere. Originally built at the turn of the century, it's been operated by the same family since 1938. Fruit trees and a garden add the grace note, and some of the bedrooms are air-conditioned. One room has a kitchenette, and all units contain mid-sized bathrooms. Fourth-floor units open onto lakeside views, and nonsmoking rooms are available.

1, av. Sainte-Luce, CH-1003 Lausanne. ℂ 021/320-23-61. Fax 021/320-39-63. www.elite-lausanne.ch. 33 units. 160SF–230SF ($88–$126.50) double. Rates include buffet breakfast. AE, DC, MC, V. Bus: 1, 3, or 5. **Amenities:** Car rental desk; tour desk; dry cleaning; nonsmoking rooms. *In room:* TV, minibar, hair dryer, safe.

Minotel Crystal Within walking distance of the Palais de Beaulieu, a congress center, this hotel is often the favorite of visiting business clients. Monsieur and Madame Fiora welcome guests to their location on a quiet pedestrian street. The bedrooms are standardized, with tidy bathrooms. There's an underground parking facility a short walk from the hotel.

5, rue Chaucrau, CH-1003 Lausanne. © 021/320-28-31. Fax 021/320-04-46. www.minotel.com. 40 units. 182SF–260SF ($100.10–$143) double; 234SF–312SF ($128.70–$171.60) triple; 275SF ($151.25) suite. AE, DC, MC, V. Parking 17SF ($9.35). Bus: 1 or 5. **Amenities:** Restaurant, bar; nearby golf course; laundry/dry cleaning. *In room:* TV, minibar, hair dryer, safe.

WHERE TO DINE

Lausanne offers a wide range of restaurants where you can find the specialties of Switzerland and the Vaud, as well as those of France, Greece, Italy, and China. Typical Swiss food is served in the Upper Town.

Try the Geneva lake fish, omble chevalier. Trout and perch from the lake are also popular; in autumn, many restaurants feature game dishes.

EXPENSIVE

La Grappe d'Or ★★★ SWISS Philippe Rochat may reign in the suburbs, but in Lausanne proper the domain of Angelika and Peter Baermann is the most sought-after citadel of food and drink. This formal French restaurant has received multiple awards from both Swiss and French gastronome societies. The cuisine doesn't religiously adhere to yesterday, but makes its own creative statement. The atmosphere is that of a rotisserie, and some of the most discriminating palates from all over the surrounding area come here to partake of the chef's latest imagination. Menus change with the seasons, and the meats are excellent, as is roebuck (in season). The seafood part of the menu is likely to include scampi, red mullet, or sea bass with fennel. Every dish is prepared with care and based on the most carefully selected ingredients.

3, rue Cheneau-de-Bourg. © 021/323-07-60. Reservations required. Main courses 40SF–80SF ($22–$44); fixed-price lunch 59SF–77SF ($32.45–$42.35), fixed-price dinner 105SF–165SF ($57.75–$90.75). AE, MC, V. Mon–Fri noon–2:15pm and 7–10pm, Sat 7–10pm. Bus: 7 or 16.

MODERATE

Café Beau-Rivage ★ SWISS Although its prices fall into the moderate range, its grandeur and elegance help it compete with the most expensive restaurants in the city. The restaurant is in a lakeside pavilion, the dining room resembling a Paris cafe, with mirrors, pillars, bay windows, and a flowery terrace. Typical tasty dishes, made only with the freshest ingredients, include steak tartare, *marmite de pêcheur* (casserole of fish), fricassée of chicken flavored with vinegar and tarragon, and tagliatelle with seafood. Sumptuous desserts can be ordered from the trolley. After 7:30pm, the place becomes an enjoyable piano bar. The cafe is open for coffee, tea, pastries, and a lighter menu Monday to Friday from 11am to 1am and Saturday and Sunday from 9am to 1am.

In the Beau-Rivage Palace, 18, place du Général-Guisan, Ouchy. © 021/613-33-33. Reservations recommended. Main courses 32SF–50SF ($17.60–$27.50); fixed-price dinner 68SF ($37.40). AE, DC, MC, V. Daily 11:30am–1am. Metro: Ouchy.

La Petite Grappe/Il Grappolino d'Oro ★ *Value* SWISS La Grappe d'Or (see above) is the most famed eatery within the city limits of Lausanne. The good news is that you can enjoy the same high-quality food here, but for less money. Oliver, the son of the founding father Peter Baermann, has opened this more informal restaurant a short walk away. It has the same quality of food, although the service and the dress are more casual. Like its parent, La Petite

Grappe adjusts its menu to take advantage of the best of any season, ranging from fresh asparagus in the spring to game in the autumn. The lake fish dishes are excellent. Try the monkfish with olive juice for example, or saddle of veal with lentils. Cardons, a delectable cousin of the artichoke, are also served when available.

15, rue Cheneau-de-Bourg. (C) 021/311-84-22. Reservations required. Main courses 32SF–50SF ($17.60–$27.50); fixed-price menu 42SF ($23.10) at lunch, 75SF–95SF ($41.25–$52.25) at dinner. AE, MC, V. Mon–Sat noon–2pm and 7–10pm.

Le Jardin d'Asie (★ CHINESE/JAPANESE/MALAYSIAN The finest Asian restaurant in Lausanne, Le Jardin celebrates the cuisine of China, Japan, and to a lesser degree, Malaysia. The setting is a pale-green-and-pink representation of a garden, with enough space between tables to permit the broadly international clientele discreet conversations. Menu items include a choice of foods from the major culinary traditions of China, as well as sushi, sashimi, and *teppanyaki* (Japanese cuisine prepared by a uniformed chef in front of your table). There's even a choice of Malay dishes, including shrimp or chicken in peanut sauce and beignets of shrimp.

7, av. du Théâtre. (C) 021/323-74-84. Reservations recommended. Main courses 20SF–28SF ($11–$15.40); fixed-price Chinese menu 40SF ($22); fixed-price Japanese menu 40SF ($22). AE, DC, MC, V. Mon–Sat 11:45am–2pm and 7–10pm. Bus: 7 or 16.

INEXPENSIVE

Buffet de la Gare CFF SWISS/FRENCH Inside Lausanne's main rail station, the brasserie is large and bustling, while the restaurant offers a secluded series of cubbyholes and nooks and more upscale service. There's little difference in price between the brasserie and the restaurant. Many find the brasserie more fun, the restaurant more sedate. Good-tasting dishes available at both include vol-au-vent with mushrooms, filets of sole "Uncle Charles," poached turbot in hollandaise sauce, veal sausages, and mignons of pork in cream sauce.

In the train station, 11, place de la Gare. (C) 021/311-49-00. Reservations recommended in the restaurant only. Main courses 22SF–55SF ($12.10–$30.25); fixed-price menu 25SF ($13.75). MC, V. Restaurant, daily 7am–midnight. Brasserie, daily 11am–midnight. Bus: 1, 3, or 5.

Pinte Besson (★ *Finds* SWISS/VAUD This is a tiny restaurant with a smoke-stained vault of hand-chiseled masonry dating from 1780. It's celebrated locally for its cheese fondues, cheese on toast, and seasonal specialties, along with dried alpine beef. Beef or horse steak is grilled and served on a slate stone. There are sidewalk tables in summer, and benches are placed outside on sunny days.

4, rue de l'Ale. (C) 021/312-72-27. Main courses 18SF–35SF ($9.90–$19.25). MC, V. Mon–Fri noon–2pm and 6pm–midnight, Sat–Sun noon–2pm. Closed Aug. Bus: 1 or 9.

NEARBY DINING

Auberge du Raisin (★★ It's set in its ways, and its staff is a bit rigid, but despite these minor drawbacks, a stopover at this verdant Relais & Châteaux will offer impeccable food and insight into upscale, *grand bourgeois* life within French-speaking Switzerland. Set on 13th-century foundations, in the center of the town of Cully, it's most famous for its restaurant, where delicate flavorings are a hallmark of chef Adolfo Blokbergen. Within a setting accented with antique paneling and an elegant sense of alpine rusticity, you can order such classic dishes as steamed supreme of pigeon with truffles, a cold consommé of lobster with fresh tarragon, ravioli stuffed with scallops and served with a caviar-enriched champagne sauce, and a poached filet mignon of veal with summer vegetables.

Although a full complement of European wines is offered, ask for one of the Swiss vintages, particularly one from the surrounding region.

There are 10 comfortable, somewhat frilly-looking bedrooms on-site, priced at 260SF to 320SF ($143 to $176) for a double, and from 450SF to 550SF ($247.50 to $302.50) for a suite. Rates include breakfast.

1, place de l'Hôtel de Ville, CH-1096 Cully. ☎ 021/799-21-31. Fax 021/799-25-01. Main courses 25SF–50SF ($13.75–$27.50). AE, DC, MC, V. Open Mon–Sat noon–2pm and 6–10pm. From Lausanne, take Route Cantonale that borders the edge of the lake, following the signs to Vevey, then turn off to follow the signs to Cully.

Hotel de Ville (formerly "Girardet") ✿✿✿ SWISS/FRENCH For years, Philippe Rochat followed dutifully in the footsteps of the founder (Frédy Girardet) of this legendary restaurant, quietly helping the grand patriarch of French cuisine prepare the thousands of upscale platters that contributed to this establishment's fame. Since 1996 and the retirement of his mentor, Switzerland's culinary patriarch, Rochat has taken over, doing a masterful job of keeping Girardet's legend alive while simultaneously updating the menu with some creations of his own. The venue for this mini-drama, which has been avidly watched by gastronomes throughout the region, is within the solid stone walls of what was originally conceived in 1929 as Crissier's Town Hall *(Hôtel de Ville)*. Assisted by his wife, Franziska (winner of the 1997 New York City marathon), he prepares succulent meals for tables of culinary aficionados who sometimes make reservations many months in advance. Specialties change frequently, according to the availability of ingredients and the inspiration of Rochat himself. Recent successes have included a ragoût of fresh quail with young vegetables, crawfish in caviar butter, duckling from the wetlands around Nantes cooked pink and prepared with Brouilly wine, preserved duckling in lemon and spices, and glazed sweetbreads with wild mushrooms. The cheese trolley that's wheeled around after the main course is absolutely spectacular.

In the Hotel de Ville, 1, rue d'Yverdon, Crissier. ☎ 021/634-05-05. Reservations essential. Main courses 55SF–110SF ($30.25–$60.50); fixed-price menu 220SF–245SF ($121–$134.75). Tues–Sat noon–2pm and 7–9pm. Closed 3 weeks in Aug and 2 weeks Dec–Jan.

LAUSANNE AFTER DARK

Few other cities in Switzerland manage to remain as cosmopolitan but relentlessly conservative as Lausanne. Consequently, you'll find lots to do, often with a Gallic insouciance, after dark. You might begin your evening hanging out in any of the cafes and bars ringing the **Espace Flon,** a cluster of restaurants and shops at place Flon. Lots of hideaways, frequented by strollers of all ages, will be here to tempt you, but one of the most appealing is **Le Grand Café,** esplanade de Mont-Benon (☎ 021/320-40-30). Here, in an American-inspired space that contains some of the glitter and razzmatazz of a Planet Hollywood (with which it's not connected) you can meet a cross section of virtually every night owl in town.

Attractive and popular discos include **Le Mad,** route de Genève (☎ 021/ 312-29-19), where the fads and preoccupations of nocturnal Paris filter quickly in from the west via an under-30 crowd. Its most visible competitor for the loyalties of the sometimes fickle disco crowd is **D Club,** 4, rue du Grand-Pont (with an entrance around the corner on rue Centrale; ☎ 021/351-51-42).

Ouchy White Horse Pub, 66, av. d'Ouchy (☎ 021/616-75-75), draws the crowds at night who in summer enjoy the terrace with views of the water. There's beer on tap, and a range of tapas and burgers are sold. It's the most authentic pub atmosphere in town.

Lausanne is also a city of culture. With Geneva it shares the Orchestre de la Suisse Romande and also occasionally hosts the legendary ballet company of Maurice Béjart. The local tourist office will advise on what's available at the time of your visit. Most performances of major cultural impact take place at the **Théâtre-Municipal Lausanne,** avenue du Theatre (© **021/310-16-00**). **Beaulieu,** at 10, av. des Bergières (© **021/643-21-11**), is also a venue for dance concerts, operas, and orchestral music presentations. Tickets can be purchased at **Billetel,** which has various locations over Lausanne. For more information contact the Théâtre-Municipal Lausanne.

2 Morges ⨀

7 miles (11km) W of Lausanne, 16 miles (26km) E of Geneva

Set against a backdrop of the Savoy Alps, the small town of Morges on Lac Léman is headquarters for the region's vineyards. Its port was built on an ancient site inhabited by prehistoric lake dwellers. Because of its elegant lakeside setting, and because of its stellar hotels and restaurants, this is one of the premier stopovers along Lake Geneva. If she were still around, you could get confirmation on that from long-time resident Audrey Hepburn. Today the town is a favorite stop for a chic set of international yachters.

ESSENTIALS

GETTING THERE   Trains run almost every 30 minutes throughout the day between Geneva and Lausanne, and most of them stop at Morges. For **rail information** call © **0900/300-300.**

Bus no. 57 runs from Lausanne to Morges. Call © **0900/300-300** for **bus schedules.** One-way transit costs 20SF ($11) from Geneva and 2.40SF ($1.30) from Lausanne.

If you're driving from Lausanne, head west toward Geneva along N1.

In addition, between late May and September, several lake steamers stop at Morges every day on their way between Geneva and Lausanne; depending on their schedule, some require a boat change at Yvoire. For information, contact the **CGN** (Compagnie Générale de Navigation), 17, av. de Rhodanie, in Lausanne (© **848-811-848**), or **Jardin Anglais,** in Geneva (© **021/614-62-00**).

VISITOR INFORMATION   The **Morges Tourist Information Office,** on rue du Château (© **021/801-32-33**), is open year-round on Monday to Saturday 9:30am to noon and 2 to 6pm.

SEEING THE SIGHTS

Baron Louis of Savoy built the **Castle of Morges** in 1286 to defend himself against the bishopric of Lausanne. The imposing bastion, which originally had a moat, was the residence of a Bernese bailiff from 1536 to 1798. It eventually passed to the canton of Vaud, which used it as an arsenal. Today, it contains the **Vaud Military Museum** (Musée Militaire Vaudois) (© **021/804-85-56**). The weapons and uniforms on display date from the late 15th century to modern times. The museum is open February to June and September to mid-December, Tuesday to Friday from 10am to noon and 1:30 to 5pm and on Saturday, Sunday, and holidays from 10am to 5pm; in July and August, Tuesday to Friday from 10am to 5pm. Admission is 7SF ($3.85).

Musée Alexis Forel ⨀, in a 15th-century patrician house at 54, Grand-Rue (© **021/801-26-47**), contains a collection of engravings, 17th- and 18th-century furniture, 18th-century silver and glassware, ancient ceramics, and antique dolls—all exhibited in an intimate setting of a former private home. The museum is open Tuesday to Sunday from 2 to 5:30pm. Admission is 5SF ($2.75) for adults, free for children.

The town's newest, and in many ways most interesting, museum is the **Pavillon Audrey Hepburn** , chemin des Plantées, in the neighboring hamlet of Tolochenaz (© **021/803-64-64**), a mile east of Morges. Take the TPM bus no. 2 to reach it or else enjoy the walk. It occupies what was originally built in the 1950s as a wood-sided schoolhouse, set within sight of the stone-sided chalet that Audrey Hepburn occupied on and off again for the last 40 years of her life. Although you can't visit the chalet itself (it's occupied by her son, Sean Ferrer), the one-room schoolhouse offers testimony to a life that incorporated Hollywood stardom with hard, long hours as an ambassador for UNICEF, replete with photos and testimonials from well-wishers throughout the world. Frankly, the scope of the actress-humanitarian's life (born in Brussels in 1929, raised in the Netherlands and England, died in Switzerland in 1993) is broader than many of her movie star fans ever realized. Within a very short walk, you can visit Ms. Hepburn's grave in the village cemetery (Cimitière de Tolochenaz). The museum is open year-round Tuesday to Sunday from 1:30 to 5:30pm. Entrance costs 10SF ($5.50) for adults and 5SF ($2.75) for seniors and children 6 to 18.

If the day is sunny, you can take one of the most lovely **bike rides** in western Switzerland beginning at Morges train station where you can rent a bike for 26SF to 32SF ($14.30–$17.60) a day. The tourist office (see above) will provide a map and help you plot your route. The trail leads from Morges to the village of Lully and goes via Bussy and Ballens to Biere. This takes you through some of the most scenic of Lake Geneva vineyards. From Biere you continue down a small valley to Begnins and then Fechy, the latter a panoramic lookout point. Eventually you reach Aubonne where you can take a second-class road via Lavigny, Villars-sous-Yens, and Lully back to Morges. The 35-mile (56km) trip takes about 5½ hours.

WHERE TO STAY & DINE

Fleur du Lac SWISS/FRENCH   Many residents of Geneva make weekend excursions to taste the unusual and imaginative food served at this beautiful restaurant on the quay beside the lake. Famous specialties include Lake Geneva perch plus imported seafood. The menu, which changes with the season, includes an unusual version of medallions of foie gras served with pistachio nuts and a sweet-and-sour sauce inspired by Asia, filet of lake perch with butter sauce and tartar sauce, rosettes of roast lamb with turnips and a butter-enhanced tarragon sauce, and poached suprême of turbot with wine/herb sauce and shellfish. Dessert might be a "fantasy of coconut." More than 250 domestic and foreign wines are available. There's an outdoor terrace facing the lake. A small bistro offers specialties of the day costing 20SF ($11) and up. The bus from Lausanne stops in back of the hotel.

The establishment also rents 29 rooms, and no two are alike. All units face south, with a view across the lake to the French Alps and snowcapped Mont Blanc. Most of the rooms have large balconies or terraces, along with phones, TVs, and such amenities as combination tub and showers, hair dryers, and trouser presses. For room and breakfast, doubles cost 228SF to 268SF ($125.40 to $147.40). One suite—for one to four guests—rents for 470SF ($258.50).

Quai Igor-Stravinsky, 70, rte. de Lausanne, CH-1110 Morges. © **021/811-58-11.** Fax 021/811-58-88. www. fleurdulac.ch. Reservations required. Main courses 38SF–58SF ($20.90–$31.90); fixed-price meal 65SF ($35.75) at lunch, 85SF ($46.75) at dinner. AE, DC, MC, V. Daily 11:30am–2pm and 6:30–10pm. Bus: 57 from Lausanne.

Restaurant de l'Union FRENCH   Set between two historic and central streets of Morges' old town, this well-recommended, appealingly old-fashioned restaurant offers well-prepared cuisine that's neither expensive nor pretentious. Prepared by members of the von Kaenel family, the food choices include a succulent version of fricassée of chanterelles. The best beef selection is *tournedos vaudois,* which is grilled on a hot stone set directly atop your table. Also look for an unusual version of horse meat with sweet peppers (a favorite with the lunch crowd eager for a quick platter of very traditional food), and grilled filet of lamb with rosemary. Everybody's favorite dessert is an idiosyncratic and very popular version of *tarte à la raisinée,* which combines the texture of a flan with that of a pastry. The restaurant is in a hotel that contains 14 simple bedrooms, all with private bathroom, TV, and phone. With breakfast included, doubles cost 146SF ($80.30).

In the Hôtel de Savoie, 7, Grand-Rue, CH-1110 Morges. ℭ **021/801-21-55.** Reservations recommended. Main courses 17SF–39SF ($9.35–$21.45); fixed-price menu 25SF–75SF ($13.75–$41.25). MC, V. Mon–Sat 11:30am–2:30pm and 6:30–11pm.

3 Nyon ⟨★⟩

14 miles (22km) E of Geneva, 17 miles (27km) SW of Lausanne

Unhurried and peaceful, Nyon has been a popular lakefront resort since the Victorian era; masses of flowers decorate its waterfront quays. In Roman times Julius Caesar used the settlement here as a military outpost for his soldiers. Between 1781 and 1813, Nyon was famous for its delicate, almost translucent porcelain.

A major stopover on the lake steamer route, Nyon is ideal for walks. You can, in fact, take a walk around the town walls known as **Promenade des Vieilles Murailles.** The walk goes along the 19th-century town walls until the promenade broadens into the **Esplanade des Marronniers** from which the most stunning panorama unfolds. You can also wander around at leisure, enjoying the flower-filled park and quays bordering the yachting harbor.

ESSENTIALS

GETTING THERE   Nyon lies directly on the rail lines that connect Geneva with Lausanne. Trains depart from both those larger cities for Nyon every 30 minutes throughout the day. Call ℭ **0900/300-300** for **train schedules.**

Nyon is connected by bus to a handful of other French-speaking towns to its northwest, few of which have railway junctions of their own. There are also bus connections from Nyon's railway station to Geneva several times throughout the day. Despite these buses, most travelers arrive in Nyon by train. For bus schedules, contact the tourist office (see below).

If you're driving, head west from Lausanne, or east from Geneva, along N1.

In addition, there are a handful of lake steamers that travel in summer (May to September) between Geneva and Lausanne, stopping briefly in Nyon. Trip time by boat from Lausanne to Nyon is 2½ hours. For information and reservations, contact **CGN** (Compagnie Général de Navigation), 17 av. de Rhodanie, in Lausanne (ℭ **0848-811-848**).

VISITOR INFORMATION   The **Nyon Tourist Information Office,** at 7, av. Viollier (ℭ **022/361-62-61**), is open May 29 to September 20, Monday to Friday from 8:30am to noon and 2 to 5:30pm, and Saturday and Sunday from 9:30am to noon and 1 to 6pm; off-season Monday to Friday from 8:30am to noon and 2 to 5:30pm.

SEEING THE SIGHTS

For an adventure off the beaten path, you can rent a **bike** for 26SF ($14.30) at the Nyon rail station and cycle to Céligny, lying midway between Coppet and Nyon. You can go all the way to Coppet in 6 miles (10km) by heading south. But spend what time you can at **Céligny,** one of the most enchanting of all lakeside villages.

Richard Burton called Céligny home during the last years of his life. There's a small port here filled with yachts and grassy lawns ideal for sunbathing. In fact, the swimming here is the best along the lake.

Later you can wander over to the village cemetery to visit the grave of the great actor and former resident. Elizabeth Taylor has told friends that she has purchased the adjacent plot next to the man she married and divorced twice.

Musée du Léman, 8, quai Louis-Bonnard (✆ 022/361-58-88), is devoted exclusively to the geography, history, marine culture, arts, and ethnography of Lake Geneva. It also contains three large aquariums, plus flora and fauna of the largest lake of Western Europe.

Musée Romain, rue Maupertuis (✆ 022/361-75-91), displays specimens of Roman architecture, as well as Roman statuary, inscriptions, mosaics, crafts, amphorae, glasswork, and coins. The basilica, which stands at one end of the forum of the Roman colony (Colonia Julia Equestris), was a public building for justice and commerce.

Entrance to either museum costs 6SF ($3.30) for adults, 3SF ($1.65) for children and students. Both museums maintain the same hours: April to October, Tuesday to Sunday from 10am to noon and 2 to 6pm (open Mondays in July and August); November to March, Tuesday to Sunday from 2 to 6pm.

WHERE TO STAY

The **Rôtisserie du XVI Siècle,** listed in "Where to Dine," below, also has rooms for rent.

Hôtel Beau-Rivage ⭐ This hotel is your best bet. Sections of this hotel were built in 1481, when an inn stood on the site welcoming pilgrims and merchants. Most of the building seen today, however, dates from around 1900. Cozy and old-fashioned, the Beau-Rivage, 7 minutes from the railroad station, was built directly on the quays in the heart of the old town. Sweeping views of the lake are available from any of the hotel's many balconies. The public rooms have been tastefully modernized in a summertime motif, which includes a series of brightly colored modern paintings. The mid-sized bedrooms are traditionally furnished, some with four-posters.

49, rue de Rive, CH-1260 Nyon. ✆ 022/365-41-41. Fax 022/365-41-65. www.hotel-beau-rivage-nyon.ch. 50 units. 240SF–380SF ($132–$209) double; from 450SF ($247.50) suite. Rates include buffet breakfast. AE, DC, MC, V. Free parking outside, 18SF ($9.90) in garage. **Amenities:** Restaurant; limited room service; laundry service. *In room:* TV, minibar, hair dryer.

WHERE TO DINE

Rôtisserie du XVI Siècle ⭐ *Finds* SWISS This is a charming old inn with good food and affordable bedrooms. The building that gives this establishment its name was constructed during the 16th century on ancient Roman foundations. After a disastrous fire in the early 1990s, this place reopened as a simple, unpretentious restaurant. The delightful cuisine might include filets of perch sautéed with almonds, an array of grilled meats, and salads. The most popular offering is a two-course *menu du jour,* which includes an appetizer and a well-stocked main course, which changes daily. The most prevalent specialties are game hen with rosemary and *entrecôte XVI Siècle,* a hefty chunk of beefsteak seasoned with local herbs and served with matchstick potatoes. This is not a site for *grande gastronomie*—instead, the food is straightforward, generous in its portions, and geared to popular tastes.

The establishment also offers 19 simple but pleasantly furnished bedrooms, 13 with private bathroom. Doubles without bathroom rent for 100SF ($55), going up to 160SF ($88) with bathroom.

Place du Marché, CH-1260 Nyon. © 022/361-24-41. Reservations recommended. Main courses 17SF–35SF ($9.35–$19.25). AE, MC, V. Mon–Sat 11:30am–2pm and 6:30–10pm.

4 Vevey ⟨★⟩

11 miles (18km) E of Lausanne, 4 miles (6km) NW of Montreux

Home of Nestlé chocolate, the resort of Vevey has been popular with British visitors since the 19th century. It's at the foot of Mount Pélerin, which you can ascend by funicular. The town, dating from Roman times, was built at the mouth of the Veveyse River and is the center of the Lavaux vineyards. In the Middle Ages it was known as an important trading post on the route from Piedmont, in Italy, to Burgundy, in France.

Rousseau's descriptions of his "sentimental rambles" in the lake district lured the first Romantic visitors. In time, English and Russian aristocrats selected the sheltered Swiss Riviera for long winter sojourns. Famous exiles to the area have included the English regicide Edmund Ludlow, the French painter Gustave Courbet, the Polish pianist Ignace Paderewski, and the Polish novelist Henryk Sienkiewicz.

As such former visitors as Henry James, Oskar Kokoschka, and even Dostoyevsky could tell you, Vevey is a great town for walks, especially its Old Town, filled with interesting restaurants, bars, and shops. You can no longer see Graham Greene or Victor Hugo on the streets, but you'll still find much that is rewarding. Stop in at the tourist office and pick up a free brochure, "On the Trail of Hemingway," that will direct you to not only the former residences of Papa but places frequented by dozens of celebrities.

ESSENTIALS

GETTING THERE Vevey lies on the major rail link between Lausanne and (via the Simplon Tunnel) the great cities of northern Italy. Dozens of trains stop here every day. Trip time from Lausanne is 15 minutes and the round-trip fare costs around 19SF ($10.45). Call the tourist office (see below) for more information.

If you're driving from Lausanne, head south along N9; from Montreux, drive northwest on N9 along the edge of the lake.

Daily from May through mid-October, about half a dozen lake steamers transit the length of Lake Geneva, stopping at Lausanne, Vevey, Geneva, and several other cities along the way. Travel time to Vevey from Geneva is almost 5 hours; from Lausanne, about 1 hour. For information, contact the **CGN** (Compagnie Générale de Navigation), 17, av. de Rhodanie, Lausanne (© **0848-811-848**).

VISITOR INFORMATION The **Vevey Tourist Office,** 29, Grand-Place (© **021/922-20-20**), is open June to mid-September, daily from 9am to 6pm; the rest of the year, Monday to Friday from 9am to noon and 1:30 to 6pm and Saturday from 9am to 4pm.

SEEING THE SIGHTS

Begin by exploring the **Grand-Place,** a mammoth market plaza, the town's nerve center and largest parking lot, facing Lac Léman. The corn exchange on the north dates from the early 19th century. As you walk in this area and along the quay, you'll enjoy views of the Savoy Alps.

For a slice of local life, head for the **Café de La Clef,** 1, rue du Théâtre (© **021/921-22-45**), where Jean Jacques Rousseau stayed in 1730. This is the landmark cafe of Vevey, and over the years it's seen a parade of Who's Who from Oona Chaplin to Le Corbusier. As you drink your libation, you can enjoy views of the pillared marketplace out front. The decor is dowdy and unfashionable, just how the habitués like it. If you're around at lunchtime, drop in for local Swiss specialties including lake fish such as perch or even a fondue in winter.

Church of St. Martin, boulevard St-Martin (no phone), dating from the 10th century, is on a belvedere overlooking the resort. It has a large rectangular tower with four turrets, and there's a good view of Vevey from the tower. Its interior contains a dusty-looking collection of excavations that, along with the church itself, are always open.

A statue by John Doubleday on the new **square Chaplin,** quai Perdonnet, commemorates the area's most illustrious former resident, Charlie Chaplin. Chaplin moved here from the United States in 1952 with his young wife, Oona O'Neill, in part to escape accusations of Communist sympathies. Except for brief interludes, he remained in Vevey until his death in 1977. When he died, he was considered a popular, unpretentious (and fabulously wealthy) local citizen. The life-size statue erected in his honor represents the little tramp in baggy pants—the character Chaplin made famous—gazing out at his favorite view of Lake Geneva and the Alps in the distance.

Chaplin actually lived in the little village of **Corsier,** above Vevey, which dates back to the 2nd century. Its church is thought to have been established by the Abbey of St. Maurice; inside you can see some 15th-century paintings. Villagers dedicated a park to their famous resident. Although the stately villa he occupied cannot be visited, the comedian is buried in the cemetery (Cimetière de Corsier), a 3-minute walk downhill from the village. Bus no. 11 or 12 goes from Vevey to Corsier.

Musée du Vieux-Vevey   This stately chateau contains two museums: the Musée Historique du Vieux-Vevey and the Musée de la Confrérie de la Vigneron (Winemakers Museum). Exhibits include 18th-century antiques and mementos of the vintners' trade, wrought-iron work, arms, pewter, tools, and some of the paraphernalia associated with the region's wine festivals. Paintings by local artists are also displayed, and there are ancient and medieval artifacts once excavated from the area around Vevey.

2, rue du Château. © **021/921-07-22.** Admission 5SF ($2.75) adults; 4SF ($2.20) students, seniors, and children 15 and under. Mar–Oct Tues–Sun 10:30am–noon and 2–5:30pm; Nov–Feb Tues–Sun 2–5pm.

Musée Jenisch   This museum was founded at the end of the 19th century, created from a bequest by Fanny Jenisch of Hamburg, who with her husband had made their home in Vevey. Today, the museum houses the Fine Arts Museum (Musée des Beaux-Arts) and the Museum of Prints (Cabinet Cantonal des Estampes). The collection is rich in paintings by Swiss artists, and features representative works of Bissier and other artists.

2, av. de la Gare. © **021/921-29-50.** Admission 12SF ($6.60) adults, 10SF ($5.50) seniors, 6SF ($3.30) students. Children 16 years and under free. Mar–Oct Tues–Sun 11am–5:30pm; Nov–Feb Tues–Sun 2–5:30pm.

Musée Suisse de l'Appareil Photographique (Swiss Camera Museum)
The only museum of its kind in Switzerland, this five-story celebration of the printed image contains examples of the machines that recorded human history from the earliest daguerreotypes to the present. The uppermost floor is devoted to a changing exposition of modern photographic art, but for aficionados of photography, the fascination here is the amazing range of cameras from the 1920s to today.

6, rue des Anciens-Fossés. ☎ 021/925-21-40. Admission 6SF ($3.30) adults; 4SF ($2.20) students, seniors, and children 15 and under. Mar–Oct Tues–Sun 11am–5:30pm. Nov–Feb Tues–Sun 2–5:30pm.

Musée de l'Alimentarium
Established in the 1980s with funds derived mostly from the charitable foundations associated with the Nestlé organization, this museum celebrates the development of foodstuffs around the world. Set near the statue of Chaplin, it's the most interactive museum in Vevey, containing lots of buttons that children (and adults) can push to release odors of sizzling foods, activate dioramas and computerized exhibitions, and begin film clips that show the preoccupation of the human race with its own survival.

Quai Perdonnet. ☎ 021/924-41-11. Admission 10SF ($5.50) adults; 8SF ($4.40) students and seniors. Children 16 and under free. Year-round Tues–Sun 10am–6pm.

WHERE TO STAY

Best Western Hôtel du Lac ⭑   This well-established hotel, affiliated with Vevey's more expensive Hôtel Les Trois Couronnes (see below), is popular because of its lakeside view and its distinct sense of old-fashioned charm. A government-rated four-star choice, it was built in 1868 but has been renovated bit by bit ever since. It has a swimming pool and a flower-studded lakeside terrace. Appropriate for a relaxing vacation beside the lake, the hotel is mostly patronized by foreign, especially British, visitors. If you read Anita Brookner's novel *Hôtel du Lac*, you might expect a grander place. Brookner took poetic license in describing its formality and refinement. Some bedrooms are better than others. Many have been updated with contemporary styling; others, however, are comfortable but vaguely dowdy, languishing back in a bygone era. The hotel restaurant, Le Chenaie, deserves its excellent reputation for Swiss and French specialties.

1, rue d'Italie, CH-1800 Vevey. ☎ 800/528-1234 in the United States, or 021/921-10-41. Fax 021/921-75-08. 56 units. 280SF–370SF ($154–$203.50) double. Rates include buffet breakfast. AE, DC, MC, V. Free parking outdoors, 15SF ($8.25) in garage. Bus: 1 or 2. **Amenities:** Restaurant; pool; tennis courts; health club; concierge; room service; laundry service. *In room:* TV, minibar, hair dryer, iron, safe.

Hôtel des Négociants   Built close to Vevey's main square in 1974, this government-rated two-star, four-story, brick-sided hotel does a thriving business in its street-level brasserie. The members of the Bertholet family are your hosts, working hard to carefully maintain the hotel when they're not catering to hungry guests in their dining room. The small guest rooms are functionally furnished but well maintained, each outfitted with a small bathroom.

27, rue du Conseil, CH-1800 Vevey. ☎ 021/922-70-11. Fax 021/921-34-24. www.hotelnegociants.ch. 23 units. 140SF–166SF ($77–$91.30) double. MC, V. **Amenities:** Restaurant. *In room:* TV.

Hôtel Les Trois Couronnes ⭑⭑⭑   This leading hotel is famous as the setting of Henry James's first popular success *Daisy Miller;* the film version, by the director Peter Bogdanovich, was also made here. The Daisy Millers still arrive today, although perhaps not as innocent as the subject of James's novella. It's located in the center of town, in a white stucco and gray stone building with noble details. Built in 1842, it still remains the grande dame, as it's so often called, of Vevey hotels. Rated five stars by the government, it has been progressively renovated over the years. The lobby has an elegant gallery with white balustrades three floors tall. The mid-sized to spacious rooms retain their 19th-century charm, the more expensive units with attractive antiques. Each accommodation comes with a luxurious private bathroom.

49, rue d'Italie, CH-1800 Vevey. © **800/223-5652** in the United States, or 021/923-32-00. Fax 021/923-33-99. 62 units. 410SF–450SF ($225.50–$247.50) double; 700SF ($385) suite. Rates include continental breakfast. AE, DC, MC, V. Bus: 1. **Amenities:** Restaurant; limited room service; laundry service. *In room:* TV, minibar, hair dryer.

ON THE OUTSKIRTS

Le Mirador 𝄞𝄞𝄞 Evocative of an elegant manor house, Le Mirador is one of the grandest spas in western Switzerland. Lying 400 meters above Lake Geneva in the heart of Swiss wine county on Mont-Pélerin, 8 miles north of Vevey, the hotel is composed of a four-story chalet and an equally luxurious balconied annex. This retreat is deluxe living in grand style, with luxurious furnishings and fine paintings. Although a favorite venue for conferences, the resort is also ideal for the spa devotee, drawn to such treatments as cellular therapy. There is no better example in Switzerland of a 21st-century resort than Le Mirador.

5, chemin du Mirador, CH-1801 Mont-Pélerin. © **021/925-11-11.** Fax 021/925-11-12. www.mirador.ch/tarifs-e.htm. 83 units. 750SF ($412.50) double. AE, DC, MC, V. **Amenities:** 2 restaurants; bar; indoor-outdoor pool; health club; elegant spa; business center; salon. *In room:* TV, minibar, hair dryer, safe.

WHERE TO DINE

La Pinte de l'Hôtel de Ville SWISS *Pinte* is old French for "bistro," but in this case it suggests an extremely simple eatery where folks often come to drink instead of eat. It's very unpretentious and small. This landmark cafe overlooks the trees and cobblestones of an old square across from the city hall, and outside tables are available in fair weather. The food is simple but good. Appetizers include *assiette valaisanne* (air-dried beef); typical main courses are steak maison, steak with mushroom sauce, and couscous. It also offers sandwiches and three kinds of fondue.

19, rue de l'Hôtel-de-Ville. © **021/921-78-80.** Reservations recommended. Main courses 14.50SF–28SF ($8–$15.40). MC, V. Mon–Fri 11:30am–2pm and 6–10pm, Sat–Sun 8am–7pm. Cafe snacks Mon–Sat 7am–midnight. Bus: 1.

Restaurant Denis Martin "Le Château" 𝄞𝄞 CONTINENTAL One of the most spectacular restaurants of Vevey occupies the street level of the town's oldest building—a baronial villa built in 1599. Inside, a pair of dining rooms offer soaring vaults composed of stone, contemporary accessories, and a noteworthy collection of modern sculpture by well-known Swiss artist André Raboud. During clement weather, a flower-studded outdoor terrace offers sweeping views over lawns and the nearby lake. Menu items change frequently, according to the inspiration of chef and owner Denis Martin, but two representative, consistently excellent specialties include duck liver served with apple chutney and spice bread; and line-caught sea bass with basil-flavored olive oil and sweet peppers. If you prefer to leave the composition of your meal to the experts, consider one of the set-price menus, the most elaborate of which is composed of 15 artfully presented mini-courses.

2, rue de Château, on the street level of the Musée Historique de Vieux Vevey. © **021/921-1210.** Reservations required. Main courses 65SF–85SF ($35.75–$46.75); set-price menus 148SF–198SF ($81.40–$108.90). AE, DC, MC, V. Tues–Sat noon–2pm and 7–10pm. Closed: Dec 23–Jan 15.

Restaurant du Raisin ✿ LYONNAIS/VAUDOIS   This is the center of gastronomy. An inn has flourished on this site since the 1880s. The real glamour of the place lies one floor above street level, in a room lined with a changing roster of paintings by local artists. Here, an intensely cultivated cuisine based on modernized Lyonnais and Vaudois dishes is served using only fresh and seasonal ingredients. The best examples include a bouquet of wild greens studded with freshwater crawfish, fava beans, and vinaigrette; an upscale stew of lobster with artichoke hearts, fresh nasturtiums, and black truffles; and sea bass with fried zucchini flowers and ratatouille-flavored butter. Dessert might be a frozen soufflé enhanced with herbed liqueur (La Grande Gruyère) from the nearby mountains.

Despite the allure of the upstairs restaurant, don't overlook the charm of the street-level brasserie, a site that wins many office workers' votes for a preferred lunch stop. Menu items here are cheap, cheerful, and flavorful, and include such platters as deboned filets of perch, veal kidneys with mustard sauce, duck breast in orange sauce, and roasted pig's trotters with lentils and sausages.

3, Grand-Place. ✆ 021/921-10-28. Reservations recommended in restaurant, not necessary in brasserie. Restaurant, main courses 40SF–56SF ($22–$30.80); fixed-price menu 48SF–80SF ($26.40–$44). Brasserie, fixed-price menu 25SF–45SF ($13.75–$24.75); platters 14SF–37SF ($7.70–$20.35). AE, DC, MC, V. Restaurant, Tues–Sat 11:30am–2:30pm and 6:30–10pm, Sun 11:30am–2:30pm. Brasserie, daily 11am–2:30pm and 6:30–10:30pm.

Taverne du Château ✿ SWISS   Built in 1681, this large stucco building is a lot more elegant today than when it was originally constructed as a farmer's grange. One of the most elaborately gentrified buildings in town, it has a large carved beam extending out over one of the top-floor windows. A pulley was attached to the beam to transport supplies to the upper floors. Over the pavement hangs a wrought-iron and gilt sign with a picture of a horse and two men fighting. Many of the menu items focus on seafood, served in well-prepared, intensely rehearsed ways. The menu might include such mouthwatering specialties as a sauté of freshwater crawfish with tomatoes and parsley, sea wolf with basil and sweet-pepper sauce, warm sautéed duck liver, a gâteau of pigeon, an aromatic rack of lamb with herbs of Provence, and chicken supreme cooked in a Pinot Noir sauce. In autumn the menu features many game dishes. For many gastronomes, this restaurant is a required stopover along Lake Geneva.

43, rue d'Italie. ✆ 021/921-12-10. Reservations required. Main courses 30SF–55SF ($16.50–$30.25); fixed-price menu 70SF–125SF ($38.50–$68.75). AE, DC, MC, V. Tues–Sat 11am–3pm and 6:30pm–midnight. Closed Sept 1–15. Bus: 1 or 2.

VEVEY AFTER DARK

At the columned marketplace in the center of town, **Café de La Clef Chez Manu,** 1 rue de Théâtre (✆ **021/921-245**), was made famous in 1730 when Jean-Jacques Rousseau used to hang out here. As for decor, the place looks lost in a time capsule back somewhere in the early part of the 20th century, but it remains Vevey's enduring favorite as a worthy hangout at all times of the day or night. The place fills up for lunch with locals devouring such dishes as perch from lake Geneva. The other much frequented spot is **Les Temps Modernes,** 6B, rue des Deux Gares (✆ **021/922-3439**), both a restaurant and a club. It's the French name for *Modern Times,* one of the most famous films made by Vevey's most famous resident, the late Charlie Chaplin. This club attracts the most diverse group of patrons, from skiers to bankers. With its junky furniture, the club occupies a warehouse-like building. If you stay for dinner, the food is excellent, although many visitors come here to enjoy live music performances— everything from hot salsa nights to concert jazz. Sometimes there's no cover unless the performers are well known, at which time a 20SF ($11) cover is imposed. Closed in July and August.

5 Montreux ★★

2 miles (3km) E of Vevey, 15 miles (24km) E of Lausanne, 62 miles (100km) E of Geneva

The chief resort of the Swiss Riviera, Montreux rises in the shape of an amphitheater from the shores of the Lac Léman. An Edwardian town with a distinct French accent, it has long been a refuge for expatriates, including the novelist Vladimir Nabokov. Known for its balmy climate, it sports a profusion of Mediterranean vegetation, which grows lushly in the town's many lakeside parks. The mountains at the town's back protect it from the winds of winter, allowing fruit trees, cypresses, magnolias, bay trees, almonds, and even palms to flourish.

The city has expanded greatly from its original 19th-century core, incorporating several former villages along the shoreline. One of these, Clarens, was used by Rousseau as the setting for his epistolary novel *La nouvelle Héloïse*. The resort enjoyed its heyday in the years just before World War I, when it had only 85 hotel beds. It hosted such distinguished visitors as Tolstoy, Flaubert, Dostoyevsky, and Ruskin. In recent times the town has revived, and today about three-fourths of the resort's 20,000 inhabitants are engaged in some touristic capacity or another.

Though the resort is favored year-round, it's most densely crowded in summertime, when traffic clogs most of the streets.

ESSENTIALS

GETTING THERE   Montreux not only lies on the famous *Orient Express* line linking Paris to Milan, but it's also connected to the link between Geneva and the Simplon Tunnel. Dozens of trains stop at Montreux every day headed in both directions. The most famous is the *Train Panoramique,* a big-windowed train with a transparent roof that links Montreux to Interlaken. Passengers who take this conveyance often continue, after a change of train, on to Lucerne in a conventional railway car. For bookings, contact **M.O.B.** (Société Montreux-Oberland-Bernois), Gare de Montreux (✆ **021/963-65-31**). For more Swiss **rail information,** dial ✆ **0900/300-300.**

If you're driving, Montreux sits in the middle of a network of superhighways linking Germany, France, and Italy with Switzerland. The divider of the traffic coming from Germany via Bern is just outside Montreux. From that vantage point, you can go either east or west across Switzerland.

In addition, Montreux is one of the stops on the east-west steamer route between Villeneuve and Geneva. Travel by lake steamer from Lausanne is about 1 hour, or about 3 hours from Geneva. Most boats depart between May and September, with limited service throughout the rest of the year. For information and bookings, contact **CGN** (Compagnie Générale de Navigation), in Lausanne (✆ **0848/811-848**).

VISITOR INFORMATION   The **Montreux Convention & Tourist Information Office,** rue du Théâtre (✆ **021/962-84-84**), is opposite the boat-landing pier. Throughout the year, it's open daily from 9:30am to 6:30pm.

SEEING THE SIGHTS

Explore the old houses and crooked streets of Old Montreux. Later, stroll along the quayside promenade by the lake. The only way to discover the charms of far-flung and widely scattered Montreux is by using up a lot of shoe leather.

The most impressive castle in Switzerland, the **Château of Chillon** ★★ (✆ **021/966-89-10**) is on the lake 2 miles south of Montreux. To reach it, you can ride trolley bus no. 1 for 2.60SF ($1.45) each way. But for many the most enthralling way to reach Chillon from Montreux is to walk along the scenery-studded 2-mile (3km) lake path. It's the grandest promenade you can take in Montreux. Most of the castle dates from the 13th century, but its oldest section is thought to be 1,000 years old. The castle was built by Peter II of Savoy and is one of the best-preserved, and most frequently photographed, medieval castles of Europe. So-called sorcerers were tried and tortured here. The most famous prisoner, François Bonivard, was described by Byron in *The Prisoner of Chillon*. Bonivard was the prior of St. Victori in Geneva, and when he supported Geneva's independence in 1532, the Catholic duke of Savoy chained him in the dungeon until 1536, when he was released by the Bernese.

The chateau is open April to September, daily from 9am to 6pm; March and October, daily from 9:30am to 5pm; November to February, daily from 10am to 4pm. It's closed Christmas and New Year's. Admission costs 7.50SF ($4.15) for adults, 3.50SF ($1.95) for children 6 to 16; it's free for children 5 and under.

Rochers-de-Naye ★★★ at 6,700 feet is one of the most popular tours along Lake Geneva. From Montreux a cogwheel train takes visitors in less than an hour up to Rochers-de-Naye. The train ascends the slopes over Lac Léman, passing **Glion,** a little resort on a rocky crag almost suspended between lake and mountains. You come to **Caux** at 3,600 feet, lying on a natural balcony overhanging the blue bowl of the lake. Finally, the peak of Rochers-de-Naye rises high in the Vaudois Alps. In the distance you can see the Savoy Alps, including Mont Blanc and the Jura Alps. At the end is an alpine flower garden, the loftiest in Europe. The train departs from the railway station of Montreux every hour during the day, beginning at 7:30am, with the last departure between 5:30 and 7pm, depending on the season. The travel time, each way, to Caux is 20 minutes. The round-trip fare between Montreux and Rochers-de-Naye is 45SF ($24.75). Holders of Swiss Rail passes or Eurail passes pay half-price. Call (✆ **021/963-6531**) for more information.

Villeneuve, the little port town at the end of the lake, is where Lord Byron wrote *The Prisoner of Chillon* in 1816. Mahatma Gandhi visited Romain Rolland when the French novelist and pacifist lived here. The town and its surrounding countryside have been painted by many artists, including Oskar Kokoschka, who once lived here. Villeneuve is a 25-minute walk from the Château of Chillon, which is visible from virtually every point in the village.

WHERE TO STAY

Many of the leading hotels of Montreux have greatly improved in recent years. Unfortunately, good budget accommodations are lacking.

EXPENSIVE

Grand Hôtel Excelsior ★★   A renowned Montreux landmark since 1903, this government-rated five-star lakeside hotel offers quiet opulence and discreet personal service. The elegant marble foyer has marquetry, a hushed sense of restraint, and Queen Anne antiques. The charm of this hotel is enhanced by oil

Montreux Jazz Festival

One of the biggest musical bashes in Europe occurs at the internationally known **Montreux Jazz Festival,** beginning the first week of July and running for 2 weeks. Everyone from Bob Dylan to B. B. King is likely to show up for the music and festivities. Ticket prices are high. If you'd like to attend a lot of the events, you can purchase a festival pass for 1,300SF ($715); otherwise, you pay from 50SF to 130SF ($27.50–$71.50) for each individual ticket. The tourist office in Montreux provides advance information and even sells tickets. For more information, call ℂ **021/623-45-67.** Tickets for many events, especially the top ones, often sell out early. If you show up and can't get a ticket, you can still enjoy "Jazz Off," some 500 hours of admission-free open-air concerts, often staged by new or wanna-be talent throughout the city. The tourist office keeps a schedule, but much of the fun is spontaneous.

paintings and baroque sculpture. The luxurious rooms are spacious, and all have lakefront balconies. Each comes with a combination tub and shower except for 11 units, which have showers.

21, rue Bon-Port, CH-1820 Montreux. ℂ 021/966-57-57. Fax 021/966-57-58. www.grandhotelexcelsior.ch. 70 units. 360SF–450SF ($198–$247.50) double; from 1,100SF ($605) suite for 2. Rates include buffet breakfast. Half board 55SF ($30.25) extra. AE, DC, MC, V. Parking 15SF ($8.25). Bus: 1. **Amenities:** 3 restaurants, bar; pool; fitness center; sauna; salon; room service; massage; babysitting; laundry/dry cleaning. *In room:* TV, minibar, hair dryer, safe.

Le Montreux Palace 𝕬𝕬𝕬   Facing the lake, this is an opulent palace originally built in 1853, and massively enlarged in 1906 into the beaux arts structure you see today. Despite being the largest hotel in Montreux, a monument visible from miles away, frequent renovations have retained its embellished ceilings, parquet floors, and crystal chandeliers. Once a favorite of Russian tsars, it later attracted Vladimir Nabokov—the author of *Lolita,* among other works—who spent long periods of creative time here. Architectural charm abounds—one room has an arched ceiling with an Art Nouveau stained-glass skylight ringed with statues of cupids and demigods. Each of the comfortably old-fashioned bedrooms, many quite spacious, has French doors and a balcony. The rooms in the rear, however, open onto the mountain and not the lake. All units come with luxurious marble bathrooms. In all, the place is elegant, bemused, blasé, and very historic.

100, Grand'Rue, CH-1820 Montreux. ℂ 021/962-12-12. Fax 021/962-17-17. www.montreux-palace.com. 235 units. 450SF–670SF ($247.50–$368.50) double; 850SF–3,500SF ($467.50–$1,925) suite. AE, DC, MC, V. Parking 5SF ($2.75). Bus: 1. **Amenities:** 3 restaurants, 2 bars; pool; nearby golf course; tennis courts; exercise room; spa; Jacuzzi; sauna; salon; room service; massage; laundry. *In room:* A/C, TV, minibar, coffeemaker, hair dryer, iron.

Royal Plaza Inter-Continental 𝕬𝕬   This is the most architecturally avant-garde hotel in Montreux. Designed in a semi-futuristic style in 1982, it rises eight floors above an enviable position beside the lake, amid gardens and pedestrian walkways accented with shrubs, lawns, and trees. Because of the slope of the hillside on which the hotel is built, the lobby is set on the hotel's third floor, but few visitors realize that until they begin to explore the hotel a bit. Most of the spacious rooms face the lake and are designed in a sleek modern decor that would suit any five-star hotel in the world. All the accommodations contain luxurious bathrooms.

97, Grand'Rue, CH-1820 Montreux. ✆ **800/327-0200** in the United States, or 021/962-50-50. Fax 021/962-51-51. 163 units. 375SF–475SF ($206.25–$261.25) double; 790SF–1,105SF ($434.50–$607.75) suite. Rates include buffet breakfast. AE, DC, MC, V. Underground parking 19SF ($10.45). Bus: 1. **Amenities:** 2 restaurants, bar; pool; fitness center; sauna; car rental; room service; laundry. *In room:* A/C, TV, minibar, hair dryer, iron, safe.

MODERATE

Grand Hôtel Suisse et Majestic ✦ This opulent, 19th-century landmark, originally built in the 1870s and renovated frequently since then, is in the heart of Old Montreux, beside the lake. Take one of the three elevators past the *trompe-l'oeil* murals to the art nouveau lobby on the top floor. From here you'll have access to a terrace with classical statuary and a panoramic view. Comfort and subdued elegance are the keys to the success of this hotel. Most of the spacious rooms have an updated Belle Epoque decor, each equipped with a luxurious bathroom.

43, av. des Alps, CH-1820 Montreux. ✆ **021/966-33-33.** Fax 021/966-33-00. 135 units. 190SF–300SF ($104.50–$165) double; 490SF–690SF ($269.50–$379.50) suite. Rates include buffet breakfast. AE, DC, MC, V. Bus: 1. **Amenities:** 2 restaurants, bar; room service; laundry/dry cleaning. *In room:* TV, minibar, hair dryer.

Hôtel Eden au Lac ✦✦ The lingering nostalgia and beautiful restoration of this hotel evoke scenes from the movie *Death in Venice,* based on a work by Thomas Mann. It's a favorite hotel in Montreux, and it's less expensive than the Palace. Situated on the lakeside promenade, it has a grand 19th-century style and a façade that resembles an Art Nouveau wedding cake. The pink-and-white neo-baroque Gatsby Bar has stained-glass windows, and there's a garden terrace with magnolias. The owners offer well-appointed, spacious rooms. The junior and senior suites are among the most opulent in Montreux.

11, rue du Théâtre, CH-1820 Montreux. ✆ **021/966-08-00.** Fax 021/966-09-00. www.edenmontreux.ch. 105 units. 320SF–420SF ($176–$231) double; 400SF–520SF ($220–$286) suite for 2. Rates include continental breakfast. AE, DC, MC, V. Parking 20SF ($11). Bus: 1. Closed mid-Dec to end of Jan. **Amenities:** 3 restaurants, bar; fitness center; room service; laundry/dry cleaning. *In room:* TV, minibar, hair dryer.

Hotel Victoria ✦✦ This Relais & Châteaux opens onto views of mountains and lakefront, and is surrounded by extensive, manicured grounds. It truly lives up to Lake Geneva's reputation as an idyllic retreat for hedonists. Expect a lot of pampering at this mansion dating from 1869. Noel Coward, the playwright, stayed here some 4 decades ago and raved about it in letters sent back to his theatrical friends in London. Following in Coward's footsteps, the Victoria has witnessed a parade of other celebrities, even royalty. "We try to make our guests feel at home," the owner, Toni Mittermair, told us, and in that stated goal he succeeds admirably. The most desirable bedrooms open onto a private balcony overlooking the lake. All the accommodations are good, however, with well-chosen furnishings, fine art, and luxurious bathrooms.

Route de Caux, CH-1823 Glion sur Montreux. ✆ **021/963-31-31.** Fax 021/963-13-51. www.montreux.ch/victoria/screen.html. 50 units. 240SF–350SF ($132–$192.50) double; 420SF–580SF ($231–$319) junior suite. AE, DC, MC, V. **Amenities:** Restaurant, bar, piano lounge; pool; tennis court; small gym; sauna. *In room:* TV, minibar, hair dryer, safe.

INEXPENSIVE

Hostellerie du Lac ✦ *Finds* This well-maintained, century-old villa is excellently located on the lakefront promenade, about a minute's walk from the casino. Here, long-time owner Roger Falconnier welcomes visitors into a cozy, nostalgic environment that artfully combines kitsch with slightly battered modern furniture, creating a calm, peaceful ambience. Some rooms have a balcony; others have purely decorative (nonworking) fireplaces.

12, rue du Quai, Ch-1820 Montreux. ℂ 021/963-32-71. Fax 021/963-1835. www.mantreux.ch. 8 units, 2 without bathroom. 85SF–95SF ($46.75–$52.25) double without bathroom, 130SF–150SF ($71.50–$82.50) double with bathroom. MC, V. Closed Jan 1–Feb 15. **Amenities:** Restaurant; nearby golf course. *In room:* TV, fridge, hair dryer.

ON THE OUTSKIRTS

Villa Kruger ★★ *Finds*   This is a real discovery and the most offbeat living choice in the area. In the leafy suburb of Clarens, a half mile north of Montreux, the villa was erected in 1874 as a vacation retreat for Paul Kruger, then president of South Africa. Today it is a boutique hotel of charm and grace, although admittedly overly decorated, a whirlpool of fringes, swags, furbelows and the like along with gilt mirrors, candelabra, Persian rugs, and antiques. You feel like you're staying at the home of your very rich aunt—not at a hotel. This luxury guesthouse lies on the shores of Lake Geneva in a superb setting. The guest rooms consist of three twins and one single, and all have private bathrooms. South African wines are served with a cuisine called "Haute Karoo," a region of South Africa often compared to Provence.

Villas Dubochet 17, CH 1815 Clarens-Montreux. ℂ **021/989-2110.** Fax 021/964-7439. www.villakruger. ch/frames/doku.html. 4 units. 300SF–450SF ($165–$247.50) double. AE, MC, V. Rates include breakfast. **Amenities:** Restaurant. *In room:* TV.

WHERE TO DINE
VERY EXPENSIVE

Le Pont de Brent ★★★ FRENCH/SWISS   The district's finest and best known restaurant is in a turn-of-the-century house near a historic bridge in the hamlet of Brent. Gérald Rabaey, the owner and chef, prepares a frequently changing array of seafood, including a soup made with mussels and leeks, Breton lobster with zucchini in a tarragon-flavored cream sauce, rabbit in mustard sauce, and roast pigeon with herbs. Succulent versions of trout, turbot, and sea bass are also featured, along with fresh mushrooms and the best fruits of any season. We could heap praise upon praise on this restaurant and still not do it justice. It is the grandest choice for dining along Lake Geneva. The combination of flavors is inspired. Inventiveness and solid technique reign supreme here. After a meal here you will proclaim you've arrived in paradise as you kidnap the chef to take him home.

In Brent. ℂ **021/964-52-30.** Reservations required. Set-price menus 180SF ($99) or 220SF ($121). MC, V. Tues–Sat noon–2pm and 7–9:30pm. Closed 3 weeks in midsummer and 2 weeks Dec–Jan. From Montreux, follow the signs to Blonary-Brent, driving 2 miles (3km) northwest of the city.

L'Ermitage ★★★ FRENCH/SWISS   Set in Montreux's lakefront suburb of Clarens, this restaurant occupies the dignified premises of a *maison bourgeoise* built in the late 19th century and surrounded with a spacious park. The celebrated chef, Etienne Krebs, owns the place along with his charming wife, Isabelle, who handles the dining room, which has welcomed everyone from the president of Switzerland to Quincy Jones. You'll dine in one of three rattan-filled rooms painted "the colors of water and sun" or on a terrace overlooking the lake. Menu items change with the seasons but always reflect fresh ingredients. Palate-pleasing examples include a casserole of foie gras with celery; filet of *fera* (a fish from the nearby lake) with capers and artichoke hearts; a salad of baby crawfish in an emulsion of tomatoes and olive oil; rosettes of roast lamb with aromatic alpine herbs; and a supreme thigh of wild duckling in a sheathing of mashed potatoes with a sauté of exotic mushrooms.

The site also maintains four rooms, priced at 230SF to 300SF ($126.50–$165), and three suites, 330SF to 420SF ($181.50–$231), with breakfast included. Each has rattan furniture and is individually decorated with taste and flair.

75, rue du Lac, CH-1815 Clarens. ℂ **021/964-44-11.** Fax 021/964-70-02. Reservations recommended. Main courses 52SF–67SF ($28.60–$36.85); fixed-price meals 65SF–160SF ($35.75–$88). AE, DC, MC, V. Daily 11:30am–2pm and 7–10pm. Closed Sun–Mon Oct–Apr and Dec 21–Jan 21. Drive a half-mile east of Montreux, following the lakefront road and signs pointing to Vevey.

EXPENSIVE

La Vieille Ferme ⚡ SWISS/INTERNATIONAL   This old stone-walled house is in the village of Chailly, in a building dating from the 13th century when it functioned as a munitions warehouse for local monks and later as a farmhouse. As such, it's one of the oldest buildings in the region. Accompanying your meal will be regional background music, which is performed almost every night. Yvan Mabillard is clearly a master chef, as revealed by his offering of succulent beef dishes, aromatic alpine lamb, chicken, rabbit, frogs' legs, tender veal, lake perch, trout, crawfish, and a velvety goose liver made into a terrine. The menu also includes gratiné of shrimp or grilled beef, and fondue *bourguignonne* and cheese fondue. The chef grills fresh fish and meat better than anyone else in the area. The arrival of large tour groups may interrupt your intimate dinner.

40, rue de Bourg, Chailly-sur-Montreux. ℂ **021/964-64-65.** Reservations required. Main courses 22SF–48SF ($12.10–$26.40); fixed-price menu 25SF–35SF ($13.75–$19.25) at lunch, 55SF ($30.25) at dinner. AE, MC, V. Wed–Sun noon–2:30pm and 7–10pm. Closed July. From Montreux, follow the signs to autoroute N1; then just before you reach the autoroute, follow the signs to Chailly-Village, a total of 2½ miles (3km) north of Montreux.

Les Magnolias ⚡ RHONE/PROVENÇAL   Despite its role as the showcase restaurant in one of the most elegant beaux arts hotels in Montreux, this is not a particularly expensive establishment—at least by Swiss standards. You'll reach it by passing through the hotel's marble lobby, but once you're inside, you'll notice a subtle nautical decor in the comfortable bar off to one side, and an emphasis on the culinary traditions of the Rhône Valley. Menu items change with the season, and might include delectable deep-fried zucchini flowers with a *mousseline* of sea wolf, a standard version of *pissaladière niçoise* (a kind of Provençal quiche), filets of perch or sole meunière, and a divine roasted salmon garnished with duck liver and herbs.

In the Grand Hôtel Excelsior, 21, rue Bon-Port. ℂ **021/966-57-57.** Reservations recommended. Main courses 25SF–35SF ($13.75–$19.25); fixed-price menu 60SF ($33). AE, DC, MC, V. Daily noon–2pm and 7–10pm. Bus: 1.

MODERATE

Restaurant Chinois Wing Wah *Kids* CANTONESE   Hearty portions of well-prepared Chinese food and relatively reasonable prices attract many families to this scarlet-and-gold dining room. The owner, originally from Hong Kong, prepares lacquered duck, twice-grilled beef, spicy shrimp, diced chicken with hot peppers, crispy roast chicken, and curried shrimp. The restaurant's name translates as "happiness."

42, Grand'Rue. (?) **021/963-34-47.** Reservations required. Main courses 25SF–35SF ($13.75–$19.25); fixed-price meal 14SF–23.50SF ($7.70–$12.95) at lunch, 45SF–76SF ($24.75–$41.80) at dinner. AE, DC, MC, V. Daily 11:30am–2:30pm and 6:30–10:30pm. Bus: 1.

INEXPENSIVE
Caveau des Vignerons SWISS   At the corner of rue di Marché, this is a tavern that has long been a local favorite. A traditional Swiss cuisine is served in a candlelit cave that is elegantly decorated with wood paneling. In this unusual atmosphere, you can order some of the best-tasting dishes in town, all reasonably priced. True devotees flock here for the horse meat which you can cook yourself at table, although those from other cultures might prefer to stick to one of the delectable Swiss specialties instead. The cave turns out some of the best cheese and meat fondues in town. You can also look for the constantly changing daily specials, and finish your selection with one of the creamy desserts.

30, rue Industrielle. (?) **021/963-2570.** Reservations recommended. Main courses 17SF–44SF ($9.35–$24.20). AE, DC, MC, V. Mon–Fri 9am–midnight, Sat 3pm–midnight. Bus: 1.

MONTREUX AFTER DARK
The major action spins around the **Casino de Montreux,** 9, rue du Théâtre (© **021/962-83-83**), but don't expect a casino where fortunes are made and lost, or even a particularly impressive architectural monument. The casino here has almost no architectural interest, set in a dull modern building in the heart of town near the lake. Despite that, it can provide some nightlife diversion in an otherwise rather dull town. Inside, you'll find a modest assortment of gaming tables, but since the limit on any official wager in Switzerland is 5SF ($2.75), gambling here is about as puritanical as gambling can be. About 200 slot machines shake, rattle, and roll, along with a handful of roulette tables. There is a small disco open nightly till 4am.

The first one in Switzerland, **Harry's New York Bar,** in Le Montreux Palace, 100, Grand Rue (© **021/962-12-12**), is the most convivial watering hole. There's a Harry's Bar in many European cities today, but this particular example—managed by one of the grandest hotels of Montreux—won't remind you of any of them. Once the home of an auto showroom, it underwent an elegant transformation with the installation of rich paneling and touches of brass and leather. The bartenders—a well-trained crew hailing from almost everywhere—mix cocktails the old-fashioned way (shaken, not stirred). Most clients come here to drink, but if you're hungry, they serve light but elegant meals.

Another popular place is **Duke's,** in the Royal Plaza Inter-Continental, 97, Grand-Rue (© **021/962-50-50**), one of the venues for the Montreux Jazz Festival. A video wall features clips from the festival. If you're celebrating, opt for the champagne, although there's an impressive range of beers for 7.50SF ($4.15).

Other hot spots after dark include **Caesar's,** 515, Grand-Rue (© **021/ 963-75-59**), known for its lakeside terrace dances and occasional cabaret; and **Pussycat Club,** 100, Grand-Rue (© **021/963-34-44**), a good place to go dancing. There's even a DJ and—get this—a sushi bar.

Geneva

G eneva is located in the Rhône Valley at the southwestern corner of Lake Geneva (or Lac Léman, in French), between the Jura Mountains and the Alps. It's the capital of the canton of Geneva, the second-smallest canton in the Swiss Confederation.

Switzerland's second-largest city has an idyllic setting on one of the biggest alpine lakes and within view of the pinnacle of Mont Blanc. Filled with parks and promenades, the city becomes a virtual garden in summer. It's also one of the healthiest cities in the world thanks to prevailing north winds that blow away all air pollution.

Geneva is surrounded by French territory, connected to Switzerland only by the lake and a narrow corridor. The city's overwhelming French influence is apparent in its mansard roofs, iron balconies, sidewalk cafes, and French signs.

1 Orientation

ARRIVING

BY PLANE The **Geneva-Cointrin Airport** (✆ 022/717-71-11), although busy, is quite compact and easily negotiated. **Swissair** (✆ 800/221-4750) serves Geneva more frequently than any other airline. **Crossair** (✆ 0848/852-230) offers the best local connections, connecting Geneva with Lugano, Zurich, and Bern, plus flying in from several European capitals. Other international airlines flying into Geneva include **Air France** (✆ 022/827-87-87), with seven flights daily from Paris; and **British Airways** (✆ 0848/40-10-10), with seven daily flights from London.

To get into the center of Geneva, there's a train station linked to the air terminal with trains leaving about every 8 to 20 minutes from 5:39am to 11:36pm for the 7-minute trip; the one-way fare is 8.40SF ($4.60) in first class and 5SF $2.75) in second class. A taxi into town will cost 30SF ($16.50) and up, or you can take bus no. 10 for 2.20SF ($1.20).

BY TRAIN Geneva's CFF (Chemins de Fer Fédéraux) train station in the town center is **Gare Cornavin,** place Cornavin (✆ 0900/300-300 for ticket information). A small tourist office branch is at the train station.

Note: When the Lausanne-Geneva railroad line was extended to Cointrin Airport, a second "main" railroad station was built here with both long-distance and intercity trains. To avoid having to make the trip back to the center from the airport, be sure you get off the train at the Cornavin station.

BY CAR From Lausanne, head southwest on N1 to the very end of southwestern Switzerland.

BY LAKE STEAMER From late May to late September there are frequent daily arrivals by Swiss lake steamer from Montreux, Vevey, and Lausanne (you can use your Eurailpass for the trip). If you're staying in the Left Bank (Old

Town), get off at the Jardin Anglais stop in Geneva; Mont Blanc and Pâquis are the two Right Bank stops. For more information, call © **022/312-52-23.**

VISITOR INFORMATION

Geneva's tourist office, the **Office du Tourisme de Genève,** is located at 3, rue du Mont-Blanc (© **022/909-70-00**). The staff provides information about the city, and can also arrange hotel reservations both in Geneva and throughout Switzerland, and refer you to other establishments specializing in car and motorcycle rentals and excursion bookings. They can also give you details about audio-guided visits to the Old Town. The tourist office is open from June 15 to September 15, Monday to Friday from 9am to 6pm and Saturday and Sunday from 8am to 5pm; the rest of the year, Monday to Saturday from 9am to 6pm.

CITY LAYOUT

Geneva is a perfect city to explore on foot. It's divided by Lake Geneva (Lac Léman) and the Rhône River into two sections: the Right Bank and the Left Bank. In addition to taking our walking tour of the highlights (see "Attractions," later in this chapter), you may rent an audio-guided tour in English from the tourist office (see above) for 10SF ($5.50). This tour covers more than two dozen highlights in the Old Town, and comes complete with cassette, player, and map. Its estimated duration is 2 hours. A 50SF ($27.50) deposit is collected prior to your receipt of a cassette player.

RIVE GAUCHE (LEFT BANK)   This compact and colorful area is the oldest section of the city. Here you'll find Old Town, some major shopping streets, the famous Flower Clock, the university, and several important museums.

Grand Rue is the well-preserved main street of Old Town. It's flanked by many houses dating from the 15th and 18th centuries. The street winds uphill from the ponts de l'Ile; at place Bel-Air it becomes rue de la Cité, then Grand Rue, and finally rue de l'Hôtel-de-Ville. Eventually it reaches **place du Bourg-de-Four**—one of the most historic squares of Geneva (Rousseau was born in a simple house at no. 40).

South of this street is **promenade des Bastions,** a greenbelt area with a monument to the Reformation; it overlooks the Arve River. Directly to the west, in the northern corner of promenade des Bastions, is **place Neuve,** which is the finest square in Geneva.

From place Neuve, you can take rue de la Corraterie, which was once surrounded by the city wall, to the Rhône and the **ponts de l'Ile.** On this bridge is the **Tour de l'Ile,** what's left of the 13th-century bishops' castle.

On the shore of Lake Geneva is the **Jardin Anglais** (English Garden) with its Flower Clock and, farther out, the **Parc La Grange** and the nearby **Parc des Eaux-Vives.**

RIVE DROITE (RIGHT BANK)   You can cross to the other side of the Rhône on any of several bridges, including pont du Mont-Blanc, pont de la Machine, pont des Bergues, and ponts de l'Ile. The Right Bank is home to Gare Cornavin, the major international organizations, and several attractive parks.

Place St-Gervais is in the St-Gervais district; this has been the area for jewelers and watchmakers since the 18th century.

Along the northern shore of Lake Geneva is **quai du Président-Wilson,** named for the U.S. president who helped found the League of Nations.

The Right Bank is surrounded by parks, from the tree-shaded promenades along the Rhône to the **Parc de la Perle du Lac, Parc Barton,** and **Parc Mon-Repos** on the outskirts.

FINDING AN ADDRESS   In a system developed during the Middle Ages, all Swiss cities, including Geneva, begin their street-numbering system with the lowest numbers closest to the old center of town. The numbers increase the farther out from Old Town you go. Even numbers are on one side of a street; odd numbers are on the other side.

MAPS   The tourist office (see above) presents visitors with a detailed and easy-to-follow free map of Geneva.

NEIGHBORHOODS IN BRIEF

Rues Basses   Rues Basses (translated either as "low streets" or figuratively as "lower town") is found between Old Town and the south bank of the Rhône. It's the major commercial and shopping district of Geneva. Its major street is rue du Rhône, although rue de la Confédération and rue du Marché are also important arteries.

Old Town (Vieille Ville)   At an altitude of 1,326 feet (398m), Old Town is the most history-rich section of Geneva. This is Left Bank Geneva, with its narrow streets, flower-bedecked fountains, and architectural blends of Gothic, Renaissance, and 18th-century features. The twin towers of the Cathedral of St. Pierre dominate Old Town, whose geographical and spiritual center is place du Bourg-de-Four.

The Promenades of Geneva   These streets almost constitute a "neighborhood" in themselves. This section of quays along both Lake Geneva and the Rhône is best experienced by walking. One of the most scenic walks is from the Parc des Eaux-Vives on the Left Bank to the Parc de Mon-Repos on the Right Bank. Along the way you'll have a clear view of Geneva's most famous and visible monument, the Jet d'Eau. Set a few inches above the surface of the lake, this powerful fountain spurts a plume of shimmering water 460 feet (138m) into the air. Except during special circumstances, such as the arrival of a foreign head of state, it operates only between March and October.

2 Getting Around

Walking is the cheapest, most practical form of transportation in Geneva. It's also the most advantageous, from a tourist's point of view. For the city's quaint Old Town, tree-shaded promenades line the lake, and you can browse many chic shops walking leisurely about Geneva. Savor the measured tempo of life here that makes this city particularly alluring to the foreign visitor.

Nevertheless, if speed is the object, you may avail yourself of the public transportation system, which is reasonably priced and as dependable as a Swiss watch.

BY PUBLIC TRANSPORTATION

For the most part, all of Geneva's public **tram and bus lines** begin at place Cornavin, in front of the main railroad station. From here, you can take bus F or 8 to the Palais des Nations.

Tickets for zone 10, a sprawling area that covers most of the urban area of Geneva, are sold at automatic vending machines located at each stop. These machines operate both with coins or by means of plastic, magnetized cards, which are sold in the form of bulk-rate passes. Tickets for zones other than zone 10, for destinations in the suburbs of Geneva, and for destinations in France, are sold by drivers on the corresponding buses.

Four **basic tickets** are provided: (1) free transportation for 1 hour in central Geneva's zone 10, with as many changes as you wish on any vehicle, for 2.20SF ($1.20); (2) a trip limited to three stops, valid for half an hour, allowing a return trip, at a cost of 1.50SF (85¢); (3) free transportation for 1½ hours in all zones of the network of Geneva, at a cost of 5SF ($2.75); and (4) a ride for 1 hour in zone 10 for children 6 to 12 as well as for seniors (women over 62 and men over 65), at a cost of 1.50SF (85ce); children 5 and under ride free.

If you plan to use the system frequently, multi-use tickets and daily cards can be purchased from agents whose addresses are listed on posts at the various stops. A wide range of these tickets are available, and often you can adapt the system to fit your particular needs. For example, a *carte journalière* (1-day ticket) for free transportation in zone 10 costs 6SF ($3.30) for as many trips and changes as you need. It's valid from the time you stamp it up to the termination of the day's service, which is around midnight.

There's also a daily ticket costing 12SF ($6.60) that includes transportation not only in zone 10, but also in zones 21, 31, and 41, which take in practically the whole network of Greater Geneva. Many worthy attractions and restaurants are in the suburbs.

These tickets and many other kinds of tickets, including combined bus/cable-car tickets that will carry you to the top of Salève mountain, the city's highest point, are available from the Geneva public transport system's agencies or from official dealers. For customer service and more information, call ℂ **022/308-34-34.**

BY TAXI

The meter on whatever cab you take in Geneva will automatically begin calculating your fare at 6.50SF ($3.60), and then add between 2.70SF ($1.50) and 3.30SF ($1.80) for every kilometer (.62 mile) you travel, depending on the time of day or night. The fare from the airport to the center of town is around 30SF ($20.10). No tipping is required. To call for a **taxi,** call ℂ **022/331-41-33** or 022/320-20-20.

BY CAR

Driving is not recommended because parking is too difficult and the many one-way streets make navigation complicated. However, should you wish to rent a car and tour Lake Geneva (see chapter 9), you'll find many car-rental companies represented in the arrivals hall of the airport or in the center of the city. Major car rental companies in Geneva include **Avis,** 44, rue de Lausanne (ℂ **022/731-90-00** or at the airport 022/929-03-30); **Budget,** 36, rue de Zurich (ℂ **022/900-24-00** or at the airport 022/798-22-52); **Hertz,** 60, rue de Berne (ℂ **022/731-12-00** or at the airport 022/798-22-02); and **Europcar,** at the airport (ℂ **022/909-69-90**).

BY BIKE

Touring the city by bicycle isn't particularly practical because of the steep cobblestone streets, speeding cars, and general congestion. However, you might want to consider renting a bike for touring the countryside around Geneva. The major rental outlet is at the baggage desk at **Gare Cornavin** (✆ **022/ 791-02-50**), where city bikes cost 26SF ($14.30) and mountain bikes rent for 35SF ($19.25).

Another major outlet, charging from 10SF to 16SF ($5.50–$8.80) per day, depending on the type of bicycle you want to rent, is **Genève Roule,** 17, place Montbrillant (✆ **022/740-13-43**). If you're interested in renting a small motor scooter or somewhat larger motorbike, head for **Horizon Motos,** 51, rue de Lausanne (✆ **022/732-29-90**), which offers motor scooter rentals for 30SF to 76SF ($16.50–$41.80) per day; and motorbike rentals for 144SF to 205SF ($79.20–$112.75) per day. You'll need to present a motorcycle driver's license (from whatever country of origin you come from is fine) for motorbike rentals, but to rent most scooters you do not require any special permits.

✐ FAST FACTS: Geneva

American Express The American Express office at 7, rue du Mont-Blanc (✆ **022/731-76-00**), is open Monday to Friday from 8:30am to 6pm and Saturday from 9am to noon. Even when the office is closed, dial the above-listed number for a recorded list of emergency numbers.

Babysitters A list of agencies offering this service is available at the tourist office. Most middle- and upper-bracket hotels will also secure an English-speaking babysitter for you, or you can call **Service de Placement de l'Université,** 4, rue de Candolle (✆ **022/329-39-70**). Call before noon if you want a sitter at night. Another option involves calling **Chaperones Rouges** (✆ **022/304-04-86**), which is the organization associated with the Red Cross that's responsible for teaching young girls about child-care rituals. Some of their students sometimes make themselves available for babysitting in either a private home or a hotel room.

Bookstore One of the largest in Geneva is the well-stocked **Payot,** 5, rue Chantepoulet (✆ **022/731-89-50**), with a good selection of books in French, German, and English.

Business Hours Most banks are open Monday to Friday from 8:30am to 4:30pm (until 5:30pm on Wednesday). Most offices are open Monday to Friday from 8am to noon and 2 to 6pm, although this can vary. It's always best to call first.

Car Rentals See "By Car," above.

Consulates If you lose your passport or have other business with your home government, go to your nation's consulate: **United States,** 7, chemin de la confédération (✆ **022/840-51-61**); **Australia,** 2, chemin des Fins (✆ **022/799-91-00**); **Canada,** 1, chemin du Pré-de-la-Bichette (✆ **022/ 919-92-00**); **New Zealand,** 2, chemin des Fins (✆ **022/929-03-50**); the **United Kingdom,** 37–39, rue de Vermont (✆ **022/918-24-00**).

Currency Exchange In a city devoted to banking and the exchange of international currencies, you'll find dozens of places to exchange money in Geneva. Three of the most visible outlets, however, are run by **UBS-SA,** one of the country's largest banking conglomerates. You'll find a branch at the **Gare Cornavin,** 10, place Cornavin (✆ **022/375-33-60**), that's open daily from 8:30am to 8:30pm; a branch at the **Cointrin Airport** that's open daily from 6:30am to 9pm; and a downtown branch at 2, rue de la Confederation (℡ **022/375-75-75**) that's open Monday to Friday from 8:30am to 4:30pm. The branches in the airport and in the railway station also house "money-automats"—you receive an equivalent amount of Swiss francs for every $20, $50, and $100 bill you insert into the machine.

Dentist English-speaking dentists are available at one of the *cliniques dentaires* at 5, rue Malombré (℡ **022/346-64-44**), Monday to Friday from 7:30am to 8pm and Saturday and Sunday from 8am to 6pm.

Doctor If you become ill and want to consult a doctor, including one who will travel to your hotel, call ℡ **022/322-20-20**; or arrange an appointment with an English-speaking doctor at the **Hôpital Cantonal**, 24, rue Micheli-du-Crest (℡ 022/372-33-11).

Drugstores Each night a different set of four drugstores stays open either till 9pm or 11pm. Call ℡ **144** or **111** to find out which drugstore will be open. One of the world's biggest drugstores, **Pharmacie Principale**, in Confédération-Centre, 8, rue de la Confédération (℡ **022/318-66-60**), offers everything from medicine to clothing, perfumes, optical equipment, cameras, and photo supplies. It's open Monday to Friday from 9am to 7pm and Saturday from 9am to 5pm.

Emergencies In an emergency, dial ℡ **117** for the police, ℡ **144** for an ambulance, and ℡ **118** to report a fire.

Eyeglasses For your eyeglass and contact lens needs, you can go to **Visi-Lab**, in the Confédération-Centre, 8, rue de la Confédération (℡ **022/ 318-66-60**).

Hospitals You can go to the **Hôpital Cantonal**, 24, rue Micheli-du-Crest (℡ **022/372-33-11**).

Internet Access You can check your e-mail at **Funet Discount Internet Café**, 44, rue de Lausanne (℡ **022/738-500-00**), near Gare Cornavin. Open Monday to Friday 9am to 9:30pm and Saturday and Sunday noon to 9:30pm.

Library The **American Library**, at 3, rue de Monthoux (℡ **022/732-80-97**), has a subscription service open to those looking for a wide variety of the latest books in English. A month's membership, the minimum allowable, costs 25SF ($16.75). A refundable deposit of 50SF ($33.50) is required before you can borrow your first book.

Lost Property Go to the **Service Cantonal des Objets Trouvés**, 7, rue des Glacis-de-Rive (℡ **022/787-60-00**), open Monday to Thursday from 8am to 4:30pm and Friday from 8am to 4pm.

Luggage Storage/Lockers Luggage can be stored and lockers rented at the main railroad station, **Gare Cornavin**, place Cornavin (℡ **0900/ 800-800**).

Newspapers/Magazines Newspapers in Geneva are printed in French, but the latest copies of the *International Herald Tribune, USA Today,* the *New York Times,* and *The Washington Post* are available at most newsstands and in large hotel newsstand kiosks. And if you're planning on moving to Geneva, or spending more than a month here, consider acquiring a copy of *The Guide to English-Speaking Geneva* which is available free at the

American Library (see above) or from the city's premier English-language bookshop, **The ELM** (English Language Media), 5, rue Versonnex (☎ 022/ 736-09-45).

Police In an emergency, call ☎ **117.** For nonemergency matters, call ☎ **022/427-84-00.**

Post Office There's a limited **Office de Poste** at Gare Cornavin, 16, rue des Gares (☎ **022/739-21-11**), open Monday to Friday from 6am to 10:45pm, Saturday from 6am to 8pm, and Sunday from noon to 8pm. A better bet is the city's main post office, **Bureau de Poste Montbrillant,** rue des Gares (☎ **022/739-21-11**), which offers a full range of telephone, telegraph, and mail-related services Monday to Friday from 8am to 10:45pm, Saturday from 8am to 10pm, and Sunday from noon to 8pm.

Restrooms You'll find public facilities at all rail and air terminals and on main squares. Otherwise, you can patronize those in cafes and other commercial establishments such as department stores.

Safety Geneva is one of the safest cities in the world, but that doesn't mean you shouldn't take the usual precautions when traveling anywhere. Protect your valuables. Car thefts have been on the rise. High-class prostitutes and confidence swindlers proliferate in Geneva to prey on the well-heeled.

Shoe Repairs An outlet of **Mr. Minit** is located in the Metro-Shopping arcade, 30, rue du Mont-Blanc (☎ **022/732-42-59**). Most repairs can be performed while you wait.

Taxes There is no special city tax, other than the 6.5% value-added tax (VAT) attached to all goods and services throughout Switzerland.

Telegrams/Telex/Fax Virtually every post office in Geneva maintains a handful of *tele-cabines* where you can pay cash for a phone call to anywhere in the world, but the densest concentration of these phones lies within the main railway station, **Gare Cornavin,** place Cornavin (it's open 24 hours a day). Within less than a block, you'll find additional phones in the **Office de Poste Montbrillant** (Cornavin Dépôt), 16, rue des Gares, 1200 Geneve 2 (☎ **022/739-24-61**), which is open Monday to Friday from 7am to 10:45pm, and Sunday from noon to 8pm. Either site can send telegrams or faxes for you.

Tipping Most restaurants and hotels, even taxis, add a service charge of 10% to 15% to your bill, so no further tipping is necessary unless you want to reward someone for a special service.

Transit Information For **train information,** call ☎ **0900/300-300** from anywhere in Switzerland. Contact the **airport** at ☎ **022/717-71-11.** For **bus information** Monday to Friday from 8am to 9pm, dial ☎ **022/308-33-11;** for information on Saturday and Sunday, call ☎ 022/308-34-34.

Useful Telephone Numbers For general telephone directory information, call ☎ **111;** for the time, ☎ **161;** for the weather, ☎ **162.**

3 Where to Stay

A truly world-class city, Geneva has lots of hotels, most of which are clustered around the railway terminal or stretched along the lakefront. But be warned—

Where to Stay in Geneva

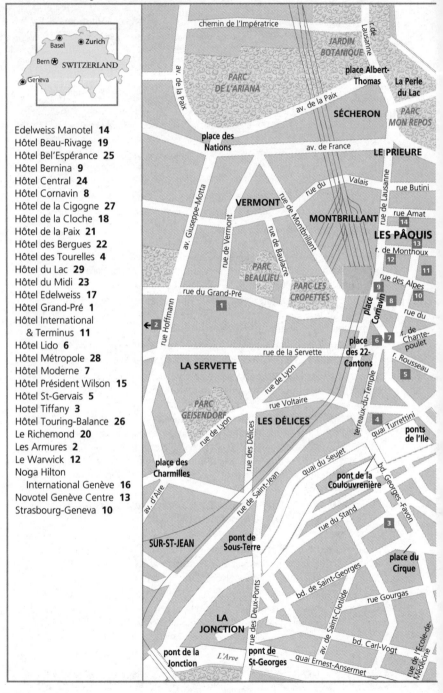

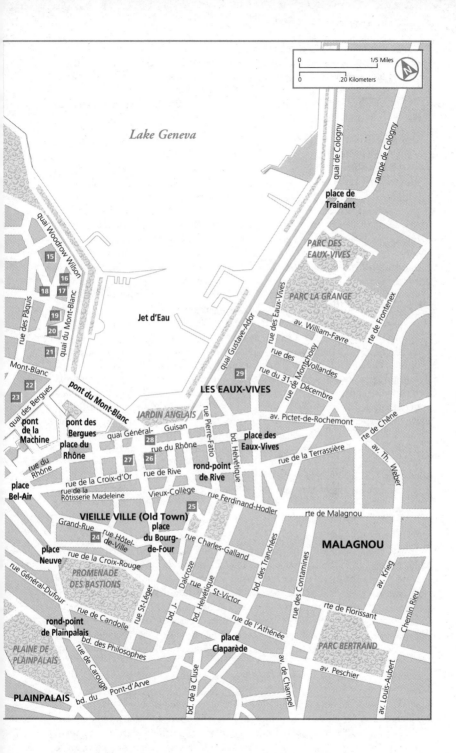

Lake Geneva

PARC DES EAUX-VIVES

PARC LA GRANGE

place de Traînant

quai de Cologny

rampe de Cologny

quai Woodrow Wilson

15

16

18 17

19

20

21

Mont-Blanc

22

23

Jet d'Eau

quai du Mont-Blanc

rue des Pâquis

quai des Bergues

pont du Mont-Blanc

pont de la Machine

pont des Bergues

place du Rhône

rue du Rhône

quai Général- Guisan

JARDIN ANGLAIS

28

rue du Rhône

27 26

rue de Rive

rue de la Croix-d'Or

rue de la Rôtisserie Madeleine

place Bel-Air

Vieux-Collège

rue Pierre-Fatio

bd. Helvétique

29

rue des Eaux-Vives

rue des Vollandes

rue du 31 Décembre

LES EAUX-VIVES

av. Pictet-de-Rochemont

place des Eaux-Vives

rond-point de Rive

rue de la Terrassière

quai Gustave-Ador

av. William-Favre

rue de Montchoisy

rte de Frontenex

rte de Chêne

av. Th. Weber

rue Ferdinand-Hodler

rte de Malagnou

MALAGNOU

VIEILLE VILLE (Old Town)

place du Bourg-de-Four

25

Grand-Rue

rue Hôtel-de-Ville

24

place Neuve

rue de la Croix-Rouge

rue Charles-Galland

bd. des Tranchées

rue des Contamines

rue Général-Dufour

PROMENADE DES BASTIONS

Dalcroze

rue J-

rue St-Victor

bd. Helvétique

rue St-Léger

bd. J-

rue de Candolle

rond-point de Plainpalais

PLAINE DE PLAINPALAIS

bd. des Philosophes

rue de Carouge

Pont-d'Arve

bd. du

PLAINPALAIS

rue de l'Athénée

place Claparède

bd. de la Cluse

av. de Champel

PARC BERTRAND

av. Peschier

rte de Florissant

av. Krieg

Chemin Rieu

av. Louis-Aubert

0 1/5 Miles
0 .20 Kilometers

N

Geneva hosts a number of international conferences and conventions, so many of its hotels are booked months in advance. And while it does incorporate dozens of expensive hotels in all different architectural styles (from the antique to the super-modern), it doesn't have very many intimate, family-run inns.

Note: Unless indicated otherwise, all rooms in hotels we've recommended below have a private bathroom.

ON THE RIGHT BANK
VERY EXPENSIVE

Hôtel Beau-Rivage ★★★ This landmark 1865 hotel, which has counted Richard Wagner among its guests, receives our highest recommendation for its traditional Victorian charm and impeccable service. However, you'll pay—and pay dearly—for the privilege of staying here or at its rival, Le Richemond (see below). In 2001 the hotel underwent extensive renovations, combining several rooms into larger units and generally upgrading both the public and the private areas. Its colorful history has included the auction of the jewels of the late duchess of Windsor; and after World War I, the treaty creating the Republic of Czechoslovakia was signed here. The most tragic event in its history, however, was the assassination of Empress Elisabeth of Austria, who was stabbed in 1898 by the anarchist Luigi Lucheni as she was leaving the hotel on her way to a lake steamer. To this day, history buffs rent the pale-blue Empress Suite. Madame Mitterrand always makes it her stopover when she's in Geneva.

The hotel was built by Jean-Jacques Mayer, who came from Stuttgart. Its most striking feature is the open, five-story lobby. The hotel also became the first in Europe to install elevators. Today it's run by the founder's great-grandson, with the help of an enthusiastic staff. The rooms are individually furnished and frequently redecorated. All front rooms have views of the Right Bank. Rooms are categorized by size, "romantic" rooms being more spacious, and "classical" rooms medium in size. Some of the romantic accommodations contain frescoes. Each unit also has a roomy private bathroom, clad in marble or tile, with robes and deluxe toiletries.

13 quai du Mont-Blanc, CH-1201 Genève. © 022/716-66-66. Fax 022/716-60-60. www.beau-rivage.ch. 97 units. 560SF–810SF ($308–$445.50) double; from 1,650SF ($907.50) suite. AE, DC, MC, V. Parking 30SF ($16.50). Bus: 1. **Amenities:** 2 restaurants, bar; room service; babysitting; laundry/dry cleaning. *In room:* A/C, TV, minibar, hair dryer.

Hôtel des Bergues ★★★ After a massive recent renovation, this bastion of luxury looks fabulous. The elegant, four-story hotel—designated a historic monument by the Swiss—once catered to the monarchs of Europe. Today it's a favorite with the international business community, diplomats, and members of European society. It has long been ranked by Institutional Investor as one of the world's top hotels. The hotel's impressive guest list has included Jean Cocteau, the duke of Edinburgh, the queen of Spain, Edward VIII, the queen of Hawaii, and Emperor Franz Joseph and Empress Elizabeth ("Sissi") of Austria. Grandly memorable from its centrally located position at the edge of the Rhône, the hotel also hosted many meetings of the League of Nations. During World War II it was known as the "hotel of the Allies," having played host to so many Allied leaders.

The hotel's efficient 130-person staff is here to serve your needs, and the public rooms are lavish. The bedrooms have Directoire and Louis Philippe furnishings. In 1997 the rooms on the second and third floors were ripped apart, some walls removed, and the dimensions made larger. Rooms ranked superior on the Bel Etage floor are the finest choices here, although all units are beautifully appointed. Lake-view rooms are more expensive. The hotel shelters two of the classiest dining rooms in Geneva: Le Pavillon and L'Amphitryon.

33, quai des Bergues, CH-1211 Genève. ☎ 022/908-70-00. Fax 022/908-70-90. www.hoteldesbergues.com. 123 units. 570SF–853SF ($313.50–$469.15) double; from 2,250SF ($1,237.50) suite. AE, DC, MC, V. Parking 35SF ($19.25). Bus: 7. **Amenities:** 2 restaurants, lounge; exercise room; sauna; room service; babysitting; laundry/dry cleaning. *In room:* A/C, TV, minibar, hair dryer, safe.

Hôtel Président Wilson ★★★   Located across a busy boulevard from the lakefront, a 5-minute drive (or a brisk walk) from the center of town, this modern hotel is sometimes mistaken for the diplomatic headquarters of some international agency. In 1994, it launched an ambitious expansion program, with the addition of a new wing and a total renovation inside and out. The guest rooms and suites are furnished with classic European styling, with extensive use of wood and rich fabrics. Luxury extras are all in place, with bidets, robes, marble bathrooms, full-length mirrors, dual basins, and elegant carpeting. Windows open onto views of Lake Geneva and Mont Blanc. Despite the good intentions of the staff, an anonymity prevails. One of the galleries displays the hotel's collection of 17th-century Gobelin tapestries.

47, quai du Président-Wilson, CH-1211 Genève. ☎ 022/906-66-66. Fax 022/906-66-67. www.hotelpwilson. com. 255 units. 310SF–540SF ($170.50–$297) double; from 750SF ($412.50) suite. AE, DC, MC, V. Parking 30SF ($16.50). Bus: 1. **Amenities:** 3 restaurants, 2 bars; pool; spa; Jacuzzi; sauna; room service; massage; babysitting; laundry/dry cleaning; nonsmoking floor. *In room:* A/C, TV, minibar, hair dryer, safe.

Le Richemond ★★★   Le Richemond, which counts some of the world's most prominent people among its guests, is the greatest hotel in Geneva. When Michael Jackson checked in, he was following in the footsteps of the famous and infamous of yesteryear, including Colette, Miró, and Chagall. Erected in 1875, the neoclassical, travertine building has wrought-iron balustrades and is situated near the lake, across from a small park. In the 19th century it was an unpretentious guesthouse, but the hotel has been transformed under the direction of the Armleder family, who have run it since the day it opened. Its public rooms look like a museum, with dozens of valuable engravings and an array of furniture dating from the days of Louis XII. Accommodations range from the most spacious in the city to medium in size; nearly half of the units here are suites, attracting all of Europe, plus international CEOs. A huge block of rooms is renovated every year and all look as good as new. This is true Grand Hotel living, with elegant fabrics, tasteful upholstery, and luxurious beds, plus spacious marble bathrooms with robes and a basket of expensive toiletries. The hotel restaurant, Le Gentilhomme Bar, is one of the finest dining establishments in Geneva (see "Where to Dine," later in this chapter).

Jardin Brunswick, CH-1211 Genève. ☎ 022/715-70-00. Fax 022/715-70-01. www.richemond.ch. 91 units. 590SF–790SF ($324.50–$434.50) double; 990SF–2,900SF ($544.50–$1,595) suite. AE, DC, MC, V. Parking 45SF ($24.75). Bus: 1. **Amenities:** 2 restaurants, bar, lounge; health club; sauna; salon; room service; babysitting; laundry/dry cleaning; nonsmoking rooms. *In room:* A/C, TV, minibar, hair dryer.

Noga Hilton International Genève ★   Located at the edge of the lake, this is the largest deluxe hotel in Switzerland, and one of the best in the Hilton chain. Depending on your taste, the hotel is either stylish and glossy, or else a bit anonymous. All the rooms are custom-designed, with beautiful wood, fabrics, and artwork, and are equipped with spacious marble bathrooms and oversized beds. The rooms overlooking the lake and the town are higher priced; those opening onto a quiet courtyard are less. The hotel has a gourmet restaurant,

Le Cygne, one of the best in Geneva (see "Where to Dine," later in this chapter), and an elegant Asian restaurant, Le Tsé-Yang.

19, quai du Mont-Blanc, CH-1211 Genève. © **800/445-8667** in the U.S. and Canada, or 022/908-90-81. Fax 022/908-90-90. www.hilton.com/geneve. 410 units. 585SF–810SF ($321.75–$445.50) double; from 1,200SF ($660) suite. AE, DC, MC, V. Parking 1SF (55¢) per hour. Bus: 1. **Amenities:** 4 restaurants, 3 bars; pool; health club; sauna; room service; massage; babysitting; laundry/dry cleaning; art gallery; small casino. *In room:* A/C, TV, minibar, hair dryer, safe.

EXPENSIVE

Hôtel Cornavin ⊕★   Few other hotels in Geneva have been as radically renovated, as frequently, as this government-rated four-star contender that stands adjacent to the railway station. Originally built in 1932, with a bland and neutral-looking facade that overlooks the bustle of Geneva's most commercial square, it was heightened in 1998 with the addition of a ninth floor that capped the original structure. That, coupled with an overhaul of each of the already existing bedrooms, produced an efficient, well-managed, business-conscious hotel. Each of the bedrooms is outfitted in tones of gray with either blue or salmon, and a sense of contemporary warmth. Each is soundproofed against the noise of the nearby traffic, and contains a neatly kept bathroom.

23, bd. James-Fazy, CH-1201 Genève. © **022/716-12-12.** Fax 022/716-12-00. www.fhotels.ch. 162 units. 295SF–360SF ($162.25–$198) double. Rates include buffet breakfast. AE, DC, MC, V. Bus: 10. **Amenities:** Lounge; room service; babysitting; laundry/dry cleaning. *In room:* A/C, TV, minibar, hair dryer.

Hôtel de la Paix ⊕★★   In terms of opulence it's a notch down from the Beau Rivage, but since its prices are less expensive and it's a lot less pretentious, many clients seek it out for those reasons. Although not in the ultra top tier, it's grand and glamorous, and after a complete overhaul, it's better than it's ever been. Royalty from Liechtenstein, Monaco, and the Netherlands, as well as international dignitaries and celebrities such as the guitarist Andrés Segovia, have stayed in this 1865 hotel directly on the lake. Designed by an Italian architect and built of stone from Meillerie, the building belonged to the kingdom of Sardinia for a long time. The main salon is a double-tiered arched extravaganza, with marble columns, elaborate Corinthian capitals, and a balustraded loggia overlooking a massive crystal chandelier. Rooms are traditionally furnished and often quite roomy, with antiques intermixed with well-chosen modern pieces. The marble and tile bathrooms are luxuriously equipped. This hotel is a member of the Leading Hotels of the World.

11, quai du Mont-Blanc, CH-1201 Genève. © **800/223-6800** in the U.S., or 022/909-60-00. Fax 022/909-60-01. www.hoteldelapaix.ch. 101 units. 450SF–590SF ($247.50–$324.50) double; 720SF–1,200SF ($396–$660) suite. AE, DC, MC, V. Parking 35SF ($19.25). Bus: 6, 8, 10, or 15. **Amenities:** 2 restaurants, bar; health club; sauna; room service; babysitting; laundry/dry cleaning. *In room:* A/C, TV, minibar, hair dryer, safe.

Hôtel Grand-Pré ⊕★ *Kids*   Set between the center of town and the airport, this modern, six-story, government-rated four-star hotel is convenient and efficient. Rooms are standardized but comfortable, most outfitted in tones of bordeaux with contemporary, uncontroversial furniture. Everything was completely renovated in 1999, including the fifth floor breakfast room and the lobby-level bar. Based on management whims and occupancy rates, discounts are sometimes granted on Friday and Saturday nights. The hotel quotes special terms for families, depending on their size, and families with kids especially appreciate the refrigerator in each room.

35, rue du Grand-Pré, CH-1201 Genève. © **022/918-11-11.** Fax 022/734-76-91. 89 units. 310SF–340SF ($170.50–$187) double; 420SF ($231) suite. Rates include continental breakfast. AE, DC, MC, V. Parking 15SF ($8.25). Bus: 8. **Amenities:** Bar, lounge; car rental; room service; laundry/dry cleaning. *In room:* A/C, TV, minibar, hair dryer.

Le Warwick ⭐ *Kids*   This contemporary hotel, located across from the train station, is a strong choice, built during the 1970s and owned and operated by a Hong Kong chain with headquarters in Paris. The abstractly modern lobby contains sweeping staircases, loggias, balconies, marble floors, and Oriental rugs. The refurbished, soundproof bedrooms each renovated in 1999 are often sunny, boldly patterned, and comfortable, with marble bathrooms. Le Warwick allows children up to 12 years of age to stay free in their parents' room. Its brasserie is open for light meals and snacks all day long.

14, rue de Lausanne, CH-1201 Genève. ℂ 022/716-80-80. Fax 022/716-80-01. www.warwickhotels.com. 169 units. 350SF–580SF ($192.50–$319) double; 1,400SF ($770) suite. AE, DC, MC, V. Parking 15SF ($8.25). Bus: 6 or 33. **Amenities:** 2 restaurants, bar; room service; babysitting; laundry/dry cleaning. *In room:* A/C, TV, minibar, hair dryer, safe.

MODERATE

Hôtel du Midi   Ideally situated on a tree-lined square near the center of Geneva, this salmon-colored, eight-story hotel reminds most visitors of an apartment building. A complete renovation in 1994 moved the reception area to the street level and added half a dozen bedrooms to the hotel's 1968 infrastructure. The windows are double-glazed to keep out the noise, and there's wall-to-wall carpeting in every room. The bedrooms contain such accessories as warming racks for towels. Bedrooms are medium in size and, although not spectacular, are exceedingly well maintained. Bathrooms are a bit cramped, but with adequate shelf space. The Hôtel du Midi manages to remain comfortable in spite of the somewhat plain appearance.

4, place Chevelu, CH-1211 Genève. ℂ 022/544-15-00. Fax 022/731-00-20. www.hotel-du-midi.ch. 90 units. 220SF–350SF ($121–$192.50) double. Rates include continental breakfast. AE, DC, MC, V. Parking 18SF ($9.90). Bus: 7. **Amenities:** Restaurant, lounge; room service; laundry/dry cleaning. *In room:* A/C, TV, minibar, hair dryer, safe.

Hôtel Edelweiss   This brown-and-white, eight-story hotel towers above its neighbors near quai du Président-Wilson. Inside, it has a rustic decor that contrasts with its modern exterior. The bedrooms are cozy and furnished with pinewood furniture crafted in a country-Swiss style. Even though in the heart of Geneva, you get provincial comfort here. Bedrooms are medium in size with sitting areas and desk space, plus first-rate mattresses and good linens. Bathrooms, although small and plain, are neatly kept. Built in the early 1960s, the hotel was last renovated in the 1990s.

2, place de la Navigation, CH-1201 Genève. ℂ 022/544-51-51. Fax 022/738-85-33. 42 units. 263SF ($144.65) double. Rates include buffet breakfast. AE, DC, MC, V. Bus: 1. **Amenities:** Restaurant, lounge; room service; babysitting; laundry/dry cleaning. *In room:* A/C, TV, minibar, hair dryer, safe.

Novotel Genève Centre *Value*   One of the most consistently reliable government-rated four-star hotels in Geneva's commercial center is this comfortable, standardized member of a France-based chain. It was originally built in the 1970s as a five-star Ramada, and consequently, bedrooms are bigger than what you'd expect at a usual Novotel. From the street, you'll step down into a stylish-looking, marble-trimmed lobby, then head upstairs to larger-than-expected, comfortably standardized bedrooms, each with a writing table favored by business travelers, and a sofa that can be transformed into an additional bed.

19, rue de Zurich, CH-1211 Genève 1. ℂ 022/909-90-00. Fax 022/909-90-01. 205 units. 230SF–410SF ($126.50–$225.50) double. AE, DC, MC, V. Bus: 1, 5. **Amenities:** Restaurant, bar; 24-hour room service; babysitting; laundry/dry cleaning. *In room:* TV, minibar, hair dryer, safe (in ⅔ of rooms).

Strasbourg-Geneva ⭐   Set close to the railway station on a dead-end street that is surprisingly tranquil, this building was originally constructed around 1900 by a nostalgic entrepreneur originally from Strasbourg. Over the years many different renovations both outside and inside have kept it looking fresh and new. The most recent overhaul occurred in 1999. Some of the more recently renovated bedrooms have wooden surfaces and pastel colors; others are comfortably and traditionally conservative. The bedrooms, as befits a turn-of-the-century hotel, range from spacious (usually on the lower floors) to a bit cramped. Each bedroom has fine linens, plus compact bathrooms lined with tile and equipped with decent plumbing. Run by a local family, this hotel had remained independent until it affiliated with Best Western in 1999.

10, rue J-J-Pradier, CH-1201 Genève. © **800/528-1234** or 022/906-58-00. Fax 022/738-42-08. www. strasbourg-geneva.ch. 53 units. 220SF–240SF ($121–$132) double; 260SF–500SF ($143–$275) suite. Rates include continental breakfast. AE, DC, MC, V. Bus: 1, 2, 3, 4, 8, 12, 13, or 44. **Amenities:** Lounge. *In room:* TV, minibar, hair dryer.

INEXPENSIVE

Hotel Bel'Espérance *(Value)*   At the gateway to Old Town, close to the lake, this is a hotel managed by The Salvation Army. It's no bare-bones hotel but a decent budget hotel with well furnished, good-sized bedrooms, accompanied by private shower or bathroom. Many rooms are suitable for up to 4 beds, and the most desirable units open onto a private balcony with a view of the Cathédrale St. Pierre. A homey, warm atmosphere prevails.

1, rue de la Vallée, CH-1204 Genève. © **022/818-37-37.** Fax 022/818-37-73. www.hotel-bel-esperance.ch. 40 units. 130SF–170SF ($71.50–$93.50) double; 150SF–180SF ($82.50–$99) triple. Rates include breakfast. AE, MC, V. Bus: 8. *In room:* TV.

Hotel Bernina   Set directly across from the Cornavin railway station, this is an old-fashioned but worthy hotel with a reputation for fair prices and relatively comfortable accommodations. Don't expect luxury. There's a Sputnik-era severity to the lobby, with furniture like what you'd expect in an airport waiting lounge, and a blasé, not particularly responsive staff. But rooms are high-ceilinged and sunny, albeit somewhat battered. They are clean, filled with angular modern furniture, and soundproofed against the noise of the traffic outside. A Pizza Hut (under separate management) lies on the ground floor of the hotel, and the restaurant congestion of the railway station is just across the square.

22, place de Cornavin, CH-1211 Genève. © **022/908-49-50.** Fax 022/908-49-51. www.bernina-geneve.ch. 77 units (72 with bathroom). 100SF–120SF ($55–$66) double without bathroom; 150SF–210SF ($82.50–$115.50) double with bathroom. Rates include breakfast. AE, DC, MC, V. Bus: 6 or 33. **Amenities:** Pizzeria. *In room:* TV.

Hôtel de la Cloche *(Value)*   This small hotel, the best bargain in Geneva, occupies the second floor of a 19th-century apartment building that rises from a narrow street behind the modern bulk of the Noga Hilton. Guests here appreciate its modest cost and unpretentious accessories, as well as its glamorous location and the easy availability of the nearby Hilton facilities. It's run by a charming and elderly widow, Madame Chabbey, who provides guests with a computerized access code to enter the building. The bedrooms are high-ceilinged, often decorated with ornate plasterwork, elegant moldings, and simple furniture. Some units look out over a quiet inner courtyard and some offer views over the lake. Rooms are spacious and cared for, designed with an eye to old-fashioned comfort. Those with private bathrooms will find rather cramped shower stalls. But most guests have to share the corridor bathrooms, which are adequate for the job and well maintained. In-room amenities are scarce; units come with a phone, but no TV.

6, rue de la Cloche, CH-1001 Genève. © 022/732-94-81. Fax 022/738-16-12. www.smpage.ch/cloche. 8 units, 5 with bathroom, shower only. 95SF ($52.25) double without bathroom, 120SF ($66) double with bathroom; 105SF ($57.75) triple without bathroom; 145SF ($79.75) quad without bathroom. AE, MC, V. Bus: 1. **Amenities:** Lounge.

Hôtel des Tourelles _(Value_   Named after the twin towers that flank the edges of its turn-of-the-century facade, this stone-sided, government-rated two-star hotel offers good value in simple, straightforward rooms that are made more palatable by high ceilings, small refrigerators and, in some cases, balconies overlooking the Rhône and its quays. Some of the bedrooms have decorative marble fireplaces dating from the year of the hotel's construction. The staff is helpful and, in some cases, charming. Units come equipped with tidy bathrooms containing showers. Breakfast is the only meal served. The only drawback to this place involves traffic noise from the busy riverside avenues adjacent to the hotel, but shutting the double-glazed windows helps muffle most of it.

2, bd. James-Fazy, CH-1201 Genève. © 022/732-44-23. Fax 022/732-76-20. destourelles@compuserve.com. 23 units. 130SF ($71.50) double. Rates include buffet breakfast. Extra bed 25SF ($13.75). AE, DC, MC, V. Bus: 1. Tram: 1, 10, or 13. **Amenities:** Lounge; laundry. _In room:_ TV.

Hôtel International & Terminus _(Kids_   This hotel lies across the street from the main entrance of Geneva's railway station, and has been directed by three generations of the Cottier family. Originally built in 1900, it was radically upgraded in 1999, with pairs of smaller rooms reconfigured into larger units especially good for families. Rated three stars by the local tourist board, the hotel has a lobby that alternates Louis-style furnishings with modern pieces. Stay here for the exceedingly good value. The small to spacious bedrooms are fitted with first-rate furnishings and the maintenance level is high. Bathrooms seemed to have been added as an afterthought, in areas not designed for them, and are a bit cramped with shower stalls. The restaurant, La Veranda, serves some of the most reasonable meals in Geneva, and also keeps the pizza ovens cauldron hot.

20, rue des Alpes, CH-1201 Genève. © 022/732-80-95. Fax 022/732-18-43. 53 units. 180SF ($99) double. Rates include continental breakfast. AE, DC, MC, V. Bus: 6, 10, or 33. **Amenities:** Restaurant; lounge. _In room:_ TV, minibar.

Hôtel Lido   This durable choice 2 blocks from the rail station was built in 1963 and completely renovated in the 1990s. This is a simple, government-rated two-star hotel with few if any frills—it's recommended for its bargain price. The small rooms are furnished in a no-nonsense functional style. All rooms come equipped with neatly kept bathrooms with shower-tub combinations. The hotel has five floors with an elevator, and room service is available during limited hours.

8, rue Chantepoulet, CH-1201, Genève. © 022/731-55-30. Fax 022/731-65-01. www.hotel-lido.ch. 31 units. 180SF ($99) double. Rates include continental breakfast. AE, DC, MC, V. Bus: 10. **Amenities:** Lounge; limited room service; laundry. _In room:_ TV.

Hôtel Moderne   Near the railroad station and the lake, this is a seven-story, rectangular, white structure, with a low-lying, glassed-in extension containing the breakfast room. The hotel was renovated in 1999, and the public rooms are modern, with Nordic furniture and abstract angles and curves. The bedrooms, each with soundproof windows, have standardized furnishings and are clean, modern, and often sunny. You'll wish the bathrooms had more room to spread out your stuff, though you'll appreciate the tidy maintenance, the up-to-date plumbing, and the clean showers. The hotel's restaurant serves only breakfast, but there's an Italian restaurant under separate management in the same building.

1, rue de Berne, CH-1211 Genève. © 022/732-81-00. Fax 022/738-26-58. www.hotelmoderne.ch. 54 units. 180SF–190SF ($99–$104.50) double. Rates include buffet breakfast. AE, DC, MC, V. Bus: 10. **Amenities:** Lounge; room service; babysitting; laundry/dry cleaning; nonsmoking rooms. *In room:* TV.

Hôtel St-Gervais   One of the simplest hotels we recommend in this guide, this place is inside an old-fashioned, vaguely nondescript building in Geneva's medieval core, a 3-minute walk from Gare Cornavin. Although it has quirky idiosyncrasies that appeal to architects and historic renovators, some guests have expressed annoyance at having to navigate their way to the upper floors with a lot of luggage. Fortunately, there's a cramped elevator on-site, but other than that, the place is minimalist but comfortable, with an emphasis on durable, functionalist furniture and a conservative (or nonexistent) color scheme of beige and brown. You get routine rooms here, and well-worn but still comfortable beds. As for plumbing, you most often have to settle for a sink, although the hotel maintains an adequate number of hallway bathrooms, which are kept very tidy. Rooms with private bathrooms are also well maintained and come equipped with shower-tub combinations.

20, rue des Corps-Saints, CH-1201 Genève. © and fax **022/732-45-72.** 26 units, 2 with bathroom. 78SF ($42.90) double without bathroom, 98SF–105SF ($53.90–$57.75) double with bathroom. AE, MC, V. Tram: 1, 3, 4, 5, or 6. **Amenities:** Bar, lounge; laundry. *In room:* No phone.

ON THE LEFT BANK
VERY EXPENSIVE

Métropole ★★★   Originally constructed around 1850, this is an imposing neoclassical building, which was used during World War II for the storage of prisoner-of-war records by the International Red Cross. In the late 1990s, its owners spent millions of francs on its complete restoration. Today, set between rue du Rhône and the Jardin Anglais, it offers views of Lake Geneva and the noisy quayside traffic from its larger rooms, and comfortably conservative bedrooms accented with wood paneling. Rooms are quite palatial, with luxurious beds and marble bathrooms equipped with deep tubs, robes, toiletries, and bidets.

34, quai du Général-Guisan, CH-1204 Genève. © **022/318-32-00.** Fax 022/318-33-00. www. swisshotel.com. 128 units. 390SF–690SF ($214.50–$379.50) double; 790SF–1,900SF ($434.50–$1,045) suite. AE, DC, MC, V. Parking 35SF ($19.25). Bus: 8. **Amenities:** Restaurant, bar; room service; babysitting; laundry/dry cleaning. *In room:* A/C, TV, minibar, hair dryer, safe.

EXPENSIVE

Hôtel de la Cigogne ★★★   Personalized and charming, this is our favorite Left Bank hotel, a chic, glamorous retreat for the discerning. This deluxe hotel was rebuilt after years of dilapidation and turned into an offbeat Relais & Châteaux that showcases designer and decorator talent. Combined with an adjoining building, the old hotel and its mate have the renovated facades of the original 18th- and 19th-century structures. With three sheltered courtyards overlooking a flowering plaza, this is one of the most tranquil hotels in Geneva. The bedrooms contain handmade mattresses, luxurious bathrooms, and bed linens embroidered with the hotel's coat of arms. Each bedroom is furnished differently, ranging from 1930s movie-mogul style to the "baron and baroness at their country place." Some units have working fireplaces.

17, place Longemalle, CH-1204 Genève. ℂ **022/818-40-40.** Fax 022/818-40-50. www.cigoghe.ch. 50 units. 420SF–540SF ($231–$297) double; 750SF–870SF ($412.50–$478.50) suite. Rates include continental breakfast. AE, DC, MC, V. Parking 25SF ($13.75). Bus: 6 or 9. **Amenities:** Restaurant; room service; laundry/dry cleaning. *In room:* A/C, TV, minibar, hair dryer, safe.

Les Armures ★★   Surpassed only by La Cigogne, this is one of the most elegant and prestigious hotels on Geneva's Left Bank. Positioned a few steps from both the Cathedral and the medieval Musée Tavel, it utterly lacks the late-19th-century grandeur of its government-rated five-star competitors across the river, on the north bank of the Rhone. Instead, you'll find a labyrinth of narrow corridors, and architectural gemstones that include beamed (and sometimes frescoed) ceilings and carefully preserved remnants of the building's origins in the 17th century. Each unit is different from its neighbors, usually with exposed brick or stone, and each alternates modern plumbing with richly detailed tilework in its bathrooms. This is not a blockbuster Belle Epoque hotel. The ambience here is cozy and well-upholstered, with an ostentation that's subtle and based for the most part on the building's sense of quirky antique charm.

1, rue Puits-Saint-Pierre, 1205 Genève. ℂ **022/310-91-72.** Fax 022/310-98-46. www.hotel-les-armures.ch. 28 units. 440SF–460SF ($242–$253) double; 495SF–565SF ($272.25–$310.75) suite. AE, DC, MC, V. **Amenities:** Restaurant, bar; babysitting; laundry/dry cleaning. *In room:* A/C, minibar, TV, hair dryer.

MODERATE

Edelweiss Manotel *Finds*   This is the most artfully folkloric hotel in Geneva, evoking the kind of cozy alpine decor that most Swiss people associate with isolated hamlets in the country's mountains. Although it was built in a seven-story boxy-looking design in 1967 and renovated in 1999, the interior of this place—including each bedroom—showcases the meticulous craftsmanship of another era. That's thanks to carefully finished pinewood paneling and country-baroque accessories that show off folkloric Switzerland at its most charming. The hotel's social centerpiece is its restaurant.

2, place de la Navigation, CH-1201 Genève. ℂ **022/544-51-51.** Fax 022/544-51-99. www.manotel.com. 42 units. 250SF ($137.50) double; 285SF ($156.75) triple. Rates include breakfast. AE, DC, MC, V. Bus: 1. **Amenities:** Restaurant, bar; concierge; massage; babysitting; laundry/dry cleaning. *In room:* A/C, TV, minibar, safe.

Hotel Tiffany ★ *Value*   This little charmer of a Belle Epoque boutique hotel lies on a Left Bank street 3 blocks south of the river and about a 12-minute stroll from the center and the lake. Although it can hardly match the style and glamour of the lakeside palaces, it is attractive in its modest way with everything from stained glass to Art Nouveau bed frames. In its category, it offers some of the most reasonable prices in Geneva, especially considering its style. Rising five floors, it has such touches as leather-clad armchairs and a summertime sidewalk cafe. Bedrooms are mid-sized with lots of extras, including soundproofing and spacious bathrooms. We prefer the rooms in the "attic," with their beams, rooftop vistas, and sloping walls.

1, rue des Marbriers, CH-1204 Genève. ℂ **022/708-1616.** Fax 022/708-1617. www.hotel-tiffany.ch. 43 units. 300SF–320SF ($187.50–$200) double; from 390SF ($243.75) suite. Buffet breakfast included. AE, DC, MC, V. Bus: 1 or 4. **Amenities:** Restaurant, English bar. *In room:* A/C, TV, minibar, hair dryer, safe.

INEXPENSIVE

Hotel Central   Set on the fifth, sixth, and seventh floor of a prominent building erected in 1924, this hotel has been a haven for cost-conscious visitors to Geneva since 1928. You'll find a very modern format, with a minimalist interior, on a street lined with banks and upscale shops. You'll register in the sixth floor reception area, containing carved antiques from Bali. (The establishment's Danish-born owner used to manage a five-star hotel there.) Know in advance that the smallest rooms have two-tiered bunk beds, toilets in alcoves off the hallway, and very little space. The more expensive rooms are bigger and more comfortable. All rooms are equipped with a shower and sink. Be alert that the reception staff is available only from 7am to 9pm, so if you're planning on a late-night check-in, make prior arrangements. Breakfast is served in the bedrooms.

2, rue de la Rôtisserie, CH-1204 Genéve. ✆ **022/818-81-00.** Fax 022/818-81-01. www.hotelcentral.ch. 30 units, 22 with private toilet. 75SF ($41.25) double without toilet; 95–150SF ($52.25–$82.50) double with toilet; 195SF ($107.25) suite. Rates include breakfast. AE, DC, MC, V. Bus: 12. *In room:* TV.

Hôtel du Lac *Value*   This small budget hotel built at the end of World War II is on the Left Bank in the old city, occupying the sixth and seventh floors of an apartment building. The Swiss-Italian managers don't pretend to offer first-class service, but they make up for it with their hospitality and their ability to speak English. If you can do without spaciousness, and if you'll settle for a somewhat worn thin mattress, you'll get one of the best values in a very expensive city. Of course, you'll have to go without a private bathroom, although the public bathrooms are quite adequate. You're given a set of decent towels, and will rarely have to line up to use one of the shower-only bathrooms. About half a dozen rooms at this hotel are rented on a long-term basis.

15, rue des Eaux-Vives, CH-1207 Genève. ✆ **022/343-36-60.** Fax 022/735-45-82. 26 units, none with bathroom. 90SF ($49.50) double; 125SF ($68.75) triple. Rates include continental breakfast. No credit cards. Bus: 9 from the train station to place des Eaux-Vives. **Amenities:** Lounge. *In room:* No phone.

AT NEARBY BELLEVUE

Hôtel La Réserve ★★★   Elegant and discreet, this prestigious government-rated five-star hotel was built at the edge of the lake in 1973 and enlarged in the mid-1980s. Because local codes wouldn't allow any structure higher than three stories, it was patterned in a vaguely neoclassical style after the many private villas that ring the lake. Set behind white walls and under a red-tile roof, it nestles within 8 landscaped acres that explode into bloom every year with thousands of tulips. It lies a 12-minute drive north of Geneva's center, beside the road leading to Lausanne, and has a setting carefully engineered for maximum peace, quiet, and (very upscale) contemplative rest. The public areas are filled with unusual art (much of it Chinese) and a mixture of conservative modern and Asian furniture. The spacious guest rooms are luxurious, with such extras as sound-proofing, fax machines, and large tile or marble bathrooms. The Chinese Tsé-Fung has the best Asian food in Geneva.

301, rte. de Lausanne, CH-1293 Bellevue-Genève. ✆ **022/959-86-88.** Fax 022/959-85-88. 115 units. 460SF–540SF ($253–$297) double; from 840SF ($462) suite. AE, DC, MC, V. Free parking. **Amenities:** 2 restaurants; bar; pool; 4 tennis courts; health club; sauna; boat rental; room service; massage; babysitting; laundry/dry cleaning. *In room:* A/C, TV, minibar, hair dryer, safe.

4 Where to Dine

Geneva is one of the gastronomic centers of Europe, with an unmistakable French influence. Genevese today take their dining seriously, and practice fine eating with consummate flair and style. Meals are frequently long, drawn-out affairs.

Naturally, Geneva serves all the typically Swiss dishes, such as filets of perch from Lake Geneva and fricassée of pork. In season, many of its restaurants offer cardoon, which is similar to an artichoke and is usually served gratiné. By all means, try the Genevese sausage, *longeole. Omble chevalier* comes from Lac Léman and is like a grayling, although some compare it to salmon.

Cheese is also a staple on the Genevese table, including such Swiss varieties as *tomme* and Gruyère, plus, in season, *vacherin* from the Joux Valley. Naturally, everything will taste better with the Perlan (white wine) and Gamay (red wine) from Geneva's own vineyards.

ON THE RIGHT BANK
VERY EXPENSIVE

Le Chat-Botté ✶✶✶ FRENCH   This grand restaurant is in one of the fanciest hotels in Geneva. Suitably decorated with tapestries, sculpture, and rich upholstery, with a polite and correct staff, it serves some of the best food in the city. There are some critics who consider it among the best restaurants of Europe. If the weather is right, you can dine on the flower-bedecked terrace, overlooking the Jet d'Eau. The meals are expensive but worth the price. The cuisine, although inspired by French classics, is definitely contemporary. Typical starters include delectable zucchini flowers stuffed with vegetables and essence of tomato; and lobster salad with eggplant "caviar," olive oil, and fresh herbs. Some of the most enticing items on the menu we've sampled include carpaccio with black olives and Parmesan cheese, poached wing of skate in an herb-flavored sauce, and oven-roasted Sisteron lamb with stuffed vegetables. The chef's best-known dish is a delicate filet of perch from Lake Geneva, which is sautéed until it's golden. Finish with one of the day's freshly made desserts, perhaps iced truffles in a nougatine casket.

In the Hôtel Beau-Rivage, 13, quai du Mont-Blanc. ☏ 022/716-69-20. Reservations required. Main courses 45SF–55SF ($24.75–$30.25). Fixed-price menus (Mon–Fri only) 60SF–145SF ($33–$79.75) at lunch, 115SF–145SF ($63.25–$79.75) at dinner. AE, DC, MC, V. Daily noon–2pm and 7–10pm. Bus: 6 or 33.

Le Cygne ✶✶✶ FRENCH   This restaurant is among the best in Geneva, with a decor of lacquered wood, beige and dark-orange velvet, and best of all, an exceptional view over the Geneva harbor to the Alps. It offers a refined cuisine with impeccable service. Plushly comfortable, Le Cygne is a showcase for the culinary skills of its outstanding chef, Philippe Jourdin. The menu changes seasonally and may offer such delightful choices as terrine of blackened chicken in a crawfish and anis-flavored aspic, served with a marinade of mushrooms in walnut oil; an earthy fish soup; smoked filet of sea bass sauced with a truffle-flavored vinaigrette; roast lamb with coriander and tomatoes stuffed with moussaka; and grilled filet of rabbit served with foie gras on a fondue of onions perfumed with fresh thyme. Five elaborate trolleys, each laden with a different roster of treats, combine to create one of the most spectacular arrays of desserts—perhaps the most spectacular—served in Switzerland.

In the Noga Hilton International, 19, quai du Mont-Blanc. ☏ 022/908-90-85. Reservations required. Main courses 40SF–65SF ($22–$35.75); fixed-price meal 61SF–81SF ($33.55–$44.55) at lunch, 79SF–139SF ($43.45–$76.45) at dinner. AE, DC, MC, V. Daily noon–2pm and 7–10:30pm. Closed 1 week in Jan, 11 days at Easter, and 3 weeks in July. Bus: 1.

Le Neptune ✶✶✶ SEAFOOD   At one of Geneva's finest seafood restaurants, the decor is intimate, intensely floral, and graced with an enormous fresco displaying an inside view of Neptune's kingdom. Although the kitchen closes on the weekend, during the week it entertains some of the most discerning palates in Geneva. The menu changes based on market conditions, but you're likely to

Where to Dine in Geneva

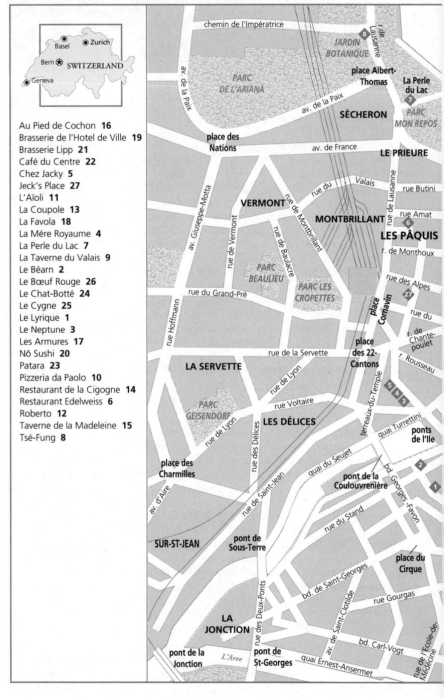

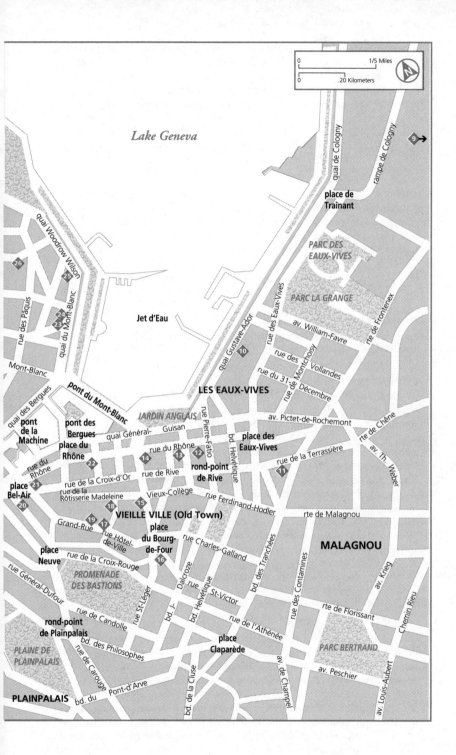

Lake Geneva

Jet d'Eau

PARC DES
EAUX-VIVES

PARC LA GRANGE

place de
Traînant

quai de Cologny

rampe de Cologny

9 →

26

25

24
23

rue des Pâquis

quai Woodrow Wilson

quai du Mont-Blanc

Mont-Blanc

pont du Mont-Blanc

quai des Bergues

pont
de la
Machine

pont des
Bergues

place du
Rhône

rue du
Rhône

place
Bel-Air

20

21

22

rue de la Croix-d'Or

rue de la
Rôtisserie Madeleine

JARDIN ANGLAIS

quai Général- Guisan

rue du Rhône

14

13

rue de Rive

rond-point
de Rive

quai Gustave-Ador

rue des Eaux-Vives

10

rue des Montchoisy

rue du 31 Décembre

LES EAUX-VIVES

av. Pictet-de-Rochemont

rue Pierre-Fatio

bd. Helvétique

place des
Eaux-Vives

12

rue de la Terrassière

11

Vollandes

rte de Frontenex

av. William-Favre

rte de Chêne

av. Th. Weber

18

15

Vieux-Collège

rue Ferdinand-Hodler

rte de Malagnou

MALAGNOU

19

17

VIEILLE VILLE (Old Town)

Grand-Rue

rue Hôtel-
de-Ville

place
du Bourg-
de-Four

16

rue Charles-Galland

place
Neuve

rue de la Croix-Rouge

PROMENADE
DES BASTIONS

rue St-Léger

bd. J.-
Dalcroze

rue
Helvétique

bd.
St-Victor

bd. des Tranchées

rue des Contamines

rue Général-Dufour

rue de Candolle

rond-point
de Plainpalais

PLAINE DE
PLAINPALAIS

bd. des Philosophes

rue de Carouge

bd. du Pont-d'Arve

PLAINPALAIS

rue de l'Athénée

place
Claparède

bd. de la Cluse

av. de Champel

rte de Florissant

av. Peschier

PARC BERTRAND

av. Krieg

Chemin Rieu

av. Louis-Aubert

0   1/5 Miles
0   .20 Kilometers

N

317

be offered such dishes as herbed vichyssoise with hazelnut oil and a dollop of foie gras, crawfish salad with a barnacle-flavored vinaigrette, cassolette of oysters seasoned with algae-flavored butter sauce, Atlantic sea bass roasted in a salt crust with thyme, filets of John Dory with a sauce made from whipped butter, and sea-urchin roe served with seafood-flavored pasta. If you're not in the mood for fish, you might enjoy such dishes as rack of Scottish lamb in puff pastry with spices and gray partridge roasted "en casserole" with autumn herbs.

In the Hôtel Mandarin Oriental du Rhône, 1, quai Turrettini. ℂ **022/909-00-06.** Reservations required. Main courses 45SF–65SF ($24.75–$35.75); fixed-price meal 68SF ($37.40) at lunch, 68SF–130SF ($37.40–$71.50) at dinner. AE, DC, MC, V. Mon–Fri noon–2pm and 7:30–10pm. Bus: 6, 8, 10, or 15.

Tsé-Fung ✦✦ CHINESE   Tsé-Fung is one of the best Chinese restaurants in Switzerland. The specialties are Pekinese, Szechuan, Cantonese, and even Mongolian, including marmite mongole, lacquered duck, and steamed fish with Chinese mushrooms. The restaurant continues to elicit adoration and salivation from is many devotees, often Asians who are frequently in Geneva on business. The chefs are so skilled here their meals might be called seductive. The healthy, clean, crisp flavors of each dish keep this restaurant an ongoing leader in its specialty niche. The restaurant is off the road to Lausanne at the Hôtel La Réserve (see "Where to Stay," earlier in this chapter) and has a terrace by the swimming pool. There's also a bar.

In the Hôtel La Réserve, 301, rte. de Lausanne. ℂ **022/774-17-41.** Reservations required. Main courses 48SF–140SF ($26.40–$77); fixed-price meal 50SF–125SF ($27.50–$68.75) at lunch, 80SF–125SF ($44–$68.75) at dinner. AE, DC, MC, V. Daily noon–2pm and 7–10pm.

EXPENSIVE

La Mère Royaume ✦ FRENCH   This is one of the oldest restaurants in Geneva, established around the turn of the century and graced with wooden paneling and stained-glass windows. The restaurant is named after a heroine who, in 1602, poured boiling stew over a Savoyard soldier's head and then cracked his skull with the kettle. With an antecedent like that, you'd expect some of the heartiest fare in Geneva, but instead the restaurant offers delicately cooked French specialties, such as *omble chevalier*—that delicate white fish from Lake Geneva—and a version of trout that has been pronounced divine. Try such tempting specialties as sea wolf in puff pastry, tender rack of lamb flavored with fresh tarragon, and in the autumn, savory game dishes such as venison and pheasant. The brasserie serves fondues, raclettes, filet of sole, shrimp with garlic, and some winning terrines.

9, rue des Corps-Saints. ℂ **022/732-70-08.** Reservations required. Brasserie, main courses 18SF–35SF ($9.90–$19.25); fixed-price menu 42SF–48SF ($23.10–$26.40). Restaurant, main courses 30SF–50SF ($16.50–$27.50); fixed-price menu 55SF–100SF ($30.25–$55). AE, DC, MC, V. Mon–Fri noon–2pm and 7–10:30pm, Sat 7–10:30pm. Bus: 4, 6, or 7. Tram: 13.

La Perle du Lac ✦ SWISS   Situated in a single-story pavilion owned by the city, this is the only restaurant in Geneva that's not separated from the waters of the lake by a stream of traffic. It's set beneath the venerable trees of Mon Repos Park, not far from the United Nations complex. Although the candlelit interior is lovely, you might want to reserve a table on the outdoor terrace in warm weather. A talented French chef prepares a marvelous mousseline of sweetbreads and champignons. Other specialties, each delectable, include line-caught, grilled sea wolf with fresh fennel and olive oil, and braised strips of fera (freshwater lakefish) flavored with saffron. Pigeon breast is another fine choice, served with duck liver and fresh apricots. Ravioli appears in an unusual version stuffed with fresh watercress. The sorbets—ask for a mixture—are superb. Year after year, meticulous cooking and the use of only the finest and freshest ingredients make this not only a satisfying choice but an eternal favorite.

128, rue de Lausanne. ℭ 022/731-79-35. Reservations required. Main courses 40SF–65SF ($22–$35.75). AE, DC, MC, V. Tues–Sun noon–2pm and 7:30–10pm. Closed Dec 22–Jan 25. Bus: 4 or 44.

MODERATE

Chez Jacky ⍟ *Finds* SWISS   This provincial bistro should be better known, although it already attracts everyone from grandmothers to young skiers en route to Verbier. It's the domain of Jacky Gruber, an exceptional chef from Valais. There's subtlety in Monsieur Gruber's cooking that suggests the influence of his mentor, Frédy Giradet, hailed as Switzerland's greatest chef before his recent retirement. You might begin with Chinese cabbage and mussels and continue with filet of turbot roasted with thyme or perhaps beautifully prepared pink duck on a bed of spinach with a confit of onions. Be prepared to wait for each course. The chef tirelessly seeks the most select produce for his imaginative and innovative dishes, and he continues to dazzle his regular clients year after year, winning new converts as well.

9–11, rue Necker. ℭ 022/732-86-80. Reservations recommended. Main courses 39SF–42SF ($21.45–$23.10); fixed-price meal 45SF ($24.75) at lunch; 58SF–86SF ($31.90–$47.30) at dinner. AE, DC, MC, V. Mon–Fri 11am–2pm and 6:30–11pm. Closed the 1st week of Jan and 3 weeks in Aug. Bus: 5, 10, or 44.

Le Boeuf Rouge LYONNAIS   Few other restaurants in Geneva's center work so hard to bring you an authentic version of the brasserie-style cuisine of Lyon. As such, you'll find such dishes as Lyonnais sausage with scalloped potatoes, chateaubriand in red wine sauce, blood sausage, and quenelles of pike-perch—any of which might be preceded by a delectable version of onion soup or green salad with croutons and bacon. The decor is appealingly kitschy, complete with lots of Art Nouveau posters and late 19th-century ceramics. The staff here is brusque, but kind.

17, rue Alfred-Vincent (corner of the rue Paquis). ℭ 022/732-7537. Reservations recommended. Main courses 29SF–49SF ($15.95–$26.95); fixed-price meal 35SF ($19.25) at lunch; 45SF–50SF ($24.75–$27.50) at dinner. AE, DC, MC, V. Mon–Fri noon–2pm and 7–10:30pm, Sat 7–10pm. Bus: 1.

Patara ⍟⍟ THAI   This is the most elegant and prestigious Thai restaurant in Geneva, occupying a street-level premises within the Beau-Rivage Hotel, and a position immediately adjacent to Le Chat Botté, one of the most elegant restaurants in town. Within a decor of teakwood carvings, Thai paintings, and soothing colors of blue-green, an impeccably dressed, mostly Thai staff will serve flavor-filled examples of the best of their country's cuisine. The best menu items include braised chicken in green curry with coconut milk; steamed sea bass in lime sauce; giant prawns with garlic and cilantro; and pan-fried filet of gilthead in a spicy basil sauce. There's also an interesting selection of food (asparagus and shiitake mushrooms in oyster sauce) for vegetarians. Dessert might include warm papaya pie with ginger-flavored ice cream.

In the Hotel Beau-Rivage, 13, quai du Mont-Blanc. ℭ 022/731-55-66. Reservations recommended. Set menu (minimum 2 diners) 85SF ($46.75) per person. Main courses 19SF–39SF ($10.45–$21.45). Mon–Fri noon–3pm, daily 7pm–midnight. Bus: 6 or 33.

INEXPENSIVE

Jeck's Place ⍟ PAN ASIAN   Near the Cornavin rail station, this place is a delight. It's like taking a culinary trip to southeast Asia, with stopovers in such places as China, Malaysia, Thailand, and India. Escaping from the traffic outside, you enter a warm and friendly enclave, where Jeck Tan of Singapore will greet you. The cuisine of Asian specialties provides temptation with every order, the trays of delicacies brought out by waitresses in sarongs. The specialties of the day will be seasoned with delicate blends of spices, notably lemongrass and curry but also chili and ganlaga (from the ginger family). It's not the dull beef sauté, for example, but a medley of delight in a sauce flavored with cloves, curry, cinnamon, coconut milk, and lemongrass. We often make a meal of the appetizers alone, including homemade steamed dumplings stuffed with a blend of pork and vegetables flavored with coriander. The house specialty, and our favorite dish, is Jeck's chicken in green curry. Another exotic treat is a delicate whiting spread with spicy lemongrass sauce and grilled on banana leaves.

14, rue de Neuchâtel. (C) 022/731-3303. Reservations recommended. Main courses 18SF–30SF ($11.25–$18.75). Special lunch platter 13SF ($8.15). Mon–Fri 11:30am–2pm and 6:30–10pm. AE, DC, MC, V. Bus: 4, 5, or 9.

ON THE LEFT BANK
EXPENSIVE

Le Béarn ★★★ FRENCH   Terribly sophisticated and terribly chic, this is a well-established culinary landmark with an impressive list of clients that includes the Aga Khan and the baron de Rothschild, along with various diplomats, politicians, and luminaries from the world of high finance and Hollywood. Jean-Paul Goddard, who is French from the Savoy region near Chambéry, and his excellent staff have created the best restaurant in the business center of Geneva. Everything is on a small scale as there are only 10 tables, and the service is personalized. The renovated interior contains two dining areas—one decorated in the Louis XVI style, the other with elegantly rustic accessories. Menu choices are carefully timed to coincide with the seasons, and include a lavish emphasis on whatever happens to be fresh (regardless of how esoteric) at the time of your visit. December, for example, will stress truffles, as many as 12 different varieties, that are used as garnishes and flavoring. Autumn game specialties include rabbit "à la Royale," a form of slow-simmered compôte bound together with blood and foie gras and served with fresh noodles. There's also roasted Scottish thrush, and such intriguing dishes as a platter with "three terrines of autumn" that combines rabbit, partridge, and thrush. Also look for delectable morels stuffed with fresh asparagus tips and such midsummer delicacies as a platter of "three gourmandises" that includes "essence" of lobster in liquid form, rillettes of crabs, and claws of Breton lobster all arranged artfully on the same plate. Desserts are appropriately stylish and sumptuous.

4, quai de la Poste. (C) 022/321-00-28. Reservations required. Main courses 30SF–65SF ($16.50–$35.75); fixed-price meal 55SF–160SF ($30.25–$88) at lunch, 90SF–160SF ($49.50–$88) at dinner. AE, DC, MC, V. Mon–Fri noon–2pm and 7:15–10pm, Sat 7:15–10pm. Closed July 15–Aug 10 and Sat June–Sept. Bus: 2, 10, or 22.

MODERATE

Brasserie de l'Hotel de Ville ★ *Finds* SWISS   This is one of the most deliberately archaic-looking restaurants in Geneva, with a reputation that goes back to 1764 and a clientele that prefers that absolutely nothing changes in either its old-fashioned decor or its choice of dishes. In spite of its look, it's rather hip and popular with the Genevois, as well as a growing number of arts-industry hipsters and affluent members of the bourgeoisie, who appreciate the place for its old-fashioned charm. Within a dining room loaded with antique or semi-antique kitsch, you'll be joined by antique dealers and clients from the local antique shops. The menu is more sophisticated and better than ever. Try the filets of freshwater lake perch meunière. Sometimes the prized fish of Lake Geneva, *omble*, is also served in a butter sauce. One old-fashioned dish remains on the menu, Longeole du val d'Arve (traditional Geneva-styled sausages flavored with cumin). You can also order such delights as rack of lamb flavored with herbs of Provence, along with a seasonal focus on asparagus, mushrooms, and game dishes. We always like to launch ourselves with a fresh dandelion salad with medallions of sautéed duck liver.

19, Grand Rue. ℂ 022/311-70-30. Reservations recommended. Main courses 33SF–48SF ($18.15–$26.40); fixed-price menus 57SF–104SF ($31.35–$57.20). AE, DC, MC, V. Daily 11:30am–11:30pm. Bus: 17.

Brasserie Lipp SWISS This bustling restaurant is named after the famous Parisian brasserie, and when you enter, especially at lunch, you'll think you've been transported to Paris. Waiters in black jackets with long white aprons are constantly rushing about with platters of food, here on the ground floor of a modern shopping complex. The menu contains a sampling of French bistro dishes.

Like its Parisian namesake, the Geneva Lipp specializes in several versions of charcuterie. You can also order three kinds of pot-au-feu and such classic dishes as a Toulousian cassoulet with confit de canard (duckling). The fresh oysters are among the best in the city. These dishes will not dazzle you with subtle nuances, and service is a bit frantic, but it appeals to all lovers of the old-fashioned French brasserie.

In Confédération-Centre, 8, rue de la Confédération. ℂ 022/311-10-11. Reservations recommended. Main courses 20SF–45SF ($11–$24.75); plats du jour 20SF ($11) lunch only; fixed-price menus 55SF–75SF ($36.85–$50.25). AE, DC, MC, V. Daily 11:45am–12:15am. Bus: 12.

Café du Centre *Kids* SWISS/CONTINENTAL This cafe is usually hysterically busy, and permeated with a kind of brusque anonymity. But despite its drawbacks, this remains very much an Old Geneva institution, established in 1871. Part of its charm comes from a location that's separated from the traffic-clogged quays by a clock tower of chiseled stone, and by dozens of flower stalls. Despite the thousands of cups of coffee and glasses of beer served here, it's more akin to a restaurant that serves drinks than a cafe that offers food. During nice weather, most of the business takes place outdoors on a terrace opening onto the square, while the rest of the year, business moves inside into a pair of street-level rooms whose nostalgic decor might remind you of an old-fashioned brasserie in Lyon. A thick, multilingual menu offers food items such as excellent versions of fresh fish as well as Wiener schnitzel, a savory version of onglet of beef, and pepper steak. Café du Centre offers an English-language menu of some 140 items—surely one of those will please your kids.

5, place du Molard. ℂ 022/311-85-86. Reservations recommended. Main courses 36SF–50SF ($19.80–$27.50); fixed-price assiette du jour 19.50SF ($10.75) at lunch Mon–Fri only. AE, DC, MC, V. Daily 7am–midnight. Tram: 12.

La Coupole SWISS This is a true brasserie—far more elegant than its Parisian namesake. The place is more popular at noon, especially with shoppers and office workers, than it is at night. Fanciful and fun, it's dotted with grandfather clocks, a bronze Venus, Edwardian palms, and comfortable banquettes. The menu is limited but well selected; the *cuisine du marché* (market place) is a delight, although many patrons stick to the standard old red-meat bistro specials such as the inevitable entrecôte.

116, rue du Rhône. ℂ 022/787-50-10. Main courses 34SF–44SF ($18.70–$24.20); fixed-price menus 52SF–72SF ($28.60–$39.60). AE, DC, MC, V. Mon–Sat 11:30am–2:30pm and 7:30pm–12:30am. Bus: 2, 9, or 22. Tram: 12.

Cheese, Cheese & More Cheese

Cheese making is an integral part of the Swiss heritage. Cattle breeding and dairy farming, concentrated in the alpine areas of the country, have been associated with the region for 2,000 years, since the Romans ate *caseus Helveticus* (Helvetian cheese). Today more than 100 different varieties of cheese are produced in Switzerland. The cheeses, however, are not mass produced—they're made in hundreds of small, strictly controlled dairies, each under the direction of a master cheese maker with a federal degree.

The cheese with the holes, known as Switzerland Swiss or Emmentaler, has been widely copied, since nobody ever thought to protect the name for use only on cheeses produced in the Emme Valley until it was too late. Other cheeses of Switzerland, many of which have also had their names plagiarized, are Gruyère, Appenzeller, raclette, royalp, and sapsago. The names of several mountain cheeses have also been copied, including *sbrinz* and *spalen,* closely related to the *caseus Helveticus* of Roman times.

Fondue   Cheese fondue, which consists of cheese (Emmentaler and natural Gruyère used separately, together, or with special local cheeses) melted in white wine flavored with a soupçon of garlic and lemon juice, is the national dish of Switzerland. Freshly ground pepper, nutmeg, paprika, and Swiss kirsch are among the traditional seasonings. Guests surround a bubbling *caquelon* (an earthenware pipkin or small pot) and use long forks to dunk cubes of bread into the hot mixture. Other dunkables are apples, pears, grapes, cocktail wieners, cubes of boiled ham, shrimp, pitted olives, and tiny boiled potatoes. Other fondues include fondue *bourguignonne* made with chunks of beef and red wine, preferably from Burgundy. Fondue *Chinois* has as its base a vegetable, herb, and meat-flavored bouillon, into which is dipped chunks of meat, usually beef, on long forks.

Raclette   This cheese specialty is almost as famous as fondue. Popular for many centuries, its origin is lost in antiquity, but the word raclette comes from the French word *racler,* meaning "to scrape off." Although raclette originally was the name of the dish made from the special mountain cheese of the Valais, today it describes not only the dish itself but also the cheese varieties suitable for melting at an open fire or in an oven.

A piece of cheese—traditionally half to a quarter of a wheel of raclette—is held in front of an open fire. As it starts to soften, it is scraped off onto one's plate with a special knife. The unique flavor of the cheese is most delicious when the cheese is hottest. The classic accompaniment is fresh, crusty, homemade dark bread, but the cheese may also be eaten together with potatoes boiled in their skins, pickled onions, cucumbers, or small corncobs. You usually eat raclette with a fork, but sometimes you may need a knife as well.

La Favola ✿ TUSCAN/ITALIAN   Don't expect anything large or standardized if you opt for a meal in this supremely ethnic, Tuscan-style restaurant. It's the best Italian restaurant in Geneva, and its most devoted habitués hail it as the best restaurant in Geneva, period. Set a few steps from the Cathédral de St-Pierre, it contains only two cramped dining rooms; the family-managed staff would be a lot more comfortable speaking Italian dialect than the clipped versions of French you're likely to hear in most other restaurants in Geneva. The menu is small and short but choice, varying with the availability of ingredients and the seasons. Look for such delightful dishes as carpaccio of beef; *vitello tonnato* (paper-thin veal with a tuna sauce); lobster salad; potato salad with cèpe mushrooms; such pastas as fresh ravioli with either eggplant or bolet mushrooms; and a luscious version of tortellini stuffed with ricotta, meat juices, red wine, and herbs. Meat and fish vary daily. Don't even think of coming here on weekends, as the place is locked tight. It contains seating for only 34 diners at a time, so advance reservations are key.

15, rue Jean-Calvin. ✆ 022/311-74-37. Reservations required. Main courses 40SF–55SF ($22–$30.25). AE, MC, V. Mon–Fri noon–2pm and 7:15–10pm. Closed 2 weeks in July–Aug and 1 week at Christmas. Tram: 12.

Les Armures ✿ *Kids* SWISS   In spite of the government-rated five-star elegance of the hotel that contains this restaurant, it is surprisingly unpretentious and affordable. Dining is possible on three different floors. The lower you go, the more animated the scene becomes. This stone building is located on a cobblestone street across from a medieval arsenal in one of the most colorful neighborhoods of the Old Town. The building was constructed in the 16th century, and this place has thrived as one of the most atmospheric restaurants since its founding in 1957. The three different fondues offered are the best in Geneva. Many Swiss children make an entire meal out of *rösti*, or Swiss-style hash browns. Other specialties include raclette and several pizza and pasta dishes. The winter-only sauerkraut garni is also a savory meal—made with several types of sausage and pork. In fact, the staff still remembers the day in January 1994 when Bill Clinton dropped in to sample their sauerkraut during a break in political negotiations. Pastas and hamburgers round out the menu here, which should make any child's palate happy.

1, rue des Puits-St-Pierre. ✆ 022/310-34-42. Main courses 20SF–45SF ($11–$24.75); fixed-price menu 48SF ($26.40). AE, DC, MC, V. Mon–Fri 8am–midnight, Sat–Sun 11am–midnight. Bus: 3 or 5.

Restaurant de la Cigogne ✿✿ CONTINENTAL   This is one of the most appealing and best-staffed restaurants on Geneva's Left Bank, with a growing clientele and a growing reputation for excellence. Classified as a member of the prestigious Relais & Châteaux group, it's housed within an opulently paneled ground-floor room of the also-recommended hotel. Cosseted, discreetly elegant, and cozy, with impeccable service, it offers a full bar, a spectacular wine list, and well-groomed cuisine. At lunch, the venue is a bit more businesslike and rapid, segueing into a more relaxed and leisurely venue at dinner. Menu items reflect whatever ingredients are in season at the time of your arrival, but are likely to include, among others, a superb ravioli of shrimp with a brunoise of vegetables and a mousseline sauce; turbot prepared *façon grand-mère;* and a delectable cordon bleu of veal stuffed with foie gras and truffles, served with a galette of polenta with Parmesan and asparagus. Desserts are rolled around aboard a spectacular-looking trolley.

In the Hotel de la Cigogne, 17, place Longemalle. ✆ 022/818-40-13. Reservations recommended. Main courses 43SF–53SF ($23.65–$29.15); set-price lunches 59SF–105SF ($32.45–$57.75); set-price dinners 105SF ($57.75). AE, DC, MC, V. Daily noon–2pm and 7–10pm. Closed Sat and Sun during July and Aug. Bus: 6 or 9.

Restaurant Edelweiss *(Kids)* SWISS This is the most famous folkloric, alpine-style restaurant in Geneva. It's set within the cellar of the also-recommended Edelweiss Manotel, an establishment that carries the alpine chalet theme into its bedrooms, and whose restaurant is the most artfully rustic within its neighborhood. Tables are lined up cozily under a very high ceiling that showcases the flagstone columns, the fluegelhorns, the cowbells, and the live folkloric bands that oom-pah-pah their way throughout the dinner hour. Rib-sticking menu items include six kinds of fondues, raclettes, roasted lamb chops with herbs, Zurich-style sliced veal in cream sauce; and several kinds of fish. If you have children, this might be a particularly worthy choice, because of the vast amounts of visual and folkloric distraction that add to the experience of dining here.

In the Edelweiss Manotel, 2, place de la Navigation. (✆ 022/544-51-51. Reservations recommended. Main courses 28SF–41SF ($15.40–$22.55); set menus 55SF ($30.25); children's platters 12SF ($6.60) each. AE, DC, MC, V. Daily 7–10:30pm. Bus: 1.

Roberto ITALIAN One of the most appealing Italian restaurants in Geneva occupies a relatively formal-looking dining room that's sheathed with wood paneling, mirrors, and a series of contemporary paintings by the restaurant's owner, Roberto Carugati. There's more here, however, than just artwork, as the food is delectable, flavored with the kind of Mediterranean sunshine that you'd expect from a midsummer trip to Italy. Menu items include such succulent pastas as tortelloni with chopped veal and a cream sauce; filets of turbot with béarnaise sauce; and scampi served with tarragon. Especially sought-after are the house versions of saltimbocca (veal with ham), osso buco (braised veal shanks), and *crespelle ai quattro formaggi* (Italian crepes with four kinds of cheeses).

10, rue Pierre Fatio. (✆ 022/311-8033. Reservations recommended. Main courses 30SF–50SF ($16.50–$27.50). AE, MC, V. Mon–Fri noon–2pm and 7:15–10pm, Sat noon–2pm. Bus: 8, 9, 12.

INEXPENSIVE

Au Pied de Cochon *(★) (Finds)* LYONNAIS/SWISS Named after a restaurant at Les Halles in Paris, this is the best place to go in Geneva for hearty Lyonnais fare if you don't mind the smoke and the noise. The setting is fin-de-siècle, with a staff dressed entirely in black and white. The bistro maintains its Lyonnais antecedents, which every Francophile knows are the most illustrious for fine brasserie-style food. A lot of young people, artists, and local workers are attracted here, as well as lawyers from the Palais de Justice across the way. The cooking is as grandmother used to prepare it, providing she came from the Lyon area. Naturally, the namesake *pieds de cochon* (pigs' feet) is included on the menu, along with tender alpine lamb, grilled angouillettes, and tripe.

4, place du Bourg-de-Four. (✆ 022/310-47-97. Reservations recommended. Main courses 27SF–40SF ($14.85–$22). AE, DC, MC, V. Daily 7:30am–2:30pm and 6:30pm–midnight (closed Sun June–Aug). Bus: 2 or 7. Tram: 12.

L'Aïoli *(Finds)* PROVENÇAL Named after the famous garlic sauce of Provence, this popular neighborhood restaurant stands opposite Le Corbusier's Maison de Verre. Something of a local secret, it offers personalized service and some of the finest Provençal cooking in town. Marius Anthoine, the owner, who hails from the Valais, founded the restaurant in 1987. An evening meal includes an appetizer, first plate, main dish, cheese, dessert, coffee, and wine (you can spend more by ordering a la carte). Among the featured dishes are lamb gigot, frogs' legs Provençal, and scampi Provençal. Monsieur Anthoine also makes a delectable pot-au-feu as well as beef ragoût. Look for the daily specials, such as a savory, Provence-derived lamb stew called *gardiane camarguaise.*

6, rue Adrien-Lachenal. ℂ 022/736-79-71. Reservations not required. Main courses 20SF–35SF ($11–$19.25); menu dégustation 73SF ($40.15). AE, DC, MC, V. Mon–Fri 11am–2:30pm and 7–10:30pm. Closed Aug. Bus: 1 or 6. Tram: 12.

Le Lyrique SWISS   Le Lyrique contains both a formal restaurant and a brasserie. The restaurant opened in 1981 but was cleverly patterned on turn-of-the-century models. It bustles with urban vitality and is very tuned to the arts and business lives of Geneva. Normally, the restaurant is completely closed on Saturday and Sunday, unless there's a special presentation at the Grand Théâtre de Genève, just a short distance away (in that event, the restaurant remains open). The brasserie, which has a terrace, is open all day but serves hot meals only during the hours mentioned below. In the restaurant, you can try such carefully prepared dishes as filet of sea wolf with grapefruit, a roulade of rabbit with pasta maison, and tagliatelle with scampi. In the brasserie, menu items include chicken supreme with ravioli and leeks, and an *assiette Lyrique,* a meal in itself that combines four vegetarian and fish dishes—tartare of salmon, tartare of vegetables, terrine of vegetables, and eggplant "caviar."

12, bd. du Théâtre. ℂ 022/328-00-95. Reservations recommended. Restaurant, main courses 25SF–40SF ($13.75–$22); fixed-price meal 50SF–62SF ($27.50–$34.10). Brasserie, main course 20SF–30SF ($11–$16.50); fixed-price menu 39SF–50SF ($21.45–$27.50). AE, MC, V. Mon–Fri noon–2pm and 6:30–10pm. Bus: 2 or 22.

Nô Sushi (Value) JAPANESE   Popular, hip, and mobbed every day at lunchtime, this is a large, high-ceilinged space devoted to a labyrinth of countertops that merge into the most bemused and whimsical Japanese restaurant in town. It would probably remind you of an old-fashioned luncheonette, except for a winding conveyor belt that exposes everything that's listed on the menu to the view of its clients. This is the only automated sushi bar in Switzerland, and as such, adds an eccentric and trend-conscious flair to a neighborhood that's better known for its relative conservatism. You'll know how much something costs by the color of the platter that contains it. You'll pluck everything except the miso soup, which is carried to your seat by a waitress, directly from the moving conveyor belt. Hot foods remain hot thanks to a candle flickering beneath. Sushi (with rice) and sashimi (without rice) choices include mullet, calamari, octopus, salmon, and tuna. There are also teriyaki dishes, tempura, and a medley of rice and noodle dishes, any of which you can combine into a full meal.

Confédération Centre, 8, rue de la Confédération. ℂ 022/810-39-73. Reservations not necessary. Sushi, sashimi, rolls, and small platters 5SF–10SF ($2.75–$5.50). AE, MC, V. Mon–Thurs 11:30am–midnight, Fri–Sat 11:30am–1am. Closed Sun. Bus: 12.

Pizzeria da Paolo ITALIAN/PIZZAS   Bustling, friendly, and completely unpretentious, this simple pizzeria offers more than 20 kinds of pizzas in a cozy, wood-sheathed setting close to the water jet that's the very symbol of Geneva. If pizzas aren't your thing (the house specialty is a Pizza Paolo, made from spinach and cheese), there is also a full complement of chicken parmigiana, stuffed and roasted turkey, fresh salads, ham dishes, and fresh fish. Don't expect glamour, just good value and some filling and very tasty Italian food.

3, rue du Lac. ℂ 022/736-3049. Reservations recommended. Pizzas 15.50SF–22SF ($8.55–$12.10); main-course platters 20SF–48SF ($11–$26.40). AE, DC, MC, V. Daily 11:45am–2pm and 6:45–11pm. Tram: 12.

Taverne de la Madeleine *(Value)* SWISS   Robust, unpretentious, and known for its no-nonsense approach to serving well-prepared, cost-conscious food, this restaurant—one of the oldest in Geneva—is set against the old city wall beside the Eglise de la Madeleine. The building is a century old, and the restaurant itself was established more than 80 years ago. If you're having difficulty finding the address, just circle the church, and the old three-story house will be on the corner of rue des Barrières. Inside are bistro tables, red cafe chairs, and a brusquely efficient staff catering to the lunchtime business crowd. The establishment is operated by a philanthropic organization that forbids the consumption of alcohol (alcohol-free beer is available). You can order a variety of well-prepared dishes. Specials include four types of pasta, vegetarian sandwiches, and such hearty fare as a big plate of osso buco with *pommes frites.* Menu items also include an émincé of Indian-style chicken with curry sauce and rice and piccata of turkey Milanese with tomato sauce and spaghetti. The kitchen also prides itself on its filet of lake perch prepared meunière style or Vevey style with exotic mushrooms.

20, rue Toutes-Ames. ✆ 022/310-60-70. Reservations recommended. Main courses 15SF–27SF ($8.25–$14.85); plat du jour 15SF ($8.25). MC, V. Sept–June Mon–Fri 7:30am–6:30pm (last food order at 4pm), Sat 9am–4:30pm (last food order at 2:30pm); July–Aug Tues–Sat 7:30am–9pm. Bus: 2. Tram: 12.

AT CAROUGE

A l'Olivier de Provençe *(★ Finds)* FRENCH   Set in Carouge, this Provençal restaurant offers some of the best dining on Geneva's perimeter. Though open throughout the year, it's especially popular in warm weather, when patrons can dine on its tree-shaded terrace. The savory dishes include flambéed versions of *loup de mer* (sea bass), ragoût of scampi, entrecôtes, *soupe de poisson,* and fresh salmon with sorrel. In autumn the restaurant is especially known for its game dishes, such as pheasant, rabbit, pigeon, and venison. A platter of guinea fowl appears in two different versions, both a supreme and a chartreuse of guinea with thighs, each served with fresh morels. In all, this is a good, bourgeois restaurant if you don't mind the slight excursion south of the city.

13, rue Jacques-Dalphin, Carouge. ✆ 022/342-04-50. Reservations required. Main courses 33SF–48SF ($18.15–$26.40); fixed-price menus 68SF ($37.40), 86SF ($47.30), and 98SF ($53.90). AE, V. Mon–Fri noon–2pm and Mon–Sat 7–10:15pm (closed Sat July–Aug). Tram: 12.

L'Ange du Dix Vins *(★)* CONTINENTAL   This is the best restaurant in Carouge, lying 3 miles south of Geneva, with a clientele that sometimes migrates from central Geneva just to dine here. Inside, you'll find an unpretentious decor that emulates old-fashioned France from the 1950s, with touches of Art Nouveau. The name derives from a complicated word game (if you speak French, ask a staff member), and the fact that the menu contains *dix vins* (10 wines) that change every few months or so. A succulent array of food items include lobster tails served with lime-flavored butter; half-cooked foie gras with fava beans; a bouillabaisse of lamb (that's right) with saffron and potatoes; and a supreme of guinea fowl with green beans and leeks. Set near Carouge's place du Marché, it places tables, parasols, and potted geraniums on the pavement during clement weather.

31, rue Jacques Dalphin. [tel.] 022/342-03-18. Reservations recommended. Main courses 28SF–42SF ($15.40–$23.10). Mon–Fri noon–2pm and 7–11pm. Closed: Sat–Sun. Tram: 12.

AT AIRE-LE-LIGNON

La Taverne du Valais *(★ Finds)* SWISS   This is the best and most appealing grill-style restaurant in the Geneva area. Loaded with alpine charm and rusticity, it lies in a quiet suburb about 4 miles southwest of central Geneva, surrounded with dining terraces and grape arbors. About 90% of the diners here opt for a charcoal brazier that's deposited directly atop your table, and upon which you'll grill whatever you order from the kitchen. The staff will bring out impeccably manicured portions of turkey, lamb, chicken, duck, fish, and/or calamari. A very fresh combination of them all is particularly succulent. With your main course come trays laden with a copious assortment of garnishes that include fruit chutneys, mustards, and tartar sauce; and sauces made from curry, paprika, basil, pimento, ginger, parsley, garlic, and red wine. Hardworking members of the Impala family are your hosts. This place has been a landmark, for both its ambience and its coziness, since 1967.

4, chemin des Sellières, Aire-Le Lignon. © 022/796-23-23. Main courses 37SF–43SF ($20.35–$23.65). AE, MC, V. Wed–Sun noon–2pm, Tues–Sun 7–10pm. Bus: 7, 18, 27.

5 Attractions

You can see most of Geneva on foot. The best way to familiarize yourself with the city, however, is by taking a walking tour, which covers all the major sights.

SUGGESTED ITINERARIES

If You Have 1 Day Begin the day by viewing the spectacular water fountain, the Jet d'Eau, and the Flower Clock in the **Jardin Anglais.** Then take a cruise of **Lake Geneva** on a steamer. Return in the early afternoon and explore the Left Bank's **Old Town.** Have dinner at a restaurant on place du Bourg-de-Four.

If You Have 2 Days Spend the first day as above. On the second day, visit some of the most important **museums** of Geneva, each completely different. It'll take a full day of sightseeing to absorb the most important: the Musée d'Art et d'Histoire, the Musée International de la Croix-Rouge et du Croissant-Rouge (Red Cross Museum), and the Palais des Nations.

If You Have 3 Days Spend the first 2 days as outlined above. On your third day, take our walking tour

of Geneva (see later in this chapter) in the morning, and in the afternoon go on one of the organized excursions to the Alps, including **Mont Blanc,** for a panoramic view.

If You Have 4 Days Spend the first 3 days as suggested above. By now you're an old hand at finding your way around Geneva, and you can use your last days for excursions. While still based in Geneva, take a lake steamer to **Lausanne** (see chapter 9). You'll have time to explore its Old Town and walk its lakeside quays at Ouchy before returning to Geneva in the evening.

If You Have 5 Days Spend days 1 to 4 as above. On the 5th day, take another lake steamer, this time to **Montreux** (see chapter 9); after visiting this lakeside resort, take a trip outside the town to see the **Château de Chillon,** immortalized by Lord Byron.

THE TOP ATTRACTIONS

In addition to the sites listed below, Geneva's other top attractions—all premier sights—are the **Jet d'Eau,** the famous fountain that has virtually become the city's symbol; the **Flower Clock,** in the Jardin Anglais, with 6,500 flowers; and **Old Town,** the oldest part of the city. All these sights, and more, are detailed in our walking tour, later in this chapter.

Geneva Attractions

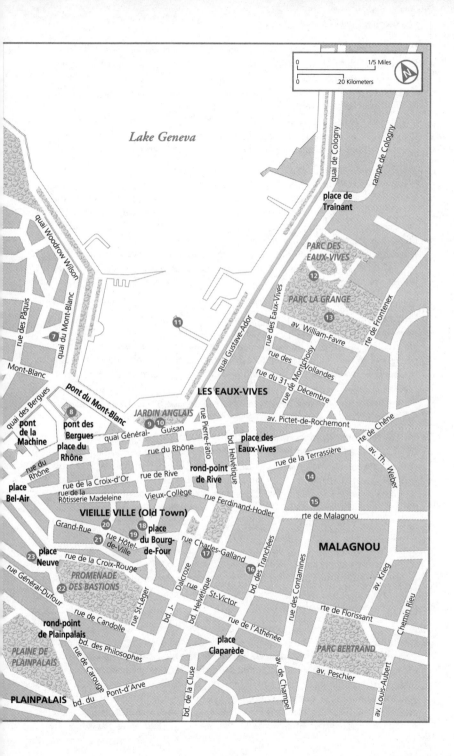

Lake Geneva

1/5 Miles
.20 Kilometers

N

quai de Cologny

rampe de Cologny

place de Trainant

PARC DES EAUX-VIVES

12

PARC LA GRANGE

13

av. William-Favre

rte de Frontenex

rue des Pâquis

quai Woodrow Wilson

quai du Mont-Blanc

7

rue des Eaux-Vives

11

quai Gustave-Ador

Mont-Blanc

pont du Mont-Blanc

LES EAUX-VIVES

rue des Vollandes

rue du 31-^e Décembre

rue de Montchoisy

av. Pictet-de-Rochemont

rte de Chêne

quai des Bergues

8

JARDIN ANGLAIS

9 10

Guisan

rue Pierre-Fatio

av. Th. Weber

pont de la Machine

pont des Bergues

quai Général-

bd. Helvétique

place des Eaux-Vives

rue de la Terrassière

place du Rhône

rue du Rhône

14

rue du Rhône

rue de la Croix-d'Or

rue de Rive

rond-point de Rive

15

place Bel-Air

rue de la Rôtisserie Madeleine

Vieux-Collège

rue Ferdinand-Hodler

rte de Malagnou

VIEILLE VILLE (Old Town)

Grand-Rue

20

18 place du Bourg-de-Four

MALAGNOU

place Neuve

23

19

rue Hôtel-de-Ville

21

rue Charles-Galland

17

rue de la Croix-Rouge

PROMENADE DES BASTIONS

22

rue St-Léger

Dalcroze

16

bd. des Tranchées

rue des Contamines

av. Krieg

rue Général-Dufour

rue de Candolle

bd. J.-

St-Victor

bd. Helvétique

rue de l'Athénée

rte de Florissant

Chemin Rieu

rond-point de Plainpalais

bd. des Philosophes

place Claparède

PARC BERTRAND

av. Louis-Aubert

PLAINE DE PLAINPALAIS

rue de Carouge

bd. de la Cluse

av. de Champel

av. Peschier

PLAINPALAIS

bd. du Pont-d'Arve

Musée Ariana ★★ Located to the west of the Palais des Nations, the Italian Renaissance building was constructed by Gustave Revilliod, the 19th-century Genevese patron who began the collection. Today it's one of the top porcelain, glass, and pottery museums in Europe. Here you'll see Sèvres, Delft faïence, and Meissen porcelain, as well as pieces from Japan and China. It's also the headquarters of the International Academy of Ceramics.

10, av. de la Paix. ℂ **022/418-54-50**. Admission: permanent collection, free; temporary exhibitions, 4.50SF ($2.50) adults; free admission for children under 18. Wed–Mon 10am–5pm. Bus: 8 or F.

MAMCO (Musée d'Art et Contemporain) ★ Some 20 years in the making, Geneva's first modern art museum opened in 1994. This prestigious showcase displays a vast collection of European and American art covering the last 4 decades. Out of some 1,000 works of art owned by the museum, only 300 are permanently on display. This space is packed with all the big names— Frankenthaler, Stela, Segal, and others. Some 1,600 square feet (480 sq. m) of space is set aside for exhibitions that change three times a year.

10, rue des Vieux-Grenadiers. ℂ **022/320-61-22**. Admission 8SF ($4.40) adults, 6SF ($3.30) children 13–18; free children 12 and under. Tues noon–9pm, Wed–Sun noon–6pm. Bus: 1 or 32.

Musée d'Art et d'Histoire (Museum of Art and History) ★★ At Geneva's most important museum, displays include prehistoric relics, Greek vases, medieval stained glass, 12th-century armor, Swiss timepieces, and Flemish and Italian paintings. The Etruscan pottery and medieval furniture are both impressive. A 1444 altarpiece by Konrad Witz depicts the "miraculous" draught of fishes. Many galleries also contain works by such artists as Rodin, Renoir, Hodler, Vallotton, Le Corbusier, Picasso, Chagall, Corot, Monet, and Pissarro.

2, rue Charles-Galland (between bd. Jacques-Dalcroze and bd. Helvétique). ℂ **022/418-26-00**. Free admission, 4.50SF ($2.50) temporary exhibitions. Tues–Sun 10am–5pm. Bus: 1, 3, 5, 8, or 17.

Musée International de la Croix-Rouge et du Croissant-Rouge (International Red Cross and Red Crescent Museum) ★ Here you can experience the legendary past of the Red Cross in the city where it started; it's across from the visitors' entrance to the European headquarters of the United Nations. The dramatic story from 1863 to the present is revealed through displays of rare documents and photographs, films, multiscreen slide shows, and cycloramas. You're taken from the battlefields of Europe to the plains of Africa to see the Red Cross in action. When Henry Dunant founded the Red Cross in Geneva in 1863, he needed a recognizable symbol to suggest neutrality. The Swiss flag (a white cross on a red field), with the colors reversed, ended up providing the perfect symbol for one of the world's greatest humanitarian movements.

17, av. de la Paix. ℂ **022/748-95-25**. Admission 10SF ($5.50) adults; 5SF ($2.75) students, seniors, and children. Wed–Mon 10am–5pm. Bus: 18, F, V, or Z.

Palais des Nations ★★ Surrounded by ancient trees and modern monuments, the buildings comprise the second-largest complex in Europe after Versailles. Up to 1936 the League of Nations met at the Palais Wilson. That year the League's headquarters was transferred to the Palais des Nations, which was inaugurated by the Aga Khan. The international organization continued minor activities through the war years until it was dissolved in 1946, just as the newly created United Nations met in San Francisco. Today the Palais des Nations is the European headquarters of the United Nations. A modern wing was added in 1973.

Fun Fact **Did You Know?**

- Geneva didn't enter the Helvetic Confederation until as late as 1815.
- Jean-Jacques Rousseau was born in Geneva in 1712, and his arch-rival, Voltaire, lived here from 1755 to 1759.
- During the Dark Ages, the kings of Burgundy made Geneva their capital.
- John Calvin, the reformer, settled in Geneva in 1536, turning it into the "Rome of the Protestants."
- Napoleon slept in the Old Town on May 9, 1800, and Geneva remained part of France until December 31, 1813.
- Geneva's annual Escalade celebration still commemorates a victory over the duke of Savoy's troops in 1602.
- Villa Montalegre in Cologny, outside Geneva, was the birthplace of the horror story *Frankenstein*.

Part of the interior is devoted to exhibitions showcasing the high-minded but ineffectual precursor of the United Nations, the League of Nations. Frequent tours, departing whenever the staff feels there are enough participants to justify conducting one, leave from the visitors' entrance at 14, av. de la Paix, opposite the Red Cross building. For information, contact the **Visitors' Service,** United Nations Office, 14, av. de la Paix (© **022/907-45-60**).

Parc de l'Ariana, 14, av. de la Paix. © **022/907-48-96**. Admission 8.50SF ($4.70) adults, 6.50SF ($3.60) students, 4SF ($2.20) for children 5 and under. July–Aug daily 9am–6pm; Sept–June daily 10am–noon and 2–5pm. Bus: 5, 8, 18, F, V, or Z.

MORE ATTRACTIONS
MUSEUMS

The Baur Collections 🐦   The collections, housed in a 19th-century mansion with a garden, constitute a private exhibit of artworks from China (dating from the 10th to the 19th century) and Japan (17th to 20th century). On display are ceramics, jade, lacquer, ivories, and delicate sword fittings.

8, rue Munier-Romilly. © **022/346-17-29**. Admission 5SF ($2.75) adults; free for children. Tues–Sun 2–6pm. Bus: 1 or 8.

Maison Tavel 🐦   Constructed in 1303 and partially rebuilt after a fire in 1334, this is the city's oldest house and one of its newest museums. The building has undergone several transformations over the centuries, before opening as a museum in 1986. The front wall is typically 17th century, with gray paint, white joints, and stone sculpted heads. The house contains a courtyard with a staircase, a 13th-century cellar, and a back garden. The museum exhibits historical collections from Geneva dating from the Middle Ages to the mid-19th century. The Magnin relief in the attic is outstanding, as is the copper-and-zinc model of Geneva in 1850, which is accompanied by a light-and-tape commentary. Objects of daily use are displayed in the old living quarters. Postcards, books, slides, and small guidebooks are available at the book stand.

6, rue du Puits-St-Pierre. © **022/418-37-00**. Free admission. Tues–Sun 10am–5pm. Bus: 3, 5, or 17.

Musée de l'Horlogerie (Watch Museum)   This town house chronicles the history of watches and clocks from the 16th century. It displays everything from sand timers to sundials, although most of the exhibits are concerned with the watches of Geneva, usually from the 17th and 18th centuries. The enameled watches of the 19th century are particularly outstanding; many have chimes that play when you open them.

15, rte. de Malagnou. ✆ 022/418-64-70. Free admission. Wed–Mon 10am–5pm. Bus: 6 or 8. Tram: 12.

RELIGIOUS MONUMENTS

The **Old Town** 🌟, or Vieille Ville, on the Left Bank, is dominated by the **Cathédrale de Saint-Pierre** 🌟, cour St-Pierre (✆ 022/311-75-75), which was built in the 12th and 13th centuries and partially reconstructed in the 15th century. Recent excavations have disclosed that a Christian sanctuary was here as early as A.D. 400. In 1536 the people of Geneva gathered in the cloister of St. Pierre's and voted to make the cathedral Protestant. The church, which has been heavily renovated over the years, has a modern organ with 6,000 pipes. The northern tower was reconstructed at the end of the 19th century, with a metal steeple erected between the two stone towers. If you don't mind the 145 steps, you can climb to the top of the north tower for a panoramic view of the city, its lake, the Alps, and the Jura Mountains.

To enter the St. Pierre archaeological site, called **Site Archéologique de St-Pierre,** go through the entrance in cour St-Pierre, at the right-hand corner of the cathedral steps. The underground passageway extends under the present cathedral and the High Gothic (early 15th-century) **Chapelle des Macchabées,** which adjoins the southwestern corner of the church. The chapel was restored during World War II, after having been used as a storage room following the Reformation. Excavations of the chapel have revealed baptisteries, a crypt, the foundations of several cathedrals, the bishop's palace, 4th-century mosaics, sculptures, and geological strata.

✆ Frommer's Favorite Geneva Experiences

Wine Tasting in the Countryside Winding your way through the rolling vineyards just outside Geneva makes for an enjoyable day's outing. Many of the best Swiss wines never leave the country, and grapes grow on slopes overlooking Lake Geneva and the Rhône. Pick up a brochure called *Discover Geneva and its Vineyards* from the tourist office and set out.

Sailing Lake Geneva The crescent-shaped lake, called Lac Léman locally, gives Geneva a resortlike ambience, stretching for 45 miles (72km). In the summer it's alive with activity: sailing, rowing, canoeing, water skiing, and more—and you can join in the fun.

Wandering Through Old Town Geneva's Vieille Ville has been called "Europe's best-kept secret." Exploring its ancient streets brings you to art galleries, antiques shops, booksellers, and tiny bistros. Follow the Grand Rue, where Jean-Jacques Rousseau was born, and wander back into time.

The cathedral and the chapel are open June to September daily from 9am to 7pm; March to May and in October daily from 9am to noon and 2 to 6pm; in January, February, November, and December daily from 9am to noon and 2 to 3pm. There is no admission charge to visit the cathedral, although donations are welcome; tower admission is 3SF ($1.65). Sunday service is held in the cathedral at 10am, and an hour of organ music is presented on Saturday at 6pm from June to September. The archaeological site is open Tuesday to Saturday from 11am to 1pm and 2 to 5pm; the admission charge is 5SF ($3.35) adults, 3SF ($1.65) students and seniors. Take bus no. 3, 5, or 17, or tram no. 12.

Next door to the cathedral is a Gothic church where Calvin preached, known as the **Temple de l'Auditoire,** or Calvin Auditorium. It was restored in 1959 in time for Calvin's 450th anniversary.

PARKS, GARDENS & SQUARES

If you walk heading north along the quays, you'll arrive at some of the lushest parks in Geneva. **Parc Mon-Repos** ★★ is off avenue de France and **La Perle du Lac** is off rue de Lausanne. Directly to the right is the **Jardin Botanique** (Botanical Garden), which was established in 1902. It has an alpine garden, a little zoo, greenhouses, and exhibitions, and can be visited free, May to September, daily from 8am to 7:30pm; and October to April, daily from 9:30am to 5pm.

You can take a boat to the other side of Lake Geneva and get off at quai Gustave-Ador. From there you can explore two more lakeside parks—**Parc la Grange,** which has the most extravagant rose garden in Switzerland (especially in June), and next to it, the **Parc des Eaux-Vives.**

When you leave the Botanical Garden on the Left Bank, you can head west, along avenue de la Paix, about a mile (about 1½km) north from the Pont du Mont-Blanc, to the Palais des Nations in the **Parc de l'Ariana.**

LES PAQUIS DISTRICT ★★

One of Geneva's most animated and elegant districts, **Les Pâquis** faces the harbor from the Right Bank of Lake Geneva. To reach it, head north along quai des Bergues, which leads into quai du Mont-Blanc. On your left, at the intersection of quai du Mont-Blanc and Gare Routière, stands the **Brunswick Monument,** the tomb of Charles II of Brunswick, who died in Geneva in 1873. The duke left his fortune to the city with the provision that it build a monument to him. Geneva accepted the fortune and modeled the tomb after the Scaglieri tombs in Verona.

Les Pâquis is a sector of cozy bistros, nightclubs, ateliers, elegant boutiques, and banks. The word *pâquis* comes from the Latin pascuum, "pasture." The cows that grazed here are long gone, but from about A.D.1330 the district consisted of a vast expanse of fields, pastures, and wastelands. It was far from the heart of the city and its protective ditches, and exposed to the permanent danger of invasion.

From the 14th century, as the city developed a stronger defense system, this unincorporated territory became safer, and more and more people made homes here. In the 15th century the Pâquis was home to potters and fisherfolk, and eventually homes and small industries began to take root.

In 1831, the French writer Chateaubriand settled at the **Hôtel des Etrangers,** 22, rue des Pâquis. From 1851 on, development was fairly rapid, with the construction of **quai du Mont-Blanc** and of the **Rotonde,** the English church. An American church was also constructed, and in 1857 **quais Pâquis** and **Eaux-Vives** were erected. Construction on the Cornavin railway station began the following year. The **Pont du Mont-Blanc** was erected in 1862. Soon, the lake promenade, the façade des Pâquis, and quai du Mont-Blanc became fashionable.

In 1873, construction began on the **Hôtel National** (Palais Wilson); from 1925 to 1936 it would house the first secretariat of the League of Nations. The Kursaal was built between 1874 and 1879. One of the most infamous events in the history of the area was the assassination of Empress Elisabeth of Austria, in 1898, at the landing stage facing the duke of Brunswick's mausoleum.

After wandering through the district with no particular fixed itinerary, visitors may tour Lake Geneva in a lake steamer. Steamers leave from quai du Mont-Blanc.

ESPECIALLY FOR KIDS

Geneva is a city with many attractions of interest to the younger set. The following are perhaps the coolest of the cool:

Visiting the **Musée International de la Croix-Rouge et du Croissant-Rouge** (Red Cross Museum) is like attending an adventure movie, as kids are enraptured by the sweep and drama of this heroic organization, which has always been near the "core of the action."

One of the best natural-history museums of Europe, the **Musée d'Historie Naturelle** delights children with its tropical birds, mammals, and exotic reptiles.

Jet d'Eau and the **Flower Clock** are exciting introductions for children. After viewing both of them, parents can take their kids for a tour by steamer on Lake Geneva.

FOR THE LITERARY ENTHUSIAST

At 25, rue des Délices, you'll find the house—now the **Institut et Musée Voltaire** (© **022/344-71-33**)—where Voltaire lived from 1755 to 1760 and from time to time after that up to 1765; he wrote part of *Candide* here. The museum displays furniture, manuscripts, letters, and portraits, as well as a terra-cotta model of the famous seated Voltaire by Houdon. The museum is open Monday to Friday from 2 to 5pm, and admission is free. Take bus no. 6, 7, 11, 26, or 27.

WALKING TOUR	GENEVA'S QUAYS & OLD TOWN

Start	Jet d'Eau.
Finish	Place du Bourg-de-Four.
Time	2 hours.
Best Times	Any sunny day.
Worst Times	Rush hours, Monday to Friday from 8 to 9am and 5 to 6pm.

Along the Quays If, like most tourists, you arrive in the summer, you might begin your discovery of the city with a long promenade along the quays of Geneva. The one sight you can't miss is the:

❶ Jet d'Eau

In the quai Gustave-Ador, this famous fountain is the trademark of the city. Visible for miles, from April to September it throws water 460 feet (138m) into the air above the lake. The Genevese call the fountain the *jeddo*. It dates from 1891, but was improved in 1951. Many cities have sent engineers to Geneva to study the workings of the fountain, although it remains a carefully guarded state secret. The fountain pumps 132 gallons of water per second into the air.

Walking Tour: Geneva's Quays & Old Town

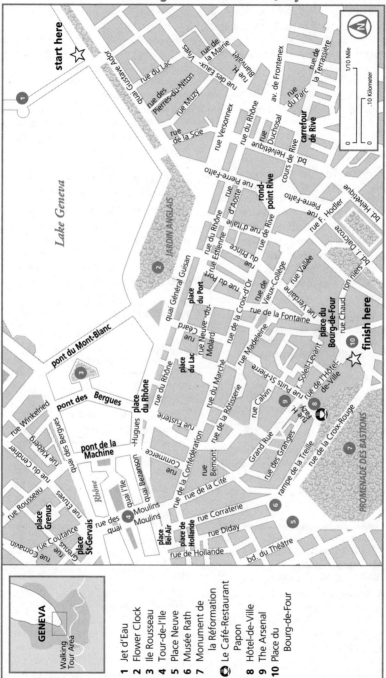

start here

finish here

Lake Geneva

Rhône

pont du Mont-Blanc

pont des Bergues

pont de la Machine

JARDIN ANGLAIS

PROMENADE DES BASTIONS

carrefour de Rive

rond-point Rive

place du Port

place du Rhône

place du Lac

place Bel-Air

place de Hollande

place Grenus

place St-Gervais

place du Bourg-de-Four

quai Gustave Ador

rue du Lac

rue des Pierres-du-Niton

rue Muzy

rue des Eaux-Vives

rue de la Mairie

rue H. Blanvalet

av. de Frontenex

rue du Parc

rue de la Terrassière

rue de la Scie

rue Versonnex

rue du Rhône

rue Duchosal

rue Helvétique

cours de Rive

bd. Helvétique

rue Pierre-Fatio

rue Pierre-Fatio

rue F. Hodler

bd. J. Dalcroze

rue d'Aoste

rue d'Italie

rue de Rive

rue Estienne

Tour du Molard

rue du Prince

rue Vieux-Collège

rue Vallée

rue Verdaine

quai Général Guisan

rue de la Croix-d'Or

rue de la Fontaine

rue Neuve-du-Molard

rue du Marché

rue de la Rôtisserie

rue Madeleine

rue Calvin

rue du Puits St-Pierre

rue Soleil-Levant

rue de l'Hôtel-de-Ville

rue Chaud-ronniers

rue de la Croix-Rouge

rue Céard

rue Fusterie

Grand Rue

rue des Granges

rampe de la Treille

rue de la Confédération

rue du Commerce

rue de la Cité

rue Bernont

rue Corraterie

rue Diday

bd. du Théâtre

rue de Hollande

quai Bezanson-Hugues

quai de l'Ile

rue des Moulins

Moulins

quai des Bergues

rue Coutance

rue Rousseau

rue du Cendrier

rue Winkelried

rue Kléberg

rue des Étuves

rue Cornavin

rue Grenus

N

1/10 Mile

0   .10 Kilometer

1 Jet d'Eau
2 Flower Clock
3 Ile Rousseau
4 Tour-de-l'Ile
5 Place Neuve
6 Musée Rath
7 Monument de la Réformation
☕ Le Café-Restaurant Papon
8 Hôtel-de-Ville
9 The Arsenal
10 Place du Bourg-de-Four

GENEVA

Walking Tour Area

Once you've seen the fountain, you'll be ready to explore the quays, with their gardens and ancient buildings. The aquatic population consists of seagulls, ducks, and swans. A fleet of small boats, called *mouettes genevoises,* shuttles visitors from one quay to another from spring until autumn.

Lying directly off quai du Général-Guisan is another Geneva landmark:

② Flower Clock

In the Jardin Anglais (English Garden), the clock's face is made of carefully landscaped beds of flowers, and it keeps perfect time! The Jardin Anglais is at the foot of the Mont Blanc Bridge, which spans the river at the point where the Rhône leaves Lake Geneva. The bridge was rebuilt in 1969.

Cross Pont du Mont-Blanc and turn left (south) along quai des Bergues on the Right Bank of Geneva until you come to the next bridge, called Pont des Bergues. If you cross this bridge you'll come to:

③ Ile Rousseau

A statue of the philosopher sculpted by Pradier in 1834 greets you here. The island, which was Rousseau's stomping ground and the site of many of his reveries, is now home to ducks, swans, grebes, and other aquatic fowl. Situated in the middle of the Rhône, it was once a bulwark of Geneva's river defenses.

Return to quai des Bergues and continue to walk left along the quay until you reach place St-Gervais and the:

④ Tour-de-l'Ile

A château was built here in 1219, although the tower is all that remains today. The château had been used as a prison and place of execution by the counts of Savoy. A wall plaque commemorates a visit by Caesar in 58 B.C. Once the fortified core of the Old Town, it bears some similarities to Paris's Ile de la Cité. You can also explore the old markets, which often exhibit the works of contemporary Genevese artists.

The walking tour of the quays is particularly good for children because the sights are outside and easily understandable. If the children get tired, however, you can take them to quai du Mont-Blanc, where they can board *le mini-train de Genève.* This 40-minute excursion will take them along the major parks and quays of Geneva. Departures April to October are daily every half hour from 9am to 5pm. Adults pay a fare of 8SF ($4.40) and children are charged 6SF ($3.30).

Through Old Town   At this point, you'll be on the doorway of Geneva's Old Town or Vieille Ville, set on the cultural Left Bank. The district is one of the most remarkable in Switzerland.

After leaving the Tour de-l'Ile, you can continue across the Rhône until you reach place Bel-Air, on the Left Bank. From here, head south for a short distance along rue de la Monnaie, which quickly becomes rue de la Cité. When that street changes its name to rue de la Tertasse, continue south along this street until you reach:

⑤ Place Neuve

This is the cultural heart of Geneva. The square has a statue of General Dufour, who was a cofounder of the Red Cross. Monuments on this square include the Grand Théâtre and the Conservatory of Music. The Grand Théâtre (opera house) was built in 1874 (see "Geneva After Dark," later in this chapter). The conservatory dates from 1858.

Also on the square is the:

⑥ Musée Rath

The museum, place Neuve (© 022/ 418-33-40), has temporary exhibitions of paintings and sculpture. It's open Thursday to Tuesday from 10am to 5pm, Wednesday from noon to 9pm, and costs 5SF ($2.75) adults, 3SF ($1.65) students and children. The museum can be reached by tram nos. 12 and 13, and bus nos. 3, 4, 5, 11, and 12.

From place Neuve, continue southeast along rue de la Croix-Rouge until you come to the:

⑦ Monument de la Réformation

The Reformation Monument was built in 1917 along a 16th-century rampart, beneath the walls of the Old Town on promenade des Bastions. The monument, which is 100 yards (91m) long, represents John Knox, Calvin, Théodore de Bèze, and Guillaume Farel—the four Genevese reformers. Other statues include Cromwell, the Pilgrim Fathers and, on either end, Luther and Zwingli.

Retrace your footsteps along rue de la Croix-Rouge until you return to place Neuve. From the square, take a sharp right and follow ramp de la Treille, which becomes rue Henri-Fazy, where you can:

TAKE A BREAK
One of the oldest and most venerated cafes of Geneva, Le Café-Restaurant Papon, 1, rue Henri-Fazy (✆ 022/311-54-28), lies near the Tour Baudet in the vicinity of the Hôtel-de-Ville. A restaurant, creperie, tearoom, and cafe, it has been entertaining drinkers and diners under its vaulted ceilings since the 17th century.

Turn right at rue de l'Hôtel-de-Ville and you'll approach the:

⑧ Hôtel-de-Ville (town hall)

The Hôtel-de-Ville is a short walk from the cathedral, and dates from the 16th and 17th centuries. Its Baudet Tower was constructed in 1455. The building, which has a cobblestone ramp instead of a staircase, has witnessed some of the city's most important diplomatic events. The Red Cross originated here in 1864.

Across from the town hall is:

⑨ The Arsenal

This arcaded structure dates from 1634. In the courtyard of the building is a cannon cast in 1683.

Continue along rue de l'Hôtel-de-Ville until you reach:

⑩ Place du Bourg-de-Four

This spot was first a Roman forum and later a medieval town square. The Palais de Justice here was built in 1707, but it has housed courts of law only since 1860. While you're in this area, you'll come across a fountain, many antiquaries' shops, and art galleries.

ORGANIZED TOURS
BUS & TRAM TOURS

If you're new in Geneva and want an easy-to-digest breakdown of the way the city is divided into various neighborhoods and districts, consider a tram tour. Departing from the south bank's Place du Rhône (May to September only), red-painted, open-sided trolley cars meander through neighborhoods that include the city's medieval center, the glossy shopping districts, and the hotel and museum-studded precincts of the river's north bank. Trams depart at 45-minute intervals every day between 9:30am and 6:45pm, last about an hour, and cost 7.90SF ($4.35) for adults and 5.90SF ($3.25) for children. For more information, contact **STT Trains Tours S.A.**, 36, bd. St-Georges (✆ **022/781-04-04**).

A 2-hour City Tour is operated daily all year by **Key Tours S.A.,** 7, rue des Alpes, square du Mont-Blanc (✆ **022/731-41-40**). The tour starts from the Gare Routière, the bus station at place Dorcière, near the Key Tours office. From November to March the tour is offered only once a day at 2pm, but from April to October two tours leave daily, at 10am and 2pm.

A bus will drive you through the city to see the monuments, landmarks, and lake promenades. In the Old Town you can take a walk down to the Bastions Park to the Reformation Wall. After a tour through the International Center, where you'll be shown the headquarters of the International Red Cross, the bus returns to its starting place. Adults pay 35SF ($19.25) and children 4 to 12 accompanied by an adult are charged 18.50SF ($10.20), while children 3 and under go free.

BOAT TOURS

The cold, clear waters of Lac Léman have attracted visitors for many generations. If you're interested in cruising on these waters (which never freeze, even in winter), at least two companies offer worthwhile tours. Your best bet involves determining how extensive you want your tour to be, and then selecting one whose duration corresponds to your schedule.

Regardless of which you select (see below), you'll enjoy sweeping waterside views of the ringing hills, bucolic calm, and some of the most famous vineyards in Switzerland, many of which seem to roll down to the historic waters. Because of bad weather and low visibility in winter, cruises only run between April and late October, and in some cases, only between May and September.

Two separate companies offer cruises along the lake. The smaller of the two, **Mouettes Genevoises Navigation,** 8, quai du Mont-Blanc (© **022/ 732-29-44**), specializes in small-scale boats carrying only about 100 passengers at a time. Each features some kind of guided (prerecorded) commentary, in French and English, throughout. An easy promenade that features the landscapes and bird life along the uppermost regions of the river Rhône draining the lake is the company's **Tour du Rhône** (Rhône River Tour). The trip originates at a point adjacent to Geneva's Pont de l'Ile, and travels downstream for about 9 miles (2 hr. and 45 min.) to the Barrage de Verbois (Verbois Dam) and back. Between April and October, departures are daily at 2:15pm, and also on Wednesday, Thursday, Saturday, and Sunday at 10am. It costs 22SF ($12.10) for adults and 15SF ($8.25) for children 4 to 12; it's free for children under 4. The same company also offers 1¼-hour tours (four times a day) and 2-hour tours (twice a day) out onto the lake. The longer tour includes a prerecorded commentary on the celebrity residences and ecology of the lake en route. These tours cost 12SF ($6.60) for the shorter tour and 22SF ($12.10) for the longer tour. No stops are made en route.

Mouette Genevoises Navigation's largest competitor, **CGN** (Compagnie Générale de Navigation), quai du Mont-Blanc (© **022/312-52-23**), offers roughly equivalent tours, in this case between May and September, that last an hour, departing four to six times a day (depending on the season) from the company's piers along quai du Mont-Blanc. Known as "Les Belles Rives Genevoises," they charge 12SF ($6.60) for adults and 6SF ($3.30) for children 6 to 16; children 5 and under ride free. Tours include prerecorded commentaries and are, frankly, about as long in duration as many short-term visitors to the city really want.

Although its hour-long cruises are popular, CGN devotes most of its time, energy, and money to hauling boatloads of commuters and sightseers between the ports that line the perimeter of the lake. They're conducted aboard larger craft that resemble seagoing ferryboats, and the experience is usually more workaday than the short cruises described above. None includes guided commentary. Despite that, many visitors appreciate the silence and the fact that CGN's larger boats each contains an attractive brasserie with uniformed waiters, starched linen, fixed-price menus at 30SF ($16.50) each, and affordably priced *assiettes du jour* (plates of the day). You can ask the sales staff at CGN to configure almost any tour along the lake that appeals to you, incorporating half-day stopovers and/or overnights in towns like Nyon, Lausanne, Vevey, Montreux,

Evian, Yvoire, and Thonon. Barring that, you can sign up for either of the prepackaged experiences (*grands et petits* tours of the lake) as described below. In most cases, CGN vessels depart from the piers beside quai du Mont-Blanc, but whenever the schedule warrants it, the departure might move 200 yards (182m) away, to the piers in the nearby Jardin Anglais.

The most comprehensive ride requires a full day: the **Tour du Grand Lac.** It departs every morning at 9am, pulls for very brief interludes into about half a dozen ports en route, and returns to Geneva that night at 8:45pm. A 2-hour stopover in Montreux, plus a leisurely lunch on board, is included as part of the experience. The round-trip circuit costs 73SF ($40.15) for adults and 36SF ($19.80) for ages 6 to 25; it's free for children 5 and under. A more recommendable, and more practical, tour is **Le Tour du Petit Lac,** which incorporates only the lower portion of the lake, including stops at Nyon (in Switzerland) and Yvoire (in France), and lasts for about half a day. It departs from quai du Mont-Blanc every morning at 9am and every afternoon at 2:30pm; another tour departs from Jardin Aylas at 10:30am. The round-trip cost is from 34SF to 47SF ($18.70–$25.85), depending on where you opt to sit in the boat (the upper level is expensive).

CGN also offers a tour that combines a lake cruise and a visit to the Château de Chillon with a return by train back to Geneva. Between June and September, a boat leaves from the Mont Blanc pier daily at 9:15am, arriving in Chillon at 2:15pm. During July and August an additional boat departs from the Jardin Anglais pier at 10:30am, arriving in Chillon around 3:50pm. Participants can visit the castle before taking a train or bus from the small station at Chillon to Montreux, and then transfer to one of the hourly trains from Montreux back to Geneva. Some visitors opt to dally in Montreux a while, perhaps remaining for lunch or dinner. The cost for the full round-trip excursion is 54SF ($29.70) in second class and 73SF ($40.15) in first class. For **more information,** call ✆ **022/312-52-23.**

A TOUR TO MONT BLANC ✿✿✿

If you have time, we highly recommend a Mont Blanc excursion, which is an all-day trip to Chamonix by bus and a cable-car ride to the summit of the Aiguille du Midi (12,610 ft/3783m). The tour leaves Geneva at 8:30am and returns at 6pm daily. Buses leave from the bus station (Gare Routière). You must take your passport with you.

Other mechanized ascents which are part of this tour are to Vallée Blanche by télécabin, an extension of the Aiguille du Midi climb, from April to October; to Mer de Glâce via electric rack railway to the edge of the glacier, from which you may descend to the ice grotto (the climb is not available in the winter); and to Le Brevent, an ascent by cable car to a rocky belvedere at 7,900 feet (22,370m), facing the Mont Blanc range. Lunch is included.

An English-speaking guide will accompany your bus tour. **Key Tours S.A.,** 7, rue des Alpes (place du Mont-Blanc; Case Postale 1745), CH-1211 Genève (✆ **022/731-41-40**), operator of the excursions, requires a minimum of eight people per trip. Tours range from 88SF ($48.40) for adults and 48SF ($26.40) for children.

6 The Active Vacation Planner

Like most cities in health-conscious Switzerland, Geneva has many sports facilities. However, locals often pursue activities outside the city. They're more interested in following their own personal sports program than they are in spectator sports, except for soccer, which is played in various stadiums. (Matches are announced in the tourist office's monthly "List of Events.")

The big spectator event of the year, a soccer tournament known as the **Bol d'Or,** takes place sometime in June (the Swiss National Tourist Office abroad will provide exact dates).

The world's most important **lake regatta** attracts approximately 600 sailboats and more than 3,500 competitors. The lake is virtually covered with white sails. It takes 7 hours for the luckiest to sail from one end to the other—and more than 24 hours for the unluckiest. But participants from all over the world swear it's worth trying.

BIKING   Cyclists consider the Geneva countryside a paradise. What could be better than a ride through forest, vineyard, and cornfield? The most passionate bikers climb Bernex's hill or cross the border into France (bring a passport). See "Getting Around," earlier in this chapter, for details about renting a bike.

GOLF   The best course is **Golf Club de Genève,** route de la Capite at Cologny (© **022/707-48-00**), which is an 18-hole course open March to December Tuesday to Sunday from 8:30am to 12:30pm and 2 to 6pm. Greens fees are 150SF ($82.50) for 18 holes. This is a private course but often allows nonmembers to play, preferably those associated with golf courses in their home countries. Always call about admission before heading here, however. There is also an on-site pro shop.

HEALTH CLUB   **Silhouette Health & Fitness,** 4, rue Thalberg (© **022/ 732-77-40**), is the most comprehensive, best-equipped, and most sociable health club in Geneva. Set very close to the grand hotels (Hotel de la Paix, Hotel Beau-Rivage, Hotel Richemond) of the Right Bank, it welcomes temporary visitors to the city for a fee of 20SF to 27SF ($11 to $14.85), depending on the day of the week and time of day you arrive. Expect everything from aerobics to free weights, with every other kind of health and exercise machine as well. It's open Monday to Friday from 9am to 9pm; Saturday and Sunday 10am to 5pm.

JOGGING   In addition to the many trails that have been laid out in the parks, you can also jog along the quays and the lakeshore beaches. The best places for jogging are Parc Bertrand, Parc des Eaux-Vives, and Parc Mon-Repos.

SAILING   This is the most popular sport in Geneva. All along the quays in the summer you'll find kiosks offering sailboats for rent.

SKIING   In the winter the people of Geneva flock to the resorts of the Haute Savoie in France, notably Chamonix and Megève. Each resort is about an hour's drive from Geneva. The smaller, lesser-known French resort of Flaine is even closer to Geneva. In Switzerland itself, the place nearest Geneva where there's good skiing is the Glacier of Les Diablerets or the resort of Champéry.

SWIMMING   In summer, swimmers usually head for the beaches along the lake. The most popular of these is **Geneva Beach** (Genève Plage), Port Noir (© **022/736-24-82**), where you can swim from 9am to 7pm for 7SF ($3.85).

TENNIS   Tennis somehow seems more invigorating in the sunshine and sometimes brisk mountain air near the French Alps. An option for tennis in Geneva would be the courts at **Le New Sporting Club,** 47, rte. de Collex (© **022/774-15-14**).

7 Shopping

From boutiques to department stores, Geneva is a shopper's dream come true. The city, of course, is known for its watches and jewelry, but it's also a good place to buy embroidered blouses, music boxes from the Jura region, cuckoo clocks from German Switzerland, cigars from Havana (not allowed into the United States), chocolate, Swiss army knives, and many other items.

Geneva practically invented the wristwatch. In fact, watchmaking in the city dates from the 16th century. Be sure to avoid purchasing a Swiss watch in one of the souvenir stores. If jewelers are legitimate, they'll display a symbol of the Geneva Association of Watchmakers and Jewelers. Here, more than in any other Swiss city perhaps, you should be able to find all the best brands, including Vacheron & Constantin, Longines, Omega, and Blancpain, to name just a few. Sometimes there are discounts on such items as cameras. Most salespeople you'll encounter speak English and are very helpful.

A shopping spree might begin at **place du Molard.** Once this was the harbor of Geneva before the water receded. Merchants from all over Europe used to bring their wares to trade fairs here in the days before merchants immigrated to richer markets in Lyon.

If you walk along rue du Rhône and are put off by the prices, go 1 block south to rue du Marché, which in various sections becomes rue de la Croix-d'Or and rue de Rive, and is sometimes referred to by locals as "la rue du Tram" because of the many trolleys which run along its length. Don't be afraid to comparison-shop in Geneva—many stores jack up prices for visitors.

Store hours vary in Geneva. Most stores are open Monday to Friday from 8am to 6:30pm and Saturday from 8am to 5pm.

ANTIQUES

Ars Nova *Finds*   By anyone's estimate, this is the best shop in Geneva for Art-Deco paintings, sculptures, furniture, carpets, and decorative accessories produced in France between 1920 and the outbreak of World War II. Owner Beatrice Hermann is an authority on the period that many connoisseurs consider sublime. The store is in the heart of Geneva's medieval core. 6, rue Jean-Calvin. ✆ 022/311-86-60.

Ernest Schmitt and Co. Antiquities   This store beautifully displays English furniture in the ground-floor rooms of an 18th-century private house. Much of the furniture is from the 18th and 19th centuries, much of it English, and there's also a wide display of antique silver from the same era. Be sure to ask the owner to take you across the cobblestone courtyard to see the other showrooms. 3, rue de l'Hôtel-de-Ville. ✆ 022/310-35-40.

AUCTIONS

The city has some of the world's most famous auction houses, with sales taking place mostly in May and November. During these periods, myriad social events accompany the auctions. Moreover, the city is an important center for the world art market and hosts prominent art and antiques dealers. Details and venues of sales appear in the tourist office's monthly "List of Events."

Antiquorum   This is the largest repository of antique time pieces in the world, with a reputation that's known to connoisseurs throughout the world. Virtually all of its inventory consists of antique jewelry and antique watches—a sure attraction in this city. Almost everything is sold at auction, rather than over the counter. The array of watches includes some of the most historically important watches in the world. 2, rue du Mont-Blanc. ℂ **022/909-28-50.**

Christie's   Geneva has always attracted some of the wealthiest tourists in the world, and to satisfy their craving for world-class art and antiques, they often attend the showcases and auctions of Christie's Auction House. Along with its leading competitor, Sotheby's (see below), it's one of the most glamorous art and antiques emporia in Europe. 8, place de la Taconnerie. ℂ **022/319-17-66.**

Sotheby's   If there's a rare medieval triptych for sale, or a unique collection of 18th-century silver, it's likely to be auctioned at Sotheby's. Rivaled in glamour only by the company's branches in Paris and London, the Geneva branch offers an insight into some of the most unusual art and art buyers in town. 13, quai du Mont-Blanc. ℂ **022/908-48-00.**

CHINA
Aux Arts du Feu   Founded in 1897, this waterside store sells fine crystal, porcelain, china, silver, and decorative objects from around the world. 18, quai du Général-Guisan. ℂ **022/311-35-21.**

CHOCOLATES
Confiserie Rohr   The aroma from this chocolate store practically pulls you in off the street. Among other specialties, you'll find chocolate-covered truffles, "gold" bars with hazelnuts, and *poubelles au chocolat* (chocolate "garbage pails"). 3, place du Molard. ℂ **022/311-63-03.** This establishment maintains another store at 42, rue du Rhône (ℂ **022/311-68-76).**

CLOTHING
Addison   This is the best men's wear store within the sprawling, multi-level shopping mall known as the Confédération Centre. Inside, you'll find salesmen who tend to remember many of their former clients, a sense of personalized intimacy, and enough suits and blazers to outfit any of the well-tailored business meetings of Geneva. Confédération Centre, rue du Marché at place Bel-Air. ℂ **022/312-33-50.**

Anita Smaga   Its garments are as expensive as they are elegant, and its clientele includes some of the best-heeled women in the world. The look is grand chic couture (and haute couture), but, depending on your taste, there might be an accessory or two appealing to your sense of whimsy. 51, rue du Rhône. ℂ **022/310-26-55.**

Chanel   Whatever a woman's taste in clothes, and whatever her age, there's nothing that makes her look better than Chanel. Despite the passage of time, the look can usually be identified at a glance, and remains dear to the hearts of stylishly mature women everywhere. This branch in the heart of Geneva's most glamorous shopping district keeps the tradition alive. 43, rue du Rhône. ℂ **022/311-08-62.**

Les Créateurs   This boutique is well known to many women who consider a sexy, black cocktail dress an essential part of their wardrobe. Within a cosmopolitan, multilingual temple to European chic, you'll find inventories by Gucci and its imitators, knitwear specialist Chacok, and Paris-based couturier Azzadine Alaïa. 100, rue du Rhône. ℂ **022/311-51-42.**

DEPARTMENT STORES
Bon Genie   Located on place du Molard, this department store sells mostly high-fashion women's clothing. Its storefront windows display art objects from

local museums alongside designer clothes. There's also a limited selection of men's clothing, as well as furniture, cosmetics, and perfumes. 34, rue du Marché. *©* 022/818-11-11.

Magazine zum Globus This is one of the largest department stores in Geneva, with many boutique-style departments that flourish inside and a self-image that's firmly patterned after the upscale Galeries Lafayette in Paris. Expect glamour, lots of upbeat cheerfulness, and departments devoted separately to travel bureaus, an agency selling theater tickets, a hairdresser, newspaper kiosks, and a bistro and sandwich shop/cafe. 48, rue du Rhône. *©* 022/319-50-50.

GIFTS

Come Prima Our favorite Geneva shop benefits from a spectacular array of gift and leather items, as organized by a hardworking entrepreneur (Myriam Krieger-Demetriadès) whose personality permeates every aspect of the place. Officially, she runs a boutique loaded with top-quality leather bags and carry-alls, as well as one-of-a-kind wooden puzzles. There are also teddy bears from Germany, folk-style cushions embroidered in Hungary, hyper-stylish umbrellas, and classically tasteful table decorations. 17, rue de la Cité (place Bémont). *©* 022/310-77-79.

Edgar Affolter's Swiss Tradition *(Value* Although this place identifies itself as a souvenir shop, its collection of watches is extensive, often at prices less expensive than you might have found within more glamorous and sophisticated-looking shops. Expect lots of cuckoo clocks, wood carvings, tablecloths, and T-shirts, as well as items from the Swiss military line of watches. 17, rue du Mont-Blanc. *©* 022/731-65-44.

JEWELRY/WATCHES

Bucherer Located opposite the Mont Blanc Bridge, this chrome-and-crystal store sells deluxe watches and diamonds. The store offers such name brands as Rolex, Piaget, Ebel, Baume & Mercier, Omega, Tissot, Rado, and Swatch. The carpeted third floor is filled with relatively inexpensive watches. You'll also find a large selection of cuckoo clocks, music boxes, embroideries, and souvenirs, as well as porcelain pill boxes and other gift items. 45, rue du Rhône. *©* 022/319-62-66.

Gübelin Jewelers Dating from 1854, this family-run establishment is known mainly for its brand-name watches, although it also sells beautiful precious stones and jewelry in 18-karat gold. You'll see two perpetual-motion clocks in the windows, giving chronological as well as astrological time, with fanciful enamel notations of the different time zones. You can also buy reasonably priced gifts, such as pen and pencil sets. 1, place du Molard (60, rue du Rhône). *©* 022/310-86-55.

L. Scherrer Located on the most prestigious street in Geneva, this elegant store, founded in 1955, sells a good selection of watches, diamonds, and gems. The polite staff caters to an elite clientele. 29, rue du Rhône. *©* 022/819-07-07.

LEATHER

Hermès Like all Hermès boutiques, this store sells purses, leather accessories, diaries, jewelry, watches, ready-to-wear clothing, furs, and, naturally, the famous Hermès scarf, priced at 370SF ($247.90) each, and tie. Everything is beautifully hand-crafted. 43, rue du Rhône. *©* 022/311-76-77.

LINENS

Leinen Langenthal Established over a century ago, this store boasts an enviable reputation for good-quality merchandise and a showroom on the city's most

The Land of Time

August 8, 1535   The Protestant Reformation arrives in Geneva. A mob forcibly evicts the Catholic archbishop who, in his haste, forgets his watch. Today it's a prime exhibit in Geneva's watch and clock museum.

1541   In the wake of the Reformation, French-born Jean Calvin introduces the Protestant work ethic and welcomes exiled Protestant craftsmen from throughout Europe. Many are watchmakers and jewelers. Alas, ostentatious jewelry is outlawed in the tightly controlled new community, and jewelers' efforts must be funneled somewhere. No zealot ever claimed that a watch wasn't an essential part of any God-fearing man's wardrobe, so the ban against jewelry formed the base of what would eventually become the premier watchmaking center in the world.

1601   A watchmaker's guild enforces rules that regulate the watchmaking industry. Obligations include public prayers before each assembly of the guild, and that each watch be signed or marked as the work of a specific craftsperson.

1707   A Swiss is appointed watchmaker to the court of the Chinese emperor K'ang-Hi in Peking. Swiss compatriots fan out across the globe, creating markets in places such as the Ottoman court in Istanbul, where business booms with baubles destined for the sultan's harem.

Around 1750   Julien Le Roy, celebrated Paris-based watchmaker to the king of France, complains bitterly that the watchmakers of Geneva are flooding southern France with "their accursed watches."

1780   Most of Geneva's St. Gervais district, behind the present-day Grand Hôtel des Bergues, and 5,000 employees are devoted to the town's biggest industry, watchmaking. The town's most expensive real-estate rentals are always on the fifth and sixth floors of cramped and narrow town houses, where the light is brightest. The neighborhood's most famous child? Jean-Jacques Rousseau, whose father trained him in Plutarch and the Roman classics by night and made watches by day.

1880   Gustav Flaubert, the greatest novelist of 19th-century France, compiles a list of pithy sayings (*Idées Réçues*). His definition of "pocket watch" was "suitable only if it was made in Geneva."

Today   Thousands of technical developments and a rigorous attention to quality have made Switzerland the leading watchmaker in the world, a title it has held for more than 400 years. Although Hong Kong and Japan produce greater numbers of watches today, Switzerland produces the greatest number of upscale watches and the most complicated watches, and receives an estimated 55% of all funds worldwide spent on consumer purchases of watches. In the 1990s, Switzerland produced 98 million watches and watch movements worth $5.3 billion (U.S.) at wholesale. You can buy everything from watches worth a millionaire's ransom to "fun watches," "disposal watches," watches designed for deep-sea diving or parachute jumping, all kinds of chronometers and measuring devices, and— newest of all—eco-watches crafted from recycled aluminum cans.

prestigious shopping street, across from the Union des Banques Suisses. Merchandise includes napery, towels, bed linens, and "table suites," some of it embroidered by hand in the Swiss lace center of St. Gallen. 13, rue du Rhône. © 022/310-65-10.

PICTURE FRAMES

Berndt's *(Finds* Never judge a picture by its frame? That's not entirely true, according to this purveyor of antique frames, any of which could suitably adorn that old-master portrait you happened to pick up on your prior trip to Geneva. The store's buyers cull the auction houses of Europe for their inventory of antique lacquered, gilded, painted, carved, or silvered frames. Most frames range in price from 2,500SF to 10,000SF ($1,375–$5,500), although some simple unpretentious ones cost 125SF ($68.75). Some of the frames at this shop are new but carefully distressed to look as antique as possible, and sell for a lot less money. 34–36, Grande-Rue. © 022/311-74-85.

SHOES

Bruno Magli This is one of the best-stocked shoe stores in Geneva, with an elegant variety of Italian shoes, purses, and accessories. Shoes for both women and men are scattered over one floor, modeled in many ways on the outfit's Fifth Avenue showroom in New York City. 47, rue du Rhône. © 022/311-53-77.

SILVER

Au Vieux Canon Its specialty is antique English silver, most of it crafted during the 19th and early 20th centuries, and most of it culled from estate sales held throughout the United Kingdom. Also look for 19th-century Viennese bronzes, depicting everything from Europe's great composers to whimsical nymphs waving garlands of flowers. Granted, you might be able to buy an equivalent item for less money if you haul it back from London, but the inventory is elegant and the setting is appropriately opulent. 40, Grande-Rue. © 022/310-57-58.

TOBACCO

Davidoff This is the most famous tobacco store in the world, with the best cigars you'll find in Europe. This is the place where the Davidoff retail empire all began. For many years, this was the business headquarters of Zino and Marthe Davidoff, White Russian émigrés who arrived in Switzerland in 1911. When they were in their 60s, with the help of a marketing expert (Dr. Schneider) from Basel, they eventually spearheaded a chain of upscale cigar stores that now extends throughout Europe and the Americas. 2, rue de Rive. © 022/310-90-41.

TOYS

Jouets Weber *(Kids* This member of a worldwide chain has been selling children's toys and adults' pastimes for at least 150 years from a location at the corner of rue de la Fontaine. Everything, from computer toys to simple playthings carved from wood by craftspeople in the Alps and Asia, is available. Adults appreciate such *jeux de société* (parlor games) as Pictionnari, priced at 79SF ($52.95), which will improve both your social skills and your French-language vocabulary. 12, rue de la Croix-d'Or. © 022/310-42-55.

8 Geneva After Dark

Geneva has more nightlife than any other city in Switzerland. Most activity centers around **place du Bourg-de-Four,** a stagecoach stop during the 19th century. In the Old Town there are lots of outdoor cafes in the summer. But if you get bored, you might consider going into France, which, because Switzerland limits bets to 5SF ($2.75), attracts most of Geneva's serious gamblers. There's gambling at Divonne, France, 12½ miles away.

THE PERFORMING ARTS

Geneva has always attracted the culturally sophisticated, including Byron, Jean-Baptiste, Corot, Victor Hugo, Balzac, George Sand, and Franz Liszt. Ernst Ansermet founded Geneva's great **Orchestre de la Suisse Romande,** whose frequent concerts entertain music lovers at **Victoria Hall.** For opera there's the 1,500-seat **Grand Théâtre,** which welcomes Béjart, the Bolshoi, and other ballet companies, in addition to having a company of its own.

For a preview of events at the time of your visit, pick up a copy of the monthly "List of Events" issued by the tourist office.

Grand Théâtre de Genève   Modeled on the Paris Opéra, this building was opened in 1879. It burned down in 1951 and was subsequently rebuilt in the same style, except for the modern auditorium, which has a seating capacity of 1,488. From September to July, it presents eight operas and two ballets, as well as recitals and chamber-music concerts. Place Neuve. ℂ **022/418-31-30.** Tickets, 25SF–148SF ($13.75–$81.40) for opera, 20SF–125SF ($11–$68.75) for ballet.

Victoria Hall   This 1,866-seat hall is the home of the celebrated Orchestre de la Suisse Romande. This is Geneva's most famous musical institution, whose interpretations have been heard throughout the world. For 50 years it was conducted by Ernst Ansermet and, through this maestro, had close associations with Igor Stravinsky. 14, rue du Général-Dufour. ℂ **022/328-81-21.** Tickets 18SF–58SF ($9.90–$31.90).

THE CLUB & MUSIC SCENE

Arthur's Club   The hyper-modern decor here is as appealing as anything else to open in Geneva in years, but despite that, the venue remains fun, unpretentious, and committed to preserving a healthy balance of clients between the ages of 18 and 45. Inside, 10 different bars manage to attract subcultures of their own, so regardless of your age or preferences you'll eventually find something or someone that appeals to you. On busy nights, expect as many as 2,500 people, many of whom dance, dance, dance, crammed inside. The location is near the Geneva airport (take bus 10 from the center). Centre I.C.C., 20, rte. des Près-Bois. ℂ **022/791-77-00.** Cover 25SF ($13.75), including first drink. Fri–Sun 11pm– 5am.

Au Chat Noir *Finds*   In the suburb of Carouges, this is the current hot spot in town, a venue for funk, rock, salsa, jazz, and some good old New Orleans blues. It's crowded on weekends but the club will take reservations. Live music is presented nightly at either 9 or 10pm. After a few drinks, you begin to fear that the car suspended from the ceiling might fall in on you. 13, rue Vautier, Carouges. ℂ **022/343-49-98.** Cover 10SF–15SF ($5.50–$8.25). Mon–Thurs 6pm–4am, Fri 6pm–5am, Sat 9pm–5am, and Sun 9am–4am. Tram: 12 from place Bel-Air in central Geneva.

Club 58   This private club does allow nonmembers to enter, although men are required to wear jackets. It has become increasingly popular with people from the developing world, many of whom have settled more or less permanently in Geneva. Occasionally the club presents some top names in show business. Drinks in the club cost 18SF to 25SF ($9.90–$13.75). Club 58 is mainly a disco, but it has a restaurant attached. 15, Glacis de Rive. ℂ **022/735-15-15.** Cover 5SF–15SF ($2.75–$8.25). Club opens daily at 10pm; restaurant opens at 8pm.

Griffin's Club Griffin's is the chic choice in Geneva. Technically it's private—you may or may not get in, depending on the mood of the management at the time of your visit. If you're "correctly dressed" and "correctly behaved," you have a good chance, more likely Monday to Thursday. The popularity of nightclubs comes and goes, but the collection of celebrities who have traipsed here reads like a who's who from the tabloids. Jackets are required for men. The decor is red and black, with lots of live plants and large paintings in the restaurant where main courses are priced at 30SF to 55SF ($16.50–$30.25). 36, bd. Helvétique. C 022/735-12-18. No cover. Restaurant open nightly 7:30pm until at least 3:30am. Disco open 11pm–5 or 6am, depending on the night of the week. July–Aug the entire premises are closed every Sun and Mon.

Le Dancing de la Coupole In one of the downtown area's most popular brasseries, La Coupole, this disco and dance hall focuses most intently on retro music of the 1960s. Whisky begins at 15SF ($8.25); beer, at 8.50SF ($4.70). Tram: 12. 116, rue du Rhône. C **022/787-50-12.** No cover. Tues–Sat 5pm–2am.

L'Interdit Hip and well-organized, with just the slightest trace of cynicism, this is a well-known pickup bar where a gentleman who's looking for female companionship will probably find it. Security is tight, and the clientele is affluent (or at least it does a realistic imitation of appearing to be so) and international. There's a prominent bar area, a dance floor, and a decorative theme that includes cavorting nymphs, satyrs, and references to ancient Greece and Rome. 18, quai du Seujet. C **022/738-90-91.** Cover 20SF ($11), including first drink. Open nightly 10:30pm–5am.

Velvet Within its genre, this is a safe and well-recommended nightclub, especially popular with tourists, but it isn't for the timid, and unless you're an unusually brazen woman or firmly attached to an attentive male escort, it's more appropriate for men. It's very heterosexual, very permissive, and loaded with working women waiting for a visitor to buy them a drink. In most instances, its tawdrier aspects are rather artfully concealed, although that's a tall order for a place where, beginning around 11pm, as many as 32 international beauties, many of them topless, begin strutting their stuff in a nonstop, informally choreographed spectacle that continues, on and off, till around 5am. It lacks the artistic flair of Crazy Horse or Moulin Rouge in Paris though. There's a restaurant and a disco on the premises, as well as a master/mistress of ceremonies who gives shape and form to the cabaret. Drinks begin at 19SF ($10.45), but usually average around 24SF ($13.20) each. 7, rue du Jeu-de-l'Arc. C **022/735-00-00.** No cover Sun–Thurs, 10SF ($5.50) Fri–Sat. Open nightly 10pm–5am. Restaurant closed Sun, but not the cabaret and bar.

THE BAR SCENE

Most bars in Geneva close at 1:30 or 2am.

Le Francis Bar This fashionable bar, often a venue for the *le tout Geneve* or "cream of the crop" of Geneva, becomes an attractive piano bar in the evening. Whisky with soda ranges from 17SF to 25SF ($9.35–$13.75). Live piano music begins at 10pm. 8, bd. Helvétique. C **022/346-32-52.**

Le Jardin *Finds* Although technically functioning as the apéritif bar for the adjacent restaurant, this place is an attractive option in its own right. Naturally, it attracts a chic and sometimes stuffy crowd, ranging from Texas ranchers to Zurich bankers to glamorous women in $50,000 furs. The Napoleon III decor includes crystal chandeliers and velvet chairs. In the Hôtel Richemond, Jardin Brunswick. ℂ 022/715-77-20.

Mr. Pickwick Pub *Value* This pub serves simple, English-style meals, but most patrons come here to drink. The paneled rooms are filled in the evening with a young crowd, who enjoy the dim lighting and American music. The place gets very crowded and can be fun. Irish coffee is a specialty, but most visitors order beer. In Geneva this pub is sometimes called the "Tower of Babble" because of all the languages spoken here (many employees of the United Nations hang out here). 80, rue de Lausanne (corner of rue Rothschild). ℂ 022/731-67-97.

THE GAY & LESBIAN SCENE

Many lesbian groups meet for political and social consciousness-raising at the **Centre Femmes Nathalie Barney** (Le Maison), 30, av. Peshier, in the district of Champel (ℂ 022/797-27-14). It's the most visible and best-organized outlet for gay women in French-speaking Switzerland, and is named for Nathalie Barney, a well-known lesbian liberationist who ran a memorable salon in Paris at the turn of the century. Several nights a week, different social and political gatherings are organized. The organization maintains a restaurant open for group dinners only on designated nights of the week and a women's bar open only on Friday and Saturday nights.

The equivalent for men is Geneva's gay switchboard, **Dialogai,** 57, av. de Wendt, in the district of Servette (ℂ 022/906-40-40). It provides multilingual information and advice to anyone who calls. On the basement level are a library, a cafe and bar, and meeting rooms for Wednesday-night dinners and Saturday-night dance parties. The organization publishes a free list of the gay bars in Geneva and French-speaking Switzerland, and is the best access to the male homosexual network of Geneva. It schedules discussion groups for gay youths and gay senior citizens, and it also offers support groups for people who are HIV positive.

Le NewLoft, 20, quai du Seujet (ℂ 020/38-28-28), is a large, campy, and convivial nightclub and cabaret that derives 90% of its business from heterosexuals, despite (or perhaps because of) an emphasis on drag acts as part of its nightly entertainment. It evokes a Carnival every night it's open, thanks partly to the hostess-related skills of its Dutch-born owner, nightlife entrepreneur Marisa Allen. It opens every day for breakfast (7:20–11am), lunch (noon to 2pm), and dinner (8–11pm) but its real heart and soul aren't visible until around 10:15pm, when the cabaret begins. Then, you'll pay a cover charge of 20SF ($11) to watch a bevy of multi-gendered entertainers, magicians, and musicians strut their stuff before an energetically appreciative audience. Set menus at dinner cost from 65SF to 120SF ($35.75–$66) per person, focusing on an international menu.

Another hot spot on the gay scene is **Thermos,** 19, rue Goetz Monin (ℂ 022/320-72-65), a basement bar that draws many local students as well as foreign visitors in pursuit of them. A summer terrace across from the bar is the scene of a Thai/Japanese restaurant, **L'Elephant & Sumo.** Later diners return to the Thermos for action in the darkened back room, which even contains a queen-size bed.

Le Kid, 99, bd. Carl-Vogt (ℂ 022/320-44-96), is a popular gay-oriented cafe and restaurant specializing in vegetarian cuisine. In the university area, it is open all day. **Le Pretexte,** 9, rue du Prince (ℂ 022/310-14-28), has a dance floor and two bars, plus a trio of areas with different themes, including Italian, baroque, and Asian. It is the most visible gay disco in town. Big and highly visible within a commercial street on the lake's southern shore, it closes whimsically whenever there isn't enough biz, and—other than every Friday and Saturday—it has erratic hours.

9 Easy Excursions from Geneva

There are many attractions in the region around Geneva. Several of the most popular places—at least around the lake—have been covered in chapter 9, on Lausanne and Lake Geneva. Refer to that chapter for highlights around the lake itself. This section will deal with the attractions that are closest to Geneva.

MONT SALÈVE 𝒢
The limestone ridge of Mont Salève (House Mountain) is 4 miles south of Geneva, in France. Its peak is at 4,000 feet (1,200m), but you'll need a passport to get near it. If you have a car, you can take a road that goes up the mountain, which is popular with rock climbers. Bus no. 8 will take you to Veyrier-Douane, on the French border, where there's a passport and Customs control. A 6-minute cable-car ride will take you to a height of 3,750 feet (1,125m) on Mont Salève. From there you'll have a panoramic sweep of the Valley of the Arve, with Geneva and Mont Blanc in the background.

CAROUGE 𝒢
Carouge, a suburb of Geneva, is a historic European town. It dates from the 18th century, when it was built by the king of Sardinia to rival Geneva. Architects from Turin supplied the Piedmontese charm. At the Congress of Vienna, in 1815, Carouge was annexed to the canton of Geneva. Once Carouge was the playground of smugglers and gold washers who panned for the precious metal in the Arve. The Genevese themselves—at least those who wanted to escape from the puritanical city—came here in search of decadence.

Switzerland now considers Carouge a national landmark because of its architecture. It can be reached from Geneva by tram 12 from the center. Begin your exploration in the Market Square, with its old fountain, plane trees, and markets. A Roman stone was imbedded in the Church of the Holy Cross. As you walk around, you'll pass the court of the count of Veyrier's palace, dating from 1783; place du Temple, with a fountain from 1857; and a Louis XVI carved door at 18, rue St-Victor.

COLOGNY
Byron and Shelley both lived in the residential suburb of Cologny, where they met at the Villa Diodati in 1816. Nine miles northeast of Geneva, the suburb is served by bus A from the city. The view of the lake and the city is especially good from the "Byron Stone" on chemin de Ruth (Ruth's Path) leading to the Byron fields.

The best time to go to Cologny is on Thursday afternoon (between 2 and 6pm), when you can visit the **Bodmeriana Library,** 19–21, rte. du Guignard (© **022/707-44-33**), a foundation established by a Zurich millionaire named Martin Bodmer. The private collection contains first editions, rare manuscripts, and objets d'art.

COPPET
Located 9 miles (15km) north of Geneva in the canton of Vaud, this little town on the western shore of Lake Geneva is one of the most interesting destinations in the region.

From Geneva's main station take the NYN train for a 20-minute ride to the Chateau de Coppet in Coppet. Tickets cost 10SF ($6.70) round-trip. If you're driving, head north from Geneva along Route 2.

Château de Coppet ⚑ (☎ 022/776-10-28) attracted some of the greatest minds of the 18th and 19th centuries. The château, which sits on a hill beside the lake, between Lausanne and Geneva, was purchased in 1784 by Jacques Necker, the rich and powerful finance minister of Louis XVI. His daughter was Madame de Staël—a great French woman of letters, who was eventually sent into exile for her opposition to Napoleon. The château is still owned by Necker's descendants. The museum contains some mementos of Madame de Staël. From April through June and September and October, the chateau is open daily from 2 to 6pm. During July and August, it's open daily from 10am to noon and from 2 to 6pm. Between November and March, it's closed. Admission costs 10SF ($5.50) for adults, 8SF ($4.40) for students and senior citizens, 5SF ($2.75) for children 6 to 16. It's free for children 5 and under.

A noteworthy local hotel, an elegant place with only 19 units and a well-recommended restaurant, is the **Hotel du Lac,** Grand-Rue, CH-1296 Coppet (☎ **022/776-15-21**).

Lucerne & Central Switzerland

Lucerne (Luzern in German) and its lake lie in the heart of Switzerland, where the tops of the mountains are covered with eternal snow and their sides flanked with glaciers. We're in William Tell country now, where the seeds that led to the Swiss Confederation were sown. It was near Brunnen, in the meadow of Rutli, that the Everlasting League of 1315 was created.

Despite the presence of many small resorts in the neighborhood, Lucerne is the district's largest and busiest city. The lake that nurtures it is the fourth largest in Switzerland, 24 miles (39km) long and (at its broadest) 2 miles (3km) wide. Geologists refer to it as the terminal basin for the nearby glaciers. The lake is known in German as Vierwald-stättersee and in French as the Lac des Quatre Cantons. Either way, it's the lake of the four cantons: Lucerne, Uri, Unterwalden, and Schwyz (from which Switzerland derives its name).

Lucerne and its lake are among the most popular tourist destinations in all of Europe. Paddle-steamers service the many cable cars and lidos (beaches) set at the edge of the water, providing sweeping views of mountains with names like Pilatus and Rigi along the way. The region is rich in panoramas, folklore, and sports such as tobogganing, skiing, hill climbing, ice-skating, and curling. The irregular geography of the brusquely vertical limestone and granite outcroppings make the shoreline one of the most romantic sites in Switzerland.

1 Lucerne ★★★

31 miles (50km) S of Zurich, 56 miles (90km) E of Bern

Lucerne is a tourist favorite partly because it embodies the storybook image of a Swiss town. Located at the north end of the lake, the city abounds in narrow cobblestone streets, slender spires and turrets, covered bridges, frescoed houses, and fountains. Its residents are quick to tell you that you're "never very far from the snow"—Mounts Rigi and Pilatus form the southern gate to the city, and the snowcapped Alps loom in the distance.

Lucerne's strategic gateway to the south and the rich markets of Italy lie between Rigi and Pilatus. The city's history has always been tied to the St. Gotthard Pass. During the 13th century, the routes leading to it were simple mule paths. By 1820, the road had been widened enough to allow the easy passage of carriages. By 1882, Lucerne had a railway tunnel. Once a satellite vassal of the Hapsburgs, in 1332 Lucerne became the first city to join the Swiss Confederation. Unlike Geneva and Zurich, Lucerne did not support the Reformation and has always remained a stronghold of Catholicism.

The city is a renowned cultural center. Richard Wagner spent several of his most productive years in Tribschen, on the outskirts of Lucerne (there's a Wagner museum here). Arturo Toscanini was a founder of the Lucerne International

Festival of Music, one of the most important musical events in Europe, which takes place annually in August and September.

The residents of Lucerne are a sports-oriented people. Every summer there are international rowing regattas on Rotsee. Swimmers go to the lido (lake beach) and golfers head for the 18-hole golf course on the outskirts. Other sports include tennis, hiking, and mountaineering. Residents seem especially fond of horse races, and there are plenty of international jumping contests.

You'll find Lucerne at its best on Tuesday and Saturday mornings, when it becomes a lively market town. The markets are sheltered by stately arcades on both banks of the Reuss River.

ESSENTIALS

GETTING THERE   Lucerne lies at the junction of four major rail lines, which connect it by fast train with every other major city of Switzerland. Travel time from Bern on one of the many express trains is 90 minutes; from Zurich, 50 minutes. Call ℂ **157-22-22** (no area code) for **rail schedules.**

If you're driving from Bern, take Route 10 north and east. From Zurich head south and west along E41, turning southwest and following the signs at the junction with N14.

VISITOR INFORMATION   The **Lucerne Tourist Office** is at Franken-strasse 1 (ℂ **041/227-17-17**). It's open in summer, Monday to Friday from 8:30am to 6pm, Saturday from 9am to 5pm, and Sunday from 9am to 1pm. During winter, hours are Monday to Friday 8:30am to noon and 2 to 5pm, Saturday 9am to 1pm.

CITY LAYOUT

Most arrivals are at the railroad station, on **Bahnhofplatz,** where trains pull in from Zurich and other parts of Switzerland. This train depot is on the south bank of the Reuss River.

If you cross a bridge from the station square, you'll be on the north bank at **Schwanenplatz** (Swan Square), which is the center of Lucerne. Also on the north bank of the Reuss is **Altstadt** (Old Town), containing many burghers' houses with oriel windows and old squares with fountains. The only way to explore this area is on foot.

Kapellgasse is a major shopping street that leads to the **Kornmarkt** (Corn Market) where you'll find the Altes Rathaus (Old Town Hall), dating back to 1602. To the west of the Kornmarkt is the **Weinmarkt** (Wine Market), a lovely old square with a much-photographed fountain.

The Kursaal, a casino-and-restaurant complex, stands at Kurplatz on **National-quai,** the major quay of Lucerne facing the lake.

From Kurplatz, Löwenstrasse leads to **Löwenplatz,** site of the Panorama, a famed canvas depicting the retreat of the French army during the Franco-Prussian War (1870 to 1871). Nearby stands the even-more-famous Löwendenkmal (Lion Monument), the town's best-known monument.

GETTING AROUND

Lucerne has an efficient network of local buses, one ride on which costs from 2SF to 5SF ($1.10–$2.75), depending on the distance you ride. Buy your tickets at automatic vending machines before you board. A ticket that's valid for a full day costs 10SF ($5.50); a ticket valid for a full week goes for 22SF ($12.10). For more information about **bus routes** within Lucerne, call ℂ **041/369-66-00.**

Bikes can be rented at the railway station for 27SF ($14.85) per day between 7am and 7:45pm daily. A bike trip along the north shore of Lake Lucerne can be one of the scenic highlights of a visit to central Switzerland. This trip can easily absorb a whole day (take along a picnic lunch). The tourist office will provide a map and you can set off from the Lucerne train station heading for St. Niklausen and Kastanienbaum in the direction of Tribschen. If you have time, visit the Richard Wagner Museum. The most beautiful stretch is along the lake to Winkel-Horw beach where you can go for a brisk lake swim if the temperature is right. The duration of this 8-mile (13km) ride, including the return to Lucerne, should take about 1½ hours.

SEEING THE SIGHTS

The best panoramas are the views from one of Lucerne's nine lookout towers. Part of the old fortifications erected along the north side of the medieval sector, they were all built in a different style between 1350 and 1408. At twilight they stand in dramatic silhouette against the sky. The nine towers are known as the **Museggturme,** but you can climb only three of them. Admission is free, and they're open only from May until the beginning of October from noon to 8pm daily. You can also take a short walk on the old outer wall of the city.

Although our only walking tour (see below) is for the independent traveler, guided walking tours are also available; see the tourist office (see "Visitor Information" above) for more details. These tours cost around 15SF ($8.25). In summer, tours depart Monday to Saturday (except holidays) at 10am; in winter, tours are conducted only Wednesday and Saturday at 9:30am.

SPECIAL EVENTS

The **Lucerne International Festival of Music** is held from August 16 to September 15. For more information, contact the International Festival of Music at Hirschmattstrasse 13, CH-6002 Luzern (© **041/226-44-00**). The **Easter Festival Lucerne** is another popular event. There's also a **summer night festival** on August 12 with fireworks, music, and festivities along the lake, as well as an annual **Carnival** before Ash Wednesday.

WALKING TOUR	LUCERNE

Start	Schwanenplatz.
Finish	Kurplatz.
Time	2½ hours.
Best Times	Any sunny day.
Worst Times	Rush hours, Monday to Friday from 8 to 9am and 5 to 6pm.

The best way to see Lucerne is on foot, going along its lakeside quays, across its old squares, and through the streets of its old town.

Start in the heart of Lucerne at:
❶ Schwanenplatz
Translated as Swan Square, it lies on the north bank of the Reuss River and is reached by crossing the bridge, the Seebrücke, from Bahnhofplatz on the south bank, site of the train station.

Adjoining the square on the west is:
❷ Kapellplatz
This is the site of St. Peter's Church. The church, the oldest in Lucerne, was built in 1178. In the center of the square is a fountain commemorating Carnival revelry in Lucerne.

From here, continue west along a major shopping street, Kapellgasse, until you reach the:

❸ Kornmarkt

This is the old Grain Exchange or "Corn Market," which is today the site of the:

❹ Altes Rathaus (Old Town Hall)

A Renaissance building from 1602, the town hall has impressive masonry, a tremendous roof, and a tall rectangular tower. The tower is a good vantage point from which to survey the crowded market scene on Tuesday and Saturday mornings.

To the left of the town hall is the:

❺ Am-Rhyn-Haus

This 17th-century building houses a Picasso collection (described below). The town house is entered at Fürrengasse 21.

After leaving the museum, follow Rathausquai east toward Schwanenplatz again, but only to cross the:

❻ Kapellbrücke (Chapel Bridge)

The symbol of Lucerne, this covered wooden footbridge can be used to cross the Reuss River, leading to the south bank. Built in 1333, the bridge is 560 feet long and crosses the river diagonally. It's one of the best-preserved wooden bridges in Switzerland, used originally for defense. There's also an octagonal Wasserturm (Water Tower), used variously as a prison, a torture chamber, and an archive. The bridge was always known for its 122 paintings that hung from its arched roof. Some of them were done in 1599 by Heinrich Wagmann, illustrating the daily activities and dress of the people. The bridge was damaged in a fire in 1993 and two-thirds of the original paintings were destroyed or severely damaged. Lucerne city officials directed that copies be made. After a $2.1-million reconstruction, this landmark bridge was reopened in the spring of 1994.

You emerge onto Bahnhofstrasse; you can continue right (west) until you see the next covered bridge across the Reuss, the:

❼ Spreuerbrücke (Mills Bridge)

Built in 1407 and restored in the 19th century, this wooden bridge spans an arm of the Reuss. Its gables are painted with the Dance of Death, a mural by Kaspar Meglinger dating from the 17th century. The mural commemorates a plague that swept through the city.

Cross the bridge and take a sharp right to reach:

❽ Mühlenplatz (Mills Square)

This square dates from the 16th century. This was the old site of Lucerne markets.

From Mühlenplatz, walk down Kramgasse (to the east) to reach the:

❾ Weinmarkt (Wine Market)

Here you'll find a lovely old square with a fountain, west of Kornmarkt. Long ago the mystery play *Confraternity of the Crown of Thorns* was performed here. Among the colorful old dwellings on the square is the Müllersche Apotheke, a "drugstore" from 1530.

Directly northeast of the Weinmarkt lies:

❿ Hirschenplatz (Stag Square)

Another landmark square of Lucerne, it's filled with restored buildings, many of them with painted facades and wrought-iron signs. In 1779 Goethe stayed at the Goldener Adler.

From Hirschenplatz, head east along Weggisgasse, which opens eventually onto Falkenplatz. From Falkenplatz, continue east along Hertensteinstrasse until you come to Löwenplatz. This is the site of:

⓫ Panorama

Panorama is one of the largest canvases in Europe, covering 11,836 square feet and curving in a circle around a central platform. Painted in 1889 by Edouard Castres and contained in a round building that was designed especially for it, it depicts the

Walking Tour: Lucerne

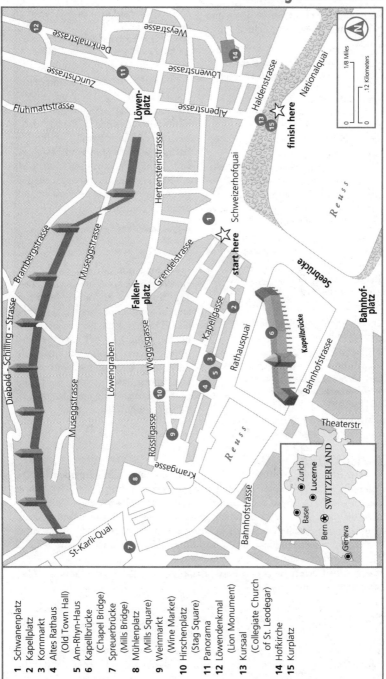

1 Schwanenplatz
2 Kapellplatz
3 Kornmarkt
4 Altes Rathaus
   (Old Town Hall)
5 Am-Rhyn-Haus
6 Kapellbrücke
   (Chapel Bridge)
7 Spreuerbrücke
   (Mills Bridge)
8 Mühlenplatz
   (Mills Square)
9 Weinmarkt
   (Wine Market)
10 Hirschenplatz
   (Stag Square)
11 Panorama
12 Löwendenkmal
   (Lion Monument)
13 Kursaal
14 Collegiate Church
   of St. Leodegar)
14 Hofkirche
15 Kurplatz

bloody retreat of the French army into Switzerland during the Franco-Prussian War.

The next stop on this tour is not immediately visible from Löwenplatz but requires a brief detour north along Denkmalstrasse. Within about a block of Löwenplatz, high above your head you'll see one of the most famous statues in Switzerland, the:

⑫ Löwendenkmal
(Lion Monument)

Carved in deep relief into the sandstone cliff above the town, the monument is an allegorical reference to the bravery of the Swiss Guards who died in the Tuileries of Paris in 1792 trying to save the life and honor of Marie Antoinette. During his grand tour of Europe, Mark Twain called the Dying Lion of Lucerne "the saddest and most poignant piece of rock in the world." Designed by the great Danish sculptor Bertel Thorvaldsen, the statue was dedicated in 1821.

Retrace your steps back to Löwenplatz, then head south along Löwenstrasse all the way to the lake and Kurplatz, a few steps east of Schwanenplatz, the site of the:

⑬ Kursaal

This spot is a casino-and-restaurant complex on Kurplatz on Nationalquai.

Above Nationalquai, view the twin towers of the Catholic:

⑭ Hofkirche (Collegiate Church of St. Leodegar)

Named after the patron saint of Lucerne, this is the most important church in the city. There was once a monastery at this site, but the present Gothic-Renaissance building dates from the 17th century. The interior has rich wrought-iron work, carvings, and a famous organ from 1640, with 4,950 pipes. Concerts are presented in the summer. The church also has a beautiful courtyard with arcades.

A good way to end the tour, you are now standing at:

⑮ Kurplatz

From here you can take in the best view of the lake from its northern rim. You can also take steamers from this area to visit various resorts along the lake. The view from here encompasses not only the lake but also the Alps from Rigi to Pilatus. The quays are lined with trees, hotels, and shops, ideal for exploring on foot. At the end of the promenade is the lido (beach), called Lucerne's "Riviera."

OTHER ATTRACTIONS

Gletschergarten (Glacier Garden)   This so-called glacier garden has 32 "potholes" that were worn into the sandstone bed of an Iron Age glacier, during the era when ice covered the surface of Lake Lucerne. Discovered and cleared of their debris in 1872, the holes measure up to 30 feet wide and almost as deep. A museum at the site contains a famous 18th-century relief map of the Alps, prehistoric remains of plant and animal life, and a Swiss homeland museum. A 12-minute film is also shown to visitors.

Denkmalstrasse 4. ℂ 041/410-43-40. Admission 9SF ($4.95) adults, 5.50SF ($3.05) children. Apr–Oct daily 9am–6pm; Nov–Mar daily 10am–5pm. Bus: 1.

Kunstmuseum (Fine Arts Museum)   The Fine Arts Museum includes many paintings by Swiss artists, dating from the 16th century to the present. Ferdinand Hodler (1835–1918) is among those represented, as well as Dufy and Utrillo. The museum also presents changing exhibits of modern-day Swiss and international art. For information about current exhibitions and events, consult the daily press or ask at the tourist office.

Tribschenstrasse 61. ℂ 041/226-78-00. Admission 10SF ($5.50) adults, 4SF ($2.20) children. Tues 10am–5pm, Wed 10am–9pm, Thurs–Sun noon–5pm. Closed late Nov to mid-Apr.

Neus Kunstmuseum (Modern Art Museum) ✿ In the culture and Convention Centre (KKL), this museum is the creation of Jean Nouvel, the most famous architect of France. In a setting near the rail station, he has created a futuristic environment for the display of mainly temporary exhibits, most of them avant-garde. There is also a permanent collection of works (which are rotated), ranging from the 15th to the 20th centuries.

The museum, in spite of a kind of neutrality, is nonetheless impressive in its architecture, especially when windows open onto panoramic vistas of urban space. In addition to a vast area to display art dramatically, there is also an art library with special literature and a spectacular terrace with views of the lake and the cityscape. Notices of the nature of temporary exhibitions are posed at the tourist office (see above).

Europlatz 1. Tel. **041/226-78-00**. Admission 10SF ($5.50) adults, 8SF ($4.40) students and children. Tues and Thurs–Sun 11am–6pm, Wed 11am–8pm.

Picasso Museum ✿ A small but choice collection of the works of Pablo Picasso is displayed on three levels, including paintings, drawings, original prints, sculpture, and ceramics from the last 20 years of the artist's life. The collection was a gift from Siegfried and Angela Rosengart, who presented the city of Lucerne on its 800th anniversary with eight masterpieces by Picasso, one for each century. Outstanding works include *Woman and Dog Playing* (1953), *Woman Dressing Her Hair* (1954), *The Studio* (1955), *Rembrandtesque Figure and Cupid* (1969), and a sculpture, *Woman with a Hat* (1961). The building, Am-Rhyn-Haus, was finished in 1618 in the Renaissance style by Walthard Am-Rhyn, mayor of Lucerne. It belonged to his descendants until 1946, when it became the property of the city.

In addition, the museum also displays some 200 of the most memorable photographs of David Douglas Duncan, one of the world's great photographers, who became famous for his combat photography of World War II for *Life* magazine. He also took countless photographs of Picasso.

Fürrengasse 21. ✆ **041/410-35-33**. Admission 6SF ($3.30) adults, 3SF ($1.65) children. Daily 10am–6pm. Bus: 1.

Richard Wagner Museum Wagner lived here from 1866 to 1872 and composed several works, including *Die Meistersinger*. Located about 2 miles (3km) from the city in the suburb of Tribschen, the museum contains some original scores and memorabilia, including letters and pictures. There's an exhibit of antique musical instruments in the summer.

Wagnerweg 27, Tribschen. ✆ **041/360-23-70**. Admission 5SF ($2.75) adults, 4SF ($2.20) children. Tues–Sun 10am–noon and 2–5pm. Closed Nov 15 to Feb. In summer, motorboats leave every hour from in front of the railroad station (rail passes are valid for this trip). Bus: 6, 7, or 8 to Wartegg.

Verkenrshaus der Schweiz (Swiss Transport Museum) ✿✿✿ This museum is the best of its kind in Europe and very popular with foreign visitors. It's located beyond the Haldenstrasse cable-car station, lying more than a mile northeast of the center and accessible via bus. All forms of transportation, old and new, are on display, including railway cars, airplanes, automobiles, ships, and spaceships. Also on display is the oldest steamboat in the country, the Riga, built in 1847. The most popular exhibition is a scale model of a Swiss railway crossing the Gotthard Pass (a dozen trains move simultaneously). The museum has recently opened many new attractions, including new rail exhibits and an adventure ride called the Gotthard Tunnel Show.

The Longines Planetarium is at the eastern end of the complex. Here you can experience the constellations, a solar and lunar eclipse, and simulated space travel. Also attached to the transport museum is the Hans Erni House, containing artwork by this well-known native son.

Lidostrasse 5. ⓒ 041/370-44-44. Admission 21SF ($11.55) adults, 19SF ($10.45) students and seniors, 12SF ($6.60) children. Apr–Oct daily 9am–6pm; Nov–Mar daily 10am–5pm. Bus: 6 or 8.

Historisches Museum Luzern (Museum of Swiss History)   Originally conceived as an arsenal for the storage of weapons in the 1560s, this building was reconfigured as a showplace for medieval and Renaissance art and sculptures in 1983. Adjacent to the surging river that flows through the center of town, this museum celebrates the arts and crafts that emerged from central Switzerland between around 1600 and 1900. One of the museum's centerpieces is the Gothic-style stone monument that once dominated the Wienerplatz, in the town center. (What you'll see there today is a copy.) Thanks to the solid wooden staircase that spirals its way around it, you'll get a close-up view of the stone-carved knights and cherubs that grace its pinnacle—a view that until previously was visible only to birds. Other exhibits trace the development of Lucerne beginning around 1300. The top floor of the museum is reserved for special (i.e. temporary) exhibits, including an overview of the way 20th-century Swiss cartoons treat medieval and mystical themes.

Pfistergasse 24. ⓒ 041/228-54-24. Admission free; special exhibitions 5–8SF ($2.75–$4.40). Tues–Fri 10am–noon and 2–5pm. Sat–Sun 10am–5pm. Bus: 2

The Bourbaki Panorama   This is the world's best replica of a 19th-century bloodbath that reinforced Switzerland's role as a neutral (non-aligned) power, and which provided the first testing ground for the then-fledging Red Cross. It commemorates an incident in the Franco-Prussian War (1870–1871) when the defeated French forces of General Charles Bourbaki (1816–1897) fled out of France into Switzerland to avoid annihilation by the Germans. In Switzerland, the starving, diseased, and disorganized French forces were disarmed by the Swiss army, then welcomed into homes throughout Switzerland for rest and recuperation from the brutal winter. Today, the event is hailed as one of the finest acts of humanitarian courage in Swiss history, and celebrated in the form of this circular painting, completed in 1881, of the bloody battlefield. Originally conceived as a Barnum & Bailey-style tourist attraction in the 19th-century, the site was converted into an auto repair shop in 1925, and the painting was "shortened" in two separate incidents that ultimately removed about 12 feet of gray sky from the top of the wraparound panorama. In 2000, the site was rebuilt, the painting cleaned, and the museum opened, with recorded narration, as a celebration of a genuinely bizarre but evocative interlude in European history. Be prepared for the recorded sounds of gunshots and cannon, dying men and horses, and a mournful but stirring account of wartime follies and heroism.

Löwenplatz 11. ⓒ 041/412-3030. Admission 6SF ($3.30), 4SF ($2.20) children 6–16. Free for children under 6. Daily 9am–6pm. Tram: 1.

NEARBY ATTRACTIONS

There are dozens of half-day and full-day excursions from Lucerne—so many that we recommend you allow at least 5 days to see the city and its environs. There are several points of interest around Lake Lucerne. Most of them can be reached by paddle-steamer along the lake. While en route, you can enjoy a panoramic view of the water and mountains. Lake Lucerne (Vierwaldstättersee) winds its way 24 miles (39km) into the alpine ranges of the heart of Switzerland.

Many excursions can be combined with a trip to the top of a mountain by cable car or funicular. Summer is the peak season.

Schiffahrtsgesellschaft Vierwaldstättersee (Lake Lucerne Navigation Co.; © 041/376-67-67) operates a flotilla of lake steamers that chug across the surface of Lake Lucerne, much to the delight of sightseers who appreciate the steep mountains rising on all sides. Round-trip passage from Lucerne to the lake's most distant point, Flüelen (a 4-hour round-trip) costs 66SF ($36.30) in first class, 44SF ($24.20) in second class, and departs from the quays opposite the Hauptbahnhof in Lucerne. In midsummer, departures begin at 8:26am, and continue every hour or so throughout the day. Wherever you decide to disembark en route, find out the departure time of the last boat back to Lucerne. Usually, the last boat from Flüelen departs before 5:46pm. All boats have a restaurant, or at least a cafeteria, on board.

The **William Tell Express** offers an opportunity to see regions of German- and Italian-speaking Switzerland in 1 full-day excursion. Between May 12 and October 24, it transports participants, as part of a 6-hour travel experience, from Lucerne, via Lugano, to Locarno. Begin with a 3-hour boat ride from Lucerne to the lakeside hamlet of Flüelen, then hop aboard a special train for a continuation of the trip across some of the most jagged and precipitous mountain scenery in the world. Seats in the first-class compartments have wider windows and skylights, while those in the less comfortable second-class cars are slightly less panoramic. A three-course meal, served aboard the lake steamer during the first part of the journey, is included in the one-way (Lucerne to Locarno) price of 66SF ($36.30) in first class and 44SF ($24.20) in second class. Reservations, preferably several days in advance, are vital. To make them, and get more information, call © 041/367-67-67. If you opt for a round-trip ticket from Lucerne to Locarno and then back to Lucerne, we advise spending at least 1 night in the Ticino before returning back to Lucerne. Round-trip tickets (Lucerne–Locarno–Lucerne) cost 70SF ($38.50) in first class and 52SF ($28.60) in second.

SHOPPING

Few other cities in Switzerland rely as heavily on the tourist trade as Lucerne, so consequently, you'll be faced with a barrage of mercantilism at virtually every street corner. Most obvious of the "heavy artillery" involves sales of wristwatches and folk handicrafts. The biggest jeweler in town is **Bucherer,** Schwanenplatz 5 (© 041/369-77-00), whose sprawling displays of luxury goods are rivaled only by the showrooms of **Gübelin,** Schweizenhofquai (© 041/410-51-42). Less consciously upscale, and more folkloric in their orientation, are the town's main outlets for handicrafts. These include **Casa Grande,** Grendel 6 (© 041/418-60-71); **Schmid-Linder,** Denkmalstrasse 9 (© 041/410-43-46); and **Leinen,** Weinmarkt 19 (© 041/410-44-33), which inventories clothing for men and women that will evoke Heidi, her grandfather, and her goatherd, Peter. Embroideries and linens for dining rooms and bedrooms are the offerings at **Sturzenneger,** Schwanenplatz 7 (© 041/410-19-58), and at **Neff,** Löwenstrasse 10 (© 041/410-19-65). Some of the pieces come from Switzerland's embroidery center of St. Gallen, others from less evocative factories in the Far East, but many are of heirloom quality.

Souvenirs of your trip to Lucerne are a lot less expensive, and a lot more workaday, at either of the town's two mass-market department stores. They are **Manor,** Nordmann & Co., Weggisgasse 5 (© 041/419-76-99); and **EPA,** Rössligasse 20 (© 041/410-19-77). Both sell housewares, clothing, school supplies, and anything you'd need to run a home. They also have a limited collection of Swiss souvenirs. More upscale, and more specifically geared to clothing for men, women, and children, is **Globus,** Pilatusstrasse 4 (© **041/227-07-07**).

Hofstetter & Berney, Schweizerhofquai 6 (© **041/410-31-06**), features a well-rounded collection of music boxes. The staff will tell you about the differences in tones, and the complexities of sounds produced by the various instruments, all of which are made in Switzerland, and which contain varying numbers of musical notes. Some of them might reproduce strains from Pachelbel's Canon, others a replica of the Austrian National Anthem.

Confiserie H & M Kurmann, Bahnhofstrasse 7 (© **041/210-19-187**), is the most distinguished pastry and chocolate shop in Lucerne. Many of the residents of Lucerne remember this shop from their childhood, when its pastries and chocolates might have been served as part of their birthday parties. Today, it's one of the few deeply entrenched big-name pastry makers in Switzerland that hasn't set up additional branches in other parts of the country. Everything is, as you'd expect, highly caloric and highly tempting.

You'll find a worthy collection of sporting equipment and outdoor clothing at **Bannwart Sport A.G.,** Weggisgasse 14 (© **041/410-45-38**).

The richly nuanced architecture of the city itself is the backdrop for the outdoor **fruit and vegetable market,** conducted during spring, summer, and autumn from both banks of the river every Tuesday and Saturday from 8am to around 1pm. Between May and October, Lucerne hosts a rowdy, somewhat disorganized **flea market** where the contents of estate sales and whatever anyone discovered in their grandmother's attic is displayed along either side of Untere Burgerstrasse. And the first Saturday of every month throughout the year, during daylight hours, artisans and craftspeople from throughout the region congregate at the **Weinmarkt** to display and sell their wares.

WHERE TO STAY

Lucerne is one of the most visited cities of Switzerland, with a wide range of hotels. But they're mostly expensive and moderate; there's a shortage of good budget hotels. Reservations are very important in the summer, when hordes of Europeans and North Americans pour into this town.

VERY EXPENSIVE

Grand Hotel National ✦✦✦   This is a monumental landmark and the former home base of Cesar Ritz. It's the most appealing hotel in Lucerne, much less stiff than the more famous but somewhat chilly Switzerland. Built "in the style of the French kings," this legend among Swiss hotels has a huge facade of gray stone, with a mansard roof and dozens of gables. Constructed in 1870, when visitors were just beginning to discover Lake Lucerne, it looks like a wing of the chateau at Versailles. Guests have included monarchs and diplomats from all over Europe. Between 1977 and 1980, the owner reconstructed this grand palace and installed modern conveniences. Following renovations in 2001, the main lobby is stately and elegant, one of the grandest in Lucerne. The predictably varied bedrooms are among the most comfortable and luxurious in the city, with thick carpets and old-fashioned charm, often with a four-poster canopied bed. Many have private balconies with a view of the lake. The bathrooms are opulent in white marble.

Haldenstrasse 4, CH-6002 Luzern. © **041/419-09-09.** Fax 041/419-09-10. www.national-luzern.ch. 96 units. 410SF–570SF ($225.50–$313.50) double; 680SF–1,000SF ($374–$550) suite. AE, DC, MC, V. Parking 35SF ($19.25). Bus: 6 or 8. **Amenities:** 4 restaurants; bar; pool; tennis courts; health club; sauna; room service; massage; babysitting; laundry/dry cleaning. *In room:* TV, minibar, hair dryer, safe.

Palace Hotel ✫✫✫   This large Belle Epoque 1906 hotel by the lake is one of the best in Switzerland, maintaining a regal air and a stiffly formal welcome. It has two towers and a mansard roof. The lobby has Ionic columns, high ceilings, and a massive chandelier. Each of the spacious guest rooms has an individual decor and is filled with luxuries and conveniences. Try, if possible, for a room on floors five and six, as they are the most up-to-date and have the most scenic views. The hotel contains many luxury extras such as splendid carpeting, sitting areas, and commodious bathrooms beautifully styled and equipped.

Haldenstrasse 10, CH-6006 Luzern. ✆ **800/223-6800** in North America, or 041/410-04-04. Fax 041/410-15-04. www.palace-luzern.com. 168 units. Apr–Oct 460SF–620SF ($253–$341) double; from 675SF ($371.25) suite. Nov–Mar 365SF–495SF ($200.75–$272.25) double; from 550SF ($302.50) suite. Half board 85SF ($46.75) extra. AE, DC, MC, V. Parking 28SF ($15.40). Bus: 2. **Amenities:** 2 restaurants, bar; small health club; sauna; room service; massage; babysitting; laundry/dry cleaning. *In room:* A/C, TV, minibar, hair dryer, safe.

Schweizerhof Luzern ✫ *Overrated*   Although it has its admirers, this hotel is formal and opulent but a bit stiff. In our view, Grand Hotel National is just as elegant and a lot more appealing. Nonetheless, the Schweizerhof remains a longtime favorite of many travelers ever since it opened in 1844. The Hauser family has owned this 19th-century "palace" since 1861 and reopened it again in 1999 following extensive remodeling and renovations. It has extended a welcome to such former guests as Napoleon III, Leo Tolstoy, Richard Wagner, and Mark Twain. It consists of three symmetrical white buildings connected by arched passageways lining the lake for at least 2 blocks; one of the buildings is rented as office space. The lobby has pink marble columns and pilasters and a cream-colored ceiling with plaster details. The Belle Epoque-style bedrooms are spacious and well furnished, and have well-maintained bathrooms. Try for a room, if possible, with a view of Lake Lucerne and the surrounding alpine range.

Schweizerhofquai 3, CH-6002 Luzern. ✆ 041/410-04-10. Fax 041/410-29-71. www.schweizerhof-luzern.ch. 107 units. Apr–Oct 455SF–495SF ($250.25–$272.25) double; 780SF–870SF ($429–$478.50) suite. Nov–Mar 330SF–410SF ($181.50–$225.50) double; 650SF–710SF ($357.50–$390.50) suite. Rates include continental breakfast. AE, DC, MC, V. Parking 20SF ($11) in garage. Bus: 1 or 24. **Amenities:** Restaurant, bar; room service; babysitting; laundry/dry cleaning. *In room:* A/C, TV, minibar, hair dryer, safe.

EXPENSIVE

Art Deco Hotel Montana ✫✫   This is one of the best government-rated four-star hotels in central Switzerland. This neoclassic hotel was originally built in 1911 as a private villa high on a hillside overlooking the lake. In the 1960s, a modern extension was added with cozy bedrooms, most of which offer views. A private funicular, departing from a point near the edge of the lake, carries clients of the hotel or its restaurants uphill to the hotel's entrance. The interior public rooms would please your Victorian great-great-grandmother, with their old-fashioned appeal of Oriental rugs, swag curtains, brocaded antique chairs and settees, and polished paneling, along with a good infusion of Art Deco styling. The bedrooms, however, are modernized, although with traditional styling, and are comfortable with firm beds and neatly kept bathrooms.

Adligenswilerstrasse 22, CH-6002 Luzern. ✆ **0800-55-23-44** in the United States, or 041/419-00-00. Fax 041/419-00-01. www.hotel-montana.ch. 65 units. May–Oct 325SF–395SF ($178.75–$217.25) double; 450SF–550SF ($247.50–$302.50) junior suite. Off-season 265SF–325SF ($145.75–$178.75) double; 345SF–455SF ($189.75–$250.25) junior suite. Rates include buffet breakfast. AE, DC, MC, V. Free parking. Bus: 6 or 8. **Amenities:** Restaurant, 2 bars; room service; babysitting; laundry/dry cleaning. *In room:* TV, minibar, hair dryer.

Chateau Gutsch ✫✫   No hotel in Central Switzerland is as imbued with a Disney-like fairytale aura as this mock castle lying at Gutschberg, at the western end of Lucerne on the road to Bern and reached by a 10-minute bus or 3SF ($1.65) cable-car ride leaving from Baselstrasse. With its steeples, turrets, and towers, this is storybook Switzerland. Aside from the mock trappings, the stunning aspect of the place is its panoramic view. If you opt for a room overlooking the lake, expect to pay twice as much. Bedrooms are only mid-sized but are well maintained and furnished. The most elegant of the accommodations are graced with four-posters and large terraces.

Klanonenstrasse CH-Luzern. ℂ **041/249-41-00.** Fax 041/249-41-91. Info@chateau-guetsch.ch. 31 units. 320SF–450SF ($176–$247.50) double, 550SF–950SF ($302.50–$522.50) suite. AE, DC, MC, V. **Amenities:** 2 restaurants, bar; pool. *In room:* TV, hair dryer.

Hotel Des Balances ✸ This tranquil government-rated four-star hotel, directly on the Reuss River, also faces the most colorful square in town, an 8-minute walk from the rail station. The elaborate gray-stone building has lots of curlicue wrought-iron balconies; the interior has high ceilings and Oriental rugs. Following massive renovations to both its interior and its facade, the hotel has emerged as one of the finest in its price range in Lucerne. Your room, likely to be decorated in soothing pastels with a freshly tiled bathroom, will open either onto a picture-postcard view of the river or (if in the rear) the historic Weinmarkt. If you're seeking a room in Altstadt, make it the Balances. Guests are permitted to drive to the hotel even though it lies in a pedestrian zone.

There's a great view of the city from the popular riverside cafe. The hotel restaurant, Rotes Gatter, is recommended separately (see "Where to Dine," below).

Weinmarkt, CH-6002 Luzern. ℂ **800/528-1234** in the United States and Canada, or 041/410-30-10. Fax 041/410-64-51. www.balances.ch. 60 units. Apr–Oct 360SF–395SF ($198–$217.25) double; 565SF ($310.75) suite. Off-season 280SF–320SF ($154–$176) double; 440SF ($242) suite. Rates include buffet breakfast. AE, DC, MC, V. Parking 27SF ($14.85). Bus: 1. **Amenities:** Restaurant, lounge; room service; babysitting; laundry/dry cleaning. *In room:* TV, minibar, hair dryer, safe.

Hotel Hermitage ✸ *(Finds* In 1990, a run-down older hotel was demolished and in its place arose this modern lakeside building with its own private beach. The Hermitage's pink-painted walls contain spacious doubles and junior suites. Each unit has a lakefront view, a private balcony, and a tastefully modern decor featuring rattan furniture. All units also contain neatly kept bathrooms. Set in a flowering suburb 2½ miles (4km) east of the center of Lucerne, the hotel (rated four stars by the Swiss government) has a cafe-terrace beside the water.

Seeburgstrasse 79, CH-6006 Luzern-Seeburg. ℂ **041/375-81-81.** Fax 041/375-81-825. www.hotel-hermitage.ch. 50 units. May–Oct 365SF ($200.75) double; 395SF ($217.25) junior suite. Nov–Apr 230SF ($126.50) double; 275SF ($151.25) junior suite. Rates include continental breakfast. AE, DC, MC, V. Free parking. Bus: 24. **Amenities:** 2 restaurants, lounge; tennis court; room service; laundry/dry cleaning. *In room:* TV, minibar, hair dryer.

Hotel Monopole & Métropole ✸ Built in 1898, this grand hotel has a carved limestone facade, wrought-iron balconies, half columns, and elaborately detailed windows. Its central location is convenient for the rail station or the lake. The mid-sized rooms are individually furnished; some are modern and others have paneling, alcove beds, and chalet chairs. All come equipped with tidy bathrooms.

Pilatusstrasse 1, CH-6002 Luzern. ℂ **041/226-43-43.** Fax 041/226-43-44. www.hotel-monopole.com. 82 units. Apr–Oct 340SF ($187) double. Nov–Mar 270SF ($148.50) double. Rates include buffet breakfast. AE, DC, MC, V. Bus: 1. **Amenities:** Restaurant, bar; room service; babysitting; laundry/dry cleaning. *In room:* TV, minibar, hair dryer.

The Hotel ⭐⭐⭐ *(Finds* In a panoramic setting in the center of the city, this is a luxurious boutique hotel, the most exclusive in Lucerne. Famed French architect Jean Nouvele designed it. Although familiar to London, this type of urban boutique hotel is new to Switzerland. Called simply "The Hotel," it is luxury personified, yet there is an artful simplicity to it. From the custom-design furnishings in wood and steel to the luscious, avant-garde cinema scenes on the guest room ceilings, every aspect of the hotel reflects Nouvele's unique touch. Some two dozen studios and suites are spread across the seven-story building. Preferred are five corner junior suites with park views on both sides. Other options include garden and park luxe suites with patio, and luxe studios with park view. Nouvele achieves his dream of "combining spirituality with elegance into a timeless design—not a matter of decor but of lifestyle."

The bathrooms are among the most luxurious in Lucerne, sexy and cool, and bamboo lovers can book a deluxe suite with a private patio planted with this exotic species—you can shower in a bamboo jungle.

French tradition with Asian refinement are reflected in the cuisine of the stylish Bam Bou restaurant.

Sempacherstrasse 14, CH-6002 Luzern. (℃ **041/226-86-86.** Fax 041/226-86-90. www.the-hotel.ch. 25 units. 390SF–460SF ($214.50–$253) double; from 510SF ($280.50) suite. AE, DC, MC, V. **Amenities:** Restaurant, bar; room service; babysitting; laundry/dry cleaning. *In room:* A/C, TV, minibar, hair dryer, safe.

MODERATE

Grand Hotel Europe A neoclassical pediment graces the white facade of this 19th-century hotel lying 1 mile east of the center on the north shore of the lake. Much-needed renovations in 1994 to 1995 have given the hotel a new lease on life. There's a row of awnings sheltering the public rooms, which face a garden. The salons contain large tapestries, Oriental rugs, and comfortable couches and chairs. Most of the rooms are spacious and well furnished, each with a firm bed and well-maintained plumbing. All units have neatly kept bathrooms.

Haldenstrasse 59, CH-6002 Luzern. (℃ **041/370-00-11.** Fax 041/370-10-31. www.europe-luzern.ch. 188 units. 260SF–295SF ($143–$162.25) double. Rates include continental breakfast. AE, DC, MC, V. Free parking. Closed Nov–Mar. Bus: 2. **Amenities:** Restaurant, bar; room service; laundry/dry cleaning. *In room:* TV, hair dryer.

Hotel Astoria ⭐ This first-class modern hotel boasts prominent horizontal rows of windows and a desirable location in the center of Lucerne, a 5-minute walk from the lake. The hotel is often patronized by business travelers and groups drawn to its modern, streamlined, and no-nonsense atmosphere. Well-maintained and well-respected, this hotel was built in three separate phases: Its main core dates from 1957, and in the mid-70s and again in 1998, two separate enlargements were added to the hotel's (quieter and calmer) back side. On-site is a hugely popular and trendy club and disco on the upper floor called The Penthouse. The subdued interior of the hotel is decorated with furniture and accessories evocative of Thailand. Each of the well-furnished rooms has a firm bed and a clean bathroom.

Pilatusstrasse 29, CH-6003 Luzern. (℃ **041/226-88-88.** Fax 041/226-88-90. 200 units. 200SF–300SF ($110–$165) double; 350SF ($192.50) suite. Rates include buffet breakfast. AE, DC, MC, V. **Amenities:** 2 restaurants, 2 bars, disco; room service; babysitting; laundry/dry cleaning. *In room:* TV, minibar, hair dryer.

Hotel des Alpes Set in Lucerne's historic core, this hotel lies in the pedestrian zone. It was originally built around 1740 as an inn for travelers. Today, behind a tall and narrow facade with restrained baroque detailing, the beneficiary of a radical renovation in the late 1970s, it continues to welcome visitors into its premises. Although the public rooms retain their old-fashioned charm, most of the mid-sized bedrooms have been streamlined and filled with vinyl and laminated pieces in the roadside-motel tradition. Rooms in the rear open onto Altstadt, and those on the upper floors sometimes have views over the low skyline of Lucerne. All of the units contain neatly kept bathrooms.

Though parking is not available on the premises, guests can leave their cars across the river at the railway station, a 5-minute walk from the hotel.

Furrengasse 3, CH-6004 Luzern. © **041/410-58-25.** Fax 041/410-74-51. www.desalpes-luzern.ch. 45 units. Apr–Oct 230SF–390SF ($126.50–$214.50) double. Nov–Mar 180SF–255SF ($99–$140.25) double. Rates include continental breakfast. AE, MC, V. Bus: 1, 2, 6, 7, and 8. **Amenities:** 2 restaurants, lounge; room service; laundry/dry cleaning. *In room:* TV, minibar.

Hotel Krone   Despite the lushly baroque facade of this middle-bracket hotel, its bedrooms are simple, well-organized, and contemporary-looking. This is the result of a radical renovation in the early 1990s that ripped apart the interior of the five-story building. The Hotel Krone is solidly positioned on one of the city's most charming medieval squares, in a neighborhood that shows off Lucerne's architectural personality. Bedrooms in back are slightly bigger than those overlooking the Weinmarkt in front, which have better views and a more intense sense of history. Each unit comes with a neatly kept private bathroom. Don't expect a deeply entrenched sense of luxury, or even a particularly large or opulent-looking lobby: In this case, the space was devoted instead to accommodations. No alcohol is served within the hotel, but there are plenty of bars and restaurants within a short walk.

Weinmarkt 12, CH-6004 Luzern. © **800/528-1234** in the U.S., or 041/419-44-0000. Fax 041/419-44-90. www.bestwestern.ch/kroneluzern. 25 units. 190SF–270SF ($104.50–$148.50) double. Rates include breakfast. AE, DC, MC, V. Bus: 1 or 2. **Amenities:** Restaurant; laundry/dry cleaning. *In room:* TV, minibar (alcohol free), hair dryer.

Hotel Schiller ☆   Although it's surrounded by other antique buildings near the railway station, the Schiller stands out with its 19th-century details and colorful awnings above the entrance. It's favored by business travelers who want to be in the commercial center of town, close to the railway station. The interior has many fine touches, including an ample use of white marble, much of which was added during a renovation in 1991. Each mid-sized room in this comfortable hotel is different; the most modern are on the fifth and sixth floors, while the more traditional fill the lower levels. The front rooms can be noisy at times. Many nonresidents patronize the hotel's drinking and eating facilities.

Pilatusstrasse 15, CH-6002 Luzern. © **041/226-87-87.** Fax 041/210-34-04. 82 units. Apr–Oct 230SF–280SF ($126.50–$154) double; 310SF ($170.50) suite. Nov–Mar 170SF–180SF ($93.50–$99) double; 240SF ($132) suite. Rates include buffet breakfast. AE, DC, MC, V. Bus: 1. **Amenities:** 2 restaurants, 2 bars; room service; babysitting; laundry/dry cleaning. *In room:* TV, hair dryer.

Hotel Zum Rebstock ☆ *Finds*   This is a historic landmark. The foundations of this hotel date from the 12th century, when the site, west of the Hofkirche and south of the Panorama, was the setting for a monastery. Surrounded by vineyards, the half-timbered building has green shutters with a brown-tile roof. In 1443, it was the headquarters of the winegrowers' guild; later it was used as a recruitment center for the Swiss mercenaries who came from this region. The rooms are small but cozily comfortable, each outfitted in a different color and decorative motif. All units contain well-maintained bathrooms. The inn offers two restaurants serving both Swiss regional dishes and international platters.

Sankt-Leodegar-Platz 3, CH-6004 Luzern. © **041/418-82-20.** Fax 041/418-82-30. 30 units. 270SF–280SF ($148.50–$154) double. Rates include buffet breakfast. AE, DC, MC, V. Parking 15SF ($8.25). Bus: 1, 2, or 7. **Amenities:** 3 restaurants, bar; room service; laundry/dry cleaning. *In room:* TV, minibar, hair dryer.

Romantik Hotel Wilden Mann ★★ This is the best choice for the nostalgia buff. Around 1900, a local entrepreneur, operating from the core of an early-16th-century tavern, began slowly but systematically buying up the historic real estate around him. The result you'll see today incorporates seven antique houses—the oldest dating from 1517—into a well-orchestrated whole. Inside, a confusing but charming labyrinth of hallways, many accented with exposed stone and beams, and, in some cases, with artfully old-fashioned paneling, lead to the cozy bedrooms. All rooms are well maintained and have neatly kept bathrooms. Here, warm colors and a sense of yesteryear combine with modern extras for winning four-star comforts.

Even if you don't stay here, consider a meal in the artfully rustic dining room (see "Where to Dine," below).

Bahnhofstrasse 30, CH-6007 Luzern. ✆ **041/210-16-66.** Fax 041/210-16-29. www.wilden-mann.ch. 50 units. 260SF–370SF ($143–$203.50) double; 330SF–410SF ($181.50–$225.50) junior suite. Rates include breakfast. AE, DC, MC, V. Bus: 2. **Amenities:** 3 restaurants, lounge; room service; babysitting; laundry/dry cleaning. *In room:* TV, minibar, hair dryer.

INEXPENSIVE

Hotel Alpha This severe-looking, white-fronted building is a 10-minute walk from the city center and rail station, near Pilatusplatz. Renovated many times since its original construction, it's one of the simplest hotels in town, offering well-scrubbed but small bedrooms with few extras and modest furnishings, although the mattresses are firm. Those units containing private bathrooms are in most cases equipped with shower-tub combinations. On the premises are two lounges, each with a TV set and a collection of newspapers.

Zähringerstrasse 24, CH-6003 Luzern. ✆ 041/240-42-80. Fax 041/240-91-31. www.hotlalpha.ch. 45 units (34 without bathroom). 98SF ($53.90) double without bathroom, 130SF ($71.50) double with bathroom; 129SF ($70.95) triple without bathroom; 164SF ($90.20) quad without bathroom. Rates include buffet breakfast. AE, MC, V. Bus: 1 or 2 to Pilatusplatz. **Amenities:** Lounge; bike rental. *In room:* No phone.

Pension Panorama *Value* One of the better bargains in Lucerne, this angular, four-story hotel, built in the 1970s, is on a hill with a sweeping view of the lake and mountains. It's a 10-minute walk from the center of the Old Town. The small rooms are reasonably comfortable and well maintained, although simply and functionally furnished. There's a communal bathroom with shower-tub combination for every four bedrooms. Only breakfast is served, but there's a kitchen for guests to prepare snacks.

Kapuzinerweg 9, CH-6006 Luzern. ✆ 041/420-67-01. Fax 041/420-67-30. www.pensionpanorama.ch. 13 units (11 without bathroom). 70SF–90SF ($38.50–$49.50) double without bathroom, 120SF ($66) double with bathroom. Rates include continental breakfast. MC, V. Free parking. Bus: 4 or 5 to Felsberg. **Amenities:** Lounge. *In room:* No phone.

Pension Villa Maria ★ *Finds* Set in a charming garden near the north shore of the lake, this family-run villa was built in 1955 and is today owned by members of the Winkler family. Part of the experience is the welcome they offer in this chalet-inspired private home with comfortably cluttered public rooms decorated in shades of red, gold, and pink. The rooms—all doubles—are clean, spacious, and comfortable with excellent beds. Those units with bathrooms have clean facilities. The establishment is located about half a mile from the center of Lucerne.

Haldenstrasse 36, CH-6002 Luzern. ✆ and fax 041/370-21-19. 10 units (4 with bathroom). 140SF ($77) double without bathroom, 150SF ($82.50) double with bathroom. Additional bed in room 30SF ($20.10) extra. Rates include continental breakfast. AE, V. Closed Nov–Feb. Free parking. Bus: 6. **Amenities:** Lounge; car-rental desk; room service; babysitting; laundry/dry cleaning. *In room:* Hair dryer.

Tourist Hotel   This budget hotel with a sage-green facade stands beside the river, a 10-minute walk from the train station. The hotel attracts young people and families to its rooms. Nine conventional units can accommodate up to four beds, and communal dormitory-style rooms are also available that contain between 4 and 10 beds each, usually stacked as bunk beds. The furnishings are in a basic, functional modern style. Many of the rooms open onto a view of the river and the faraway mountains of Pilatus and Titlis. Rooms with private bathrooms have clean quarters and mostly contain shower-tub combinations. All units have hot and cold running water. There's a dining room as well as a lounge on the premises. Because the hotel lies in a pedestrian zone, it's hard to find parking.

St. Karliquai 12, CH-6004 Luzern. ℂ 041/410-24-74. Fax 041/410-84-14. www.touristhotel.ch. 9 units, 6 with bathroom; 100 dormitory beds. 112SF ($61.60) double without bathroom, 160SF ($88) double with bathroom; 138SF ($75.90) triple without bathroom, 180SF ($99) triple with bathroom; 180SF ($99) quad without bathroom, 240SF ($132) quad with bathroom; 30SF–33SF ($16.50–$18.15) dorm bed. Those with ISIC card get a 10% discount. Rates include buffet breakfast. AE, MC, V. Bus: 2 or 9. **Amenities:** Restaurant, lounge; laundry. *In room:* TV.

Zum Weissen Kreuz   Parts of this antique inn date from the 1400s, and although a complete renovation of the premises was completed in 1987, the site still exudes a nostalgic sense of yesteryear. The small bedrooms are scattered over five floors connected by an elevator, and in some cases a scattering of old-fashioned, turn-of-the-century furnishings can be found. All units have tidily kept bathrooms equipped with shower stalls. Its location near the Picasso Museum and the Kornmarkt adds to its appeal. Behind its white-fronted exterior lies the unpretentious Al Forno restaurant and pizzeria. *Warning:* Don't look for the entrance of this hotel on Furrengasse, as it's positioned on the side street, Badergasse.

Furrengasse 19 (entrance on Badergasse), CH-6004 Luzern. ℂ **041/418-82-20.** Fax 041/418-82-30. www. hotel-wkreuzch. 22 units. 150SF–195SF ($82.50–$107.25) double. Rates include breakfast. AE, DC, MC, V. Bus: 1, 4, or 5. **Amenities:** Restaurant, lounge; laundry/dry cleaning. *In room:* TV.

WHERE TO DINE

Lucerne has some of the finest restaurants in Switzerland, in a wide range of prices, so don't confine yourself to your hotel at mealtime.

EXPENSIVE

China Restaurant Li-Tai-Pe ✪ BEIJING/CHINESE   This long-standing Chinese restaurant was founded in 1965 by "grande dame" Margaret Chi Tsun, whose late husband was once an aide to General Chiang Kai-shek. Margaret Chi Tsun is assisted by her daughter, Greta Chi, a modern-day businesswoman with ties to the New World and to Hong Kong. Although fickle fame has passed on, it's still here and serving many of the same excellent dishes it always did. Located on a narrow street in the old town, the restaurant has two levels and is decorated with Asian artifacts and somber lighting. Many sweet-and-sour dishes are offered, such as codfish, pork, or crispy chicken. Two especially good dishes are chicken Kung Bao (made with peanuts and chili) and stewed beef with crispy rice. *Boaling* are dumplings with different fillings, a choice appetizer. You might also begin with egg-blossom soup, to be followed by beef with tomatoes or chicken with green peppers.

Furrengasse 14. ℂ **041/410-10-23.** Reservations recommended. Main courses 30SF–44SF ($16.50–$24.20); fixed-price lunch 23SF ($12.65); fixed-price dinners 45SF–63SF ($24.75–$34.65). AE, DC, MC, V. Daily 11:30am–2:30pm and 6–11pm. Bus: 1 or 2.

Marc Zimmermann ★★★ CONTINENTAL If the snobby reception around here isn't a turn-off, you'll find the grandest cuisine of Lucerne served at this castle-like hotel, the Chateau Gutsch (see previous recommendation). If you follow in the footsteps of such legendary diners here as Thomas Mann or Charles Chaplin, you'll be rewarded with one of the grandest meals and grandest views in Central Switzerland. (On-site is another less desirable restaurant, 1001 Nacht, with authentic Indian cuisine.) The chef, Zimmermann, personally shops for only the freshest and finest of ingredients, which are shaped into dishes of culinary finesse and perfection. Sometimes plates arriving at your table look like works of art. Expect seasonal variations but anticipate such appetizers as quail ballotine or lobster salad with avocado and chervil, or perhaps a chartreuse of green asparagus and calf's sweetbreads. Soup aficionados should delight in the frog leg soup with fresh morels. Roasted pike-perch with a spicy oil arrives at your table looking delectable, or else you may prefer a meat or poultry dish such as roasted Challans of duck in a honey lime sauce. Several specialties such as knuckle of milk lamb from the Pyrenees are served only for two.

In Chateau Gutsch, Kanonenstrasse. ℭ **041/249-41-41.** Reservations required. Main courses 48SF–58SF ($26.40–$31.90). Fish menu 98SF ($53.90); castle menu 98SF ($53.90). Menu surprise (2 dinners only) 145SF ($79.75) per person. AE, DC, MC, V. Daily 11:30am–2pm and 6:30–10:30pm.

Old Swiss House ★ SWISS/FRENCH This half-timbered building near the Lion Monument is one of the most photographed attractions in the area. This crowd-pleaser—often filled with groups—is a mandatory stopover on a dining tour of Lucerne, and has been since it started attracting a horde of British visitors in 1859. To its credit, it has endured and outlasted everything else, with the food remaining good. The restaurant is decorated in 17th-century style, with porcelain and antique glass, hand-carved oak doors, wooden stairways, leaded- and stained-glass windows with heraldic panes from 1575, antique silver, and old pewter. There are also original oil paintings throughout the house. Perhaps the most outstanding item of the entire collection is a handmade porcelain stove from 1636, in the Knight's Room. The house has a long bar near the entry, private banquet rooms upstairs, and a dining room downstairs. In fair weather you can have lunch on the terrace. There's a city parking lot 200 yards away. Waitresses wear regional dress and speak several languages.

One of the dishes this place does best is an elegant version of Wiener schnitzel—a bestseller here for more than 40 years—that's pan-fried aboard a trolley that's wheeled alongside your table. Freshwater fish (fera, omble chevalier, pike-perch) from the nearby lake are excellent too, as well as turbot meunière, filet of beef stroganoff, calf's liver, roasted rack of baby lamb from Scotland, and sliced veal in cream sauce.

Löwenplatz 4. ℭ **041/410-61-71.** Reservations recommended. Main courses 20SF–45SF ($11–$24.75) lunch, 38SF–59SF ($20.90–$32.45) dinner. Fixed-price lunches 32SF–69SF ($17.60–$37.95), fixed-price dinner 69SF ($37.95). AE, DC, MC, V. Tues–Sun 11:30am–midnight. Closed 3 weeks in Feb. Bus: 1.

Stadtkeller ★ SWISS This is a crowd pleaser. Although there's been an inn in the cellar of Lucerne's town hall since 1685, none of its earlier versions has placed such a heavy emphasis on Swiss folklore. In a cavernous cellar lined with antique accessories, you can enjoy hearty alpine meals whose flavors are enhanced by doses of folk music, which begins at 12:15pm at lunch and at 8pm during dinner. Depending on your tastes, you'll find the experience harmless or just a bit corny, although many visitors consider it the Swiss equivalent of a beer hall in Munich. The most economical way to enjoy the place is simply to order a half liter of beer, with a supplemental charge that's imposed whenever music is playing. But to really get into the experience, consider the heaping platters of smoked pork with sauerkraut, pork or veal sausages with rösti, several kinds of schnitzel with mushrooms, or roulade of beef with new potatoes. Folk music is featured *only* from March to October.

Sternplatz 3. (?) **041/410-47-33.** Reservations recommended. Main courses 30SF–58SF ($16.50–$31.90); fixed-price lunch 45SF ($24.75); fixed-price dinner 65SF ($35.75). Music surcharge of 10SF ($5.50) for dinner and 8SF ($4.40) for lunch is imposed on a la carte meals and drinkers only. AE, MC, V. Apr–Oct daily noon–1:30pm and 7:30–10:15pm; Nov–Mar Tues–Sat noon–1:30pm and 7:30–10:15pm.

MODERATE

Hofstube ✿ SWISS/FRENCH   This flourishing restaurant is in the Hotel Zum Rebstock, next to a building used as a guildhall for Lucerne winegrowers in the Middle Ages. The 1920s-style entrance hall is filled with valuable Art Deco pieces. This is a historic Swiss-style restaurant, with two different dining rooms, both folkloric and charming. The older is the Hofstube; the slightly newer dining area is the Hofegge, which is the site of an elaborate Sunday brunch from 8am to 4pm. Beyond the dining area is a large, illuminated courtyard, where additional tables are set up on warm summer nights. The menu, a classic blend of Swiss and French traditions, usually includes an impressive array of terrines, delicious lake trout, suckling veal with spinach, filet of pork and beef in a cognac sauce, and veal and sultanas in puff pastry.

In the Hotel Zum Rebstock, Sankt-Leodegar-Platz 3. (?) **041/410-35-81.** Reservations recommended. Main courses 15SF–40SF ($8.25–$22). AE, DC, MC, V. Mon–Sat 7am–midnight, Sun 8am–midnight. Bus: 1, 2, 5, or 7.

La Bonne Cave *Finds* SWISS/ITALIAN   At least some of the charm of this place involves its emphasis on wine, rather than on beer, as is the case with many of its nearby competitors. Set under the medieval stone vaulting of a building in the old town, directly beside the river, it offers more than 140 vintages of wine— many of them Swiss, French, or Italian, displayed on wooden racks above a cobble-covered floor. You can always select a bottle from the wine shop here, which will be uncorked in the restaurant and served without any supplemental fees, at prices less than you might have expected in a grander restaurant. But if you want as broad-based an exposure to as many wines as possible, consider several glasses of different vintages. Wine is king but the kitchen also turns out plates of good-tasting food. Menu items include platters of either Italian antipasti or an assortment of Swiss cheese; shrimp marinated in olive oil; *vitello tonnato,* beefsteak tartare; and platters of air-dried alpine beef.

Rathausquai 1. (?) **041/410-45-16.** Reservations not necessary. Salads 9SF ($4.95), main courses 19.50SF–36SF ($10.75–$19.80), wines 5.40SF–7.30SF ($2.95–$4) per glass. AE, MC, V. Bar and wine shop daily 9am–midnight; food daily 11am–10:30pm.

Rotes Gatter ✿✿ SWISS/INTERNATIONAL   At this previously recommended hotel in Altstadt, opening onto the historic Weinmarkt, is one of the city's exceptional restaurants. The building housing it was the town jail back in 1369, but it was converted into a restaurant in 1519. Its terrace, with a view of the river Reuss, is one of the most hotly contested seats in town on a balmy summer night. Its refined nouvelle-inspired cuisine attracts both locals and visitors.

The decor is a stylish combination of medieval masonry, 19th-century wrought iron, and postmodern, hi-tech lighting. Try such tempting dishes as freshwater crabs grilled with feta cheese and marinated herbs; filets of pike-perch with olive oil and artichoke hearts; roasted rabbit stuffed with chanterelles and basil; Sisteron lamb in puff pastry with olive oil and thyme juices; and breast of chicken stuffed with shrimp and dill, on a bed of marinated sweet peppers.

In the Hotel des Balances, Weinmarkt. (C) 041/418-28-28. Reservations recommended. Main courses 35SF–49SF ($19.25–$26.95), set menus 72SF–85SF ($39.60–$46.75). AE, DC, MC, V. Daily 11:30am–1:30pm and 6–10pm.

Wilden Mann Stübe/Burgerstübe ☆ SWISS/CONTINENTAL   The Burgerstübe, the older of the two dining rooms, dates from at least 1517. Set on the ground floor of the Romantik Hotel, both dining rooms have carefully maintained paneling and antique touches that include coffered ceilings painted with the coats of arms of each of Lucerne's leading families. The food items are rich and succulent, often inspired by the tastes of Old Switzerland. Examples include Wildermann pastete, crafted from filet of beef cooked in its own juices and encased in puff pastry; Küglipastete, a shank of veal in a cream sauce with mushrooms in a puff-pastry cone with peas and carrots; hashed Zürich-style veal served with rösti; and breast of veal cooked "Luzern style," with a cream-based kidney sauce. More conventional menu items include chateaubriands, steaks, and roast rack of lamb with rosemary sauce. In midsummer, seating expands onto a flowering outdoor terrace overlooking one of the Old Town's historic squares.

In the Romantik Hotel Wilden Mann, Bahnhofstrasse 30. (C) 041/210-16-66. Reservations recommended. Main courses 18SF–50SF ($9.90–$27.50); fixed-price lunch 18SF–45SF ($9.90–$24.75), fixed-price dinner 60SF ($33). AE, DC, MC, V. Daily 10:30am–midnight (limited menu 2–6pm and after 10pm). Closed for 2 weeks in July. Bus: 2.

INEXPENSIVE

Rathaus Brauerei Restaurant _Finds_ SWISS   This is one of the few establishments in Lucerne that brews its beer on-site. They usually include at least four, whose individual characteristics vary according to the season, but which will usually feature the most popular brand, Rathaus Bier, a blond lager that's available year-round; as well as wheat beer; a dark beer known as _dunkel;_ and the heaviest, darkest, and strongest of all, _bok._ You'll find the place under the arcades of the riverfront promenade, close to the northern terminus of the city's well-known covered bridge, immediately beneath the exhibitions of the Picasso Museum. You can dine in the open air, or head inside to a series of medieval vaults which shelter the polished copper of the fermentation vats. Menu items reflect the savory, hearty dishes that seem to go well with beer, including schnitzels, lamb steak, Swiss sausage (of veal or pork), and grilled chicken breast filets, as well as deep-fried pike-perch.

Unter den Egg 2. (C) 041/410-52-57. Reservations not necessary. Main courses 13.70SF–34.50SF ($7.55–$19); beer 3.40SF–7.40SF ($1.85–$4.05). AE, MC, V. Apr–Sept Tues–Sat 8am–12:30am, Sun–Mon 9am–12:30am. Oct–Mar daily 11:30am–12:30am.

Restaurant Fritschi _Value_ SWISS   There's absolutely nothing pretentious about this beerhall/brasserie, where clients have been soaking up suds and enjoying filling platters of traditional food since 1602. The building that contains it has an outrageously colorful replica of a medieval fresco on its facade, and an interior pair of dining rooms, one of which contains a bar, and both of which are sheathed in richly intricate marquetry. Menu items—all familiar to your Swiss greatgrandmother—include four kinds of pork schnitzel; entrecote of beef; sliced veal with a mushroom-flavored cream sauce; and sliced veal with morels. There is also a selection of fondues, any of which seem to taste better during cold weather.

Sternenplatz 5. (C) 041/410-16-15. Reservations recommended. Main courses 16.90SF–31.50SF ($9.30–$17.35). MC, V. Daily 11:30am–11pm. Bus: 1 or 2.

Schiffrestaurant Wilhelm Tell SWISS Built in 1908, this lake cruiser (*Schiff* is German for "ship") sailed boatloads of happy passengers from one end of Lake Lucerne to the other. After it was replaced by newer ships in the late 1960s, it was transformed into a floating restaurant in 1972. Now permanently moored at one of the quays, it's usually ringed with a colony of swans, which feed off the scraps thrown overboard. Drinks and snacks are served on outdoor cafe tables in the bow area, where you can have a beer or coffee throughout the day. A formal restaurant is found under the low ceiling of the aft section, where fine food is served with alert attention. The ship's engine, brightly polished and set behind glass, is on display as a work of industrial art. The well-chosen menu might include excellently prepared filets of perch or sole prepared seaman's style, chopped chicken breast with smoked ham and bits of apple in a calvados sauce with rösti, and flavorful grills of succulent veal and beef.

Landungsbrücke 9. ℂ **041/410-23-30.** Reservations recommended. Main courses 18SF–45SF ($9.90–$24.75); fixed-price lunch 17.50SF–20.50SF ($9.65–$11.30). AE, MC, V. Daily 10am–midnight. Closed Jan–Feb. Bus: 2.

Vinotek Opus *Finds* CONTINENTAL Set within a pair of interconnected medieval buildings, one side of which opens onto views of the river, this wine bar rocks and rolls in one of the most irreverent formats in town. It's understood that you'll come here for at least one glass (and perhaps several) of the Swiss and foreign wines served. You can also order platters of Serrano-style smoked ham, Italian soft cheese marinated in olive oil with garlic, *vitello tonnato,* a tartare of smoked salmon, and gazpacho studded with smoked mussels. There are even some experimental dishes such as Asian lasagne "Shanghai" (with Asian vegetables, shiitake mushrooms, snow peas, tofu, and soy sprouts), or red snapper in red curry sauce, as well as more mainstream platters such as fried perch filets or roulades of rabbit filet. The cellar contains more than 650 types of wine. Sprawling and convivial, the place offers seating in two dining rooms, at tables beside two different bars, and a wide terrace beside the river overlooking the Old Town.

Bahnhofstrasse 16. ℂ **041/226-4141.** Reservations not necessary. Platters 18SF–38SF ($9.90–$20.90); wine 6SF–9SF ($3.30–$4.95) per glass. AE, DC, MC, V. Bars daily 8am–midnight; kitchen daily 11:30am–11:30pm.

Wirtshaus Galliker *Finds* SWISS Generous portions of unpretentious, well-prepared food are served amid a rustic decor and an often-rowdy atmosphere of fun-loving Luzerners out for a night of gluttonous drinking and smoking. The house itself was first mentioned in documents in 1681. Back then it was a private residence, but it became a restaurant in 1800 and was purchased in 1856 by the Galliker family, whose members still run it. They're especially proud of their small garden in back with space for 28 diners. The waitresses, some of whom might look like your Swiss-German grandmother if you had one, keep the suds and the regional fare flowing. The cuisine is a sort of Lucerne soul food, everything from tripe in white-wine sauce to calf's head, with sweetbreads from nearly all barnyard animals. Farm-style bratwurst seasoned with caraway seeds is consumed along with chunky bread in mass quantities. Less esoteric favorites include beef Stroganoff and thinly sliced calf's liver sautéed in butter with herbs and served with rösti. Fruity desserts are a summer favorite. If you're sharing a table, it's polite to wish your fellow diners *guten appetit.*

Schützenstrasse 1. ℂ **041/241-10-02.** Reservations required. Main courses 22SF–45SF ($12.10–$24.75). AE, DC, MC, V. Tues–Sat 9:30am–midnight. Closed the last 2 weeks of July and 2 weeks in Aug. Bus: 2.

LUCERNE AFTER DARK

The most sophisticated entertainment is found at **Vegas,** the lavishly redecorated new casino at the Luzern Casino, Haldenstrasse 6 (ℂ **041/418-56-56**).

You can try your luck at 140 slot machines. You're limited, however, to only 5SF ($2.75) per bet. On the second floor, you can indulge in a few rounds of boule. Other options here include strip shows at the Red Rose Night Club/Cabaret, and folklore shows in Le Chalet, with traditional music, dances, and costumes, as well as yodeling, alphorn (a large horn) playing, and flag throwing.

On a more cultural note, if you speak German, you can attend performances at the **Stadttheater,** Theaterstrasse 2 (℅ **041/210-66-18**). Directly on the lake on the rail station side of town, it's the home of Luzern's major theater group. Operas in their original language are also staged here. The Allgemeine Musikgesellschaft Luzern is the local resident orchestra, presenting performances at the **Kunsthaus,** Frohburgstrasse 6, from October to June, or at the Kultur und Kongress Zentrum (see below). For more information, call ℅ **041/210-50-50.**

In the late 1990s, the city of Lucerne inaugurated one of the most dramatically modern, large-scale buildings in central Switzerland, the **Kultur und Kongress Zentrum** (KKZ), Europaplatz 1 (℅ **041/226-7070**), as a glittering showcase to corporate conventions and the performing arts. Poised behind the railway station in starkly modern contrast to the spires and alpine architecture of the rest of Lucerne, its controversial shape might remind newcomers of an enchanted "music box" that glitters with acres of glass and metal panels in shades of forest green, dark blue, and red. It was designed with a spectacular copper-sheathed roof by noted Parisian architect Jean Nouvele. Its auditoriums have some of the best acoustics in central Europe, thanks to rotating panels behind the stage. Expect heavy use of this site for classical, rock, and heavy metal concerts. (For ticket information about the concerts that will be presented here, check out the posters in front of the building, or call the concert hall itself at ℅ **0848/800-800** or 0900/552-225.) There's also a snack bar and cafe on the premises.

If you like Swiss folkloric presentations, head for the **Stadtkeller,** Sternenplatz (℅ **041/410-47-33**), which has good food and presents a program of traditional Swiss entertainment, complete with alphorns, cowbells, national costumes, throwing, and yodeling. Presentations are March to October, daily from 8 to 10:30pm.

Other episodes of Swiss folklore can be experienced aboard the **Night Boat Luzern,** Seestrase 106 (℅ **041/319-49-78**), a cruiser that departs from Pier 6 in front of Lucerne's railway station. It operates every night, business permitting, between May and September, departing at 8:45pm and returning at 10:15pm. Advance reservations are required. In most cases, members of a folk musical group perform on board, and there's also a restaurant serving Swiss alpine food. If you opt for the cruise with dinner, the combined cost is around 97SF ($53.35). The boat ride without dinner costs 54SF ($29.70).

The Altstadt or Old Town always brims with pubs and cafes, of which **Mr. Pickwick's Pub,** Rathausquai 6 (℅ **041/410-59-27**), is the most authentic-looking, and the most popular, British pub in Lucerne, with a sudsy, woodsy-looking decor that's awash with Brits, beer, and anyone else who simply wants to toss back a pint or two from a riverfront location near the northern end of the old town's covered bridge. It generally stays open nightly until 1am, which is very late by the standards of Lucerne.

If you're tired of yodeling and want south-of-the-border spice, head for **Cucaracha,** Pilatusstrasse 15 (℅ **041/226-87-87**), for a night of nachos, burritos, and Coronas. Many hotels have more subdued bars, especially the **National,** Haldenstrasse 4 (℅ **041/419-09-09**), which has a glossy American-type bar, and the **Palace Hotel,** Haldenstrasse 10 (℡ **041/416-16-16**), which has two American-style bars. The most ultra-cool place in Lucerne is **The Lounge Bar at The Hotel,** Sempacherstrasse 14 (℡ **041/226-86-86**).

P-1 the Club, on the top floor of the Hotel Monopol, Pilatusstrasse 1 (℡ **041/220-13-15**), is our favorite nightclub in Lucerne. We say that partly because it's crowded with the kinds of hip and available people you can talk to, and partly because it boasts one of the most dramatic physical settings of any nightclub in Switzerland. To reach it, you'll wait in line on the lobby level of the Monopole & Metropole hotel, a Belle-Epoque beauty that sits across the plaza from the railway station. An attendant will funnel clients, in elevator-sized blocks, into a lift that will haul you to a point beneath the hotel's ornate copper-sheathed cupola. Here, recently released dance music, three bars, and a pair of outdoor terraces combine to create an instant party ambience that virtually everyone finds invigorating. By all means, climb to the club's highest point for open-air views of Lucerne that are among the best in the city. Incidentally, this nightclub's name (P1) derives from a simplification of its address (Pilatusstrasse 1).

The Loft, Haldenstrase 2 (℡ **041/410-92-44**), is a serious contender for the title of the most hip and with-it nightclub in a town that's loaded with worthy competition. Music is a sophisticated blend of whatever you might have expected in London or Los Angeles, and the crowd is young and beautiful. The decor includes at least two bar areas, and a balcony that overlooks a high-tech dance floor ringed with free-standing candelabrum, whose candles seem to flicker in rhythm to the music. There is a cover charge of 10SF to 15SF ($5.50–$8.25).

A counterculture bar is the **Bläch-Bar,** in the fairly conservative Hotel Flora, Seidenhofstrasse (℡ **041/229-7979**). Outfitted in Mephistophelean colors of blood red and black, and studded with iron sculptures representing the various demons of hell, it specializes in trance music, house music, and sounds favored by punk-rockers in their 20s and 30s. A definite departure from too strict a diet of yodeling and Swiss folklore, it can be a lot of fun. The terrace of the **Penthouse Bar** at the Hotel Astoria, Pilatusstrasse 29 (℡ **041/226-88-88**), offers a panoramic view over the rooftops of the city and the dramatic mountainscape beyond. Large sofas are an invitation to linger. On weekends, live DJs keep everybody in a party mood. Also at the same hotel is the **Pravda Dance Club,** one of the city's best venues for meeting other young people. Exotic drinks in a romantic Kasbah-like setting can be ordered at the **Casablanca Bar** at the Hotel Schiller, Pilatusstrasse 15 (℡ **041/226-87-87**).

Heaven, Burgerstrasse 21 (℡ **041/210-41-43**), is Lucerne's only gay bar, and as such, it attracts people (mostly men) from many of the hamlets of central Switzerland. Don't expect too much—the venue can be glum, and overall, you'll get a sense that most of the clients would rather be partying in say, Hamburg or Berlin. Overall, you might be happiest here if you define the place as a distinctive but low-energy local pub where most of the clients happen to be gay, German-speaking, and Swiss.

EASY EXCURSIONS FROM LUCERNE

Lake Lucerne is known for its scenery and the many Old-World villages along its shores. Many poets have praised the area's beauty. You may be lucky enough to stay in a hotel room that commands a view of the lake.

Lake steamers and mountain railways can get you to most points of interest around Lake Lucerne. Boat cruises are free if you have a Eurail or InterRail pass.

Mountain railways can whisk you to elevations of 10,000 feet (3,000m) or more in a very short time. Our first adventure will be a major mountain excursion to Mount Pilatus, a 7,000-foot (2,100m) summit overlooking Lucerne.

MOUNT PILATUS ✫✫✫

Pilatus-Kulm is located 9 miles (15km) south of Lucerne. Its German name derives from an old legend: During medieval times, it's said, the city fathers of Lucerne banned travel up the mountain because they thought that its slopes were haunted by the ghost of Pontius Pilate; they feared that Pilate would be angered by intrusive visitors and cause violent storms. For many years after the ban was finally lifted, only a few souls were brave enough to climb the mountain. Queen Victoria made the trip in 1868. Today, the ascent to Pilatus is one of the most popular excursions in Switzerland.

Between May and November, weather permitting, the cog railway operates between Alpnachstad, at the edge of the lake, and the very top of Mount Pilatus. From the quays of Lucerne, take a lake steamer for a scenic 90-minute boat ride to Alpnachstad. If you have a rail pass, remember that it will be valid on this steamer.

At Alpnachstad, transfer to the electric cog railway, which runs at a 48° gradient—the steepest cogwheel railway in the world. Departures are every 45 minutes daily 8:50am to 4:30pm May to September only. At Pilatus-Kulm you can get out and enjoy the view. There are two mountain hotels and a belvedere offering views of Lake Lucerne and many of the mountains around it. For the descent from Mount Pilatus, some visitors prefer to take a pair of cable cars—first a large cabin-style téléphérique, then a small gondola. The cable cars end at Kriens, a suburb of Lucerne. Here you can take bus no. 1, which will carry you into the heart of Lucerne. The round-trip fare on the cog railway and cable car is 78.20SF ($43), 50% off for children under 16.

A similar excursion to Pilatus is possible in the winter, but because the cog railway is buried in snow, you must alter your plans. You'll have to ascend and descend by cable car, which many visitors find exhilarating. From the center of Lucerne, take bus no. 1 from the Bahnhof to the outlying suburb of Kriens. At Kriens, transfer to a cable car that glides over meadows and forests to the village of Fräkmüntegg, 4,600 feet (1,380m) above sea level. The trip takes half an hour. At Fräkmüntegg, switch to another cable car, this one much more steeply inclined than the first. A stunning feat of advanced engineering, it swings above gorges and cliffs to the very peak of Mount Pilatus (Pilatus-Kulm). Unlike the cog railways, these cable cars operate year-round. The round-trip ride by cable car from Kriens to Fräkmüntegg costs 78.20SF ($43).

For information, consult the staff at the city's tourist office or call ✆ **041/ 329-1111.** They're well informed about these excursions, as are the desk personnel at most of Lucerne's hotels.

RIGI ✫✫✫

For another panoramic view from a hilltop belvedere, go to Rigi, 15 miles east of Lucerne. The view from Rigi is different from that atop Mount Pilatus, so if you see both you won't be replicating your experience. Pilatus offers the more panoramic vista, but the view from Rigi is more beautiful. By most accounts, Rigi (5,900 ft./1,680m) is the most famous mountain view in the country. However, you might be disappointed if the weather's not clear. Rigi is called the "island mountain" because it appears to be surrounded by the waters of lakes Lucerne, Zug, and Lauerz. It's accessible by two cog railways and a cableway.

Adventurous visitors making the "grand tour" in the 19th century spent the night at Rigi-Kulm to see the sun rise over the Alps. Victor Hugo called it "an incredible horizon . . . that chaos of absurd exaggerations and scary diminutions." Later, Mark Twain also climbed to the top to see the sun rise across the Alps. But he was so exhausted, as he relates in *A Tramp Abroad,* that he collapsed into sleep, from which he didn't wake until sunset. Not realizing that he had slept all day, he at first recoiled in horror, believing that the sun had switched its direction and was actually rising in the west. This experience continues to be one of nature's loveliest offerings in all of Europe. For those wanting to partake of the tradition, many hotels are perched on the mountainside.

You can travel to the mountain by taking a 55-minute trip by lake steamer from Lucerne to Vitznau, a small resort on the northern shore of the lake. The rack railway from Vitznau to Rigi-Kulm was the first cog railway in Europe, built in 1871. You can also approach the mountain from Arth-Goldau, which is on the southern shore of Zug Lake. The Arth-Goldau cog railway to Rigi-Kulm opened in 1876. The maximum gradient is 21°. Both cog railways cost 68.50SF ($37.70) for the round-trip. It's possible to go up one way and come down the other if you want to see both sides of the mountain. The trip from Vitznau takes 40 minutes and the trip from Arth-Goldau lasts 35 minutes. There are a dozen departures a day in season. An alternative ascent is strongly advocated by the local tourist office. Begin at the quays in Lucerne, and take a lake steamer to Vitznau. From here, after a stroll through the town, go to the top of Rigi Kulm by cog railway and admire the view from the top. Then descend halfway down the mountain via the same cog railway, getting off midway at Rigi Kaltbad. Here you'll switch to the Rigi Seilbahn cable car, which will carry you the rest of the way downhill, a 15-minute downhill walk from the hamlet of Wiggis. You can begin this trip daily between 8am and around 2pm, which is the last reasonable departure time, if you want to see the sights and return to Lucerne before dark. The tourist office or a staff member at the phone listed below will recite the available times of departures. Many visitors, however, find that the most convenient departure time from Lucerne is at 8:32am and again at 10:32am. For more information about anything to do with ascents of Mount Rigi, call the **Lucerne Tourist office** at © **041/399-87-87.** The ascents described in this section are possible only from March to October.

DIETSCHIBERG 🏵🏵

The best view of Lucerne and its lake can be enjoyed from Dietschiberg, at 2,065 feet (619m). Board the cable car on Haldenstrasse in Lucerne. The trip takes about half an hour. You can also see Pilatus and Rigi from a belvedere platform.

GÜTSCH

One sweeping panorama of the region that's easily accessible from the center of Lucerne (and doesn't involve a full day's excursion) is the mountain plateau of Gütsch, 1,715 feet (514m) above sea level. Board a short funicular on Baselstrasse for the 10-minute ride. At the top is a belvedere platform beside the Hotel Château Gütsch, which takes in the city, the lake, and the snowcapped Alps. The funicular departs in both directions every 10 minutes throughout the year, beginning at 8:30am and terminating every night at midnight. Every day from 12:45 to 1:15pm there's a 30-minute lunch break for the operators. The ride costs 3SF ($1.65) one-way. For more information, call the **Château Gütsch** (© **041/249-41-00**).

Impressions

We were soon tramping leisurely up the leafy mulepath, and then the talk began to flow, as usual. It was twelve o'clock noon, and a breezy, cloudless day; the ascent was gradual, and the glimpses from under the curtaining boughs, of blue water, and tiny sail boats, and beetling cliffs, were as charming as glimpses of dreamland.

—Mark Twain, on "Climbing the Rigi"

MOUNT TITLIS ✸✸

Mount Titlis, which is visited as an excursion from the little resort of Engelberg, is the highest point from which you can get a view over central Switzerland. The summit is always covered by snow and ice; there's an "ice cave," in addition to a glacier trail. The view from the belvedere, at 9,900 feet (2,970m), takes in the Jungfrau and the Matterhorn, as well as Zurich and Basel on a clear day. There's a summer ski run with a ski lift. There are also two restaurants: the **Panorama Restaurant Titlis** (℗ **041/639-50-88**), at 10,000 feet (3,000m), and the **Gletscher-Restaurant Stand** (℗ **041/639-50-85**), at 8,040 feet (2,412m).

To get to the summit, you take a funicular and three cable cars. The last stage of the cable-car trip is the most spectacular, as you're taken right over the glacier. Visitors with respiratory problems may want to forgo this trip because of the thinness of the air at such elevations. The terminal at the summit (which is referred to in some time-tables as Kleintitlis, or Little Titlis) has an observation lounge and a large sun terrace.

To get to Titlis from Lucerne's Bahnhof, drive or take a train to Engelberg; the round-trip costs 75SF ($41.25). Then to reach the summit take the cable cars that run daily beginning at 8:30am, with the last one back at 4:40pm. In winter, skiers use this connection to get to the higher slopes. For more information and schedules, call ℗ **041/639-50-50** or 041/639-50-61.

2 Bürgenstock ✸✸

10 miles (16km) SE of Lucerne

The most luxurious resort in the region, Bürgenstock is situated above Lake Lucerne on a 6-mile (10km) limestone ridge. The late Audrey Hepburn, Sophia Loren, and many other movie stars have lived here, swelling the resort's international reputation for glamour. Bürgenstock is lower in altitude than other resorts in the region, reaching only 1,640 feet (492m) on its northern side; the southern edge of town gently slopes through fertile pastureland to the Stans Valley.

ESSENTIALS

GETTING THERE   About a dozen trains make the 40-minute trip from Lucerne to Kehrsiten-Bürgenstock every day. From Kehrsiten-Bürgenstock, you transfer to a steeply ascending cog railway (its gradient is 45%) that departs every 25 to 45 minutes throughout the day for the 7-minute ascent to Bürgenstock. Call ℗ **0900/300-300** for **rail schedules.**

In the summer, frequent **lake steamers** (℗ **041/367-67-67**) leave from the quays in the center of Lucerne, taking 30 minutes to reach the pier at Kehrsiten. From here, passengers transfer to the cog railway.

Since the road to Bürgenstock is winding and treacherous, it's better to go via the lake steamer or train as outlined above. However, if you insist on driving, head south from Lucerne on N8 to Stansstad and, from here, take a steep and narrow, often-dangerous road east for 3 miles (5km) until you reach Bürgenstock.

VISITOR INFORMATION   There are no street names, so follow hotel directional signs. The **Bürgenstock Tourist Office** (© **041/610-55-45**) is open from 8am to 6pm.

EXPLORING THE AREA

When in Bürgenstock you can forget about museums and a lot of man-made attractions. What you do is walk and walk and absorb the mountain panoramas. One of the great walks of central Switzerland, the **Bürgenstock-Felsenweg trail,** begins here. Allow about 2½ hours for the walk from Bürgenstock high above Lake Lucerne to the village of Ennetbürgen.

Begin at the upper funicular station at Bürgenstock, heading east past the Palace Hotel. Then turn left and strike out. Along the way you'll be treated to stunning views of Lake Lucern and even Pilatus.

At the **Hammetschwand Lift** you can interrupt your walk to enjoy a ride on the highest free-standing lift in Europe. You're taken to a lookout point 3,697 feet (1,127m) above sea level, where the view stretches all the way to the Swiss Alps to the south. Afterward you enter a series of short tunnels and pass the historic chapel of St. Jost, erected in 1733 as the tomb of a hermit from the Middle Ages. Heading down the slopes, you eventually reach the village of Ennetbürgen with its ferry dock where you can board vessels to take you to other towns along Lake Lucerne.

WHERE TO STAY & DINE

Bürgenstock Hotels ★★★   This is one of the most exclusive hotels in Europe, and also the largest privately owned hotel complex in Switzerland. Set in a 12-acre private park, it consists of three separate buildings: the Grand Hotel (opened in 1873), the Palace Hotel (opened in 1904), and the Park Hotel (opened in 1888 but demolished and rebuilt in a plush, modern style in 1991). The public rooms of each of the three hotels abound in art treasures, including works by Rubens, van Dyck, Tintoretto, and Brueghel. The furniture is worthy of a modern-day Versailles, and many different fireplaces throw off a welcoming glow. The bedrooms are traditionally furnished, spacious for the most part, and well maintained with luxurious appointments. All units have very well-kept bathrooms. In the summer, a battalion of gardeners keeps the grounds immaculate and flowering.

Ch-6363 Bürgenstock. © 800/874-4002 in the United States, or 041/612-90-10. Fax 041/612-90-11. www.buergenstock-hotels.ch. 183 units. Grand and Palace hotels, 410SF–440SF ($225.50–$242) double. Park Hotel, 460SF–580SF ($253–$319) double; from 770SF ($423.50) suite. Rates include continental breakfast. AE, DC, MC, V. Free parking. All closed Nov–Mar. **Amenities:** 5 restaurants, 2 bars; 2 pools; 9-hole golf course; 2 tennis courts; health spa; sauna; room service; massage; babysitting; laundry/dry cleaning. *In room:* TV, minibar, hair dryer, safe.

Hotel Fürigen   Located on a wooded hillside high above the lake, this resort hotel has white walls and a red-tile roof with gables and towers. Completely renovated in 1991, it offers mid-sized, comfortable bedrooms with excellent beds and good views. All rooms also come equipped with tidy bathrooms. The hotel operates two restaurants on the lake, one serving Greek dishes, the other Italian.

CH-6363 Bürgenstock. © 041/610-00-60. Fax 041/610-27-24. www.hotel-fuerigen.ch. 82 units, 2 suites. 290SF ($159.50) double; 320SF ($176) suite. Rates include buffet breakfast. Half board 50SF ($27.50) per person extra. AE, DC, MC, V. Free parking. **Amenities:** 2 restaurants, bar; pool; tennis courts; fitness center; sauna; Turkish bath; room service; babysitting; laundry/dry cleaning. *In room:* TV, hair dryer, safe.

Waldhotel Bürgenstock *Value*   This is a far more affordable and democrat-ically priced hotel than the Bürgenstock Hotels' bastion of luxury accommo-dations. There has been a hotel at this site since 1895. The present modern building was constructed after the previous hotel burned in 1958. The new ver-sion has an elegantly paneled lounge, an elevator, and a narrow terrace with a view of the snowy mountains. Most of the spacious rooms have balconies, all have firm beds, and those with private bathrooms are for the most part equipped with shower-tub combinations. The hotel is accessible by a single-lane road that winds through an alpine meadow dotted with huts and 19th-century chalets.

The Waldheim also offers a less expensive alternative to dining at the Bür-genstock Hotels.

CH-6363 Bürgenstock. ℂ **041/611-03-83.** Fax 041/610-64-66. www.waldhotel-buergenstock.ch. 55 units, 10 without bathroom. 310SF ($170.50) double without bathroom, 360SF–410SF ($198–$225.50) double with bathroom. Rates include continental breakfast. AE, DC, MC, V. Free parking. Closed Dec 27–Jan 3. **Amenities:** Restaurant; pool; health club; sauna; steam room; children's center; room service; babysitting; laundry/dry cleaning. *In room:* TV, minibar, hair dryer, safe.

3 Weggis ⁄★⁄★

19 miles (30km) E of Lucerne

The lakeside resort of Weggis is on the sunny side of Mount Rigi, one of three holiday centers (Vitznau and Gersau are the others) that offer the kind of mild climate found in favored parts of Italy. Weggis and the other resorts are about an hour's walk or a 5-minute drive apart. Well-tended garden promenades stretch for several miles along the lakeshore. Mark Twain stayed here in 1897.

Of the three resorts, Weggis is the most preferred. It's usually the first port of call for steamers from Lucerne and is also easily accessible from the international St. Gotthard railway line, although it's not on the main traffic route.

Many excursions are possible from early spring to late autumn. You can take the aerial cableway up to Rigi-Kaltbad (4,756 ft./1,427m), a mountain health resort behind Weggis. This is great walking country, not only on the promenade quays but on the slopes of the Rigi, which are planted with vines. Even some almost tropical species of vegetation grow here. In addition, mountain transport links Weggis with the Rigi Railways.

ESSENTIALS

GETTING THERE   Several **lake steamers** (ℂ **041/367-67-67**) depart from the quays of Lucerne for Weggis every day, requiring about 45 minutes for the transfer. Once you reach Weggis, a local bus run by the village transports you (in the summertime only) from the lakefront to the upper reaches of the town.

Though Weggis is not directly accessible by rail, the railway junction of Kuss-nacht lies 6 miles from Weggis. From Kussnacht, buses depart for the 10- to 13-minute ride to Weggis.

If you're driving from Lucerne, drive east on Route 2, along the northern rim of Lake Lucerne, cutting south on Route 2b at the signposted turnoff to Weggis.

VISITOR INFORMATION   The **Weggis Tourist Office** (ℂ **041/390-11-55**) is open Monday to Friday from 8am to 6pm, Saturday and Sunday 9am to 2:30pm. (Off-season, the office remains closed on weekends.) If you'd like to go biking along the banks of Lake Lucerne, you can stop in here and rent a bike for the day for 26SF ($14.30).

WHERE TO STAY & DINE

Hotel Albana 🏠 This hotel is outclassed only by the Beau Rivage (see below). The most prestigious hotel at Weggis, the Hotel Albana was built in the Art Nouveau style in 1896 and has been run by the Wolf family since 1910. One of the public rooms, with a grand piano and a 10-foot (3m) Meissen ceramic stove, looks almost baronial. Heavy brass chandeliers hang from the frescoed ceiling, and large rococo mirrors reflect the wood paneling. The mid-sized bedrooms are modernized with excellent beds. Many have good views of the nearby lake. The best food at the resort is served in the Panorama Restaurant, which has large windows and a terrace above the lake. The decor of the hotel's Jazz Bar was inspired by Matisse; on some nights it offers live music.

CH-6353 Weggis. ⓒ 041/390-21-41. Fax 041/390-29-59. www.albana-weggis.ch. 57 units. 240SF–360SF ($132–$198) double. Half board 58SF ($31.90) extra. Rates include buffet breakfast. AE, DC, MC, V. Closed Dec 15–Jan 15. **Amenities:** Restaurant, bar, lounge; sauna; bike rental; room service; babysitting; laundry/dry cleaning. *In room:* TV, minibar, hair dryer, safe.

Hotel Beau-Rivage 🏠🏠 One of the attractions of this 1908 hotel is its expanse of manicured lawn, which reaches down to the lake near the boat landing. The view of the mountains from here is exhilarating. The symmetrical hotel has a series of wrought-iron balconies, and the traditional and spacious rooms are comfortably furnished with wood, brass, and pastel shades. Comfortable bedrooms open onto panoramic lake and mountain views.

CH-6353 Weggis. ⓒ **041/392-79-00.** Fax 041/390-19-81. www.beaurivage-weggis.ch. 41 units. 210SF–330SF ($115.50–$181.50) double; 340SF–400SF ($187–$220) suite. Half board 48SF ($26.40) extra. Rates include continental breakfast. AE, DC, MC, V. Free parking. Closed late Oct to Mar. **Amenities:** Restaurant, bar; pool; room service; laundry/dry cleaning. *In room:* TV, minibar, hair dryer.

Hotel Central am See This old-fashioned resort hotel, built with six large gables and many smaller ones, stands on a shady peninsula with a swimming pool near the lake. Constructed in 1912 and completely renovated in 1995, it offers an interior with traditional furniture and an elevator carrying clients to the well-maintained, rather stark bedrooms, most of which offer a view of the lake and mountains. All units come equipped with tidy bathrooms containing showers. The hotel has a greenhouse-style restaurant, the Winter Garden, overlooking the lake.

CH-6353 Weggis. ⓒ **041/392-09-09.** Fax 041/392-09-00. www.central-am.see.ch. 35 units. Oct to mid-May 210SF–280SF ($115.50–$154) double. Mid-May to Sept 230SF–310SF ($126.50–$170.50) double. Rates include breakfast. AE, DC, MC, V. Parking 10SF ($5.50). Closed Nov 9–Jan 15. **Amenities:** 2 restaurants, bar; pool; bike rental; room service; babysitting; laundry/dry cleaning. *In room:* TV, hair dryer.

Hotel Rössli *Value* Completely renovated in 1997, this century-old hotel with elaborate shingles occupies the most desirable lakefront position at the center of the resort town, facing a tranquil square with flowers, statues, and a fountain. The hotel has ornate wood balustrades and russet-colored shutters. The renovated interior is modern, with a decor of wrought iron, wicker chairs, and hanging lamps. The Nölly family offers pleasant mid-sized rooms with attractive furniture and neatly kept bathrooms. You'll also find a sidewalk cafe in front.

CH-6353 Weggis. ⓒ **041/390-11-06.** Fax 041/390-27-26. www.wellness-roessli.ch. 60 units. 200SF–220SF ($110–$121) double. Half board 30SF ($16.50) extra. Rates include buffet breakfast. AE, DC, MC, V. Free parking. Closed Nov–Mar. **Amenities:** Restaurant, lounge. *In room:* TV.

4 Vitznau ⟨★⟩

16 miles (26km) E of Lucerne, 2½ miles (4km) SE of Weggis

Vitznau is located on a different bay of Lake Lucerne, at the foot of the Rigi. At 1,446 feet (439m), it offers an alpine panorama that's mirrored in the lake. It's an hour's drive from Zurich.

Sports vacations are especially popular in Vitznau from April to October. Facilities include swimming in the lake, indoor and outdoor pools, and tennis courts. There are also many inviting hiking trails—ideal for long walks—in the meadows, woodlands, and mountains.

The Vitznau-Rigi railway starts at Vitznau along the shores of Lake Lucerne, on the south side of Mount Rigi. The railway terminates at Kulm peak, after passing through the mountain stations of Rigi-Kaltbad-First, Rigi Staffelhöehe, and Rigi Staffel. In the summer, old-fashioned steam trains travel on this stretch of electric rack-and-pinion railway. Pause to enjoy the beauty of the resort before heading up to the mountain. Departures are every 30 minutes.

ESSENTIALS

GETTING THERE   The only rail line servicing Vitznau is a local alpine train connecting it to such panoramic points as Rigi-Kulm and Rigi-Kaltbad. Call ⟨✆⟩ 0900/300-300 for **rail schedules.**

Buses depart for Vitznau from the Küssnacht railway station, which is reached from Lucerne by train every hour, requiring about 45 minutes, including a stopover in Weggis. Some of the buses continue to Gersau, where there's a connection to Brunne. For **bus schedules** and information, call ⟨✆⟩ 041/367-67-67.

Ferries depart for Vitznau from the quays of Lucerne every hour in summer and about every 2 hours in winter. The trip takes about 1 hour. Call ⟨✆⟩ 041/ 367-67-67 for more information.

If you're driving, the resort is reached by first passing through Weggis (see section 3, earlier in this chapter), then continuing along route 2b south to Vitznau, a very short drive along the lake.

VISITOR INFORMATION   The **Vitznau Tourist Board,** in the town center (⟨✆⟩ 041/398-00-35), is open November to Easter Monday to Saturday from 9am to noon and 1 to 6:30pm. From Easter to June and September to October, hours are Monday to Friday 8:30am to noon and 1 to 6:30pm, Saturday 9am to noon. July and August, the office is open Monday to Friday 9am to 6:30pm, Saturday 9am to 2pm, and Sunday 9am to noon.

EXPLORING THE AREA

If you'd like to enjoy the pleasures of the lake itself, both paddleboats and motorboats are for rent at **Anker Travel,** Zihlstrasse (⟨✆⟩ 041/397-17-07). It's also possible to swim in the bay here, although the temperatures are a mite chilly for those from sunnier climes.

If you're biking down from Vitznau, you can tour the entire right bank of the lake by **Route 2,** which runs all the way to Altdorf (see section 6 below).

WHERE TO STAY & DINE

Hotel Rigi   Although the service from the staff may leave you as cold as an alpine lake, this is a clean and decent place that can be recommended for its economy. About a block from the boat-landing dock, the hotel is a century-old monument within the town center, although rooms have been kept fairly up-to-date.

Finds An Idyllic Swimming Hole

To escape from the crowds along Lake Lucerne, we'll let you in on a secret. At the very southeastern tip of Lake Lucerne is the narrow and splendid inlet lake, the **Urnersee,** which attracts fewer visitors than the resorts along Lake Lucerne even though it's no less majestic or beautiful. In fact, this is the more remote, the wildest, and the loveliest part of the whole of Lake Lucerne. A natural rock obelisk, called **Schillerstein,** rises some 85 feet (25m) out of the Urnersee, dedicated to Friedrich von Schiller, the author of _Wilhelm Tell._

Units come in a variety of shapes and sizes and are comfortable, with firm beds and good maintenance. Opt, if available, for one of the corner bedrooms that open onto their own private balconies and a view of the lake. Don't expect many in-room amenities outside of a telephone and private bathrooms.

Haupstrasse, CH-6354 Vitznau. © **041/397-2121.** Fax 041/397-1825. www.rigi-vitznau.ch. 36 units. 130SF–190SF ($71.50–$104.50) double. Rates include breakfast. AE, DC, MC, V. **Amenities:** Restaurant, lounge; room service; laundry/dry cleaning.

Park Hotel Vitznau ★★★   One of the most elegant waterside havens along the Lucerne Riviera, this Belle Epoque hotel offers lavish living. It was designed by architect Karl Koller and built in 1902 at the foot of Mount Rigi. A wing added in 1985 maintains the spirit of the original "fairytale castle." Today's hotel grew out of a simple 1866 B&B that once attracted such wanderers as Mark Twain and Victor Hugo. The spacious bedrooms have been completely renovated, with marble-clad bathrooms and such thoughtful extras as heated towel racks. The bathtubs with showers have been dubbed "pharaonic." English chintz, both in draperies and upholstery, give the rooms a summery look. Try for one of the seven or so lake-view rooms on the first floor in the older section, each of which has a sprawling lakefront terrace. Rooms 121 and 123 are most frequently requested, since they have particularly large terraces. Ceilings within the hotel's public areas are particularly high and grand, each a decorative throwback to the late-19th-century age of hotel design. There's also a sun terrace with parasols. The a la carte restaurant, Quatre Cantons, with a lakeside terrace, is one of the finest French restaurants in Switzerland.

Kantonstrasse, CH-6354 Vitznau. © **041/399-6060.** Fax 041/399-6070. www.parkhotel-vitznau.ch. 112 units. 470SF–620SF ($258.50–$341) double; from 1,000SF ($550) suite. Rates include buffet breakfast. AE, DC, MC, V. Free parking. Closed Oct 21–Apr 22. **Amenities:** 3 restaurants, bar; 2 pools; 2 tennis courts; health club; sauna; free bikes; water-skiing; room service; babysitting; laundry/dry cleaning. _In room:_ TV, minibar, hair dryer.

5 Brunnen ★★

28 miles (45km) SE of Lucerne

Brunnen is a popular vacation resort in the canton of Schwyz. It's located at the foot of Fronalpstock, in a beautiful inlet at the southern end of Lake Lucerne, where you find the Urnesee (or Lake Uri), one of the most beautiful lake sites in Switzerland. There's a fine view of the two lakes and the Alps from the quays. The resort is about an hour's drive from Zurich's Kloten International Airport.

ESSENTIALS

GETTING THERE   Some of the local trains running between Zurich and Lugano or Locarno in Switzerland's deep south stop in Brunnen, although some require changes in such towns as Goschenen. Call ☎ **0900/300-300** (no area code) for **rail schedules.**

A mini-armada of buses commutes dozens of times every day from Schwyz to both the waterfront and the railroad station at Brunnen, requiring only about 12 minutes for the one-way passage. Other buses travel from Brunnen to the beginning of the cable car that ascends to Morschach. For **bus schedules** and information, call ☎ **041/390-11-33.**

Several lake steamers depart from the quays of Lucerne for Brunnen throughout the day, with more frequent service scheduled during midsummer. Travel time from Lucerne to Brunnen ranges from 2 to 2½ hours. For more information, call ☎ **041/367-67-67.**

From Lucerne, drive to the resorts of Weggis and Vitznau (see sections 3 and 4, earlier in this chapter), then continue southeast along Route 2b until you reach Brunnen.

VISITOR INFORMATION   The **Brunnen Tourist Office,** Bahnhofstrasse 32 (☎ **041/825-00-40**), is open Monday to Friday from 8:30am to noon and 1 to 6pm. July and August the office is also open on Saturday from 9am to noon and from 1:30 to 4pm.

EXPLORING THE AREA

What you do here is walk along the shady **lakeside quays** ⋆⋆, among the country's most scenic parts, taking in views of the wild and remote lake, the Urnesee.

The Legend of William Tell

One of the most famous names in Swiss history, linked with that country's struggle for liberty, concerned a William Tell, who may never have existed. But to the Swiss he is very real, the father who with his crossbow hit the apple that the tyrannical Austrian bailiff of Uri, Gessler, had placed on the head of his son.

When Gessler allegedly asked Tell why he had brought a second arrow, Tell told him he intended it for Gessler if he had hit his son instead of the apple. Furious, Gessler had Tell dragged to his boat at the northwestern shore of Lake Lucerne. A storm came up and Gessler released Tell from his fetters, hoping that his strong arms could save the boat party. Tell escaped and waited on the shore near Gessler's castle. When Gessler arrived, Tell hit him with an arrow straight through the heart. Or so the story goes.

First found in a ballad, the tale dates from at least before 1474. Over the years various authors have smoothed away inconsistencies and rounded out the tale. But it was Schiller's play in 1804 that gave the tale worldwide renown.

Alleged proofs of the actual existence of a William Tell break down hopelessly upon scholarly examination. For example, entries in the parish registers are forgeries. One document which alleged that 114 men in 1338 had been "personally acquainted" with Tell didn't surface until 1759—no doubt a fake.

Tellskapelle or the Tell Chapel stands today as a monument to the legend, lying at the Lake of the Four Cantons between Sisikon and Flüelen.

The views of the lake from the quays are stunning, taking in the awesome Uri-Rotstock, twin peaks with a small glacier.

The area around Brunnen—so beloved by Hans Christian Andersen—is the cradle of the Confederation and abounds in reminders of the country's history, including archives in Schwyz where the Confederation documents are displayed, and the Federal Chapel in Brunnen.

This is also William Tell country. Around the year 1250, several families left Raron in the Valais and crossed the Alps to establish new homes in desolate Schächental/Uri. Records confirm that the Tell family helped found the settlement. According to folk legend, William Tell was the hero of a decisive battle in 1315 and reportedly died in 1350. Historians, however, have no proof of these events.

Nevertheless, the Swiss honor the man who shot an apple off the head of his brave young son with a bow and arrow in a test of prowess. Many visitors travel to Sisikon, just south of Brunnen, to see the **Tell Chapel,** which was restored in 1881; the chapel contains records from the early 16th century and paintings by Stückelberg.

NEARBY ATTRACTIONS   Brunnen is the starting point of **Axenstrasse,** the stunning panoramic road—a masterpiece of engineering—leading south to the St. Gotthard Pass. It goes along the rim of Lake Uri (Urnersee), in and out of subterranean passageways and galleries carved out of the mountain. Brunnen is also a base for excursions by ship, mountain railway, bus, and train to points around Lake Lucerne.

WHERE TO STAY & DINE

Hotel Bellevue   Built in the 1800s and completely renovated in 1995, this baroque hotel at the edge of the lake offers cozy, old-fashioned comfort. Werner Achermann and his family offer well-maintained rooms, most with carpeting and all with well-maintained bathrooms. Some units are wheelchair accessible. The hotel also has a sun terrace.

Axenstrasse 2, CH-6440 Brunnen. ℂ 041/820-13-18. Fax 041/820-38-89. www.bellevue-brunnen.ch. 46 units. 240SF–260SF ($132–$143). Half board 30SF ($16.50) per person extra. Rates include continental breakfast. AE, DC, MC, V. Free parking. Closed Nov–Apr. **Amenities:** Restaurant, bar, lounge; laundry/dry cleaning. *In room:* TV, minibar.

Hotel Elite   ⟨Value⟩   Built in 1964, this lakeside hotel lies behind a facade of beige wood, with large balconies and a terrace by the water shaded by clipped sycamores. You must be a guest to enjoy the sixth-floor terrace with a panoramic view. The public rooms are dignified and modern, while the mid-sized bedrooms, decorated in earth tones, have comfortable beds and neatly kept bathrooms. The hotel chef offers a number of specialties from the grill; a special feature is the fresh fish from Swiss lakes.

Axenstrasse 1, CH-6440 Brunnen. ℂ 041/820-10-24. Fax 041/820-55-65. www.hotel-elite-brunnen.ch. 45 units. 130SF–180SF ($71.50–$99) double. Rates include buffet breakfast. AE, DC, MC, V. Parking 5SF ($2.75). Closed Nov–Mar 1. **Amenities:** Restaurant, lounge; laundry/dry cleaning. *In room:* TV.

Seehotel Waldstätterhof   ⋆⋆   One of the few government-rated five-star hotels opening onto the lake, the Waldstätterhof offers old-style comfort. The symmetrical white building has a mansard roof and a series of balconies overlooking the lake. Plenty of modern comforts have been installed since the hotel opened in 1870; it was last renovated in 1992. Each of the well-furnished and spacious rooms offers a well-maintained bathroom. The public rooms are grand and the dining room has fanciful chandeliers. The grounds are well kept and free of traffic and include a private beach on the lake. There's also a terrace restaurant, rotisserie, and stube. The Lake Lucerne steamers stop nearby, and the Schiller Memorial Stone can be seen on the opposite shore of the lake. The hotel is open year-round.

Waldstätterquai 6, CH-6440 Brunnen. ⓒ 041/825-06-06. Fax 041/825-06-00. www.walderstaetterhof.ch. 104 units. 310SF–390SF ($170.50–$214.50) double; 560SF–720SF ($308–$396) suite. Half board 50SF ($27.50) extra. Rates include buffet breakfast. AE, DC, MC, V. Free parking outside, 10SF ($5.50) in garage. **Amenities:** 3 restaurants, bar; tennis court; health club; sauna; room service; babysitting; laundry/dry cleaning. *In room:* TV, minibar, hair dryer, safe.

6 Altdorf

34 miles (54km) SE of Lucerne

Altdorf is the town where the William Tell legend is said to have taken place. A statue of the Swiss national hero stands in the main square. The key to the St. Gotthard Pass, Altdorf is north of the Alps and 2 miles (3km) south of where the Reuss River flows into the Urnesee. It's the capital of the canton of Uri and the starting point of the road over the Klausen Pass. The most scenic way to get to Altdorf from Lucerne is to ride a lake steamer to Flüelen and transfer to a bus. The total trip takes about 3 hours. Call the tourist office (see below) for more information.

ESSENTIALS

GETTING THERE   Several daily trains make the 27-minute trip to Altdorf from the region's biggest railway junction, Arth-Goldau, on their way south to Chiasso and eventually Milan. Call ⓒ **0900/300-300** for **rail schedules.**

The bus routes coming into Altdorf connect the town with mountain hamlets, which usually have no railway junctions of their own. In the summer a handful of buses connect it with Zurich's Hauptbahnhof, sometimes with a transfer in Flüelin. Travel time from Zurich is about 1½ hours. For bus schedules and information, call ⓒ 041/618-85-55.

If you're driving from Brunnen on Lake Lucerne, continue south along N4.

VISITOR INFORMATION   The **Altdorf Tourist Office** (ⓒ **041/872-04-50**) is open Monday to Friday from 9 to 11:30am and 1:30 to 5:30pm; Saturday, 9 to 11:30am.

SEEING THE SIGHTS

The famous **William Tell statue** is in front of the early-19th-century town hall and a tower dating from the Middle Ages. The monument was created by Richard Kissling in 1895; it was this image, engraved on a postage stamp, that became familiar to people all over the globe.

Altdorf is set in a scenic area of central Switzerland that makes for good biking. You can rent a bike at the train station (ⓒ 041/870-10-08). You can also rent mountain bikes and motorbikes at **Mototreff,** Flüelerstrasse 20 (ⓒ **041/ 870-97-37**). Armed with a good map from the tourist office, set out on your adventure.

NEARBY ATTRACTIONS   The road to the Klausen Pass leads to **Bürglen,** one of the oldest hamlets in Uri. Snowdrifts block the pass from October to May. Bürglen, according to legend, was the birthplace of William Tell. The **Tell Museum,** Hauptstrasse (ⓒ 041/870-41-55), contains documents and mementos relating to the early history of Switzerland. The museum is in a Romanesque tower adjacent to the parish church. It's open April to June and September and October, daily from 10 to 11:30am and 1:30 to 5pm; in July and August, daily from 9:30am to 5:30pm. Admission is 5SF ($2.75) for adults, 1.50SF (85¢) for children 15 and under.

WHERE TO STAY & DINE

Goldener Schlüssel *Value*   The best of the lot is this five-story, government-rated three-star hotel in the center of town. A historic inn dating from the 19th century, it faces a tiny medieval plaza and is distinguished by a wrought-iron sign bearing a golden key (goldener Schlüssel). The hotel's accessories include a handful of original paintings. The bedrooms are cozy and comfortably furnished and those units with bathrooms have clean showering facilities.

The hotel's well-reputed restaurant serves a cuisine based on all-Swiss recipes and local ingredients.

Schützengasse 9, CH-6460 Altdorf. ✆ 041/871-10-02. Fax 041/870-11-67. 25 units, 18 with bathroom. 110SF–120SF ($60.50–$66) double without bathroom, 170SF–195SF ($93.50–$107.25) double with bathroom; 290SF ($159.50) suite. Half board 45SF ($24.75) per person extra. Rates include buffet breakfast. AE, DC, MC, V. Free parking. **Amenities:** Restaurant, lounge; room service. *In room:* TV.

Hotel Bahnhof *Finds*   Anna Niederberger and her family own this small, well-established tourist hotel that resembles a private house, with a modern addition in front. Built in 1880, it still retains many of its old-fashioned and somewhat quirky architectural details. It has dated furniture, and all rooms have a sink. The accommodations are small but pleasantly paneled and comfortable, with good beds.

CH-6460 Altdorf. ✆ 041/870-10-32. Fax 041/870-99-32. 28 units (none with bathroom). 85SF ($46.75) double. Rates include continental breakfast. No credit cards. Free parking. **Amenities:** Restaurant, lounge. *In room:* No phone.

7 Amsteg

9 miles S of Altdorf, 4 miles S of Erstfeld

This traditional stop on the St. Gotthard route is a good base for walks and mountain excursions. Amsteg is at the mouth of the Maderanertal. In the distance you can see a tall viaduct, which holds the tracks of the St. Gotthard railway.

ESSENTIALS

GETTING THERE   Train service was discontinued to the rarely used Amsteg railway station several years ago, so railway passengers headed for Amsteg get off at the hamlet of Erstfeld. From here the Swiss railway system operates shuttle service, by bus, at hourly intervals throughout the day for the price of 4SF ($2.20) per person each way. For information on both the **railway** and the **shuttle,** call ✆ 0900/300-300.

VISITOR INFORMATION   Amsteg does not have a tourist office. The tourist office (✆ 044/2-28-88) of Altdorf, just north of Amsteg, is open Monday to Friday 9 to 11:30am and 1:30 to 5:30pm; Saturday, 9 to 11:30am.

WHERE TO STAY & DINE

Hotel Stern und Post *☆*   This is the most colorful and atmospheric hotel in Amsteg. It has been managed since 1734 by members of the Tresch family, who established it as part of their administration of the local branch of the then-private Swiss Postal system. After 1850, when the Swiss Postal System became a branch of the national government, the family maintained this hotel in addition to nearby lodgings for more than 400 horses, most of which were used for hauling mail and supplies over the nearby Gotthard Pass. Today, under the administration of Elizabeth Tresch, this hotel retains many of its ornate

19th-century antiques, moldings, doors, and decorative accessories. Some of the bedrooms are furnished with Victorian-style beds and lots of gingerbread, with high ceilings and nostalgic reminders of another era. Rooms containing private bathrooms have well-equipped facilities; there are only sinks with running water in those without. Public areas, discreetly modernized and enlarged and—in newer wings—pierced with panoramic windows, have gray-green walls and reminders of the hotel's earliest origins. The in-house restaurant, which seats up to 40 guests, will spoil you with a plentiful cuisine and well-chosen wines from their private cellar.

CH-6474 Amsteg. © **041/883-14-40.** Fax 041/883-02-61. www.sternpostch. 20 units, 14 with bathroom. 103SF–20SF ($56.65–$66) double without bathroom; 180SF–240SF ($99–$132) double with bathroom. 50SF ($27.50) supplement for half board per person. (3 nights' minimum stopover required for half board.) Rates include breakfast. Parking: 8SF ($4.40) per night. AE, DC, MC, V. Closed: Jan to mid-Mar. **Amenities:** Restaurant, bar; room service; babysitting; laundry/dry cleaning.

8 Andermatt ★

31 miles (50km) SE of Lucerne

At the crossroads of the Alps, Andermatt is a sports center known for its long, sunny days in winter. It's in the Urseren Valley, at the junction of two alpine roads—the St. Gotthard highway and the road to Oberalp and Furka. Visitors flock here for the valley's scenic grandeur, best absorbed by hiking in summer or cross-country skiing in winter.

ESSENTIALS

GETTING THERE   Andermatt lies directly on a secondary rail line connecting Chur with Lucerne, where further connections can be made on express trains to the rest of Switzerland. Travel time from Lucerne is about 1¾ hours. Call © **0900/300-300** for **rail schedules.**

Three or four buses travel daily from the bus junction of Airola to Andermatt. To Airola, buses funnel in every day from Basel, Lucerne, Zurich, and Lugano, with connections to such other resorts as Brig and Oberwald. For **bus schedules** and information, call © **081/949-20-34.**

If you're driving from Amsteg, continue south along N2.

VISITOR INFORMATION   The **Andermatt Tourist Office,** on Gotthardstrasse 2 (© **041/887-14-54**), is open Monday to Saturday from 9am to noon and 2 to 5:30pm.

EXPLORING THE AREA

Andermatt is a good base for hikes across the mountain passes, including the St. Gotthard Pass and the Furka Pass. In the winter, skiers flock to Gemsstock, Natschen, Oberalp, and Winterhorn. In winter, the town offers 10 lifts, five cable cars, 12½ miles (21km) of cross-country trails open November to May, and 35 miles of downhill runs. Intermediate to advanced skiers are attracted to the resort. Safety devices help protect against snowdrifts and avalanches. Other sporting facilities include a Swiss Ski School, an ice-skating and curling rink, an indoor swimming pool, and squash courts. Sleigh rides are also offered.

Andermatt is one of the best places in central Switzerland for mountain biking in summer. Rent mountain bikes from **Christen Sport,** Gotthardstrasse 55 (© **041/8871251**).

South of Andermatt, the **St. Gotthard Pass** ★, at 6,920 feet, provides a link between the Grisons and the Valais Alps. It's one of the most stunning and scenic passes in Switzerland, used by merchants and messengers as far back as the early Middle Ages. The road through the pass was built in the 18th and 19th centuries atop a much older footpath; it's still the shortest route between the two watersheds that fall away on either side. A 9-mile-long (15km) railway tunnel burrows under the peak of the St. Gotthard massif; nearby, the St. Gotthard road tunnel, opened in 1980, is the longest one in the world. There's no toll along the 10-mile (16km) route, which is open year-round. (The road high above it closes during heavy snowfalls.)

If you don't have a car, you can take either the postal bus over the pass or the train through the tunnel. The postal bus leaves from Andermatt and goes to Airolo daily between mid-April and September 21. Departures from Andermatt are at 9:35am and 12:30pm. The last bus back leaves Airolo at 5pm. In winter the pass is closed and postal buses can't get through, but you could take the train to Göschenen and from there continue by train to Airolo. Trains run through the tunnel frequently, the only way for trains to cross this mountain-pass area. For **train information** and schedules, call ✆ **0900/300-300.**

The 20-mile **Furka Pass Road** 🌟🌟🌟 going from Gletsch to Andermatt takes about 2½ hours and is one of the most scenic rides in Europe. Begin the trip at Gletsch at 580 feet (174m). As you drive along you'll have panoramic views of the Rhone Glacier, and both the Bernese and Valais Alps. The pass at 7,975 feet (2,392m) is the highest shelf of the towering longitudinal furrow, dividing the Swiss Alps from the rail junction at Martigny to the town of Chur. In 1982 a railway tunnel, a stunning feat of modern engineering, opened the pass between the villages of Oberwald and Realp. Going through the barren valley of Garschen and bordering the foothills of Galenstock, a mountain peak, the road comes to the severe Urseren Valley before passing through the villages of Realp, Hospental, and finally Andermatt, where you might want to spend the night.

WHERE TO STAY & DINE

Hotel Aurora   Although this hotel presents a modern and unassuming facade to the world outside, the pleasant and warmly decorated interior and the hands-on management of its owners (the Christen family) make a stay here worthwhile. Built in 1969, it's a well-managed, government-rated three-star hotel, lying at the southern edge of the village, within a 5-minute walk of the town center. Each small room has touches of pine paneling, a firm bed, and a neatly kept bathroom.

CH-6490 Andermatt. ✆ **041/887-16-61.** Fax 041/887-00-89. 26 units. 130SF–150SF ($71.50–$82.50) double; 156SF–177SF ($85.80–$97.35) triple. Rates include breakfast. AE, MC, V. Free parking. Closed May and Nov. **Amenities:** Restaurant, bar; sauna; room service, laundry/dry cleaning. *In room:* TV.

Hotel Drei Könige und Post 🌟   This old and fabled inn still puts up wayfarers. There has been a series of inns at this site since 1234, and Goethe spent the night at one of them in 1775. This family-run hotel, built since then, was renovated in 1977. There's a cafe terrace in front of this white-walled chalet with buttressed eaves and brown shutters. Regional Swiss dishes are served in the hotel restaurant. The Renner family offers well-furnished paneled rooms, 10 of which have balconies. Rooms range from small to mid-sized, and each is exceedingly comfortable with traditional furnishings. All units are equipped with well-maintained bathrooms.

Gotthardstrasse 69, CH-6490 Andermatt. ✆ **041/887-00-01.** Fax 041/887-16-66. www.dreikoenige.ch. 20 units. 160SF–240SF ($88–$132) double. AE, DC, MC, V. Free parking. Closed Apr 15 to May and Nov to Dec 15. **Amenities:** Restaurant, lounge; fitness center; Jacuzzi; sauna; Turkish bath; room service; babysitting; laundry/dry cleaning. *In room:* TV, minibar, hair dryer.

12

The Grisons

Of all the Swiss cantons, the Grisons is both the largest and the least developed. Its German name is Graubunden; to the Romansh-speaking population it's Grischun, and the Italians call it Grigioni. Grisons is the French (and English) name, although French is rarely spoken in this canton.

This sparsely settled, easternmost Swiss region is very mountainous, and contains 140 square miles (225 sq. km) of glaciers. One-fifth of the canton's total area is covered with forests. The region contains the sources of the Rhine and Inn (En in Romansh) rivers, which form the major valleys of the canton. Juf, at nearly 7,000 feet (2,100m) above sea level, is the highest permanently inhabited village in the Alps. Even the 150 or so valleys of the Grisons lie at high altitudes, between 2,953 and 6,562 feet (886 and 1,969m), and the region's highest peak, Bernina, reaches 13,285 feet (3,986m). The alpine scenery here differs from that of other areas of Switzerland in altitude as well as topography—the air is clear and invigorating, which has led to the establishment of many health centers in the Grisons. The height makes it cooler at night, but it enjoys the extra daytime warmth of other southern cantons.

The Grisons was once a territory of Rhaetia, peopled by Celtic tribes in pre-Christian times. In 15 B.C., the Romans conquered the Rhaetians, began colonization, and built alpine roads. The Germanic Franks entered the Roman provinces in the 3rd century and established themselves along the Rhine. They and their successors,

the Ostrogoths, introduced Teutonic influences into the Roman territories they seized, gradually changing the language of the inhabitants to Germanic dialects, especially in the northern regions. As a result, German is spoken today by about half the Grisons population, mainly around Davos and Chur, the capital of the canton. About a sixth of the people of the Grisons—those living in the south—speak the language of their next-door neighbor, Italy.

The people of the upper valleys of the Rhine and the Inn were isolated enough to resist Germanic influences, and today they still cling to their ancestral tongue, Romansh—the language of a third of the Swiss living in the Grisons. Both the dialect spoken in the Engadine (Ladin) and that spoken in the Vorderrhein Valley (Surveltisch) are derived from the Latin of Rhaetia. The centuries altered it, so that today it sounds rather like Spanish spoken with a German accent. In 1938, Romansh officially became the fourth of the Swiss national languages.

The Grisons was one of the last regions of Switzerland to benefit from busy commerce with the rest of the country. Cars were forbidden on all roads until 1927, and even today it's illegal to drive cars in Arosa after nightfall. This ban on the use of roads helped to popularize the Rhaetian railway, whose narrow-gauge trains cross the region along hairpin turns and through dozens of tunnels. Today this railway, as well as the postal buses that crisscross the district, provide panoramas of a harsh and sometimes-bleak landscape.

The peasants of this canton banded together in 1395 to form the Ligue Grise (Gray League), from which the name Grisons is derived. Two other such leagues were formed in the area to oppose Hapsburg domination. In 1803 the three leagues formed a single canton, which joined the Swiss Confederation. The belief system of the Protestant Reformation, however, was adopted by only part of the canton, and today sections of it remain staunchly Catholic.

Since the 1950s, much of the Grisons has earned its living from tourists, who visit for the skiing and the small villages, as well as the local red and "green" wines (vetliner), the exquisite embroidery, and the handwoven linens still produced in many mountain homes.

1 Chur (★

76 miles (122km) SE of Zurich, 37 miles (59km) W of Davos

The capital of the Grisons, Chur is the oldest town in Switzerland. According to recent excavations, the area had been inhabited as early as 3000 B.C. The Romans established a settlement in 15 B.C., naming it Curia Rhaetorum. In 450 B.C., a recently Christianized Chur became the see of a bishop. The town still has a bishop, but he no longer has the power of his medieval predecessors, who ruled virtually every aspect of life in Chur until 1526.

Set at an elevation of 1,955 feet (586m), Chur lies near the head of the Rhine Valley, surrounded by towering mountains. The Plessur River, a tributary of the Rhine, flows through the center of town. Chur is at the natural junction of several of the most important routes from Italy over the alpine passes and as a result incorporates both Italian and Rhaetian influences.

Favored by visitors, who appreciate the wilderness surrounding it, Chur is the largest mercantile center between Zurich and Milan. It's also an important rail center, a terminal for several of the most scenic railway lines in Switzerland: the narrow-gauge rail line to St. Moritz (the Rhätische Bahn), the Chur-Arosa line, the *Glacier Express,* the *Palm Express,* and the *Bernina Express.* You might also go to Splügen, said to have the prettiest mountain-pass village in the area.

Chur also offers a variety of sports facilities. Summer sports include hiking and swimming at **Sportanlagen Obere** (② 081/254-42-88). In the winter, skiers have access to the top 20 ski areas surrounding Chur, some of which reach 9,000 feet (2,700m) and are only 1½ hours away.

Chur's Old Town is best discovered on foot. City officials have made it easy for you by imprinting red-and-green footprints on its sidewalks to help you on your way. The route outlined by the city is the most scenic and most historic. You travel at your own pace, just following in the footsteps of others. In addition, the tourist office (see "Essentials," below) provides personally guided tours leaving on Monday at 2:30pm, but only February to October.

ESSENTIALS

GETTING THERE   The town is the end of some international lines, such as the standard-gauge railway from Sargans. It's also the starting point for the narrow-gauge line to St. Moritz, known as the Rhätische Bahn. The Chur-Arosa line and the *Glacier Express* also start here. Chur also has frequent train connections from Zurich. Call ② **0900/300-300** for **rail schedules.**

Chur lies near the terminus of several bus lines, which link its railway facilities with some of the villages scattered throughout the nearby valleys. The two

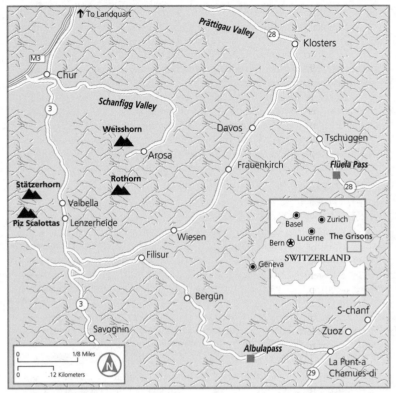

most prominent of these are Davos and St. Moritz, where bus connections can be made to Munich, across the German border. For **bus schedules** and information, call ℂ **081/254-40-60**.

If you're driving, Chur is about 90 minutes from Zurich along N3 (later N13), and easily reached by expressway.

VISITOR INFORMATION   The **tourist office** is located at Grabenstrasse 5 (ℂ **081/252-18-18**), and is open Monday 1:30 to 6pm, Tuesday to Friday 8am to noon and 1:30 to 6pm, and Saturday 9am to noon.

SEEING THE SIGHTS

You'll want to spend as much time as possible in Chur, to see the legacies left by the many emperors, kings, armies, and traders who have marched through here. In the medieval sector, you'll come across squares with flower-bedecked fountains and narrow streets, along with elegant houses and many towers.

The **cathedral of Chur** ⭐, Hof 19 (ℂ **081/252-23-12**), was built between 1151 and 1282 on an ancient foundation and was renovated extensively in the 19th century. Inside, the high altar displays a 15th-century gilded-wood triptych in the Gothic style, the largest of its kind in Switzerland. To visit the **Dom Treasury,** you'll have to apply to the sacristan at building no. 2 on the square (ℂ **081/252-92-50**). The admission cost varies depending on the exhibition, but the permanent collection includes many treasures dating from the 3rd century up to the 20th century, including medieval reliquaries of St. Lucius.

Near the cathedral, the baroque **Bishop's Palace** was built in 1732 and is still the private residence of a bishop. The palace opens onto Hofplatz—site of a Roman fort.

The town also has a museum worth visiting:

Bündner Kunstmuseum (Fine Arts Museum)   Known as the Villa Planta, this museum, set in a park, displays paintings and sculptures by many well-known Grisons artists. Some of the works are by Giovanni, Segantini, Angelica Kauffmann, Ferdinand Hodler, and Cuno Amiet, as well as by Alberto and Augusto Giacometti. You'll also find works by Ernst Ludwig Kirchner (1880–1938), the German painter and leader of the Brücke school of expressionists.

Postplatz. ℂ **081/257-28-68**. Admission 10SF ($5.50) adults, 7SF ($3.85) students. Children 16 and under free. Tues–Wed and Fri–Sun 10am–noon and 2–5pm, Thurs 10am–noon and 2–8pm.

WHERE TO STAY
EXPENSIVE

Duc de Rohan ⚘   The government-rated four-star Duc de Rohan is the best hotel and restaurant (see "Where to Dine," below) in Chur. One part of the hotel is a white-walled neoclassical villa with elaborate lintels, while the other section is modern. Many of the public rooms contain rococo and 19th-century antiques set in pastel-colored niches. The spacious bedrooms are comfortable and conservative, with excellent furnishings and efficiently organized mid-sized bathrooms.

Masanserstrasse 44, CH-7000 Chur. ℂ **081/252-10-22**. Fax 081/252-45-37. www.deuderohan.ch. 34 units. 140SF–160SF ($77–$88) double with street view, 150SF–180SF ($82.50–$99) double with garden view. Rates include buffet breakfast. AE, DC, MC, V. Free parking outdoors, 20SF ($11) inside. **Amenities:** Restaurant; pool; exercise room; sauna; room service; massage; laundry service. *In room:* TV, minibar, hair dryer.

Hotel Stern ⚘⚘   Like most members of the Romantik chain, this historic hotel is filled with authentic antiques. You know you're in for a special experience when you arrive. If notified in advance, the hotel will send a classic 1933 Buick to pick you up at the rail depot. The outside of the hotel looks like a giant strawberry mousse with white shutters. The interior has pine paneling—some of which dates from 1677—and vaulted or timbered ceilings. The modern and well-maintained bedrooms have 19th-century regional country antiques and are each fitted with a comfortable bathroom. Special grace notes include a rooftop terrace and a fireplace lounge.

Reichsgasse 11, CH-7000 Chur. ℂ **081/252-35-55**. Fax 081/252-19-15. www.romantichotels.ch/chur. 56 units. 220SF–290SF ($121–$159.50) double. Rates include buffet breakfast. AE, DC, MC, V. Free parking outdoors, 15SF ($8.25) inside. **Amenities:** Restaurant; limited room service; laundry service. *In room:* TV, minibar (in some).

MODERATE

Hotel Chur   The Chur lies in the center of town near the Old Town and about a 10-minute walk from the rail station. This imposing building with arched windows and fifth-floor gables contains three restaurants and comfortable, well-furnished bedrooms, each with a nice-sized bathroom.

Welschdörfli 2, CH-7000 Chur. ℂ **081/252-21-61**. Fax 081/253-34-92. www.hotel-chur.ch. 54 units. 155SF–170SF ($85.25–$93.50) double. Rates include buffet breakfast. AE, DC, MC, V. Free parking. **Amenities:** 3 restaurants, bar; limited room service; laundry service. *In room:* TV, minibar, hair dryer.

Hotel Freieck   Built originally in 1575, this is an old favorite. It has been renovated countless times since. Clinging stubbornly to tradition, the hotel, in the center of town, boasts a facade decorated with drawings of grapevines, a sundial, and two lions. The renovated mid-sized bedrooms contain simple furniture and comfortable bathrooms, mainly with shower. The Stockman family, however, places more emphasis on its dining rooms, which range from a rustic stucco room with massive beams and vaulting to a paneled contemporary room.

Reichsgasse 44–50, CH-7002 Chur. © **081/252-17-92.** Fax 081/253-34-19. www.freieck.ch. 37 units. 165SF ($90.75) double. Rates include buffet breakfast. AE, DC, MC, V. Free parking 7pm–8am. **Amenities:** Restaurant, bar; limited room service; laundry service. *In room:* TV.

INEXPENSIVE

Hotel Drei Könige ⚓   This historic hotel is at the entrance to the Old Town. The building's foundation dates from at least the 14th century. Excavations in the hotel cellar unearthed a collapsed tunnel that had led to the bishop's palace at the opposite end of the old city. The Schällibaum family has managed the hotel since 1911; over the years they've welcomed royalty, high-ranking politicians, and world-famous artists. The Drei Könige Hall on the premises used to be part of a monastery and, later, the seat of government.

Except for a handful of budget accommodations under the eaves, the well-scrubbed mid-sized rooms have comfortable furniture, including good beds, and the standard amenities such as up-to-date plumbing with an equal mixture of showers or tubs. The hotel has one of the most popular restaurants in town (see "Where to Dine," below).

Reichsgasse 18, CH-7002 Chur. © **081/252-17-25.** Fax 081/252-17-26. www.dreikoenige.com. 37 units, 28 with bathroom. 125SF ($68.75) double without bathroom, 145SF–170SF ($79.75–$93.50) double with bathroom. Rates include continental breakfast. AE, DC, MC, V. Parking 12SF ($6.60). **Amenities:** Restaurant, bar; access to nearby health club and golf course; limited room service; laundry service. *In room:* TV, minibar, hair dryer, iron.

Hotel Toms Räblüta ⚓⚓ (Finds   Taking over a 15th-century building, two men (both named Tom) now run the hippest hotel in town, thanks to their restoration skills and their keen sense of inn-keeping. The hotel was built in 1483 in the middle of the Old Town. Set in front of a fountain, it has blue shutters and colorful window ornamentation. The inside is paneled, with chandeliers, leaded-glass windows, and hunting trophies. The two Toms have breathed new life into the white stucco bedrooms, with modern furnishings and small private bathrooms with new tubs or showers. The most romantic way to live here is garret style in a top-floor bedroom, sleeping under sloping rafters and enjoying panoramic views over the Altstadt (Old Town) rooftops. Only some of the bedrooms have a private phone.

Pfisterplatz 1, CH-7000 Chur. © **081/267-13-57.** Fax 081/257-13-58. www.toms.ch. 9 units. 130SF–180SF ($71.50–$99) double. Rates include buffet breakfast. AE, MC, V. **Amenities:** 2 restaurants, bar; laundry service. *In room:* TV.

WHERE TO DINE
EXPENSIVE

Duc de Rohan ⚓ SWISS/MEDITERRANEAN   Many Swiss consider the dining room in the previously recommended Hotel Duc de Rohan the best restaurant in town—and we concur. Meals are served in Europeanized comfort in the restaurant or on a garden-style outdoor terrace. Drinks are available adjacent to the restaurant, in a cellar whose baronial granite fireplace juts into the cozy bar area. Carefully prepared specialties include a variety of seafood dishes and homemade ravioli.

Masanserstrasse 44. © **081/252-10-22.** Reservations recommended. Main courses 25SF–45SF ($13.75–$24.75). AE, DC, MC, V. Mon–Sat 11:30am–2pm and 6–9:30pm.

MODERATE

Hotel Stern Restaurant ⭐ GRISONS   Walter Brunner's previously recommended hotel is known for serving some of the most authentic Grisons recipes in eastern Switzerland. At this historic 1677 hotel, the restaurant is wrapped in time-worn *arvenholz,* a rich wood paneling. Regional wine is served in pewter pitchers and waiters are in folk costumes. This may sound corny, but somehow it works.

When we call the cuisine traditional, we're referring to great-grandmother style. For example, begin with barley soup or air-dried beef on a wooden plate. The rye bread from Puschlav that accompanies most dishes is scented with anise and butter. Lake trout is poached and flavored with Riesling, and vegetarian meals are also prepared. *Bizochels sursilvans* are country-style flour dumplings with bacon and potato pieces, onions, cheese, and melted butter. Dessert might be walnut ice cream with damsons.

Reichsgasse 11. ℂ 081/252-35-55. Reservations recommended. Main courses 19SF–49SF ($10.45–$26.95); fixed-price lunches 17SF–20SF ($9.35–$11); regional gourmet menu 76SF ($41.80). AE, DC, MC, V. Daily 9am–midnight.

Toms Räblüta ⭐⭐ FRENCH/ITALIAN/SWISS   Originally built as a guildhall in the 1400s, this is one of the most enduring and historic restaurants in Chur. Amid accessories that evoke alpine Switzerland of long ago, you can order the roast breast of goose in a cabbage-and-kirsch sauce, appetite-satisfying pork filets with apples and hazelnuts, or a classic calves' liver in wine with rösti. An appealing appetizer is the stuffed trout in a saffron sauce.

Pfisterplatz. ℂ 081/252-17-13. Reservations recommended. Main courses 15SF–29SF ($8.25–$15.95); fixed-price menus 40SF–81SF ($22–$44.55). AE, DC, MC, V. Wed–Mon 7am–midnight, Tues 5pm–midnight.

INEXPENSIVE

Hotel Drei Könige SWISS   The Weinstube, on the first floor, is covered with worn paneling, whose nicks and scratches only add to the character of the room. Don't expect haute cuisine here. Instead you get soul-satisfying food prepared with honest ingredients handled in an efficient and straightforward manner. Meals are served amid hunting trophies, collections of medals, and old photographs.

Usteria, one floor above street level beside the reception desk, is the more formal restaurant. The Schällibaum family welcomes some of Chur's most prominent citizens. Sometimes the chef prepares a double entrecôte *marchand de vin* or a chateaubriand Henri-IV. You can also order more standard fare, such as *pot-au-feu* (meat stew) and polenta with cheese.

Reichsgasse 18. ℂ 081/252-17-25. Main courses 19SF–35SF ($10.45–$19.25); fixed-price meal 29SF ($15.95). AE, DC, MC, V. Weinstube, daily 10am–2pm and 5pm–midnight. Usteria, daily noon–2pm and 6:30–9pm.

CHUR AFTER DARK

The hot spot in town is **Giger Bar,** Comercialstrasse 23 (ℂ 081/253-75-06). The Oscar-winning H. R. Giger, a native of Chur and set designer on the movie *Alien,* was responsible for creating this 1980 bar with its Starship *Enterprise* aura.

2 Arosa ⭐⭐⭐

19 miles (30km) E of Chur

Arosa, one of the highest of the alpine resorts (6,000 ft/1,800m above sea level), lies in a sheltered basin above the Schanfigg Valley. The most popular resort in the Grisons after Davos and St. Moritz, it basically consists of one main street

(Poststrasse) lined with hotels and shops. Though parts of the village date from the 14th century, the resort has a modern and contemporary look. If St. Moritz is too ultra-chic for you, Arosa may be your answer. Both visitors and the hotels that house them tend to be low-key and family-oriented, often favoring ski jackets over dinner jackets. Arosa lures the family trade through such attractions as kindergartens for children.

ESSENTIALS

GETTING THERE   Trains connect Chur and Arosa at the rate of one per hour during the day (trip time: 1 hr.). Trains from Zurich take 3 hours to reach Arosa. Call © **0900/300-300** for **rail information** and schedules. Zurich is the nearest airport to Arosa.

If you're driving the 19-mile (31km) drive from Chur in good weather, allow at least an hour, as the road is steep, with hairpin curves. Don't make the drive in icy weather. Instead, take the narrow-gauge railway that has been in operation since World War I.

VISITOR INFORMATION   Poststrasse is the main traffic artery through the center of town; visitors can follow hotel and restaurant directional signs.

The **Arosa Tourist Bureau,** Poststrasse (© **081/378-70-20**), is open in the winter Monday to Saturday from 9am to 6pm and Sunday from 10am to noon and 4 to 5:30pm, and in the summer Monday to Friday from 8am to noon and 2 to 6pm, and Saturday from 9am to 1pm and 2 to 4pm.

GETTING AROUND   Cars are restricted, except vehicles entering or leaving town. Even so, you won't be stranded without transportation, as a free local city bus makes frequent runs throughout the day from Unterseeplatz (in the lower reaches of town) to the railroad station and to most of the chairlifts and cable-car departure points in the resort's heights.

Taxis are always available. In the winter, a **"Night Express"** (© **081/378-7020** or 081/378-6757) taxi service runs continually from 8pm to 2am, charging 5SF ($2.75) per trip. The vehicles are marked NIGHT EXPRESS and can be stopped for boarding or getting off anywhere along the way.

FUN IN THE GREAT OUTDOORS

Skiing is the big attraction in Arosa, but summer activities and other winter sports, such as tobogganing and horse-drawn sleigh rides on the Arlenwald road, are also popular. Tennis, squash, bowling, and golf can all be played year-round at inside facilities. Walks can be taken over 18 miles (30km) of easy and varied trails kept open in the winter. In addition, guided walks are conducted from June to October, both in the morning and in the afternoon. The tourist office (see above) will supply details and trail maps. Visits are possible to a chapel from the 1400s, a cheese maker, and a local museum.

Arosa draws an international crowd to its ski slopes, offering 40 miles of the best ski runs in the Grisons. It also has the Swiss Ski School, which, with 100 instructors, is one of the best ski schools in Switzerland.

Skiing is popular in the Obersee area at the eastern edge of the resort, whose focal point—reached by cable car—is the **Weisshorn** ⋒⋒ (8,704 ft/2,611m). During the day, cable cars leave for the Weisshorn at the rate of one every 20 minutes. You first make the ascent to the middle station, Larn Mittle, at 6,640 feet (1,992m), from which there are panoramas of Arosa. From the top station is one of the grandest views in eastern Switzerland, taking in a vast panorama of the Grison Alps. Even Chur can be viewed to the northwest, at the foothills of the Calanda mountain peak.

To the west, skiers take the Hörnli gondola, reaching Hörnligrat (8,180 ft/ 2,454m) in about 16 minutes. Drag lifts at Hörnligrat fan out, taking skiers to the top of several different ski slopes.

The **Swiss Ski School** (© 081/377-11-50) provides skiing lessons for both adults and children, and private ski instruction is available from the **Grison Association of Private Ski Instructors Arosa** (© 081/377-15-56).

Intermediate, advanced, and professional skiers come to Arosa because of its proximity to the slopes on either side of the valley formed by the Weisshorn and the Hörnli mountains. Access to the 47 miles (76km) of marked downhill runs on either side of the valley is made possible by at least 16 cable cars, some chair-lifts, and a network of buses that make frequent runs up and down the valley floor. A ski pass that provides access to all of this costs 102SF ($56.10) for 2 days, 220SF ($121) for 5 days, and 265SF ($145.75) for 7 days. The cost for children is 90SF ($49.50) for 2 days, 112SF ($61.60) for 5 days, and 135SF ($74.25) for 7 days. Other passes that allow access to the ski slopes as far away as Davos, Klosters, Flims, and Lax are available, as well as some of the slopes in the Engadine, but only in increments of 90 days at a time.

Arosa offers some of the best horseback riding in eastern Switzerland. Visit the stables at **Fuhrhalterei,** Wierhof (© 081/377-41-96), which are open through-out the year. The Messner family usually has a dozen or so horses on hand, each willing to carry you across scenic local trails for 29SF ($15.95) per hour. You must call them at least a day in advance to make arrangements. The stables lie just outside the center adjacent to a local campground.

SHOPPING

The best way to get an overview of the diversity of Arosa's shops is to stroll up and down its main street, Poststrasse. If you're looking for equipment or cloth-ing that will keep you competitive in this sport-conscious town, head for **Sprecher Sports,** Poststrasse (© 081/377-12-06); **Carmena Sport,** Poststrasse (© 081/377-12-05); the winter only **Bananas Sport** (© 081/377-15-51), in the building that houses the departure point for the Weisshorn cable car; or **Schatz Sport,** Poststrasse (© 081/377-18-14), near the Hotel Kulm. If it's Grisons souvenirs you're looking for, head for **Vital,** Poststrasse (© 081/ 377-12-77), or **Banker,** Poststrasse (© 081/377-16-90). Other than that, your best bet is to simply wander along either side of the street.

WHERE TO STAY

Most of Arosa's hotels are modern and expensive. In the peak winter season reservations are imperative. Most hotels in Arosa demand a minimum stay of 7 to 10 days over the Christmas holidays. In the summer it's much easier to find accommodations.

VERY EXPENSIVE

Arosa Kulm Hotel ★★★   This government-rated five-star hotel, built in the 1970s, is one of the two leading hotels here, surpassed only by the Grand Hotel (see below). A simple guest house stood here in 1882. Surrounded by rushing streams, and close to the departure point of one of the cable cars rising into the surrounding mountains, the hotel is large, glamorous, and contemporary, with well-insulated, spacious, and exceedingly comfortable bedrooms plus deluxe bathrooms. It was partially renovated in the early 1990s. The decor combines warm tones with pinewood paneling. Almost everyone stays here on half board, which is, for the most part, required. At Christmastime, prices go even higher than those mentioned below.

CH-7050 Arosa. ℂ **081/378-88-88.** Fax 081/378-88-89. www.arosakulm.ch. 137 units. Winter 440SF–910SF ($242–$500.50) double; from 770SF ($515.90) suite for 2. Off-season 240SF–420SF ($160.80–$281.40) double; from 460SF ($308.20) suite for 2. Rates include half board. AE, DC, MC, V. Closed Apr 14–June 13 and Sept 13–Dec 5. **Amenities:** 5 restaurants, 2 bars; pool; tennis courts; exercise room; sauna; concierge; room service; massage; babysitting; laundry service. *In room:* TV, minibar, hair dryer, iron, safe.

Tschuggen Grand Hotel ✿✿✿ With its potted palms, distressed tortoise-shell wallpaper, and brass-framed mirrors, this modern high-rise could be in the pages of *Architectural Digest*. It's one of the most glamorous hotels in the Swiss Alps. The hotel looks down over Arosa from a hillside position that emphasizes its modern, rectangular design. No attempts were made to duplicate traditional chalet architecture, and the interior is richly outfitted with some of the most opulent accessories in Arosa. The spacious rooms are handsomely decorated and beautifully kept. Each week there are two *soirées élégantes*, for which evening dress is compulsory. The winter season starts at the first of December, with Arosa's traditional ski weeks, and continues until the first of April.

CH-7050 Arosa. ℂ **081/378-99-99.** Fax 081/378-99-90. www.tschuggen.ch. 129 units. 490SF–680SF ($269.50–$374) double; 770SF–1,570SF ($423.50–$863.50) suite for 2. Rates include buffet breakfast. AE, DC, MC, V. Parking 30SF ($16.50). Closed Apr 3–Dec 2. **Amenities:** 4 restaurants, bar; pool; fitness room; sauna; salon; bowling alley; room service; kindergarten with nurse; laundry service. *In room:* TV, minibar, hair dryer, safe.

EXPENSIVE

Golfhotel Hof Maran ✿ Set high in an alpine meadow, about a mile from the center of Arosa, this mountain chalet is rustically decorated with beamed ceilings, carpeting in autumnal colors, and comfortable armchairs. Many of the handsomely furnished mid-sized bedrooms have balconies for year-round tanning. Accommodations come in varied styles although the overall effect is exceedingly comfortable alpine traditional.

In Maran, Nord CH-7050 Arosa. ℂ **081/378-5151.** Fax 081/378-51-00. 53 units. Winter 450SF ($247.50) double. Summer 250SF ($137.50) double. Rates include breakfast. AE, DC, MC, V. Closed Apr 11–June 2 and Sept 15–Dec 17. **Amenities:** 2 restaurants, bar; golf course; 5 tennis courts; saunas; skating rink; room service; babysitting; laundry service. *In room:* TV, minibar, hair dryer.

Hotel Eden ✿ Hotel Eden, in the center of Arosa, is surrounded by pine trees, near the cable car and ski lift. It has five floors of weathered balconies and sun-streaked planking over white walls. The hotel interior is brightly colored, whimsical, and very comfortable. This is an aggressively marketed hotel with a flair for entertaining non-Swiss clients with or without their children. The public rooms have marble floors, Oriental rugs, hanging lamps, and wall-to-wall carpeting. Each of the spacious and comfortably furnished bedrooms has a private bathroom. The rooms with southern exposure have balconies. Write to the hotel well in advance for reservations.

CH-7050 Arosa. ℂ **081/378-71-00.** Fax 081/378-71-01. 76 units. 180SF–280SF ($99–$154) standard double; 400SF ($220) designer double. Rates include breakfast. AE, DC, MC, V. Free parking. Closed Apr–Dec. **Amenities:** 2 restaurants, bar; gym; Jacuzzi; sauna; skating rink; ski school; children's playroom; room service; babysitting; laundry service. *In room:* TV, minbar, hair dryer.

Hotel Panorama Raetia ✿ In the heart of the resort town, a short walk from Oberseeplatz, this plain but solid government-rated three-star hotel is known for its lack of pretense, good management, and realistic prices. On the bank overlooking the heart of town, the hotel offers a panoramic view from its oldest core, which dates from 1893. Its newer wing is from the architecturally undistinguished 1950s. On the premises is a small library, and the hotel offers transport to the rail station. The public areas are more for relaxing than style setting, and the mid-sized bedrooms are either traditional or sterile and modern, each with a tidy bathroom.

CH-7050 Arosa. © **081/377-02-41.** Fax 081/377-2279. 40 units. 250SF–440SF ($137.50–$242) double. Rates include half board. AE, DC, MC, V. Closed Apr 19–Dec 22. **Amenities:** Restaurant, bar; game rooms; billiards room; room service; laundry service. *In room:* TV.

Waldhotel-National Hotel ★★★ This sylvan retreat, although not as elegant as the Tschuggen Grand or the Arosa Kulm, is the most tranquil and isolated retreat at the resort. Set in a forest, this generously proportioned building was designed with symmetrical wings extending from a central core. Originally the Waldhotel was a sanatorium, and later it became a military hospital. In the public rooms, accessories include apricot-colored stencils decorating the arched ceilings, a beautifully carved and embellished booth resembling a church pulpit, and decorative ovens sheathed in ceramic tiles. The mid-sized to spacious bedrooms are comfortably and attractively furnished, with price level determined by the view. Rooms facing south open onto a view of Arosa, and those looking north open onto a vast woodland.

CH-7050 Arosa. © **081/378-55-55.** 93 units. Winter 490SF–540SF ($269.50–$297) double; 650SF–970SF ($357.50–$533.50) suite for 2. Summer 250SF–270SF ($137.50–$148.50) double; 390SF–430SF ($214.50–$236.50) suite for 2. Children 5 and under stay free in parents' room; children 6–12 are charged 50% of the adult rate. Rates include half board. AE, DC, MC, V. Closed Apr 20–June 26 and Sept 14–Dec 5. **Amenities:** Restaurant; pool; gym; room service; massage; laundry service. *In room:* TV, hair dryer.

MODERATE

Hotel Alpina ★ *Finds* Finally we've found a hotel in Arosa that looks from the outside like the type of old-fashioned chalet that's always associated with Switzerland. The balconies have hand-carved railings and trimwork. There's a terraced garden, and near the entrance a Swiss flag flaps in the mountain breeze. Our favorite rooms are up under the eaves. All the accommodations have recently been renovated without losing any of their alpine charm, and each comes with a private bathroom. The public rooms are filled with furniture painted in alpine designs, baroque clocks, and traditional chairs and couches.

CH-7050 Arosa. © **081/377-16-58.** Fax 081/377-37-52. 35 units. Winter 320SF–360SF ($176–$198) double. Summer 230SF–260SF ($126.50–$143) double. Rates include half board. AE, DC, MC, V. Free parking outdoors, 8SF–12SF ($4.40–$6.60) indoors. Closed late Apr to mid-June and mid-Nov to Dec 6. **Amenities:** Restaurant, bar; room service; laundry service. *In room:* TV, hair dryer.

INEXPENSIVE

Arve Central Originally built about a century ago and remodeled many times since then, this hotel is set back from the main street but still very much in the center of the action. It's located only a short walk from the train station. Some of the pleasant bedrooms have balconies crafted from weathered wood and are attractively furnished with a collection of upholstered settees and wooden chalet chairs. The rooms in the rear, however, have no balcony and don't open onto a view. Its French restaurant is known for serving some of the best meals in town.

CH-7050 Arosa. © **081/378-52-52.** Fax 081/378-52-50. 48 units. Winter 270SF–380SF ($148.50–$209) double. Off-season 156SF–174SF ($85.80–$95.70) double. Rates include half board. AE, DC, MC, V. Parking 8SF–14SF ($4.40–$7.70). **Amenities:** 2 restaurants; fitness center; Jacuzzi; sauna; room service; laundry service. *In room:* TV, minibar, hair dryer.

Hotel Streiff *Value* A government-rated three-star hotel, this establishment is set at the edge of a forest, somewhat away from the center of Arosa. Trails, cable cars, and chair and ski lifts are all nearby. All of the small to mid-sized rooms have a well-organized private bathroom. The bedrooms are comfortably furnished and snug. The dining room features five-course evening meals, highlighting various regions of Switzerland.

CH-7050 Arosa. 🕿 **081/378-71-71.** Fax 081/378-71-78. www.streiff.ch. 41 units. Winter 240SF–360SF ($132–$198) double. Summer 160SF–240SF ($88–$132) double. Rates include half board. No credit cards. Closed Apr 15–June 30 and Sept 1–Dec 15. **Amenities:** Restaurant; limited room service. *In room:* TV, hair dryer, safe.

Vetter *Value*   Centrally located a few steps from the railroad station and the Tschuggen cable car, this hotel offers glassed-in verandas, open porches, and wooden balconies. The interior is a mix of wrought iron and wood beams, enlivened by pithy bits of wisdom stenciled in German above a masonry fireplace. Everything is clean and comfortable. Many of the accommodations lack a private bathroom; the hallway facilities, however, are adequate and well maintained. Furnishings are generally ragtag unless you get one of the time-mellowed antique rooms in wood paneling. Some units open onto views of woodlands; others face the busy street and town center. The rooms without bathroom are among the best bargains in Arosa in the winter ski season.

CH-7050 Arosa. 🕿 **081/377-17-02.** Fax 081/377-49-19. 28 units, 15 with bathroom. 150SF–210SF ($82.50–$115.50) double without bathroom, 180SF–230SF ($99–$126.50) double with bathroom. Rates include buffet breakfast. No credit cards. Parking 3SF ($1.65). Closed Apr 9–Nov 30. **Amenities:** Laundry service.

WHERE TO DINE

Most guests book into the Arosa resort hotels on a board basis. Nearly all the major restaurants are in hotels—hence the shortage of well-known independent dining spots. However, if you can break away from your hotel for a main meal, you may want to try one of the places below.

Stueva-Cuolm ⚑ ITALIAN/CONTINENTAL   This log building belongs to the nearby Kulm Hotel, but it takes its true flavor from its managers, Armando Solaro and Raffaelo Limone. Mr. Solaro worked for several years as the personal chef of the Aga Khan—an experience that helps him serve his international clientele. The restaurant is a few steps from the inner-Arosa Tschuggen chairlift, near the top of the village. One side of the cozy room overlooks the spectator seats around one of the village's ice-skating rinks. In sunny weather, you can dine outside. The *daube de boeuf* specialty is marinated for a full day before it's served with spinach and fresh vegetables. Other continental specialties are also well prepared.

Poststrasse. 🕿 **081/378-88-88.** Reservations required. Main courses 30SF–45SF ($16.50–$24.75). AE, DC, MC, V. Dec 6–Apr 14, daily 11:45am–2:30pm and 7–10:30pm. Closed Apr 15–Dec 5.

Zum Wohl Sein ⚑⚑⚑ SWISS/CONTINENTAL   This gourmet enclave offers the most famous dining experience in Arosa, partly because it seats only 20 diners and partly because the hotel that contains it is a comfortably homey property with few upper-class pretensions. Beat Carduff, the owner and chef, prepares a fixed-price menu that changes every night of the week and features seven distinguished courses—it has received awards from many publications, including *The Wine Spectator.* In a cozy retreat lined with the rich patina of old paneling and dozens of hunting trophies, you can enjoy a meal that, when we visited, included a terrine of fresh goose liver, venison bouillon redolent with alpine herbs, ravioli stuffed with seasoned wild game cock, rock lobster with a mousseline sauce, organically grown veal with a risotto of wild mushrooms, selections from a platter of unpasteurized hard and soft alpine cheeses, and a light vanilla cream with wild strawberries. The staff advises that you schedule

4 hours to fully appreciate the languorous attention the meal deserves. Selections from a list containing more than 1,300 vintages of wine usually accompany your meal, but are not included in the all-inclusive price.

The hotel that contains this place was built in the 1930s, is now under management by its third generation of the original owners, and has 31 bedrooms outfitted in a conservative style with lots of blond paneling. Each has a TV and telephone, and rents, double occupancy, depending on the room and the season, for 250 to 350SF ($137.50–$192.50). Full board is included in the price, with meals consumed in the hotel's conventional restaurant, not in the gourmet temple described above. Zum Wohl Sein, incidentally, translates roughly as "to your health."

In the Hotel Anita, Höhepromenade, CH-7050 Arosa. © 081/377-11-09. Fax 081/377-36-18. Reservations required. Fixed-price menu 120SF ($66). AE, DC, MC, V. Wed–Sat dinner only, at 8pm. Closed Apr 15–Dec 5.

AROSA AFTER DARK

Almost every vacationer in Arosa spends at least a half hour playing the small-scale slot machines at the Spielcasino Arosa or **Arosa Casino** in the Kursaal on Poststrasse(© **081/378-70-50**), which opens every day, year-round, from noon to 3am, along with its own bar. Expect a low-energy, not particularly animated crowd with desultory croupiers tending to their appointed roulette and black-jack tables. More interesting, and in the same building, is the **Ristorante Bejazzo,** an Italian eatery that's open only during busy seasons for lunch and dinner. The casino's undisputed highlight, however, is its disco, **Nuts,** a glossily modern haven for drinkers and dancers that's open every day in midsummer and midwinter between 9:30pm and at least 3am. Entrance is free.

Another amusing after dark choice is the **Kitchen Klub** of the Hotel Eden (© **081/378-7106**), in the center of Arosa. This dance club is inside what functioned, at the turn of the 20th century, as an actual kitchen. The old pots and pans are still there. This place starts to fill up after dinner on winter nights, and the DJ, sitting on top of old refrigerators keeps the music lively. At the **Hotel Obersee**, Aussere Poststrasse (© **081/3771949**), some of the best live bands in Arosa are booked into its small Halli-Galli in winter. Call to see what's happening (if anything) before heading here.

Two night spots are near the railway station. The winter-only **Tschuetta Dancing,** on Poststrasse (© **081/377-19-49**), is a cellar-level disco/dance bar where entrance is free and drinks begin at 10SF ($6.70) each throughout the year. Across the street is **Gada,** Poststrasse (© **081/377-17-66**), a bar and disco whose decor emulates that of an antique chalet. The Post Hotel, on Poststrasse, offers a handful of stubes, a pizzeria, and **The Crazy Club** (© **081/378-50-00**), where drinks flow and a cabaret act features attractive women who strip in ways that tease and titillate but rarely get really down and dirty. A sometime competitor, offering cabaret only during midwinter's high season, most nights between 9pm and 3am, is the bar in the **Hotel Seehof** (© **081/377-15-41**), which is otherwise just a quiet and rather conventional bar. Entrance to both sites is free.

3 Klosters ✶✶

8 miles (13km) N of Davos, 27 miles (43km) E of Chur, 18 miles (29km) E of Landquart

Life at this 4,000-foot-high (1,200m) village in the Prattigau Valley has changed greatly from 1222, when a cloister was founded here. Many visitors prefer the intimacy and hospitality of Klosters to the carnival-like atmosphere of Davos.

Unlike some of its neighbors (most notably St. Moritz), Klosters has few unattractive structures. All its buildings are constructed in the chalet style, giving the town a pleasing architectural harmony. Local residents claim that the sport of tobogganing originated here.

The main road to Davos runs through Klosters, and the two resorts have been known to compete aggressively for the tourist franc. Famous past visitors include Sir Arthur Conan Doyle and Robert Louis Stevenson, who is said to have finished *Treasure Island* here. In the heyday of tax benefits, Klosters became known as "Hollywood on the Rocks." It still attracts an international crowd of movie people. It has also been given a royal seal of approval by the king and queen of Sweden, who visit regularly; but invariably generating more publicity were Prince Charles and the late Princess Diana, who for many years considered it one of their favorite Swiss resorts.

ESSENTIALS

GETTING THERE   There are frequent express trains between Zurich and the railway junction at Landquart. From Landquart, connecting trains depart about once an hour for Klosters on secondary rail lines. Call © **0900/300-300** for **rail information** and schedules.

If you're driving from Zurich, head south on the N3 expressway until you reach Landquart, at which point you cut southeast along Route 28.

VISITOR INFORMATION   Some roads in the center have street names; others outside the town don't, but establishments can easily be found by following directional signs. The **Klosters Tourist Board,** in the center of town (© **081/ 410-20-20**), is open in the winter Monday to Saturday from 8:30am to noon and 2 to 6pm and Sunday from 9:30 to 11:30am and 3:30 to 6:30pm; and in the summer Monday to Friday 8:30am to noon and 2:30 to 6pm, and Saturday 8:30am to noon and 2:30 to 5pm.

GETTING AROUND   A city bus, **bus A,** makes frequent runs from Klosters-Dorf (the railroad station) to the base of the town's ski lifts, passing virtually every building in town on the way.

SKIING & OTHER OUTDOOR FUN

Some of the finest downhill skiing in the world is here, with slopes for beginners as well as for the most advanced skiers. A kindergarten will look after the very young while you hit the slopes. The most populous part of Klosters, centered around the railway station, is called **Klosters-Platz** (square). A smaller, less populated neighborhood—site of the resort's excellent ski school—lies about a mile to the north and is called **Klosters-Dorf** (village).

The region contains two principal areas for skiing or hiking, the more popular of which is the **Gotschna-Parsenn.** To reach it, board the Gotschnagrat cableway in Klosters-Platz; the cable car carries more than 50 skiers up to the 7,545-foot (2,263m) Gotschnagrat elevation. In the peak season, especially around February, expect lines. A series of cableways, a chairlift, and 18 ski lifts hook up with the Davos-Parsenn skiing areas, where your highest point will be Weissflühgipfel (9,260 ft./2,778m). The Parsenn area is world renowned and has some of the longest runs in Europe. It offers more than 14 different cableways and ski lifts, plus more than 85 miles (137km) of well-kept runs.

The other major area, **Madrisa,** dates from the 1960s. To reach it, you go to Dorf via a bus, which leaves from Klosters-Platz every 30 minutes. From Dorf, the Klosters-Albeina gondola will take you to a height of 6,323 feet (1,897m). Then, by drag lift, known as the Schafügﬂi, you rise to 7,850 feet (2,355m).

Nontransferable R.E.G.A. (season) tickets are priced according to the number of days you plan to ski. For ski passes for the whole area, refer to "Davos Ski Passes" (see "The Active Vacation Planner" in section 4 on Davos, later in this chapter).

Horse sleighing, curling, and skating are popular sports for those who don't ski. Ask at the tourist office (see "Essentials," above) about the various venues for these activities.

In the summer, Klosters is in the center of fine hiking grounds. The Madrisa and Gotschna-Parsenn cable cars will carry you to starting points on both sides of the valley for hikes on well-marked trails through woods and alpine meadows. In Klosters, you can also enjoy tennis, squash, and swimming in a heated pool.

SHOPPING

Most of the shops are sports oriented. The best stocked include **Grischa-Sport,** Bahnhofstrasse 12C (✆ **081/422-18-55**); **Barbell,** Landstrasse 185 (✆ **081/422-12-69**); and **Adrist,** Alte Bahnhofstrasse 4 (✆ **081/410-20-80**). Galleries abound but the two devoted to various works of Graubünden artists are **Alexis Art Gallerie,** Talstrasse 1 (✆ **081/422-36-37**), and **Gallerie 63,** Doggilochstrasse 28 (✆ **081/422-27-04**).

WHERE TO STAY

Some hotels in Klosters are not on street plans, but directional signs point the way from the center.

VERY EXPENSIVE

Hotel Pardenn ★★★ A luxurious resort complex, often host to the rich and famous, this government-rated five-star deluxe hotel offers tradition, comfort, atmosphere, and a feeling of graciousness—a winning combination for which you'll pay plenty. The terrace overlooks the well-landscaped lawn. Inside is a green-marble, circular staircase. Many of the small to mid-sized accommodations have pine paneling, while others contain flowery carpets and Louis XV-style armchairs. Try, if possible, for a room with a balcony facing south. The rooms are well accessorized although the bathrooms are often small.

Monbielerstrasse, CH-7250 Klosters. ✆ **081/422-11-41.** Fax 081/422-40-06. www.pardenn.ch. 65 units. Winter 305SF–440SF ($167.75–$242) double, 505SF ($277.75) junior suite. Summer 240SF–310SF ($132–$170.50) double, 390SF ($214.50) junior suite. Rates include breakfast. AE, DC, MC, V. Free parking outside, 15SF ($8.25) in a garage. Closed Apr 3–June 24 and Sept 12–Dec 18. **Amenities:** 2 restaurants, bar; pool; gym; sauna; salon; room service; massage room; laundry service. *In room:* TV, minibar, hair dryer.

Piz Buin Hotel ★★★ This government-rated five-star hotel is the most modern and elegant in Klosters. It's located in the heart of the village, just a stroll away from the Gotschna lift, which takes you straight to the skiing and hiking area of Parsenn. The hotel, built in 1984, is designed like a chalet. The large yet cozy rooms are all equipped with two beds and a balcony, plus a luxurious bathroom. In winter no singles are rented, and doubles are only available by the week, with reservations running from Saturday to Saturday.

Alte Bahnhofstrasse 1, CH-7250 Klosters. ✆ **081/423-33-33.** Fax 081/423-33-34. 53 units. Winter (per week, including half board) 2,610SF–3,900SF ($1,435.50–$2,145) double. Summer (per night, including full board) 290SF ($159.50) double. AE, DC, MC, V. Closed Apr 18–June 26 and Oct 16–Dec 3. **Amenities:** Restaurant, bar; pool; gym; Jacuzzi; sauna; Turkish baths; room service; massage; laundry service. *In room:* TV, hair dryer, safe.

EXPENSIVE

Chesa Grischuna ★★★ This country inn in the center of Klosters is the most celebrated of its kind in the whole resort area. Set behind a lavishly decorated facade and rebuilt in 1938 on the foundation of an 1890 farmhouse, this government-rated four-star hotel has hosted some of the most illustrious personalities of Europe. Prices are high for what you get (there are even some rooms without bathroom), but since this hotel is on the see-and-be-seen circuit it can command and get a lot of francs. It's a six-story chalet whose various levels are curiously staggered in a series of ascending planes. The small to mid-sized rooms are for the most part paneled in local pine and fir, and are both elegant and cozy. All come with a firm bed, and television is available upon request. The overflow from the main house is lodged in a comfortable annex nearby where the rooms are more spacious. The hotel is famous for its chic restaurant.

Bahnhofstrasse 12, CH-7250 Klosters. (C) 081/422-22-22. Fax 081/422-22-25. www.chesagrischuna.ch. 26 units, 18 with bathroom. 220SF–330SF ($121–$181.50) double without bathroom, 310SF–490SF ($170.50–$269.50) double with bathroom. Rates include half board. AE, DC, MC, V. Free parking. Closed late May to mid-July and mid-Oct to mid-Dec. **Amenities:** Restaurant, bar; room service; massage; babysitting; laundry service. *In room:* TV (on request), hair dryer.

Silvretta Park Hotel 🏆   Opened in 1990, this government-rated four-star hotel lies opposite Silvretta Park with its cross-country ski runs and ice rink for skating, hockey, and curling. It's within walking distance of the Gotschna lift connecting the Parsenn skiing area with Klosters. Designed in a typical Swiss-chalet style, it offers modern and mid-sized rooms in a countrified style, each containing an elegant bathroom. Facilities include a balcony or terrace.

CH-7250 Klosters. (C) **081/423-3435.** Fax 081/423-3450. www.silvretta.ch. 108 units. Winter 494SF–530SF ($271.70–$291.50) double; 408SF–800SF ($273.35–$536) suite for 2. Summer 340SF–370SF ($187–$203.50) double; 494SF–530SF ($271.70–$291.50) suite for 2. Rates include half board. AE, DC, MC, V. Garage 15SF ($8.25) in winter, 10SF ($5.50) in summer. Free parking outside in summer, 5SF ($2.75) in winter. **Amenities:** 3 restaurants, bar, disco; pool; fitness center; Jacuzzi; sauna; Turkish bath; salon; room service; massage; babysitting; laundry service. *In room:* TV, minibar, hair dryer, safe.

MODERATE

Bad Serneus Kur- und Sporthotel *Value*   This well-managed and cozy government-rated three-star hotel is one of the most visible buildings in Klosters' suburb of Bad Serneus, 3½ miles (6km) north (and downhill) from Klosters. Consequently, despite the fact that the rooms are cozy, well maintained, and comfortable, prices are somewhat lower than in the heart of Klosters. Each unit comes either with private tub or a shower bathroom. When snowfalls are deep, clients can ski here from Klosters; they'll have to take a short bus ride, with their equipment, for access to the resort's ski lifts. Older, and solidly built of heavy slabs of wood painted yellow with black shutters, the hotel was enlarged and upgraded in 1987, and contains public rooms with wooden beams, regional-style stenciling, and blazing fireplaces. In summer guests can stroll in nearby flower-filled meadows.

Bad Serneus, CH-7250 Klosters. (C) **081/422-14-44.** Fax 081/422-22-51. 52 units. Winter 350SF ($192.50) double. Summer 300SF ($165) double. Rates include half board. AE, DC, MC, V. Closed Apr 10–May 15 and Oct 25–Dec 20. **Amenities:** Restaurant; pool; sauna; limited room service; massage facilities; laundry service.

INEXPENSIVE

Hotel-Pension Büel   This is a simple and completely unpretentious government-rated two-star hotel with stucco walls, brown trim, and balconies. Inside, it's clean, well-scrubbed, and rustic, with blazing midwinter fireplaces and, in most cases, flagstone floors and knotty-pine ceilings. Rooms are small and basic yet cozily comfortable with good beds and tidy maintenance. Fifteen units come with private shower, the rest with tubs. The owners are members of the Hongler family.

CH-7252 Klosters-Dorf. ℂ **081/422-26-69.** Fax 081/422-49-41. www.hotelbuel.ch. 18 units. Winter 160SF–190SF ($88–$104.50) double. Summer 130SF–140SF ($71.50–$77) double. Rates include breakfast. Half board 22SF ($12.10) per person extra. AE, MC, V. Closed May and Nov. **Amenities:** Restaurant. *In room:* TV.

Hotel Rustico *Value*   In the center of Klosters-Platz, this small, snug oasis is run by Marion Thous. More than a century old, the house has been restored and turned into a government-rated three-star hotel with modern comforts. The well-furnished bedrooms have a bathroom or shower and firm beds. The restaurant offers excellent food, and service is personalized and attentive. A lounge with a fireplace overlooks the terrace. The staff can arrange various sporting activities. Singles are not available in winter, and weekly reservations (7 days and nights) are required from December 6 to 19, January 10 to 24, and March 15 to April 4. In these same time periods, the hotel offers two ski packages. Rates vary depending on the season, and include half board, ski instruction, ski rental, and lift tickets.

CH-7250 Klosters. ℂ **081/422-12-12.** Fax 081/422-53-55. www.mypage.bluewin.ch/rustico. 12 units. Winter 236SF–296SF ($129.80–$162.80) double; summer 170SF–220SF ($93.50–$121) double. Rates include breakfast. Half board 65SF ($35.75) per person extra. MC, V. Closed June and Nov. **Amenities:** Restaurant, bar; sauna; billiards room. *In room:* TV, minibar, hair dryer, safe.

WHERE TO DINE

Alte Post SWISS/FRENCH   Master chef John M. Ehrat-Flury pampers the palate with regional specialties in this roadside chalet outside town that's decorated with game trophies and ceramics. In the autumn he prepares carefully selected game and fish dishes with the freshest ingredients. Guests dine in the restaurant or the intimate grillroom, where meats are grilled over an open fire. It's a fun, informal place and has long been a celebrity favorite. Guests enjoy such winning fare as smoked trout with juniper, suprême of salmon with pink peppercorns, and fresh mushrooms in a nest of homemade noodles.

Doggilochstrasse 136, Klosters-Aeuja. ℂ **081/422-17-16.** Reservations required. Main courses 40SF–48SF ($22–$26.40); menu dégustation 83SF ($45.65). AE, DC, MC, V. Wed–Sun 11:30am–2pm and 6–11pm. Closed May and Nov.

Chesa Grischuna ★★★ INTERNATIONAL   This restaurant is so popular that celebrities often book tables a year in advance. Some of its famous patrons have included Truman Capote, Rex Harrison, Audrey Hepburn, the Aga Khan, Winston Churchill, Deborah Kerr, and Queen Juliana of the Netherlands. More recent celebrities have included the author John Irving. The restaurant has attractively decorated alpine walls and a scattering of unusual portraits. Part of the reason for its persistent popularity is the warm welcome from the Guler family, and, of course, the food. Specialties prepared with the freshest and best of ingredients include a *crêpe suedoise* stuffed with shrimp, chicken livers in puff pastry on a bed of leeks, grilled salmon with white butter and tomato sauce, and rack of lamb. In the summer you can eat outside.

Bahnhofstrasse 12. ℂ **081/422-22-22.** Reservations required in winter. Main courses 28SF–52SF ($15.40–$28.60); fixed-price meal 33SF ($18.15) at lunch, 74SF ($40.70) at dinner. AE, DC, MC, V. Winter daily 7am–midnight; off-season, daily 11:30am–2pm and 6:30–10pm. Closed late May to July and mid-Oct to mid-Dec.

Hotel Wynegg Restaurant *Finds* SWISS   This restaurant is set on the ground floor of a 20-room hotel built in 1878, and the hotel is noted for its kitchens, partly because of the hard work of the owner, Ruth Guler, the niece of the owner of the prestigious Chesa Grischuna. The hotel came into prominence after Prince Charles chose this modest place for a discreet afternoon drink with one of his cousins. The restaurant—clean, cozy, and straightforward—offers simple but well-prepared meals, which might include local air-dried beef, hearty soups, entrecôtes, and an especially good veal steak with rösti. The decor is alpine kitsch with cuckoo clocks and checkered tablecloths.

The rooms are strictly no-frills, costing 90SF ($49.50) per person nightly in a double without private bathroom, 122SF ($67.10) per person nightly in a double with private bathroom; all rates include breakfast.

Landstrasse 205, CH-7250 Klosters. ✆ **081/422-13-40.** Fax 081/422-41-31. Reservations required. Main courses 30SF–45SF ($16.50–$24.75). AE, DC, MC, V. Daily noon–2pm and 6–10pm. Closed Apr 15–Dec 15.

Walserstube ★★★ SWISS   The Walserstube's Beat Bolliger entertains everybody from celebrities such as Prince Andrew to regular folks, and has been doing so since 1981. The time-worn and alpine-seasoned building materials came in part from an old Grisons farmhouse, and the restaurant and cafe are paneled with this wood. Art objects and antiques are used discreetly throughout the place. The location is right on the main street of town with often-heavy traffic in the peak summer and winter seasons. His cuisine is a winning combination of fresh ingredients and the best culinary skills. As you sit under the restaurant's massive wood beams and alpine carvings, you might begin with a duckling foie gras or a yogurt mousse with seasonal fruit. In season, asparagus is featured and prepared in a variety of elegant ways. The fish is special here, including salmon with onions, a fricassée of lobster, and trout grilled and served with ratatouille. You can also order excellent meat dishes, among them Scottish lamb seasoned with thyme.

Although acclaimed as the leading restaurant of Klosters, the Walserhof also offers 11 elegant rooms. In winter, with breakfast included, charges range from 290SF to 395SF ($159.50–$217.25) in a double. In summer doubles are 230SF to 260SF ($126.50–$143).

In the Walserhof Hotel, CH-7250 Klosters-Platz. ✆ **081/410-29-29.** Fax 081/410-29-39. Reservations required in peak season. Main courses 45SF–59SF ($24.75–$32.45); fixed-price menus 85SF–146SF ($46.75–$80.30). AE, DC, MC, V. Daily 11:30am–2pm and 6–11pm. Closed late Apr to mid-June and late Oct to early Dec.

4 Davos ★★★

15 miles (24km) E of Chur, 7 miles (11km) S of Klosters

Along with St. Moritz and Zermatt, Davos has some of the finest sports facilities in the world, as well as a diversified choice of après-ski entertainment. The variety of activities makes it a favorite vacation spot for the chic and wealthy as well as for the hundreds of ordinary folk just out to have a good time in the mountains.

The name Davos (first Tavauns, later Dafaas) entered written history in 1160 in a document in the Episcopal archives of Chur. In 1289 a group of families from the Valais established homes here. In 1649 the town bought its freedom from Austria.

The two sections, Davos-Platz and Davos-Dorf, were once separate entities, but in the past 25 years or so, construction on the land between the two has served to join them, making Davos today somewhat larger than St. Moritz.

The canton of Davos is the second largest in Switzerland. The high valley that contains it is surrounded by forest-covered mountains that shelter it from rough winds. The area thus has a bracing climate, which has proved ideal for a summer-and-winter resort. Davos first entered the world limelight as a health resort

Kirchner: The Tormented Genius

Ernst Ludwig Kirchner was born in Aschaffenburg, Germany, in 1880. He studied architecture in Dresden and in 1905 was a cofounder of an expressionist group, Die Brücke, which was disbanded in 1913. The artist moved to Berlin in 1911, and it was there that his body of work reached its zenith. His highly personal paintings were noted for their sharp, vivid colors, their eroticism, and their psychological tension.

Physically and mentally scarred by his confrontation with Berlin and his experiences in military service, he tried several sanatoriums before deciding on Davos in 1917. First on the Stafelalp, later in the house In den Lärchen, and finally on the Wildboden, he produced a unique body of work. In Nazi Germany, in 1936, his paintings were withdrawn from museums and labeled "degenerate art." As a result of the defamation of his character and his oeuvre, he fell into a deep depression that ended in suicide in 1938. His grave and that of his longtime companion, Erna, are located in the Davos forest cemetery.

For a look at this artist and his work, visit the **Davos Kirchner Museum,** Ernst Ludwig Kirchner Platz (© **081/413-22-02**). Entrance to the museum is 8SF ($4.40) for adults and 6SF ($3.30) for children. From Christmas to Easter and mid-July to September, it's open Tuesday to Sunday from 10am to 6pm; the rest of the year, Tuesday to Sunday from 2 to 6pm.

in the 19th century, when Dr. Alexander Spengler prescribed mountain air for his tuberculosis patients. He brought the first summer visitors here in 1860 and the first winter ones 5 years later. There are still several sanatoriums in the area.

Thomas Mann used Davos, at the foot of the Zauberberg (Magic Mountain), as the setting for his famous novel *The Magic Mountain.* He visited the resort when his wife went there briefly in 1913 for her health, seeing it as a symbol of the general malaise that afflicted Europe on the eve of World War I. Robert Louis Stevenson wrote the last seven chapters of *Treasure Island* here between 1881 and 1882, as he, too, tended his consumptive wife. Another writer, Sir Arthur Conan Doyle, engaged in a daring run on skis over the Furka Pass to Arosa. Unfortunately, the much-celebrated villa-hotel where all three writers stayed, Am Stein, contains only private apartments and cannot be visited.

The German painter Ernst Ludwig Kirchner (1880–1938) lived at Davos from 1917 until his death. He was a leading exponent of the expressionist movement.

In addition to being a well-known summer-and-winter vacation resort, Davos is also a health spa, a sports center, and an important venue for international meetings. Whether you're a hiker, mountain biker, downhill or cross-country skier, hang-glider, or ice-sports fan, Davos is an ideal place. Many nonathletes visit just for the relaxation. There's a wide choice of hotels, restaurants, bars, and discos, plus museums and concert and theater performances.

ESSENTIALS

GETTING THERE   Trains from Zurich usually require a transfer in the provincial railway junction of either Landquart or Filisur, where secondary rail lines continue on to Davos. Throughout the day, trains travel to Davos from both these towns every hour. The nearest airport is Zurich's Kloten, but the trip involves three different trains and two transfers. For information about **train schedules,** call ℭ **0900/300-300.**

Bus lines connect Chur with Munich, stopping at Davos and several other mountain towns along the way, but they usually require transfers. Call the tourist office (below) for more information.

If you're driving, proceed to Klosters (see section 3, earlier in this chapter), then continue south on Route 28 to Davos.

VISITOR INFORMATION   The **Davos-Dorf Tourist Office** is at Promenade 67 (ℭ **081/415-21-21**), open Monday to Friday from 8:30am to 6pm, with telephone service until 7pm; on Saturday it's open from 8:30am to 4pm, and on Sunday (Christmas to Easter only) from 10am to noon.

CITY LAYOUT   The town's two sections, **Davos-Platz** (5,118 ft/1535m) and **Davos-Dorf** (5,128 ft/1538m), are linked by a boulevard flanked by boutiques, shops, hotels, and cafes. This thoroughfare is the famous **Promenade,** which takes the one-way traffic flow from Dorf to Platz (beware, however, if you're driving, as buses go in both directions). The lower artery, **Talstrasse,** runs along the railroad tracks, linking the train station in Davos-Platz with the station in Davos-Dorf.

Not all roads in Davos have street names, but there are signs pointing the way to all the hotels and restaurants. Public children's **playgrounds** are found in the Kurpark in Davos-Platz and opposite the lower terminal station of the Parsenn funicular at Davos-Dorf.

GETTING AROUND   Yellow-and-white buses run along the major arteries from Davos-Dorf to Davos-Platz, making scheduled stops near all the main hotels and restaurants. In winter the buses depart daily every 10 minutes from 7am to 11:20pm; in summer departures are every 20 minutes. A single ride costs 2.50SF ($1.70).

> **Tips   A Free Ride**
>
> Any resident of any hotel or guest house in Davos showing proof of that occupancy, having paid the room tax, can ride on town buses for free.

The postal bus leaves from the Davos-Platz railroad station. Organized excursions are available on the postal buses; for information, go to the nearest post office.

SEEING THE SIGHTS

Among the old buildings to be seen in Davos-Platz are the parish **Church of St. John the Baptist,** with a nave dating from 1280 to 1285. The church, now restored, was completed in 1481. It stands east of the train station along Talstrasse. A window in the choir is by Augusto Giacometti. The adjoining **Rathaus** (town hall) has been extensively restored. Its paneled Grosse Stube (Great Chamber) dates from 1564.

In Davos-Dorf, you can visit the 14th-century **Church of St. Theodulus.** At Museumstrasse 1 is the **Altes Pfründhaus** (Old Prebend House), the town's only surviving example of a medieval burgher's domicile, now sheltering a minor local museum, the **Heimatmuseum** (ℭ **081/416-26-66**), which traces the history of the resort town through a collection of objects and documents relating to its past. It's open June 6 to October 10 on Wednesday, Friday, and Sunday from 4 to 6pm, although special tours can be arranged in other months by contacting the museum or the tourist office. Adult admission is 5SF ($3.35); children are charged 2SF ($1.10).

THE ACTIVE VACATION PLANNER

SKIING   Recreational skiing began here in 1888, but Davos first appeared on the world sports stage in 1899, when a large ice rink was opened for the world figure-skating and the European speed-skating championship competitions. In the same year the Davos-Schatzalp funicular and the Schatzalp toboggan run were inaugurated. Now Davos is one of the best ski regions in the world.

On both sides of the valley, you're faced with five large ski areas, of which the most noted is the **Parsenn-Weissflüh.** Some experts say that this is the finest ski area in Europe. To reach it, take the Parsennbahn (railway) from Davos-Dorf to **Weissflühjoch** (8,740 ft/2,622m), the gateway to the major ski area, with a huge number of runs in every category; there are a few downhill ski runs leading back to Davos that are suitable for only the most skilled skiers.

From Weissflühjoch, where there's a restaurant, take the cableway to **Weissflühgipfl** ✦✦ (9,260 ft/2,778m). It takes about an hour from Davos-Dorf. From there you can reach the celebrated Kublis run to the north.

Davos shares its snow with nearby Klosters, where you can also ski, but cable cars and T-bar lift service may keep you happy with the ski opportunities nearer to Davos. Beginners are advised to stick to Rinerhorn, the Strela slopes, or perhaps Pischa, where, if you're graded "intermediate" by your ski school instructor, you may be directed to Jakobshorn.

The ski facilities around Davos aren't the most widespread and far-flung in Switzerland, but they nonetheless incorporate enough challenges to keep intermediate and expert skiers engrossed. Most visitors opt for **Davos's Top Ski Pass,** also known as the **Davos/Klosters R.E.G.A. Ski Pass,** which includes access to five different ski regions around Klosters and Davos. Together, they incorporate 200 miles (322km) of marked ski runs, and access to three funiculars, 10 cable cars, four gondolas, and 39 other mechanical conveyances designed to haul you and your equipment uphill. It also includes free rides on the railway cars from Küblis, a nearby hamlet surrounded by snowfields, back uphill to Davos. Adults pay 121SF ($66.55) for a 2-day pass, 243SF ($133.65)for a 5-day pass, and 312SF ($171.60) for a 7-day pass. Children 6 to 16 are granted reductions of around 35%, and children 5 and under ride free.

OTHER SPORTS   Several winter sports besides skiing are offered here as well. For information on curling, contact the **Davos Curling Club/Davos-Village Curling Club,** Promenade 46, Davos-Platz (✆ 079/610-24-54). Two hours of curling, including instruction, cost 35SF to 40SF ($19.25–$22) per person.

If you're interested in ice-skating on the **Natureisbahn,** Davos-Platz, the largest natural ice rink in Europe, phone the Davos-Dorf Tourist Office (see "Essentials," above), which manages the rink. Admission costs 6SF ($3.30) for adults, 4SF ($2.20) for children. Prices are 1SF (55¢) less for holders of the Guest Card, which is presented to all hotel guests. The rink is usually open from December to February, depending on weather conditions. Davos-Platz also has a huge artificial ice rink, and both are open daily from 10am to 4pm. In addition to this natural ice-skating rink midway between Davos-Platz and Davos-Dorf, there are at least two other ice-skating venues. For any information about ice skating, contact the tourist office (see above).

Many Davos sports facilities can be used in both the winter and the summer. It has first-class tennis courts, sailing and windsurfing on Lake Davos, swimming, and horseback riding. There's an 18-hole golf course, **Golf Club Davis** (✆ 081/

465-634), with a weekday greens fee of 80SF ($44) that includes a golf cart; on weekends, the fee goes up to 100SF ($55). If you're staying in accommodations at Davos, there's a 10SF ($5.50) discount. Golf clubs can be rented for an additional 30SF ($16.50) a day. For further information and reservations, call 🕐 081/ 416-56-34). There's also a large indoor ice rink if you want to keep your skills and your skates sharp during the summer months.

Davos has an impressive **Tennis & Squash Center,** on Clavadelerstrasse in Davos-Platz (🕐 081/413-31-31), which is open daily from 8am to 10pm. Prices depend on when you play, day or night. Court rental from 4:30 to 9:30pm is 26SF ($14.30) for an indoor or outdoor court.

Want to go swimming? Call **Hawlbad,** Promenade 99, next to the Kongress (🕐 081/413-64-63), for information on either indoor swimming in winter or outdoor swimming in the summer. Adults pay 6.50SF ($3.60), children are charged 3.50SF ($1.95), and students between the ages of 16 and 25 pay 4.50SF ($2.50), all of which includes changing-room facilities. With use of the mixed sauna included, adults pay 13SF ($7.15).

HIKING & WALKING   Well-marked and -maintained footpaths and mountain trails give access to meadows, pastures, woods, and mountains both close to and far away from Davos. A 280-mile (451km) network of pathways follows brooks, crosses alpine meadows, and leads to remote hamlets, allowing you to explore the side valleys of Sertig, Dischma, and Flüela. Davos mountain railways provide access to five different walking areas and to the most rewarding vantage points around Davos. The tourist office (see "Essentials," above) will supply more details.

SHOPPING

Davos is not obsessed with Swiss folklore but you'll find lots of emphasis on cutting-edge sports equipment and clothing. Check out **Ettinger Sport,** Promenade 1053, Davos-Dorf (🕐 081/410-12-12); or its less comprehensive counterpart at the opposite end of the resort, **Angerer Sport,** Promenade 49, Davos-Platz (🕐 081/413-66-72).

Souvenirs of your stay in the Grisons are most conveniently acquired at **Pfister Holzladen,** Promenade 121A, Davos-Dorf (🕐 081/416-40-60), or **Trauffer Souvenirs,** Promenade 78, Davos-Platz (🕐 081/413-55-78). **Bennetton** sells casual men's and women's clothes at Promenade 62, in Davos-Platz (🕐 081/ 413-49-50). If you're looking for etchings, oil paintings or watercolors, or lithographs created by artists from the region and from everywhere else as well, head for any of the oft-changing exhibitions at either of the resort's most noteworthy art galleries, **Galerie Iris-Wazzau,** Promenade 79, Davos-Platz (🕐 081/413-31-06), or **Galerie Eule Art,** Promenade 41, Davos-Platz (🕐 081/413-15-00).

WHERE TO STAY
IN DAVOS-PLATZ
Very Expensive

Steigenberger Belvédère 🕐🕐🕐   This light-gray neoclassical building on the main road of Davos-Platz is a world-famous resort hotel originally built around 1875. It was purchased in the 1980s by the Steigenberger chain. The interior has a series of intricately carved fireplaces, ornate ceilings, a well-polished bar, and both contemporary and Victorian armchairs. Guests have a choice of modern, Belle Epoque, or regionally decorated rooms, many with furniture crafted from a local wood called *arvenholz.* A few, however, are rather dull in decor. It's worth visiting the pool for the murals even if you don't swim;

Finds **Hiking Without Luggage**

Three Grisons vacation resorts—Arosa, Lenzerheide-Valbella, and Davos—have joined forces to create a "Hiking Without Luggage" program. It's intended for hikers who enjoy walking from one resort to another but don't want to be bothered by luggage. Instead, your luggage is delivered to your next hotel for you, an arrangement made by various hotels. Either a 4- or a 7-day program can be booked. The most popular departure point is Davos. Two vouchers for the use of mountain railways are included in the program.

There are two hiking routes between Arosa and Davos to choose from. The easier one is via the Sapün, and the more challenging and loftier route is via the Tritt. Both paths lead to the Strela Pass. You can either take the Schatzalp/Strela mountain railway to get to Davos or continue on foot. The 4-day program, including 3 nights' accommodation, is available for 270SF to 525SF ($148.50–$288.75). Children from 12 to 16 years are eligible for a 30% discount, children from 6 to 11 years get a 50% discount, and children under 6 years are free. Included in the price is breakfast, luggage transfer, one ascent or descent in a mountain railway for each day's hike, and the relevant maps and route descriptions.

For more information, call the **Davos Tourist Office** (📞 **081/415-21-21**).

a Tahitian lagoon with flamingoes and lifelike jungle plants sway in the imaginary breeze, and seem to grow right out of the pool.

Promenade 89, CH-4270 Davos-Platz. 📞 **800/223-5652** in the United States and Canada, or 081/415-60-00. Fax 081/415-60-01. www.steigenberger.ch. 141 units. Winter 424SF–523SF ($233.20–$287.65) double; from 723SF ($397.65) suite for 2. Summer 360SF–490SF ($198–$269.50) double; from 650SF ($357.50) suite for 2. Rates include breakfast. Half board 55SF ($30.25) extra person. AE, DC, MC, V. Parking 35SF ($19.25) in winter, 25SF ($13.75) in summer. Closed Apr 10–Aug 27 and Oct 15–Nov 24. **Amenities:** 2 restaurants, bar; pool; tennis courts; sauna; salon; room service; massage; babysitting; laundry service. *In room:* TV, minibar, hair dryer, iron, safe (in some).

Expensive

Hotel Europe ✿ This longtime favorite is near the tourist office and the Schatzalp-Strela funicular. Right in the heart of Davos-Platz, the hotel lies just a few steps from the lifts, a few yards from the ice rink, and only 5 minutes from the golf greens. It was built in 1868, and is thus the oldest of the resort's big hotels. The present building is a flat-roofed, white stucco structure. The formal interior is decorated with Oriental rugs and hunting trophies. Rooms are not at all lavish, with laminated furniture, but they are well equipped with double glazing, tiled bathrooms (generally with tubs), and twin beds with firm mattresses. Opt, if possible, for a unit with a balcony facing south.

Promenade 63, CH-7270 Davos-Platz. 📞 **081/413-59-21**. Fax 081/413-13-93. 64 units. Winter 360SF–490SF ($198–$269.50) double; from 810SF ($445.50) suite for 2. Off-season 204SF–300SF ($112.20–$165) double; from 590SF ($324.50) suite for 2. Rates include buffet breakfast. AE, DC, MC, V. Parking 15SF ($8.25) in winter, 10SF ($5.50) in summer. Bus to stop 10. **Amenities:** 3 restaurants, 3 bars; pool; tennis courts; fitness room; sauna; salon; room service; babysitting; laundry service. *In room:* TV, minibar, hair dryer.

Kongress Hotel Davos ✿ This first-class hotel is a bit far from the center of town. Most guests, however, are willing to sacrifice proximity for the view of the Landwasser River and snowfields in winter or green Davos mountains in summer. The hotel, which opened in 1982, is inside the Convention Center, in the same building as the indoor swimming pool complex. Virtually all the sports facilities of Davos are close by. In addition, a public bus stops in front of the hotel for frequent rides to the ski runs. The mid-sized bedrooms are smartly furnished.

Promenade 94, CH-7270 Davos-Platz. ℭ **081/417-11-22.** Fax 081/417-11-23. 80 units. Winter 275SF–375SF ($151.25–$206.25) double. Off-season 200SF–240SF ($110–$132)double. Rates include breakfast. Half board 25SF ($13.75) per person extra. AE, DC, MC, V. Free parking outdoors; 5SF ($2.75) in garage in summer, 12SF ($6.60) in winter. Closed Apr 13–May 10. Bus to stop 10. **Amenities:** Restaurant, bar; sauna; concierge; room service; laundry service. *In room:* TV, minibar, hair dryer, safe.

Morosani Posthotel ⚡ Set at the gateway to the Promenade in Davos-Platz, this is a landmark which has been efficiently run for more than a century by the Morosani family. The hotel consists of three buildings connected by a rustically decorated underground tunnel. The cozy lobby has an open fireplace, and bedrooms are spacious. From Christmas to New Year's the hotel requires a minimum stay of 12 nights.

Promenade 42, CH-7270 Davos-Platz. ℭ **081/413-74-74.** Fax 081/413-70-60. 86 units. Winter 460SF–530SF ($253–$291.50) double. Summer 320SF–390SF ($176–$214.50) double. Winter rates include half board; summer rates include breakfast. AE, DC, MC, V. Free parking outdoors, 12SF ($6.60) in garage. Closed Apr 15–May 30 and Oct 5–Dec 6. Bus to stop 9. **Amenities:** Restaurant, bar; pool; sauna; playground; room service; babysitting; laundry service. *In room:* TV, minibar, hair dryer.

Moderate

Hotel Ochsen At the southwestern edge of the resort, close to the railway station, this is an unpretentious hotel which was originally built around 1900. It's a traditional, rustic, family-managed place, centrally located near the Jakobshorn cableway, skating rink, convention center, public swimming pool, bus station, and shops. The lobby and comfortable bar are tastefully decorated with leather furnishings and Oriental rugs. The bedrooms are well kept and many of them are quite large. Some of the upper rooms open onto views of the Jakobshorn.

Talstrasse, 10, CH-7270 Davos-Platz. ℭ **081/413-52-22.** Fax 081/413-76-71. 47 units. Winter 330SF ($181.50) double; summer 178SF ($97.90) double. Rates include buffet breakfast. Half board 35SF ($19.25) per person extra in winter, 28SF ($15.40) extra in summer. AE, DC, MC, V. Parking 12SF ($6.60). **Amenities:** Restaurant, bar; limited room service; laundry service. *In room:* TV, minibar.

Zur Alte Post ⚡ *Value* This is a pretty, pink-fronted building with hints of baroque country charm and a history that includes a stint during the late 1600s as the town's post office. Philip Charles, sometimes in cooperation with the local chairlift authorities, offers guests good value in a small-scale setting adjacent to the town hall, set back from the resort's main promenade. The bedrooms are rather small, even cramped in some cases, and feature pinewood furniture, good beds, and private bathrooms with showers. Request a room with a view over the mountains; others look out onto rather dull street scenes. The public areas include a cozy bar favored by locals, and at least three antique dining rooms. The oldest of them, Tavaasar Schtuba—open only in wintertime—is a 16th-century fantasy loaded with Swiss folklore and elaborate woodwork.

Berlistutz 4, CH-7270 Davos-Platz. ℭ **081/413-54-03.** Fax 081/413-54-03. 20 units. Winter 380SF ($209) double; summer 110SF ($60.50) double. Summer rates include breakfast; winter rates include half board and use of a ski pass valid throughout the Upper Engadine. AE, MC, V. Free parking. Dining room (but not the hotel) closed May–June and Nov. **Amenities:** Bar; limited room service; laundry service. *In room:* No phone.

IN DAVOS-DORF
Very Expensive

Flüela Hotel ⚡ More than a century after its opening, this thick-walled, solidly built hotel is still managed by the Gredig family. Its unadorned beige facade conceals an elegantly rustic and cozy interior with comfortable and well-furnished bedrooms, each fitted with cozy appointments and state-of-the-art plumbing. In recent years, many rooms have been redone; some have been enlarged into suites.

Bahnhofstrasse 5, CH-7260 Davos-Dorf. ✆ **081/410-17-17.** Fax 081/410-17-18. www.fluela.ch. 73 units. 500SF–750SF ($275–$412.50) double; from 680SF ($374) junior suite. Rates include half board. AE, DC, MC, V. Parking 15SF ($8.25). Closed Apr and May, Oct 7–Nov 24. **Amenities:** 2 restaurants; bar; sauna; Turkish bath; concierge; salon; room service; massage; babysitting; dry cleaning. *In room:* TV, minibar, hair dryer, safe.

Moderate

Hotel Dischma *Value* This is a well-recommended government-rated three-star hotel with modern amenities and a location in the heart of Davos-Dorf, near the Parsenn funicular; the Pischa bus stop is about a 5-minute walk away. The small to mid-sized bedrooms are renovated although still rustic; you don't check in here for style but for value. Nonetheless, there is much comfort, including firm beds and excellently maintained plumbing.

Promenade 128, CH-7260 Davos-Dorf. ✆ **081/416-33-23.** Fax 081/416-32-88. 27 units, 19 with bathroom. Winter 182SF ($100.10) double without bathroom, 210SF ($115.50) double with bathroom. Summer 178SF ($97.90) double without bathroom, 205SF ($112.75) double with bathroom. Rates include buffet breakfast. AE, DC, MC, V. Free parking outdoors, 12SF ($6.60) in garage. Bus to stop 5. **Amenities:** 2 restaurants, 2 bars; limited room service; laundry service. *In room:* TV, minibar.

Parsenn Sporthotel In the heart of Davos-Dorf, across the road from the Parsennbahn, this is a large and substantial Grisons chalet whose facade is covered in intricate stencils. Built in 1907 and enlarged in 1972, it sits beside a large parking lot and near a cluster of gas stations, not far from the base of several ski lifts. The ceilings of the public rooms are beamed or vaulted, sheltering a mountain-rustic decor with few frills. The mid-sized bedrooms are comfortable—some are newer than others—furnished in a pinewood chalet style. Half of them are equipped only with showers, the rest with a tub and shower combination.

Promenade 152, CH-7260 Davos-Dorf. ✆ **081/416-32-32.** Fax 081/416-38-67. www.hotelparsenn.ch. 40 units. 295SF–330SF ($162.25–$181.50) double; 370SF ($203.50) junior suite for 2. Rates include half board. AE, MC, V. Closed Easter to early Dec. **Amenities:** restaurant, bar. *In room:* TV, hair dryer.

Inexpensive

Hermann Hotel *Value* One of the most reliable cost-conscious hotels in town sits on the main street of Davos-Dorf, near the edge of the town facing Klosters. Originally built about a century ago, and completely renovated in 1985, it's a simple, four-story building with a flat roof and—at least on the outside—very few of the architectural adornments usually associated with an old-fashioned chalet. Inside, you'll find a cozy, simple decor, a clientele that appreciates the inexpensive half-board supplements, and very simple bedrooms outfitted with lots of varnished pine. Two-thirds of the rooms contain small, shower-only private bathrooms; occupants of the other units will find the corridor bathrooms adequate.

Dorfstrasse 23, CH-7260 Davos-Dorf. ✆ **081/416-17-37.** Fax 081/416-35-73. 30 units, 20 with bathroom. 100SF–160SF ($55–$88) double without bathroom; 132SF–190SF ($72.60–$104.50) double with bathroom. Rates include breakfast. Half board 15SF ($8.25) extra per person per day. Parking 10SF ($5.50). MC, V. Closed Sept 20–Dec 20 and Apr to late June. **Amenities:** Restaurant (open only to residents on half-board), bar.

Hotel Bûnda Modern and well-maintained, and set within a short walk from the Davos-Dorf railway station and the lake, this hotel consists of two buildings, each interconnected via an underground passageway. Built in 1964 and 1995, respectively, they contain, cozy, relatively spacious bedrooms, with those in the newer annex looking somewhat more contemporary than their old-fashioned counterparts in the other building. Each unit contains a private shower-only bathroom.

Museumstrasse 4, CH-7260 Davos-Dorf. ℂ **081/416-3757.** Fax 081/416-6416. 31 units. www.buenda.ch. 152SF–330SF ($83.60–$181.50) double. Rates include breakfast. Supplement for half board 15SF ($8.25) per person. AE, DC, MC, V. Closed mid-Apr to early June. **Amenities:** 2 restaurants (one reserved for hotel residents), bar; steam room; sauna; fitness room. *In room:* TV, minibar, hair dryer, safe.

IN DAVOS-LARET

Hübli's Landhaus *Finds*   Built a century ago as a relay station 3 miles (5km) from the center of Davos, on a traffic-filled highway between Davos and Klosters, Hübli's is one of the region's best little hotels for the money. The dynamic owners put most of their energy into the excellent restaurant (see "Where to Dine," below), although there's a selection of small bedrooms connected to the restaurant by a tunnel. The rooms have earth-tone fabrics and furniture and exposed hardwoods, and are known for their coziness and their vaguely folkloric references. Rooms are equally divided between those with tub baths and those with shower. In the height of midwinter the hotel provides free transportation to the ski lifts of Davos.

Kantonsstrasse, CH-7265 Davos-Laret. ℂ **081/417-10-10.** Fax 081/417-10-11. 20 units, 14 with bathroom. Winter 174SF ($95.70) double without bathroom, 235SF–255SF ($129.25–$140.25) double with bathroom. Summer 144SF ($79.20) double without bathroom, 164SF ($90.20) double with bathroom. Rates include breakfast. Half board 25SF ($13.75) per person extra. AE, DC, MC, V. Free parking. Closed Apr–June and Nov 9–Dec 15. Travel 2 miles north of Davos-Dorf along Route 28 toward Klosters. **Amenities:** Restaurant; limited room service. *In room:* TV.

WHERE TO DINE
EXPENSIVE

Bündnerstübli SWISS   The walls and the ceiling of this cozy place are covered with local pine, giving it a rustic look. The menu, appropriately, reads like a history book of local recipes, some of whose names will require a staff member to translate. One example is "Maluns," potatoes served with applesauce and local cheese. Other dishes are fondue with grated potatoes, a richly flavored barley soup, and a daily farmer's menu with large portions of reasonably priced, well-prepared food.

Dischmastrasse 8, Davos-Dorf. ℂ **081/416-33-93.** Reservations required. Main courses 20SF–50SF ($11–$27.50); 4-course fixed-price menu 84SF ($46.20). AE, DC, MC, V. Tues–Sun 11:30am–2pm and 5–11pm. Closed May–June and Nov. Bus to stop 5.

Hübli's Landhaus ★★★ CONTINENTAL   This is the finest and most sophisticated restaurant in Davos, with a reputation throughout Switzerland that draws many clients to its position 3 miles (5km) east of town, beside the highway leading to Klosters. Inside the solid white walls of what was built a century ago as a relay station for the Swiss postal service, you'll find a handful of artfully simple dining rooms and superb cuisine. Felix and Anne-Marie Hübli offer specialties that change with the seasons and the availability of the ingredients. Examples include a terrine of foie gras served with a salad of artichokes, lobster bisque, filet of turbot with lemon-flavored cream sauce, veal chop with chanterelle-flavored cream sauce, and roast duckling with blackberry sauce. Dessert might be a parfait of Peruvian mangoes, or perhaps a gratin of fresh summer berries served with passion fruit sorbet.

Kantonstrasse, Davos-Laretz. ℂ **081/417-1010.** Reservations recommended. Main courses 38SF–60SF ($20.90–$33); fixed-price lunch 48SF ($26.40), fixed-price dinner 76SF ($41.80). AE, DC, MC, V. Tues–Sun 11:30am–2pm and 6:30–9:30pm. Closed Apr 20–June 1 and Nov to Dec 10, and at lunch in winter.

Restaurant Pöstli SWISS   In winter this elegant room offers live music from 5 to 5:30pm and 8:30pm until closing time. In summer live music begins at 6pm and lasts until closing. Many guests follow dinner here with a later sojourn to the Pöstli Club, which is open in winter and also has live bands. The restaurant has a bar as well as a more formal seating area. Your choice in tasty platters is extensive—a different fresh fish daily or something classic, such as *tafelspitz* (boiled beef Viennese style). Other selections are veal liver with polenta, venison in a hunter's sauce, filet of U.S. beef with mushrooms, and rack of lamb with braised cabbage.

In the Morosani Posthotel, Promenade 42, Davos-Platz. © 081/413-74-74. Reservations required. Main courses 40SF–60SF ($22–$33); 5-course fixed-price menu 85SF ($46.75). AE, DC, MC, V. Daily 11am–2pm and 6:15pm–1am. Closed Apr 15–May 30 and Oct 5–Dec 6, and Sun and Mon in summer. Bus to stop 9.

Vinikus ★★ INTERNATIONAL   This is the kind of restaurant where a top-notch international banker might entertain some of the firm's clients during any of the conferences held in Davos-Platz. Formal, contemporary-looking, and elegant, it's outfitted with lots of varnished oaks that contrast with all-black accessories, and a view through big windows of the town's main street and its mountains. Members of the Kempf family (David cooks, his wife Jutte tends to the dining room) have been your hosts since 1992, often proposing set-price menus with which wine is included. These change every day, but usually include selections from Germany, Italy, and Austria, which go well with the sophisticated cuisine. Memorable examples include sliced veal with mushrooms, cream sauce, and rösti; duck breast with red currant sauce and rice; veal steak or venison in a walnut crust with chestnut or basil-flavored noodles; or roast veal with ratatouille. Every day, expect a tempting array of fresh pastas and vegetarian dishes.

Promenade 119. © 081/416-5979. Reservations required. Main courses 25SF–55SF ($13.75–$30.25); set-price menus (dinner only) with wine 125SF–145SF ($68.75–$79.75). AE, MC, V. Wed–Sun 11am–2pm and 6–11pm. Closed May–June.

MODERATE

Bistro Gentiana et Café des Artistes SWISS   Housed in a gold-colored building opposite the Hotel Schweizerhof in the center of town, this restaurant is the only authentic bistro in Davos. It's known for its 10 different types of fondue dishes, as well as for its unusual list of dishes prepared with snails. Unpretentious and bustling, the establishment serves ample portions of air-dried beef and ham, as well as inexpensive daily specials. Its choice of desserts includes local pears in cinnamon syrup, honey-flavored ice cream, and chocolate mousse. Wines are sold by the carafe. Don't overlook the pair of upstairs dining rooms, whose focal point is a blue-toned painting by the German artist Ernst Ludwig Kirchner, a former resident of Davos.

Promenade 53, Davos-Platz. © 081/413-49-21. Reservations required. Main courses 18SF–42SF ($9.90–$23.10); fondues 24SF–27SF ($13.20–$14.85). AE, DC, MC, V. Daily 11am–11pm. Closed Wed in summer. Bus to stop 5.

13

The Engadine

The Valley of the Inn (or En, as the locals call it in Romansh) stretches for 60 miles (97km), from the Maloja Plateau (5,955 ft/1,786m) to Finstermünz. All of the villages here except Sils lie at a higher altitude than the plateau. The highest is St. Moritz, at 6,036 feet (1,811m).

The Engadine is enclosed by great mountain ranges with meadows and forests on the steep hillsides. The villages are built of stone, originally as a protection against the fires that swept the narrow windy valleys. The whitewashed houses in the villages, known for their larders, often have sgraffito decorations, with mottoes and heraldic devices. The population is of Rhaeto-Romanic heritage and is mostly Protestant.

From the Maloja Pass, the road runs northeast through the Upper Engadine, where the clear mountain skies and dry, light breezes make the area popular in both summer and winter. Since the 19th century, when the Upper Engadine became fashionable for its "air cure," it has developed into a winter-sports resort, highlighted by St. Moritz.

The two major attractions of the Lower Engadine, where the valley is narrower and more heavily forested, are the mineral springs of Scuol and the Swiss National Park, a 55-mile (89km) wildlife sanctuary.

St. Moritz is the major rail terminus for the valley. For **information** and schedules, call ✆ **0900/300-300.** From here you can make bus or rail links to other villages of the Engadine.

EXPLORING THE REGION BY CAR

The Lower Engadine is reached from Davos over the Flüela Pass (7,818 ft/ 2,345m) and the Ofen Pass (7,050 ft/2,115m). Four major passes lead into the Upper Engadine: Maloja (5,955 ft/1,786m), Julier (7,493 ft/2,248m), Albula (7,585 ft/2,275m), and Bernina (7,621 ft/2,286m). The upper valley contains several lakes, including that of St. Moritz.

If you have time to drive only one of these passes, and weather conditions are right, make it the **Bernina Pass** ★★, a 2-hour, 34-mile (55km) drive between St. Moritz and Tirano in Italy. This pass is one of the most spectacular in Europe, and is most often blocked by snow from October to May. Since the pass is not cleared at night, it is best to start out in daytime.

Leave St. Moritz in the direction of Pontresina. Along the way you'll pass by **Muottas Muragl,** from which you can stop and take a funicular to an altitude of 8,048 feet (2,414m), where you'll be rewarded with the most stunning view of the Upper Engadine Gap. The panorama also takes in a chain of lakes lying between St. Moritz and Maloja. From the top of the station you can take some of the most dramatic mountain walks in eastern Switzerland, enjoying the alpine flora and fauna.

The road passes by Pontresina, a resort, and continues until the **Chünetta Belvedere** at 6,835 feet (2,050m). You cannot drive all the way to the top of the belvedere but still have to go 1 hour on foot. At the belvedere the spectacular peaks of the Bernina Massif, including Piz Bernina and Piz Morteratsch, lie before you.

As you continue along you'll pass another sign directing you to the **Diavolezza,** another spectacular belvedere at 9,076 feet (2,723m) that includes a 15-minute journey by cable car. Diavolezza is the starting point of one of the most famous glacier runs in the world. See "Pontresina," later in this chapter, for more information.

After crossing the Bernina Pass, where there are clear views of the Piz Cambrena and its glacier, you come to **Alp Grüm** at 6,860 feet (2,058m), overlooking the Palü Glacier and the Poschiavo Valley. Going through the resort of Poschiavo you arrive finally at **Tirano** on the downward slope, passing through tobacco fields and vineyards. At Tirano you will have arrived on Italian soil.

THE ENGADINE OUTDOORS

You don't come to this rugged part of Switzerland to stay in your hotel room all day, not with a wilderness out there to explore. After leaving the chic resorts such as St. Moritz, you enter wild, untamed scenery.

For hikers, the **Swiss National Park Service** (② 081/856-13-78) maps out a group of panoramic half- or full-day adventures into the choicest and most scenic of its wilderness land holdings. Many of these take you along rugged and often steep mountain trails so you should be in good shape. All major villages and resorts in the Engadine also offer signposted and well-maintained hiking trails and footpaths. Visit local or regional tourist offices to learn more. All maps and information are available at the Zuoz Tourist Office (see "Essentials" below), where the helpful staff will help plan an outdoor itinerary suitable to your specific interests.

For one of the **great walks** in the Engadine, you can take in vistas of four highland lakes at 5,904 feet (1,771m) above sea level. Even at this high altitude the walk is like traversing the floor of a valley. The walk begins at Maloja and goes for 8.6 miles (13.85km) to the resort of Silvaplana. Allow some 3 to 3½ hours for this alpine stroll. From Maloja traverse the eastern or southern tier of Lej da Segl. The route is well marked leading you to Segl-Maria, one of the most charming old Romansh villages. Eventually you reach the resort of Silvaplana. As you walk along you'll be following in the footsteps of Nietzsche, who lived in this area and often took this walk "to think."

For serious **mountaineering,** the **Bergsteigerschule La Margna** at Sils/Silvaplana has a mountaineering school with guided tours. One day of instruction for beginners costs 300SF ($165). Call ② **081/828-88-15** to arrange for an appointment and to get prices and listings of scheduled climbing trips. In Pontresina, **Bergsteigerschule Pontresina** (② **081/842-64-44**) also offers mountaineering programs.

Great Express Trains

From Zurich, the *Glacier Express* climbs over the Alps from St. Moritz to Zermatt in the Valais. The *Engadine Express* also goes from Chur through the Swiss National Park into the Lower Engadine. The *Palm Express* is a 2-day itinerary that combines rail and bus routes, taking visitors from St. Moritz to either Brig in the west or Zermatt in the shadow of the Matterhorn. Bookings on this route include a hotel night en route. The scenery along this run is some of the more spectacular in Switzerland. For information and seasonal availability, call **Rail Europe** at ② **800/438-7245**.

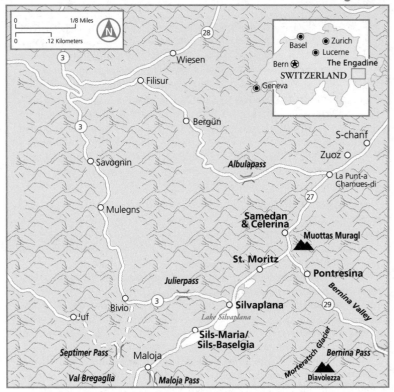

White-water expeditions are possible on the river En, but only between May and October. A half-day's outing where you'll shoot the rapids in a rubber-sided raft is priced at 100SF ($55), but cost can vary depending on the options you select. A full day's excursion goes for 150SF ($82.50). For more information about this, contact **Swissraft Engadine** (℘ 081/911-52-50), in Scuol, or any local tourist office within the Engadine.

It's also possible to go **riding** in the Engadine. The best stables are in St. Moritz (see section 3, later in this chapter).

The Engadine is known for its steep, river-eroded canyons, the sides of which rise vertiginously upward on either side. An outfit that can help direct you through some of the steepest of these is **St. Moritz Experience,** CH-7512 Champfer (℘ **081/833-77-14**). For 176SF ($96.80) per day, they'll include transportation, use of all equipment, and instruction on how to navigate up and down the edges of canyons and valleys whose microclimates are softer and gentler than those on the wind-swept upper regions nearby. The same outfit will take you on an 8-hour glacier and rock hike for around 105SF ($57.75) per person.

1 S-Chanf & Zuoz (★)

30 miles SE of Davos, 12 miles NE of St. Moritz

These two Engadine resorts with a combined population of under 2,000 residents offer attractive, and less expensive, alternatives to St. Moritz, located to the southwest.

ESSENTIALS

GETTING THERE   About 17 local trains travel daily from St. Moritz. They arrive first at Zuoz and then continue to S-Chanf, 15 to 20 minutes away, respectively, with one-way tickets priced at 8SF ($4.40) and 9SF ($4.95). For **rail information** and timetables, call © **0900/300-300.**

By car from St. Moritz, drive northeast along Route 27.

VISITOR INFORMATION   The **Zuoz Tourist Office** is in Zuoz on the main street, Via Maistra (© **081/854-15-10**). Most of the year, it's open Monday to Friday from 9am to noon and from 3 to 6pm. During the low season, it's open Monday to Friday from 3 to 5pm. There's a smaller tourist office in **S-Chanf,** on Via Maistra (© **081/854-22-55**). We would advise you to contact the office in Zuoz first. For information on transportation by bus between the two villages, contact the tourist office, or call © **081/834-90-90.**

EXPLORING THE TOWN
IN ZUOZ

This old-world village, once the chief population center of the Engadine, is located by the Inn River, amid alpine meadows and lush forests. Most of the 1,200 inhabitants of Zuoz speak Romansh.

This is the best-preserved village in the Upper Engadine, with the most striking collection of Engadine houses to be found anywhere in the valley. The best-known is the famed **Planta House** (two houses actually), on the **main square** ✦✦ of the village, with an outdoor staircase and a rococo balustrade. The Planta family, historically important in the region, built most of the spectacular structures in town. This privately owned house cannot be entered by tourists.

Another stop that merits a visit is the **village church.** Inside, look for the severed-bear's-paw theme—a heraldic symbol of the Plantas that also appears on a fountain in the main square. Augusto Giacometti designed some of the church's modern stained-glass windows.

A fledgling summer resort, Zuoz offers a wealth of activities from horseback riding to summer skiing. At 5,740 feet above sea level, this minor winter-sports center has a **ski school** (© **081/850-17-17**) for beginners, including children, as well as for those more advanced in the sport. The school is only open for business during midwinter. The most experienced skiers will gravitate to the heights of the Piz Kesch region or else journey by train to St. Moritz.

Numerous cross-country tracks lead through Zuoz in all directions, and the village is the finishing point of the Engadine ski marathon. Curling, ice skating, and sledding are other winter sports pursued here.

IN S-CHANF

At 5,100 feet, this village with a most unusual name is a summer and winter resort at the entrance to the **Swiss National Park** ✦✦✦. This park, which covers a landmass of 280 square miles (174 sq. km), is the only one of its kind in Switzerland. Hunting is strictly forbidden within its precincts, as it is viewed as a nature preserve and shelter for alpine flora and fauna. Entrance to the park is free, and it's greatly appreciated in midwinter as a cross-country ski zone and in summer as a hiking destination.

WHERE TO STAY & DINE
IN ZUOZ

Posthotel Engiadina ✦   The most visible and prestigious hotel in Zuoz is a beautifully preserved, pink neo-baroque structure that was built 125 years ago as a lodging for passengers on the Swiss postal routes. Public rooms remain faithful to the style of the original construction, but they've been charmingly updated with murals and all the modern conveniences you'd expect from a government-rated four-star hotel. At least one of the parlors contains antiques, Art Deco chandeliers, and an unusual collection of antique clocks. Bedrooms are more modern than the building's elaborate exterior would suggest. Recently renovated, they're conservative, cozy, and tasteful, with tiled bathrooms equipped mostly with well-maintained shower-tub combinations. The two in-house restaurants produce some of the finest cuisine in the area, specializing in international and regional foods. A glass of ruby vintage Veltliner goes wonderfully with their Engadine sausage.

CH-7524 Zuoz. © **081/854-10-21.** Fax 081/854-33-03. www.hotelengiadina.ch. 42 units. 134SF–316SF ($73.70–$173.80) double; 296SF–348SF ($162.80–$191.40) junior suite. Rates include breakfast. Half board, if clients remain for a minimum of 3 days, 38SF ($20.90) per person per day. AE, DC, MC, V. Closed Apr–May and mid-Oct to mid-Dec. **Amenities:** 2 restaurants, 2 bars; pool; tennis court; sauna; room service; laundry. *In room:* TV, hair dryer.

IN S-CHANF

Hotel Scaletta *finds*   Originally built in 1624 as a relay station for passengers and horses struggling over the Engadine passes, this hotel evokes old Europe. It's one of the most immediately recognizable buildings in S-Chanf, thanks to a gray-green antique facade that's accented with sgraffito, on a tiny square a few steps from the village church. The five rooms in the oldest section are the most charming, thanks to antique paneling, high ceilings, and somewhat larger dimensions. More contemporary-looking bedrooms, comfortable and well-maintained but without the patina or antiques of the others, lie within a wing that was added to the original hotel in the late 1980s. All units contain neatly kept bathrooms equipped with showers. The hotel's in-house restaurant serves Swiss cuisine at reasonable prices. This is one of the few hotels in the region, incidentally, that remains open throughout the year.

Via Maistra 52, Ch7525 S-Chanf. © **081/854-03-04.** Fax 081/884-05-06. www.hotelscaletta.ch. 20 units. 160SF–165SF ($88–$90.75) double. Rates include breakfast. Half board 32SF–58SF ($17.60–$31.90) per person. AE, DC, MC, V. **Amenities:** Restaurant, bar; curling rink; babysitting. *In room:* TV, minibar, safe.

2 Samedan ⊕ & Celerina ⊕

2 miles (3km) NE of St. Moritz, 3 miles (5km) NW of Pontresina

These twin resorts are virtually at the doorstep of St. Moritz and are sometimes referred to as suburbs of St. Moritz. But that's a somewhat demeaning label, as Samedan and Celerina have individual characters.

Samedan, originally a Roman settlement, survived to become a principal village of the Upper Engadine. Over the years many well-known Swiss families have made their homes here. Seek out the Planta House (the same family who made its mark on Zuoz) and note its large roof and impressive library of Romansh works.

Celerina (about 5,675 ft/1,702m), a hamlet on the Inn River, has long been overshadowed by its more celebrated neighbors. But for those in search of local color, Celerina (Schlarigna in Romansh) is an ideal choice as a winter or summer resort. Known for its charming Engadine houses, this little village on a sunny plain is sheltered from bitter winds.

ESSENTIALS

GETTING THERE   Almost 20 **trains** depart from St. Moritz every day, stopping 4 minutes later in Celerina and 7 minutes later in Samedan. Trains also run from Chur to Samedan. For information call © **0900/300-300.**

Buses running from St. Moritz to Lugano are not scheduled to stop at Celerina and Samedan; usually, however, if you let the driver know that you'd like to get off at either point, he'll stop for you. Buses making the run between Pontresina and St. Moritz (there are two to five buses a day, depending on the season) stop regularly at Samedan.

If you're **driving** from St. Moritz, head northeast along Route 27.

VISITOR INFORMATION   The **Celerina Tourist Office** (© **081/ 830-00-11**) and the **Samedan Tourist Office** (© **081/852-54-04**) provide information about the area. Both offices are open Monday to Friday from 8:30am to noon and 2 to 6pm; June to September and December to April, it's also open Saturday from 9 to 11am and 3 to 5pm.

EXPLORING THE AREA
IN SAMEDAN

The village (5,160 ft/1,548m) has its own ski lift and ice-skating rink, plus a ski school. In the summer it's ideal for mountain walks and for climbing. The tourist office will provide maps. Visitors can fish or play tennis and golf. When there's snow, it's possible to take a horse-drawn sleigh to St. Moritz in less than an hour, and all mountain transportation can be reached in a short time.

IN CELERINA

Celerina has an old Romanesque church, **St. John's** (San Gian), with a painted ceiling dating from 1478.

The Cresta run, a mecca for bobsledders, starts from St. Moritz and terminates near Celerina. The village also has ice rinks for curling and skating, a toboggan run, and a ski school. Winter Celerinade packages for skiing, cross-country, and curling are offered, as well as summer Celerinade guided mountain-bike tours with a picnic included.

Several interesting **conducted tours** are offered in the summer through the tourist office. An experienced guide will take you on an explorative tour through the Swiss National Park, or you can join a botanical excursion to see alpine flowers in bloom. Strenuous geological and mineralogical tours are also offered, and you can make an exciting journey from the Diavolezza over the glacier to Morteratsch. The latter tour is offered only in the spring and summer.

Celerina is known for its belvederes and panoramic views. One such view is of **Piz Nair,** at 10,837 feet (3,251m). To reach it, you can take a cable car from St. Moritz, departing every 20 minutes daily from 8:30am to 4pm. You'll ride from St. Moritz to Corviglia. At Corviglia, you board another cable car between Corviglia and Piz Nair. The round-trip passage for this ride is 42SF ($23.10) for adults and 23SF ($12.65) for children. The circular panorama takes in the Bernina summits. For information call © **081/839-80-15.**

You can also visit **Muottas Muragl** (8,040 ft/2412m). From the lower station at Punt Muragle, funicular departures are about every 30 minutes. The round-trip fare is 26SF ($14.30) for adults and 13SF ($7.15) for children. You'll have views of the Upper Engadine gap, and in the distance you can see the peaks of the Bernina massif. You'll probably see ibex and marmots as you take mountain walks. For information call © **081/842-83-08.**

WHERE TO STAY
IN SAMEDAN

Hotel Bernina ✿   Built in 1865, the Bernina maintains much of its original grandeur. The entire edifice is painted pale pink, with Italianate detailing over the windows. The comfortable mid-sized bedrooms are furnished in a rustic Engadine style, with patterned carpeting and big windows. On the premises, guests can enjoy a summer terrace and a private park. Nine units contain only a shower, while the rest have a tub and shower combination.

CH-7503 Samedan. ✆ **800/528-1234** in the United States and Canada, or 081/852-12-12. Fax 081/ 852-36-06. www.hotel-bernina.ch. 57 units. Winter 282SF–370SF ($155.10–$203.50) double. Summer 230SF–270SF ($126.50–$148.50) double. Rates include buffet breakfast. Half board (3-day minimum stay) 60SF ($33) per person extra. Children 6–12 are charged 50% of the adult rate. AE, DC, MC, V. Free parking outdoors, 15SF ($8.25) in garage. Closed May and Nov. **Amenities:** 2 restaurants, bar; tennis court; sauna; tour desk; car-rental desk; room service; laundry. *In room:* TV, minibar, hair dryer.

Hotel Chesa Quadratscha ✿   Almost a match for the Bernina (see above), this hotel is a choice of the traditionalist. This hotel grew out of an Engadine private home built in the 1870s. A modern wing was added during a massive enlargement of the house a century later. The lobby retains most of the paneling and elaborate murals of the original 19th-century construction, and one of the dining rooms, the Arvenstübli (see "Where to Dine," below), has one of the most beautifully crafted wood ceilings in town. The alpine bedrooms are comfortably furnished and have balconies and a view of the mountains.

CH-7503 Samedan. ✆ **081/852-42-57**. Fax **081/852-51-01**. 30 units. 250SF–280SF ($137.50–$154) double. Rates include half board. DC, MC, V. Parking 15SF ($8.25) Closed mid-Apr to June 15 and mid-Oct to mid-Dec. **Amenities:** 2 restaurants; sauna; limited room service; massage; laundry service. *In room:* TV, minibar, hair dryer.

IN CELERINA

Cresta Palace Hotel ✿✿   This grand building dates from the turn of the century. The inside contains several public rooms, including a bar and an elegant restaurant. The bedrooms, which come in a variety of shapes and sizes, are brightly colored and often include rustic pine furnishings, along with a good-sized bathroom.

Hauptstrasse, CH-7505 Celerina. ✆ **081/836-56-56**. Fax 081/836-56-57. www.crestapalace.ch. 98 units. Winter 350SF–490SF ($192.50–$269.50) double. Summer 270SF–370SF ($148.50–$203.50) double. Rates include breakfast. Half board 40SF ($22) per person extra. AE, DC, MC, V. Parking 15SF ($8.25) in winter, 10SF ($5.50) in summer. Closed May and Oct 12–Dec 20. **Amenities:** Restaurant, bar; pool; 2 tennis courts; gym; sauna; steam room; room service; massage; laundry. *In room:* TV, minibar, hair dryer.

Hotel Cresta Kulm ✿   The famous Cresta run and the St. Moritz-Celerina bobsled run come to an end in front of this government-rated four-star hotel, operated by Gerd E. and Christine Wagner-Lenz, the owners. Set off the main road, the sunny building is unusually designed, with modern curves, well-crafted stone floors, and white stucco walls. The bedrooms are attractively furnished and roomy.

Hauptstrasse, CH-7505 Celerina. ✆ **081/830-80-80**. Fax 081/830-80-81. www.hotel-cresta-kulm.ch. 43 units. Winter 400SF–440SF ($220–$242) double; summer 280SF–320SF ($154–$176) double. Rates include half board. AE, DC, MC, V. Free parking. Closed May and Nov. **Amenities:** Restaurant, bar; limited room service; laundry service. *In room:* TV, minibar, hair dryer.

Hotel Misani ⓥalue   A cost-conscious, government-rated two-star hotel, this establishment maintains some of the amenities offered at more expensive three-star hotels. At the edge of the village, it was built before 1900 but was completely renovated in 1992. The hotel is one of the few at the resort to remain open all year. It consists of an old Engadine inn and a newer 1993 annex that contains 15 of the hotel's 35 rooms. The sunny bedrooms are more comfortable and more modernized in the newer wing, although traditionalists still prefer the older rooms, which are also cheaper. Some of the units contain complete tub and shower bathrooms, others showers only. The Arvenstübil/Stuvetta (see "Where to Dine" below) is one of the finest restaurants in town.

Hauptstrasse, CH-7505 Celerina. ℂ **081/833-33-14.** Fax 081/833-07-97. 35 units. 170SF–240SF ($93.50–$132) double. Rates include breakfast. AE, DC, MC, V. Parking 5SF ($2.75) outdoors, 12SF ($6.60) indoors. Closed Apr and Nov. **Amenities:** 2 restaurants; limited room service; babysitting (by arrangement); laundry service. *In room:* TV.

WHERE TO DINE

Arvenstübli/Stuvetta ✯ SWISS   The restaurant's paneling and elaborate pinewood ceiling are remnants of a villa originally built on this site in 1870. Today a polite staff serves an array of well-prepared dishes, including a *darne* of salmon, a "turban" of sole with shrimp, a platter containing three different filet mignons, quail with truffles, and an array of succulent grills. If for any reason the Arvenstübli is full or closed, dinner is served in an adjacent room, the Stuvetta.

In the Hotel Quadratscha, Samedan. ℂ **081/852-42-57.** Reservations recommended. Main courses 26SF–50SF ($14.30–$27.50). DC, MC, V. Daily noon–2pm and 6–11:30pm. Closed Apr 21–June 9 and Oct 19–Dec 19.

3 St. Moritz ✯✯✯

50 miles (80 km) S of Davos, 46 miles (74 km) SE of Chur, 126 miles (202 km) SE of Zurich

St. Moritz is the *ne plus ultra* of winter glamour—a haven for German and Italian aristocracy and the jet-setters who come in February and March. Long a favorite of movie stars, it also attracts internationally prominent people in politics, the world of finance, and the arts. St. Moritz may well be the most fashionable resort in the world.

Not all its visitors, however, are prestigious. The author Peter Viertel wrote that St. Moritz attracts "the hangers-on of the rich . . . the jewel thieves, the professional backgammon players and general layabouts, as well as the high-class ladies of doubtful virtue (if such a thing still exists)."

On the southern side of the Alps in the Upper Engadine, at an altitude of 6,000 feet (1,800m), St. Moritz (San Murezza in Romansh) was originally known for its mineral springs, which were discovered, probably by the Celts, some 3,000 years ago. From Roman times through the Middle Ages visitors came here in the summer to experience the curative powers of the spring waters. The hamlet first appears in written history in an official document referring to the sale of the Upper Engadine by a count to the bishop of Chur in 1138. It was first referred to as a spring by the Swiss-born alchemist and physician known as Paracelsus.

Use of the spring waters was a summer pursuit. It was not until 1834 that the first winter guest stayed in the area. The earliest skiers appeared on the Upper Engadine scene in 1859 (the natives thought they were nutty), and in 1864 a pension owner, Johannes Badrutt, brought a group of English people to St. Moritz to spend the winter, starting what has grown into a flood of tourism.

ESSENTIALS

GETTING THERE   St. Moritz is linked by rail (through a complicated series of tunnels) to the rest of Switzerland via Chur, with other links to such non-Swiss population centers as Milan and Munich. Travel time by train from Chur

ⓒ THE *GLACIER EXPRESS*

The most famous of Switzerland's railway lines, the *Glacier Express* ★★★ connects the highest peaks and glaciers of the southeastern Alps with those of the southwestern Alps. When the train link opened in 1928, the danger of winter blizzards and snow drifts required that many of the most isolated mountain bridges be dismantled every October and then reassembled the following May. As a result, in the winter trains were rerouted on a lengthy detour through Zurich and northern Switzerland. In 1982 an 8-mile-long (13km) tunnel was drilled beneath the Furka mountain, and today trains run uninterrupted across the mountains all year long. The route is one of the most spectacular in the world, with 91 viaducts and tunnels and 291 bridges along the way. There's one daily train that runs between the regions in the winter; in summer, with its longer hours of sunlight, there are two and, in rare cases, three trains per day.

The one-way trip from Zermatt to St. Moritz takes 7½ hours and costs 239SF ($131.45) in first class and 147SF ($80.85) in second class. En route, many travelers opt to disembark in the medieval trading city of Chur to spend the night. From Chur, convenient connections can be arranged to Davos and all points east, including many towns in the alpine regions of Austria.

Advance seat reservations are required for the comfortably upholstered coaches with restaurant cars. Note that the Swiss Pass will cover the full fare on the *Glacier Express,* but because part of the route is administered by a different organization from the rest of the Swiss Rail network, holders of any travel pass in the Eurailpass family, including Youthpass and Flexipasses, will be charged about half the total fare. For information call ⓒ **081/833-59-12.**

For more information, contact any Swiss National Tourist Office, or the **Swiss Center,** 608 Fifth Ave., New York, NY 10020 (ⓒ **212/757-5944**).

is 2 hours. St. Moritz is also the end point of the world-famous *Glacier Express,* which links Zermatt, in the southwest, with St. Moritz, in the southeast. For **rail information** and schedules, call ⓒ **0900/300-300.**

St. Moritz is linked by bus to Chur, Davos, and Pontresina, each of which is easily reachable via bus connections from Munich. Call the tourist office (see below) for further information.

By car from Zurich, take N3 (later N13) to Chur and, once there, head southwest along Route 3.

VISITOR INFORMATION   The St. Moritz tourist office, **Kur- und Verkehrsverein,** via Maistra 12 (ⓒ **081/837-33-33**), will answer many of the questions a visitor might have. It's open in midsummer and midwinter, Monday to Saturday from 8am to 6pm, Sunday from 4 to 6pm; off-season, Monday to Friday from 9am to noon and 2 to 6pm, and Saturday from 9am to 1pm.

SEEING THE SIGHTS

Engadine Museum ⚘   This museum offers a glimpse of the history of St. Moritz and the Engadines. You'll learn about the *sgraffito* (designs in plasterwork) on Engadine buildings and local styles of architecture, and see a collection of Engadine antiques and regional furniture. The elegantly decorated state room shows how nobility in the area lived. Artifacts from the Bronze Age, when Druids lived in the land, are also on display, including the 3,000-year-old encasement of the spring of Mauritius. St. Moritz stands on a former "mystic place" of the Druids.

Via dal Bagn 39. ℂ **081/833-43-33.** Admission 5SF ($2.75) adults, 2.50SF ($1.40) children. June–Oct Mon–Fri 9am–noon and 2–5pm, Sun 10am–noon; Dec–Apr Mon–Fri 10am–noon and 2–5pm, Sun 10am–noon. Closed May and Nov. Bus: 1.

Segantini Museum   Housed here are works by the artist Giovanni Segantini (1858–99), who lived in the Engadine (Maloja) during the last years of his life. The artist is known for his technique termed divisionism; his most important work is a triptych called *Birth, Life, Death*, which is exhibited at the museum, among other important pictures.

Via Somplaz 30. ℂ **081/833-44-54.** Admission 10SF ($5.50) adults, 7SF ($3.85) students, 3SF ($1.65) children. Tues–Sun 10am–noon and 3–6pm. Closed Oct 21 to Nov and May. Bus: 1.

THE ACTIVE VACATION PLANNER

The tourist office has complete details about the various activities in the area. Although skiing is the premier sport, other winter-sports activities, including curling, ice-skating, tobogganing, bobsledding, and an early form of ice hockey, were enjoyed by most winter visitors in the last part of the 19th century.

SKIING

The world's oldest ski school is at Moritz-Dorf, founded in 1927. A total of five ski complexes encircles St. Moritz, the nearest being Corviglia-Piz Nair, which has some challenging, mile-long (2km) runs back to the base. There's an abundance of snow in winter on 250 miles (402km) of downhill ski runs, 100 miles (161km) of cross-country ski trails, and the Olympic ski-jumping hill.

Corvatsch, at 5,800 feet (1,740m), is known for its bowl skiing. **Corviglia** has broad runs attracting fledgling and intermediate skiers and is the base for skiing **Piz Nair** *✦✦*, the highest skiable mountain at 10,837 feet (3,251m), with a vertical drop of 4,748 feet (1,424m). Nearby, in Pontresina, a neighbor resort (see the next section), are the steep **Piz Legalb** and **Diavolezza,** with skiing for all levels of experience, including a run over the Morteratsch Glacier. All five mountains can be skied on one lift pass.

The upper Engadine region, of which St. Moritz plays the pivotal role, has 54 mechanical ski lifts, 217 miles (349km) of marked ski slopes, 7 ski schools, and an estimated 700 ski instructors who come and go semi-nomadically from season to season. A general ski pass costs 56SF ($30.80) for adults, 52SF ($28.60) for children 16 to 20, and 28SF ($15.40) for children 6 to 15. Various other ski passes are also sold, including a popular 6-day pass, which costs 261SF ($143.55) for adults, 242SF ($133.10) for those ages 16 to 20, and 113SF ($62.15) for children ages 6 to 15. These rates include unlimited use of all ski lifts and slopes in the Engadine region. Telephone **AGOB** at ℂ **081/830-00-00** for more information about cable cars and ski lifts in the Engadine region.

The groomed and tracked cross-country runs in the Upper Engadine valley include a tame 1-mile (2km) loop near the cross-country center; trails are laid out between the valley resorts. A 1-mile segment is lit for night skiing. The Engadine cross-country ski marathon is a major annual event. Instruction in cross-country skiing, available in groups on Monday, Wednesday, and Friday from 11am to 1pm, costs 35SF ($19.25) for one half-day lesson, and 90SF

($49.50) for three half-day lessons. A full day's cross-country excursion, as part of a large group, costs 45SF ($24.75). For more information, contact the **Schweizer Langlaufschule St. Moritz** (✆ **081/833-62-33**).

RIDING

Although this is the only riding stable in St. Moritz, **Reithalle,** via Ludains 3 (✆ **081/833-57-33**), has earned the respect of competitors throughout eastern Switzerland. Set within a 10-minute walk from the town center, it has about eight sturdy horses that are well used to life in the harsh alpine climate. A half-hour rink ride costs 55SF ($30.25); an hour's ride, either in the rink or in the nearby forest, costs 75SF ($41.25), and a 3-hour (half-day) tour out in the surrounding mountainsides and valley costs 140SF ($77) per person. Don't overlook horseback riding as a midwinter diversion. Since the horses need to be exercised throughout the calendar year, you're likely to be led across untrammeled snowfields of pristine beauty, and even take leisurely treks across the surface of a frozen lake. Dress accordingly—the wind-chill factor for midwinter horse treks is fierce.

OTHER WINTER SPORTS

Horse racing on the frozen lake of St. Moritz is also popular, or you can take rides on the natural-ice bobsled run. There are 30 curling rinks, winter golf played on the frozen lake, and tobogganing on the Cresta run. Indoor tennis and squash can be played as well.

If you're interested in **curling** but don't know how, you can have a first training session free (40 min.). Individual **curling lessons** thereafter cost 45SF ($24.75) for 45 minutes. Call ✆ **081/833-45-88** for details. The curling rink is the A1 Parc rink on via Maistra.

A bobsled ride costs 200SF ($110), but you get your picture taken, a drink, and a certificate in addition to the ride. Bobsled rides occur at the town's **Olympic Bobsled Run** on via Maistra (✆ **081/830-02-00**).

SUMMER SPORTS

In the summer, visitors are offered cultural programs and sports activities. Windsurfing at St. Moritz and on the lakes of nearby resorts has boomed in popularity. If you're already experienced, rental of equipment for 2 hours costs 35SF ($19.25) If you're a beginner, or if you just want to brush up on your technique, private lessons are available, costing 265SF ($145.75) for 10 lessons. Call **Windsurfschule St. Moritz** (✆ **081/828-92-29** or 081/833-44-49) for information. Sailing on the area's 25 lakes is also possible.

The closest golf course lies in Samedan, 4½ miles (7km) down the valley. This is a 6,587-yard (5,994m) par-72 course. Greens fees for a full day are 95SF ($52.25) and club rental is 32SF ($17.60) a day. Golfing is available from the end of May to the beginning of October, daily from 7am until 7pm, depending on the weather. In July and August, the course often stays open later. Call **Samedan/St. Moritz Golfplatz** (✆ **081/852-52-26**) for more information.

For tennis and squash information, consult the **Corviglia Tennis Center** in St. Moritz-Bad (✆ **081/833-15-00**). Rates for tennis are 25SF ($13.75) per hour outdoors and 30SF ($16.50) per hour indoors during the summer, or 46SF ($25.30) per hour for winter indoor tennis. Rental of one racquet and balls is 3SF ($1.65), and two racquets and balls rent for 5SF ($2.75). Squash courts run 20SF ($11) for 45 minutes in summer and 26SF ($14.30) for the same period of time in winter. The center is open daily from 8am to 10pm.

Fishing, in season between May 15 and September 15, requires the purchase of a fishing license, available only to interested parties aged 16 or older. A passport and another form of picture identification are required to get a fishing license, which costs 84SF ($46.20) 1 day, 220SF ($121) for 1 week, and 320SF ($176) for 15 days. Equipment and bait are also available. For more information about **fishing** in the area, call ✆ **081/833-67-52.**

SPAS

The spa section of this resort town is called **St. Moritz-Bad,** where you can take mud and carbon-dioxide mineral-water baths, physical therapy, and physiotherapy while you enjoy the stimulating alpine climate in a modern **Health Spa Center** (✆ **081/833-30-62**), next to the Parkhotel Kurhaus. The spa opened in 1976. From Roman times to now, "taking the waters" has been a popular pursuit for those seeking natural curative treatment for relief from pain and stress. The charge for every treatment at the spa is lower for residents of any of the town's hotels or apartments. If a client presents a "guest card" (proof of residence—and payment of a room tax), treatments cost 88SF ($48.40) for a 50-minute massage and 35SF ($19.25) for an hour-long soak within a mineral-rich "carbonic bath."

SHOPPING

Most of St. Moritz's shops line either side of the steeply inclined **via Maistra,** and most of the horrendously upscale ones vie with one another for proximity to the town's most spectacularly expensive hotel, **Badrutt's Palace** (✆ **081/837-10-00**), near the corner of via Serlas. On its premises you'll find boutiques for Gianni Versace, Prada, Jil Sander, Bulgari, and Louis Vuitton, as well as enough upscale shops for watches and jewelry to outfit a prosperous royal court. But if it's well-designed sports equipment you're looking for, or relatively durable clothing that will shelter you from the fierce Engadine weather, head for any of the following shops: **Boom Sports,** via Tegiatscha 5 (✆ **081/832-22-22**); **Corviglia Sports,** via Maistra 21 (✆ **081/833-44-77**); and **Ender Sport,** via Maistra 26 (✆ **081/833-35-36**).

The region produces lots of folkloric crafts that might commemorate your stay in the Engadine. The town's main outlet for all sorts of wood carvings, including depictions of gnarled native Engadiners in Swiss costumes, is **Ettlin,** via Rosatsch 7 (✆ **081/832-17-07**). More broad-based in its folkloric inventories, with ceramics, glassware, textiles, and wrought iron, is the souvenir and artifacts shop **Grischuna,** via dal Bagn 54 (✆ **081/833-42-36**).

The town's largest jeweler, and the one that saturates the high-season market with more advertising campaigns than any other in town, is **Bucherer,** via Maistra 17 (✆ **081/833-31-03**). Finally, the town's largest emporium for chocolates is **Merkur,** via Serlas 26 (✆ **081/833-57-26**).

WHERE TO STAY

St. Moritz offers several different types of accommodations, with dozens of hotels, boardinghouses, and chalet-style apartments. But because it's expensive, you may prefer one of several neighboring resorts, such as Pontresina, Silvaplana, S-Chanf, Zuoz, Samedan, or Celerina, all of which are covered in this chapter. The following hotels are in the heart of St. Moritz.

VERY EXPENSIVE

Badrutt's Palace Hotel ★★★ This architectural hodgepodge of mock Gothic has been at the center of St. Moritz society for decades. Society isn't what it was, but today's glitzy and the ritzy still fill its vast precincts—that is, if they can afford the lethal tariffs. However, for those on the winter see-and-be-seen circuit, this flamboyant edifice remains an enduring symbol of wealth, prestige, and conspicuous consumption. Set in the center of town behind a chiseled stone facade and a series of mock-fortified towers, the Palace was built at the turn of the century by Caspar Badrutt. Over the years the chic and famous have come through the doors of the Palace, including the shah of Iran, Greta Garbo, and Aristotle Onassis. Almost no "name" arriving today can match the roster of yesterday. The hotel's Great Hall soars in Gothic dimensions above twin black-marble fireplaces, clusters of antique furniture, and massive bouquets of flowers. Except for some special suites and spacious doubles, most of the rooms are fairly standardized and "international" in styling. You're paying more for the address than the room if you lodge here.

Via Serlas 27, CH-7500 St. Moritz. ℂ 800/223-6800 in the United States and Canada, or 081/837-10-00. Fax 081/837-29-99. www.badruttspalace.com. 240 units. Winter 700SF–1,700SF ($385–$935) double; 4,000SF ($2,200) suite. Summer 500SF–1,100SF ($275–$605) double; 2,000SF ($1,100) suite. Rates include breakfast. AE, DC, MC, V. Parking 20SF ($11). Closed early Apr to late June and Sept 16 to mid-Dec. Bus: 1. **Amenities:** 5 restaurants, 3 bars; pool; 4 tennis courts; gym; sauna; room service; babysitting; laundry service. In room: TV, minibar, hair dryer, iron, safe.

Carlton Hotel 🐦 Owned by the Grand Hotel Tschuggen of Arosa, this is an elaborate, ocher-colored château that was originally built for Nicholas II, the last tsar of Russia, in 1913. With a view of the lake and the mountains, it's one of the loveliest hotels in St. Moritz—luxurious, but without the glitzy consumption of Badrutt's Palace. One particularly spectacular sitting room has tall, narrow fireplaces with neoclassical designs. The bedrooms are well-furnished and spacious with white marble bathrooms.

Via Badrutt, Dorf, CH-7500 St. Moritz. ℂ 081/836-70-00. Fax 081/836-70-01. www.carlton-stmoritz.ch. 105 units. Winter 540SF–1,020SF ($297–$561) double; 850SF–2,600SF ($467.50–$1,430) suite for 2. Summer 380SF–640SF ($209–$352) double; 600SF–1,400SF ($330–$770) suite for 2. Rates include half board. AE, DC, MC, V. Parking 25SF ($13.75) in winter, 5SF ($2.75) in summer. Closed Apr 6–June 19 and Sept 12–Dec 2. Bus: 1. **Amenities:** 2 restaurants, bar; pool; health club; sauna; salon; room service; massage; babysitting; laundry/dry cleaning. In room: TV, minibar, hair dryer, safe.

Kulm Hotel 🐦🐦🐦 We prefer this tranquil bastion of luxury even to the Palace itself. These three elegant buildings, the oldest of which was erected in 1760, were taken over in 1856 by Joseph Badrutt, who was the first to encourage British vacationers to come to the Alps. In 1878 it became the first building in Switzerland to have electricity, and it was the center of the Olympic Games in 1928 and 1948. Over the years the Kulm has hosted royalty from all over the world, including the kings and queens of industry and entertainment. It still draws a sedate clientele, those who deliberately shun the most ostentatious Badrutt's Palace. The public rooms are beautifully paneled, with vaulted ceilings. The spacious bedrooms are grand classics, with traditional furnishings, generous closet space, and luxury beds; tiled bathrooms have dual marble basins, heated towel racks, and robes. A large part of the city's world-famous bobsled run, the Crest run, and the curling rinks of St. Moritz are on hotel property.

Via Veglia 18, Dorf, CH-7500 St. Moritz. ℂ 800/223-5695 in the United States and Canada, or 081/ 836-80-00. Fax 081/836-80-01. www.kulmhotel-stmoritz.ch. 190 units. Winter 640SF–976SF ($352–$536.80) double; 1,300SF–1,600SF ($715–$880) suite. Summer 385SF–630SF ($211.75–$346.50) double; from 850SF ($467.50) suite. Rates include breakfast. AE, DC, MC, V. Parking 11SF ($6.05) in garage in summer, 20SF ($11) in winter. Closed mid-Apr to June and mid-Sept to mid-Dec. Bus: 1. **Amenities:** 3 restaurants, 2 bars; pool; tennis court; gym; spa center with sauna; ice-skating rink; curling rink; children's playroom; salon; room service; massage; laundry. In room: TV, minibar, hair dryer.

Suvretta House ⊛ Set about a mile from the resort town, this five-star government-rated hotel offers a relaxed clientele, a grand decor, and a highly individual style. It is slightly more luxurious than Badrutt's Palace, though it doesn't quite reach the lofty peaks of the Kulm. It was built in 1912 on a plateau surrounded by mountains and lakes. Its Edwardian facade has two neo-medieval towers and a baroque central gable that has become the hotel's trademark. Except for areas of richly grained oak paneling and Engadine sgraffito, the interior is covered with plaster and pierced with an endless series of vaulted arches. The spacious guest rooms in traditional or alpine style are luxurious without being glitzy. The roomy bathrooms are tiled. It's surrounded with more land than any other hotel in St. Moritz and offers a private ski lift.

Via Chasellas 1, CH-7500 St. Moritz. ℂ **081/836-36-36.** Fax 081/836-37-37. www.suvrettahouse.ch. 210 units. Winter 580SF–1,520SF ($319–$836) double; summer 440SF–1,120SF ($242–$616) double. Rates include half board. AE, DC, MC, V. Parking 20SF ($11) in winter, 15SF ($8.25) in summer. Closed Apr 2–June 24 and Sept 3–Dec 12. **Amenities:** 2 restaurants, 2 bars; pool; driving range; 3 tennis courts; gym; sauna; ice-skating rink; curling rinks; game room; children's playground; concierge; salon; room service; massage; babysitting; laundry service. *In room:* TV, hair dryer, safe.

EXPENSIVE

Hotel Albana ⊛ A hotel was first established here in 1644; the current property has been managed by the Weinmann family since 1971. This is a popular hotel, painted a salmon color with white trim and decorated with regional designs and an occasional hunting trophy. The mid-sized to spacious bedrooms usually have ceiling beams or elaborate paneling and occasionally a regional armoire. They also contain elegant bathrooms with tub and shower (20 with shower only).

Via Maistra 6, CH-7500 St. Moritz. ℂ **800/528-1234** in the United States and Canada, or 081/833-31-21. Fax 081/836-61-62. www.albana.ch. 72 units. Winter 330SF–500SF ($181.50–$275) double. Summer 300SF–350SF ($165–$192.50) double. Rates include breakfast. Half board 35SF ($19.25) per person extra. AE, DC, MC, V. Parking 15SF ($8.25) in garage in winter, 10SF ($5.50) in summer. Bus: 1. **Amenities:** Restaurant, bar; gym; Jacuzzi; sauna; room service; massage; babysitting; laundry. *In room:* TV, minibar, hair dryer, safe.

Hotel Crystal ⊛ A short walk from the Corviglia cogwheel train, this large white-painted building looks oddly futuristic compared to the 19th-century structures around it. The interior combines comfortable alpine rusticity of knotty-pine cabinets and ceiling beams with wall-to-wall carpeting and informal furniture. All the mid-sized bedrooms are accented with either Swiss pine or walnut paneling. Each accommodation was carefully renovated in 1999. In 1997, a cavernous 3,400-square-foot (3,100 sq. m) fitness center was added in the basement of the hotel. The lobby and some of the rooms have also been enlarged, although the rustic alpine decor is still intact.

Via Traunter Plazzas 1, CH-7500 St. Moritz. ℂ **081/836-26-26.** Fax 081/836-26-27. www.crystalhotel.ch. 73 units. Winter 350SF–590SF ($192.50–$324.50) double; 790SF ($434.50) junior suite; 1,050SF–1,500SF ($577.50–$825) suite. Summer 290SF–370SF ($159.50–$203.50) double; 460SF ($253) junior suite; 670SF–900SF ($368.50–$495) suite. Rates include breakfast. AE, DC, MC, V. Closed Apr–May and Oct 10 to Nov. Bus: 1. **Amenities:** Restaurant, bar; health club; sauna; Turkish baths; room service; massage; babysitting; laundry. *In room:* TV, minibar, hair dryer, safe.

Hotel Schweizerhof ⊛⊛ This government-rated four-star establishment is still owned by the von Gugelberg family, and has been since it was built in 1896. Staid and traditional, it's well maintained (last renovated in 1997) and continues in its upscale tradition. It's a favorite of many clients who prefer its somewhat-dated Victorian overlay to the more obvious five-star hotels in town. It's also one of the few hotels of its size and stature remaining open year-round. The best units are on the fifth floor, which dates from the 1970s. This is where all the suites and the best doubles have views to the south. The least expensive accommodations are those facing north, which also lack tubs. What makes this hotel exceptional is its personal service, along with its array of drinking and dining choices.

Via dal Bagn 54, Dorf, CH-7500 St. Moritz. (C) **081/837-07-07.** Fax 081/837-07-00. 85 units. Winter 370SF–510SF ($203.50–$280.50) double; 650SF ($357.50) suite for 2. Summer 290SF–440SF ($159.50–$242) double; 490SF ($269.50) suite. Rates include breakfast. Half board 35SF ($19.25) (3 night minimum). AE, DC, MC, V. Free parking outdoors, 19SF ($10.45) in garage. Bus: 1. **Amenities:** 3 restaurants, 2 bars; health club; sauna; room service; massage; laundry service. *In room:* TV, minibar, hair dryer, safe.

Monopol-Grischuna ✹✹   Set above a busy street, this 3-decades-old stucco building offers elegant public rooms furnished with French pieces, oil paintings, and well-polished wood detailing. Half of the usually spacious bedrooms are designed around Louis XV and Louis XVI or rustic furniture, while the other half have been renovated in a modern Swiss style, with lots of wood and updated bathroom fixtures.

Via Maistra 17, Dorf, CH-7500 St. Moritz. (C) **081/833-44-33.** Fax 081/837-04-05. www.monopol.ch. 66 units. Winter 350SF–520SF ($192.50–$286) double; 490SF–650SF ($269.50–$357.50) suite. Summer 280SF–320SF ($154–$176) double; 450SF ($247.50) suite. Rates include breakfast. AE, DC, MC, V. Closed mid-Apr to mid-May and mid-Oct to Dec 9. Bus: 1. **Amenities:** Restaurant, 2 bars; pool; fitness center; sauna; room service; massage; babysitting; laundry service. *In room:* TV, minibar, hair dryer.

Posthotel ✹   In the heart of St. Moritz, this year-round government-rated four-star hotel was built in 1908 and today places more emphasis on hospitality than on stylish furniture and conspicuous opulence. There's a blazing midwinter fireplace. The comfortably furnished and sometimes quite spacious bedrooms each have well-maintained bathrooms, mostly with showers. Those on the uppermost floor have private balconies and a view of the lake. The two different sections of the hotel, built on either side of a steeply inclined street, are connected by a covered passageway over the cobblestone pavements.

Via dal Vout 3, Dorf, CH-7500 St. Moritz. (C) **081/832-21-21.** Fax 081/833-89-73. www.posthotel-stmoritz.ch. 70 units. Winter 220SF–550SF ($121–$302.50) double; 680SF ($374) suite for 2. Summer 180SF–360SF ($99–$198) double; 400SF ($220) suite for 2. Rates include breakfast. Half board 35SF ($19.25) extra. AE, DC, MC, V. Parking 15SF ($8.25). Closed mid-Apr to mid-May and mid-Oct to mid-Dec. Bus: 1. **Amenities:** Restaurant, bar; sauna; Jacuzzi; steam bath; room service; massage; laundry/dry cleaning. *In room:* TV, minibar, hair dryer, safe.

MODERATE

Hotel Eden ✹   A pleasant hotel whose architecture evokes a Tuscan villa, this establishment was built more than a century ago and has been in the Degiacomi family for some 40 years. It doesn't cost as much as either of its more glamorous neighbors, the Kulm and Badrutt's Palace. The Eden, which opens onto a tiny but charming plaza in the center of town, is filled with pinewood paneling and family antiques. Each of the simple and modernized mid-sized bedrooms has tasteful, conservative furniture, and all units come with a mid-sized private bathroom (some with complete tubs). Breakfast is the only meal served here.

Via Veglia 12, CH-7500 St. Moritz. (C) **081/833-61-61.** Fax 081/833-91-91. 36 units. Winter 265SF–397SF ($145.75–$218.35) double. Summer 166SF–275SF ($91.30–$151.25) double. Rates include buffet breakfast. MC, V. Free parking. Closed mid-Apr to mid-June and mid-Oct to mid-Dec. Bus: 1. **Amenities:** Room service; massage; babysitting; laundry. *In room:* Hair dryer, iron, safe.

Hotel Languard-Garni ✹✹ *Finds*   Built a century ago as the private home of the owner of the nearby Kulm Hotel, this much-enlarged and -altered property lies just off the main street of town. It's run by a conservative Swiss staff and the Trivella and Rico family, who display their family's ski awards (one of their sons,

Roberto, was a champion in 1978) in a glass case by the reception desk. The hotel's pine-paneled interior is well maintained and very charming, with a breakfast room that overlooks the valley and the lake. Some of the small to mid-sized accommodations have private balconies, and all have private bathrooms, of which all but five have a combination tub and shower.

Via Veglia 14, CH-7500 St. Moritz. © 081/833-31-37. Fax 081/833-45-46. www.languard-stmoritz.ch. 22 units. Winter 230SF–476SF ($126.50–$261.80) double. Summer 160SF–260SF ($88–$143) double. Rates include buffet breakfast. AE, DC, MC, V. Free parking. Closed May and Nov. Bus: 1. **Amenities:** Limited room service; massage; laundry. *In room:* TV, hair dryer, safe.

Hotel Waldhaus am See ★★ *Finds*   Built in 1880 as a tavern, this building was later expanded into a private home by a Swiss industrialist and now resembles a castle. You can dine in one of three lovely rooms, the largest of which has access to a sheltered sun terrace and views over the lake. Helen and Claudio Bernasconi-Mettier, the hosts, offer comfortably conservative mid-sized rooms with firm beds and good plumbing. All units contain a private bathroom, mostly with shower, although some come with combination tub and shower. The most desirable accommodations open onto views of the lake.

Via Dimiej 6, CH-7500 St. Moritz. © 081/833-76-76. Fax 081/833-88-77. www.waldhaus-am-see.ch. 54 units. Winter 340SF–420SF ($187–$231) double. Summer 270SF–300SF ($148.50–$165). Rates include half board. AE, DC, MC, V. Free parking outside, 15SF ($8.25) in garage. **Amenities:** 3 restaurants, bar; sauna; steam bath; massage; laundry/dry cleaning. *In room:* TV, minibar, hair dryer, safe.

INEXPENSIVE

Hotel Belvedere *Finds*   Set close to the lake in St. Moritz-Bad, this hotel was built around 1905 and has been renovated slowly and gradually ever since by the Hermann family, who continue to run it today. It's a simple, relatively unknown hotel, but a worthy choice in high-priced St. Moritz. The Belvedere has a pleasant earth-colored lobby, with warm textiles and lots of wood. The small rooms are simply but comfortably furnished, each with a private bathroom, mainly with showers, although some also contain tubs.

Via dal Bagn 5, Bad, CH-7500 St. Moritz. © 081/833-39-05. Fax 081/833-94-92. www.belvedere-hotel.ch. 30 units, 15 with bathroom. Winter 250SF ($137.50) double without bathroom, 290SF–410SF ($159.50–$225.50) double with bathroom. Summer 210SF ($115.50) double without bathroom, 230SF–320SF ($126.50–$176) double with bathroom. Rates include breakfast. Half board 30SF ($16.50) per person extra. AE, MC, V. Free parking. Closed Apr 15–June 15. Bus: 1. **Amenities:** Restaurant; limited room service.

Hotel National ★   Few other hotels in St. Moritz recall conservative mountain-style Switzerland as evocatively, or as rigidly, as this one, built a century ago. Other than an occasional refurbishment, very little changes around here. The outside has neoclassical details and wrought-iron balconies, while the interior has a scattering of Oriental rugs, informal furniture, and comfortable but small bedrooms. The family-run hotel is opposite a large indoor swimming pool. Its restaurant serves Swiss and French dishes along with various specialties from the different sections of Italy.

Via de l'Ova Cotschna 1, CH-7500 St. Moritz. © 081/833-32-74. Fax 081/833-32-75. 18 units, 15 with bathroom. Winter 270SF–310SF ($148.50–$170.50) double. Summer 200SF–230SF ($110–$126.50) double. Rates include breakfast. AE, MC, V. Closed Apr 15 to May and Oct 15 to Nov. Bus: 1. **Amenities:** Restaurant; pool (nearby). *In room:* No phone.

WHERE TO DINE

Although meals may be included in the cost of your hotel room, you may want to sample the selections at other hotels and restaurants. There are also dozens of fashionable *konditoreien* (coffeehouses).

VERY EXPENSIVE

Chesa Veglia ★★ INTERNATIONAL   *Chesa* means "house" in Romansh, and that's exactly what this Engadine-style building once was. Built in 1658 of stone, stucco, and wood, it retains much of its original paneling and carving, as well as entire rooms composed of architectural remnants from local houses. It's the only authentic Engadine house left in St. Moritz. You'll enter through a massive arched oak door. Inside, you'll find three restaurants, each on a different floor. The **Chadafo Grill** (open daily at lunch and dinner, but only in winter) cooks your meat over a wood fire that's visible from the dining room. The **Patrizier-Stube** serves tasty regional specialties at lunch and dinner. The **Hayloft,** the least expensive and least formal of the three, is a pizzeria with a wood-stoked oven. Local musicians will probably be playing in the Chadafo Grill. In all sites except the pizzeria, expect a wide choice of international dishes, from Italian (*saltimbocca*) to Hungarian (goulash) to Russian (chicken Kiev). Try the grilled scampi or trout meunière. The desserts are equally elegant, including soufflès and mousses. It's owned and operated by the Palace Hotel.

Via Veglia 2, Dorf. © 081/837-28-00. Reservations required. Main courses 34SF–65SF ($18.70–$35.75). AE, DC, MC, V. Daily 11:30am–3pm and 6:30pm–midnight. Closed Apr 15–June 21 and Sept 20–Dec 3. Bus: 1.

Jöhri's Talvo ★★★ ENGADINE/FRENCH   Established in 1992 inside the solid pine-sheathed walls of a 350-year-old Engadine house, this restaurant is St. Moritz's most upscale dining option. It lies in the center of the satellite village of Champfèr, a 10-minute walk from the western periphery of St. Moritz. The much-praised cuisine manages to blend both regional recipes (as filtered by the owner's French training) with the skillful preparation of upscale ingredients. For example, the menu lists different preparations of North Atlantic lobsters and scallops in wine sauce. Our personal favorite is a whole turbot cooked in a salt crust, which is broken open at tableside, then served with an array of garnishes and dressings. A fixed-price fish menu is available with or without a garnish of lobster and caviar, and foie gras is flown in from western France.

Better suited to the cold, high-altitude climate, however, are a range of regional dishes derived from time-honored Engadine traditions. These include *capuns* (spinach-flavored pasta cooked with cold-weather greens in consommé and served with truffles); *puschlav* ("poor man's soup," prepared with consommé and enriched with flour); and lamb raised in nearby meadows prepared with mustard sauce, mountain herbs, and sautéed potatoes. The restaurant's owners, Roland and Brigitte Jöhri, are highly conscientious and devote lots of attention to their unusual cuisine.

Via Gunels 15, Champfèr. © 081/833-44-55. Reservations recommended. Main courses 44SF–85SF ($24.20–$46.75); fixed-price menu 68SF–85SF ($37.40–$46.75) lunch only; 120SF–248SF ($66–$136.40) dinner; fixed-price fish menu from 162SF ($89.10). AE, DC, MC, V. Daily 11am–11pm (closed Mon–Tues in summer). Closed Easter to June 14 and Oct 15–Dec 18.

Restaurant Le Relais ★★ SWISS/ASIAN   In olden times, you might see such luminaries as the Aga Khan, Alfred Hitchcock, or even the shah of Iran dining here. Today's diners, even though arriving by Learjet or Rolls-Royce, don't have such pedigrees, but they still gravitate to this vast restaurant, with its draperies and chandeliers. Long accustomed to catering to the most demanding palates in the world, the chefs here have long ago perfected their craft. Each dish manages to have a distinct personality, and the cookery is virile and self-assured. The menu listings include fresh oysters, smoked trout, risotto with exotic mushrooms, julienne of veal with white-wine sauce, saddle of roebuck, and an array of desserts. For men, dark suits are necessary at night.

In Badrutt's Palace Hotel, via Serlas 27. ℂ **081/837-10-00**. Reservations required. Main courses 55SF–100SF ($30.25–$55); fixed-price meal 90SF–100SF ($49.50–$55) at lunch, fixed-price meal 100SF–150SF ($55–$82.50) at dinner. AE, DC, MC, V. Main dining room, daily 12:15–3pm and 7:30–10pm. Grill room, daily 12:30–2:30pm and 8–11pm. Closed early Apr to late June and Sept 16 to mid-Dec. Bus: 1.

EXPENSIVE

La Marmite ★★ SWISS   This woodsy lunch establishment is the best high-altitude restaurant in the Grisons. It can be reached only by funicular. The Mathis family offers excellent service and a varied menu. There's also a less expensive cafeteria on the premises that in midwinter is usually crowded with skiers. The region's choicest ingredients turn up in such dishes as creamed venison soup, fresh duck liver with truffles, calves' foot in a truffle sauce, and a bone-warming bouillon—perfect for a cold day—flavored with marrow, vegetables, sherry, and meat.

Corviglia Bergstation. ℂ **081/833-63-55**. Reservations recommended. Main courses 30SF–74SF ($16.50–$40.70). AE, DC, MC, V. Daily 8:30am–5:30pm. Closed Apr 15–Dec 15. Reached by Corviglia funicular.

Landgasthof Meierei ★★ SWISS   Built a century ago as a relay station for the Swiss postal service, today it houses four dining rooms, which have in days of yore served the shah of Iran, the playboy industrialist Günther Sachs, Picasso, the Aga Khan, and King Farouk of Egypt. Those heady glory days are but a local legend as the place has become solidly bourgeois today. Considering the glamorous clientele that the place has attracted, it serves an earthy and simple menu, ranging from local sausage served with potato salad to veal filets with varied sauces and several fish dishes.

No diner is allowed to drive a car along the difficult-to-navigate service roads that reach the restaurant. You can hire a taxi or a horse-drawn sleigh, the latter costing up to 86SF ($47.30) for four passengers. Our recommendation is that you park your car in the public parking lot near the edge of the lake, just below the Hotel Waldhaus am See, and walk the 20-minute lakeside promenade to the restaurant. The footpath has been carefully paved, and there are only a few slopes to negotiate. Before you set out, it's advisable to phone the restaurant to confirm that it's open.

There are seven cozy alpine rooms rented here costing from 230SF to 340SF ($126.50–$187) for a double or from 300SF to 480SF ($165–$264) for a suite, including breakfast.

Via Dimiej 52. ℂ **081/833-20-60**. Reservations required. Main courses 18SF–50SF ($9.90–$27.50). AE, MC, V. Tues–Sun 10am–2:30pm and 6:30–9:30pm. Closed Apr 15–June 15 and Oct 8–Dec 15.

Rôtisserie des Chevaliers ★ FRENCH   This exquisitely paneled grillroom, in one of the most historic hotels in St. Moritz, offers a cozy ambience that's especially suited to cold weather. The delectable menu is likely to include terrine and goose liver, grilled sea bass flambé, baby turbot prepared "Marseille style," and a unique stuffed veal à la Hotel Kulm. Dishes are most often based on what's the freshest and best produce available in any given season.

In the Hotel Kulm, via Veglia 18, Dorf. ℂ **081/836-80-00**. Reservations required. Main courses 40SF–65SF ($22–$35.75). AE, MC, V. Daily noon–3pm and 7pm–midnight. Closed May–Nov. Bus: 1.

MODERATE

Lapin Bleu SWISS/FRENCH/ITALIAN   Half-board guests of the hotel usually dine upstairs in the elegant grillroom, but in many ways we prefer the warm, wood-lined decor and the polite service of the street-level tavern. Specialties from the hearty alpine kitchen include steak tartare with egg; grilled filet steak;

chateaubriand with béarnaise sauce, potato croquettes, and vegetables; and fondue *bourguignonne* or *chinoise*. Liver, pork, and several preparations of veal, pasta, and seafood, including lobster, are also served. Many residents of St. Moritz come here to dine, a good sign.

In the Hotel Steffani, Sonnenplatz 1. © **081/836-96-96**. Reservations required in winter. Main courses 20SF–52SF ($11–$28.60); fixed-price meal 33SF ($18.15) at lunch, 48SF ($26.40) at dinner. AE, DC, MC, V. Daily 11:30am–11:30pm. Bus: 1.

Restaurant Acla ★ *Finds* SWISS/INTERNATIONAL   Situated in the Hotel Schweizerhof, this "little house on the mountain"—as its name is translated from Romansh—serves Swiss specialties and international dishes in a rustically appealing and rather formal ambience. In summer, during clement lunch hours, service is on a flowering outdoor terrace called Il Restaurant Giardino; Acla is closed, only to reopen in time for dinner. Prices in Il Giardino are slightly lower than those in Acla. Summer specialties include such dishes as filet of perch with tomato crust and olive-oil sauce with grilled zucchini; sautéed guinea fowl breast with summer vegetables and semolina-mushroom slices; and filet of veal with basil-cream sauce, leaf spinach, and fine noodles. In winter, main courses include salmon with strips of celery, morels and truffle sauce, served with early potatoes; cereal risotto with asparagus; grilled zucchini and tomato ragoût; or chateaubriand with béarnaise sauce. You can also order classic dishes like the famous *tafelspitz* (the boiled beef of Vienna) served with apple-horseradish and chive sauce, or blinis with caviar and smoked salmon. Trout is from the Inn River.

In the Hotel Schweizerhof, via del Bagn 54, Dorf. © **081/837-07-07**. Reservations recommended. Main courses 24SF–55SF ($13.20–$30.25). AE, DC, MC, V. Daily noon–2pm and 7–9:30pm. Bus: 1.

Veltliner-Keller SWISS/ITALIAN   It functions as a cafe and tavern throughout the day, but it's at its best for dining in the evening, when the rustically informal premises welcome many of the town's professional ski-and-see crowd. The menu includes mushroom salads, trout with mushrooms, spaghetti, and a wide selection of meats and fish, along with a savory risotto. Desserts include just about every in-season fruit in Europe. This is a very simple and very ethnic Swiss place, the quintessential local tavern preferred by many of the locals, some of whom are hotel workers.

Via dal Bagn 11. © **081/833-40-09**. Reservations required. Main courses 20SF–40SF ($11–$22). AE, DC, MC, V. Daily noon–3pm and 6–11:30pm. Bus: 1.

INEXPENSIVE

Hanselmann   Originally established in the mid-1800s, this tavern and tearoom has grown to occupy a much-embellished building decorated with sgraffito. Today, it's one of the best and most inexpensive places in town for breakfast or lunch. It's owned by Fritz Mutschler, grandson of the original founder. From the German-language breakfast menu, you might choose an omelet, an egg-and-cheese dish, or a country platter piled high with Black Forest ham and Valais rye rolls. Other dishes include Welsh rarebit and smoked salmon with buttered toast. The upstairs restaurant opens at 11:30am. The place is also popular with the après-ski crowd.

Via Maistra 8. © **081/833-38-64**. Reservations accepted only for lunch. Main courses 16SF–39SF ($8.80–$21.45); breakfast 6SF–23SF ($3.30–$12.65); fixed-price breakfast 15.50SF ($8.55); fixed-price lunch 25.50SF ($14.05). MC, V. Christmas–Feb and July–Aug, daily 7:30am–7pm; Mar–June and Sept–Christmas, Wed–Mon 7:30am–7pm. Bus: 1.

Restaurant Cascade ITALIAN   Next door to the Hotel Steffani, this restaurant offers Italian recipes. With its etched-glass mirrors and bentwood chairs, it's popular with a young, informally dressed crowd for drinks as well as food. Good-tasting dishes include carpaccio, *saltimbocca* (veal with ham), and gnocchi Piedmont style, but mainly it specializes in pastas and entrecôtes.

Via Somplaz 6, Dorf. © **081/833-15-22.** Reservations required in winter. Main courses 25SF–45SF ($13.75–$24.75). AE, DC, MC, V. Daily 6:30–11pm. Closed May–June. Bus: 1.

Restaurant Engadina *Value* SWISS   In the direct center of St. Moritz-Dorf, across the street from the town hall, is this old-fashioned family dining room that's uncharacteristic for St. Moritz. You get good value for your money here. Pleasant, comfortable, and simple, it consists of two hunter-style rooms filled with trophies and alpine accents, such as pinewood tables and paneling. There's even an outdoor wooden deck for drinking and dining if the weather is right. Selections include carpaccio, *petite marmite* (a famous Parisian soup made with lean pieces of meat and vegetable stock), fondues (with cheese or champagne), grilled steaks, goulash, and snails in garlic butter. The food is robust and hearty—no one ever accused the chefs of being too imaginative, but this is the type of chow the locals love.

Piazza da Scoula 2. © **081/833-32-65.** Reservations recommended. Main courses 22SF–45SF ($12.10–$24.75). AE, DC, MC, V. Summer Mon–Sat noon–2pm and 6:30–10pm; winter Mon–Sat 10am–10pm. Bus: 1.

ST. MORITZ AFTER DARK

Few other resorts are as depressing off-season as St. Moritz, where very few of the local entrepreneurs even pretend to be interested in doing business. But as the midwinter and midsummer seasons get underway, you'll find lots of warm cubbyholes in St. Moritz, often in hotels whose bars are inspired by the Romansh sgraffito that's so prevalent in the region. Many are eminently appropriate for a quiet and cozy drink, and some, as noted below, make special efforts to attract drinking and sometimes dancing clients from other hotels.

One of the best examples of this is the **Hotel Schweizerhof,** via dal Bagn 54 (© **081/837-07-07**), where three separate bars provide a labyrinth of nightlife options that range from the subdued to the rowdy. They include the **Muli Bar,** with North American–style country-western music; the **Stübli,** which divides its energies between cozy folkloric platters, a resident musician, and foaming steins of beer; and the **Piano Bar,** where melodies are tinkled out by visiting pianists from throughout Europe.

If you want to indulge in some small-stakes gambling, consider dropping into the somewhat dull **Casino St. Moritz,** via Maistra 28 (© **081/832-10-80**), where slot machines and roulette tables never accept a bet of more than 5SF ($3.35) at a time. Open daily in midwinter and midsummer from 8pm till the crowd thins out, it has a small bar inside, and a usually lackluster set of night owls, probably newcomers, who eventually drift on to more exciting venues. **Bobby's Pub,** via dal Bagn 52 (© **081/833-47-67**), is everybody's favorite English-style pub, replete with *faux* Victoriana and beers from throughout Europe, including Merrie Olde England. A well-entrenched staple on the nightlife circuit is **Vivai's Disco,** in the Hotel Steffani, Sonnenplazt 1 (© **081/836-96-96**). Here, despite an antique-looking entrance etched in Engadine-style line drawings, the music is contemporary and the decor is intimately lit and modern. Depending on whether there's live music, entrance costs 15SF to 30SF ($8.25–$16.50), which usually includes the first drink.

More expensive, and much more posh, are the disco and bar facilities in **Badrutt's Palace Hotel,** via Serlas 27 (© **081/837-10-00**). Most visible of these is the **King's Club Disco,** where outsiders can mingle with the rich and famous, or more likely the wanna-bes, in a mock-medieval decor that reverberates with the sound of recently released dance music. Jackets and ties aren't required. Cover is between 30SF and 45SF ($16.50–$24.75), depending on the season and night of the week, and includes the first drink. Quieter, somewhat less manic bars and watering holes, all of them relentlessly upscale, are scattered throughout other parts of the hotel as well.

4 Pontresina ⋆⋆

4 miles (6km) E of St. Moritz, 53 miles (85km) SE of Chur, 130 miles (208km) SE of Zurich

Pontresina (5,916 ft/1,775m) doesn't have the fame of St. Moritz, but it offers some of the best hiking and mountaineering in the Engadine. Its long hours of sunshine in the winter, and its access to all the noted ski sites in the greater St. Moritz area, make Pontresina an attractive alternative to the more expensive town. Situated in the Upper Engadines on the road to the Bernina Pass, at the mouth of the Bernina Valley, it's surrounded by larches, stone pines, and the Alps. From Pontresina, you also have views of what's called the "glacier amphitheater" of the Roseg Mountains.

Originally a 19th-century summer resort, Pontresina has become a leading ski resort, known for its famous ski runs, cross-country skiing tracks, and a family-friendly venue that's less expensive and less forbidding than more glamorous St. Moritz. The village today is filled with hotels and shops and has much old Engadine architecture.

ESSENTIALS

GETTING THERE   From Zurich, via Chur, a train arrives in Pontresina every hour throughout the day until 9pm (until 10pm on Friday, Saturday, and Sunday). There's also a train arriving every hour from St. Moritz. For **train schedules,** call ℂ **0900/300-300** or the railway station in Pontresina (ℂ **081/ 842-63-37**).

In the winter, a "sportbus" runs between St. Moritz and Pontresina every 30 minutes daily from 7:30am to 6:30pm. Tickets can be purchased at the post office or directly on the bus. Each way costs 6SF ($3.30); for information call the **bus station** in St. Moritz (ℂ **081/837-67-63**).

If you're driving from St. Moritz, head northeast along Route 27, then cut southeast at the junction with Route 29.

VISITOR INFORMATION   In lieu of street names, follow hotel or restaurant directional signs. The **Pontresina Tourist Office** (ℂ **081/838-83-00**) is open Monday to Friday from 8:30am to noon and 2 to 6pm. During high season, it is also open Saturday 9am to noon and 3 to 6pm; Sunday 2 to 6pm.

EXPLORING THE AREA

The Engadines provide a wealth of hiking tours that combine rides on cable cars or gondolas with sometimes strenuous hikes across rocky or, in some cases, glacial terrain. The most spectacular of these is the **Diavolezza tour** ⋆, which reaches a maximum height of 9,076 feet (2,723m), and which includes views of—and if you opt for it, hikes over—as many as two separate glaciers. To access it, travel by road for 4½ miles (7km) south of Pontresina, following the signs to the Bernina Pass until you reach the lowest station of the Diavolezza cable car, and climb aboard for a head-spinning 15-minute ascent to the top. One-way transit costs 19SF ($10.45) for adults and 9.50SF ($5.25) for children; the round-trip cost for adults is 30SF ($16.50) and 15SF ($8.25) for children. If it's winter, you can ski back down to the valley, or—more precariously (and this is only for experts)—you can negotiate down the face of the glacier to the hamlet of Morteratsch. The better bet occurs in summer, when you can take a guided hike along the surface of the glacier as part of a 4- to 5-hour tour that's recommended only for the fit and hardy. (Don't even consider this without the proper equipment, including sturdy boots with rubber treads, sunglasses, sunscreen, and protection against the rain and sometimes howling winds, even during midsummer.) A guide waits for participants every day, from May to September, at the top of the Diavolezza cable car, at noon. Participation in the walking tour costs 25SF ($13.75) for adults, and 15SF ($8.25) for children under 12. For more information about the Diavolezza hiking tour, contact the tourist offices of any of the surrounding towns and villages, including St. Moritz, Silvaplana, and Pontresina, or the **Pontresina Mountaineering School** (Bergsteigerschule Pontresina; ℂ **081/838-83-33**).

Another of the region's panoramic eyries, in this case one that's more conveniently reached than the above-recommended Diavolezzo, is **Alp Languard,** whose chairlifts will carry you to a height of 8,500 feet (2,550m). You'll access it from a hillside above the rest of the town that's within walking distance. A one-way ticket costs 15SF ($8.25) and a round-trip ticket 22SF ($12.10). Ascents are continuous during daylight hours throughout the year. For more information, contact **Sesselbahn Languard** at ℂ **081/842-62-55.**

The area's chief attraction is **Muottos Muragl** ★★★, a mountain whose peak is reached by funicular. The excursion begins in Pontresina, where you board a bus that travels 2 miles (3km) downhill in the direction of Samedan, to a final destination at the base of the funicular, Punt Muragl. The funicular ride takes 15 minutes to reach a platform set at 8,048 feet (2,414m) above sea level. From it you'll see the Upper Engadine Gap, with the mountain ranges of Piz Julier and Piz Rosatsch on either side. If the day is clear, you can also see the lakes between Maloja and St. Moritz. The excursion, including bus rides, costs 26SF ($14.30) round-trip, but a one-way ticket is available as well, for 13SF ($7.15). For information in Pontresina, call the tourist information center or inquire at the reception desk of your hotel. For information about the funicular, contact **Standseilbahn Muottos Muragle** at ℂ **081/842-83-08.**

WHERE TO STAY
VERY EXPENSIVE

Grand Hotel Kronenhof ★★★   This is the grandest hotel in town and has been run by the same family since the 1850s. Set in the center of the Pontresina, behind iron gates and a circular driveway, the Kronenhof is decorated with Corinthian columns and vaulted, frescoed ceilings. Its oldest section dates from 1848; the impressive details are from 1898 and include such baroque accessories as gilt, baby-pink cherubs, alluring nymphs, darkwood pine, restored murals, and even the original parquet floors. The mid-sized to spacious bedrooms are renovated as need dictates. Many are individually decorated with traditional Biedermeier pieces; others are in soothing pastels.

CH-7540 Pontresina. ℂ **081/842-01-11.** Fax 081/842-60-66. www.kronenhof.com. 85 units. Winter 460SF–540SF ($253–$297) double; 1,350SF ($742.50) suite for 2. Summer 385SF–495SF ($211.75–$272.25) double; 910SF ($500.50) suite for 2. Rates include breakfast. Half board 55SF ($30.25) extra per person. AE, DC, MC, V. Parking 20SF ($11) Closed Mar 27–June 24 and Oct–Dec 18. **Amenities:** 2 restaurants, 2 bars; 2 pools; 2 tennis courts; sauna; bowling; ice-skating rink; room service; massage; babysitting; laundry. *In room:* TV upon request, minibar, hair dryer, safe.

EXPENSIVE

Hotel La Collina & Soldanella ✦   This establishment is composed of two connected hotels, one built just after the turn of the century (the government-rated three-star Soldanella) and the other during the 1970s (the four-star La Collina). Many loyal clients deliberately opt for rooms in the Soldanella, knowing that the facilities of the better-rated La Collina are at their disposal, including La Collina's elegant dining room. Clients for either property register in the lobby of La Collina before heading through a network of hallways and covered passageways to their respective buildings. Regardless of which of the areas you select, bedrooms are comfortable, and the public rooms are cozy and elegant, with Oriental carpets and a scattering of regional antiques.

CH-7504 Pontresina. ☎ 081/842-01-21. Fax 081/842-79-95. www.collina.ch. 46 units (28 in La Collina, 18 in Soldanella). In La Collina, 300SF–380SF ($165–$209) double. In Soldanella, 240SF–320SF ($132–$176) double. Rates include half board. AE, DC, MC, V. Free parking outdoors, 15SF ($10.05) in garage. Closed May and Oct 18–Dec 20. **Amenities:** Restaurant; limited room service; laundry service. *In room:* TV, minibar, hair dryer.

Hotel Schweizerhof ✦   The Schweizerhof is from 1910, but it was so drastically modernized in 1975 that old-time visitors hardly recognize it; much of its roofline (including the towers and turrets) was removed. Yet it remains a huge, comfortable hotel. The mid-sized rooms are well furnished and comfortable, and the corner bay-windowed doubles open onto views to the southwest. All the bathrooms are neatly maintained, 45 units equipped with a tub-shower combination, the rest with a private shower.

CH-7504 Pontresina. ☎ 081/842-01-31. Fax 081/842-79-88. www.schweizerhofpontresina.ch. 70 units. Winter 320SF–480SF ($176–$264) double. Summer 310SF–430SF ($170.50–$236.50) double. Rates include breakfast. Half board 43SF ($23.65) per person extra. AE, DC, MC, V. Parking 15SF ($8.25). Closed Apr 13–June 11 and Oct 17–Dec 10. **Amenities:** Restaurant; bar; exercise room; Jacuzzi; sauna; steam bath; room service; massage; laundry service. *In room:* TV, minibar, hair dryer, safe.

MODERATE

Hotel Bernina *Value*   The members of the Schmid family welcome you to their hotel with old-fashioned hospitality. The hotel is not particularly historic, but it offers good value and cozy comfort in an often-forbidding landscape. Recently tiled mid-sized bathrooms (mainly with combination tub and shower), pinewood furnishings, and flower prints make the bedrooms inviting after renovation. The most panoramic views are from the corner doubles with private balconies. The dining room is decorated with panels of local wood, and the hotel's popular restaurant has excellent a la carte specialties. It's a place where the locals from the ski school meet in the winter.

CH-7504 Pontresina. ☎ 081/838-86-86. Fax 081/838-86-87. www.hotelbernina.ch. 47 units. 190SF–310SF ($104.50–$170.50) double. Rates include breakfast. AE, DC, MC, V. Parking 15SF ($8.25) in winter, 10SF ($5.50) in summer. Closed Apr 15–June 1 and Oct 3–Dec 16. **Amenities:** 2 restaurants; bar; steam bath; sauna; limited room service; massage; laundry service. *In room:* TV, minibar, hair dryer, safe.

Hotel Garni Chesa Mulin   Mr. and Mrs. Schmid and their staff go out of their way to make guests feel welcome in this quiet, centrally located hotel. The public rooms are filled with plants, which serve to accentuate the wood paneling. The large, airy bedrooms have comfortable furnishings, and in all except for six units, full bathrooms come with tub and shower combination (the remaining with shower).

CH-7504 Pontresina. ☎ 081/838-82-00. Fax 081/838-82-30. www.chesa-mulin.ch. 30 units. Winter 200SF–250SF ($110–$137.50) double. Summer 170SF–210SF ($93.50–$115.50) double. Rates include buffet breakfast. AE, DC, MC, V. Free parking outside, 9SF ($4.95) in garage nearby. Closed May and Nov. **Amenities:** Restaurant; sauna; limited room service; laundry. *In room:* TV, minibar, hair dryer (on request), safe.

WHERE TO DINE
EXPENSIVE

Hof Restaurant ⭐ CONTINENTAL/SWISS One of the most reliable dining rooms in town occupies a stone-floored room whose walls are accented with reproductions of medieval-looking sgraffito and big windows that overlook surrounding landscapes. The menu, geared for the high altitude, hearty climate outside, features generous portions of regional recipes that reflect the local traditions of both Switzerland and nearby Austria and Italy. Examples include pork filets with lemon sauce; lamb cutlets with balsamic vinegar sauce; carpaccio of veal or beef; air-dried *bundnerfleisch* (a type of beef); different preparations of salmon and trout; and the classic dish of Vienna, *tafelspitz,* the boiled beef with horseradish sauce. Dessert might include rich chocolate cake or flambéed raspberries with cream.

In the Hotel Schweizerhof. © **081/842-01-31.** Reservations recommended. Main courses 31SF–45SF ($17.05–$24.75); fixed-price lunch 27SF–45SF ($14.85–$24.75); fixed-price dinner 45SF ($24.75). AE, DC, MC, V. Daily 11am–11pm. Closed mid-Apr to mid-June and mid-Oct to mid-Dec.

MODERATE

Kronenstübli ⭐⭐ SWISS/FRENCH/ITALIAN The restaurant at the Grand Hotel Kronenhof is one of the most popular spots in town, serving the finest cuisine. It's filled with valuable pieces of brass and pewter; the wood paneling is from the mid-19th century. The cuisine is fresh flavored, inventive, and prepared with time-tested skill. You might enjoy turbot suprême with a bouquet of saffron flowers, veal mignons with a foie-gras mousse, or a Wiener schnitzel so large that it overflows the edges of the plate. For dessert, you might try the fried ice cream.

In the Grand Hotel Kronenhof. © **081/842-01-11.** Reservations required. Main courses 22SF–45SF ($12.10–$24.75). AE, DC, MC, V. Daily noon–2:30pm and 7–11pm. Closed Mar 27–June 24 and Oct–Dec 18.

Restaurant Sarazena *(Finds* SPANISH/ARABIC/ITALIAN One of the most unusual restaurants in the region utterly rejects an emphasis on Swiss cuisine, promoting instead a savory blend of Mediterranean styles that's a welcome relief from a constant diet of alpine food. The setting is a 250-year-old Engadine farmhouse with soaring granite arches—a testimonial to the solid building techniques of long ago. During clement weather, the restaurant expands onto an outdoor terrace. Arabic dishes include roasted chicken with cumin and saffron, falafel, and hummus. Italian dishes include succulent versions of spaghetti with garlic and shrimp and a peppery version of penne with smoked salmon. Iberian specialties feature paella and thin-sliced *jamon de Serrano.* After around 10:30pm, recorded disco music plays, and some diners actually get up and dance. This is not a disco; "night bar with music" better suits the vibe here.

In the town center. © **081/842-63-53.** Reservations recommended. Main courses 25SF–41SF ($13.75–$22.55). AE, DC, MC, V. Tues–Sat 6pm–midnight. Closed late Apr to mid-June and late Oct to mid-Dec.

INEXPENSIVE

Restaurant Locanda CONTINENTAL This restaurant provides intimate, vaulted rooms, where guests gather on snowy nights for classic raclette and fondues. Of course, other good-tasting fare, such as pastas, fresh trout, steaks, and various schnitzels, are also offered. The service is efficient.

In the Hotel Bernina. ℂ **081/838-86-86.** Reservations recommended. Main courses 15SF–45SF ($8.25–$24.75); fixed-price menu 40SF–48SF ($22–$26.40). AE, DC, MC, V. Daily 9am–midnight. Closed Apr 15–June 1 and Oct 3–Dec 16.

5 Silvaplana ⟨★⟩

4 miles (6km) SW of St. Moritz

Situated on Lake Silvaplana, in sight of Lake Champfèr, within a 10-minute drive of St. Moritz, the little village of Silvaplana (5,900 ft/1,770m) is at the foot of Piz Corvatsch (11,338 ft/3,401m), at the beginning of the Julier Pass.

Built around a late Gothic parish church, whose stone walls were completed in 1491, the hamlet of Silvaplana is one of the most unspoiled resort towns in the Engadine.

ESSENTIALS

GETTING THERE   Silvaplana is not serviced by any railroad. Local residents usually take the bus or drive to the railway station at St. Moritz for most of their transportation needs.

A flotilla of yellow postal buses make runs every 15 minutes in winter, and every 30 minutes in summer, from the St. Moritz railroad station to the center of Silvaplana at a cost of 2.50SF ($1.40) each way. The *Palm Express* bus also travels through Silvaplana as part of its twice-per-day route from Lugano to St. Moritz. One-way transit from Lugano to St. Moritz costs 63SF ($34.65) each way. For information on either of these forms of buses, contact the **bus station** in St. Moritz at ℂ **081/837-67-64.**

If you're driving from St. Moritz, head southwest along Route 27 for 10 minutes.

VISITOR INFORMATION   There are no street names in Silvaplana, but signs appear frequently to point the way to specific hotels, restaurants, and sites of interest. Between October and May, the **Silvaplana Tourist Office** (ℂ **081/ 838-60-00**) is open Monday to Friday from 8:30am to noon and from 1:30 to 6:30pm, and Saturday from 9am to noon. Between June and September, it's open Monday to Friday from 1:30am to 6pm, and Saturday from 9am to noon.

EXPLORING THE AREA

Swimming, hill climbing, riding, fishing, and even windsurfing on Lake Silva-plana are available in the summer. A range of cross-country trails and hiking paths are situated around the lake of Silvaplana.

Whether you're a skier, a mountaineer, a nature lover, or just a sightseer, you may want to visit **Corvatsch.** From Silvaplana, go across the narrow neck of water where Lake Champfèr and Lake Silvaplana join and take an aerial cable car at Surlej. In just 15 minutes, you'll reach the mountain station, from which you have a view of the lakes, meadows, forests, and villages of the Upper Enga-dine. From the lookout terrace you take in a panorama of what appears to be an infinity of mountain peaks, with the giant glacier of the Bernina group seem-ingly close enough to touch.

From December to May, skiers are presented with nearly 50 miles of ski runs covered with deep, powdery snow, while in the summer, you can ski on the granular ice of the glacier. Ski lifts, the most visible of which is the **Corvatsch Bergbahn** (ℂ **081/838-73-73**), carry skiers to the glacier throughout the year. It charges round-trip fares of 34SF ($18.70) for adults and 17SF ($9.35) for children.

The town's ski school, **Skischule Corvatsch** (© **081/828-86-84** for information), which is open only from December to May, charges 85SF ($46.75) per hour for private lessons.

WHERE TO STAY
EXPENSIVE

Hotel Albana ★★ This year-round hotel, a government-rated four-star choice and the best at the small resort town, stands on medieval foundations. Designed with beamed ceilings and a stone fireplace, it also has half-timbered walls and regional stenciling throughout. The mid-sized bedrooms are modern and inviting. The best accommodations are those with private balconies facing south.

CH-7513 Silvaplana. © **081/828-92-92.** Fax 081/828-81-81. 36 units. Winter 230SF–450SF ($126.50–$247.50) double. Summer 140SF–225SF ($77–$123.75) double. Rates include buffet breakfast. AE, DC, MC, V. Parking 15SF ($8.25) in garage in winter, 8SF ($4.40) in summer. **Amenities:** Restaurant; pool; gym; Jacuzzi; sauna; steam bath; concierge; room service; laundry service. *In room:* TV, minibar, hair dryer, safe.

MODERATE

Hotel Julier Palace In the heart of Silvaplana, this hotel consists of a red-fronted, turn-of-the-century chalet (the Hotel Julier) connected to a smaller, yellow-fronted annex that was added in the 1980s. The bedrooms in the annex are a bit larger than those in the Julier and more modern in their decor. The hotel is family-operated, with a good knowledge of foreign languages and customs. Large areas of both buildings were renovated during the early 1990s. All units come with mid-sized private bathrooms, mainly with shower.

CH-7513 Silvaplana. © **081/828-96-44.** Fax 081/828-81-43. 45 units. Winter 280SF–400SF ($154–$220) double. Summer 180SF–260SF ($99–$143) double. Rates include buffet breakfast. Half board 30SF ($20.10) per person extra. AE, DC, MC, V. Free parking outdoors, 12SF ($6.60) in garage. Closed Apr 17–June 15 and Oct 20–Dec 15. **Amenities:** Restaurant, bar; limited room service; laundry service. *In room:* TV.

Hotel Sonne This is a good government-rated two-star hotel with a sense of bourgeois charm that it takes very, very seriously. In the center of the village, this four-story building is decorated with flower boxes, monochromatic regional designs, and neoclassical details. The rustically modern interior has settees in the salon and old-fashioned wallpaper and paneling in the dining rooms. The small rooms are well maintained and comfortably furnished.

CH-7513 Silvaplana. © **081/828-81-52.** Fax 081/828-80-21. 45 units, 31 with bathroom. 140SF–180SF ($77–$99) per person double without bathroom, 170SF–230SF ($93.50–$126.50) per person double with bathroom. 50% reduction for children under 12. Rates include breakfast. Half board 28SF ($15.40) extra per person. AE, DC, MC, V. Free parking. **Amenities:** 2 restaurants; bar; limited room service; laundry service. *In room:* TV (on request), minibar.

INEXPENSIVE

Hotel Chesa Grusaida This government-rated two-star hotel, an Engadine house with white walls and a gently sloping roof, was built in the 1980s with lots of Swiss alpine charm and warmth. Located in the middle of a grassy lawn, it's popular with skiers. The rustic interior is crisscrossed with ceiling beams. The small rooms are comfortable and cozily furnished, each with an excellent mattress and private bathroom, most with showers.

CH-7513 Silvaplana. © **081/828-82-92.** Fax 081/828-94-09. 16 units. Winter 200SF ($110) double; summer 160SF ($88) double. Rates include breakfast. AE, DC, MC, V. Free parking. Closed May–June 15 and Oct 20–Dec 15. **Amenities:** Restaurant; limited room service. *In room:* TV (in some), minibar.

WHERE TO DINE

Le Gourmet ⚅ SWISS   The dining room in the Hotel Albana is the best choice in Silvaplana. It has a richly appealing decor of wrought iron, heavy timbers, and striped fabrics. The chef prepares such tempting specialties as medaillons of pork with grapes and nuts, sweetbreads in an artichoke sauce with a purée of asparagus, filet of lamb with black truffles, and filet of red mullet with saffron and fresh morels.

The hotel also maintains a less glamorous second-floor dining room, the Spunta Grischun, which offers Engadine dishes, main courses costing 26SF to 29SF ($14.30–$15.95).

In the Hotel Albana. ℂ **081/828-92-92.** Reservations recommended. Main courses 45SF–60SF ($24.75–$33); fixed-price menu 60SF–108SF ($33–$59.40). AE, DC, MC, V. Daily noon–1:30pm and 7:30–10pm. Closed Apr 22–June 20.

14

Lugano, Locarno & the Ticino

If you don't normally think of palm trees in Switzerland, you haven't seen the Ticino. Also called the Tessin, it's the Swiss Riviera—the retirement fantasy of thousands of Swiss living in the northern cantons. Although Italian is the major language, German and French (as well as English) are also widely spoken.

A visitor could spend at least 2 weeks just touring the valleys of the Ticino. Officially, the canton begins at Airolo (the southern exit of the St. Gotthard Tunnel), but most visitors head for the district's major resorts of Locarno, Lugano, and fast-rising Ascona. Lugano and Locarno share the shores of lakes Lugano and Maggiore with Italy. Relations between Switzerland and Italy, however, weren't always peaceful. The Ticino was basically carved out of the Duchy of Milan by Swiss soldiers and staunchly defended in several bloody battles.

The name of the canton is taken from the Ticino River, a tributary of northern Italy's Po River. The balmy climate produces subtropical vegetation, which thrives in gardens famous throughout Switzerland. The district's weather is almost addictive between March and November, but the rest of the year can be cold and damp.

The proximity of Italy manifests itself in the Ticino's architecture and cuisine. Many buildings are made of stone and are proportioned like structures in Lombardy or Tuscany. Also, in many cases, a trattoria will be owned by a Swiss-German husband and a Swiss-Italian wife, so that their cuisine ends up being a concession to each other's culinary traditions.

Sometimes getting to the Ticino is part of the fun. One of the most dramatic ways to arrive is over the **Simplon Pass** ★★, a journey that stretches from the German-speaking town of Brig in Switzerland and, after crossing the pass, descends to the Italian border town of Domodossola, a distance of some 40 miles (64km). The pass owes its origins to Napoleon, who demanded a low-altitude pass 6,500 feet (1,950m) above sea level through which artillery could be transported. This pass is often closed between December and early May because of bad road conditions. At those times automobiles are transported onto flatbed trains, which are carried through one of the longest railway tunnels in the world, the Simplon Tunnel. The tunnel stretches for 12 miles (20km). But when the pass is open it affords one of the most panoramic mountain views in Europe.

Rail passengers can also arrive dramatically by taking the ***Bernina Express*** ★★★, a 4-hour trip that begins in Zurich and ends in Italy. As you near the town of Chur you will be awed by the rugged peaks around you, but before the end of the journey, as you near the Italian border town of Tirano, you will see palm-lined lakefronts. This is the only express train that crosses the Alps with no tunnels, and, as such, it is one of the steepest railway lines in the world. At Tirano, the end of the rail run from Zurich, you can make easy bus connections on to Lugano. For more information about the *Bernina Express,* call **Rail Europe** at © **800/438-7245.**

14 miles (22km) E of Locarno, 22 miles (35km) N of Lugano, 120 miles (192km) S of Zurich, and 260 miles (416km) W of Geneva

The opening of the St. Gotthard Tunnel made this once-remote Swiss town on Italy's side of the Alps very accessible. Bellinzona is known for the beauty of its old city and the nearby hills, as well as for the hospitality of its inhabitants.

Because of its location astride the best of the ancient military and trade routes between Rome and its colonies in the north, the town is believed to be of Roman origin. It was later occupied, along with the rest of the Ticino, by both the Celts and the Ligurians. Records of the town date from A.D. 590. As the strategic key to the passes of St. Gotthard, San Bernardino, and Lucomagno, Bellinzona loomed large in the history of Lombardy. In the 8th century it was owned outright by the bishop of Como, and ownership went back and forth between Como and Milan in the 13th and 14th centuries. By 1798 it had become the capital of its own canton, Bellinzona, in the Swiss Confederation. Five years later it was incorporated into the newly formed canton of the Ticino, where it has remained ever since, serving as the canton's capital.

Saturday morning is a good time to visit here to see the lively outdoor market, between 7 and 11:30am. Peddlers, vendors, country people, artisans, and townsfolk converse in Italian over the wares.

ESSENTIALS

GETTING THERE   Bellinzona is the easiest destination to reach in the Ticino. Every train from the north of Switzerland stops here, as Bellinzona lies on the Brussels–Basel–Zurich–Milan international line. Indeed, every day one or another regional or international train stops here about once every 30 minutes. For **rail information** and schedules, call © **0900/300-300.**

The nearest airport is at **Lugano-Agno,** 30 minutes from Bellinzona by train.

If you're driving from Zurich, continue along the N2 expressway through the St. Gotthard Tunnel into the Ticino. N2 continues southeast to Bellinzona.

VISITOR INFORMATION   The **Bellinzona Tourist Bureau,** Viale della Stazione (© **091/825-21-31**), is open Monday to Friday from 8am to 6:30pm and Saturday from 9am to noon.

EXPLORING THE AREA

Bellinzona has three castles dating from the 13th to the 15th century: the Schwyz, the Unterwald, and the Uri.

Castle of Uri ⚝ (Castelgrande or San Michele, in Italian; © **091/825-81-45**), built in 1280, is the most ancient and the largest castle in town. To reach the castle, take an elevator from piazza del Sole in the town center. In addition to the elevator, there are signposted paths from piazza Collegiata and piazza Nosetto for those who'd like to take one of the most scenic walks in the area. The castle was restored in 1991 with a historical section and a small numismatic museum. The castle contains a restaurant (see "Where to Dine," below), a banquet room, and

---

Finds **Bellinzona Blues**

In late June hordes from throughout Switzerland gather in Bellinzona for the annual **Blues Festival,** where free concerts are staged in squares. Some of the biggest names in blues have appeared here, and the tourist office (see "Essentials," above) will supply the details, which change every year.

---

a congress hall. It's open daily from 10am to 6pm. Admission is 4SF ($2.20) for adults; 2SF ($1.10) for children, students, and seniors 65 or over.

The most outstanding of the three medieval fortifications is the **Schwyz Castle** *★★* (Castello di Montebello; © **091/825-13-42**). It has a 13th-century chateau with a courtyard, as well as several 15th-century additions. Today, it's a minor museum of history and archaeology. To get here by car, start from viale Stazione and follow the steep ramp up to this huge citadel. It's open daily from 10am to 6pm, and admission is 4SF ($2.20) for adults; 2SF ($1.10) for children, students, and seniors 65 or over.

Castle of Unterwald *★* (Castello di Sasso Corbaro; © **091/825-55-32**) was built in 1479. It can be reached by the same road that goes up to the Schwyz (see above). The view from the terrace here is the finest in Bellinzona. You'll see not only the lower valley of the Ticino but Lake Maggiore as well. The castle hosts temporary exhibitions. Open only April to October, Tuesday to Sunday from 10am to 6pm, the castle's admission price is 4SF to 5SF ($2.70–$3.35) depending on the exhibit.

Also worth visiting is the collegiate **Church of Sts. Peter and Stephen,** dating from the 16th century. It's a fine Renaissance structure, with a richly embellished baroque interior. The location is across from Castelgrande.

Guided walking tours of Bellinzona, its Old Town, and its castles are available upon request at the tourist office (see "Essentials," above).

SHOPPING

Pick up a map from the tourist office in the center of the Old Town. A look at the map will direct you to **Villa dei Cedri** (© **091/826-28-27**), Bellinzona's municipally owned art gallery founded in 1985. The gallery contains private art donated to the city but also mounts temporary exhibitions. In back is an enclosed garden and grounds where the townfolk grow their own small crop of local Merlot, bottles of which are offered for sale in the gallery. It's open Tuesday to Sunday from 10am to noon and 2 to 5pm; closed January and February. Admission is 8SF ($4.40) for adults; 6SF ($3.30) for students, children, and seniors 65 or over.

WHERE TO STAY

Albergo Unione The best hotel in town is a plain-looking white building with a pink-marble extension with balconies. It's surrounded by gardens, some with fountains. The government-rated three-star hotel offers modernized, mid-sized rooms with flowered carpets, tiles, firm beds, and up-to-date plumbing, mainly with private showers, although some units also offer tub baths.

Via Général Guisan 1, CH-6501 Bellinzona. © 091/825-55-77. Fax 091/825-94-60. www.albergo-unione.ch. 33 units. 196SF ($107.80) double. Rates include breakfast. AE, DC, MC, V. Closed Dec 20–Jan 20. **Amenities:** Restaurant, bar; limited room service; laundry. *In room:* TV, minibar.

WHERE TO DINE

Castelgrande ✦ TICINESE/ITALIAN   Located in the largest and most ancient castle in Bellinzona (see "Exploring the Area," above), this restaurant might be predictably overrun with camera-toting tourists getting off tour buses. But unlike restaurants installed in most European castles, the upstairs dining room here is decidedly upmarket. Downstairs, there's an informal grotto with terrace, which serves less expensive Ticino and Italian dishes, while the more formal upstairs room features gourmet specialties. When dining in this second-level room, men are advised to wear a jacket.

The restaurant is not only the most luxurious in appointments in town, it also serves the best food. The cuisine combines that of the Ticino region with dishes inspired by sunny Italy. Game is a feature, and the wine list is particularly extensive. Try such dishes as pigeon with onions in a sweet-and-sour sauce, or if it's autumn, perfectly cooked quail with porcini mushrooms. The chef's imagination is reflected in such dishes as goose liver accompanied by blueberries. Guests can ask for a table in the cavelike interior or, if the weather is right, for one on the large terrace.

Salita al Castello. ℂ **091/826-23-53.** Reservations recommended. Main courses 35SF–50SF ($19.25–$27.50). AE, DC, DISC, MC, V. Tues–Sun noon–2:30pm and 6:30–10pm.

Locanda Orico ⊀⊀⊀ ITALIAN/FRENCH This is one of the best restaurants in the Ticino, serving a refined cuisine based on market-fresh ingredients. The inn lies in a stately town house at the foot of Castelgrande in the center of Bellinzona. The chef, Lorenzo Albrici, was once a student of Frédy Girardet, hailed as one of the greatest chefs of Europe. The fixed-price lunch menu (35SF/$19.25) is the town's great dining bargain. An array of warm and cold appetizers is there to tempt you, ranging from house-marinated salmon in a sweet and sour sauce to carpaccio of duck liver flavored with sea salt. Baked shrimp are also a starter, floating in an Andalusian gazpacho. Main courses, which are especially delightful, are filet of freshwater lake perch stuffed with green leafy vegetables and filet of roasted veal with rosemary-flavored butter. For dessert, there is nothing better than a symphony of fresh fruit au gratin, flavored with Grand Marnier. This place represents grand provincial dining at its best.

via Orico 13. ℂ **091/825-15-18.** Reservations recommended. Main courses 38SF–46SF ($20.90–$25.30). AE, DC, MC, V. Open Tues–Sat 11:30am–2pm and 6:30–11pm.

2 Locarno ⊀⊀

14 miles (22km) W of Bellinzona, 25 miles (40km) N of Lugano

This ancient town at the north end of **Lake Maggiore** ⊀⊀⊀ is a vacation resort known for its mild climate. The rich Mediterranean vegetation includes camellias, magnolias, mimosa, wisteria, azaleas, and oleander in the spring. Olives, figs, and pomegranates also flourish in this climate.

Locarno entered world history in 1925 when an international conference held here resulted in a series of agreements known collectively as the Locarno Pact. It was in Locarno that the former enemies of World War I, seeking to reorder the affairs of Europe, committed themselves to a peaceful coexistence. Locarno was chosen over Lucerne, reportedly, because the mistress of the French representative wanted the meeting to be held on Lake Maggiore. The "spirit of Locarno," however, did not last long; within a decade the participants were again arming for war.

If you take the electric railway between Locarno and the Simplon Pass, you'll pass through the Centovalli, named for the hundred valleys that slope toward the river. There are many charming villages on the banks of this river. At Carnedo, in Italy, the railway climbs up to the plateau of Santa Maria Maggiore, a wide, barren, and solitary district that stretches for about 6 miles (10km) at 2,800 feet (840m) above sea level. A steep descent leads down to the railway junction of Domodossola. This international railway serves as a link between the Gotthard and the Simplon lines. The bridges are technological wonders.

ESSENTIALS

GETTING THERE The nearest airport is at Lugano (see section 4, later in this chapter), 45 minutes away by train.

The Locarno–Domodossola electric railway links Locarno with the Italian town of Domodossola. From here, you can continue to Brig in the Rhône Valley, through the Simplon Tunnel. Railway lines connect Brig with Lake Geneva and Bern through the Lotschberg Tunnel. Direct trains from Lausanne or Bern take 4 hours to reach Locarno. From the other direction, through the St. Gotthard Tunnel, Locarno is 14 miles (23km) west of Bellinzona by rail. For **rail information** and schedules, call ℂ **0900/300-300.**

Locarno sits atop the bus routes that connect Ascona with Lugano, and they continue on to many different mountain villages to the northeast until arriving at Chur. For more details about bus transportation, call the tourist office (see below).

After driving through the St. Gotthard Tunnel and reaching Bellinzona on the N2 expressway, take Route 13 west to reach Locarno.

VISITOR INFORMATION   The **Locarno Tourist Bureau,** on largo Zorzi (ℂ **091/751-03-33**), is open March to October, Monday to Friday from 8:30am to 7pm and Saturday from 10am to 4pm; November to February, Monday to Friday from 9am to 12:30pm and 2 to 6pm.

SEEING THE SIGHTS

Start your walk around town at **piazza Grande,** the main square. On the north side the arcades are filled with shops. You can find antiques, art, Swiss and Italian handicrafts, and high fashion from Milan.

From piazza Grande, follow the curvy via Francesco Rusca to the Old Town. Along the way, you can visit the **Castello Visconti,** piazza Castello 2 (ℂ **091/ 756-31-80**). This structure is all that survives from a late-medieval castle in which the dukes of Milan lived. It was severely damaged in 1518. Today the castle contains a Museum Civico, which displays many Roman artifacts excavated in the area. It's open only April to October, daily from 10am to 6pm. Admission is 6SF ($3.30).

The most important sight in Locarno is the **Santuario della Madonna del Sasso** ✦ (ℂ **091/743-62-65**), on a wooded crag above the resort in the hamlet of Orselina. Hearty visitors and devout pilgrims can climb to the church, at an elevation of 1,165 feet. However, we recommend the funicular, which leaves every 15 minutes from 7am to 11pm. The round-trip fare is 5.60SF ($3.10) for adults, 4SF ($2.20) for children. The church was founded in 1480 after a friar, Bartolomeo da Ivrea, reportedly saw a vision of the Virgin. It was reconstructed in 1616. The basilica contains much artwork, including Bramantino's *Flight into Egypt* (1520). In a museum next door to the basilica hang masterpieces by such artists as Raphael. Another masterpiece, painted in 1870, is *Christ Carried to the Sepulcher* by Antonio Ciseri. This procession scene is most often described as "Caravaggiesque." The stunning **panoramic view** ✦ can be taken in from the loggia, opening onto the rooftops of Locarno with Lake Maggiore in the distance. The grounds are open March to October, daily from 7am to 10pm, closing at 9pm off-season. The museum is open only April to October, Monday to Friday from 2 to 5pm and Sunday 10am to noon and 2 to 5pm. Only the museum charges admission: 3SF ($1.65) for adults, 2SF ($1.10) for children.

The Locarno Tourist Bureau (see "Essentials," above) sponsors a **walking tour** every Tuesday from March to October at 9:45am. In July and August, the walking tour costs 5SF ($2.75); in other months, 10SF ($5.50). That fee includes not only viewing, but also concise verbal histories of many of the town's old buildings and a drink at tour's end, usually in a nearby casino. Inquire at the office for more details.

One of our favorite pastimes is to go **biking** along the way. At the train station (Piazza Stazione. ℂ **091/743-65-64**), you can rent bikes for 21SF ($11.55) per day, with mountain bikes going for 29SF ($15.95) per day. Bikes can be rented daily from 5:45am to 9pm.

Fleeing the city (not that you would want to), you can take a postal bus (630) to the village of **Sonogo** in just 1 hour. At the end of the ride you'll be in the midst of towering peaks in one of the Ticino's most scenic valleys, **Val Verzasca.** After getting off the bus, take the first left and let the yellow signs direct you to **Lavertezzo,** across shaded glens and riverbeds through perfect and bucolic valley scenery. Allow about 3½ hours to go from Sonogo to Lavertezzo. Should you tire at any time, you can take one of the postal buses that run through the valley.

THE GAMBAROGNO RIVIERA ✸✸✸
The Gambarogno Riviera, with its characteristic Ticinese villages, spreads along Lake Maggiore's left shore for about 6½ miles (11km) to the Italian border. It begins at Contone, at the foot of the Monte Ceneri, and includes part of the Piano di Magadino (plain of Magadino) as well as the wildlife refuge, Bolle di Magadino, in a delta formed by the Ticino River.

The lush vegetation, the green chestnut forests, and the iridescent colors of the lake ranging from azure to emerald green give a uniqueness to this well-preserved region. Thanks to its Mediterranean climate, the annual temperatures average 59°F. In summer the weather is ideal for all aquatic sports. The riviera isn't just a lakeshore, but a steep mountain sloping up from the lake. On one side it is crowned by Monte Tamaro, at 6,500 feet (1,950m) above sea level, and on the other by Monte Gambarogno, at 5,700 feet (1,710m). It is this latter mountain that gives its name to the region. There's a panorama of the Alps from Monte Rosa on the west to the chain of Ticinese Alps on the north.

The region is riddled with some 125 miles (201km) of **footpaths.** The Locarno Tourist Bureau (see "Essentials," above) distributes a map indicating every trail; this map also outlines various itineraries with the time that it takes to cover them.

One path indicated on the map provides access to the whole area, from the mouth of the Ticino River to the village of Magadino, from which the biological cycles of local species can be observed. More than 300 different kinds of birds alone live and nest in this tangle of vegetation. The tourist office at Locarno also offers guided visits in a **rowboat** every Monday and Thursday. The staff at Locarno will provide more details.

SHOPPING
Most of the merchandise that's for sale in Locarno is practical instead of glittery. There is a cluster of fashionable boutiques along piazza Grande, the centerpiece of the town's shopping district, but overall, shoppers usually do best by wandering through the sprawling spaces of the town's three department stores. These are **Globus,** piazza Grande (© **091/756-39-39**), where a worthy collection of local handicrafts and Swiss souvenirs is for sale; the somewhat less upscale but just as comprehensive **Mannore,** piazza Grande (© **091/756-86-99**); and **Migros,** via Franchini 21 (© **091/756-88-11**). Migros is known in other corners of Switzerland only as an American-style grocery-store chain, but in Locarno the store sells Italian and Swiss food, wine, and specialty goods such as prosciutto, as well as hardware, clothing, souvenirs of the region, and virtually everything else you'd expect in a major department store.

Does your proximity to Italy make you thirsty for the fruits of the grape? Two family-run vineyards lie within 2 miles (3km) of Locarno, and sell bottles of their products from the premises. They are **Delea,** signposted in the hamlet of Losone, a short drive north of Locarno (© **091/791-08-17**), and **Matasci,** signposted in the hamlet of Tenero (© **091/735-60-11**). Each produces both white and red wines, all of which are for sale.

WHERE TO STAY

Locarno has many good hotels that accommodate travelers on their way to or from Italy. You can also spend a pleasant vacation along the lake here.

EXPENSIVE

Grand Hotel Locarno ★★ *Kids*   This very grand hotel opened in 1876 to celebrate the inauguration of the St. Gotthard railway line; nearly half a century later it provided accommodations for some of the most important leaders of Europe during the Locarno conference. The hotel sits amid gardens in the middle of town, facing the lake. You get grand comfort here. The salons on the main floor are capped with Belle Epoque frescoes of flowers, cherubs, and mythological figures. The hotel is large, well managed, and comfortable, with the best and most expensive rooms facing the lake. The hotel's activities for children make it a family favorite.

Via Semplone 17, CH-6000 Locarno-Muralto. © **091/743-02-82.** Fax 091/743-30-13. www.grand-hotel. locarno.ch. 80 units. 250SF–340SF ($137.50–$187) double. Half board 35SF ($19.25) extra. Rates include buffet breakfast. AE, DC, MC, V. Free parking. Closed Jan 6–Mar. **Amenities:** Restaurant; bar; pool; tennis court; children's center; room service; babysitting; laundry. *In room:* TV, minibar, hair dryer, safe (in some).

Hotel La Palma au Lac ★   Dating from the mid-1950s (and looking it), this balconied hotel of six- and seven-story buildings faces the lake, and is a particular favorite of clients who were young when Queen Elizabeth was. Sun chairs and chaise longues are set up on the terrace. The updated public rooms are decorated with oil paintings and tapestries and retain their 19th-century grace. The elegantly furnished and spacious bedrooms have an Italian flair, and units with private balconies overlook the lake.

Viale Verbano 29, CH-6600 Locarno-Muralto. © **091/735-36-36.** Fax 091/735-36-16. www.ramada-treff.ch. 68 units. 280SF–340SF ($154–$187) double; from 430SF ($236.50) suite. Rates include buffet breakfast. AE, DC, MC, V. Free parking outside. **Amenities:** 2 restaurants; bar; limited room service; massage; babysitting; laundry. *In room:* TV, minibar.

Hotel Orselina ★★★   Guests enjoy a dramatic view from this peaceful five-story oasis in a suburb north of town, accessible by funicular from Orselina. Situated on a hillside, it resembles a Spanish parador. The lake is visible in the distance. Its sloping lawns, shaded loggias, and many-tiered subtropical gardens may cause you to linger for a month at this tranquil retreat. It's got everything but a lakeside location. The mid-sized to spacious rooms are well furnished and comfortable, each with a firm French bed and a balcony facing south. Those in the newer wing are more up to date, although all the accommodations are warmly inviting.

Via Santuario 10, CH-6600 Orselina-Locarno. © **091/735-44-44.** Fax 091/735-44-66. www.orselina.com. 74 units. 398SF–448SF ($218.90–$246.40) double; 524SF–542SF ($288.20–$298.10) suite. Rates include half board. DC, MC, V. Outdoor parking 5SF ($2.75); garage parking 8SF–12SF ($4.40–$6.60). Closed Nov 6– Feb 25. **Amenities:** Restaurant; bar; 2 pools; tennis court; health club; Jacuzzi; sauna; limited room service; laundry service. *In room:* TV, minibar, hair dryer, safe (in some).

Hotel Reber au Lac ★★★   This elegantly patrician hotel is the grandest resort at Locarno and has been run by the Reber family since it opened in 1886. A genteel favorite, it shuns ostentation for solid, gracious, bourgeois comfort. Spacious gardens surround the hotel, and some of the structure, notably the west wing, has been modernized. Some of the best rooms, those with frontal views of the lake, remain the way things used to be. Regardless of your room assignment, each unit is generally spacious and all are well furnished with well-maintained plumbing. A bathing beach and private pier are also on the premises.

Viale Verbano 55, CH-6600 Locarno-Muralto. ℂ 091/735-87-00. Fax 091/735-87-01. www.hotel-reber.ch. 61 units. 270SF–410SF ($148.50–$225.50) double; 480SF–590SF ($264–$324.50) suite. Rates include buffet breakfast. Half board 45SF ($24.75) per person extra. AE, DC, MC, V. Parking 10SF ($5.50) in private garage. **Amenities:** 3 restaurants, bar; pool; sauna; limited room service; massage; laundry. *In room:* TV, minibar, hair dryer, safe (in some).

MODERATE

Hotel Beau-Rivage   Solid comfort and a return to yesterday are hallmarks of this turn-of-the-century hotel, the best choice to take your most conservative aunt to. A Doric colonnade supports the sun terrace over the main entrance. Above the colonnade, the white facade has wrought-iron balconies decorated with flowers. The interior is elegant, with vaulted ceilings, salmon-colored marble floors, and a few neoclassical gilt-edged mirrors. The mid-sized bedrooms are decorated in typical Ticino style with natural-wood furnishings; many have private balconies overlooking the lake. All the bathrooms come with shower, and some also contain tubs. The postcard-type scenic views are often better than the lake-view rooms themselves, some of which are boxlike and sparsely furnished.

Viale Verbano 31, CH-6602 Locarno-Muralto. ℂ 091/743-13-55. Fax 091/743-94-09. www.treff-hotels.ch. 50 units. 240SF–260SF ($132–$143) double. Rates include buffet breakfast. Half board 30SF ($16.50) extra. AE, DC, MC, V. Free parking. Closed Nov to mid-Mar. **Amenities:** Restaurant; room service; laundry. *In room:* TV, minibar.

Hotel Belvedere ★★ *Finds*   Set on a steep hillside in the upper heights of Locarno, this ocher-colored neoclassical hotel is a beautifully landscaped retreat. It was built in 1910 on the foundations of a 300-year-old house. Reopened in 1990 after 4 years of total restoration, it offers modernized comforts and sweeping views of the lake from each of its streamlined and contemporary bedrooms. All but three of its bedrooms have a private balcony, and 20 of the accommodations come with bathrooms with private showers, while the rest have combination tub and showers.

Via ai Monti della Trinità 44, CH-6601 Locarno. ℂ 091/751-03-63. Fax 091/751-52-39. www.belvedere-locarno.ch. 80 units. 270SF–326SF ($148.50–$179.30) double; 408SF–600SF ($224.40–$330) suite. Rates include buffet breakfast. Half board 40SF ($22) per person extra. AE, DC, MC, V. Parking 15SF ($8.25). Take Locarno's only funicular, departing from via Ramogna near the lakefront, to its 2nd stop (Belvedere), a few steps from the hotel. **Amenities:** 2 restaurants, bar; pool; health club; Jacuzzi; limited room service; massage; laundry. *In room:* TV, minibar, hair dryer, safe.

Remorino Hotel-Garni ★ *Finds*   In a secluded residential area a short walk from the center of town, this vastly improved hotel lies only 2 minutes from the lakeside promenade. For almost 3 decades it has been owned by the Kirchlechner-Qualizza family, who now personally direct the management. All the bedrooms have new furnishings along with immaculately maintained bathrooms, 10 of which come only with shower. Try if possible for a bedroom facing the lake. The garden is especially inviting, with its Mediterranean plants such as camellia, magnolia, and olive and palm trees.

Via Verbano 29, CH-6648 Minusio-Locarno. ℂ 091/743-10-33. Fax 091/743-74-29. www.remorino.ch. 25 units. 248SF ($136.40) double. Rates include buffet breakfast. AE, V. Free parking outdoors, 12SF ($6.60) in garage. Closed Nov–Feb. **Amenities:** Pool; laundry service. *In room:* TV, minibar, hair dryer, safe.

Rosa Seegarten *Value*   For good value in Locarno, try this old-fashioned, cream-colored hotel on the lake, a 3-minute walk from the train station. Half board is encouraged. Meals are served on a lakeside terrace under a grape arbor. This is the largest terrace in town, capable of seating between 150 and 200 people. All the comfortable but functionally furnished small rooms have a toilet and shower.

Viale Verbano 25, CH-6600 Locarno. © **091/743-87-31.** Fax 091/743-50-02. 37 units. 180SF–290SF ($99–$159.50) double. Rates include buffet breakfast. Half board 35SF ($19.25) per person extra. AE, DC, MC, V. Free parking. Closed Nov–Mar 15. **Amenities:** Restaurant. *In room:* TV.

INEXPENSIVE

Hotel dell'Angelo *Finds*   In the center of the action, this hotel at the end of piazza Grande could be a winning choice even if you're not staying here to save money. Reconstructed in 1976, it grew up over the ruins of a building from the late 17th century. Arches on the ground floor and balconies trimmed in iron grace its facade. As with many bargain rooms, the furnishings are sparse—with much use of Formica—but they're clean and comfortable nevertheless. Freshly starched linens and immaculately scrubbed tile, shower-only bathrooms complete with bidets make the rooms more appealing. In contrast to the bedrooms, some of the public lounges are more enticing, with paintings and antiques adding a grace note. The hotel's terrace features views of the town.

Piazza Grande 1, CH-6600 Locarno. © **091/751-81-75.** Fax 091/751-82-56. www.hotel-dell-angelo.ch. 50 units. 140SF–197SF ($77–$108.35) double. Rates include buffet breakfast. AE, DC, MC, V. Parking 12SF ($6.60). **Amenities:** Restaurant. *In room:* TV.

WHERE TO DINE

Several Locarno restaurants also rent rooms. They're sometimes noisy because of all the restaurant activity going on in the same building, but they are bargains and centrally located. At least you won't have to worry about appointing a designated driver for the evening. Choices include the **Cittàdella** and the **Ristorante Zurigo.**

EXPENSIVE

Centenario ✫✫✫ FRENCH/ITALIAN   There is no finer dining in Locarno than that found here, not even in the restaurants of the most deluxe hotels. The dining room, with austere white walls and straight-back chairs, has a simplicity that contrasts with the colorful creations of Gérard Perriard. The menu is based on fresh ingredients from the market. Seasonal specialties—and delightful ones at that—include sea bass with fennel, foie gras of duck with salad, filet of roebuck with mushrooms, roast guinea fowl with sauerkraut and truffles, and shrimp St. Jacques. For an unusual first course, ask for a cold consommé of quail eggs garnished with caviar.

Lungolago 17, Muralto. © **091/743-82-22.** Reservations required. Main courses 32SF–60SF ($17.60–$33); fixed-price meal 56SF–129SF ($30.80–$70.95). AE, DC, MC, V. Tues–Sat noon–2pm and 7–10pm. Closed 3 weeks in Feb and 3 weeks in July.

Restaurant Cittadella ✫ MEDITERRANEAN   Located in the center of the Old Town, this restaurant complex is separated from the narrow cobblestone street by a granite arcade draped with vines. The downstairs trattoria has timbered ceilings, stucco walls, and an informal ambience. Upstairs is a chic enclave of *cuisine moderne* deftly and imaginatively prepared. Specialties include a gooseliver terrine and a salad of large shrimp with nuts and mango. A mixed grill with saltwater and freshwater fish is delicious.

If you don't object to the often-noisy streets of the historic Old Town, you'll find 10 simply furnished bedrooms upstairs renting for 160SF ($88) for a double, including a buffet breakfast.

Via Cittadella 18, CH-6600 Locarno. ℭ **091/751-58-85.** Fax 091/751-77-59. Reservations required. Restaurant (upstairs), main courses 35SF–45SF ($19.25–$24.75); fixed-price gourmet menu 76SF ($41.80). Trattoria (downstairs), main courses 28SF–38SF ($15.40–$20.90); pizzas 15SF–20SF ($8.25–$11). AE, DC, MC, V. Daily noon–1:30pm and 7–10pm (June–July closed on Mon).

MODERATE

Restaurant La Carbonara SWISS/ITALIAN   There's a well-stocked bar near the entrance of this restaurant, separated from the dining room by a glass partition. The stucco walls are decorated with original paintings and copper pots. Patrons of this restaurant are regaled with full-flavored dishes perfectly prepared. Specialties include veal kidney with grappa and mushrooms, *saltimbocca* (veal with ham), and a large pasta menu, featuring macaroni with four different types of cheese. Other dishes include **braciola alla pizzaiola** (stuffed beef in a tomato sauce), grilled shrimp, and 15 types of pizza.

Piazza Stazione. ℭ **091/743-67-14.** Reservation not required. Main courses 20SF–50SF ($11–$27.50); fixed-price menu 22SF–25SF ($12.10–$13.75). AE, DC, MC, V. Daily 11:30am–2pm and 6:30pm–midnight.

Ristorante Zurigo ⭐ SWISS/ITALIAN   One of the finest places to dine on a summer night is on this restaurant's flagstone terrace, which is dotted with chestnut trees and festive lights. A loyal clientele enjoys savory Italian food right on the lakefront. The restaurant is part of a turn-of-the-century, Mediterranean-style hotel with balconies and shutters. Specialties include a platter piled high with three types of succulent pasta. The menu also includes risotto verde, *saltimbocca* (veal with ham), and tender grilled beefsteak. For dessert, the zabaglione is superb.

Zurigo also offers 27 comfortably furnished rooms, each with shower bathroom and private balcony, for reasonable prices. Double rooms cost 190SF to 242SF ($104.50–$133.10) and contain a minibar and TV .

Viale Verbano 9, CH-6600 Locarno. ℭ **091/743-16-17.** Fax 091/743-43-15. Reservations recommended. Main courses 30SF–50SF ($16.50–$27.50). AE, DC, MC, V. Daily 11am–11pm.

LOCARNO AFTER DARK

Nightlife in Locarno might not impress you, as it's a lot quieter here than in larger, and more extroverted, Ticino cities such as Lugano. So either haul yourself off to Lugano for the night, or drag out your dinner and have a nightcap in the bar at your hotel. If this idea doesn't particularly appeal to you, you might opt for a stroll along the lakefront, stopping perhaps at the **Café Debarcadero,** lungolago G. Motta (ℭ **091/751-05-55**), which stays open every night till midnight. Debarcadero also offers pizzas and pastas for 12SF to 16SF ($6.60–$8.80). Another option is the cozy bar in the **Hotel Arcadia,** lungolago G. Motta (ℭ **091/756-18-18**), where potted palms, rattan furniture, and black-and-pink marble flooring evoke a Caribbean hideaway. Piano music sometimes accompanies the liquor.

A site where you'll probably be able to strike up a conversation is **Bar La Bussola,** the social centerpiece of the nearby hamlet of Muralto (ℭ **091/743-60-95**), about a mile south of Locarno. A congenial competitor is the bar tucked away next to the dining room of the previously recommended **Ristorante La Carbonara** (ℭ **091/743-67-14**).

One of the best piano bars is the **Palm'Arte** at the Hotel La Palma au Lac, viale Verbano 29, Locarno-Muralto (ℭ **091/735-36-36**).

If you're intrigued with gambling, you might decide to spin the small-stakes wheel of fortune at the town's obscure and rather dull casino, the **Kursaal Locarno,** largo Zorza (ℭ **091/751-15-35**). Open every day of the year but

Christmas, from 4pm to 2am Sunday to Thursday and to 4am on Friday and Saturday, it offers a small bar area, lots of noisy slot machines, and croupiers at blackjack and roulette tables whose maximum bet cannot exceed 5SF ($2.75).

3 Ascona ⟨★

2½ miles (4km) SW of Locarno, 26 miles (42km) NW of Lugano

Once a tiny fishing port, Ascona has swiftly developed into a resort to rival nearby Locarno. Located snugly on Lake Maggiore, it has long been a popular rendezvous point for painters, writers, and celebrities. Lenin found the place ideal, as did Isadora Duncan and Carl Jung. Rudolf Steiner, Hermann Hesse, and Paul Klee also lived here. Today Ascona is one of the most popular destinations in the Ticino.

New developments have obscured much of the Old Town cherished by these famous people, but the heart of Ascona is still worth exploring—although you'll use up a lot of shoe leather. It has colorful little shops, art galleries (some good, some of the souvenir variety), and antiques stores.

Because of its mild climate, Ascona has subtropical vegetation. Flowers bloom year-round. Facilities include a golf course, a *lido* (beach), and a *Kursaal* (casino).

ESSENTIALS

GETTING THERE   Ascona has no railway station of its own, so most train passengers disembark at nearby Locarno and transfer to a bus or taxi for the short ride to Ascona. Locarno has good connections to the region's major railway junction of Bellinzona, which has frequent express train connections from Milan and Zurich. For **rail information** and schedules, call ℂ **0900/300-300.**

A handful of buses connect Ascona with the railroad junction of Locarno, a short distance to the northeast. The bus ride takes 15 minutes, and departures are every 15 minutes and cost 2.40SF ($1.30) one-way. For bus information, call Locarno's tourist office (see "Essentials," in section 2, earlier).

If you're driving, continue west from Locarno along Route 13.

The best way for many to get around Ascona and the rim of the lake itself is by bike, which can be rented at **Facci Claudio,** via Ascone 12 (ℂ **091/791-13-41**). The cost, depending on the bike, ranges from 17SF to 20SF ($9.35–$11) per day. Hours are Monday to Saturday 8:30am to noon and 2:30 to 6pm, Sunday 8:45 to 11:45am only.

VISITOR INFORMATION   The **Ascona Tourist Board,** in Casa Serondine, piazzetta San Pietro (ℂ **091/791-00-90**), is open Monday to Friday from 9am to noon and 1:30 to 6pm, Saturday from 10am to noon and 1:30 to 4pm.

SEEING THE SIGHTS

Coliegio Pontificio Papio, off via Cappelle, has one of the most beautiful Renaissance courtyards in Switzerland. Dating from 1584, the building has two-story Italianate loggias. The **Chiesa Santa Maria della Misericordia** is part of the cloisters of the Collegio Pontificio Papio. Built at the end of the 14th century, it contains one of the largest late Gothic frescoes in Switzerland.

Casa Serodine (also called Casa Borrani), which lies off piazza G. Motta, was built in 1620 and has one of the most richly embellished facades of any secular structure in the country.

Museo Comunale d'Arte Moderna, via Borgo 34 (ℂ **091/756-31-85**), has both changing exhibitions of modern art and a permanent collection, the latter including works by Klee and Utrillo. It is open March to December Tuesday to

Saturday 10am to noon and 3 to 5pm, Sunday 10am to noon, charging adults 7SF ($3.85); students, seniors, and children 4SF ($2.20).

Near the town, **Isole di Brissago** ⚐, off the shore of Lake Maggiore, contains a botanical garden of Mediterranean and subtropical flora. The gardens can be reached by boat not only from the center of Ascona but also from other lakeside locales, including Locarno. Boats depart Ascona daily at 9:30am and run throughout the day, with the last departure from the island back to Ascona at 5:20pm. The ride takes 10 minutes and costs 22SF ($12.10). Admission to the botanical park is an additional 7SF ($3.85).

You can also visit the little village of **Ronco** ⚐⚐ along the corniche road west, an 11-mile trip. This very Mediterranean-type village is on a slope in one of the most charming settings in all of the Ticino. Erich Maria Remarque, the German author of *All Quiet on the Western Front,* lived here and is buried in the cemetery of the little church.

SHOPPING
Ascona doesn't place much emphasis on the sale of cutesy souvenirs, and as such, you'll have to look hard for shops selling only handicrafts. You'll find postcards and a limited array of smaller, less impressive items imported directly from Italy at newsstands and kiosks in the town's pedestrian zone, which is centered around via Borgo and its offshoots. More prevalent, however, are stylish shops selling luxury goods such as crystal at **Baccarat,** via Orelli (© **091/791-21-38**). For upscale, Milan-inspired clothing for women, the best shop is **Jiuditta,** in the Galleria della Carra (© **091/791-20-19**). More intriguing are any of the town's roster of antiques dealers and art galleries. The town's most appealing antiques store, **Monna Lisa,** via Collegio 6 (© **091/791-45-52**), is managed by Hans-Peter Lehmann and his English/Irish wife, Liz. Inside, you'll find a worthy collection of china, silver, paintings, and furniture. For insights into what painters and sculptors in the Ticino are doing, head for **A.A.A.** (Associazione Artisti Asconese), Carra dei Nasi (© **091/791-11-44**), where exhibitions of works by mostly Ticino-based artists are changed every 4 to 5 weeks. Everything you'll see inside is for sale.

WHERE TO STAY
Bus no. 31 from Locarno services most of the hotels below.

VERY EXPENSIVE
Albergo Casa Berno ⚐⚐ *(Finds* Built into a hillside on a forest road above the town, this deluxe hotel with several balconied wings is a gem of a retreat. Its good-sized rooms are comfortably furnished—some of them with elegant Louis XVI-style chairs. Each room has a concrete balcony with a southern exposure, and all are equipped with beautifully maintained bathrooms. The view extends from Bellinzona (see section 1, earlier in this chapter) to the Islands of Brissago.

Via G. Madonna, CH-6612 Ascona. © 091/791-32-32. Fax 091/792-11-14. www.casaberno.ch. 62 units. 408SF–480SF ($224.40–$264) double, 540SF ($297) junior suite. Rates include half board. AE, DC. MC. V. Free parking. Closed late Oct to Feb. **Amenities:** Restaurant, bar; pool; sauna; room service; massage; babysitting; laundry. *In room:* TV, minibar, hair dryer.

Castello del Sole ⚐⚐⚐ The grandest hotel in Ascona is surrounded by a large park and green meadows. This peaceful haven is near the Maggia River, at the point where it flows into Lake Maggiore. It has the atmosphere of a private estate, 1½ miles (2km) from the center of town. There's an antique palazzo, with many courtyards. The spacious public rooms have vaulted ceilings, granite columns, and marble terraces. The rooms, which come in various shapes and sizes, have balconies and beautiful furniture, along with deluxe bathrooms. The suites are in a building east of the main hotel. Located nearby is the 18-hole golf course Locarno.

Via Muraccio 142, CH-6612 Ascona. (C) **091/791-02-02.** Fax 091/792-11-18. www.castellodelsole.com. 98 units. 510SF–640SF ($280.50–$352) double; 880SF ($484) junior suite; 1,300SF ($715) deluxe suite. Rates include continental breakfast. Half board 40SF ($22) per person extra. AE, DC, MC, V. Free parking. **Amenities:** 2 restaurants; 2 pools; golf course nearby; 7 tennis courts; fitness center; sauna; salon; room service; massage; laundry. *In room:* TV, minibar, hair dryer, safe.

Hotel Ascolago 🛫 This is a large concrete-block hotel with an angular facade and a roofline inspired by a Chinese pagoda. It's ideally located in the center of town, in a park with flowers and sculpture. A portico by the entrance looks as if it was designed by Le Corbusier. Many of the spacious bedrooms have been upgraded and are fairly stylish, decorated with subtle pastels and rosewood pieces, while others linger in the stuffy, fussy mode. Each room, however, is comfortable, with rows of awning-shaded balconies opening onto views of the garden and the lake.

Via Albarelle, CH-6612 Ascona. (C) **091/791-20-55.** Fax 091/791-42-26. 17 units. 420SF–460SF ($231–$253) double. Rates include half board. MC, V. Free parking. Closed Nov 15–Dec 15. Bus: 31 from Locarno. **Amenities:** Restaurant, bar; 2 pools; sauna; sailing school; windsurfing equipment; room service; laundry service. *In room:* TV, minibar, hair dryer.

Relais & Château Hotel Giardino 🛫🛫🛫 Although this atmospheric Mediterranean villa is one of four government-rated five-star hotels in Ascona, it's the most romantically appealing. Set about a quarter of a mile from the heart of town, connected by an antique shuttle bus that makes hourly runs back and forth, this glamorous, Mediterranean-styled villa was built on a large plot of land in 1986. Today, its structure incorporates Portuguese and Italian tilework, Veronese marble, antique Swiss panels imported from very old *weinstubes* in Zurich, and some of the most sophisticated interior decor in the region. The spacious bedrooms are cozy and plushly accessorized. Most alluring of all is the lavish garden (*il giardino*), whose illuminated lily pond is covered with a moveable stage for the entertainment, which is sometimes provided after 8pm.

Via Segnale 10, CH-6612 Ascona. (C) **091/791-01-01.** Fax 091/792-10-94. www.giardino.ch. 72 units. 690SF–730SF ($379.50–$401.50) double; 610SF ($335.50) double with 3-night minimum stay; 910SF–950SF ($500.50–$522.50) suite. Rates include half board. AE, DC, MC, V. Free parking. Closed Nov 2–Mar 13. **Amenities:** 2 restaurants, bar; pool; tennis courts; health club and spa with Jacuzzi, sauna, steam bath; room service; babysitting; laundry. *In room:* TV, minibar, hair dryer, safe.

EXPENSIVE

Hotel Acapulco au Lac 🛫 This hotel may not win any architectural prizes, but its location is winning, standing on a terrace hewn out of the cliffs. Unlike most other hotels at the resort, there's no road separating this establishment from the waters of the lake. You park your car on the roof before heading down to the reception area. The rooms on the south side contain a balcony opening onto a view of the lake. The furnishings are comfortable and cozy in the rather small rooms, which are each equipped with a bathroom with private shower (some with tubs as well). Behind the hotel are many hiking paths.

Via Cantonale, Porto Ronco, CH-6612 Ascona. (C) **091/791-45-21.** Fax 091/792-19-51. acapulco@niko.ch. 45 units. 214SF–320SF ($117.70–$176) double; 400SF ($220) suite. Rates include buffet breakfast. Half board 38SF ($20.90) per person extra. AE, DC, MC, V. Free parking. Closed Nov 3–Mar 8. Bus: 21 to Porto Ronco. **Amenities:** Restaurant, bar; pool; room service; laundry. *In room:* TV, minibar, hair dryer.

Hotel Sasso Boretto ⚘   The entire balconied structure of this hotel seems to be set on top of concrete columns. Glass windows frame the ground floor, which is surrounded by redbrick terraces and Mediterranean trees. Most of the bedrooms are decorated in warm, monochromatic tones of brown and beige. The larger ones show Italian flair; the smaller ones are less dramatic but cozy and comfortable nonetheless, with well-maintained bathrooms.

Via Locarno 45, CH-6612 Ascona. ✆ 091/791-71-15. Fax 091/786-99-00. 50 units. 340SF ($187) double. Rates include continental breakfast. Half board 40SF ($22) per person extra. AE, DC, MC, V. Parking 15SF ($8.25). Closed Jan 5–Mar 19. Bus: 31 from Locarno. **Amenities:** 2 restaurants, bar; pool; health club; sauna; room service; laundry. *In room:* TV, minibar, hair dryer.

Seeschloss-Castello ⚘⚘ *(Finds*   This gem will appeal to romantics. The tower was built in 1250 by a countess of Milan from the Ghiriglioni family. It served as the fortified dwelling of the family, which eventually controlled most of the navigation on the lake. Today palms and palmettos surround the flagstone terrace leading to the stone entryway. Pull the wrought-iron bell handle for assistance. The lobby is filled with antiques, and the spacious rooms are well maintained and comfortable, with private bathrooms with shower or else combination tub and shower. The best rooms, certainly the most romantic, are those in the tower. These are ideal for both honeymooners and off-the-record weekenders.

Piazza G. Motta, CH-6612 Ascona. ✆ **091/791-01-61.** Fax 091/791-18-04. www.castello-seeschloss.ch. 46 units. 308SF–388SF ($169.40–$213.40) double; 528SF ($290.40) double in the tower. Rates include buffet breakfast. Half board 38SF ($20.90) per person extra. AE, DC, MC, V. Free parking outdoors, 18SF ($9.90) in garage. Closed Nov to mid-Mar. Bus: 31 from Locarno. **Amenities:** Restaurant, bar; pool; room service; laundry. *In room:* TV, minibar, hair dryer.

MODERATE

Albergo Elvezia au Lac   This hotel lies in the heart of the resort town with a cobblestone terrace facing the lake and an indoor dining room just behind it. The upper-story terrace is ringed with vines. Each room, ranging from small to medium, is priced according to its panorama over the lake and whether it has a balcony or terrace looking inward to the city. All units come with a private bathroom with shower, some containing tub baths as well.

Piazza G. Motta 15, CH-6612 Ascona. ✆ **091/791-15-14.** Fax 091/791-00-03. 20 units. 226SF–255SF ($124.30–$140.25) double. Rates include continental breakfast. AE, DC, MC, V. Parking 20SF ($11). Closed Nov–Mar. Bus: 31 from Locarno. **Amenities:** Restaurant; limited room service; laundry. *In room:* TV, minibar.

Tamaro du Lac ⚘ *(Finds*   A welcome is painted in Latin above the huge arch leading into the flagstone reception hall of the original core of this gracious lakefront hotel, which was formerly an abbey. Farther on is a sky-lit central courtyard, with vines growing over the massive vaults of the arcade surrounding it. In the early 1990s, a comfortable, very quiet annex was added a few steps from the main building. The owners have decorated the interior with antiques and some romantic artifacts. The bedrooms, although lacking great style, are comfortably furnished and extremely well maintained, each with a private shower (some with tubs).

Piazza G. Motta 35, CH-6612 Ascona. ✆ 091/785-48-48. Fax 091/791-29-28. www.hotel-tamaro.ch. 51 units, 41 with bathroom, in main building; 10 units all with bathroom, in annex. 220SF–280SF ($121–$154) double with bathroom, 130SF–150SF ($71.50–$82.50) double without bathroom. Rates include breakfast. Half board 30SF ($16.50) per person extra. AE, DC, MC, V. Parking 12SF ($6.60) in private garage, 8SF ($4.40) in private parking outside. Closed Nov 15–Mar. Bus: 31 from Locarno. **Amenities:** Restaurant; limited room service; laundry service. *In room:* TV (in some). No phone in some.

INEXPENSIVE

Hotel la Perla   This white-walled hotel is located in a residential area away from the lake. Its small rooms have balconies with a good view of the mountains, and each comes with private bathroom. Note that there are three extra double rooms separated from the hotel with private bathrooms, but without balconies, costing 150SF to 180SF ($82.50–$99).

Via Collina 14, CH-6612 Ascona. ℂ 091/791-35-77. Fax 091/791-79-62. www.castelgate.net/la perla. 38 units. 220SF ($121) double. Rates include buffet breakfast. AE, DC, MC, V. Parking 7SF ($3.85). Bus: 31 from Locarno. Amenities: Restaurant; pool; limited room service; laundry. In room: TV, minibar.

WHERE TO DINE

The harbor of Ascona is lined with many restaurants. Most guests dine outside during the summer, by the lake. There are also many fine restaurants on the cobblestone streets of the Old Town.

EXPENSIVE

Aphrodite/Hostaria Giardino ★★★ FRENCH/ITALIAN These two restaurants are in the most desirable deluxe hotel in Ascona, about a quarter of a mile from the center of town. Aphrodite, the more elegant and formal, requests that men wear jackets and ties for meals served on a flowering terrace within view of a water garden and plenty of greenery. Menu specialties change every week but include perfectly prepared modern choices, such as tartare of salmon with caviar cream, filet of duckling with port sauce and dried figs, and pasta dishes such as triangolo pasta stuffed with minced lamb. The chef prepares 16 different fixed-price menus whose composition changes daily, based on the seasonal ingredients available.

The Hostaria Giardino is in a cozy environment reminiscent of a mountain hideaway, with old-fashioned menu items similar to what your Italian-Swiss grandmother might have prepared for you when you were a child. Portions are copious.

In the Relais & Châteaux Hotel Giardino, via Segnale. ℂ 091/791-01-01. Reservations recommended. Aphrodite, main courses 35SF–55SF ($19.25–$30.25); fixed-price menu (only on Sun) 145SF ($79.75). Hostaria Giardino, main courses 25SF–35SF ($13.75–$19.25). AE, DC, MC, V. Aphrodite, daily 12:30–2pm and 7–9:30pm. Hostaria Giardino, Wed–Sun 7–11pm. Closed Nov 13–Mar 10.

MODERATE

Al Pontile ITALIAN/FRENCH Many of the restaurants along the quays look alike and have similar menus, but the decor here, with a darkly rustic interior and hanging straw lamps, seems a little warmer and more intimate than elsewhere. The food is better too. The menu might include quail with risotto, osso buco, and *saltimbocca* (veal with ham), in addition to a variety of good pasta dishes. Fish dishes include scampi, sole, and salmon. For dessert, we recommend one of the homemade pies.

Longalago G. Motta 31. ℂ 091/791-46-04. Reservations required. Main courses 35SF–45SF ($19.25–$24.75); meat fixed-price menu 72SF–79SF ($39.60–$43.45); fish fixed-price menu 62SF–68SF ($34.10–$37.40). AE, MC, V. Daily 11:30am–2:30pm and 6–9pm (Jan–Mar closed Mon).

Al Torchio ITALIAN The first room of this rambling restaurant offers a rustic decor, red candles, and designs painted on the plaster walls. On a warm night you might continue past the American-style salad bar in the back and turn left into the vine-covered courtyard. The well-prepared menu might include calves' liver Venetian style, filet of lamb, a divine risotto with porcini mushrooms, a winter fondue, and a succulent spaghetti with clams. An especially delectable dish is homemade tagliolini stuffed with pulverized fish and shrimp and served with a tomato sauce flavored with olive oil and fresh herbs. For dessert, try the *gelato misto* (a mixed selection of ice cream) or a sorbet with vodka. There's a garden-style piano bar in a summery courtyard.

Contrada Maggiore 1. ✆ **091/791-71-26.** Reservations recommended. Main courses 18SF–38SF ($9.90–$20.90); fixed-price menu 30SF–52SF ($16.50–$28.60). AE, MC, V. Daily noon–2pm and 6–10pm. Winter closed Tues.

Ristorante Borromeo ✦ SWISS/ITALIAN Dating from around 1350, this former monastery and Catholic school is one of the most popular restaurants in the region, noted for its outdoor terrace. Local residents flock to its three rustic rooms with high ceilings. The kitchen staff is versatile, knowing how to prepare the best of both the Italian and Swiss kitchens. They use very fresh ingredients and don't oversauce. The menu might include risotto Milanese with saffron, a mixed grill, piccata marsala, trout, scampi, and an especially good osso buco. On our recent rounds, we especially enjoyed *saltimbocca* (veal with ham), served with a potato-based gnocchi.

Via Collegio 16. ✆ **091/791-92-81.** Reservations recommended. Main courses 24SF–45SF ($13.20–$24.75); fixed-price lunch 25SF ($13.75). AE, DC, MC, V. Daily noon–2pm and 6–10pm. Closed Mon–Tues Nov to mid-Mar.

INEXPENSIVE

Osteria Nostrana *Value* PIZZA/PASTA This is one of the most active harborfront restaurants in Ascona, with sidewalk tables overlooking the lake and its fashionable promenade. The rustically comfortable dining room serves the town's best and most reasonably priced pastas and pizzas. They also feature daily specials, sometimes as many as 15 per day, depending on the season and what's good at the market. The best pasta is the spaghetti *alla carbonara* (with meat sauce), although the linguine *ai fruitti di mare* (with shellfish) is a close runner-up, as is the fusili with heavy cream and ham. For a superb pizza, opt for the Siciliana with anchovies and black olives or the *prosciutto e funghi* (ham and mushrooms).

Lungolago G. Motta. ✆ **091/791-51-58.** Reservations not necessary. Pasta and pizzas 14SF–22SF ($7.70–$12.10). AE, DC, MC, V. Summer daily 9am–1am. Winter daily 10am–11:30pm. Bus: 31 from Locarno.

ASCONA AFTER DARK

Ascona is quiet and calm, with not nearly as energetic a night scene as, say, nearby Lugano. Despite that, discos that will happily invite you in include the **Al Lago,** via Moscia 2 (✆ **091/791-06-03**). Set beside the lake, and catering to a crowd that includes usually friendly folks up to the age of 50, it's open only on Friday and Saturday nights beginning at 11pm, and charges 12SF ($6.60) for entrance and the first drink. Its newer competitor is **Disco Memphis,** Ascona, via Lido (✆ **091/792-24-75**), a high-energy, high-profile site where the music is hot and the room temperature is even hotter. It functions as a conventional bar Sunday to Thursday and as a disco/dance hall every Friday and Saturday beginning at 10:30pm. Entrance is usually free; the first drink is 6SF ($3.30). A likable bar favored by those seeking live music is **Lello Bar,** via Aerodromo 3 (✆ **091/791-13-74**). Finally, an establishment noted for its ability to provide feminine companionship for unaccompanied men is **Happyville,** contrada Fontanelli (✆ **091/791-49-22**), where a tiny dance floor is a lot less important than the seductively lit stage. Strip shows are usually presented nightly beginning around 11:30pm.

4 Lugano ✦✦✦

20 miles (32km) S of Bellinzona, 143 miles (229km) S of Zurich

Lugano is a Swiss town with an Italian flavor. The Italian influence is evident in the city's cafes, sunny piazzas, cobblestone streets, and arcades. It's a city designed for walking. You can wander at leisure, exploring its historic old streets.

Lugano is built along the shore of **Lake Lugano** ✸✸✸, which the Italians call Lake Ceresio. The peaks of San Salvatore and Monte Brè loom on opposite sides of town. The low mountains protect it from cold alpine winds, and the climate is ideal from March to November. As the cultural center of the Ticino, Lugano has attracted many artists and casual visitors.

ESSENTIALS

GETTING THERE   The airline **Crossair,** Aeroporto Lugano (℡ **091/ 610-12-12**), provides air links between Lugano and several major cities in Switzerland (Zurich, Bern, Basel, Geneva), in Italy (Rome, Florence, Venice), and in France (Paris, Nice). Taxis await visitors at the Lugano airport for the 10-minute ride to the center of Lugano.

Lugano is a major stop along the rail lines that connect Milan with Zurich. As such, trains from all parts of Switzerland arrive throughout the day and night. For **rail information** and schedules, call ℡ **0900/300-300** or call the Lugano rail station at ℡ **091/923-66-91.** Rail passengers arrive at the Lugano railroad station, piazzale della Stazione, which is in the center of the city, west of piazza Indipendenza. If your luggage is light, you can walk to many of the hotels; if not, you can take one of the taxis waiting outside the station.

Lugano is linked by bus to dozens of hamlets in the Ticino that lack rail connections. There are also long-range buses that come from Italian cities: Como (trip time: 30 min.), Venice (trip time: 5 hr.), and Milan (trip time: 90 min.). From the rest of Switzerland, however, most visitors arrive by train.

If you're driving, pass through the St. Gotthard Tunnel and continue south along N2, via Bellinzona, all the way to Lugano.

GETTING AROUND   An explanation of fares and ticket machines can be found in a brochure distributed by the tourist office and the Public Transport Board, **Azienda Comunale dei Trasporti,** via Carducci (℡ **091/800-71-11**).

You must purchase a ticket before boarding a **bus** or a **train.** If you're caught without one, you may have to pay a 55SF ($30.25) fine. You can purchase a 1-day ticket from automatic ticket machines for 5.50SF ($3.05). This ticket allows you unlimited travel for 24 hours from the moment you purchase it. It includes the Funicular Lugano-Main Street SBBM, but not line 12, Lugano-Brè.

For **taxi service** call ℡ **091/922-88-33.**

The town of Lugano and the lakefront itself are ideal for **bikers.** You can rent a bike at the railway station in Lugano (℡ **091/923-66-91**), at ticket window no. 1. Prices begin at 27SF ($14.85) per day, depending on the type of bicycle.

VISITOR INFORMATION   The **Lugano Tourist Office** is at riva Albertolli 5 (℡ **091/921-46-64**), open Monday to Friday from 9am to 6:30pm, Saturday from 9am to 12:30pm and from 1:30 to 5pm, and Sunday from 10am to 2pm.

CITY LAYOUT   The center of town is **piazza Riforma,** dominated by a neo-classical city hall constructed in 1844. From here you can explore the ancient streets of the Old Town on foot.

Lugano is built along several lakeside quays, of which **riva Albertolli, riva Vincenzo Vela,** and **riva Antonio Caccia** are the most important. They are ideal for long, leisurely walks. They run from piazza Cassarate to piazza Paradiso.

Other major squares of Lugano, also by the lake, are **piazza Riziero Rezzonico** and **piazza Alessandro Manzioni,** the latter with gardens.

The biggest park of Lugano, also opening onto the lake, is the **Parco Civico,** site of the Casino, the Palazzo dei Congressi, and the town's large swimming pool.

Directly east of the center is **Castagnola,** a suburb and site of the Villa Favorita, with its celebrated collection of art.

Towering over Lugano are two hills, **Monte San Salvatore,** at 2,992 feet (898m), and **Monte Brè,** at 3,061 feet (918m). They're ideal for full- or half-day excursions.

SEEING THE SIGHTS

The city tourist office (see "Essentials," above) offers a **walking tour** with a guide on Tuesday at 9:30am, April to October. These free tours depart from the Chiesa degli Angioli at piazza Luini, but confirm details with the tourist office on Monday the day before the tour.

IN TOWN

Parco Civico ✿✿ is the city park along Lake Lugano. It contains the Palazzo dei Congressi (the convention center), the Casino, and the Villa Ciani art museum. Outdoor concerts are presented in the summer.

Cattedrale di San Lorenzo (St. Lawrence), via Cattedrale, in the Old Town, was originally a Romanesque church. It was reconstructed in the 13th and 14th centuries and overhauled in the 17th and 18th centuries. It has three outstanding Renaissance doorways and a baroque interior. Look for the 16th-century tabernacle at the end of the south aisle; it was designed by the Rodari brothers of Maroggia.

The other important church is the **Chiesa di Santa Maria degli Angeli** (Church of St. Mary of the Angels), piazza Luini, located on the south side of the resort. This church was built at the end of the 15th century and is known throughout the Ticino for its **frescoes** ✿✿ by Bernardino Luini, the Lombard painter. His huge fresco *The Crucifixion* dates from 1529. Many critics have compared the beauty of his work to that of Leonardo da Vinci. John Ruskin found an "unstudied sweetness" in Luini's work. The church was occupied by Franciscans until 1848.

NEARBY ATTRACTIONS

The best way to discover the small lakeside villages around Lugano is to rent a bike at the train station (see above) and set off to explore. Arm yourself with a good map from the tourist office and head for the **nature reserve** of Origlio Lake, proceeding to Ponte Capriasca, where you can visit a **parish church** with a copy of Leonardo da Vinci's *Last Supper.* From here you can continue to the villages of **Tesserete** and **Colla** along the left valley side of Cassarate, going through the woods with a marked trail to **Sonvico.** On your way back to Lugano you'll pass through the idyllic villages of **Dino, Ponte di Valle,** and finally Lugano. In all, the trip takes in about 23 miles (37km) and can be done in about 4 hours.

Swiss Miniature Village *Kids*   Small replicas of the major buildings in Switzerland are displayed along a labyrinth of asphalt paths. There's also a miniature of the twin castles in Sion. You can purchase an official guidebook for detailed explanations. This attraction is especially popular with children.

Via Cantonale, Melide-Lugano. ℂ **091/640-10-60.** Admission 12SF ($6.60) adults, 7SF ($3.85) children 15 and under. Daily 9am–6pm. Closed Nov to mid-Mar. Take a train from Lugano Village.

Fondazione Thyssen-Bornemisza (Villa Favorita) ✿✿   This 17th-century building once contained one of the world's greatest private art collections. The collection belongs to Baron Hans Heinrich Thyssen-Bornemisza, who made world headlines when he sold his stunning collection of old masters to the Prado in Madrid for $350 million. In this luxuriously furnished villa, a significant collection of "leftover" art was left behind in Switzerland to delight visitors, including 19th- and 20th-century European and American paintings and water-colors by artists such as Bierstadt, Church, Homer, Whitteredge, Chasnick, Ernst, Hopper, Marin, Molde, Pollock, Rozanoa, and Wyeth. Recently several masterpieces from German expressionism—works by Heckel and Kirchner—and some 19th-century American paintings, notably works by Moran and Bierstadt, have been integrated into the permanent collection. But to see the astonishing collection of Dürers, van Goghs, Rembrandts, and other old masters that used to hang here, you'll have to fly to Madrid. Castagnola lies to the east of Lugano.

In addition to regular hours, the villa hosts one or two temporary exhibitions a year, when it's open Tuesday to Sunday at the same hours.

Viale Castagnola. ℂ 091/972-17-41. Admission 10SF ($5.50) adults, 6SF ($3.30) children. Fri–Sun 10am–5pm. Closed Nov–Mar. Bus: 1.

Villa Heleneum   Lying 2½ miles (4km) northwest of Lugano, this landmark building is along the much-frequented walk to Gandria. It contains the Museum of Extra-European Cultures, which exhibits objects from Oceania, Indonesia, and Africa. The collection was donated by Serge Brignoni, an exponent of the surrealist movement. There's also a center for ethnographic studies, as well as a library annexed to the museum.

Via Cortivo 24, Lugano-Castagnola. ℂ 091/971-73-53. Admission 7SF ($3.85) adults, 4SF ($2.20) children. Wed–Sun 10am–5pm. Bus: 1.

THE ACTIVE VACATION PLANNER

Water sports are popular in Lugano; you can also bike or play golf and tennis.

BOATING   You can rent rowboats and motorboats along the lakefront.

SAILING   Go to **Circolo Velico,** Lago di Lugano, Foce Cassarate (ℂ 091/972-62-98), which charges 35SF to 50SF ($19.25–$27.50) per hour or 50SF to 100SF ($27.50–$55) for a day, depending on the size of the boat.

SCUBA   Try **Lugano-Sub,** G. Bucher, corso Elvezia 3 (ℂ 091/994-37-40).

SWIMMING   The **Lido** (ℂ 091/971-40-41) is a sandy stretch of beach along the lake. You can also relax on the lawn or eat at the cafeteria on the ter-race. Admission to the Lido is 7SF ($3.85) for adults, 5SF ($2.75) for children 6 to 14, and 1SF (55¢) for children under 6. Rental of a cabana costs another 6SF ($3.30). The beach is open in the summer daily from 9am to 7:30pm.

In addition, many hotels have heated pools, some with salt water.

WATERSKIING   The **Club Nautico-Lugano,** via Calloni 9 (ℂ 091/649-61-39), between Lugano and Melide, charges 150SF ($82.50) per hour, instruction included.

WINDSURFING   You can windsurf on the lake at **Club Nautico-Lugano,** via Calloni 9 (ℂ 091/649-61-39), between Lugano and Melide. The cost is 17SF ($9.35) per hour.

SHOPPING

Its role as capital of Italian-speaking Switzerland almost guarantees that Lugano's selection of merchandise will include a cosmopolitan blend of Teutonic and Mediterranean merchandise. Most of it can be viewed along either side of the resort's main shopping street, **via Nassa.** The richest trove of handicrafts is avail-able at **Bottega dell'Artigiano,** via Canova 18 (ℂ 091/922-81-40). Managed and maintained by the Cooperativa per l'Artigianato Ticinese, a quasi-governmental organization for the promotion of old-fashioned handicrafts, it offers textiles, wood carvings, pottery, and metalware, most of them made in the Ticino. The largest branch of the most interesting toy store in Switzerland, **Franz Carl Weber,** is at via Nassa 5 (✆ **091/923-53-21**). Here, all sorts of low-tech and high-tech toys (with the notable exception of war toys and toy guns, which the chain does not stock) are designed to appeal to children, teenagers, and in some cases, adults.

You'll find five floors of department-store shopping at everybody's favorite large store, **Innovazione,** piazza Dante (✆ **091/912-71-71**). A roughly equivalent department store, with some gift items and more of an emphasis on food-stuffs, groceries, hardware, and housewares, is **Migros,** via Pretorio 15 (✆ **091/923-58-21**). If you're looking for chocolates and pastries, head for a bakery that many locals remember from their childhood, **Münger,** via Luvini 4 (✆ **091/985-69-43**).

WHERE TO STAY

Lugano has hotels in all price categories. Many are located in the suburbs of Paradiso, Cassarate, and Castagnola.

VERY EXPENSIVE

Hotel Splendide Royal ✮✮✮ The splendor of the 19th century is evident in the elegant architecture of this mansard-roofed hotel. Built in 1888, the Splendide Royal has welcomed many famous people (and even a few infamous ones). Maria, queen of Romania; Vittorio Emanuele di Savoia; George Bush Sr.; and Sophia Loren have stayed here. The public rooms are decorated with columns, crystal-and-gilt chandeliers, Venetian furniture, and Oriental rugs. Guests have a choice of bedrooms, either in the flowery rooms of the original landmark wing, where some rooms contain ceiling frescoes, or in the 1983 modern wing, where the decoration is in soft colors and the furnishings in a stream-lined beech. The swimming pool is shaped like an oyster, and there's a rock garden.

Riva A. Caccia 7, CH-6900 Lugano. ✆ **091/985-77-11.** Fax 091/985-77-22. www.splendide.ch. 100 units. Mar 15–Oct, 520SF–650SF ($286–$357.50) double; from 1,300SF ($715) suite. Nov–Mar 14, 420SF–480SF ($231–$264) double; from 950SF ($522.50) suite. Rates include continental breakfast. Half board 70SF ($38.50) per person extra. AE, DC, MC, V. Free parking outdoors, 30SF ($16.50) in garage. Bus: 1 or 9. **Amenities:** Restaurant, bar; pool; sauna; room service; massage; babysitting; laundry/dry cleaning. *In room:* TV, mini-bar, hair dryer, safe.

Príncipe Leopoldo & Residence ✮✮✮ This extravagant mansion lies on a panoramic hill site, Collina d'Oro (Golden Hill), in an exclusive neighborhood overlooking the lake. The villa was built in 1868 as the home of Prince Leopold, of Austria's von Hohenzollerns. After World War I it was sold to a Swiss indus-trialist. In 1986 the villa was transformed into the Ticino's smallest luxury hotel, with an understated Italian style. Today it's our favorite hotel in Lugano. There's a modern addition with a two-story atrium and a cascade of illuminated water. The suites have beige travertine trim, and each spacious room has a terrace over-looking the lake and the suburb of Paradiso. The hotel has more amenities and services than any other in the Ticino, including deluxe toiletries, well-lit vanity mirrors, pressing facilities, even complimentary shoe shines. The hotel restau-rant is one of the finest and most elegant in the Ticino (see below).

Via Montalbano 5, CH-6900 Lugano. ✆ **091/985-88-55.** Fax 091/985-88-25. www.leopoldo.ch. 70 units. 380SF–760SF ($209–$418) double; from 900SF ($495) suite. Rates include buffet breakfast. AE, DC, MC, V.

Parking 20SF ($11). **Amenities:** 2 restaurants, bar; pool; fitness center; Jacuzzi; sauna; business center; minibus transportation, including airport pickups; room service; massage; babysitting; laundry/dry cleaning. *In room:* A/C, TV, minibar, hair dryer, safe.

EXPENSIVE

Grand Hotel Eden ★★   Among the finest hotels in Lugano, the Eden is large and contemporary, with balconies overlooking the lake. Rated five stars by the government, it has a sun terrace built over the lake, with cafe tables and chaise lounges. Guests have a choice of lodging in two buildings; the main building directly on the lake contains more spacious and better appointed accommodations and is naturally more expensive. There is also a quite good annex with comfortable rooms lacking panoramic lakeside vistas. Each unit contains a luxurious, spacious bathroom.

Riva Paradiso 1, CH-6900 Lugano-Paradiso. ℂ **091/993-01-21.** Fax 091/985-92-50. www.grandhoteleden.ch. 120 units. Main building 396SF–440SF ($217.80–$242), from 1,200SF ($660) suite. Annex 540SF ($297) double, from 1,000SF ($550) suite. Rates include buffet breakfast. Half board 58SF ($31.90) per person extra. AE, DC, MC, V. Parking 18SF ($9.90). Bus: 1, 2, or 9. **Amenities:** 2 restaurants, bar; 2 pools; room service; babysitting; laundry. *In room:* A/C, TV, minibar, hair dryer, safe.

Grand Hotel Villa Castagnola au Lac ★★★   The beauty of this ocher, Mediterranean-style villa across the street from the lake is enhanced by its exotic trees and plants—even banana trees, no less. The public rooms contain marble or parquet floors; some have large fireplaces in consonance with their baronial decor. Each spacious bedroom is uniquely and luxuriously furnished, decorated tastefully in Mediterranean styling. The manager has instructed his staff to pay attention to even the smallest detail to make guests feel at home. All rooms open onto views of the lake and the subtropical park, and all but eight contain a splendid bathroom with tub and shower (the rest with shower).

Viale Castagnola 31, CH-6906 Cassarate. ℂ **091/973-25-55.** Fax 091/973-25-50. www.slh.com/villcast. 93 units. 420SF–500SF ($231–$275) double; from 630SF ($346.50) suite. Rates include buffet breakfast. Half board 60SF ($33) per person extra. AE, DC, MC, V. Free parking outdoors, 10SF ($5.50) in garage. Bus: 1. **Amenities:** Restaurant, bar; pool; indoor golf; 2 tennis courts; fitness center and spa with sauna and Turkish bath; water sports rentals; salon; room service; massage; laundry. *In room:* TV, fridge, hair dryer, safe.

Romantik Hotel Ticino ★★ *Finds*   The central courtyard of this former 15th-century convent is covered with a glass ceiling for year-round comfort. In front of the narrow hotel is one of the most charming squares in the Old Town. Antique cupboards and chests are in the stairwell. Each of the small bedrooms is uniquely furnished, usually with 19th-century provincial pieces. They are exceedingly comfortable with well-maintained plumbing.

Piazza Cioccaro 1, CH-6901 Lugano. ℂ **091/922-77-72.** Fax 091/923-62-78. www.romantic-hotels.com. 18 units. 440SF–480SF ($242–$264) double; 680SF ($374) suite. Rates include buffet breakfast. AE, DC, MC, V. Parking 25SF ($13.75). Bus: 1 or 2. **Amenities:** Restaurant, bar; health club; room service; laundry. *In room:* A/C (in half), TV (on request), minibar, hair dryer.

MODERATE

Holiday Inn Lugano Center   This first-class chain hotel was built in 1975 out of concrete and glass and is today one of the finest hotels on the outskirts of Lugano. The seven-story high-rise is near the Lugano–Sud exit from the main highway. Many of the public rooms have red leather accents and wood trim. The show-place salon has French-style armchairs, Oriental rugs, and large windows with a view of the garden. The bedrooms are quite comfortable and well equipped.

Via Geretta 15, CH-6902 Lugano-Paradiso. ℂ **091/986-38-38.** Fax 091/986-38-39. holidayinn@bluewin.ch. 92 units. 280SF–300SF ($154–$165) double; from 320SF ($176) suite. Half board 45SF ($24.75) per person extra. AE, DC, MC, V. Free parking outdoors, 13SF ($7.15) in garage. Bus: 1 or 9. **Amenities:** Restaurant, bar; 2 pools; health club; 2 saunas; room service; laundry. *In room:* A/C, TV, fridge, minibar, hair dryer, safe, trouser press.

Hotel du Lac *Value* Architecturally bandboxy and lacking style, this hotel nonetheless offers much comfort and good value. Owned by the Kneschaurek family since 1920, it was reconstructed in the early 1960s. Renovated and improved over the years, it enjoys a lakefront location with its own private swimming area in front. All the mid-sized to spacious bedrooms have been updated with the installation of improved plumbing with combination tub and shower bathrooms. All open onto lakeside vistas; the most desirable accommodations—and the most tranquil—are on the sixth floor.

Riva Paradiso 3, CH-6902 Lugano-Paradiso. (C) 091/994-19-21. Fax 091/994-11-22. www.dulac.ch. 53 units. 336SF–370SF ($184.80–$203.50) double, 550SF ($302.50) suite. Rates include buffet breakfast. AE, DC, MC, V. Parking 10SF ($5.50). **Amenities:** Restaurant; pool; exercise room; Jacuzzi; sauna; room service; babysitting; laundry. *In room:* TV, minibar, hair dryer, safe.

INEXPENSIVE

Albergo Domus Garni This redbrick building with balconies is on the main road from Lugano to Paradiso, about a mile from the center of Lugano. The attractive and spacious interior is decorated with potted palms and Oriental rugs. The uncluttered bedrooms have large windows and a lighthearted, southern decor, with an equal mixture of private showers or combination tub and shower bathrooms.

Riva Paradiso 24A, CH-6902 Lugano-Paradiso. (C) 091/994-34-21. Fax 091/993-02-69. www.hoteldomus.ch. 30 units, 24 with bathroom. 110SF ($60.50) double without bathroom; 150SF–170SF ($82.50–$93.50) double with bathroom. Rates include buffet breakfast. AE, DC, MC, V. Free parking outdoors, 15SF ($8.25) in garage. Closed Dec–Feb. Bus: 9. *In room:* TV, minibar, hair dryer (on request), safe.

Carlton Hotel Villa Moritz ★★ *Finds* Peace and quiet are assured at this hotel, as it's located in a park a good distance from the main road. The Wernli–Sigrist family manages several 19th-century buildings clustered near a swimming pool surrounded by flagstones. The hotel also benefits from being on the sunny side of Mount Brè. The bedrooms are comfortably furnished with traditional styling. The public rooms are modern, with stone accents around the bar. Public buses transport guests to the center of Lugano in 10 minutes.

Via Cortivo 9, CH-6976 Lugano-Catagnola. (C) 091/971-38-12. Fax 091/971-38-14. www.carlton-villa-moritz.ch. 55 units. 190SF–208SF ($104.50–$114.40) double. Rates include buffet breakfast. AE, MC, V. Parking 11SF ($6.05). Closed from the end of Oct to Mar 23. Bus: 1. **Amenities:** Restaurant, bar; pool; room service; laundry. *In room:* TV.

Hotel Marina *Value* This is a government-rated three-star hotel with a flat roof and symmetrical rows of concrete balconies. The entrance hall is attractively austere, with a marble floor. The public rooms have pastel colors, tile floors, and flowered curtains. The congenial Schreiber family offers good bedrooms with large windows, wooden furniture, and comfortable beds, plus homey knick-knacks. Each unit comes with a private bathroom with shower, although some also contain tubs. It's good value all around.

Via Generale Arcioni 20, CH-6900 Lugano-Cassarete. (C) 091/971-45-12. Fax 091/970-26-19. 30 units. 130SF–145SF ($71.50–$79.75) double. Rates include buffet breakfast. AE, DC, MC, V. Bus: 2. Parking 10SF ($5.50). *In room:* TV, minibar.

Post Hotel Simplon The Post Hotel Simplon is located in the outlying suburbs of Lugano-Paradiso. In the 1990s it was renovated and became more expensive as a government-rated three-star hotel. Rooms range from small to medium in size, and they are functionally furnished, with tiled shower bathrooms (some with tubs). Breakfast is the only meal served at the hotel.

Via Generale Guisan 12, CH-6902 Lugano-Paradiso. © 091/994-44-41. Fax 091/994-12-21. 29 units. 150SF–170SF ($82.50–$93.50) double. Rates include buffet breakfast. AE, DC, MC, V. Free parking. Closed Oct 15–Mar. In room: TV, hair dryer.

WHERE TO DINE
EXPENSIVE

Principe Leopoldo ★★★ INTERNATIONAL Excellent regional and international cuisine are combined with a luxury setting in three rooms to make award-winning meals. The chef creates memorable dishes here, especially his divine risottos, one made with Gorgonzola and pears, another a green risotto with lobster and fresh herbs. The chef will dazzle you with his steamed sea bass filet with fresh tomatoes or his roasted turbot with Mediterranean "perfumes." We were also dazzled with his *saltimbocca* of rabbit with fresh mushrooms and his young duck breast roasted with lemon. Some dishes such as roasted Scottish lamb with fine herbs are prepared only for two. Hors d'oeuvres are the finest at the resort, everything from a quail salad with peaches and walnuts to lobster medallions on a carpaccio of fennel and oranges. Although the menu is international, it is strongest on Ticinese and Mediterranean dishes. Each tantalizing course comes with superb wines in perfect condition.

In the Villa Principe Leopoldo & Residence, Via Montalbano 5. © 091/985-88-55. Reservations required. Main courses 45SF–55SF ($24.75–$30.25). AE, DC, MC, V. Daily noon–2:30pm and 7–9:30pm.

Ristorante al Portone ★ SWISS/ITALIAN If you enjoy Italian-style modern cuisine, head for this sophisticated restaurant managed by chef Roberto and Doris Galizzi. As with all *cuisine moderne,* many of the combinations sound bizarre, but the taste is usually sensational. Large scampi with curry and mango and the sole "in the style of Roberto" are veritable palate pleasers. If you order the most expensive fixed-price menu (see below), you can *lascia fare à Roberto*—leave it up to Robert, the chef. You'll rarely be disappointed. Roberto is known for putting his own culinary spin on even the most traditional of Italian dishes. The desserts are also exceptional. Regrettably, the restaurant closes in August at the peak of the tourist invasion.

Viale Cassarate 3. © 091/923-55-11 or 091/923-59-88. Reservations required. Main courses 45SF–56SF ($24.75–$30.80); business lunch 58SF ($31.90); fixed-price menu 110SF–145SF ($60.50–$79.75). AE, DC, MC, V. Tues–Sat noon–2pm and 7:30–9:30pm. Closed Jan 1–10 and mid-July to mid-Aug.

Ristorante Santabbondio ★ *Finds* MEDITERRANEAN Its amiable, hardworking staff refers to the restaurant as a much-renovated, century-old grotto, but they're using the word to describe a rustic farmhouse (ca. 1862) rather than a cave. It's less than a mile south of Lugano, midway between the town center and the airport. Menu choices are based on a solid and well-intentioned respect for *cuisine du marché,* incorporating a roster of market-fresh specialties that changes every day. In a setting suitable for up to 50 diners at a time, outfitted in Tuscan-made terra-cotta tiles and tones of green and white, you'll enjoy some of the most sophisticated cuisine in the district. Examples include tartare of salmon served with a parfait of tomatoes and shrimp, Scottish grouse roasted in aged balsamic vinegar, scallops in a ginger-flavored orange-and-basil sauce, grilled filets of turbot with capers, and medallions of goat with wine sauce. Martin Dalsass is the well-rehearsed chef.

Via Fomelino. ✆ **091/993-23-88.** Reservations recommended. Main courses 55SF–63SF ($30.25–$34.65); 7-course dinner menu *degustazione* 174SF ($95.70). AE, DC, MC, V. Tues–Fri noon–2:30pm and 7:30–10:30pm, Sat 7:30–11pm, Sun noon–2:30pm; July–Aug closed on Sun. Closed 1st week in Jan.

MODERATE

Locanda del Boschetto ⭐ *Value* SWISS/ITALIAN   Some residents of Milan say that it's cheaper to make the trip here than to eat at home. The place doesn't spend much money on decor, other than some rustic alpine wood, and no one puts on airs here. Service is direct in the sort of no-frills trattoria style. Guests can watch the chef cook beef and fish over the glowing coals. He produces a simple but flavor-filled cuisine, which includes a mixed grill of local fish, spaghetti with clam sauce, grilled calves' liver, and several succulent beef dishes. The well-known restaurant is in a wooded area near the highway.

Via Boschetto 8. ✆ **091/994-24-93.** Reservations recommended. Main courses 27SF–51SF ($14.85–$28.05). AE, DC, MC, V. Tues–Sun noon–2pm and 7–10pm. Closed 15 days in Nov. Bus: 1 or 2.

Mövenpick Ristorante Parco Ciani MEDITERRANEAN/INTER-NATIONAL   Guests select from two distinct dining areas, decorated in soft pastel tones with a bright atmosphere. One of the dining rooms has bentwood armchairs, while the other contains reproductions of Empire-style antiques. Located at the edge of a city park, the concrete block structure has irregular balconies and large windows. The menu is one of the largest in the center of town. The cookery is internationally acceptable rather than creatively innovative. Begin with a minestrone made with fresh vegetables, or sample carpaccio. Many guests, particularly those from south of the border (in Italy) prefer to begin their meal with one of the many pasta dishes, including tagliatelle, spaghetti, pappardelle, tortellini, and even a risotto. One risotto served with artichokes is delectable. The chef wisely allows you to order three different sizes of pasta, depending on your appetite. A salad buffet is offered, and every night at least three vegetarian main courses are featured. Many dishes are made with curry, the fish of the day is often grilled, and for the carnivore there's an ample selection ranging from veal T-bones to U.S. Angus entrecôtes.

In the Palazzo dei Congressi, piazza Indipendenza. ✆ **091/923-86-56.** Reservations recommended. Main courses 20SF–48SF ($11–$26.40). AE, DC, MC, V. Daily 11:30am–11:30pm. Bus: 1, 8, or 9.

Ristorante Orologio ITALIAN/INTERNATIONAL   The Orologio occupies the ground floor of a buff-colored building with restrained detailing and leaded-glass windows. The restaurant has 19th-century French-provincial chairs and an ice chest displaying salads and condiments. Amusing illustrations advertise the dishes—a mermaid draws your attention to the fish courses, although the menu features more meat courses. Vincenzo Campanile and his family offer five kinds of spaghetti, four kinds of scampi, osso buco, smoked fish, Ticino minestrone, and a springtime celebration of seasonal vegetables. In September and October there's an emphasis on game and mushroom dishes such as the filet of venison with porcini mushrooms or the platter of venison for two. Pheasant dishes are also well prepared. Of all the restaurants we've recommended in Lugano, this one draws the most mixed reaction. Some locals swear by it and some foreign visitors sound its praise; others would have preferred to be sent elsewhere.

Via Nizzola 2. ✆ **091/923-23-38.** Reservations recommended. Main courses 30SF–55SF ($16.50–$30.25). AE, DC, MC, V. Mon–Sat noon–2:30pm and 7–10:30pm. Bus: 1 or 2.

INEXPENSIVE

Antica Osteria ITALIAN/FRENCH   Set adjacent to the lakefront, in Locarno's satellite hamlet of Muralto, this unpretentious, easy-to-like trattoria has occupied this stone-sided house for at least a century. Hearty meals are served in a trio of rustic, Ticinese-style dining rooms, with additional seating available on a terrace that juts out toward the lakefront. Menu items include homemade pastas such as spaghetti bolognese, or a succulent version of spaghetti Antica Osteria that's sauced with meat, mushrooms, and tomatoes; medaillons of veal with mushrooms; and escalope of veal prepared with marsala sauce, piccata style, or Milanese style. Also look for a roster of very fresh lake fish, fried simply, with butter. Wines for the most part consist of hearty Ticino-derived versions of reds, especially Merlots, and fruity whites.

Via dei Pescatori 8, Muralto. ℂ 091/743-87-94. Reservations recommended. Main courses 25SF–35SF ($13.75–$19.25); fixed-price lunch 28SF ($15.40). MC, V. Wed–Sun noon–2pm and 6–10pm; Mon and Tues noon–2pm.

Grotto dei Pescatori ★ *Finds* ITALIAN   Inaccessible by car, the only way to reach this isolated restaurant is by boat, so consequently a meal here will also involve a scenic cruise along the lake. It's set within a 5-minute walk of the hamlet of Caprino (site of only about five houses) in what was built in the 1920s as a rough-and-ready bar for the region's fishers. Over the years, it has evolved into the full-fledged, endlessly charming hideaway you'll see today. The kitchens here are set within a grotto, with food being hauled out to a lakeside terrace. Many of the day's delectable specials are written on a blackboard. Examples include a succulent version of very fresh lake perch served as simply as possible, with a sage-flavored butter sauce. Other specialties include lake fish prepared carpione-style (braised and then cold-marinated in white wine vinegar) and buckwheat polenta with beef braised in red wine.

Caprino. ℂ **091/923-98-67.** Reservations recommended on weekends. Main courses 18SF–25SF ($9.90–$13.75). MC, V. May–Sept daily 11am–11pm. From the Imbarco Giardino piers in Lugano's Piazza Riforma, take any of the boats operated by the **Navigazione Lago di Lugano** (ℂ 091/971-52-23), whose final destination is Gandria, and get off at the Caprino/Grotto dei Pescatori stop. Boats depart at 90-min. intervals and charge 12SF ($6.60) round-trip.

La Tinera ★ *Value* SWISS/ITALIAN   A familiar array of Italian specialties are served at budget prices in this basement trattoria in the center of the historic Old Town. No one bothers to dress up here, as families, often Italian, mingle with visitors for the day, each "tucking in" plenty of the regional fare served in generous portions. Fresh pasta dishes, risotto, and a robust selection of grilled meats are cooked the same as in grandmother's day. No one would want to change a thing. Regional wine is served in ceramic carafes.

Via dei Gorini 2 (off piazza Riforma). ℂ **091/923-52-19.** Main courses 14SF–32SF ($7.70–$17.60). AE, MC, V. Mon–Sat 11:30am–2pm and 6:30–10pm. Bus: 1 or 2. Or walk down via Pessina. Closed last week of July and first 3 weeks of Aug.

Osteria Ticinese da Raffaele ★ TICINESE/ITALIAN   Set on the northern outskirts of Lugano, about 1½ miles (2.4km) from the center, this is a family-run restaurant which has thrived in this spot since the 1970s. It contains room for only 35 diners at a time, divided among three small, rustically charming dining rooms. Menu items change with the seasons, and are likely to include homemade versions of tagliatelle with garlic, oil, and fresh broccoli; penne with salmon and perhaps vodka sauce; and a wide array of such succulent grilled meats as filets of lamb or beef, pork, fresh fish, and scampi. Salads are very fresh, the welcome is warm, and there's a sense of culinary pride throughout.

Via Pazzalino 19. ℂ **091/971-66-14.** Reservations recommended. Main courses 22SF–41SF ($12.10–$22.55). AE, MC, V. Mon–Fri noon–2:30pm and 6:30–9:30pm, Sat 6:30–9:30pm. Bus: 8 or 9.

NEARBY DINING & LODGING

Motto del Gallo ★★ *Finds* MEDITERRANEAN For a visual treat, visit this baroque house practically bursting with atmosphere. There's a collection of antiques and the tables are covered with lace. The restaurant is in a 15th-century hamlet that alone is worth the trip—8 miles (13km) from Lugano on the road to Bellinzona. The excellent menu features a selection of homemade pastas, including green tagliolini with scampi. Two types of risotto are offered, one of them cooked delectably in champagne. Fresh fish looms large on the menu, including a selection of "fruits of the sea" gratinée with zabaglione. Main meat dishes are likely to include a veal mignon, veal kidneys cooked with sherry, a mixed medley of meats, or perhaps alpine-style lamb roasted aromatically with fresh herbs. Instead of dessert, such as one of the cold soufflés, many diners prefer to end their meal with a regional cheese of the Ticino. The wine list includes some 500 wines from all over the world.

If you're looking for a romantic place to spend the night, there are three well-maintained suites here, which cost 235SF ($129.25) for two, including breakfast.

CH-6807 Taverne. ℂ **091/945-28-71.** Fax 091/945-27-23. Reservations required. Main courses 29SF–49SF ($15.95–$26.95); business lunch 55SF–65SF ($30.25–$35.75); menu *degustazione* 108SF ($59.40); menu *gastronomico* 135SF ($74.25). AE, DC, V. Mon–Sat noon–2pm and 7–10pm. Closed Dec 23–Jan 20. Take the unnumbered bus or local train marked Taverne.

LUGANO AFTER DARK

Lugano reigns as the center of the Ticino's nightlife circuit, with options that attract local residents from quieter towns throughout the district. Two of the most obvious options involve visits to either of the two casinos described below.

CASINOS

Casino Kursaal Since the Kursaal—unlike the Casino Municipale, below—is on Swiss soil, the highest bet allowed on its premises is 5SF ($2.75). This after-dark rendezvous is a small-stakes casino, a bar, a movie theater, a disco, a restaurant, and an occasional venue for live entertainment. The disco, Prince, on the second floor, is open Wednesday to Sunday nights from 11pm to 4am. Casino open daily noon–4am. Parco Civico. ℂ **091/923-55-01.** Cover: casino, none; disco, 20SF–30SF ($11–$16.50), including first drink.

Casino Municipale This casino lies on Italian soil, across the lake from Lugano, only 20 minutes away by ferry. The casino is a glittering establishment, filled with an international clientele and such games as blackjack and chemin de fer, along with the inevitable slot machines. Here, in Italy, gambling stakes are unlimited. Oddly, however, despite the casino's location, the currency is Swiss. Patrons must show a passport and must have a jacket, tie, and shirt on—a policy that's strictly enforced.

The casino is in the village of Campione, which, because of the vagaries of 19th- and 20th-century politics and because of the rugged terrain around it, is completely surrounded by Switzerland. Even its telephone area code is the same as Lugano's. Long ago, the imperial fiefdom of Campione was presented to a Milanese monastery and it has remained Italian ever since. The men of Campione were famous for their stonework, and many buildings in Milan are a testament to their skill. Take a moment to admire their handiwork in some of the local buildings. Piazzale Milano 1, Campione, Italy. ℂ **091/640-11.** Cover 15SF ($8.25). Daily 3:30pm–2:15am; slot machines open at 1:45pm.

OTHER NIGHTLIFE OFFERINGS

Other than gambling, you'll find a dense roster of bars and cafes, many of them lining the edges of the historic center's most famous square, piazza Riforma. One of the most interesting is the **Café Olimpia** (© **091/922-74-88**), an elegant stone building with hundreds of chairs set out in front and a focus on live music some evenings. A few steps away is the **Café Tango** (© **091/922-27-01**), more like a bar than a traditional cafe, where an Argentine motif (and recorded music) often attracts clients from everywhere in Europe. Everybody's favorite English pub (where only a few of the staff and clients actually come from Britain) is the **Pub Pave,** riva Albertolli 1 (© **091/922-07-70**). Here, in a setting lined with faux Victoriana, you'll find at least 50 different beers and a panoramic position adjacent to the edge of the town's lake. If you ever wondered about South American expatriates and where they happened to live in Switzerland, head no farther than the **Mango Club,** piazza Duarte 8 (© **091/922-94-38**). Here, almost everybody will know how to salsa and merengue, probably better than you, and with a more convincing grasp of *español* as it's spoken in Colombia and the Dominican Republic. Originally established in 1995 and now a fixture on the nightlife circuit of the Ticino, it's open every night beginning at 10pm, with many of the guests arriving after 12:30am. Cover, which includes the first drink, costs 12SF ($6.60).

Titanic, via Cantonale, pambio-Noranco (© **091/985-60-10**), attracts the young and hip to the largest dance club in the Ticino. The cover charge usually begins at 12SF ($6.60). Go late. The club lies off the A2 exit for Lugano-Sud.

If strip-tease *artistes* are your thing, consider **Dancing Cécil,** riva Paradiso, in the nearby suburb of Lugarno-Paradiso (© **091/994-97-24**), at the hotel Vittoria. It's open daily from 10pm.

5 Morcote ⋆⋆

7 miles (11km) S of Lugano, 25 miles (40km) S of Bellinzona

Morcote is one of the most idyllic villages of Switzerland. Its arcaded houses and old streets are built on the southern slopes of Monte Arbostora, at 2,755 feet (826m). Cypresses and vineyards grow on the mountain.

ESSENTIALS

GETTING THERE   Several buses depart from Lugano every day for Morcote (trip time: 30 min.).

Throughout the summer about a dozen boats make the trip every day from Lugano to Morcote, with many intermediary stops along the way. Depending on the schedule, trip time is between 50 minutes and 2 hours. The round-trip boat fare is 28SF ($15.40). In the winter boats continue to run, but on a less frequent schedule.

For both bus and boat schedules and information, contact the tourist office, below.

If you're driving from Lugano, head south along Route A4.

VISITOR INFORMATION   Morcote now has its own tourist information office in the center (© **091/996-11-20**). Office hours are Monday to Friday from 8am to 12:30pm and 1:30 to 6pm.

SEEING THE SIGHTS

Chiesa di Madonna del Sasso dates from the 15th century; it was reconstructed later, however, and given a baroque overlay. It has some memorable 16th-century frescoes. A staircase with more than 400 steps leads down to the village and the lake, and the cemetery contains the remains of many famous people.

Scherrer Park (☎ **091/996-21-25**) contains typical Ticino trees and plants, as well as sculpture and architecture. Some of the sculpture is from the Far East. Admission is 7SF ($3.85) for adults without a guide or 12SF ($6.60) with a guide, 5SF ($2.75) students and seniors, 1SF (55¢) children 10 and under. It's open March to October, daily from 9am to 5pm.

WHERE TO STAY

Carina Carlton ★★   This hotel is imbued with an Italian-style facade, with pink-and-cream trim and lime-green shutters. Such lighthearted contrast of colors also marks the lobby, which is decorated with Oriental rugs. The hotel's several terraces are filled with potted plants and small tables. A structure of whimsical design, it was once owned by the architect Gaspare Fossati (d. 1883), a native of Morcote, who was known for his renovations of Saint Sophia in Constantinople (present-day Istanbul). Some of the awards he received from the Ottoman sultan are displayed in the lobby. The Carina Carlton offers mid-sized bedrooms filled with provincial furniture (some of it antique).

Via Cantonale, CH-6922 Morcote. ☎ **091/996-11-31**. Fax 091/996-19-29. 21 units. 200SF–240SF ($110–$132) double; 300SF ($165) suite. Rates include continental breakfast. Half board 46SF ($25.30) per person extra. AE, DC, MC, V. Closed Oct 27–Mar 6. **Amenities:** Pool; limited room service; laundry. *In room:* TV, minibar, hair dryer, safe.

Hotel Rivabella   If you want to escape from the most congested part of Morcote, try this Italian-style country house farther down the lakefront. Beneath the terrace built out over the water, sailboats and motorboats are moored. Flower boxes on the rustic covered porch are filled with begonias and geraniums. The Iannelli family offers comfortable small to mid-sized rooms with provincial furniture, including private bathrooms with shower (some with tub). The more expensive rooms are larger and have a lake view.

Via Cantonale, CH-6922 Morcote. ☎ **091/996-13-14**. Fax 091/996-16-52. 14 units. 100SF–160SF ($55–$88) double. Rates include continental breakfast. Half board 29SF ($15.95) extra per person. AE, V. Free parking. Closed Nov to Mar 15.

WHERE TO DINE

One long-enduring dining favorite along the lake, **La Voile d'Or** ★★ (in the Hotel Olivella an Lac, Nord-Est. ☎ **091/996-1001**), was closed for renovations as this book went to press. However, the restaurant (featuring a constantly changing menu based on the freshest of market ingredients) is slated to reopen in the summer of 2002, just in time for diners to enjoy its intimate atmosphere and impeccable service amidst an oasis of lawns, flowers, and elegant terraces.

Bella Vista ★★★ *Finds* CONTINENTAL   On a belvedere towering over Lake Lugano, this is a cozy restaurant of charm and grace. It is clearly the outstanding dining choice of the area, lying in the vineyards of Vico Morcote. The restaurant is housed in two typical Ticinese buildings that date back at least three centuries. In summer, terrace dining with a panoramic view is preferred, or, in cooler weather, perhaps you'd like a table in front of the fireplace. The Schwarzer family, your hosts, are demanding in their standards and are accustomed to pleasing some of the most discerning palates in both Switzerland and northern Italy. The menu is spectacular and many dishes come as a surprise—those lobsters flown in are the same type the Bush family enjoys in Maine, for example. The homemade pasta dishes don't get much better than those served here.

You might also consider Bellavista as a hideaway place to stay. It rents 11 charmingly furnished bedrooms with tub and shower and such amenities as a minibar. Guests can also enjoy the sun terrace and solarium. Doubles rent for 150SF to 200SF ($82.50–$110), with suites going for 330SF ($181.50). You can arrive early for a drink at the bar or a walk in the garden.

Strada de Vigh 2, CH-6921 Vico-Morcote. ✆ **091/996-1143**. Reservations required. Main courses 29SF–38SF ($15.95–$20.90); fixed-price menus 75SF ($41.25), 85SF ($46.75), 95SF ($52.25). AE, DC, MC, V. July–Sept daily 6:30–9:30pm and Tues–Sun noon–1:30pm. Oct–Nov and Feb–June Tues 6:30–9:30pm and Wed–Sun noon–1:30pm and 6:30–9:30pm. Closed Dec–Jan. Lies 1¼ miles (2km) south of Melide.

Ristorante della Posta SWISS/ITALIAN   Established in 1863, this restaurant features two terraces staggered back from each other overlooking the lake. It operates from the center of Morcote. Waiters scurry with food-laden trays from the kitchen across the street. The setting is charming, but the traffic makes it somewhat hectic. Delectable specialties include risotto with mushrooms, osso buco with polenta, fresh lake fish, and real Italian pizza. Fresh fish is the chef's specialty, and it's most often served grilled. There are also several different preparations of fresh mushrooms offered nightly, and the veal cutlet Milanese is always reliable.

Via Cantonale. ✆ **091/996-11-27**. Main courses 28SF–48SF ($15.40–$26.40); pizza 18SF–28SF ($9.90–$15.40). AE, DC, MC, V. Daily 11am–midnight. Closed Nov to mid-Mar.

Liechtenstein

With a history going back to the 14th century, Liechtenstein is a wonderful land of fairy-tale castles, chalets decorated with geraniums, Rhine meadows, and small villages high in the Alps. One of the castles is inhabited by the reigning prince.

Nestled snugly beside Austria and separated from Switzerland by the Rhine River, it's one of the smallest independent sovereign states of Europe, along with San Marino in Italy and Andorra in the Pyrenees. The entire country is only about 16 miles (26km) long and 4 miles (6km) wide.

Liechtenstein is famous for its finely engraved postage stamps, which are treasured by collectors the world over. The stamps illustrate the country's religion (predominantly Roman Catholic), monarchy, art, history, landscape, nature, and leisure activities. Stamps provide 25% of the government's income, and new series are being introduced all the time. There's a postal museum in Vaduz, the capital of the principality.

Although commonly regarded as remote, Liechtenstein is actually very accessible from eastern Switzerland. A number of good roads link the two countries, and there are no border formalities or Customs stops. There are guards at the Austrian border, but they rarely stamp visitors' passports.

The ideal way to explore Liechtenstein is to simply wander around. Every village in the tiny principality has a network of hiking and walking routes, which the locals themselves put to good use. Marked hiking routes cover 93 miles (150km) in the alpine area and 74 miles (119km) in the valley, which, considering the country's size, takes up a huge chunk of the land space.

Malbun and Steg are ideal starting points for mountain tours, and Gaflei and Planken (the tiniest hamlet in the country) are departure points for the Drei Schwestern area. The tourist office (see below) distributes a pamphlet outlining the best hiking trails throughout the Unterland (Lower Country), the Oberland (Upper Country), and the alpine region.

Guided half- or full-day tours are arranged every Thursday in summer by the **Liechtenstein Alpine Association.** Routes depend on weather conditions and are published on the Saturday preceding the tour in the local newspapers under a column headed "Wanderungen des Liechtensteiner Alpenvereins." For information and registration, contact the guide given in the announcement.

1 About Liechtenstein

ORIENTATION

GEOGRAPHY   The Rhine River forms Liechtenstein's western boundary; the Swiss canton of St. Gallen is on the other bank. To the east is the Austrian province of Vorarlberg, and to the south are the Grisons of Switzerland. Liechtenstein is cradled by the **Drei Schwestern** (Three Sisters) mountains.

PEOPLE   About 32,000 citizens live in 11 communes (comparable to Switzerland's cantons). Most—more than 80%—are Roman Catholic and of German ancestry. They enjoy one of the highest standards of living in the world and pay very little in taxes. Unemployment is rare.

The country's prosperity, however, is a relatively recent development. Many old-timers remember the hardships of World War I, when the country was virtually cut off from food supplies because of blockades. The social and economic growth since the end of World War II has exceeded that of any other Western nation. Today Liechtenstein is one of the most highly industrialized countries in Europe. The industry is hardly noticeable, however, because the factories and workshops are dispersed among orchards, meadows, and woodlands. There are no smokestacks, with their pollution from fumes. One of the industrial specialties is the production of false teeth.

Liechtenstein has a rich cultural life, supported by royal patrons and the cooperation of neighboring countries. Though open to foreign influences, through commerce and cultural exchanges as well as through tourism, Liechtenstein maintains its unique national identity by severely restricting citizenship. Any foreigner wishing to become a citizen must first be approved by a majority of the commune he or she intends to live in; then his application must be approved by parliament, and then by the monarch. The process is obviously meant to discourage to immigration.

LANGUAGE   Most residents of Liechtenstein, who are largely of Austrian origin, speak a German dialect. English is also understood throughout the country.

GOVERNMENT   The Principality of Liechtenstein is a constitutional hereditary monarchy with a unicameral parliament (Diet). The state power is vested in the prince and the people. The prince's powers are passed on through hereditary succession to the throne and are independent of the will of the people. The people also have political power and must work together with the prince, according to the constitution.

Members of the parliament are chosen for 4 years by general elections. The right to vote is universal (women received the right to vote in 1984), secret, and direct. Public referendum is an important right of all citizens. Any law passed by the Diet that is not declared urgent may be put to referendum. The constitution also assures freedom of speech, freedom of the press, and freedom of assembly.

Liechtenstein has a prime minister and four councilors, appointed by the prince for a 4-year term. They act as a link between the prince and the Diet. In 1969 the principality celebrated its 250th anniversary.

ESSENTIALS

GETTING THERE   The nearest airport is **Kloten International Airport** outside Zurich, about 80 miles (130km) to the west of Vaduz. There are both train and bus transportation into Liechtenstein from Zurich.

Many express trains pass through Liechtenstein, but none stop there. You can take a train from Zurich to Sargans or to Buchs in nearby Switzerland. Call ℂ **0900/300-300** for **rail schedules.** At both Sargans and Buchs you'll find good bus connections to Vaduz and other communes in Liechtenstein.

If you're driving from Zurich, head southwest along N3 until you reach the junction with N1, then take N1 north to the turnoff for Vaduz.

ℂ *FAST FACTS:* **Liechtenstein**

Currency The Swiss franc is legal tender in Liechtenstein; the exchange rate is the same as in Switzerland (see "Money" in chapter 2).

Documents Required All travel documents recognized by Swiss authorities are valid in Liechtenstein. However, you'll encounter the formalities of any Western European border crossing if you enter through Austria.

Holidays Public holidays are January 1 (New Year's Day), January 6 (Epiphany), February 28 (Mardi Gras), Good Friday, Easter Monday, May 1 (Labor Day), May 25 (Feast of the Ascension), June 5 (Whit Monday), June 15 (Corpus Christi), August 15 (Feast of the Assumption), September 8 (Nativity of Our Lady), November 1 (All Saints' Day), December 8 (Feast of the Immaculate Conception), December 25 (Christmas), and December 26 (Boxing Day).

Information For further information about the principality, contact the **Liechtenstein National Tourist Office,** Städtle 37 (P.O. Box 139), FL-9490 Vaduz, Liechtenstein (ℂ **00423/232-14-43**). This office is open July to August, Monday to Friday from 8am to 5:30pm; and the rest of the year, Monday to Saturday from 8am to noon and 1:30 to 5:30pm.

Mail The postage rates are the same as in Switzerland (see "Fast Facts: Switzerland," in chapter 2). But you must, of course, use Liechtenstein stamps.

Medical Needs Doctors and dentists take turns handling emergency calls (the names of those currently available are published in the Saturday and Sunday newspapers). Your hotel will put you in touch with an English-speaking doctor or dentist. Phone ✆ **144** for an ambulance.

Telephone Until recently, calls to Liechtenstein were considered the same as calls to a region of Switzerland, and were accessible via Switzerland's country code (41). A recent electronic change-over altered the rules and now treats calls to Liechtenstein as calls to an independent country that's separate from Switzerland. To call Liechtenstein from the U.S., dial whatever international prefix your long-distance carrier requires (usually **011**), followed by Liechtenstein's country code **00423,** followed by the seven-digit local number. To call Liechtenstein from anywhere in Switzerland or anywhere else in the world, dial whatever international prefix is required at the phone you happen to be using, followed by the country code for Liechtenstein (00423), followed by the seven-digit local number.

2 Vaduz ✶

80 miles (130 km) E of Zurich, 24 miles (38km) E of Chur

Vaduz (pronounced Va-*dootz*) is the capital of the Principality of Liechtenstein. Vineyards surround this little town (pop. about 5,000) at the foot of the royal family's castle. The rural commune, known for its good wines, is also very hospitable and sociable to visitors. The capital is most often visited on a brief stopover—just time enough to buy some of the famous postage stamps and record the visit to this tiny country in your passport. But as the capital of one of the last vestiges of the Holy Roman Empire and the seat of the only German-speaking monarchy in the world, Vaduz merits a closer look, at least time to walk its streets and visit some of its museums.

ESSENTIALS

GETTING THERE   See "Essentials" in "About Liechtenstein," above.

VISITOR INFORMATION   The **Vaduz Tourist Office** is at Städtle 37 (✆ **00423/232-14-43**). It's open July to August, Monday to Friday from 8am to 5:30pm; and the rest of the year, Monday to Saturday from 8am to noon and 1:30 to 5:30pm.

SEEING THE SIGHTS

Traffic is allowed one-way on the main street, **Städtle.** Also at the center of Vaduz is the **Rathaus** (town hall). The post office is across the street. Vaduz offers a wide range of sports and entertainment. Facilities include a miniature golf course, tennis courts, and a large swimming pool.

   One of the best ways to get around not only Vaduz but other parts of the country itself is to rent a bike or a small motorcycle. Rentals are possible at **Bike Garage,** Triesen 10 (✆ **00423/390-03-90**). The cost is 20SF ($11) per day for the average bike.

The prince's castle, **Schloss Vaduz,** dates from the 12th century. The oldest parts are the keep and the buildings on the east side. The castle was burned down by Swiss troops in 1499 and rebuilt at the beginning of the 16th century. It has round bastions at the northeast and southwest corners. Once a bleak and gloomy fortress, the castle is now much improved. The private interior contains lavish furnishings, antiques, and priceless artwork. Although the public is not welcome inside, the exterior of the fortress is surely worth seeing. The climb along the wooded footpath takes 20 minutes and starts between the Hotel Real and the Hotel Engel. There's a sweeping vista from the grounds of the castle.

In the upper village, on the road to the castle, is the **Red House.** This was the seat of the vassals of the counts of Werdenberg during the Middle Ages. The house was acquired along with the vineyard by the Monastery of St. Johann in the Toggenburg.

Liechtenstein State Art Collection ★★ The princes of the House of Liechtenstein have been art collectors since the 17th century. Their treasures were in a palace in Vienna until 1940, when Prince Franz Joseph II decided to display his collection in his own country. The collection occupies two floors of a gallery above the tourist office. The works by Rubens are among the greatest in the world. They include *The Toilet of Venus* and a cycle of nine large paintings illustrating the history of a Roman consul. Many of the pictures on exhibit are reproduced on Liechtenstein's famous stamps. The art collection is the country's most outstanding attraction and the highlight of a trip to Liechtenstein.

Städtle 37. ☏ **00423/235-03-00.** Admission 8SF ($4.40) adults; 5SF ($2.75) students, seniors, children 10–16. Free for children 10 and under. Tues–Sun 10am–5pm; Thurs open till 8pm.

Postal Museum Philatelists and other admirers come from all over the world to see the Liechtenstein stamps. The collection includes the stamps of the Universal Postal Union, printing plates, and postal documents. Liechtenstein's first stamp dates from 1912. The museum was opened in 1930.

Städtle 37. ☏ **00423/236-61-05.** Free admission. Daily 10am–noon and 1–5pm.

SHOPPING

If there's any flash and glitter in Liechtenstein at all, it appears only in very subdued form. You might especially notice this during your shopping excursions, which are best limited to central Vaduz, a neighborhood that can never really escape the sense of being a somewhat overgrown village. Liechtenstinian handicrafts are best ferreted out at **Timeless A.G.,** Herrengasse 1, Vaduz (☏ **00423/ 385-41-14**). Here, black and white marble that's mined in Balzers, Liechtenstein's southernmost hamlet, is sold in the form of clocks, vases, ashtrays, tabletops, picture frames, and virtually everything else. An outlet that sells gift items from Liechtenstein, Austria, Italy, and Switzerland is **L'Atelier,** Städtle 36 (☏ **00423/232-46-88**). Its merchandise, as selected by the outfit's long-time owner, Hélène de Marchi, includes lamps, dolls, hand-painted silks, stoneware, pewter, sculpture, and other handmade objects.

Liechtenstein has been famous since the turn of the century for its rustic and durable pottery, produced in natural-looking colors such as blue, beige, and yellow, in factories that lie within a 10-minute drive of Vaduz. The larger of the principality's two factories for stoneware is **Schaedler Keramik A.G.,** which straddles Hauptstrasse (☏ **00423/373-14-14**), the main street of the hamlet of Nendeln, 5 miles north of Vaduz. Its only real competitor, at least within the principality, is the somewhat smaller outfit **Haas Kunst Keramik A.G.,**

Zollstrasse 70, in the nearby hamlet of Schaan (℡ **00423/232-18-83**). Both firms maintain sales outlets on their premises and present pottery-making demonstrations to anyone who's interested.

The principality's premier outlet for wines produced by vineyards belonging to the prince is the **Hofkellerei des Fürsten Liechtenstein,** Feldstrasse, Vaduz (℡ **00423/232-10-18**). Set in a solid, not particularly imaginative-looking building that's owned by the prince, it stockpiles the fruits of his family's vineyards, most of which are either in the principality or in Lower Austria (Niederösterreich) just across the border. Look for both whites and reds, and a somewhat heavy-handed emphasis on the organization's royal connections.

Don't overlook the Liechtenstinian postal service—an entity that produces more stamps than are ever used to actually mail letters—as a shopper's mecca. One of the busiest emporiums in the principality is the bureaucratic-looking kiosk in the main post office, **Postwert Zeichenstelle der Regierung,** Städtle, FL-9490 Vaduz (℡ **00423/236-64-44**). Here stamps that commemorate Liechtenstein's history, botany, zoology, and achievements are sold to avid collectors, and even to folk who never thought they were collectors.

WHERE TO STAY
Most of Liechtenstein's hotels are in the capital.

VERY EXPENSIVE
Park Hotel Sonnenhof ✫✫✫   The finest hotel in the principality is among the finest in Europe. Diplomatic receptions are held here frequently. Built in the late 19th century, the hotel has been modernized into a streamlined chalet, with balconies and awnings. The garden is beautiful, and the spacious, elegant rooms are handsomely decorated and furnished with luxury beds and state-of-the-art plumbing, including luxurious tub and shower combinations in all but three (shower only).

Mareestrasse 29, FL-9490 Vaduz, Liechtenstein. ℡ 00423/232-11-92. Fax 00423/232-00-53. www.relais chateaux.ch/sonnenhof. 29 units. 360SF–450SF ($198–$247.50) double; 430SF–480SF ($236.50–$264) junior suite. Rates include buffet breakfast. Half board 75SF ($41.25) per person extra. AE, DC, MC, V. Free parking outdoors, 15SF ($8.25) in garage. **Amenities:** Restaurant; pool; nearby tennis courts; gym; sauna; room service; laundry. *In room:* TV, minibar, hair dryer, safe.

MODERATE
Gasthof Löwen ✫   Set on the highway within a pleasant and well-cultivated garden, this is the oldest inn (established in 1380) in Liechtenstein. Few others evoke old-fashioned alpine life as effectively as this one, thanks to its antique rooms outfitted with furniture that was originally crafted around 1920, and a clear, clean color scheme of stark white offset with varnished paneling. Bedrooms come in a variety of sizes and shapes, but all are comfortably Middle Europa, with dowdy furniture, soft beds, crisp linens, and plumbing that still works (often noisily).

Herrengasse 35, FL-9490 Vaduz, Liechtenstein. ℡ 00423/238-11-44. Fax 00423/238-11-45. www.hotels.li/loewen. 7 units. 250SF–320SF ($137.50–$176) double. Rates include breakfast. AE, DC, MC, V. From Vaduz, take the bus marked "Feldkirch." **Amenities:** Restaurant; bar; limited room service; laundry service. *In room:* TV, minibar, hair dryer, safe.

Hotel Engel   An unassuming and unpretentious hotel, this small inn lies on the main street of Vaduz, a roadway filled with summer tourist buses. The owners run a welcoming hotel, and 12 of the 17 rooms have flower-festooned balconies overlooking the action. All the mid-sized accommodations have bright colors and newly tiled bathrooms with private shower or tub. The hotel is modern outside and decorated with rustic artifacts inside. In addition, it has the only Chinese restaurant in the country, plus an international restaurant.

Städtle 13, FL-9490 Vaduz, Liechtenstein. *(C)* **00423/236-17-17.** Fax 00423/233-11-59. 20 units. 153SF–175SF ($84.15–$96.25) double. Rates include continental breakfast. AE, DC, MC, V. Free parking. **Amenities:** 2 restaurants; limited room service. *In room:* TV, minibar.

Hotel Real ★★   Rich in tradition, this well-maintained hotel is on the main street, below the wooded bluff on which the palace of the prince is built. Although known primarily for its restaurant, it is a superlative choice for its luxurious bedrooms as well. The facade is decorated with flower boxes in the summer. The spacious rooms are well maintained and comfortable and have been renovated in a modern style, with deluxe mattresses and beautifully maintained private bathrooms, equally divided between those with private shower and those with tub and shower combination. The hotel restaurant serves the best food in the principality (see "Where to Dine," below).

Städtle 21, FL-9490 Vaduz, Liechtenstein. *(C)* **00423/232-22-22.** Fax 00423/232-08-91. www.relais chateauch/real. 13 units. 240SF–270SF ($132–$148.50) double; 370SF–430SF ($203.50–$236.50) suite. Rates include continental breakfast. AE, DC, MC, V. **Amenities:** Restaurant; laundry service. *In room:* TV, minibar, hair dryer.

INEXPENSIVE
Hotel Garni Landhaus Prausch   Located a 5-minute walk east from the town center, this structure dates from 1917, when it was built as the home of a conservative and prosperous burger. Today it retains the solid and well-grounded aura of its original function. The public areas are covered with flagstone floors, while the small bedrooms have wall-to-wall carpeting and durable, reliable country-style furnishings, including private bathrooms with showers (some with tubs).

Zollstrasse 16, FL-9490 Nendeln, Liechtenstein. *(C)* **00423/232-46-63.** Fax 00423/232-54-86. www.hotels.li/garni. 22 units. 140SF ($77) double. Rates include breakfast. AE, DC, MC, V. Free parking. Closed Oct–Mar. **Amenities:** Pool; Jacuzzi; sauna. *In room:* TV, minibar.

WHERE TO DINE
EXPENSIVE
Restaurant Real ★★★ CONTINENTAL   The royal family are frequent guests here—their castle looms above the restaurant, which is on the main street of Vaduz. There are cafe tables and chairs outside. The dining rooms have paneling and lighting fixtures shaped like grape garlands. You'll appreciate the well-polished ambience of understated prosperity. The chefs hired here are the finest in the principality. They always choose the very finest ingredients, which they fashion into delectable platters with razor-sharp techniques. There is a certain charm and fragrance connected with every dish. The menu might include bouillabaisse, scampi ravioli, a gratin of seafood, *tafelspitz* (boiled beef), veal piccata, or perhaps a perfectly done Wiener schnitzel.

Städtle 21. *(C)* **00423/232-22-22.** Reservations required. Main courses 39SF–75SF ($26.15–$50.25); fixed-price 6-course meal 152SF ($83.60). AE, DC, MC, V. Daily 11:30am–2pm and 6:30–10pm.

Restaurant Torkel ★ *Finds* SWISS   The prince owns this charming country inn on the site of an old winepress. It's in the royal vineyards on the outskirts of town; park your car and follow the signs a short distance to a low-lying building. The cuisine, never accused of being overly imaginative, is satisfying and most filling, a true regional flavor of central Europe. Seasonal specialties are likely to include veal dishes, filet goulash Stroganoff, freshwater fish in Riesling sauce, and "Torkelsteak." Noodle and rösti dishes are also offered. Wine is available from the royal cellars, including a house variety of the local sparkling wine (Sekt). The menu changes every day, offering only what is fresh at the market.

Hintergasse 9. ℂ 00423/232-44-10. Reservations recommended. Main courses 35SF–60SF ($19.25–$33). AE, DC, MC, V. Mon–Fri noon–1:30pm and 6:30–9pm, Sat 6:30–9:30pm.

MODERATE

Chinatown CHINESE   The only Chinese restaurant in the principality is on the second floor of the Hotel Engel, recommended above. There's a terrace for fair-weather dining. Chinese cooks were brought in from Hong Kong, and many of the good-tasting dishes show a Cantonese influence. Fish and poultry dishes are excellent.

In the Hotel Engel, Städtle 13. ℂ 00423/236-17-17. Reservations recommended. Main courses 24SF–40SF ($13.20–$22); fixed-price menu 60SF–70SF ($33–$38.50). AE, DC, MC, V. Daily 11am–2pm and 6–10pm.

INEXPENSIVE

Old Castle Inn GERMAN/AUSTRIAN/SWISS   Locals gather at the long, half-timbered bar to drink and gossip, and German folk music or background pop music is played. You'll be able to see the castle from the leatherette banquettes that surround the wooden tables. Outside is a terrace with a striped canopy and geraniums around the border. The menu is changed daily. There's a good selection of wurst and steak dishes, or you might choose one of the cold dishes or well-stuffed sandwiches. There are different kinds of "schnitzel" available, each platter served with *pommes frites* and a salad. The menu also includes such standard fare as minestrone, spaghetti, lasagna, hamburger, and veal liver Venice style.

Aeulestrasse 22. ℂ 00423/232-10-65. Reservations not required. Main courses 15SF–35SF ($8.25–$19.25) . AE, DC, MC, V. Daily 8am–1am.

VADUZ AFTER DARK

Conservative—and according to its critics, drab—Liechtenstein can't even begin to compete with the nightlife options of larger cities in Switzerland. Your best bet will probably involve retiring early after a nightcap at either your hotel bar or one of the spots mentioned below. Discos aren't really a factor here. Noteworthy bars, however, include the **Vanini Bar,** a youthful, high-energy meeting place in the Hotel Adler, Herrengasse (ℂ **00423/232-21-31**); the **Apero-Bar,** a site associated with the Restaurant Wolff, Städtle (ℂ **00423/232-23-21**); and **Schwefl's Bar,** Austrasse (ℂ **00423/233-20-20**).

3 The Unterland

Formed by the Rhine Valley, Liechtenstein's Unterland, or Lower Country, is at the foot of the Drei Schwestern (Three Sisters) mountains. It contains eight villages along the slopes of the Eschnerberg and five parishes: Ruggell, Schellenberg, Eschen-Nendeln, Gamprin-Bendern, and Mauren-Schaanwald. The landscape is a rugged mix of wooded hills, meadows, and clean brooks. Agricultural and industrial development has not been allowed to damage the environment.

The **Eschnerberg Historical Trail** is an extensive network of footpaths. The Eschnerberg hills were a refuge for prehistoric settlers, offering an islandlike setting in the marshy Rhine Valley. The marshes have since been drained. A hike along these trails is both pleasant and informative. You'll learn the history of the people who have lived in this region.

All the villages recommended below are on the postal-bus route from Vaduz. The tourist office will provide a map outlining the various routings and transportation connections possible.

SCHELLENBERG

This second-smallest parish in the principality (pop. 577) also has the smallest surface area. It was already settled when the New Stone Age began. Some of the Iron Age artifacts displayed in the National Museum in Vaduz were unearthed here. The Herren (nobles) von Schellenberg built two castles here in the Middle Ages. One of the castles, the **Obere Burg Schellenberg,** has been restored and offers a good view. Schellenberg is a starting point for the Eschnerberg Historical Trail.

MAUREN-SCHAANWALD

These two villages are a mile apart, in a parish covering only 3 square miles (5 sq. km). Mauren is one of the most beautiful sights in Liechtenstein. It was called Muron in 1178 and today is known as the "Village of the Seven Hillocks." The remains of Roman baths and a second-century farmhouse or outbuilding have been excavated here. The village is also known for its fine church, dating from 1787. The meadows and woodlands between Mauren and Schaanwald have been designated a bird sanctuary. The preserve contains a conservation pond and a nature trail. The villages are on the Schaan-Feldkirch road leading to Austria.

GAMPRIN-BENDERN

This small parish along the Rhine has picture-postcard charm. The two hamlets on the west spur of Eschnerberg are rich in archaeological discoveries. Excavations have shown that the area was inhabited continuously from about 2500 B.C. to the Roman era. Discoveries around Gamprin have yielded many clues about the culture of the New Stone Age. The remains of a farm and a small church dating from A.D. 55 have been found on the hill on which the **Bendern church** stands today. This church belonged to the Convent of Schanis (St. Gallen) from 809 to 1177 and to the Monastery of St. Luzi (Chur) from 1200 to 1816. After the Reformation, the St. Luzi monks built a larger structure, which included the abbot's quarters.

It was at Bendern's **Kirchhügel** that the men of the lowlands swore loyalty to the prince of Liechtenstein in 1699. It's very scenic and includes a fitness track, a history trail, and a campground. The **Mariengrotte** (Mary's Grotto), at Bendern, is the only shrine of its kind in the country.

ESCHEN-NENDELN

Eschen was first mentioned in the Carolingian land registry in 850 under the name Essane, derived from the Celtic word *esca,* meaning "by the water." The water refers to the Esche, a nearby brook. Flint artifacts from the Middle Stone Age, about 5000 B.C., have been found here, and New Stone Age settlements have been excavated at Malanser and Schneller. The upper part of Eschen, **Schönbühl,** is one of the country's most attractive residential areas.

The parish includes the village of **Nendeln,** in which the foundation of a Roman villa and a prehistoric settlement have been discovered. Nendeln lies 3 miles (5km) northeast of Schaan, on Route 16.

There are several buildings worth visiting in the area. The **Pfründhaus** is a prebend structure, where the clergy lived. The **Holy Cross Chapel,** on the

Rofenberg, was formerly a place of public assembly. The restored **church at Eschen** has the original walls of the old church laid bare. Other churches include **St. Sebastian's Chapel** and the **Rochus Chapel**. Liechtenstein's first industrial enterprise was a **tile factory** founded at Nendeln in 1836. For a century it was the only industrial plant in the Unterland.

There's a pool in Eschen, and a health trail in Nendeln. You can also enjoy the peaceful mountain footpaths of the Eschnerberg trail.

WHERE TO STAY & DINE

Hotel Engel   This is one of two hotels with the same name (Hotel Engel; see "Where to Stay" in section 2) in Liechtenstein, a fact that causes lots of confusion to visitors arriving in the principality for the first time. A 10-minute drive north from Vaduz, near the principality's biggest ceramic factories (recommended separately in "Shopping" in section 2), the hotel has a dark, modern facade and a large, antique winepress in the yard. Seasonal flowers and plants add freshness to the public areas, a fact that appeals to some local residents, who like to congregate in the hotel on Sunday mornings. The mid-sized bedrooms are simple, durable, and very clean; 10 have a phone and TV. All the units are equipped with a private bathroom with shower (some with tubs).

Churer Strasse 36, FL-9485 Nendeln, Liechtenstein. © 00423/373-31-31. Fax 00423/373-12-60. 17 units. 147SF–172SF ($80.85–$94.60) double; 199SF ($109.45) minisuite. Rates include breakfast. AE, DC, MC, V. Closed Feb 14–28 and Sept 15–Oct 2. **Amenities:** Restaurant. *In room:* TV (in some), phone (in some).

4 The Oberland

The Oberland, or Upper Country, of Liechtenstein was the former estate of the count of Vaduz. It consists of Vaduz and five parishes or communes: Planken, Schaan, Triesen, Triesenberg, and Balzers. Although the area is in the south of Liechtenstein, it's still known as the Upper Country because of topography. The Unterland (Lower Country), to the north, is filled with meadows and hills gently rising from the Rhine Valley, while the Oberland, from Planken on south, consists of higher country, reaching up to the Liechtenstein Alps.

In the shadow of the Drei Schwestern mountains, the Oberland abounds in woodlands and mountain trails, alpine flowers, and protected animal species. Settlements founded by Swiss immigrants some 700 years ago still retain their ancient traditions. There are plenty of opportunities for recreation throughout the region, but the alpine portion is the best place for winter sports.

All the villages and hamlets below are reached by postal bus from Vaduz. Pick up a map at the tourist office in Vaduz (see "Essentials," in section 2, earlier), where you can also learn about possible routings and schedules.

Planken is the starting point for excursions to the **Drei Schwestern** (Three Sisters) area. From here, you'll have an outstanding panoramic view of the Rhine Valley and the Swiss mountains extending from Pizol to Lake Constance. There's a chapel dedicated to St. Joseph containing copies of old masters and a bronze cross by Georg Malin.

SCHAAN

Located on the Arlberg railway line, Schaan is the country's main communications center. It's located at the foot of the Drei Schwestern, just 2 miles (3km) west of Vaduz. The Carolingian land registry (ca. A.D. 831) lists Liechtenstein's second-largest parish under the name Scana. Archaeologists have discovered the remains of a Roman fort, two Roman legionnaires' helmets from the 1st century A.D., and an Alemannic decorative shield from the 6th or 7th century. The 12th-century **Romanesque church** is worth a visit.

There's a **sports center** (© **00423/233-35-25**) near a forest, offering tennis courts, a health center, an indoor swimming pool, public baths, and a children's playground. You can also hike in the mountains.

The **Theater a Kirchplatz** (© **00423/237-59-69**) is one of the important cultural centers of the region. It presents international artists.

WHERE TO STAY & DINE

Dux Hotel   This Iberian-style country house is very superior for a tourist-class hotel. Built in 1924, it has a large sun terrace and long wrought-iron balconies. The rugged mountains loom in the background, and there are several old oak trees on the lawn. The comfortable mid-sized rooms have wood ceilings and modern amenities, including private bathrooms with shower (some with tubs). The recently renovated hotel is accessible to wheelchairs.

Duxweg 31, FL-9494 Schaan, Liechtenstein. © 00423/232-17-27. Fax 00423/232-48-78. 10 units. 120SF–135SF ($66–$74.25) double. Rates include continental breakfast. MC, V. Free parking. Closed Feb and the first 3 weeks of Sept. **Amenities:** 3 restaurants, bar; tennis court; gym; sauna; limited room service; laundry. *In room:* TV, minibar.

Hotel Linde *Value*   This is the town's hotel bargain. The semibaroque facade has a single ornate gable and a pumpkin-colored extension. Well-pruned hedges shield the sun terrace from the street traffic. The clean and comfortable, although small, rooms are functionally furnished. The hotel's restaurant (closed on Sunday) serves a very limited but reasonably priced menu.

Feldkircherstrasse 1, FL-9494 Schaan, Liechtenstein. © 00423/232-17-04. Fax 00423/232-09-29. 23 units. 126SF ($69.30) double. Rates include continental breakfast. AE, MC, V. Free parking. Closed Dec 1–Jan 15. **Amenities:** Restaurant. *In room:* TV, minibar, hair dryer, safe.

Hotel Sylva im Sax *Finds*   This little chalet in the woods is so inviting that you may want to anchor here for the night and make the easy commute to Vaduz. It's about a block above the main road. A mother and daughter, Friederecke and Sylva Eberle, offer well-furnished mid-sized rooms and a sauna. The largest room is laid out for business travelers and includes a fax machine and a second telephone. The restaurant serves some of the best food in the area.

Saxgasse 6, FL-9494 Schaan, Liechtenstein. © 00423/232-39-42. Fax 00423/232-82-47. 8 units. 170SF–195SF ($93.50–$107.25) double. Rates include continental breakfast. MC, V. Free parking. **Amenities:** Restaurant; sauna; limited room service; laundry service. *In room:* TV, minibar, hair dryer.

Schaanerhof   This is a modern hotel with a pink-and-white facade and balconies on several sides. The interior is comfortable and warm, and the bedrooms are well furnished and maintained. The main dining room serves Italian, Austrian, and Asian dishes, with a revolving monthly menu featuring different cuisines of the world.

In der Ballota 3, FL-9494 Schaan, Liechtenstein. © 00423/232-18-77. Fax 00423/233-16-27. 28 units. 170SF ($93.50) double. Rates include buffet breakfast. AE, V. Free parking. Closed Dec 22–Jan 8. **Amenities:** Restaurant; pool; gym; sauna; Turkish bath; limited room service; laundry. *In room:* TV, minibar, hair dryer.

TRIESENBERG

The largest parish of Liechtenstein has stretches of woodland, scrub, farmland, and pasture. High above the Rhine Valley is the village Triesenberg, containing about 2,000 inhabitants, reached by taking a hill road out of Vaduz. The road is filled with steep bends but offers extensive views. The farming community is developing into a center for light industry and tourism.

Triesenberg, like Planken, was settled in the late 13th century by Swiss immigrants from the Valais. Many of the parish residents wear colorful regional garb. Modern materials and methods are used to build the houses, but the style dates from the early 14th century. The influence of the Valais is evident. The restored town hall is elegant, and the community center contains a local museum and exhibition of wood engravings.

At 2,600 feet (780m), Triesenberg is a good base for excursions to the Liechtenstein Alps. Fine highways and well-tended hiking trails lead from Triesenberg to the alpine resorts: Masescha (4,100 ft/1,230m), Silum (5,000 ft/1,500m), Gaflei (5,000 ft/1,500m), Malbun (5,250 ft/1,575m), and Steg (4,600 ft/1,380m). Steg is on the way to Malbun and features the Valuna–Lopp cross-country skiing center and a ski lift. The half-mile-long Gnalp-Steg tunnel connects the valley with the alpine area.

WHERE TO STAY & DINE

Hotel Kulm   Spring blossoms cascade down the balconies of this centrally located hotel with a pink and light-grained wood facade. It offers a wide view of the valley, with a sidewalk cafe in front. The interior is a mix of rustic and modern styles. The furniture is comfortable in the well-maintained bedrooms, half of which contain a private bathroom with shower, the others with combination tub and shower.

Dorfzentrum, FL-9497 Triesenberg, Liechtenstein. ℂ 00423/237-79-79. Fax 00423/237-79-78. www.kulma hotels.li. 20 units. 142SF–162SF ($78.10–$89.10) double. Rates include continental breakfast. Half board 31SF ($17.05) per person extra. AE, DC, MC, V. Free parking. **Amenities:** 2 restaurants. *In room:* TV, minibar.

Hotel Steg   This well-kept hotel, run by the Lamperts, is north of Triesenberg on the road to Steg. The hotel was originally built 200 years ago and has been renovated frequently since, most recently in the late 1980s. It's a rather underpublicized and unpretentious choice. The small rooms are simple but generally adequate. In addition to the regular doubles, there are two dormitories, one for 10 occupants, another for 5 occupants. Corridor bathrooms are well maintained and uncrowded.

FL-9497 Steg/Triesenberg, Liechtenstein. ℂ 00423/263-21-46. Fax 00423/263-21-47. 11 units, none with bathroom; 7 dorm beds. 80SF ($44) double; 25SF ($13.75) dorm bed. Rates include continental breakfast. Half board 25SF ($13.75) extra. MC, V. Free parking. Closed Apr 15–May 15 and Nov 15–Dec 15. **Amenities:** Restaurant. *In room:* No phone.

Nürnberger's Hotel Martha Bühler ★ *(Finds)*   This is our favorite hotel in the upper reaches of Liechtenstein. This establishment was founded in 1976 by Martha Tschikof-Bühler, the first woman from Liechtenstein to compete in the Winter Olympic Games, in Grenoble (1968) and Sapporo (1972). She no longer has anything to do with this inn, which is now owned by Mr. Nürnberger. The hotel is next to a baroque tower and offers a sweeping view of the valley. The public rooms are filled with elaborate wood detailing and warmly inviting colors and textures. The paneled bedrooms are cozy and well furnished, each with a balcony plus a private bathroom with shower (some with tubs). The restaurant (closed on Monday) serves a limited menu of well-prepared Liechtensteiner specialties.

FL-9497 Triesenberg, Liechtenstein. ℂ 00423/237-47-77. Fax 00423/237-47-70. 16 units. 160SF ($88) double; 220SF ($121) suite. Half board 28SF ($15.40) per person extra. AE, DC, MC, V. Free parking. Closed 2 weeks in Nov. **Amenities:** Restaurant, bar; room service; laundry. *In room:* TV.

MASESCHA

Hikers and mountaineers prefer this small resort village 2 miles (3km) north of Triesenberg. The hamlet is perched high above the Rhine Valley. You can admire the cliffs, woods, lush meadows, and clear mountain brooks of this alpine world. In the village you should see **Theodul's Chapel,** a restored medieval church.

MALBUN

Fast rising as a winter ski area, Malbun, 9 miles (15km) north of Vaduz, is the center of winter sports in Liechtenstein, with ski lifts, chairlifts, a ski school, and hotels with indoor swimming pools. You can take the chairlift up to the **Bettlerjoch Peak,** at 6,900 feet (2,070m). The prince of Wales and Princess Anne learned to ski here many winters ago. In the summer this is an ideal starting point for mountain walks.

WHERE TO STAY & DINE

Alpenhotel ✿ *Finds*   This is one of the oldest hotels in Malbun, in the same family since 1908. It's filled with charming details, such as chandeliers made from deer antlers. The wooden ceilings are painted with alpine floral designs and the heavy timbers are carved with regional reliefs. Jacob and Elsa Vögeli-Schroth are eager to please. There are a modern annex and a covered swimming pool. The attractive restaurant serves savory food.

Malbun, FL-9497 Triesenberg, Liechtenstein. ✆ 00423/263-11-81. Fax 00423/263-96-46. 30 units. Winter 160SF–180SF ($88–$99). Summer 140SF ($77) double. Rates include buffet breakfast. Half board 25SF ($13.75) per person extra. AE, DC, MC, V. Free parking. Closed Apr 15–May 15 and Nov to mid-Dec. **Amenities:** Restaurant; pool; limited room service; laundry. *In room:* TV, minibar.

Hotel Malbunerhof ✿   This government-rated four-star chalet—the best in town—is near the ski lifts. The timbered lounge has a fireplace and stucco walls decorated with farm implements. The small to mid-sized rooms are comfortable and well furnished in a modern but not stylish way. The restaurant serves excellent meals in a homey atmosphere.

Malbun, FL-9497 Triesenberg, Liechtenstein. ✆ 00423/263-29-44. Fax 00423/263-95-61. www.schwaerzler-hotels.com. 29 units. Winter 246SF–330SF ($135.30–$181.50) double; 360SF ($198) junior suite for 2, 420SF–500SF ($231–$275) junior suite for 4. Summer 230SF–260SF ($126.50–$143) double; 305SF ($167.75) junior suite for 2, 390SF–440SF ($214.50–$242) junior suite for 4. Rates include half board. AE, DC, MC, V. Free parking. Closed Apr 16–May 19 and Oct 16–Dec 19. **Amenities:** Restaurant; bar; pool; sauna; bowling alley; room service; laundry service. *In room:* TV, minibar, hair dryer.

Appendix: History 101

AT THE CROSSROADS OF EUROPE   Despite its "neutral" image, Switzerland has a fascinating history of external and internal conflicts. Its strategic location, at the crossroads of Europe, made it an irresistible object to empire builders from Roman times. There's even evidence that prehistoric tribes struggled to hold tiny settlements along the great Rhône and Rhine rivers.

The first identifiable occupants were the Celts, who entered the alpine regions from the west. The Helvetii, a Celtic tribe, inhabited a portion of the country that became known as Helvetia. The tribe was defeated by Julius Caesar when it tried to move into southern France in 58 B.C. The Romans conquered the resident tribes in 15 B.C., and peaceful colonization continued until A.D. 455 when the barbarians invaded, followed later by the Christians. Charlemagne (742–814) conquered the small states, or cantons, that occupied the area now known as Switzerland and incorporated them into his realm, which later became the Holy Roman Empire. In the years that followed, Switzerland became a battleground for some of the major ruling families of Europe, especially the Houses of Savoy, the Habsburgs, and the Zähringen.

BIRTH OF THE CONFEDERATION   The Swiss have always guarded their territory jealously. In 1291 an association of three cantons formed the Perpetual Alliance—the nucleus of today's Swiss Confederation. To be rid of the grasping Hapsburgs, the Confederation in 1439 broke free of the Holy Roman Empire. It later signed a treaty with France, a rival power, agreeing to provide France with mercenary troops. This led to Swiss fighting Swiss in the early 16th century. The agreement was ended around 1515, and in 1516 the confederates declared their complete neutrality.

THE REFORMATION   The Protestant Reformation created bitter conflicts in Switzerland between those cantons defending papal Catholicism and those embracing the new creed of Protestantism. Ulrich Zwingli, who like Martin Luther had converted from the Catholic faith, led the Swiss Reformation, beginning in 1519. He translated the Bible into Swiss-German and reorganized church rituals. The Protestant movement was spurred by the 1536 arrival in Geneva of John Calvin, who was fleeing Catholic reprisals in France.

Geneva became one of the most rigidly puritanical strongholds of Protestantism in Europe, fervently committed to its self-perceived role as the New Jerusalem. The spread of Calvinism led to the coining of the French term "Huguenot," a corruption of the Swiss word Eidgenosse (confederate).

After Zwingli died in a religiously motivated battle in 1531, the Swiss spirit of compromise came into play and a peace treaty was signed, allowing each region the right to practice its own faith. Today, 55% of the Swiss define themselves as Protestant, 43% as Roman Catholic, and 2% as members of other faiths.

Despite the deep divisions within the Confederation created by the Reformation, the confederates managed to stay together by adopting a pragmatic approach to their religious and political differences. Such an approach to national issues, based on compromise, remains one of the cornerstones of the Swiss political system. Later, during the Thirty Years' War (1618–48), the Swiss remained neutral while civil wars flared around them.

INDUSTRIALIZATION & PO-LITICAL CRISES Turning to economic development, Switzerland in the 18th century became the most industrialized nation in Europe. A rapid population growth, however, created social problems, widening the division between the new class of wealth and the rest of the population. Popular uprisings occurred, but it was only after the French Revolution that they had an effect, causing the Swiss Confederation to collapse in 1798.

Under French guardianship, progressives moved to centralize the constitution of the Swiss Republic. This pull toward centralization clashed with the federalist traditions of the semi-independent cantons. In 1803, Napoleon Bonaparte established a confederation with 19 cantons, but when he fell from power, Swiss conservatives revived the old order. Much of the social progress resulting from the Napoleonic period was reversed and the aristocrats had their former privileges restored to them.

The present Swiss boundaries were fixed at the Congress of Vienna in 1814–15. In 1848 a federal constitution was adopted and the capital established at Bern.

The federal state, by centralizing responsibility for such matters as customs dues and the minting of coins, created conditions favorable to economic progress. The construction of a railway network and the establishment of a banking system also contributed to Switzerland's development. Both facilitated the country's export industry, consisting chiefly of textiles, pharmaceuticals, and precision machinery.

NEUTRALITY THROUGH TWO WORLD WARS During World War I (1914–18), Switzerland maintained its neutrality from the general European conflict but experienced serious social problems at home. As

Dateline

- 15 b.c. The Romans conquer the Helvetii and other resident alpine tribes.
- a.d. 455 Barbarian invasions begin.
- 742–814 Charlemagne incorporates much of what is now Switzerland into his enormous empire.
- 1291 Three cantons form the Perpetual Alliance, the germ of today's Swiss Confederation.
- 1439 The Confederation breaks free of the Holy Roman Empire (dating from 962).
- 1516 The confederates (Eidgenossen) proclaim their neutrality in Europe's conflicts.
- 1798 The French Revolution brings an invasion of radical forces and ideas, and the old Confederation collapses.
- 1803 Napoleon Bonaparte establishes a new 19-canton confederation, with relatively enlightened social policies.
- 1814–15 The Congress of Vienna guarantees the national boundaries and neutrality of Switzerland.
- 1848 The Swiss adopt a federal constitution, still in force today; Bern is recognized as the capital.
- 1914 Switzerland declares its neutrality at the outbreak of World War I.
- 1918 Swiss workers stage the only general strike the country has ever known.
- 1920 Switzerland joins the League of Nations, offering space for a headquarters at Geneva.
- 1939 Fearing an invasion by Nazi Germany, the country orders a total mobilization of its air and ground forces.
- 1939–45 Remaining neutral, despite its laundering of Nazi gold, Switzerland becomes a haven for escaping prisoners of war and avoids direct conflicts.
- 1948 Switzerland introduces broad-based social reforms, including the funding of old-age pensions.
- 1986 The Swiss electorate votes against membership in the United Nations.
- 1992 By a close vote, the Swiss reject ties to an economically integrated Europe.

continues

purchasing power fell and unemployment rose dramatically, civil unrest grew. One cause of bitterness was that Swiss men conscripted into the army automatically lost their jobs. In November 1918, workers, dissatisfied with their conditions, called a general strike, the first and only one in Switzerland's history. The strike led to

- 1996–97 Critics around the world attack Switzerland's role as a World War II banker for the Nazi war effort.
- 1998 Three Swiss banks agree to a $1.25 billion fund to be distributed among Holocaust victims.
- 2000 Swiss voters agree to closer EU link.

the introduction of proportional representation in elections. In the 1920s, a 48-hour work week was introduced and unemployment insurance was improved.

In 1920, Switzerland joined the League of Nations and provided space for the organization's headquarters at Geneva. As a neutral member, however, it exempted itself from any military action that the League might take.

In August 1939, on the eve of World War II (1939–45), Switzerland, fearing an invasion, ordered a mobilization of its defense forces. But an invasion never came, even though Switzerland was surrounded by Germany and its allies. It proved convenient to all the belligerents to have, in the middle of a continent in conflict, a neutral nation through which they could deal with each other. Switzerland was also successful in deterring a Nazi invasion by indicating to Hitler that it was determined to defend itself. It managed to convince Nazi Germany that any invader would pay in blood for every foot of ground gained in Switzerland.

The sense of neutrality remains so strong that even as recently as 1986 the Swiss voted, in a national referendum, against membership in the United Nations. Switzerland, however, did join the United Nations Educational, Scientific, and Cultural Organization, contributing to its Third World development funds.

Switzerland's political isolationism of the postwar years coincided with a period of unprecedented financial and industrial growth. Many social-welfare programs were introduced, unemployment was virtually wiped out, and the country moved into an enviable position of wealth and prosperity.

INTO THE FUTURE In 1992, the Swiss rejected the opportunities offered by the economic integration of Europe, preferring their traditional isolation and neutrality. A referendum in December 1992 vetoed the government's attempt to seek full membership in the EU. But the vote was close: 50.3% against and 49.7% in favor.

All six French-speaking cantons backed the plan, while all but one of the German-speaking cantons opposed it. This revealed a rather dangerous split in a multicultural country's aspirations and political hopes. The plan for European integration was favored not only by the government, but also by bankers, labor leaders, intellectuals, and most industrialists. However, it was overwhelmingly rejected by the small rural communities that form much of the Swiss landscape.

Fear of a flood of refugees might have made the final decision for many Swiss, who have looked in horror at the onslaught of workers from abroad pouring into Germany and creating disharmony.

In 1996 and 1997, headlines proclaimed Switzerland a banker for Nazi gold. In July of 1997 teams from three major U.S. accounting firms moved into 10 Swiss banks to begin an independent inquiry into funds that may have belonged to Holocaust victims.

The Clinton administration accused Switzerland of prolonging World War II by acting as banker to Nazi Germany. But authorities in Bern quickly rejected the accusation as "unsupported" and termed Washington's assessment "one-sided." Reeling from these charges, Switzerland faced new accusations that its wartime weapons industry profited from—and favored—Hitler's Germany in arms trading worth millions of dollars.

The Swiss government ordered its banks to preserve any remaining records of their dealings with Nazi Germany. But in January 1997 a Swiss security guard at the Union Bank of Switzerland halted the destruction of documents from the wartime era, including some that appeared to deal with the forced auctions of property in Berlin during the 1930s.

In 1998 three Swiss banks agreed to pay $1.25 billion to Holocaust survivors, hoping to settle the claims of thousands of survivors whose families lost assets in World War II.

In May of 2000, Swiss voters by a 67% majority broke with their long-held isolationism and approved agreements with the EU that will link this tiny alpine nation more closely with its neighbors such as Austria, Germany, France, and Italy. The government hopes that the bilateral accords will be a first step toward eventual Swiss membership in the union.

Index

See also Accommodations index, below.

Be
a click
ahead
on your way
to
Switzerland:
MySwitzerland.com

FROMMER'S® COMPLETE TRAVEL GUIDES

Alaska
Amsterdam
Argentina & Chile
Arizona
Atlanta
Australia
Austria
Bahamas
Barcelona, Madrid & Seville
Beijing
Belgium, Holland & Luxembourg
Bermuda
Boston
British Columbia & the Canadian
  Rockies
Budapest & the Best of Hungary
California
Canada
Cancún, Cozumel & the Yucatán
Cape Cod, Nantucket &
  Martha's Vineyard
Caribbean
Caribbean Cruises & Ports of Call
Caribbean Ports of Call
Carolinas & Georgia
Chicago
China
Colorado
Costa Rica
Denmark
Denver, Boulder & Colorado Springs
England
Europe
European Cruises & Ports of Call
Florida
France

Germany
Great Britain
Greece
Greek Islands
Hawaii
Hong Kong
Honolulu, Waikiki & Oahu
Ireland
Israel
Italy
Jamaica
Japan
Las Vegas
London
Los Angeles
Maryland & Delaware
Maui
Mexico
Montana & Wyoming
Montréal & Québec City
Munich & the Bavarian Alps
Nashville & Memphis
Nepal
New England
New Mexico
New Orleans
New York City
New Zealand
Nova Scotia, New Brunswick &
  Prince Edward Island
Oregon
Paris
Philadelphia & the Amish Country
Portugal
Prague & the Best of the Czech
  Republic

Provence & the Riviera
Puerto Rico
Rome
San Antonio & Austin
San Diego
San Francisco
Santa Fe, Taos & Albuquerque
Scandinavia
Scotland
Seattle & Portland
Shanghai
Singapore & Malaysia
South Africa
South America
Southeast Asia
South Florida
South Pacific
Spain
Sweden
Switzerland
Texas
Thailand
Tokyo
Toronto
Tuscany & Umbria
USA
Utah
Vancouver & Victoria
Vermont, New Hampshire
  & Maine
Vienna & the Danube Valley
Virgin Islands
Virginia
Walt Disney World & Orlando
Washington, D.C.
Washington State

FROMMER'S® DOLLAR-A-DAY GUIDES

Australia from $50 a Day
California from $70 a Day
Caribbean from $70 a Day
England from $75 a Day
Europe from $70 a Day

Florida from $70 a Day
Hawaii from $80 a Day
Ireland from $60 a Day
Italy from $70 a Day
London from $85 a Day

New York from $90 a Day
Paris from $80 a Day
San Francisco from $70 a Day
Washington, D.C., from $80
  a Day

FROMMER'S® PORTABLE GUIDES

Acapulco, Ixtapa & Zihuatanejo
Alaska Cruises & Ports of Call
Amsterdam
Aruba
Australia's Great Barrier Reef
Bahamas
Baja & Los Cabos
Berlin
Big Island of Hawaii
Boston
California Wine Country
Cancún
Charleston & Savannah
Chicago
Disneyland

Dublin
Florence
Frankfurt
Hong Kong
Houston
Las Vegas
London
Los Angeles
Maine Coast
Maui
Miami
New Orleans
New York City
Paris

Phoenix & Scottsdale
Portland
Puerto Rico
Puerto Vallarta, Manzanillo &
  Guadalajara
San Diego
San Francisco
Seattle
Sydney
Tampa & St. Petersburg
Vancouver
Venice
Virgin Islands
Washington, D.C.

FROMMER'S® NATIONAL PARK GUIDES

Family Vacations in the National
  Parks
Grand Canyon

National Parks of the American
  West
Rocky Mountain
Yellowstone & Grand Teton

Yosemite & Sequoia/
  Kings Canyon
Zion & Bryce Canyon

FROMMER'S® MEMORABLE WALKS

Chicago	New York	San Francisco
London	Paris	

FROMMER'S® GREAT OUTDOOR GUIDES

Arizona & New Mexico	Northern California	Vermont & New Hampshire
New England	Southern New England	

SUZY GERSHMAN'S BORN TO SHOP GUIDES

Born to Shop: France	Born to Shop: Italy	Born to Shop: New York
Born to Shop: Hong Kong,	Born to Shop: London	Born to Shop: Paris
Shanghai & Beijing		

FROMMER'S® IRREVERENT GUIDES

Amsterdam	Los Angeles	San Francisco
Boston	Manhattan	Seattle & Portland
Chicago	New Orleans	Vancouver
Las Vegas	Paris	Walt Disney World
London	Rome	Washington, D.C.

FROMMER'S® BEST-LOVED DRIVING TOURS

Britain	Germany	New England
California	Ireland	Scotland
Florida	Italy	Spain
France		

HANGING OUT™ GUIDES

Hanging Out in England	Hanging Out in France	Hanging Out in Italy
Hanging Out in Europe	Hanging Out in Ireland	Hanging Out in Spain

THE UNOFFICIAL GUIDES®

Bed & Breakfasts and Country	Florida with Kids	New Orleans
Inns in:	Golf Vacations in the	New York City
California	Eastern U.S.	Paris
New England	The Great Smokey &	San Francisco
Northwest	Blue Ridge Mountains	Skiing in the West
Rockies	Inside Disney	Southeast with Kids
Southeast	Hawaii	Walt Disney World
Beyond Disney	Las Vegas	Walt Disney World for
Branson, Missouri	London	Grown-ups
California with Kids	Mid-Atlantic with Kids	Walt Disney World for Kids
Chicago	Mini Las Vegas	Washington, D.C.
Cruises	Mini-Mickey	World's Best Diving Vacations
Disneyland	New England & New York	
	with Kids	

SPECIAL-INTEREST TITLES

Frommer's Adventure Guide to Australia & New Zealand
Frommer's Adventure Guide to Central America
Frommer's Adventure Guide to India & Pakistan
Frommer's Adventure Guide to South America
Frommer's Adventure Guide to Southeast Asia
Frommer's Adventure Guide to Southern Africa
Frommer's Britain's Best Bed & Breakfasts and Country Inns
Frommer's France's Best Bed & Breakfasts and Country Inns
Frommer's Italy's Best Bed & Breakfasts and Country Inns
Frommer's Caribbean Hideaways

Frommer's Exploring America by RV
Frommer's Gay & Lesbian Europe
Frommer's The Moon
Frommer's New York City with Kids
Frommer's Road Atlas Britain
Frommer's Road Atlas Europe
Frommer's Washington, D.C., with Kids
Frommer's What the Airlines Never Tell You
Israel Past & Present
The New York Times' Guide to Unforgettable Weekends
Places Rated Almanac
Retirement Places Rated

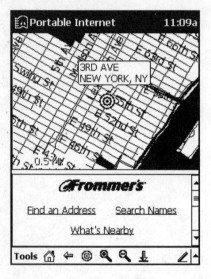